Good Housekeeping

COOKERY
BOOK

Good Housekeeping

COOKERY BOOK

The cook's classic companion

PAVILION

NOTES

- Both metric and imperial measures are given for the recipes. Follow either set of measures, not a mixture of both, as they are not interchangeable.

- All spoon measures are level.
  1 tsp = 5ml spoon; 1 tbsp = 15ml spoon.

- Ovens and grills must be preheated to the specified temperature.

- Use sea salt and freshly ground black pepper unless otherwise suggested.

- Fresh herbs should be used unless dried herbs are specified in a recipe.

- Medium eggs should be used except where otherwise specified. Free-range eggs are recommended.

- Note that some recipes contain raw or lightly cooked eggs. The young, elderly, pregnant women and anyone with an immune-deficiency disease should avoid these because of the slight risk of salmonella.

(B) Bread Machine Recipe

(V) Vegetarian Recipe

Published in the United Kingdom in 2014 by
Pavilion
1 Gower Street
London
WC1E 6HD

This edition published 2014 for Index Books

The Good Housekeeping website is
www.goodhousekeeping.co.uk

10 9 8 7 6 5 4 3 2 1

ISBN 978-1-909815-89-6

A catalogue record for this book is available from the British Library.

Reproduction by Mission Productions Ltd, Hong Kong
Printed and bound by Toppan Leefung Printing Ltd, China

This book can be ordered direct from the publisher at
www.pavilionbooks.com

Contents

Foreword

It seems like we're surrounded by recipes these days. Recipes on the internet, recipes in newspapers and on the television and, of course, in your favourite magazines. But few of us have the time or the money to waste on super-complicated food ideas that may or may not work – how do you edit all this information so that you're guaranteed a successful outcome every time?

What's needed is a cooking bible that you can turn to time and time again. A book filled with recipes, all of which have been developed and triple-tested so you know they will work. Recipes that will become family favourites and handed down to future generations. Recipes that will be your go-to signature dish whenever you need to impress. And recipes you'll simply love to make when you fancy a relaxing afternoon in the kitchen – just you, the radio, a cup of tea and a mixing bowl!

Since its first publication in 1948, the *Good Housekeeping Cookery Book* has served four generations of cooks and has sold more than two million copies. Today, with so much choice around us, its classic, essential easy-to-follow recipes are more important than ever and I'm delighted it has been updated to celebrate the 90th birthday of the Good Housekeeping Institute.

Happy cooking and I hope you enjoy your cookery book for many, many years to come.

Lindsay Nicholson
Editorial Director
Good Housekeeping

The Good Housekeeping Institute and the Cookery Book

The Good Housekeeping Institute was created in 1924 to provide readers of *Good Housekeeping* magazine with expert consumer advice and delicious, easy-to-follow recipes. These ideals still hold true today. The *Good Housekeeping Cookery Book* is the Institute's famous classic cookbook and is now established as the cooks' ultimate bible. This edition has been updated for the 21st-century cook, while keeping faith with the traditions and precision of the original book. Every recipe published in this book has been rigorously triple-tested by the Good Housekeeping Institute experts so that you can cook any dish with confidence.

Stocks
and Stuffings

Stocks

Well-flavoured stocks form the basis of soups, sauces, stews and many other savoury dishes. You will find an extensive range of ready-made stock products in most supermarkets and these have improved significantly in recent years, but the flavour of a good home-made stock is incomparable. Stocks are easy to make.

Fishmongers are usually only too happy to let you have fish bones and trimmings; similarly poulterers and butchers will generally supply chicken carcasses and other bones. Any stock that is not required for immediate use can be frozen in manageable quantities. To save freezer space, you can boil the stock to reduce the volume by half and concentrate the flavour before freezing.

The characteristics of a good stock are clarity and a fine flavour. Guard against over-seasoning, as boiling concentrates the flavour and saltiness. Fat and impurities will make a stock cloudy, so these should always be removed by skimming the surface from time to time during cooking. If possible, use a conical sieve to strain the stock and allow the liquid to drip through; avoid pressing any vegetables in the sieve or you will lose clarity.

Once strained, cool the stock quickly, ideally over a bowl of chilled water, then chill. A thin, solid layer of fat will form on the surface of most stocks; just lift it off the stock with a slotted spoon. Bring the stock to the boil before use.

If you haven't the time to make your own stock, opt for one of the better ready-made alternatives. Fresh stocks available in cartons from the chilled cabinet, liquid stock concentrates and vegetable bouillon powder are preferable to powdered stock cubes. These are still inclined to be strong and salty so, if you use them, do so sparingly, or choose a low-salt variety.

Vegetable Stock

Makes 1.1 litres (2 pints)
Preparation time 10 minutes
Cooking time 35 minutes

225g (8oz) onions, roughly chopped
225g (8oz) celery sticks, roughly chopped
225g (8oz) trimmed leeks, roughly chopped
225g (8oz) carrots, roughly chopped
2 bay leaves
a few fresh thyme sprigs
1 small bunch of parsley
10 black peppercorns
½ tsp sea salt

1 Put the onions, celery sticks, leeks and carrots into a large pan.
2 Add 1.7 litres (3 pints) cold water, the herbs, black peppercorns and salt. Bring slowly to the boil and skim off any scum. Partially cover the pan and simmer for 30 minutes; check the seasoning.
3 Strain the stock through a fine sieve into a bowl and allow to cool. Cover and keep in the fridge for up to three days. Use as required.

NUTRITION PER 100ml (3½fl oz)
5 cals | trace fat (trace sats) | 1g carbs | 0.2g salt Ⓥ

Basic Bone Stock

Makes about 900ml–1.1 litres (1½–2 pints)
Preparation time 10 minutes
Cooking time about 3 hours

900g (2lb) meat bones, fresh or from cooked meat, chopped
2 onions, chopped
2 celery sticks, chopped
2 carrots, chopped
1 tsp salt
3 black peppercorns
bouquet garni (1 bay leaf, a few fresh parsley and thyme sprigs)

1 Put all the ingredients in a pan with 2 litres (3½ pints) water. Bring to the boil and skim off any scum. Cover and simmer for about 3 hours. Strain the stock and, when cold, remove all traces of fat.

Cook's Tip
If using a pressure cooker, add the bones and 1.4 litres (2½ pints) water, bring to the boil and skim. Add the remaining ingredients. Bring to High 6.8kg (15lb) pressure and cook for 1–1¼ hours (cook in 1.7 litres (3 pints) water for 2 hours if you are using marrow bones). Reduce the pressure at room temperature.

NUTRITION PER 100ml (3½fl oz)
12 cals | 1g fat (trace sats) | 1g carbs | 0.5g salt

Chicken Stock

Makes 1.1 litres (2 pints)
Preparation time 10 minutes
Cooking time about 2 hours

225g (8oz) onions, roughly chopped
150g (5oz) trimmed leeks, roughly chopped
225g (8oz) celery sticks, roughly chopped
1.6kg (3½lb) raw chicken bones
bouquet garni (2 bay leaves, a few fresh parsley and
  thyme sprigs)
1 tsp black peppercorns
½ tsp sea salt

1 Put the vegetables into a large pan with the chicken
bones, 3 litres (5¼ pints) cold water, the bouquet garni,
peppercorns and salt. Bring slowly to the boil and skim
the surface. Partially cover the pan and simmer gently for
2 hours; check the seasoning.
2 Strain the stock through a fine sieve into a bowl and cool
quickly. Cover and keep in the fridge for up to three days.
Remove the fat from the surface and use as required.

Cook's Tip
Instead of chicken bones, you can use a large boiling
chicken – obtainable from selected butchers and poulterers.
Or use the poultry giblets, if they are available.

NUTRITION PER 100ml (3½fl oz)
10 cals | 1g fat (trace sats) | 1g carbs | 0.2g salt

Fish Stock

Makes 900ml (1½ pints)
Preparation time 10 minutes
Cooking time 35 minutes

900g (2lb) fish bones and trimmings
2 carrots, chopped
1 onion, chopped
2 celery sticks, sliced
bouquet garni (1 bay leaf, a few fresh parsley and
  thyme sprigs)
6 white peppercorns
½ tsp sea salt

1 Wash and dry the fish bones and put into a large pan.
2 Add the vegetables to the pan together with 900ml
(1½ pints) cold water, the bouquet garni, peppercorns and
salt. Bring slowly to the boil and skim the surface. Cover
and simmer gently for about 30 minutes.
3 Strain the stock through a fine sieve into a bowl and
check the seasoning. Cool quickly, cover and keep in the
fridge for up to two days. Use as required.

TRY SOMETHING DIFFERENT
Court Bouillon To make this enriched fish stock, add
150ml (¼ pint) dry white wine and 3 tbsp white wine
vinegar at step 2.

NUTRITION PER 100ml (3½fl oz)
5 cals | trace fat (trace sats) | 1g carbs | 0.2g salt

Basic Gravy

Makes about 300ml (½ pint)
Preparation time 2 minutes
Cooking time 2–3 minutes

1 Pour (or skim) off the fat from a corner of the roasting
tin, leaving the sediment. Add 300–450ml (½–¾ pint)
vegetable water, or chicken, vegetable or meat stock.
2 Heat gently, stirring to scrape up the sediment, and boil
steadily until the gravy is a rich brown colour.

TRY SOMETHING DIFFERENT
Rich Wine Gravy Deglaze the tin with 150ml (¼ pint) red
or white wine, or 90ml (3fl oz) sherry or other fortified wine,
and bubble for 2 minutes before adding the stock or water.
For a sweeter gravy, add 2 tbsp redcurrant jelly with the wine.

Thick Gravy Sprinkle 1–2 tbsp flour into the tin and cook,
stirring, until browned, then gradually add the liquid and
cook, stirring, for 2–3 minutes until smooth and thickened.

Cook's Tips
• Gravy is traditionally served with roast meat or poultry.
• If possible, make the gravy in the roasting tin while the
  joint (or bird) is resting. This will incorporate the meat
  juices that have escaped during roasting.
• A little gravy browning can be added to intensify the
  flavour and colour.

NUTRITION PER 100ml (3½fl oz)
10 cals | 2g fat (1g sats) | 1g carbs | 0.2g salt

Stuffings

A moist, tasty stuffing will enhance the flavour of poultry and game birds; it will also improve their appearance by helping to plump the bird into a neat shape. Boned joints of meat, whole boned fish, and vegetables such as peppers, aubergines and large tomatoes, lend themselves perfectly to stuffing, too.

Most stuffings are based on breadcrumbs, rice, sausage meat, oatmeal or suet, with added flavouring ingredients and beaten egg or other liquid to bind the stuffing together. If required, the dry ingredients can be mixed together in advance, but the liquid should be added shortly before use. Stuff the bird (or meat or fish) just before cooking, and weigh after stuffing in order to calculate the cooking time.

When stuffing poultry, stuff the neck end only to ensure sufficient heat penetration through to the body cavity. The stuffing swells during cooking as it absorbs juices from the meat, poultry or fish, so don't pack it in too tightly or it may spill out. Cook any surplus stuffing in a separate baking dish.

Herb and Lemon Stuffing

Serves 4
Preparation time 10 minutes
Cooking time 10 minutes, plus cooling
Sufficient for a 1.4kg (3lb) oven-ready chicken

40g (1½oz) butter
1 small onion, chopped
1 garlic clove, crushed
75g (3oz) white breadcrumbs
2 tbsp freshly chopped flat-leafed parsley
2 tbsp freshly chopped tarragon or thyme
finely grated zest and juice of 1 small lemon
1 medium egg yolk
salt and ground black pepper

1 Melt the butter in a small pan, add the onion and garlic, and fry gently for 7–10 minutes to soften. Tip into a bowl and leave to cool.
2 Add the breadcrumbs, chopped herbs, lemon zest and juice, then stir in the egg yolk to bind the stuffing. Season well with salt and ground black pepper.

Cook's Tip
Keep the spent lemon halves to put into the cavity of the bird for extra flavour.

NUTRITION PER 100ml (3½fl oz)
150 cals | 10g fat (6g sats) | 12g carbs | 1.1g salt Ⓥ

Chestnut Stuffing

Serves 10
Preparation time 15 minutes
Cooking time about 50 minutes
Sufficient for a 4.5–5.4kg (10–12lb) oven-ready turkey

450g (1lb) fresh chestnuts, slit on one side, or 225g can whole chestnuts (unsweetened), drained and chopped
25g (1oz) butter
2 onions, chopped
350g (12oz) fresh breadcrumbs
75g (3oz) shredded suet
3 tbsp creamed horseradish
1 tsp lemon juice
salt and ground black pepper

1 For fresh chestnuts, preheat the oven to 200°C (180°C fan oven) mark 6. Bake for 10 minutes or until the skins crack. Peel when cool. Simmer in salted water for 20 minutes until tender. Drain and chop.
2 Melt the butter and fry the onions just until soft. Take off the heat and stir in the remaining ingredients.
3 Fry gently, stirring, for 15–20 minutes, or bake in an ovenproof dish at 200°C (180°C fan oven) mark 6 for 30–35 minutes covered, then 15 minutes uncovered. Cool.

TRY SOMETHING DIFFERENT
Sausage Meat and Chestnut Stuffing Mix 225g (8oz) fresh breadcrumbs, 450g (1lb) pork sausage meat, grated zest of 1 orange, 1 tsp dried sage, and salt and pepper in a large bowl. Drain and chop a 400g can whole chestnuts in water. Add to the bowl and bind with the juice of 1 orange.

NUTRITION PER 100ml (3½fl oz)
285 cals | 11g fat (5g sats) | 45g carbs | 1g salt

Spicy Sausage Stuffing

Serves 8
Preparation time 10 minutes
Cooking time 10 minutes, plus cooling
Sufficient for a 4.5kg (10lb) oven-ready turkey

350g (12oz) spicy Italian-style pork sausages
125g (4oz) butter
2 onions, chopped
225g (8oz) oatmeal
1 tsp finely chopped fresh thyme
salt and ground black pepper

1 Skin the sausages and break up the meat in a bowl.
2 Melt the butter in a pan, add the onions and cook gently for 7–10 minutes until soft and golden, then mix in the oatmeal and thyme. Leave to cool.
3 Add the mixture to the sausage meat and mix well, seasoning generously with salt and pepper.

NUTRITION PER 100ml (3½fl oz)
400 cals | 29g fat (12g sats) | 28g carbs | 1.5g salt

Mushroom and Cashew Nut Stuffing

Serves 10
Preparation time 15 minutes
Cooking time 15 minutes, plus cooling
Sufficient for a 4.5kg (10lb) oven-ready turkey

2 onions, finely chopped
50g (2oz) butter
450g (1lb) brown-cap mushrooms, roughly chopped
4 tbsp freshly chopped parsley
75g (3oz) salted cashew nuts, toasted and roughly chopped
125g (4oz) fresh white breadcrumbs
2 large eggs, beaten
salt and ground black pepper

1 Fry the onions in the butter for 8 minutes until soft and golden. Add the mushrooms and fry for 4–5 minutes until the moisture has evaporated. Mix in the parsley, nuts and breadcrumbs. Cool. Add the eggs, season and mix well.

NUTRITION PER 100ml (3½fl oz)
140 cals | 9g fat (4g sats) | 11g carbs | 0.7g salt Ⓥ

Sage and Onion Stuffing

Serves 4
Preparation time 10 minutes
Cooking time 10 minutes, plus cooling
Sufficient for a 1.4kg (3lb) oven-ready chicken

1 tbsp oil
75g (3oz) onion, chopped
125g (4oz) pork sausage meat
1 tbsp finely chopped fresh sage
salt and ground black pepper

1 Heat the oil in a frying pan, add the onion and cook gently for 7–10 minutes until soft and golden.
2 Turn into a bowl and leave to cool.
3 Add the sausage meat and sage to the cooled onion mixture and stir to blend. Season the mixture with salt and pepper and stir again.

NUTRITION PER 100ml (3½fl oz)
150 cals | 13g fat (4g sats) | 4g carbs | 1.3g salt

Wild Rice Stuffing

Serves 10
Preparation time 5 minutes
Cooking time 45 minutes
Sufficient for a 5kg (11lb) oven-ready goose

125g (4oz) wild rice
225g (8oz) rindless streaky bacon, cut into strips
2 red onions (about 225g/8oz), peeled and finely chopped
75g (3oz) dried cranberries
1 medium egg, beaten
salt and ground black pepper

1 Put the rice, 900ml (1½ pints) cold water and ¼ tsp salt in a pan. Bring to the boil, partially cover and simmer for 45 minutes until tender. Drain and cool.
2 Dry-fry the bacon until just brown, then put in a bowl. Fry the onions until soft. Add the cranberries and cook for 1–2 minutes, then mix with the bacon and cool. Add the rice, egg and seasoning, then stir throughly to combine.

NUTRITION PER 100ml (3½fl oz)
146 cals | 6g fat (2g sats) | 18g carbs | 0.9g salt

Sauces
and Dressings

Sauces

A certain mystique is attached to sauce-making, but all that is really needed is a little time, patience and your undivided attention. Essentially, a sauce should always complement and enhance the dish it is accompanying. The flavours of the sauce must never be so overpowering that they mask the intrinsic flavours and textures of the accompanying dish.

Roux-based sauces, such as béchamel, are probably the most familiar of all. These are based on equal quantities of butter and flour, which are cooked together. First the butter is melted, then the flour is mixed in and the resultant roux is cooked before the liquid is added. For a classic white béchamel sauce, the roux is cooked but not coloured; for a blond sauce, such as velouté, the roux is cooked until biscuit-coloured; for a brown sauce, such as espagnole, the roux is cooked until brown.

The classic French emulsified sauces, such as hollandaise, Béarnaise and beurre blanc, rely on the reduction of liquids to give an intense flavour, and the addition of either butter or eggs to enrich and thicken. These sauces are a little more difficult to make because of their tendency to separate, but using a blender or food processor simplifies the process and is relatively foolproof.

Emulsified sauces are best made shortly before serving and kept warm over a pan of hot water.

Some sauces are thickened towards the end of preparation. Last-minute thickeners include arrowroot, cornflour and beurre manié (butter and flour kneaded together in equal quantities).

Other popular sauces included in this chapter are tomato sauces, pesto, salsa verde and classic British favourites, such as apple sauce, mint sauce and cranberry sauce; also gravies, savoury butters, custard and other sweet sauces to accompany desserts.

Allow yourself sufficient time to make a sauce – it is invariably working in haste that results in a lumpy or curdled sauce. If a roux-based sauce becomes lumpy, just whisk or beat vigorously; if this doesn't work, pass through a sieve, or whiz in a blender or food processor.

An emulsified sauce that shows signs of curdling can often be rescued by adding an ice cube to the sauce and whisking the mixture thoroughly.

Most sauces can be prepared in advance and reheated carefully when required. Cover the surface closely with damp greaseproof paper as soon as the sauce is made, to prevent a skin from forming on standing.

Béchamel Sauce

Makes 300ml (½ pint)
Preparation time 5 minutes, plus infusing
Cooking time 5 minutes

300ml (½ pint) semi-skimmed milk
1 onion slice
6 peppercorns
1 mace blade
1 bay leaf
15g (½oz) butter
15g (½oz) plain flour
salt and ground black pepper
freshly grated nutmeg

1 Pour the milk into a pan. Add the onion slice, peppercorns, mace and bay leaf. Bring almost to the boil, then remove from the heat, cover and leave to infuse for about 20 minutes. Strain through a fine sieve.
2 To make the roux, melt the butter in a pan, stir in the flour and cook, stirring, for 1 minute without colouring.
3 Remove from the heat and gradually pour on the infused milk, whisking constantly.

4 Season lightly with salt, pepper and grated nutmeg. Return to a gentle heat and cook, stirring constantly, until the sauce is thickened and smooth. Simmer gently for 2 minutes, stirring constantly.

TRY SOMETHING DIFFERENT
Cheese (Mornay) Sauce Off the heat, stir 50g (2oz) finely grated Gruyère or mature Cheddar and a large pinch of mustard powder or cayenne pepper into the finished sauce. Heat gently to melt the cheese, if necessary.
Onion (Soubise) Sauce Sauté 1 large, finely diced onion in a little butter over a low heat for 10–15 minutes until softened. Stir the sautéed onion into the sauce at step 4.
Parsley Sauce Stir in 2 tbsp freshly chopped parsley at step 4.
Simple White Sauce Omit the flavouring ingredients and infusing stage, and just stir the cold milk into the roux.
Thick (Binding) Sauce Increase the butter and flour to 25g (1oz) each with the same quantity of liquid.

NUTRITION PER 75ml (5 tbsp)
75 cals | 4g fat (3g sats) | 7g carbs | 0.8g salt (V)

Hollandaise

Serves 6
Preparation time 20 minutes
Cooking time 8 minutes

4 tbsp white wine vinegar
6 black peppercorns
1 mace blade
1 onion slice
1 bay leaf
3 medium egg yolks
150g (5oz) unsalted butter, at room temperature,
  cut into pieces
2 tbsp single cream (optional)
lemon juice to taste
salt and ground white pepper

1 Put the vinegar, peppercorns, mace, onion slice and bay leaf into a small pan. Bring to the boil, then boil to reduce to 1 tbsp liquid. Dip the base of the pan in cold water to stop further evaporation. Put to one side.
2 Put the egg yolks into a heatproof bowl with 15g (½oz) of the butter and a pinch of salt. Beat until well combined, then strain in the reduced vinegar.
3 Put the bowl over a pan of barely simmering water and whisk for 3–4 minutes until the mixture is pale and beginning to thicken.
4 Beat in the remaining butter, a piece at a time, until the mixture begins to thicken and emulsify. Make sure each addition of butter is incorporated before adding the next. Do not allow the mixture to overheat or the eggs will scramble and split. Take off the heat.
5 Whisk in the cream, if you like. Season with salt and pepper and add a little lemon juice to taste. Serve at once.

Cook's Tips
• Hollandaise is a wonderfully rich sauce to serve with hot or cold vegetables, such as asparagus and globe artichokes, poached fish and shellfish.
• If the sauce shows signs of curdling, add an ice cube and whisk thoroughly; the hollandaise should re-combine.
• To make hollandaise in a food processor, melt the butter and allow it to cool until tepid. Put the strained reduced vinegar, egg yolks and salt in the processor bowl and process for 10 seconds. With the motor running, add the melted butter in a thin steady stream through the feeder tube and process until emulsified. Finish the sauce as in step 5, above.

NUTRITION PER SERVING
230 cals | 24g fat (14g sats) | trace carbs | 0.8g salt Ⓥ

Béarnaise Sauce

Serves 4
Preparation time 20 minutes
Cooking time 8–10 minutes

4 tbsp white wine vinegar or tarragon vinegar
2 shallots, finely chopped
6 black peppercorns
a few fresh tarragon sprigs, chopped
2 medium egg yolks
75g (3oz) butter, at room temperature, cut into pieces
2 tsp freshly chopped flat-leafed parsley or chervil (optional)
salt and ground white pepper

1 Put the vinegar, shallots, peppercorns and tarragon into a very small pan. Bring to the boil, then boil to reduce to 1 tbsp liquid. Dip the base of the pan in cold water to stop further evaporation. Leave to cool, then strain.
2 Beat the egg yolks and reduced vinegar together in a heatproof bowl.
3 Put the bowl over a pan of barely simmering water and whisk for 3–4 minutes until the mixture is pale and beginning to thicken.
4 Beat in the butter, a piece at a time, until the mixture begins to thicken and emulsify. Make sure each addition of butter is incorporated before adding the next. Do not allow the mixture to overheat or the eggs will scramble and split. Take off the heat.
5 Season with salt and pepper to taste. Stir in the chopped herbs, if you like.

Cook's Tips
• If the sauce shows signs of curdling, add an ice cube and whisk thoroughly; the sauce should re-combine.
• Serve this classic butter sauce with grilled meats, especially beef and lamb steaks.

NUTRITION PER SERVING
180 cals | 18g fat (11g sats) | 2g carbs | 0.9g salt Ⓥ

Beurre Blanc

Serves 4
Preparation time 5 minutes
Cooking time 5 minutes

3 tbsp white wine vinegar
3 tbsp white wine
2 shallots, finely chopped
225g (8oz) butter, chilled and cut into small cubes
salt and ground black pepper

1 Put the vinegar, white wine and shallots into a very small pan. Bring to the boil, then boil to reduce to 1 tbsp liquid.
2 Over a low heat, whisk in the butter, a piece at a time, until the sauce begins to thicken as the butter melts. Move the pan on and off heat to avoid overheating.
3 If you like a smooth sauce, pass the sauce through a sieve. Season with salt and pepper to taste.

TRY SOMETHING DIFFERENT
Herb Beurre Blanc Add 2 tbsp freshly chopped herbs, such as tarragon, chives or chervil, to the finished sauce.
Red Wine Sauce Use 6 tbsp red wine instead of the white wine and vinegar.

Cook's Tips
• If the sauce shows signs of curdling, add an ice cube and whisk thoroughly; the sauce should re-combine.
• Serve with poached or grilled fish and poultry.

NUTRITION PER SERVING
420 cals | 46g fat (29g sats) | 2g carbs | 1.5g salt Ⓥ

Mild Curry Sauce

Serves 4
Preparation time 5 minutes
Cooking time 20 minutes

50g (2oz) butter
1 onion, finely chopped
3–4 tsp mild curry powder
3 tbsp plain flour
450ml (¾ pint) milk or half stock and half milk
2 tbsp mango or apple chutney, roughly chopped
salt and ground black pepper

1 Melt the butter in a pan, add the onion and fry gently until golden.
2 Stir in the curry powder and cook for 3–4 minutes. Add the flour and cook gently for 2–3 minutes.
3 Remove the pan from the heat and gradually stir in the milk or stock and milk mixture. Bring to the boil slowly and continue to cook, stirring, until the sauce thickens.
4 Add the chutney and seasoning. Reheat the sauce gently before serving.

Cook's Tip
Curry sauce is useful when you want to make a curry in a hurry, and it makes good use of leftovers of meat, poultry and fish.

NUTRITION PER SERVING
245 cals | 13g fat (8g sats) | 28g carbs | 1.5g salt Ⓥ

Barbecue Sauce

Serves 4
Preparation time 5 minutes
Cooking time about 25 minutes

50g (2oz) butter
1 large onion, chopped
1 tsp tomato purée
2 tbsp red or white wine vinegar
2 tbsp Worcestershire sauce
2 tsp mustard powder
salt and ground black pepper

1 Melt the butter in a pan, add the onion and sauté gently for 10 minutes or until softened. Stir in the tomato purée and cook, stirring, for 2 minutes.
2 Mix together the wine vinegar, Worcestershire sauce, mustard powder, salt and pepper in a bowl, stir in 150ml (¼ pint) water, then add to the pan. Bring to the boil, stirring, then simmer gently for 10 minutes until thick, stirring occasionally.

Cook's Tip
Serve with barbecued or grilled chicken, sausages, burgers or chops.

NUTRITION PER SERVING
110 cals | 10g fat (7g sats) | 4g carbs | 1g salt

Bread Sauce

Serves 8
Preparation time 10 minutes
Cooking time 15 minutes

1 onion, quartered
4 cloves
2 bay leaves
450ml (¾ pint) milk
150g (5oz) fresh white breadcrumbs
½ tsp freshly grated nutmeg, or to taste
50g (2oz) butter
200ml (7fl oz) crème fraîche
salt and ground black pepper

1 Stud each onion quarter with a clove. Put the onion, bay leaves and milk into a pan. Heat very gently on the lowest possible heat for 15 minutes.
2 Remove the onion and bay leaves, then add the breadcrumbs, nutmeg and butter, and stir to combine. Add the crème fraîche and season with salt and pepper to taste. Serve warm.

NUTRITION PER SERVING
210 cals | 16g fat (11g sats) | 13g carbs | 0.8g salt Ⓥ

Apple Sauce

Serves 4
Preparation time 10 minutes
Cooking time 10 minutes

450g (1lb) cooking apples, such as Bramleys
25g (1oz) butter
2 tbsp sugar, or to taste

1 Peel, core and slice the apples and put into a pan with 2–3 tbsp water. Cover and cook gently for 10 minutes, stirring occasionally, or until soft and reduced to a pulp.
2 Beat with a wooden spoon until smooth, then pass through a sieve, if you prefer a smooth sauce. Stir in the butter and enough sugar to taste. Serve warm.

Cook's Tip
This sauce is traditionally served with roast pork and goose, to cut the richness of the meats.

NUTRITION PER SERVING
110 cals | 5g fat (3g sats) | 17g carbs | 0.1g salt Ⓥ

Creamy Mushroom and Wine Sauce

Serves 6
Preparation time 10 minutes
Cooking time 20 minutes

2 tbsp oil
2 shallots or 1 onion, finely diced
175g (6oz) button or cup mushrooms, sliced
150g (5oz) mixed wild mushrooms, sliced
2 garlic cloves, crushed
150ml (¼ pint) white wine (see Alcoholic Drinks and
  Vegetarians on page 489)
200ml (7fl oz) crème fraîche
2 tsp freshly chopped thyme
salt and ground black pepper

1 Heat the oil in a pan, add the shallots or onion and cook gently for 10 minutes. Add the mushrooms and garlic, and cook over a high heat for 4–5 minutes until tender and all the moisture has been driven off.
2 Pour in the wine, bring to the boil and let it bubble until reduced by half.
3 Add the crème fraîche, 100ml (3½fl oz) water and the seasoning. Bring to the boil and bubble for 5 minutes or until the liquid is slightly thickened and syrupy.
4 Add the chopped thyme, adjust the seasoning to taste and serve the sauce immediately.

TRY SOMETHING DIFFERENT
Light Wine Sauce Replace the crème fraîche with red wine for a lighter sauce.

Cook's Tip
This sauce is particularly good with pan-fried steak or chicken.

NUTRITION PER SERVING
190 cals | 18g fat (10g sats) | 3g carbs | 0.4g salt Ⓥ

Cranberry Sauce

Serves 8
Preparation time 30 minutes
Cooking time 1 hour 5 minutes, plus chilling

2 tbsp olive oil
450g (1lb) red onions, thinly sliced
grated zest and juice of 1 large orange
1 tsp coriander seeds, lightly crushed
¼ tsp ground cloves
1 bay leaf
150g (5oz) dark muscovado sugar
150ml (¼ pint) red wine
450g (1lb) cranberries

1 Heat the oil in a medium pan, add the onions and cook gently for 5 minutes. Add the orange zest and juice, coriander seeds, ground cloves, bay leaf, sugar and red wine. Bring to the boil, then reduce the heat and simmer gently for 40 minutes.
2 Add the cranberries, bring back to the boil, then simmer for 20 minutes. Cool and chill until required.
3 Bring to room temperature before serving.

Cook's Tip
Serve this tangy relish with a traditional Christmas turkey.

NUTRITION PER SERVING
140 cals | 3g fat (trace sats) | 26g carbs | 0g salt Ⓥ

Fresh Tomato Sauce

Serves 4
Preparation time 10 minutes
Cooking time 30 minutes

900g (2lb) vine-ripened tomatoes, roughly chopped
2 tbsp extra virgin olive oil
2 garlic cloves, crushed
grated zest of 1 lemon
1 tsp dried oregano
2 tbsp freshly chopped basil
a pinch of sugar, or to taste (optional)
salt and ground black pepper

1 Put the tomatoes, oil, garlic, lemon zest and oregano into a pan. Bring to the boil, then reduce the heat, cover and simmer gently for 20 minutes.
2 Add the chopped basil, salt and pepper to taste and a little sugar, if required. Simmer, uncovered, for a further 10 minutes or until the sauce is slightly thickened.
3 If you like a smooth sauce, pass through a sieve and reheat before serving.

Cook's Tip
This sauce is good with meat loaf.

NUTRITION PER SERVING
100 cals | 7g fat (1g sats) | 8g carbs | 0.6g salt Ⓥ

Cumberland Sauce

Serves 4
Preparation time 10 minutes
Cooking time 10 minutes, plus cooling

finely pared zest and juice of 1 orange
finely pared zest and juice of 1 lemon
4 tbsp redcurrant jelly
1 tsp Dijon mustard
4 tbsp port
a pinch of ground ginger (optional)
salt and ground black pepper

1 Cut the citrus zests into fine julienne strips and put into a small pan. Add enough cold water to cover, bring to the boil, then reduce the heat and simmer for 5 minutes. Drain.
2 Return the citrus zests to the pan with the orange and lemon juices, redcurrant jelly and mustard and heat gently, stirring, until the jelly has dissolved. Simmer for 5 minutes, then add the port.
3 Leave to cool. Season with salt and pepper to taste, and add a little ginger if you like.

Cook's Tip
Serve this sauce cold, with gammon.

NUTRITION PER SERVING
70 cals | 0g fat | 15g carbs | 0.7g salt Ⓥ

Anchovy Sauce

Serves 4
Makes 300ml (½ pint)
Preparation time 5 minutes
Cooking time about 10 minutes

15g (½oz) butter
15g (½oz) plain flour
150ml (¼ pint) milk
150ml (¼ pint) fish stock
1–2 tsp anchovy essence
a squeeze of lemon juice
red food colouring (optional)
salt and ground black pepper

1 Melt the butter in a pan, stir in the flour and cook gently for 1 minute, stirring.
2 Remove the pan from the heat and gradually stir in the milk and stock. Bring to the boil slowly and continue cooking, stirring all the time, until the sauce comes to the boil and thickens.
3 Simmer very gently for a further 2–3 minutes, stirring.
4 Stir in anchovy essence to taste, the lemon juice and a few drops of red food colouring to tint it a pale pink, if you like. Season with salt and pepper.

Cook's Tip
Serve hot with plaice, brill or turbot.

NUTRITION PER SERVING
58 cals | 4g fat (2g sats) | 5g carbs | 0.7g salt

Mint Sauce

Serves 4
Preparation time 10 minutes, plus standing

1 small bunch of mint, stalks removed
1–2 tsp golden caster sugar to taste
1–2 tbsp wine vinegar to taste

1 Finely chop the mint leaves and put into a bowl with the sugar. Stir in 1 tbsp boiling water and set aside for about 5 minutes to dissolve the sugar.
2 Add the wine vinegar to taste. Leave to stand for about 1 hour before serving.

Cook's Tip
This sauce is the classic accompaniment to roast lamb.

Horseradish Cream

Serves 4
Preparation time 5 minutes

2 tbsp grated fresh horseradish
2 tsp lemon juice
2 tsp sugar
a pinch of mustard powder (optional)
150ml (¼ pint) double cream

1 Mix together the horseradish, lemon juice, sugar and mustard, if you like.
2 Whip the double cream until it forms soft peaks, then fold in the horseradish mixture.

Cook's Tip
The classic accompaniment to roast beef.

NUTRITION PER SERVING
10 cals | trace fat (0g sats) | 2g carbs | 0g salt Ⓥ

NUTRITION PER SERVING
198 cals | 20g fat (13g sats) | 3g carbs | trace salt Ⓥ

Tartare Sauce

Makes 150ml (¼ pint)
Preparation time 5 minutes, plus standing

150ml (¼ pint) Mayonnaise (see page 29)
1 tsp freshly chopped tarragon or snipped fresh chives
2 tsp chopped capers
2 tsp chopped gherkins
2 tsp freshly chopped parsley
1 tbsp lemon juice or tarragon vinegar

1 Put all the ingredients in a bowl and mix well.
2 Leave to stand for at least 1 hour before serving, to allow the flavours to blend.

Cook's Tip
Traditionally served with fried or poached fish.

NUTRITION PER TEASPOON
1 cal | 0g fat | trace carbs | trace salt ⓥ

Tomato Ketchup

Makes 1.1 litres (2 pints)
Preparation time 30 minutes
Cooking time 1 hour

2.7kg (6lb) ripe tomatoes, sliced
225g (8oz) sugar
300ml (½ pint) spiced vinegar (see Pickled Onions, page 482)
1 tbsp tarragon vinegar (optional)
a pinch of cayenne pepper
1 tsp paprika
1 tsp salt

1 Put the tomatoes in a pan and cook over a very low heat for about 45 minutes, stirring frequently, until they cook down to a pulp. Bring to the boil and cook rapidly, stirring frequently, until the pulp thickens.
2 Press the pulp through a nylon or stainless steel sieve, then return the pulp to the pan and stir in the remaining ingredients. Simmer gently until the mixture thickens.
3 Pour the ketchup into warm, sterilised bottles. Seal and label, and store in a cool, dark place for up to one year.

NUTRITION PER TEASPOON
24 cals | 0.1g fat (trace sats) | 6g carbs | 0.1g salt ⓥ

Fresh Pesto

Serves 4
Preparation time 10 minutes

50g (2oz) fresh basil leaves
1–2 garlic cloves
25g (1oz) pinenuts
6 tbsp extra virgin olive oil, plus extra to store
2 tbsp freshly grated Parmesan (see Vegetarian Cheeses, page 228)
a squeeze of lemon juice (optional)
salt and ground black pepper

1 Roughly tear the basil and put it into a mortar with the garlic, pinenuts and a little of the oil. Pound with a pestle to a paste. Alternatively, purée in a food processor to a fairly smooth paste.
2 Gradually work in the rest of the oil and season with salt and pepper to taste. Transfer to a bowl.
3 Stir in the Parmesan, check the seasoning and add a squeeze of lemon juice, if you like.

4 Store in a screw-topped jar, covered with a thin layer of oil, in the fridge for up to three days.

TRY SOMETHING DIFFERENT
Coriander Pesto Replace the basil with coriander leaves. Add 1 seeded and chopped chilli (see Cook's Tips, page 69) with the garlic, if you like. Omit the Parmesan.
Rocket Pesto Replace the basil with rocket leaves. Add 1 tbsp freshly chopped parsley at step 3.
Sun-dried Tomato Pesto Replace half the basil with 50g (2oz) sun-dried tomatoes in oil, drained and roughly chopped. Use a blender or food processor to work the ingredients together to a paste.

NUTRITION PER SERVING
250 cals | 26g fat (4g sats) | 1g carbs | 0.7g salt ⓥ

Salsa Verde

Serves 4
Preparation time 5 minutes

a small handful of fresh parsley, about 40g (1½oz)
6 tbsp fresh white breadcrumbs
5 tbsp olive oil
1 tsp capers, rinsed and drained
1 gherkin
2 tbsp lemon juice
1 tbsp snipped fresh chives
salt and ground black pepper

1 Put all the ingredients, except the seasoning, into a blender or food processor and process until they are thoroughly combined.
2 Turn into a bowl and season with salt and pepper to taste. Store in the fridge for up to five days.

Cook's Tip
This piquant, fresh-tasting sauce is good with pork schnitzel and grilled meats.

NUTRITION PER SERVING
190 cals | 17g fat (2g sats) | 8g carbs | 1g salt

Flavoured Butters

Serves 4
Preparation time 5 minutes

125g (4oz) unsalted butter, at room temperature
flavourings of your choice (see below)

1 Make sure the butter is at room temperature to make it easier to work. Beat in your chosen flavouring(s) by hand or using a food processor.
2 Turn on to clingfilm, shape into a log, wrap tightly and chill in the fridge for at least 1 hour.

Cook's Tip
A slice of flavoured butter makes an excellent quick alternative to sauces for serving with grilled meats, fish and all kinds of vegetables. They need to be prepared several hours in advance to allow time to chill and become firm enough to slice.

TRY SOMETHING DIFFERENT

Add the following flavourings to 125g (4oz) butter:
Anchovy Butter Add 6 mashed anchovy fillets.
Blue Cheese Butter Add 50g (2oz) blue cheese.
Citrus Butter Add the finely grated zest of 1 lemon, or 1 orange or 1 lime. Season with salt and pepper to taste.
Garlic Butter Add 1 crushed garlic clove and 2 tsp freshly chopped parsley or chervil.
Herb Butter Add 2 tbsp freshly chopped mixed herbs, such as flat-leafed parsley, chervil and tarragon, plus a squeeze of lemon juice.
Horseradish Butter Mix in 2 tbsp creamed horseradish.

Fresh Vanilla Custard

Serves 8
Preparation time 20 minutes
Cooking time 10 minutes, plus cooling if needed

600ml (1 pint) whole milk
1 vanilla pod, split lengthways, or 1 tsp vanilla extract
6 large egg yolks
2 tbsp golden caster sugar
2 tbsp cornflour

1 Pour the milk into a pan. Scrape the vanilla seeds into the milk and add the pod, or add the vanilla extract. Slowly bring to the boil. Turn off the heat immediately and set aside to infuse for 5 minutes. Remove the vanilla pod, rinse and dry, then put in a jar of sugar to make vanilla sugar.
2 Put the egg yolks, sugar and cornflour in a bowl and whisk together. Gradually whisk in the warm milk.
3 Rinse the pan and pour the mixture back in. Heat gently, whisking constantly, for 2–3 minutes until the custard thickens enough to thinly coat the back of a wooden spoon. Serve immediately or cover the surface closely with damp greaseproof paper, then cover with clingfilm and chill.

Cook's Tip
If you have prepared the custard in advance and want to serve it warm, microwave on medium for 2 minutes, stir, then microwave for a further 2 minutes.

NUTRITION PER SERVING
120 cals | 8g fat (3g sats) | 10g carbs | 0.1g salt Ⓥ

Sabayon Sauce

Serves 6
Preparation time 15 minutes
Cooking time about 10 minutes, plus chilling

75g (3oz) golden caster sugar
3 medium egg yolks
125ml (4fl oz) double cream
grated zest and juice of 1 lemon

1 Put the sugar and 125ml (4fl oz) water into a small pan over a low heat until the sugar has dissolved. Increase the heat to high and boil for 7–8 minutes or until the syrup registers 105°C/220°F on a sugar thermometer (and looks very syrupy with large pea-size bubbles).
2 Meanwhile, whisk the egg yolks in a small bowl until light and fluffy. Gradually pour in the hot syrup in a thin stream, whisking continuously. Continue to whisk until the mixture is thick, mousse-like and cool.
3 In a separate bowl, whip the cream until it forms stiff peaks, then add the lemon zest and juice, and whip again to form soft peaks. Gently fold the citrus cream into the mousse mixture.
4 Cover and chill in the fridge until required. Whisk well before serving.

Cook's Tip
Serve as an alternative to vanilla custard, with grilled fruit and other desserts.

NUTRITION PER SERVING
170 cals | 12g fat (6g sats) | 14g carbs | trace salt Ⓥ

Butterscotch Sauce

Serves 6–8
Preparation time 5 minutes
Cooking time 10 minutes

50g (2oz) butter
75g (3oz) light muscovado sugar
50g (2oz) golden caster sugar
150g (5oz) golden syrup
125ml (4fl oz) double cream
a few drops of vanilla extract
juice of ½ lemon

1 Put the butter, sugars and golden syrup in a heavy-based pan over a low heat and stir occasionally until melted together and smooth. Cook gently, stirring, for 5 minutes.
2 Take off the heat and slowly stir in the double cream. Add the vanilla extract and lemon juice. Stir over a low heat for 1–2 minutes until smooth. Serve hot or cold.

Cook's Tip
Serve poured over ice cream or steamed or baked puddings.

NUTRITION PER SERVING
230 cals | 12g fat (8g sats) | 32g carbs | 0.1g salt

Caramel Sauce

Serves 6
Preparation time 5 minutes
Cooking time 10 minutes

50g (2oz) golden caster sugar
150ml (¼ pint) double cream

1 Melt the sugar in a small heavy-based pan over a low heat until liquid and golden in colour. Increase the heat to medium and cook to a rich, dark caramel.
2 Immediately take off the heat and pour in the cream in a slow steady stream, taking care, as the hot caramel will cause the cream to boil up in the pan.
3 Stir over a gentle heat until the caramel has melted and the sauce is smooth. Serve hot or cold.

Cook's Tip
Serve poured over ice cream or steamed or baked puddings.

NUTRITION PER SERVING
150 cals | 12g fat (8g sats) | 9g carbs | trace salt Ⓥ

Rich Chocolate Sauce

Serves 6
Preparation time 5 minutes
Cooking time 5 minutes

125g (4oz) dark chocolate (at least 70% cocoa solids), broken into pieces
2 tbsp light muscovado sugar
25g (1oz) unsalted butter

1 Put the chocolate into a small pan with the sugar and 150ml (¼ pint) water. Stir over a low heat until the chocolate has melted and the sugar has dissolved, then bring to the boil, stirring constantly.
2 Simmer gently for 1 minute, then remove from the heat and stir in the butter until melted and combined.

TRY SOMETHING DIFFERENT
Chocolate and Grand Marnier Sauce Omit the sugar. Add 2 tbsp Grand Marnier (or other liqueur of your choice) to the sauce with the butter.

Cook's Tip
Serve poured over ice cream, profiteroles, or steamed or baked puddings.

NUTRITION PER SERVING
150 cals | 12g fat (6g sats) | 10g carbs | trace salt Ⓥ

Coffee Sauce

Serves 4
Preparation time 5 minutes
Cooking time 3 minutes

5 tsp instant coffee powder
1½ tsp arrowroot
175g can evaporated milk
2 tbsp light soft brown sugar

1 Mix the coffee powder and arrowroot to a smooth paste with a little water, then make up to 150ml (¼ pint) with more water.
2 Pour into a pan, add the evaporated milk and sugar, and slowly bring to the boil, stirring. Simmer for 1 minute.

Cook's Tip
Serve poured over ice cream, plain cakes, or steamed or baked puddings.

NUTRITION PER SERVING
102 cals | 4g fat (3g sats) | 14g carbs | 0.2g salt Ⓥ

Lemon or Orange Sauce

Serves 4
Preparation time 10 minutes
Cooking time 15 minutes, plus cooling

grated zest and juice of 1 large lemon or orange
1 tbsp cornflour
2 tbsp sugar
a knob of butter
1 medium egg yolk (optional)

1 Put the fruit zest and juice in a pan and make up to 300ml (½ pint) with water. Put the cornflour and sugar in a bowl and add just enough of the liquid to make a smooth cream.
2 Bring the remaining liquid to the boil, then pour on to the blended mixture, stirring constantly. Put back in the pan and bring to the boil over a low heat, stirring until the sauce thickens and clears. Add the butter.
3 Cool, then beat in the egg yolk, if you like, and reheat, stirring, without boiling.

Cook's Tip
Serve the sauce with pancakes, plain cakes or steamed or baked puddings.

NUTRITION PER SERVING
91 cals | 3g fat (2g sats) | 15g carbs | trace salt Ⓥ

Raspberry Coulis

Serves 4
Preparation time 10 minutes, plus chilling

225g (8oz) raspberries
2 tbsp Kirsch or framboise eau de vie (optional)
icing sugar to taste

1 Put the raspberries into a blender or food processor with the Kirsch or eau de vie, if you like. Whiz until they are completely puréed.
2 Transfer the purée to a fine sieve, and press and scrape it through the sieve until nothing is left but the pips.
3 Sweeten with icing sugar to taste and chill until needed.

TRY SOMETHING DIFFERENT
Use different soft fruits and liqueurs; for example, try crème de cassis with blackcurrants or Amaretto with apricots.

Cook's Tip
Serve with ice cream or meringues.

NUTRITION PER SERVING
32 cals | trace fat (trace sats) | 6g carbs | trace salt Ⓥ

Chantilly Cream

Serves 8
Preparation time 10 minutes, plus chilling

300ml (10½fl oz) double cream
1 tbsp golden caster sugar
finely grated zest of 1 orange (optional)

1 Whip the cream with the sugar until it forms soft peaks. Fold in half the grated orange zest, if you like. Cover and chill until needed.
2 Serve the Chantilly Cream sprinkled with the remaining orange zest, if you like.

Cook's Tips
• Use to sandwich meringues or serve with fruit and jelly.
• Flavour the Chantilly Cream with 2 tbsp Grand Marnier to serve with Christmas pudding.

NUTRITION PER SERVING
180 cals | 17g fat (12g sats) | 4g carbs | trace salt

Crème Pâtissière

Makes 450ml (¾ pint)
Preparation time 15 minutes, plus infusing
Cooking time 5 minutes, plus cooling

300ml (½ pint) milk
1 vanilla pod, split lengthways, or 1 tsp vanilla extract
3 medium egg yolks, beaten
50g (2oz) golden caster sugar
2 tbsp plain flour
2 tbsp cornflour

1 Pour the milk into a heavy-based pan. Scrape the vanilla seeds into the milk and add the pod, or add the vanilla extract. Slowly bring to the boil, take off the heat and leave to infuse for 10 minutes. Discard the pod (or rinse and dry and use to flavour vanilla sugar).
2 Meanwhile, whisk the egg yolks and sugar together in a bowl until thick and creamy, then whisk in the flour and cornflour until smooth. Gradually whisk in the hot milk, then strain back into the pan.
3 Slowly bring to the boil, whisking constantly. Cook, stirring, for 2–3 minutes until thickened and smooth.
4 Pour into a bowl, cover the surface with a round of wet greaseproof paper and leave to cool.

Cook's Tip
Use as a filling for fruit flans and other pastries.

NUTRITION PER SERVING
120 cals | 4g fat (2g sats) | 8g carbs | trace salt Ⓥ

Brandy Butter

Serves 8
Preparation time 10 minutes, plus chilling

150g (5oz) unsalted butter, at room temperature
150g (5oz) golden icing sugar, sifted
3 tbsp brandy

1 Put the butter into a bowl and whisk to soften. Gradually whisk in the icing sugar, pouring in the brandy just before the final addition. Continue whisking until the mixture is pale and fluffy, then spoon into a serving dish.
2 Cover and chill until needed. Remove from the fridge 30 minutes before serving.

TRY SOMETHING DIFFERENT
Rum Butter Cream 75g (3oz) butter until pale and soft. Gradually beat 75g (3oz) soft brown sugar into the butter, then add 4 tbsp rum a few drops at a time, taking care not to allow the mixture to curdle. Finally stir in the grated zest of ½ lemon and a squeeze of lemon juice. The finished sauce should be pale and frothy.

Cook's Tips
• Serve with Christmas pudding.
• For a light, fluffy texture, whisk the brandy butter using an electric mixer just before serving.

NUTRITION PER SERVING
230 cals | 16g fat (10g sats) | 20g carbs | 0.3g salt Ⓥ

Dressings

A salad is rarely complete without a dressing. Whether it's a piquant vinaigrette, a creamy mayonnaise or just a squeeze of lemon or lime juice, it is invariably the dressing that pulls all the ingredients together.

There are two main types of salad dressings: oil and vinegar or citrus dressings, and creamy dressings, which are usually mayonnaise-based. The proportion of oil to vinegar in the former is largely a matter of personal taste. In general, about six parts oil to one part vinegar works best, but if you prefer a more acidic dressing, perhaps four parts oil to one part vinegar.

Oils and vinegars form the basis of most salad dressings. For best results, use the correct oil, and/or vinegar, for the particular dressing.

Oils and Vinegars

OLIVE OIL

Olive oil comes in a range of flavours and styles, from zingy, pungent extra virgin to light, mild olive oil. Extra virgin olive oil – cold pressed and from a single estate – is the premium type. A good extra virgin olive oil can be used with great effect in salads. It is particularly good drizzled liberally over raw vegetables, tomatoes or salad leaves, with just a little lemon juice or balsamic vinegar. Light or mild olive oil is the best choice for making mayonnaise, where extra virgin oil would be too overpowering.

FLAVOURED OILS

These add character to salad dressings. You can buy ready-made flavoured oils or make your own. Try the following simple ideas:
Fresh herb oil needs to be used within a day so only make it in small quanities. To make this, put 15g (½oz) freshly chopped mixed herbs (such as basil, chervil, chives and parsley) in a bowl, pour on 150ml (¼ pint) extra virgin olive oil and set aside to infuse for 2–3 hours.
Chilli and garlic oil will spike up a salad. To prepare, put the peeled cloves from a whole head of garlic into a small pan with 300ml (½ pint) mild olive oil and 1 small red chilli, seeded and very finely chopped (see Cook's Tips page 69). Heat gently for 5–6 minutes until the garlic is golden. Cool, then strain into a clean bottle.

NUT OILS These are excellent in salads. Ranging from mild to strong, they include groundnut or peanut, hazelnut, walnut, almond and sesame oils. Sesame oil is used in very small amounts, often blended with groundnut or even vegetable oil.

BALSAMIC VINEGAR

Dark and aromatic, this Italian vinegar has an exquisite mellow, sweet and sour flavour and lends a good depth and character to salad dressings. Traditionally matured in oak casks for anything between five and` 20 years, balsamic vinegar is expensive, but a little goes a long way – a few drops can transform a salad.

CIDER VINEGAR

This is milder than wine vinegar and works well in salad dressings where a subtle acidity is required.

FLAVOURED VINEGAR

Wine vinegars can be flavoured with aromatic herbs, fruits, spices, and even flower petals. Better wine vinegars, such as Champagne and sherry vinegars, need nothing to enhance their natural flavours. Of the fruit vinegars, raspberry vinegar is the most popular, although you can also buy strawberry, blackberry and peach vinegars. To make your own herb vinegar, immerse a few herb sprigs, such as rosemary or thyme, in a bottle of red or white wine vinegar, or cider vinegar. Leave in a cool, dark place to infuse for two to three weeks. Strain and re-bottle, adding a fresh herb sprig, if you like.

WINE VINEGAR

This is the strongest natural vinegar, with an average acidity of 6.5 per cent, and contains no preservatives. Special varieties include pale yellow Champagne vinegar, Rioja red wine vinegar with a deep mellow flavour, and full-bodied, nutty brown sherry vinegar.

French Dressing

Makes 100ml (3½fl oz)
Preparation time 10 minutes

1 tsp Dijon mustard
a pinch of sugar
1 tbsp white or red wine vinegar
90ml (6 tbsp) extra virgin olive oil
salt and ground black pepper

1 Whisk the mustard, sugar, vinegar and seasoning together in a bowl, then gradually whisk in the olive oil until the dressing is amalgamated and thickened.

TRY SOMETHING DIFFERENT

Balsamic Dressing Omit the mustard and sugar. Use balsamic vinegar instead of wine vinegar.
Garlic Dressing Whisk 1 crushed garlic clove into the dressing.
Herb Dressing Use only ½ tsp mustard. Replace the vinegar with lemon juice and add 2 tbsp freshly chopped mixed herbs, such as parsley, chervil and chives.
Honey and Lemon Dressing Use lemon juice instead of vinegar, 1 tsp clear honey in place of the sugar, and wholegrain rather than Dijon mustard.

Cook's Tip
Instead of whisking, just put all the ingredients in a screw-topped jar and shake well to combine.

NUTRITION PER SERVING
110 cals | 11g fat (2g sats) | trace carbs | 0.4g salt (V)

Mayonnaise

Makes 300ml (½ pint)
Preparation time 10 minutes

2 medium egg yolks, at room temperature
2 tsp lemon juice or white wine vinegar
1 tsp Dijon mustard
a pinch of sugar
300ml (½ pint) light olive oil
salt and ground black pepper

1 Put all the ingredients except the oil and seasoning into a food processor or blender. Season, then blend briefly until pale and creamy.
2 With the motor running, pour the olive oil through the feeder tube in a steady stream until the mayonnaise thickens. Thin to the required consistency, if necessary, with a little hot water.
3 Store the mayonnaise in a screw-topped jar in the fridge for up to three days.

TRY SOMETHING DIFFERENT

Aïoli Put 4 crushed garlic cloves into the processor with the egg yolks, 1 tbsp lemon juice and ½ tsp salt and process, as in step 1, until evenly combined. Continue as step 2.
Garlic and Basil Mayonnaise Add 1 crushed garlic clove at step 1. Fold 2 tbsp freshly shredded basil into the mayonnaise at the end.
Herb Mayonnaise Fold in 2 tbsp freshly chopped herbs, such as chives, chervil, basil, tarragon or coriander.
Lemon Mayonnaise Use lemon juice rather than wine vinegar. Add 1 tsp grated lemon zest and an extra 1 tbsp lemon juice at the end.
Mustard Mayonnaise Stir in 4 tbsp Dijon mustard at the end of the recipe.
Thousand Island Dressing Add 2 tsp tomato purée, 2 tbsp chopped stuffed olives, 2 tsp finely chopped onion, 1 chopped hard-boiled egg and 1 tbsp chopped parsley to the finished mayonnaise.

Cook's Tips
• The ingredients must be at room temperature.
• If eggs are used straight from the fridge the mayonnaise is liable to curdle.
• To make mayonnaise by hand, mix the egg yolks, mustard, sugar and seasoning in a bowl, then whisk in the oil, a drop at a time to begin with, then in a slow, steady stream. Finally, add the lemon juice or vinegar.

NUTRITION PER SERVING
110 cals | 12g fat (2g sats) | trace carbs | 0.2g salt

Herbs, Spices and Flavourings

Herbs

Fresh herbs lend a superb flavour to all kinds of dish. Their flavour is derived from essential oils in the leaves and stems, which are released when the herb is heated, crushed or chopped. Herbs may be chopped before they are added to a dish, or used whole. The more delicate herbs, such as parsley, chervil and tarragon, should be added towards the end of cooking, while tougher varieties, such as rosemary and thyme, are added at the start. Ideally, pick fresh herbs just before using, or use soon after purchase.

Dried herbs work well in cooked dishes, such as casseroles, but they are generally not suitable for use in salads. Dried herbs have a stronger flavour than fresh ones and should be used more sparingly: if substituting dried for fresh herbs, use one-third of the amount specified. Dried herbs keep best in airtight jars away from the light. They will retain their flavour for about six months.

Angelica
All parts of this tall plant are used for flavouring, although only the young candied stem is available commercially. Crystallised angelica stems are used to decorate cakes, pastries and desserts. The root is good for stewing with acid fruits such as rhubarb. Angelica leaves can be chopped and used to flavour salads or fish dishes.

Basil
This popular Italian herb has a distinctive aroma and flavour. The delicate leaves are easily bruised by chopping, so it's better to tear or shred them with your fingers. Basil has a natural affinity with tomatoes, but goes well with most salads, grilled meat and green vegetables. It also forms the basis of the classic Italian sauce, pesto. This herb has a short growing period during the summer and needs plenty of sun, but it is sold fresh all year round.

Bay leaves
Shiny and smooth, bay leaves are highly aromatic, so one or two leaves are sufficient to flavour a dish. Bay leaves are used in marinades, casseroles, soups and stocks, and to flavour infusions of milk for use in sauces such as béchamel. Bay is one of the classic ingredients of a bouquet garni. You can buy sprigs, freeze them in a plastic bag and use straight from the freezer.

Chervil
A delicate, sweet-flavoured herb with attractive serrated leaves, chervil is used in a similar way to the more popular herb, parsley. It will enhance many vegetables, especially new potatoes, as well as all kinds of salads, and egg, cheese, fish and chicken dishes. Chervil is also one of the classic components of the French *fines herbes*. It is an excellent choice as a flavouring for butter sauces, such as hollandaise, and makes a pretty garnish.

Chive
This member of the onion family has long narrow, green leaves and purple flowers. The leaves are used to flavour salads, sauces and dressings, and as a garnish. A hardy perennial, this herb is easy to grow in the garden and in containers. To use, snip the chives into short lengths with scissors.

Coriander
Pungent and intensely flavoured, this herb is an important culinary flavouring, especially in Indian and Thai dishes. It is sold in pots, bunches and packs. It resembles flat-leafed parsley but has more rounded leaves. The plant is also grown commercially for its seeds, which taste quite different and are used as a spice. Aromatic coriander leaves are often used with spices, especially in Middle Eastern, Asian and Mexican dishes, as well as in salads and soups.

Curry leaves
These shiny, spiky leaves have a fresh-tasting flavour akin to curry powder. They are used as a herb in cooking, most often added whole, but sometimes chopped first. Curry leaves often feature in curries from southern India, and the fresh or dried leaves can be used sparingly to flavour soups and stews. Sold fresh in bunches, curry leaves can be frozen in a plastic bag, and added to dishes as and when required.

Dill
This fragrant hardy annual is grown for its feathery leaves (also known as dill weed) and for its seeds, which are dried and used as a spice. Dill leaves have a slightly sharp, yet sweet flavour, which complements fish and shellfish dishes perfectly, and it is the classic flavouring in gravad lax (Scandinavian smoked salmon). Dill is also added to salads, omelettes, chicken dishes and used as a garnish.

Fennel
This herb resembles dill and is a member of the same family, but it has a sweet anise flavour, which is quite different. Both the feathery leaves and seeds are used. Fennel is a classical flavouring for fish – especially oily fish, as it counteracts the richness. It also works well in marinades, soups and vegetable dishes.

Lemongrass
A tall, hard grass with pale green leaves, lemongrass has a distinctive lemony aroma and taste. It is used in Thai and other South-east Asian dishes to flavour soups, chicken, fish and meat dishes, and can also be used to flavour puddings. The stems are usually bruised to release their flavour and added whole before cooking, then removed. Or, the tough outer leaves are removed and the rest chopped. Dried and powdered lemongrass is also available.

Lime leaves, kaffir
The leaves of the kaffir lime tree have a highly aromatic lime flavour and are frequently used in Thai and Malaysian dishes. They are available from selected supermarkets and Asian food stores, and freeze successfully.

Lovage
This herb has an intense peppery flavour, akin to celery. Lovage leaves are best used sparingly to enhance the flavour of robust soups and meat stews. A little chopped lovage will add an unusual tang to salads and cold roast beef sandwiches.

Marjoram
There are three forms of this aromatic herb: sweet marjoram, pot marjoram and wild marjoram, which is better known as oregano. Pot marjoram has a more powerful flavour than sweet marjoram but it is used in a similar way: to flavour pizzas, savoury flans, sausages, marinades, stuffings and roasts, such as game and pork. It is also good to add flavour to vegetables.

Mint
Among the many mints available are peppermint, spearmint, pineapple mint, lemon mint and apple mint. Most varieties have a powerful flavour and should be used sparingly. Mint is the perfect partner to potatoes, peas and many other vegetables, and fresh mint sauce or jelly is the classic accompaniment to lamb. The leaves are used to embellish wine and fruit cups, fruit salads and other desserts. It is widely available and very easy to grow.

Mixed herbs, dried
Sold in jars, mixed dried herbs are used for seasoning soups and casseroles. The combination usually includes parsley, sage, thyme, marjoram and tarragon. Dried herbs are only suitable for adding to dishes at the start of cooking.

Oregano (wild marjoram)
Also called wild marjoram, the herb oregano and its close relative, marjoram, are largely interchangeable in dishes, although oregano is more aromatic and strongly flavoured. It is used with meat, sausages, soups, pizzas, pasta sauces and other Italian dishes, tomatoes, in salads, with cooked vegetables, and in egg and cheese dishes.

Parsley
Both the flat-leafed and curly-leafed varieties of this common herb are widely available. Flat-leafed parsley has a more pronounced flavour and is generally preferred. Parsley stalks are always included in a bouquet garni and chopped parsley is a classic ingredient of *fines herbes*. Chopped parsley leaves are used in all kinds of savoury dishes, including sauces, soups, salads, stuffings and herb butters, with vegetables, chicken, ham, fish and shellfish, and also as an attractive garnish.

Rosemary
This pungent herb with its spiky leaves is the classic partner to lamb. Rosemary sprigs are usually added whole to a dish and taken out before serving, for a more subtle flavour. Finely chopped leaves are used sparingly, and usually as the sole herb. Rosemary sprigs are used in marinades for meat, fish and poultry, and to flavour roast and barbecued meats. Finely chopped rosemary can be added to pizza and bread doughs, stuffings, cakes and biscuits.

Sage
This soft-leafed herb has a strong, distinctive taste. Garden sage has pale grey-green leaves, but there are many other varieties, including purple sage and variegated sage. It is the classic flavouring for roast pork, and is used to enhance other meat dishes, especially liver and sausages, casseroles, stuffings, salads, egg and cheese dishes. As it has a powerful flavour, sage should be used sparingly. Melted butter flavoured with fresh sage leaves is delicious on pasta, gnocchi and vegetables.

Tarragon
Of the two main species of this herb, French tarragon is far superior in flavour and texture to the Russian variety. Tarragon is a strongly flavoured herb with important culinary uses. It is a component of *fines herbes* and is often added to tartare, hollandaise and béarnaise sauces. Tarragon is also used to flavour wine vinegar, marinades, fish and chicken dishes, savoury butters and sauces.

Thyme
Of the many varieties of this important herb, garden and lemon thyme are the most common. Thyme has a distinctive flavour and is one of the classic ingredients in a bouquet garni. It can be rubbed over beef and lamb before roasting, and used to flavour casseroles, soups, stuffings, bread sauce, carrots, onions and mushrooms. Lemon thyme is especially good in stuffings, and in fish dishes. Thyme is also used to flavour oils and vinegars.

Aromatics

GARLIC

Although not a herb, garlic is an important aromatic flavouring, often used in conjunction with fresh herbs. It is the most pungent member of the onion family. There are three main varieties: white, red and pinkish-purple. Garlic is widely used to enhance the flavour of savoury dishes. Raw garlic is used in marinades, salads and dressings. During cooking, the flavour of garlic becomes mellow and sweet. Choose firm garlic bulbs and pull off individual cloves as required.

Spices

Most spices come from hot countries. They are the dried parts of aromatic plants and may be the fruit, bark, seed, root or flower bud. Once rare and expensive commodities, they are now everyday flavouring ingredients. Most spices are sold dried, either whole or ground.

For optimum flavour, buy whole spices and grind them yourself – using a pestle and mortar, or an electric spice grinder – rather than buying ready-ground spices. If possible, grind the spice just before use. An electric coffee grinder can be used, but should then be reserved for this purpose. An electric blender is suitable for larger quantities. Ground spices may be fried in oil before adding other ingredients such as vegetables and meat.

Buy spices in small quantities, as their flavour deteriorates relatively quickly. Keep them in small, airtight glass jars, coloured if possible, and away from light, as this adversely affects their flavour. Discard any that are not used within a year of purchase.

Dry-frying spices

Spices are often toasted in a dry heavy-based frying pan to mellow their flavour and lose any raw taste. They can be dry-fried individually or as mixtures. Put the hardest ones, such as fenugreek, into the pan first and add softer ones, like coriander and cumin, after a minute or so. Stir until evenly browned. Cool, then grind, or crush.

Allspice
Also called Jamaica pepper, allspice is sold as small dried berries or ready ground. The whole spice is an ingredient of pickling spice. It tastes like a mixture of cloves, cinnamon and nutmeg. Allspice can be used whole in marinades, meat dishes, pickles, chutneys and with poached fish. Ground allspice is added to meat and vegetable dishes, cakes, milk puddings and fruit pies.

Aniseed (anise)
These small seeds have a strong, distinctive flavour. They are used mainly to flavour cakes and biscuits, but also in salad dressings, with red cabbage, in cheese, fish and shellfish dishes. Aniseed is the main flavouring in Pernod, anisette and ouzo.

Caraway seeds
These small brown seeds have a sharp, liquorice-like taste that is widely appreciated in central European and Jewish cookery. Caraway seeds are primarily used for flavouring cakes, biscuits and breads; they also add flavour to sauerkraut, vegetables, cheese dishes, sausages and pork.

Cardamom
Available both as small green and large black pods containing seeds, cardamom has a strong aromatic quality and should be used sparingly. Add cardamom pods whole and remove before serving, or extract the seeds and use these whole or grind them to a powder just before use. Cardamom is a component of most curry powders. It is also used in pickles, beef and pork dishes, with roasted vegetables, to infuse custards and rice puddings, and in baking.

Cayenne
This spice is made from small, hot, dried red chillies. It is always sold ground as cayenne pepper and is sweet, pungent and very hot. Use it sparingly to flavour meats, barbecue sauces, eggs, fish, vegetables, cheese sauces, pastry and vegetable soups. Unlike paprika, cayenne pepper cannot be used for colouring as its flavour is too pronounced.

Chilli powder/chilli seasoning
Fiery hot chilli powder is a spice that is used cautiously in Mexican dishes, Indian curries, pickles, chutneys, ketchups, soups, tomato dishes, casseroles, spaghetti and meat sauces. Some brands, often called mild chilli powder or chilli seasoning, are a mixture of chilli and other flavourings, such as cumin, oregano, salt and garlic; these are therefore considerably less fiery than hot chilli powder. Adjust the quantity you add to dishes accordingly.

Cinnamon
The dried, rolled bark of a tropical evergreen tree, cinnamon is available as sticks and powdered. It has a sweet, pungent flavour. Cinnamon sticks have a more pronounced flavour than the powder, but they are difficult to grind at home, so buy ready-ground cinnamon for use in sweet, spicy baking. Use cinnamon sticks to flavour meat casseroles, vegetable dishes, chutneys and pickles, with chocolate and to infuse fruit compotes, custards, hot drinks, mulled wine and fruit punches.

Cloves
Sold whole and ground, cloves have a distinctive, pungent flavour. They are used mainly to flavour apple dishes, Christmas pudding, mincemeat, bread sauce, pumpkin, mulled wine, and to stud whole baked gammon and onions. In general, whole cloves are best removed from a dish before serving.

Coriander seeds
The mild, sweet, orangey flavour of coriander seeds tastes quite different from the herb. Sold whole or ground, coriander is an ingredient of most curry powders and of pickling spice. It is a typical flavouring in many spicy Moroccan, Middle Eastern and Indian meat and vegetable dishes. It is also very good in home-made chutneys and pickles.

Cumin seeds
The strong, slightly bitter taste of cumin is improved by toasting. Sold whole as seeds, or ground, cumin is an ingredient of curry powders and some chilli powder mixtures. Cumin is also used to flavour pickles, chutneys, cheese dishes, soups, cabbage, rice, Middle Eastern dishes, marinades and fruit pies.

Curry pastes
These ready-made mixtures contain spices, fresh chillies, onion, ginger and oil. Many different varieties of curry pastes are available, including Thai red curry paste and special Indian curry pastes.

Curry powder
Bought curry powders are readily available, but for optimum flavour make your own.
Put the following spices into an electric blender or grinder: 1 tbsp each cumin and fenugreek seeds; ½ tsp mustard seeds; 1½ tsp each black peppercorns, poppy seeds and ground ginger; 4 tbsp coriander seeds; ½ tsp hot chilli powder and 2 tbsp ground turmeric. Grind to a fine powder. Store the curry powder in an airtight container and use within one month.

Fenugreek seeds
Small, hard fenugreek seeds have a distinctive aroma and slightly harsh, hot flavour. An ingredient of commercial curry powders, fenugreek is also used in chutneys, pickles and sauces, but rarely as the only spice.

Five-spice powder
A powerful, pungent ground mixture of star anise, Szechuan pepper, fennel seeds, cloves and cinnamon or cassia, five-spice powder is used sparingly in Chinese cooking. It is added to Chinese red-cooked meats, roast meat and poultry, marinades and stir-fries.

Garam masala
Sold ready prepared, this Indian spice mix is aromatic rather than hot. To make your own garam masala, grind together 10 green cardamom pods, 1 tbsp black peppercorns and 2 tsp cumin seeds.

Ginger

The root of ginger has a hot, fairly sweet taste and is sold in various forms as fresh root ginger or dried, and in dried ground form. Root ginger needs to be cooked to release its true flavour – peel, slice and use in curries, sauces, chutneys and in Chinese cooking. Ground ginger is used in curries, sauces, preserves, cakes as well as sprinkled on melon. Stem ginger is also preserved in syrup or crystallised and used to flavour sweet dishes.

Harissa

A hot mixture of chilli and up to 20 spices, harissa can be bought in powder and paste form.

To make harissa: grill 2 red peppers until charred, cool, then skin, core and seed. Put 4 seeded, roughly chopped red chillies into a food processor with 6 peeled garlic cloves, 1 tbsp ground coriander and 1 tbsp caraway seeds. Process to a rough paste. Add the grilled peppers, 2 tsp salt and 4 tbsp olive oil. Whiz until smooth. Store in a screw-topped jar, covered with a thin layer of olive oil. Use within two weeks.

Horseradish

A root of the mustard family, horseradish has a hot, biting, pungent taste and is used raw, but sparingly. It is sold ready-grated in jars. Creamed horseradish is the classic relish for roast beef and is excellent with oily fish; it is sold in jars or you can make your own (see page 21).

Juniper berries

These small purple-black berries have a distinctive scent, with a hint of pine. They should be crushed before being added to a dish to release their maximum flavour. Use juniper berries with game, venison, pork, in marinades and casseroles with those ingredients, and in pâtés and sauerkraut. Juniper is also a flavouring agent in gin.

Mace

The outer covering of the nutmeg, mace is bright red when harvested and dries to a deep orange colour. It is sold as blades (useful for infusing) or ground. It has a sweeter, more delicate flavour than nutmeg but it is more expensive. Use mace in mulled wine and punches, potted meat, fish dishes, béchamel sauce, soups, meat stews, milk puddings and fruit compotes.

Mustard seeds

There are three types of mustard seed: black, brown and white (or yellow). The darker seeds are the more pungent. Most ready-prepared mustards are a combination of the three. The seeds are either left whole (as in wholegrain mustard) or ground, then mixed with liquid such as wine, vinegar or cider. English mustard is sold dry as well as ready-mixed. As a condiment, mustard is served with sausages, steaks, ham, gammon and cheese; it is also used to flavour dressings and sauces.

Nutmeg

This seed of the nutmeg fruit has a distinctive, nutty flavour. It is sold whole or ground, but is best bought whole, as the flavour of freshly grated nutmeg is far superior. Use it in creamy soups; sprinkled on buttered corn, spinach, carrots and beans; in cheese dishes; with chicken and veal; in custards, milk puddings, Christmas pudding, biscuits and cakes.

Paprika

A sweet mild spice, paprika is always sold ground to a red powder. It is good for adding colour to pale egg and cheese dishes. Some varieties, particularly Hungarian, are hotter than others. Use it in salads, fish, meat and chicken dishes, with veagetables, on canapés and in goulash. Produced from oak-smoked red peppers, smoked paprika has an intense flavour and a wonderful smoky aroma, which lends an authentic flavour to paella; it is also excellent with potatoes, fish and chicken dishes.

Pepper

There are several forms: green, black and white. Green or unripe berries have a mild flavour and are used whole in pâtés, with duck and other rich meats, in casseroles and sauces. They are sometimes lightly crushed. Black pepper has a strong, pungent, hot flavour and is best used freshly ground to season dishes. White pepper is more aromatic and less hot in flavour. Its main use is in light-coloured dishes and sauces that would be spoiled by dark flecks.

Pink peppercorns
Unrelated to the pepper plant, pink peppercorns are the dried berries of a shrub from South America. These attractive, peppery berries are used in small quantities to flavour pâtés, poultry and game dishes. If consumed in large quantities, they are mildly toxic.

Poppy seeds
The small hard, black seeds from the opium poppy, poppy seeds have a nutty flavour and no narcotic effect. Poppy seeds are used to add flavour and enhance the appearance of breads, biscuits and cakes; dips and spreads; salads and dressings; they are also used in curry powder. Creamy-coloured poppy seeds are also available.

Saffron
The most expensive of all spices, saffron is the dried stigma of the saffron crocus flower. It has a subtle flavour and aroma, and imparts a hint of yellow to foods. Powdered saffron is available, but it is the whole stigmas, called saffron strands or threads, which give the best results. A generous pinch is all that is needed to flavour and colour dishes such as bouillabaisse, chicken soup, rice, paella, fish sauces, breads and cakes.

Star anise
Attractive, dried, star-shaped fruit of an evergreen tree native to China, star anise is red-brown in colour with a pungent aniseed flavour. It is used whole to flavour Chinese meat stews and steamed fish. One star anise is sufficient to flavour a large quantity. Ground star anise should be used sparingly; it is a component of Chinese five-spice powder.

Szechuan pepper
Also called anise pepper, this hot aromatic spice is made from the dried red berries of a Chinese tree. It is one of the ingredients of Chinese five-spice powder.

Tamarind
Dark brown, with a fresh, acidic flavour, tamarind is the pulp that surrounds the seeds within the large pods of the Indian tamarind tree. It is sold dried and compressed into blocks. To use, break off pieces and soak 1 tbsp dried tamarind pulp in 4 tbsp warm water for 20 minutes, then strain the liquid through a sieve, pressing to extract the juice. Use to add a sour flavour to chutneys, sauces and curries. Ready-made tamarind paste is available in jars from larger supermarkets.

Turmeric
This bright spice resembles ginger and is a member of the same family, although it is rarely available fresh. The orange flesh is commonly dried, then ground and sold in powdered form. Turmeric powder has an aromatic, slightly bitter flavour and should be used sparingly in curry powder, pickles, relishes and rice dishes.

Vanilla
These pods are the long, thin, dried, black seed pods of a climbing orchid, which are sold whole. Natural vanilla extract is also obtainable. You can also buy vanilla bean paste: pure vanilla with natural vanilla seeds in a paste form. To release the seeds from the pod, slit the pod in half lengthways, then run the point of a knife along the central core to extract the seeds. To make vanilla sugar, leave a vanilla pod in a jar of caster sugar to impart its flavour. To flavour custards, sweet sauces, ice creams and other creamy desserts, put a whole or split pod in the milk or cream to infuse. The vanilla pod can be rinsed, dried and used again.

Flavourings and Essences

Included here are a selection of common bottled flavourings and essences, although wines and other alcoholic drinks also have a culinary role. True essences are made by naturally extracting the flavour from the food itself; flavourings are synthetic and tend to be cheaper and more potent. Both flavourings and essences are intensely flavoured and frequently only a few drops are needed in a recipe.

Almond essence

Made from bitter almonds, this is used in baking, usually to reinforce the flavour of almonds in the recipe. Synthetic flavouring is widely available, but most supermarkets stock real almond essence, which is far superior.

Angostura bitters

Its secret formula includes cinnamon, cloves, citrus peel, nutmeg, prunes, quinine and rum. Used to flavour drinks and aperitifs, such as Pimm's, it can also be added to casseroles, fruit salads, puddings and cakes.

Orange flower water

This potent, colourless flavouring liquid is distilled from the flowers of the Seville orange. Orange flower water is used sparingly to flavour cakes, biscuits, pastries and desserts.

Oyster sauce

A thick, dark brown Chinese sauce, which is both sweet and salty. It is widely used in Asian dishes, especially stir-fries, and is available from supermarkets as well as Asian stores.

Peppermint oil

Similar to peppermint essence, peppermint oil is made from the concentrated oil from the natural plant. The oil is mostly used for making sweets.

Plum sauce

Chinese plum sauce is made from plums, vinegar, salt and sugar. It has a sweet, salty and fruity flavour and is traditionally served with Peking duck, or as a dipping sauce with crispy deep-fried snacks.

Rose water

A highly fragrant rose-flavoured water, which is either distilled from rose petals or prepared from rose oil. It is used sparingly in baking and desserts, Turkish delight and other Middle Eastern recipes.

Soy sauce

A light or dark brown sauce with a salty, sweetish taste, made from boiled and fermented soya beans and used in Asian cookery. Light soy sauce is lighter and less salty and strong. Japanese soy sauce is light and refined.

Tabasco

This fiery hot sauce is based on red chillies, spirit vinegar and salt, and prepared to a secret recipe. A dash of Tabasco may be used to add a kick to soups, casseroles, sauces, rice dishes and tomato-based drinks.

Tahini

A creamy-textured paste, tahini is made from finely ground sesame seeds. It is widely used in Middle Eastern dishes and is sold in jars in larger supermarkets and delicatessens.

Thai fish sauce

Known as nam pla in Thailand, this highly pungent sauce adds a distinctive taste to Asian dishes. It is obtainable from most supermarkets, although light soy sauce can be substituted if necessary.

Vanilla extract

True vanilla extract is taken from vanilla pods and is superior to the widely available vanilla flavouring, made from an ingredient in clove oil. It is used to enhance sweet dishes, sometimes to bring out the flavour of chocolate.

Soups

Soups

There is nothing quite as comforting as a flavourful home-made soup that makes the most of seasonal ingredients. The secret of a great-tasting soup is invariably a well-flavoured home-made stock, but if you are short of time, use one of the fresh stock products available from supermarkets. Chunky hot soups are the obvious choice for winter starters, and several of the recipes in this chapter are substantial enough to serve as a meal in themselves – especially if you increase the quantities and serve them with lots of warm, crusty bread. For summer starters, choose lighter soups – a chilled soup is the ideal refreshing choice for a hot day. For best results, use really fresh ingredients in prime condition. A blender or a food processor is a great help when making creamy soups.

Garnishes and accompaniments

Adding a complementary finishing touch will enhance the flavour as well as the appearance of a fresh soup. Smooth soups, in particular, benefit from a contrasting swirl of cream or crème fraîche and, perhaps, a sprinkling of pepper or paprika.

Top robust soups with Parmesan shavings or a sprinkling of freshly grated Gruyère, Parmesan, Pecorino or Cheddar cheese. Try stirring a spoonful of Fresh Pesto (see page 22) into hearty vegetable potages; this also works well with tomato soups. Ring the changes with classic, sun-dried tomato, coriander or rocket pesto.

Citrus butters make a tasty garnish (see page 23). Thinly slice the butter and top each portion of soup with a few slices – it will melt deliciously into the soup as you serve it.

Croûtons

This classic garnish for soups is very easy to make. Remove the crusts from 3 or 4 thick slices of day-old white bread, then cut into 2.5cm (1in) squares. Heat a 2.5cm (1in) depth of oil in a frying pan, then fry the bread cubes, turning constantly, until crisp and golden. Remove and drain on kitchen paper.

Use flavoured bread, such as walnut or sun-dried tomato bread, to make savoury croûtons. Preheat the oven to 200°C (180°C fan oven) mark 6. Toss the flavoured bread cubes in oil – such as walnut or sun-dried tomato (from a jar of sun-dried tomatoes) – and put into a shallow roasting tin. Bake in the oven for 15 minutes or until golden, then drain on kitchen paper.

Chunky bread slices can also be just toasted and then cut into cubes. Croûtons can be prepared ahead, allowed to cool, then stored in an airtight container.

To serve, warm through in the oven.

Fresh herbs

A simple sprinkling of fresh herbs will enliven most soups. Fresh herb flowers can also make a pretty and unusual garnish. Chop the herbs just before serving, and choose a herb that complements that flavour of the soup – for example, basil with tomato, chives with creamy soups, or coriander with Asian-style soups.

Melba toast

This wafer-thin, brittle toast is traditionally served with soups and pâtés. Preheat the oven to 180°C (160°C fan oven) mark 4. Toast 3 or 4 slices of soft-grain bread lightly on both sides. Quickly cut off the crusts, split each slice horizontally in two and scrape off any doughy bits. Sprinkle with Parmesan and paprika, if you like.

Spread the slices on a baking sheet and bake in the oven for about 10 minutes or until golden and curled.

Melba toast can be prepared ahead, cooled then stored in an airtight tin.

To serve, warm through in the oven.

Bruschetta

This Italian favourite goes well with most soups. Grill thick slices of day-old rustic bread, such as ciabatta, lightly on both sides. Immediately rub all over with a peeled garlic clove, pressing into the bread so the aromatic oil from the garlic soaks into the bread. Drizzle with a little extra virgin olive oil and serve.

Parmesan crisps

These crisps are made from melted Parmesan cheese and complement fresh-tasting creamed soups. See Cook's Tips page 45 for the recipe.

Chicken and Dumpling Soup

Serves 6
Preparation time 20 minutes
Cooking time 25 minutes

1½ tbsp olive oil
1 onion, finely chopped
2 carrots, finely diced
3 celery sticks, finely diced
1 garlic clove, crushed
1.6 litres (2¾ pints) chicken stock
500g (1lb 2oz) skinless chicken thigh
  fillets, cut into finger-size strips
1 leek, trimmed and sliced into rings

For the dumplings
100g (3½oz) plain flour
½ tsp baking powder
a large handful of fresh
  parsley, chopped
5 tbsp semi-skimmed milk
salt and ground black pepper

1 Heat ½ tbsp of the oil in a large pan and gently fry the onion, carrots and celery for 10 minutes or until softened. Stir in the garlic and cook for 1 minute.
2 Pour in the chicken stock and bring to the boil. Add the chicken and leek, bring back to the boil, then reduce the heat and simmer for 6 minutes or until the chicken is cooked through and the vegetables are just tender.
3 Meanwhile, put the flour into a medium bowl. Stir in the baking powder, three-quarters of the parsley and plenty of seasoning. Add the remaining oil and the milk and stir together until just combined to make a rough, slightly sticky dough.
4 Drop small teaspoonfuls of the dumpling mixture into the simmering stock and leave to cook for about 4 minutes (the dumplings will swell up, so don't be tempted to make them too big). Check the seasoning. Ladle the soup and dumplings into warmed soup bowls, garnish with the remaining parsley and serve.

NUTRITION PER SERVING 29 cals | 12g fat (3g sats) | 18g carbs | 0.2g salt

---

Classic Soup Dumplings

Serves 4
Preparation time 10 minutes
Cooking time 15–20 minutes

125g (4oz) self-raising flour, plus extra to dust
50g (2oz) shredded suet
salt and ground black pepper

1 In a bowl, mix the flour, suet and seasoning with sufficient cold water to make an elastic dough.
2 Divide into about 16 portions and, with lightly floured hands, roll into small balls.
3 Add to any soup and simmer for 15–20 minutes.

TRY SOMETHING DIFFERENT
Flavour these dumplings with any of the following:

• 25g (1oz) finely grated Cheddar
• ½ finely chopped small onion
• 1 tbsp freshly grated Parmesan
• ½ tsp mild curry powder or paprika
• 1 tbsp chopped watercress
• 1½ tsp freshly chopped parsley or snipped fresh chives
• 1 tsp freshly chopped tarragon
• ½ tsp mixed dried herbs
• 1 tbsp drained canned sweetcorn
• 1 tsp caraway seeds

Cream of Mushroom Soup

Serves 4
Preparation time 15 minutes, plus soaking
Cooking time 40 minutes

15g (½oz) dried porcini mushrooms
50g (2oz) butter
1 large onion, chopped
1 garlic clove, crushed
1 tbsp freshly chopped sage
700g (1½lb) chestnut mushrooms, or mixed chestnut and flat
  mushrooms, chopped
750ml (1¼ pints) vegetable stock
150ml (¼ pint) crème fraîche
a pinch of freshly grated nutmeg
salt and ground black pepper
snipped fresh chives to serve

1 Put the dried mushrooms into a bowl, pour on 150ml
(¼ pint) boiling water and set aside to soak for 20 minutes.
Remove the porcini with a slotted spoon; strain the liquid
and keep to one side. Chop the mushrooms and set aside.
2 Melt half the butter in a pan, add the onion, porcini,
garlic and sage, and fry for 10 minutes or until softened
and lightly golden. Add the remaining butter, then add
the fresh mushrooms and increase the heat. Stir-fry for
5 minutes or until the mushrooms are browned.
3 Stir in the reserved porcini liquid and stock. Bring to the
boil, then reduce the heat, cover the pan and simmer gently
for 20 minutes.
4 Transfer to a blender or food processor and whiz until
smooth. Return to the pan.
5 Stir in most of the crème fraîche and season with
nutmeg, salt and pepper to taste. Reheat the soup gently.
Spoon into warmed bowls and add a swirl of crème fraîche
and a sprinkling of snipped chives to each portion. Serve
at once.

NUTRITION PER SERVING 290 cals | 26g fat (11g sats) | 8g carbs | 0.8g salt Ⓥ

Cream of Watercress Soup

Serves 6
Preparation time 15 minutes
Cooking time 30 minutes

250g (9oz) watercress
50g (2oz) butter
1 onion, finely chopped
700g (1½lb) potatoes, cut into small pieces
900ml (1½ pints) milk
900ml (1½ pints) vegetable stock
6 tbsp single cream
salt and ground black pepper
Parmesan Crisps (see Cook's Tip below and Vegetarian
  Cheeses, page 228) to serve (optional)

1 Trim the watercress and discard the coarse stalks.
Reserve a few sprigs to garnish, then roughly chop the rest.
2 Melt the butter in a large pan, add the onion and cook
gently for 8–10 minutes until soft. Add the potatoes
and cook for 1 minute, then pour in the milk and stock,
and bring to the boil. Reduce the heat and simmer for
15–20 minutes until tender.
3 Take the pan off the heat. Stir in the chopped watercress,
then transfer to a blender and purée, in batches, until
smooth. Pour the soup into a clean pan, then add the
cream and season with salt and pepper. Heat through, then
serve garnished with the reserved watercress sprigs and a
Parmesan crisp, if you like, with the remaining Parmesan
crisps on the side.

Cook's Tip

PARMESAN CRISPS Preheat the oven to 200°C (180°C fan
oven) mark 6 and line two baking sheets with baking
parchment. Put heaped tablespoonfuls of freshly grated
Parmesan on to the sheets, spacing them well apart, and
spread each one out. Sprinkle with poppy seeds and bake
for 5–10 minutes until lacy and golden. Leave on the
baking sheet for 2–3 minutes to firm up slightly, then
transfer to a wire rack to cool.

NUTRITION PER SERVING 251 cals | 13g fat (8g sats) | 26g carbs | 0.4g salt Ⓥ

French Onion Soup

Serves 6
Preparation time 25 minutes
Cooking time 1 hour 10 minutes

2 tbsp olive oil
6 large onions, about 1.6kg (3½lb), finely sliced
2 tsp fresh thyme leaves, plus extra to garnish
500ml (17fl oz) dry cider
1 tsp caster sugar
1.5 litres (2½ pints) good-quality vegetable stock
6 small slices white bread
150g (5oz) Gruyère cheese, grated (see Vegetarian Cheeses,
  page 228)
salt and ground black pepper

1 Gently heat the oil in a large pan. Add the onions, thyme
and a large pinch of salt. Bring to the boil, then cover
the pan and cook over a low heat for 30 minutes, stirring
occasionally or until the onions are soft.
2 Pour in the cider and add the sugar. Turn up the
heat and bubble, stirring frequently, until the cider has
evaporated and the onions are well caramelized. This will
take 30–40 minutes.
3 Add the stock and heat through. Check and adjust the
seasoning.
4 Preheat the grill to medium. Put the bread on a baking
tray and lightly toast both sides under the grill. Divide the
cheese equally among the toasts and grill until melted and
bubbling.
5 To serve, spoon the soup into warmed soup bowls. Top
each bowl with a cheese toast and garnish with thyme
leaves and black pepper.

NUTRITION PER SERVING 287 cals | 13g fat (6g sats) | 2g carbs | 0.5g salt Ⓥ

Broccoli and Goat's Cheese Soup

Serves 6
Preparation time 10 minutes
Cooking time 20 minutes

50g (2oz) butter
2 onions, chopped
1 litre (1¾ pints) vegetable stock
700g (1½lb) broccoli, broken into florets, stout stalks peeled
  and chopped
1 head of garlic, separated into cloves, unpeeled
1 tbsp olive oil
150g (5oz) goat's cheese
salt and ground black pepper

1 Preheat the oven to 200°C (180°C fan oven) mark
6. Melt the butter in a pan over a gentle heat. Add the
onions, then cover the pan and cook for 4–5 minutes until
translucent. Add half the stock and bring to the boil. Add
the broccoli and bring back to the boil, then cover the pan,
reduce the heat and simmer for 15–20 minutes until the
broccoli is tender.
2 Meanwhile, toss the cloves of garlic in the oil and tip
into a roasting tin. Roast in the oven for 15 minutes or
until soft when squeezed.
3 Leave the soup to cool a little, then add the goat's cheese
and purée in batches in a blender or food processor until
smooth. Return the soup to the pan and add the remaining
stock. Reheat gently on the hob and season to taste with
salt and pepper.
4 Ladle the soup into warmed bowls, squeeze the garlic
cloves out of their skins and scatter over the soup, add a
sprinkling of black pepper and serve.

TRY SOMETHING DIFFERENT
• Double the quantity of goat's cheese if you prefer a
  stronger flavour.
• Instead of goat's cheese, substitute a soft garlic cheese for
  a really garlicky flavour.
• Try it with chicken or turkey stock for a non-vegetarian
  option.

NUTRITION PER SERVING 220 cals | 16g fat (10g sats) | 8g carbs | 0.5g salt Ⓥ

Fresh Tomato Soup with Basil

Serves 6
Preparation time 15 minutes
Cooking time 40 minutes

50g (2oz) butter
2 onions, thinly sliced
900g (2lb) tomatoes
3 tbsp plain flour
900ml (1½ pints) chicken stock
2 tbsp tomato purée
1½ tsp freshly chopped basil or ½ tsp dried, plus basil sprigs
    to garnish
150ml (¼ pint) single cream (optional)
salt and ground black pepper

1 Melt the butter in a pan, add the sliced onions and fry
gently until golden brown, stirring occasionally.
2 Meanwhile, halve the tomatoes, then scoop out the seeds
into a sieve placed over a bowl. Press the seeds to remove
all the tomato pulp and juice. Discard the seeds and put
the juice aside.
3 Remove the pan from the heat and stir in the flour, then
return it to the heat and cook gently for 1 minute, stirring.
Remove from the heat again and gradually stir in the stock,
then return to the heat and bring gently to the boil, then
continue to cook, stirring, until thickened.
4 Stir in the tomato purée, herbs and the tomatoes with
the reserved juice, and season with salt and pepper. Cover
the pan and simmer gently for about 30 minutes.
5 Leave the soup to cool slightly, then sieve or purée in
a blender or food processor. Strain through a sieve into a
clean pan and reheat gently. Taste and adjust the seasoning
if necessary.
6 Ladle the soup into individual soup bowls, garnish with
basil and swirl a little cream through each bowl just before
serving, if you like.

NUTRITION PER SERVING 193 cals | 12g fat (8g sats) | 18g carbs | 0.6g salt

Carrot and Coriander Soup

Serves 6
Preparation time 15 minutes
Cooking time about 30 minutes

40g (1½oz) butter
175g (6oz) trimmed leeks, sliced
450g (1lb) carrots, sliced
2 tsp ground coriander
1 tsp plain flour
1.1 litres (2 pints) vegetable stock
150ml (¼ pint) single cream
salt and ground black pepper
a few coriander leaves, roughly torn
  to serve

1 Melt the butter in a large pan, add the leeks and carrots, stir, then cover the pan and cook gently for 7–10 minutes until the vegetables begin to soften but not colour.

2 Stir in the ground coriander and flour and cook, stirring, for 1 minute.
3 Add the stock and bring to the boil, stirring. Season with salt and pepper, then reduce the heat, cover the pan and simmer for about 20 minutes or until the vegetables are tender.
4 Leave the soup to cool a little, then purée in batches in a blender or food processor until quite smooth.
5 Return to the pan and stir in the cream. Taste and adjust the seasoning. Reheat gently but do not boil.
6 Ladle into warmed bowls, scatter with torn coriander leaves and serve.

NUTRITION PER SERVING 140 cals | 11g fat (7g sats) | 10g carbs | 0.2g salt Ⓥ

Minestrone with Pesto

Serves 4
Preparation time 10 minutes
Cooking time 45 minutes

2 tbsp olive oil
1 small onion, finely chopped
1 carrot, chopped
1 celery stick, chopped
1 garlic clove, crushed
2 tbsp freshly chopped thyme
1 litre (1¾ pints) hot vegetable stock
400g can chopped tomatoes
400g can borlotti beans, drained and
  rinsed
125g (4oz) minestrone pasta
175g (6oz) Savoy cabbage, shredded
salt and ground black pepper
Fresh Pesto (see page 22), toasted
  ciabatta and extra virgin olive oil
  to serve

1 Heat the oil in a large pan, add the onion, carrot and celery and fry for 10 minutes or until soft. Add the garlic and thyme and fry for 2–3 minutes.
2 Add the hot stock, tomatoes and half the borlotti beans to the pan and bring to the boil. Mash the remaining beans and stir into the soup, then reduce the heat and simmer for 20 minutes. Add the minestrone pasta and cabbage and simmer for a further 10 minutes.
3 Taste and adjust the seasoning, then ladle the soup into four warmed bowls and serve with a dollop of fresh pesto on top and with slices of toasted ciabatta drizzled with extra virgin olive oil on the side.

NUTRITION PER SERVING 334 cals | 11g fat (3g sats) | 47g carbs | 1.5g salt Ⓥ

Mulligatawny Soup

Serves 4
Preparation time 10 minutes
Cooking time 40 minutes

3 streaky bacon rashers, rind removed,
    finely chopped
550g (1¼lb) chicken portions
600ml (1 pint) chicken stock
1 carrot, sliced
1 celery stick, chopped
1 apple, cored and chopped
2 tsp curry powder
4 peppercorns, crushed
1 clove
1 bay leaf
1 tbsp plain flour
150ml (¼ pint) milk
50g (2oz) long-grain rice, cooked, and
    crusty bread to serve

1 Fry the bacon in a pan until the fat runs but without browning. Add the chicken and brown well. Drain on kitchen paper and pour off the fat.
2 Return them to the pan with the stock, carrot, celery, apple and flavourings. Bring to the boil, reduce the heat, cover and simmer for 30 minutes or until the chicken is tender.
3 Remove the chicken, cool a little, then cut off the meat and return it to the soup. Discard the clove and bay leaf, and reheat the soup gently.
4 Mix the flour with a little cold water. Add to the soup with the milk and reheat without boiling.
5 Ladle into warmed bowls, add some rice and serve with crusty bread.

NUTRITION PER SERVING 252 cals |
13g fat (4g sats) | 7.3g carbs | 0.9g salt

Curried Parsnip Soup

Serves 6
Preparation time 20 minutes
Cooking time 50 minutes

40g (1½oz) butter
1 onion, sliced
700g (1½lb) parsnips, peeled, cored and
    finely diced
1 tsp curry powder
½ tsp ground cumin
1.1 litres (2 pints) chicken or vegetable
    stock
150ml (¼ pint) single cream, plus extra
    to garnish
salt and ground black pepper
paprika to serve

1 Melt the butter in a large pan, add the onion and fry gently for 5–7 minutes or until soft. Add the parsnips and fry for about 3 minutes.
2 Stir in the curry powder and cumin, and cook for a further 2 minutes.
3 Add the stock and season to taste with salt and pepper. Bring to the boil, then reduce the heat, cover the pan and simmer for 35 minutes or until the vegetables are tender.
4 Leave the soup to cool a little, then purée in batches in a blender or food processor until smooth.
5 Return the soup to the pan and taste and adjust the seasoning. Add the cream and reheat gently but do not boil.
6 Ladle the soup into warmed bowls, swirl in a little cream, then sprinkle with paprika and serve.

NUTRITION PER SERVING 184 cals |
12g fat (7g sats) | 17g carbs | 0.2g salt

Borscht

Serves 4
Preparation time 10 minutes
Cooking time 45 minutes, plus chilling

6 small raw beetroot, about 1kg
  (2¼lb), peeled
2 onions, chopped
1.1 litres (2 pints) beef stock
2 tbsp lemon juice
6 tbsp dry sherry
salt and ground black pepper
150ml (¼ pint) soured cream or natural
  yogurt and snipped fresh chives or dill
  to garnish

1 Grate the beetroot coarsely and put into a pan with the onions, stock and seasoning. Bring to the boil, then reduce the heat, cover the pan and simmer for about 45 minutes.
2 Strain, discarding the vegetables, then add the lemon juice and sherry to the liquid. Taste and adjust the seasoning. Leave to cool, then chill in the fridge.
3 Serve well chilled, garnished with a whirl of soured cream or yogurt and snipped chives or dill.

NUTRITION PER SERVING 220 cals | 8g fat (5g sats) | 27g carbs | 2.4g salt

---

Pea and Ham Soup

Serves 4
Preparation time 10 minutes
Cooking time 15 minutes

1 tbsp oil
1 onion, chopped
750g (1lb 11oz) frozen peas
1 litre (1¾ pints) chicken stock
2 × 200g (7oz) unsmoked gammon
  steaks, fat trimmed
1 tbsp freshly chopped chives, plus
  extra to garnish
4 tsp half-fat crème fraîche
ground black pepper
crusty bread to serve

1 Heat the oil in a large pan and fry the onion for 10 minutes or until softened but not coloured.
2 Stir in the peas and chicken stock and bring to the boil. Add the gammon steaks and simmer for 5 minutes or until cooked through.
3 Lift out the gammon and set aside on a board. Whiz the soup in a blender or food processor until completely smooth (in batches, if necessary). Meanwhile, shred the gammon into fine pieces, discarding any fat.
4 Return the soup to the pan, reheat gently and add the shredded gammon and the chives. Check the seasoning.
5 Spoon into warmed soup bowls and garnish with some crème fraîche, extra chives and black pepper. Serve with crusty bread.

NUTRITION PER SERVING 373 cals | 13g fat (4g sats) | 20g carbs | 2.3g salt

Mexican Bean Soup

Serves 6
Preparation time 15 minutes
Cooking time 25 minutes

4 tbsp olive oil
1 onion, chopped
2 garlic cloves, chopped
a pinch of dried chilli flakes
1 tsp ground coriander
1 tsp ground cumin
½ tsp ground cinnamon
900ml (1½ pints) vegetable stock
300ml (½ pint) tomato juice
1–2 tsp chilli sauce
2 × 400g cans red kidney beans
2 tbsp freshly chopped coriander
salt and ground black pepper
lime butter to serve (optional, see Citrus Butter, page 23)
coriander leaves, roughly torn to garnish

1 Heat the oil in a large pan, add the onion, garlic, chillies
and spices and fry gently for about 5 minutes or until
lightly golden.
2 Add the stock, tomato juice, chilli sauce and beans with
their liquid. Bring to the boil, then reduce the heat, cover
the pan and simmer gently for 20 minutes.
3 Leave the soup to cool a little, then purée in batches in
a blender or food processor until very smooth.
4 Return the soup to the pan. Stir in the chopped
coriander and heat through, then season to taste with salt
and pepper.
5 Ladle the soup into warmed bowls. Top each portion
with a few slices of lime butter, if you like, and scatter with
torn coriander leaves.

NUTRITION PER SERVING {without lime butter} 184 cals | 8g fat (1.2g sats) | 21g carbs | 1.3g salt ⓥ

Simple Vegetable Soup

Serves 4
Preparation time 10 minutes
Cooking time 40 minutes

2 tbsp oil, or 1 tbsp oil and 25g (1oz)
  butter
1–2 onions, finely chopped
1–2 garlic cloves, crushed (optional)
450g (1lb) chopped mixed vegetables,
  such as leeks, cauliflower, potatoes,
  celery, fennel, parsnips, canned
  tomatoes (chopped finely or into
  larger dice for a chunky soup)
  and peas
1.1 litres (2 pints) vegetable stock
crusty bread to serve (optional)

1 Heat the oil or oil and butter in a
large pan, add the onions and fry until
soft. Add the garlic, if you like.
2 Add the chopped mixed vegetables
and the stock. Bring to the boil, then
reduce the heat and simmer for
20–25 minutes until the vegetables
are tender. Add the peas and simmer
for 5 minutes or until heated through.
3 Leave chunky, partially purée or
blend until smooth, if you like.
Reheat and serve with crusty bread,
if you like.

NUTRITION PER SERVING 114 cals |
6g fat (1g sats) | 13g carbs | 1.5g salt Ⓥ

Lentil and Bacon Soup

Serves 6 as a main course
Preparation time 10 minutes
Cooking time 1 hour 40 minutes

175g (6oz) red lentils
1.7 litres (3 pints) chicken stock
1 garlic clove, crushed
1 clove
200g (7oz) lean bacon rashers, rind
  removed, diced
225g can tomatoes
1 onion, chopped
450g (1lb) potatoes, diced
2 tbsp lemon juice
salt and ground black pepper
crisply fried bacon strips, freshly
  chopped parsley, grated cheese or
  croûtons to garnish

1 Put the lentils, stock garlic, clove,
bacon, tomatoes, onion, and salt and
pepper in a large pan. Bring to the
boil, then reduce the heat, cover the
pan and simmer for 1 hour or until
the lentils are soft.
2 Add the potatoes and cook for
a further 20 minutes or until tender.
3 Remove and discard the clove.
Allow the soup to cool slightly, then
purée in a blender or food processor
until smooth.
4 Return the soup to the pan, add the
lemon juice and reheat gently. Taste
and adjust the seasoning, then garnish
with bacon strips, chopped parsley
and grated cheese.

NUTRITION PER SERVING 209 cals |
3g fat (1g sats) | 32g carbs | 1.6g salt

Scotch Broth

Serves 4
Preparation time 15 minutes
Cooking time 1 hour

1 tbsp vegetable oil
250g (9oz) lamb neck fillets, cut into 2cm (¾in) cubes
2 parsnips, roughly chopped
2 carrots, roughly chopped
1 onion, finely chopped
1 potato, peeled and finely diced
3 smoked streaky bacon rashers, finely sliced
125g (4oz) pearl barley
1 litre (1¾ pints) lamb stock
75g (3oz) frozen peas
a small handful of parsley, finely chopped
salt and ground black pepper

1 Heat the oil in a large flameproof casserole over a high heat. Add the lamb and fry until browned all over, in batches, if necessary, to stop the lamb from sweating rather than browning.
2 Add the parsnips, carrots, onion, potato and bacon and fry for 3–5 minutes until hot and golden.
3 Add the pearl barley and mix well. Pour in the stock and stir well, scraping any sticky goodness from the bottom of the casserole. Bring to the boil, then cover the pan, reduce the heat and simmer gently for 40–50 minutes until the lamb is tender.
4 Stir in the peas, heat through gently, then check the seasoning and add salt and pepper to taste. Transfer to individual bowls, garnish with parsley and serve.

NUTRITION PER SERVING 4258 cals | 20g fat (7g sats) | 45g carbs | 1.4g salt

Cock-a-Leekie Soup

Serves 8
Preparation time 30–40 minutes
Cooking time 1 hour 20 minutes

1.4kg (3lb) oven-ready chicken, including giblets if available
2 onions, roughly chopped
2 carrots, roughly chopped
2 celery sticks, roughly chopped
1 bay leaf
25g (1oz) butter
900g (2lb) leeks, trimmed and sliced
125g (4oz) ready-to-eat prunes, sliced
Classic Soup Dumplings (see page 43), made with the
  addition of 2 tbsp freshly chopped parsley and 2 tbsp
  freshly chopped thyme
salt and ground black pepper
freshly chopped parsley to garnish

1 Put the chicken into a pan in which it fits quite snugly,
then add the chopped vegetables, bay leaf and chicken
giblets. Pour in 1.7 litres (3 pints) water and bring to
the boil, then reduce the heat, cover the pan and simmer
gently for 1 hour.
2 Meanwhile, melt the butter in a large pan. Add the leeks
and fry gently for 10 minutes or until softened.
3 Remove the chicken from the pan and leave until cool
enough to handle. Strain the stock and put to one side.
Strip the chicken from the bones and shred roughly. Add
to the stock with the prunes and softened leeks.
4 Make the dumplings and lightly shape the dough into
2.5cm (1in) balls. Bring the soup just to the boil and
season well with salt and pepper. Reduce the heat, add
the dumplings and cover the pan. Simmer for about
15–20 minutes until the dumplings are light and fluffy.
Serve the soup sprinkled with chopped parsley.

Cook's Tip
Make the stock a day ahead, if possible, then cool
overnight. The following day, remove any fat from the
surface before using.

NUTRITION PER SERVING 280 cals | 4g fat (1g sats) | 40g carbs | 0.2g salt

Bouillabaisse

Serves 4
Preparation time 15 minutes
Cooking time 45 minutes

1kg (2¼lb) mixed fish fillets and
  shellfish, such as red mullet, John
  Dory, monkfish, red snapper, whiting,
  cleaned mussels in shells (see Cook's
  Tips, page 95), large cooked peeled
  prawns and crab claw meat
a pinch of saffron
3 tbsp olive oil
1 onion, sliced
1 leek, trimmed and sliced
2 celery sticks, sliced
2 garlic cloves, crushed
400g can plum tomatoes, or skinned,
  seeded flavourful fresh ones, chopped
  (see page 277)
bouquet garni (1 bay leaf, a few fresh
  parsley and thyme sprigs)
1 strip of orange zest
1 tbsp sun-dried tomato paste
½ tsp fennel seeds
1.1 litres (2 pints) fish stock
2 tbsp freshly chopped parsley
1 tbsp freshly chopped thyme
salt and ground black pepper
crusty bread to serve

1 Cut the fish fillets into bite-sized pieces.
2 Put the saffron into a small bowl, pour on 150ml (¼ pint) boiling water and leave to soak.
3 Heat the oil in a large pan, add the onion, leek, celery and garlic, and cook until softened. Add the tomatoes, bouquet garni, orange zest, sun-dried tomato paste and fennel seeds, and cook for a further 1–2 minutes.
4 Add the fish stock together with the saffron and its soaking liquid. Season with pepper and a little salt and bring to the boil. Reduce the heat and simmer for about 30 minutes.
5 Add the fish pieces and mussels (not the prawns or crab claws) and cook for about 5–6 minutes until the fish is just cooked and the mussels have opened; discard any mussels that remain closed.
6 Stir in the chopped herbs, prawns and crab claw meat. Heat through and serve in warmed bowls with plenty of crusty bread.

Cook's Tip
This classic French fish soup originates from Marseilles. If possible, buy whole fish and fillet them yourself, using the bones and trimmings to make a flavourful stock (see page 11).

NUTRITION PER SERVING 330 cals | 13g fat (1g sats) | 9g carbs | 1.5g salt

Smoked Haddock Chowder

Serves 4
Preparation time 15 minutes
Cooking time 25 minutes

25g (1oz) butter
2 onions, chopped
125g (4oz) smoked streaky bacon
  rashers, rind removed, chopped
600ml (1 pint) whole milk
225g (8oz) potatoes, cut into 1cm
  (½in) cubes
3 celery sticks, thinly sliced
198g can sweetcorn, drained
450g (1lb) skinless smoked haddock
  fillet, cut into 8 pieces
salt and ground black pepper
crusty bread to serve

1 Heat the butter in a large, wide pan, add the onions and fry for 3 minutes.

Add the bacon and cook for a further 5 minutes or until it is no longer pink.
2 Add the milk and 600ml (1 pint) boiling water, then season with 1 tsp salt and plenty of pepper. Add the potatoes and celery, and cook for 5 minutes.
3 Stir in the drained sweetcorn and gently lower in the haddock. Cover the pan and cook for 10 minutes or until the fish is just cooked. Serve in individual bowls, with crusty bread.

TRY SOMETHING DIFFERENT
Serve the chowder topped with croûtons (see page 59) and plenty of freshly chopped parsley.

NUTRITION PER SERVING 410 cals | 20g fat (10g sats) | 26g carbs | 4.2g salt

Leek and Potato Soup

Serves 4
Preparation time 10 minutes
Cooking time 45 minutes

25g (1oz) butter
1 onion, finely chopped
1 garlic clove, crushed
550g (1¼lb) leeks, trimmed and
  chopped
200g (7oz) floury potatoes, sliced
1.3 litres (2¼ pints) hot vegetable stock
crème fraîche and snipped fresh chives
  to garnish

1 Melt the butter in a large pan, add the onion and cook over a low heat for 10–15 minutes until soft. Add the garlic and cook for a further 1 minute. Add the leeks and cook for 5–10 minutes until softened. Add the potatoes and toss with the leeks.
2 Pour in the hot stock and bring to the boil, then reduce the heat and simmer the soup for 20 minutes or until the potatoes are tender.
3 Leave the soup to cool a little, then purée in batches in a blender or food processor until smooth.
4 To serve, reheat the soup gently. Ladle into warmed bowls and garnish with crème fraîche and chives.

NUTRITION PER SERVING 117 cals | 6g fat (4g sats) | 13g carbs | 0.1g salt Ⓥ

Gazpacho

Serves 6
Preparation time 20 minutes, plus chilling
Cooking time 10 minutes

1 medium cucumber, peeled, seeded and coarsely chopped
450g (1lb) fully ripened tomatoes, skinned, seeded and
  chopped (see page 277)
100g (3½oz) green pepper, cored, seeded and chopped
50–100g (2–3½oz) onions to taste, chopped
2 garlic cloves, chopped
3 tbsp olive oil
3 tbsp white wine vinegar
450ml (¾ pint) tomato juice
2 tbsp tomato purée
salt and ground black pepper
ice cubes and 1 green pepper, cored, seeded and finely diced
  to serve

For the croûtons
4 thick slices white bread, crusts removed
50g (2oz) butter

1 Mix all the gazpacho ingredients together in a large
bowl, seasoning with ¼ tsp salt. Purée the mixture in
batches in a blender or food processor until smooth.
2 Return the soup to the bowl, cover the pan and chill for
at least 2 hours.
3 To make the croûtons, cut the bread into cubes. Heat the
butter in a large frying pan and sauté the bread cubes over
a medium heat, stirring frequently, until golden on all sides.
Remove and drain the croûtons on kitchen paper.
4 Just before serving, add a few ice cubes to the soup.
Serve each portion garnished with diced green pepper and
the croûtons.

Cook's Tip
This Spanish iced soup is wonderfully refreshing in hot
weather. Drop in a few ice cubes just before serving to
make it as cold as possible.

NUTRITION PER SERVING 220 cals | 14g fat (5g sats) | 21g carbs | 1.4g salt Ⓥ

Dips, Canapés and Nibbles

Dips

Serve these dips with warm pitta bread fingers, corn chips, breadsticks or an assortment of crudités (vegetable sticks), such as strips of celery, fennel, cucumber, courgette, peppers and carrots, blanched asparagus tips and cauliflower florets, and cherry or baby plum tomatoes.

Tzatziki

Serves 8 • **Preparation time** 10 minutes

1 cucumber
300g (11oz) Greek yogurt
2 tsp olive oil
2 tbsp freshly chopped mint
1 large garlic clove, crushed
salt and ground black pepper
pitta bread and vegetable sticks to serve

1 Halve, seed and dice the cucumber and put into a bowl.
2 Add the yogurt and oil. Stir in the chopped mint and garlic, and season with salt and pepper to taste. Cover and chill in the fridge until ready to serve.
3 Serve with warm pitta bread and vegetable sticks.

NUTRITION PER SERVING
50 cals | 4g fat (2g sats) | 1g carbs | 0.4g salt Ⓥ

Hummus

Serves 6 • **Preparation time** 15 minutes

400g can chickpeas, drained and rinsed
juice of 1 lemon
4 tbsp tahini
1 garlic clove, crushed
5 tbsp extra virgin olive oil
salt and ground black pepper
pitta bread or toasted flatbreads to
  serve

1 Put the chickpeas, lemon juice, tahini, garlic and oil in a blender or food processor. Season generously with salt and pepper, then whiz to a thick paste.
2 Spoon the hummus into a bowl, then cover and chill until needed.
3 Serve with warm pitta bread or toasted flatbreads.

TRY SOMETHING DIFFERENT
Black Olive Hummus (pictured) Stir 25g (1oz) roughly chopped pitted black olives and 1 tsp paprika into the hummus paste. Sprinkle with a little extra paprika and oil, if you like. Serve with carrot sticks and breadsticks.

NUTRITION PER SERVING 170 cals | 14g fat (2g sats) | 7g carbs | 0.7g salt Ⓥ

Taramasalata

Serves 6 • **Preparation time** 15 minutes

100g (3½oz) country-style bread, crusts removed
75g (3oz) smoked cod roe
2 tbsp lemon juice
100ml (3½fl oz) light olive oil
ground black pepper
pitta bread or toasted flatbreads to serve

1 Put the bread into a bowl, cover with cold water and leave to soak for 10 minutes. Drain and squeeze out most of the water.
2 Put the smoked cod roe in a bowl, cover with cold water and soak for 10 minutes, then drain and remove the skin.
3 Put the roe in a blender or food processor with the bread and whiz for 30 seconds. With the motor running, pour in the lemon juice and oil, and whiz briefly to combine. Season with pepper to taste.
4 Spoon into a bowl, cover and chill until needed. Serve with warm pitta bread or toasted flatbreads.

NUTRITION PER SERVING
180 cals | 15g fat (2g sats) | 7g carbs | 0.3g salt

Guacamole

Serves 6 • **Preparation time** 10 minutes

2 ripe avocados
2 small tomatoes, seeded and chopped
  (see page 277)
juice of 2 limes
2 tbsp extra virgin olive oil
2 tbsp freshly chopped coriander
salt and ground black pepper
tortilla chips, or pitta bread and
  vegetable sticks to serve

1 Cut the avocados in half, remove the stones and peel away the skin. Tip the flesh into a bowl and mash roughly with a fork.
2 Quickly add the tomatoes, lime juice, oil and chopped coriander. Mix well and season with salt and pepper to taste. Cover and chill until ready to serve.
3 Serve the guacamole with tortilla chips or warm pitta bread and vegetable sticks.

NUTRITION PER SERVING
160 cals | 16g fat (3g sats) | 2g carbs | 0.4g salt ⓥ

Blue Cheese Dip

Serves 6 • **Preparation time** 5 minutes

150ml (¼ pint) soured cream
1 garlic clove, crushed
175g (6oz) blue Stilton cheese (see Vegetarian Cheeses
  on page 228)
juice of 1 lemon
salt and ground black pepper
snipped chives to garnish
vegetable sticks to serve

1 Put the soured cream, garlic, Stilton and lemon juice into a blender or food processor and whiz to a smooth paste.
2 Transfer to a serving dish and chill until required. Check the seasoning, sprinkle with chives and serve with a selection of vegetable sticks.

TRY SOMETHING DIFFERENT
Use Dolcelatte instead of Stilton cheese.

NUTRITION PER SERVING
170 cals | 15g fat (7g sats) | 1g carbs | 1g salt ⓥ

Tapenade

Serves 4 • **Preparation time** 5 minutes

3 tbsp capers, rinsed and drained
75g (3oz) pitted black olives
50g can anchovy fillets in oil, drained
100ml (3½fl oz) olive oil
2 tbsp brandy
ground black pepper
vegetable sticks or grilled vegetables and toasted French
  bread to serve

1 Put the capers, olives and anchovies into a blender or food processor and whiz briefly to chop.
2 With the motor running, add the oil in a steady stream. Stir in the brandy and season with pepper to taste. Transfer to a serving bowl.
3 Serve the tapenade with raw vegetable sticks and/or grilled vegetables and toasted French bread.

NUTRITION PER SERVING
270 cals | 26g fat (2g sats) | trace carbs | 2.3g salt

Dried Tomato Pesto

Makes 180g (6¼oz)
Preparation time 10 minutes

100g (3½oz) sun-dried tomatoes in oil, drained weight
20g pack fresh basil leaves
1 small garlic clove, roughly chopped
25g (1oz) pinenuts, toasted (see Cook's Tip, page 312)
4–6 tbsp olive oil, plus extra to store
25g (1oz) Pecorino, grated (see Vegetarian Cheeses
  on page 228)
salt and ground black pepper

1 Blend the tomatoes, basil, garlic and pinenuts to a purée.
2 Gradually add enough of the oil to make a loose but not too sloppy paste. Stir in the cheese. Season with salt and pepper to taste.

Cook's Tip
This will store in the fridge for up to one month in a sterilised jar – cover the top with a layer of olive oil.

NUTRITION PER SERVING
84 cals | 8.3g fat (1.3g sats) | 8g carbs | 0.3g salt Ⓥ

Red Pepper and Feta Dip

Makes about 375g (13oz) (25 tbsp)
Preparation time 5 minutes

290g jar roasted red peppers, drained
200g (7oz) feta cheese (see Vegetarian Cheeses, page 228),
  crumbled
1 small garlic clove
1 tbsp natural yogurt
toasted pitta bread to serve

1 Put all the ingredients into a blender or food processor and whiz until smooth.
2 Serve the dip with strips of toasted pitta bread.

NUTRITION PER SERVING
32 cals | 3g fat (1g sats) | 1g carbs | 0.3g salt Ⓥ

Canapés and Nibbles

Dips, canapés and savoury finger foods, such as spiced nuts and marinated olives, are perfect for drinks parties, as they can be made ahead. Simply warm canapés through prior to serving. Allow about 10 canapés per person, with nuts, olives, dips and 'dunks' as extras. A colourful serving plate of crudités with a selection of dips always looks attractive.

Lemon and Rosemary Olives

Serves 6 • **Preparation time** 15 minutes, plus 24 hours chilling

a few fresh rosemary sprigs, plus extra to garnish
1 garlic clove
175g (6oz) mixed black and green Greek olives
pared zest of 1 lemon
2 tbsp vodka (optional)
300ml (½ pint) extra virgin olive oil

1 Soak the rosemary and garlic in boiling water for 2 minutes, then drain. Put in a jar with the olives, lemon zest and vodka, if you like. Cover with oil, cover and chill for at least 24 hours.
2 To serve, remove the olives from the oil and garnish with sprigs of fresh rosemary. Use within one week.

Cook's Tip
Use the leftover oil in salad dressings and marinades.

NUTRITION PER SERVING
300 cals | 36g fat (5g sats) | 0g carbs | 1.2g salt Ⓥ

Cocktail Rolls

Serves 10
Preparation time 20 minutes

200g (7oz) smoked salmon slices
100g (3½oz) cream cheese or goat's cheese
1 tbsp dill-flavoured mustard or creamed horseradish
1 large courgette
about 2 tbsp hummus
200g (7oz) prosciutto (see Cook's Tip, page 76)
about 2 tbsp fruity chutney, such as mango
1 small bunch of chives, finely chopped
1 roasted red pepper, finely chopped
ground black pepper

1 Lay the smoked salmon on a sheet of greaseproof paper. Spread with a thin layer of cheese, then a layer of mustard or horseradish, and roll up.
2 Using a vegetable peeler, pare the courgette into long, wafer-thin strips. Lay the strips on a board, spread with cheese, then hummus, and roll up.
3 Lay the prosciutto on a board. Spread thinly with cheese, then with the chutney, and roll up.
4 Stand the rolls on a greaseproof paper-lined baking sheet (trimming the bases if necessary), cover with clingfilm and chill for up to 8 hours.
5 About 2 minutes before serving, top each roll with a little cheese. Dip the salmon rolls into the chopped chives, the prosciutto rolls into the red pepper and the courgette rolls into coarsely ground black pepper.

NUTRITION PER SERVING 117 cals | 7g fat (3g sats) | 4g carbs | 1.7g salt

Red Pepper Pesto Croûtes

Serves 24
Preparation time 20 minutes
Cooking time 15–20 minutes

1 thin French stick, sliced into 24 rounds
olive oil to brush
Fresh Pesto (see page 22)
4 pepper pieces (from a jar of marinated peppers), each sliced into 6 strips
pinenuts to garnish

1 Preheat the oven to 200°C (180°C fan oven) mark 6. Brush both sides of the bread slices with oil and put on a baking sheet. Cook in the oven for 15–20 minutes.
2 Spread 1 tsp pesto on each croûte, top with a pepper strip and pinenuts, and serve.

NUTRITION PER SERVING 90 cals | 5g fat (1g sats) | 10g carbs | 0.3g salt

Mozzarella Nibbles

Makes 30
Preparation time 15 minutes

2 × 125g tubs mozzarella bocconcini, drained (see Cook's Tips)
75g (3oz) thinly sliced Parma ham, cut into strips
400g (14oz) pitted black and green olives, halved
125g (4oz) roasted artichokes, cut into small pieces
125g (4oz) roasted peppers, cut into small pieces
1 bunch of fresh basil leaves

1 Wrap each mozzarella ball in a piece of Parma ham. Push a halved olive on to a cocktail stick, then add a piece of artichoke, a piece of pepper, a basil leaf, then a wrapped mozzarella ball. Repeat to make about 30 nibbles.

2 Serve immediately or cover and chill for up to 1 hour.

Cook's Tips
- Bocconcini are mini mozzarella balls – the perfect bite-size nibble. They are available from Italian delis and good supermarkets. Alternatively, replace with two regular mozzarella balls, cubed.
- For vegetarians, omit the ham.
- Instead of artichokes, use halved cherry tomatoes.

NUTRITION PER SERVING 41 cals | 3g fat (1g sats) | 1g carbs | 0.9g salt

Sweet Chilli Prawns

Makes 30
Preparation time 20 minutes, plus overnight marinating

30 large cooked peeled prawns, about 250g (9oz)
150ml bottle sweet chilli sauce
grated zest and juice of ½ lime
3 tbsp freshly chopped basil
½ cucumber, about 15cm (6in) long
2 tbsp clear honey

1 The night before serving, mix the prawns, 2 tbsp of the chilli sauce, the lime zest and juice, and the basil in a small non-metallic bowl. Cover with clingfilm and chill overnight.
2 Up to three hours before serving, use a vegetable peeler to pare along the length of the cucumber to make 15 thin strips. Cut each strip of cucumber in half widthways.
3 Thread each piece of cucumber on to a cocktail stick in a concertina shape, then add a marinated prawn. Cover the skewers with clingfilm and chill until ready to serve.
4 To serve, spoon the remaining chilli sauce into a small serving bowl and stir in the honey. Pile the prawn and cucumber skewers on to a large serving plate and serve with the chilli sauce for dipping.

TRY SOMETHING DIFFERENT
- Use fresh coriander instead of basil.
- Instead of prawns, use cooked and peeled crayfish tails.

NUTRITION PER CANAPÉ 16 cals | trace fat (0g sats) | 1g carbs | 0.1g salt

Cheese Straws

Makes 24
Preparation time 10 minutes, plus chilling
Cooking time 18–20 minutes, plus cooling

200g (7oz) self-raising flour, sifted, plus extra to dust
a pinch of cayenne pepper
125g (4oz) unsalted butter, diced and chilled,
  plus extra to grease
125g (4oz) Parmesan, finely grated (see Vegetarian Cheeses,
  page 228)
2 medium eggs
1 tsp ready-made English mustard
sesame and poppy seeds to sprinkle

1 Put the flour, cayenne and butter into a food processor
and pulse until the mixture resembles breadcrumbs.
(Alternatively, rub the butter into the flour and cayenne in
a large bowl by hand, until it resembles fine crumbs.) Add
the Parmesan and mix in.
2 Crack one egg into a bowl. Separate the other egg, put
the white to one side and add the egg yolk to the bowl
with the whole egg. Mix in the mustard. Add to the flour
mixture and mix together. Tip on to a board and knead
lightly for 30 seconds, then wrap in clingfilm and chill for
30 minutes.
3 Preheat the oven to 180°C (160°C fan oven) mark 4.
Grease two baking sheets. Roll out the pastry on a lightly
floured surface to a 23 × 30cm (9 × 12in) rectangle, cut out
24 straws and carefully twist each straw twice. Put on the
baking sheets.
4 Beat the reserved egg white with a fork until frothy, and
brush over the cheese straws, then sprinkle with the sesame
and poppy seeds. Bake for 18–20 minutes until golden.
5 Remove from the oven and cool for 5 minutes, then
transfer to a wire rack and leave to cool completely.

NUTRITION PER SERVING 96 cals | 6.5g fat (4g sats) | 6.3g carbs | 0.3g salt Ⓥ

Devils on Horseback

Makes 8
Preparation time 10 minutes
Cooking time 15 minutes

8 blanched almonds
olive oil
8 large ready-to-eat prunes, stoned
4 thin streaky bacon rashers, rinded
8 rounds of bread, about 5cm (2in) in diameter
50g (2oz) butter
salt and cayenne pepper
watercress to garnish

1 Preheat the grill. Fry the almonds for 2–3 minutes in
a little oil, until they are golden brown, then toss in a little
salt and cayenne pepper. Put an almond in the cavity of
each prune.
2 Stretch the bacon rashers with the back of a knife, cut
in half and roll around the prunes. Secure with a wooden
cocktail stick or small skewer and cook under a medium
grill, turning, until all the bacon is golden brown.
3 Meanwhile, fry the bread for 2–3 minutes in the butter,
until golden. Put a prune on each piece, garnish with
watercress and serve at once.

TRY SOMETHING DIFFERENT
Angels on Horseback Omit the almonds and prunes and
replace with 8 oysters sprinkled with cayenne pepper and
lemon juice. Put one roll on top of each croûte of bread
and bake in the oven at 200°C (180°C fan oven) mark 6
for 15 minutes or until the bacon is lightly cooked. Serve at
once, garnished with watercress.

NUTRITION PER SERVING 128 cals | 9g fat (4g sats) | 9g carbs | 0.5g salt

Chicken Satay Skewers

Serves 4
Preparation time 30 minutes, plus chilling and soaking
Cooking time 8–10 minutes

1 tbsp coriander seeds
1 tbsp cumin seeds
2 tsp ground turmeric
4 garlic cloves, roughly chopped
grated zest and juice of 1 lemon
2 bird's eye chillies, finely chopped (see Cook's Tips)
3 tbsp vegetable oil
4 boneless, skinless chicken breasts, about 550g (1¼lb),
 cut into finger-length strips
salt and ground black pepper
½ cucumber, cut into sticks to serve

For the satay sauce
200g (7oz) salted peanuts
1 tbsp molasses sugar
½ lemongrass stalk, chopped
2 tbsp dark soy sauce
juice of ½ lime
200ml (7fl oz) coconut cream

1 Put the coriander and cumin seeds and the turmeric
into a dry frying pan and heat for 30 seconds. Tip into
a blender and add the garlic, lemon zest and juice,
chillies, 1 tbsp oil and 1 tsp salt. Whiz for 1–2 minutes
to a thick paste.
2 Put the paste into a large shallow non-metallic dish, add
the chicken and toss everything together. Cover and chill
in the fridge for at least 20 minutes or up to 12 hours.
3 To make the satay sauce, put all the ingredients into a
food processor and add 2 tbsp water. Whiz to make a thick
chunky sauce, then spoon into a dish. Cover and chill.
Meanwhile, soak 24 bamboo skewers in water for at least
20 minutes.
4 Preheat the barbecue or grill until hot. Thread the
chicken on to the skewers, drizzle with the remaining
oil and cook for 4–5 minutes on each side until cooked
through. Serve with the satay sauce and the cucumber.

TRY SOMETHING DIFFERENT
Replace the chicken in the main recipe with pork
tenderloin or beef rump.

Cook's Tips
• Chillies vary enormously in strength, from quite mild to
 blisteringly hot, depending on the type of chilli and its
 ripeness. Taste a small piece first to check it's not too hot
 for you.
• Be extremely careful when handling chillies that you do
 not touch or rub your eyes with your fingers, as they
 will sting. Wash knives immediately after handling
 chillies for the same reason. As a precaution, use rubber
 gloves when preparing them, if you like.

NUTRITION PER SERVING 687 cals | 51g fat (21g sats) | 11g carbs | 2.1g salt

Tangy Chicken Bites

Makes 48
Preparation time 10 minutes

2 × 50g packs mini croustades
about 275g (10oz) fruity chutney, such
  as mango
2 roast chicken breasts, skinned, torn
  into small pieces
250g carton crème fraîche
a few fresh thyme sprigs

1 Put the croustades on a board.
Spoon about ½ tsp chutney into each
one. Top with a few shreds of chicken,
a small dollop of crème fraîche and
a few thyme leaves. Transfer the
croustades to a large serving plate and
serve them immediately.

TRY SOMETHING DIFFERENT
• Use mini poppadoms as the base
  instead of croustades.
• Replace the chutney with a spoonful
  of cranberry sauce.
• Instead of roast chicken, use turkey.

NUTRITION PER SERVING 43 cals |
2g fat (1g sats) | 4g carbs | 0.1g salt

Smoked Salmon Blinis

Makes 16
Preparation time 5 minutes

3 tbsp crème fraîche
16 small blinis or 125g pack
  (see Cook's Tips)
125g (4oz) thinly sliced smoked
  salmon
1 tbsp freshly snipped chives
lemon wedges to serve

1 Spread crème fraîche on to the
blinis, then fold the salmon loosely
on top. Sprinkle with chives and serve
with lemon wedges to squeeze over.

Cook's Tips
• Originally from Russia, blinis
  are bite-size yeast pancakes; they
  can be topped with a variety of
  ingredients to make perfect party
  canapés and are available from most
  supermarkets.
• Instead of blinis, use small pieces of
  pumpernickel or rye bread.
• Instead of smoked salmon, use
  hot-smoked salmon flakes. Put the
  salmon flakes, crème fraîche and
  a little ground black pepper into
  a bowl and mix gently. Put 1 tsp
  of the mixture on to each blini,
  sprinkle with chopped chives and
  serve immediately.

NUTRITION PER BLINI 43 cals |
3g fat (1g sats) | 2g carbs | 0.3g salt

Buckwheat Blinis

Makes 30
Preparation time 15 minutes
Cooking time 30 minutes

225g (8oz) buckwheat flour, sifted (see Cook's Tip)
225g (8oz) plain flour, sifted
2 tsp caster sugar
a large pinch of salt
2 × 7g packs fast-action dried yeast
3 medium eggs
700ml (24fl oz) warm milk
1 tbsp sunflower oil, plus extra for frying
lumpfish roe and dill to garnish
soured cream and pickled herring to serve

1 Put the flours in a large bowl with the sugar and salt.
Stir in the yeast. Make a well in the centre and add 2 whole
eggs and 1 yolk, putting the white aside for later.
2 Gradually blend in the milk to make a smooth batter.
Stir in the oil. Cover with clingfilm and leave for 1 hour.
3 Heat a large heavy-based frying pan over a medium–low
heat. Put the egg whites into a clean, grease-free bowl and
whisk until they form stiff peaks. Fold them carefully into
the yeast mixture.
4 When the pan is hot, add a splash of oil and carefully
wipe around the base with a thickness of folded kitchen
paper. Pour in a couple of spoonfuls of mixture to make
a 7.5–8cm (3–3¼in) circle. When bubbles come to
the surface, turn and cook the other side until golden.
Continue with the remaining mixture, putting the cooked
blinis into a warmed oven between sheets of greaseproof
paper as you go.
5 Serve topped with soured cream and pickled herring, and
garnished with lumpfish roe and dill.

Cook's Tip
You can find buckwheat in major supermarkets, delis and
health-food shops. Alternatively, swap wholemeal flour for
the buckwheat.

NUTRITION PER BLINI 80 cals | 2g fat (0.5g sats) | 14g carbs | 0.1g salt

Starters

Mixed Italian Bruschetta

Serves 6
Preparation time 25 minutes

1 long thin French stick
400g can butter beans, drained and rinsed
a small handful of fresh mint, shredded
zest and juice of ½ lemon
2 tbsp extra virgin olive oil, plus extra to garnish
seeds from ½ pomegranate
150g (5oz) cherry tomatoes, quartered
200g (7oz) mozzarella bocconcini, halved (see Cook's Tips,
  page 66)
1 tbsp Fresh Pesto (see page 22)
2 tbsp freshly chopped basil, plus extra leaves to garnish
a small handful of rocket
6 slices bresaola
15g (½oz) freshly shaved Parmesan
75g (3oz) roasted red pepper, sliced
2 tbsp Tapenade (see page 63)
salt and ground black pepper

1 Cut the bread diagonally into 24 slices and toast in
batches. Mash together the butter beans, mint, lemon zest
and juice and oil. Season to taste with salt and pepper and
stir through most of the pomegranate seeds. Set aside.
2 In a separate bowl, stir together the cherry tomatoes,
mozzarella bocconcini, pesto and basil.
3 To assemble, spoon the bean mixture on to six toasts and
garnish with the remaining pomegranate seeds. Top
a further six with the mozzarella mixture and six with
rocket, bresaola and Parmesan. Drizzle with the oil. For
the final six bruschetta, put a few slices of roasted pepper
on each toast. Add a little tapenade and garnish with
a basil leaf.

NUTRITION PER SERVING 398 cals | 15g fat (7g sats) | 47g carbs | 2.5g salt

Cheesy Stuffed Mushrooms

Serves 1
Preparation time 10 minutes
Cooking time 10 minutes

1 tsp unsalted butter
1 large flat mushroom
a small handful of chopped spinach
½ garlic clove, finely chopped
15g (½oz) breadcrumbs
15g (½oz) vegetarian Cheddar, grated
  (see Vegetarian Cheeses, page 228)
1 medium egg yolk
1 tbsp freshly chopped parsley
salt and ground black pepper

1 Heat the butter in a small frying pan until foamy. Meanwhile, pull out the stalk from the mushroom and finely chop the stalk.
2 Add the whole mushroom to the pan and fry for 5 minutes, turning once or until tender. Transfer to a small ovenproof dish, smooth side down.
3 Add the chopped mushroom stalk to the pan with the spinach and garlic. Season with salt and pepper. Fry for a few minutes until the spinach has wilted.
4 Meanwhile, stir together the breadcrumbs, grated cheese, egg yolk and parsley. Pile the spinach mixture on top of the mushroom and top with the breadcrumb mixture.
5 Grill for 2–3 minutes until golden and bubbling.

NUTRITION PER SERVING 243 cals | 16g fat (8g sats) | 12g carbs | 0.8g salt Ⓥ

Classic Prawn Cocktail

Serves 6
Preparation time 20 minutes

450g (1lb) cooked peeled king prawns
125g (4oz) iceberg lettuce, thinly
  shredded
6 tbsp Mayonnaise (see page 29)
3 tbsp tomato ketchup
finely grated zest of 1 lemon, plus
  lemon wedges to serve
a few dashes of Tabasco sauce to taste
a few large pinches of paprika
  (optional)
½ cucumber
salt and ground black pepper
Melba toast or bread to serve (optional)

1 Lay the prawns out on kitchen paper and pat dry. Put into a large bowl and add the shredded lettuce, mayonnaise, tomato ketchup, lemon zest, Tabasco and paprika, if you like. Stir to combine, then season with salt and pepper as necessary.
2 Slice the cucumber half into equal rounds, as thinly as possible.
3 Use the cucumber to line the glasses, then spoon in the prawn mixture. Garnish with some black pepper and a sprinkle of paprika, if you like. Serve with lemon wedges, and Melba Toast or bread, if you like.

NUTRITION PER SERVING 174 cals | 12g fat (2g sats) | 3g carbs | 0.8g salt

Sizzling Scallops with Pancetta and Sage

Serves 6
Preparation time 15 minutes
Cooking time 15 minutes

1 tbsp sunflower oil
150g (5oz) pancetta, diced
6 sage leaves, finely shredded
18 scallops (with or without the corals),
  cleaned
balsamic vinegar to garnish
1 punnet cress to garnish
salt and ground black pepper

1 Heat half the oil in a large frying
pan over a medium heat and fry the
pancetta for 8 minutes or until golden.
Add the sage leaves and fry for a
further 1 minute. Tip the mixture and
any oil into a bowl. Cover with foil to
keep it warm.
2 Pat the scallops dry with kitchen

paper and season well with salt and
pepper. Heat the remaining oil in the
pancetta pan, turn up the heat to high
and fry the scallops for 4 minutes,
turning halfway through or until they
are lightly golden and feel springy
when pressed.
3 Divide the scallops among small
serving plates, then spoon the
pancetta mixture and any oil around
them. Dot with balsamic vinegar and
scatter the cress over the top to serve.

Cook's Tip
You can fry the scallops as close
together as you like – it helps them
stay straight rather than tipping over.

NUTRITION PER SERVING 175 cals |
10g fat (1g sats) | 3g carbs | 1.0g salt

Melon and Parma Ham

Serves 4
Preparation time 10 minutes

900g (2lb) cantaloupe melon, chilled
8 thin slices Parma ham
juice of 1 lemon
ground black pepper

1 Cut the melon in half lengthways
and scoop out the seeds. Cut each half
into four wedges.
2 With a sharp knife and a sawing
action, separate the flesh from the
skin, keeping the flesh in position on
the crescent of skin.
3 Cut across the flesh into thick,
bite-sized slices, then push them
alternately in opposite directions to
make an attractive pattern.
4 Roll up each slice of ham into a
cigar shape. Put on serving dishes

with the melon wedges, and sprinkle
with lemon juice and pepper.

Cook's Tip
Prosciutto is Italian dry-cured ham.
It is available from Italian delis and
most supermarkets. Parma ham is a
type of prosciutto, but other types are
less expensive.

NUTRITION PER SERVING 83 cals |
1g fat (0.4g sats) | 12g carbs | 0.7g salt

Smoked Salmon Parcels

Serves 8
Preparation time 35 minutes
Cooking time 5–6 minutes

8 large scallops or 16 small queen scallops with corals
   attached, about 300g (11oz) total weight
2 large ripe avocados, peeled and stones removed
1 large garlic clove, crushed
6 small spring onions, finely chopped
1 green chilli, seeded and chopped (see Cook's Tips, page 69)
1½ tbsp grapeseed oil
grated zest and juice of 1 lime, plus extra to squeeze
8 large slices smoked salmon, about 400g (14oz) total weight
   and 23cm (9in) in length
salt and ground black pepper
rocket leaves and lime wedges to garnish

For the coriander dressing
25g (1oz) fresh coriander sprigs
1 small garlic clove, crushed
50ml (2fl oz) grapeseed oil
1 tbsp lime juice

1 To make the coriander dressing, put all the ingredients
in a blender and process until smooth.
2 To make the parcels, remove any tough membranes from
the scallops and season with salt and pepper. Put them in
a steamer and cook for about 5 minutes or until the flesh
is just white. (Alternatively, put the scallops on a heatproof
plate, cover with another plate and steam over a pan of
simmering water for about 3 minutes on each side. Drain
and set on kitchen paper to cool.)
3 Put the avocados, garlic, spring onions, chilli, oil and
lime zest and juice in a bowl. Mash the avocado with
a fork, mix well and season with salt and pepper.
4 Lay the salmon on a worksurface, put a large scallop
or two small ones on each slice and spoon some avocado
mixture on top. Roll the salmon around the filling. Put the
parcels on serving plates and squeeze over a little lime juice.
Drizzle with the coriander dressing and serve with rocket
and lime wedges.

NUTRITION PER SERVING 209 cals | 12g fat (2g sats) | 3g carbs | 2.3g salt

Potted Prawn Pâté

Serves 4
Preparation time 15 minutes, plus chilling

225g (8oz) cooked peeled prawns
75g (3oz) butter, softened
2 tsp lemon juice
4 tsp freshly chopped parsley
salt and ground black pepper
cooked peeled prawns and lemon slices to garnish
French bread to serve

1 Finely chop the prawns. Beat them into 50g (2oz) butter with the lemon juice, parsley, salt and pepper.
2 Spoon into a serving dish and level the surface. Melt the remaining butter and pour over the prawn mixture. Chill in the fridge for 1 hour. Garnish with prawns and lemon slices. Serve with French bread.

NUTRITION PER SERVING
195 cals | 16g fat (10g sats) | 0.1g carbs | 3.1g salt

Chicken Liver Pâté

Serves 4
Preparation time 15 minutes
Cooking time 10 minutes, plus chilling

700g (1½lb) chicken livers
75g (3oz) butter
1 onion, finely chopped
1 large garlic clove, crushed
1 tbsp double cream
2 tbsp tomato purée
3 tbsp dry sherry or brandy
4 bay leaves to garnish (optional)
hot toast fingers or French bread to serve

1 Trim away any sinews and fat from the livers, then rinse and pat dry. Melt the butter in a frying pan over a low heat, then increase the heat and fry the livers for 5 minutes or until just coloured; do not overcook or they will toughen.
2 Reduce the heat and add the onion and garlic. Cover the pan and cook the mixture for 5 minutes. Tip the contents of the pan into a bowl and cool.
3 Transfer to a food processor or blender with the cream, tomato purée and sherry or brandy, and whiz until smooth.
4 Pack the pâté into four 150ml (¼ pint) individual dishes and cool until firm. Top with bay leaves, if you like. Chill the pâté for at least 2 hours, or even better overnight.
5 Serve with hot toast fingers or French bread.

TRY SOMETHING DIFFERENT
Pack the pâté into a 450g (1lb) loaf tin. After chilling, cut it into chunky slices to serve.

NUTRITION PER SERVING
420 cals | 28g fat (14g sats) | 6g carbs | 0.7g salt

Smoked Mackerel Pâté

Serves 6
Preparation time 10 minutes, plus chilling

275g (10oz) smoked mackerel
50g (2oz) butter, softened
3 tbsp creamed horseradish sauce
2 tbsp single cream
ground black pepper
fresh parsley sprig to garnish

1 The day before you want to serve, skin the mackerel and discard the bones. Mash the flesh in a bowl.
2 Mix the butter with the fish and add the horseradish sauce and cream. Season with pepper. Salt is not usually needed as the fish is quite salty.
3 Spoon the mixture into a serving dish, cover tightly and chill until required.
4 Leave the pâté at room temperature for 30 minutes before serving. Decorate the surface of the pâté with indentations made using a blunt-edged knife and garnish with a parsley sprig.

TRY SOMETHING DIFFERENT
Herby Mackerel Pâté Cream together 125g (4oz) butter, 2 tbsp freshly chopped parsley and 1 tsp lemon juice and beat well. In a 600ml (1 pint) dish, layer the mackerel mixture and parsley butter, beginning and ending with a thick layer of mackerel.

NUTRITION PER SERVING
249 cals | 23g fat (8g sats) | 2g carbs | 1.2g salt

Chunky Pâté with Port

Serves 8
Preparation time 25 minutes, plus setting
Cooking time about 1½ hours, plus cooling

350g (12oz) boneless belly pork, rind removed,
  roughly chopped
1 large skinless chicken breast, about 150g (5oz)
225g (8oz) chicken livers, trimmed
1 large duck breast, about 200g (7oz), skinned and chopped
  into small pieces
125g (4oz) rindless streaky bacon rashers, diced
3 tbsp port or brandy
1 tbsp freshly chopped rosemary
2 tbsp green peppercorns
salt and ground black pepper
crusty bread to serve

To finish
a few bay leaves
2 tsp powdered gelatine
150ml (¼ pint) white port or sherry

1 Preheat the oven to 170°C (150°C fan oven) mark 3.
Coarsely mince the belly pork in a food processor, retaining
some small chunks. Mince the chicken breast in the
processor, then mince the chicken livers.
2 Mix all the meats together in a large bowl with the port
or brandy, 1 tsp salt, some pepper, the chopped rosemary
and green peppercorns.
3 Pack the mixture into a 1.1 litre (2 pint) terrine and
stand it in a roasting tin containing 2.5cm (1in) boiling
water. Cover with foil and cook in the oven for 1 hour.
4 Remove the foil and arrange a few bay leaves on top of
the pâté. Cook for a further 30 minutes or until the juices
run clear when the pâté is pierced in the centre with a
sharp knife or skewer.
5 Drain the meat juices into a small bowl and leave to
cool. Skim off any fat, then sprinkle over the gelatine and
leave until softened. Stand the bowl in a pan of gently
simmering water until the gelatine has dissolved. Stir in
the port or sherry. Make up to 450ml (¾ pint) with water,
if necessary.
6 Pour the jellied liquid over the pâté and chill until set.
Store the pâté in the fridge for up to two days. Serve with
crusty bread.

NUTRITION PER SERVING 344 cals | 22g fat (8g sats) | 3g carbs | 0.7g salt

Salmon and Mackerel Terrine

Serves 8
Preparation time 20 minutes, plus chilling

350g (12oz) smoked salmon, in long slices
200g (7oz) full-fat cream cheese
125g (4oz) hot-smoked mackerel, skinned and flaked
finely grated zest of 1–2 lemons to taste
2 tbsp freshly chopped dill
25g (1oz) cornichons, finely chopped
300ml (½ pint) double cream
salt and ground black pepper
lemon wedges and bread or Melba toasts to serve

1 Line a 900g (2lb) loaf tin with clingfilm, allowing the excess to hang over the edges. Then line the tin with some of the salmon slices so there are no gaps.
2 Put the cream cheese and mackerel into a food processor and whiz until well combined. Empty into a bowl and stir in the lemon zest, dill, cornichons, a little salt and plenty of pepper.
3 In a separate bowl, lightly whip the cream until it just holds its shape, then fold through the fish mixture.
4 Spoon the filling into the lined tin and press down. Fold over any overhanging salmon, then cover the filling with the remaining salmon. Fold over the clingfilm, then wrap the whole tin well in clingfilm. Chill for at least 4 hours or ideally overnight.
5 To serve, peel off the clingfilm to expose the top layer of salmon. Put a serving plate over the terrine, then invert. Lift off the tin and peel off the clingfilm. Serve in slices with lemon wedges and bread or Melba toasts.

NUTRITION PER SERVING 413 cals | 39g fat (18g sats) | 0.5g carbs | 2.1g salt

Chicken and Vegetable Terrine

Serves 8
Preparation time 40 minutes, plus chilling
Cooking time 1 hour 2 minutes, plus chilling

900g (2lb) chicken joints
1 small slice of white bread, crusts removed
450ml (¾ pint) double cream, chilled
1 small bunch of watercress, trimmed
125g (4oz) small young carrots
125g (4oz) French beans, trimmed and stringed
275g (10oz) peas in the pod, shelled
75g (3oz) small even-sized button mushrooms
200g (7oz) can artichoke hearts, drained
butter to grease
salt and ground black pepper
rocket leaves to garnish (optional)

For the sauce
225g (8oz) ripe tomatoes, skinned and quartered
  (see page 277)
125ml (4fl oz) vegetable oil
50ml (2fl oz) white wine vinegar
75ml (2½fl oz) tomato purée

1 Cut all the chicken flesh away from the chicken bones; discard the bones, skin and fat. Finely mince the chicken and the bread. Chill for 30 minutes. Stir the cream into the chicken mixture with salt and pepper to taste.
2 Mix one-third of the chicken mixture with the watercress. Cover both bowls and chill for 2 hours.
3 Preheat the oven to 170°C (150°C fan oven) mark 3. Cut the carrots and beans into neat matchstick pieces, 2.5cm (1in) by 3mm (⅛in). Blanch the carrots, beans and peas for 2 minutes in separate pans of boiling water. Drain.
4 Trim the mushroom stalks level with the caps. Cut the mushrooms across into slices 5mm (¼in) thick. Dice the artichoke hearts into 5mm (¼in) pieces.
5 Grease and base line a 1.1 litre (2 pint) lidded terrine dish. Spread half the watercress and chicken mixture over the base of the terrine. Arrange the carrots in neat crossways lines over the top, then spread one-quarter of the chicken mixture carefully over the carrots.
6 Lightly seasoning the vegetables as they are layered, sprinkle the peas over the chicken mixture in the dish and put another thin layer of chicken mixture on top. Next, put the mushrooms in crossways lines and top with the remaining watercress and chicken mixture. Arrange the

artichokes on top, cover with half the remaining chicken mixture, arrange the beans in crossways lines, and cover with the remaining chicken mixture.
7 Put a double sheet of greased greaseproof paper on top and cover tightly with the lid. Put the terrine in a roasting tin with water to come halfway up the side. Cook in the oven for 1 hour or until firm.
8 Cool a little, drain off any juices, then invert the terrine on to a serving plate. Cool, then chill for 1 hour.
9 Meanwhile, to make the sauce. Purée the tomatoes with the oil, vinegar, tomato purée and seasoning. Rub through a sieve. Chill lightly before serving, then garnish with some rocket leaves, if you like.

NUTRITION PER SERVING 616 cals | 54g fat (23g sats) | 8g carbs | 0.6g salt

Shellfish
and Fish

Shellfish

Shellfish are prized for their delicate flavours and textures, especially the excellent species that are caught off the UK coastline – including lobsters, crabs and scallops.

Shellfish can be divided into three main categories: crustaceans, molluscs and cephalopods. Crustaceans – lobsters, crabs, crayfish, prawns, shrimps and so on – have hard external skeletons, segmented to allow for movement.

Molluscs live inside one or two hard shells (valves). Cockles, winkles and whelks are univalves. The bivalves include mussels, clams, oysters and scallops.

Cephalopods, namely squid, octopus and cuttlefish, belong to the mollusc family, but they do not have external shells; the clear plastic-like quill inside squid is effectively an internal shell.

Choosing shellfish

Always buy shellfish from a reputable fishmonger or supermarket fresh fish counter with a high turnover of stock and prepare it within 24 hours. Most seafood from supermarkets has been previously frozen, so don't re-freeze it. It is unwise to gather shellfish yourself, unless you are sure the area is free from pollution; molluscs are particularly susceptible to pollution and can carry diseases.

When choosing molluscs, select those with tightly closed, undamaged shells. Mussels, clams, scallops and oysters that are sold fresh are still alive and an open shell may indicate that the shellfish is far from fresh. A sharp tap on the shell should persuade it to close up if it's alive, if not discard it. Similarly, univalves should withdraw back into their shell when prodded.

When buying cooked shellfish, such as lobster, crab and prawns, make sure the shells are intact. Lobsters and crabs should feel heavy for their size and have a fresh aroma. Any unpleasant smell is an indication that the shellfish is past its best. When choosing cephalopods, such as octopus and squid, look for those with firm flesh and a smell of the sea.

Crustacea

A large family of shellfish, crustacea are characterised by an external skeleton and jointed limbs. They include crabs, lobsters and shrimps.

Molluscs

These are a highly diverse group of shellfish including bivalves, gastropods and cephalopods:

Bivalves With a hinged, two-piece external shell, this group of shellfish includes mussels and oysters.

Gastropods have snail-like shells and include whelks, winkles, conch, abalone and limpets.

Cephalopods are classed as shellfish, although most do not have an obvious external skeleton and have a modified body that includes tentacles or arms, such as squid, cuttlefish and octopus. The 'shell' is in the form of a hard, transparent internal quill.

Buying shellfish

Shellfish have seasons and although some are available all year round, others are harder to find. Weather conditions can affect availability and therefore cost. When buying crustaceans they should smell sweet and fresh and be moist. Crabs, lobsters and langoustines are best when sold live for home cooking and should feel heavy for their size.

When buying molluscs, look for those with shells that are smooth and shiny. The shells of oysters, scallops, clams and mussels should be shut, or should close when tapped. Some shellfish are always sold live. This includes all the bivalves except scallops, which are sometimes removed from their shells and cleaned. Live crabs, lobsters and crayfish should display plenty of movement, with snapping claws or pincers. When buying precooked shellfish, such as langoustines, prawns and crab, buy from a reputable supplier. Use all shellfish on the day of purchase.

Frozen shellfish

Apart from scallops, prawns and other frozen shellfish, are sold raw or cooked. Shellfish can be cooked from frozen.

Preparing and cooking shellfish

Stir-fry This method is best suited to pieces of firm shellfish, prawns or squid. Toss the prepared fish in a little oil, with spices and aromatics, in a wok for 1–2 minutes until just cooked through. Prawns are cooked when they turn pink. Do not overcook them or they will be tough.

Sear Use for firm-fleshed shellfish such as scallops. Heat a little oil in a frying pan until very hot, then cook briefly for about 1 minute on each side, to give it a flavourful crust on the outside while the centre remains tender.

Deep-fry Use for all shellfish. Prepare the fish and a coating (which can be batter, seasoned flour, or flour, egg and breadcrumbs). Heat vegetable oil in a deep-fryer to

180°C or until a cube of bread browns in 40 seconds. Coat the shellfish, then carefully lower into the oil a few pieces at a time and cook until crisp and golden. Remove using a slotted spoon. Drain on kitchen paper.

Grill Marinate the shellfish, or season and brush with oil, then grill on both sides until just cooked through.

Braise Best suited to shellfish such as prawns. Prepare a tomato sauce, then add the prepared shellfish. Spoon the sauce over to cover and simmer gently for 5–10 minutes until just cooked through. It will need only a few minutes.

Steam Season and/or marinate the shellfish, then put into a dish that will fit into a bamboo steamer. Put the steamer into a pan or wok over boiling water. Steam for 10–15 minutes until firm and just cooked through.

Preparing prawns

1 To shell prawns, pull off the head and put to one side. Using pointed scissors, cut through the soft shell on the belly side.
2 Prise the shell off, leaving the tail attached. (Add to the head to be used for making stock.)
3 Using a small sharp knife, make a shallow cut along the length of the back. Using the point of the knife, remove and discard the black vein (the intestinal tract) that runs along the back.
4 To 'butterfly' the prawn, cut halfway through the flesh lengthways from head to tail, and open up the prawn.

Preparing crabs

1 Live crabs must be humanely killed before cooking. Put the crab into the freezer for 5 minutes, then put belly-up on a board. Plunge a large cook's knife straight down into the crab's head, between or just below the eyes. Put into a pan of boiling water and cook for 5 minutes per 450g (1lb), or steam for 8 minutes per 450g (1lb).
2 To serve whole, simply set on the table with crackers and crab picks for diners to use themselves.
3 To remove the cooked meat for a recipe, put the crab on a board, with the belly facing up. Twist off the legs and claws. Lift off and discard the 'apron' (tail) – long and pointed in a male, short and broad in a female. Pull the body out of the shell and remove and discard the feathery gills and grey stomach sac. Cut the body into pieces and pick out the meat using your fingers and a crab pick or small knife. Scrape the brown meat from the shell, keeping it separate from the white meat. If there is roe in a female, keep that separate, too.

4 Crack the claws with the back of a large knife, and pull out the meat in a single piece or in large chunks.

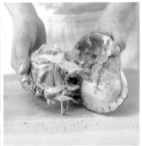

5 Cut through the shells of the legs with scissors, then cut through the opposite side. Pull off the shell halves to expose the meat and remove.

Preparing lobsters

1 To kill a lobster humanely before grilling, boiling or baking, put it into the freezer for 5 minutes. Then put it on a chopping board and hold the body firmly. Take a large cook's knife and plunge it straight down into the lobster's head, right between or just below the eyes. (It is inhumane to simply plunge it into boiling water or to put it into cold water and then bring it up to the boil.)
2 To cook the lobster whole, put it in a large pan of boiling water and cook for 15–20 minutes (see Cook's Tip, page 92).
3 If you are going to split the raw lobster for grilling or baking, cut the freshly killed lobster right through the head, then cut all the way down the length of the tail to split it in two. Remove the head sac, which lies just behind the eyes, and discard. If you wish, you can remove the black coral (tomalley) and the green intestine, which lie inside the back of the shell just behind the head sac, or they may be left in place for cooking.
4 If you want the tail meat in one piece, split the head to where the tail begins, then use scissors to cut through the soft shell of the belly, down to the tail.

5 Pull the tail meat out with your fingers. Clean the head as in step 3. Cut off the claws and spiny legs. Crack the claws with a hammer or lobster cracker and remove the meat. Save the shells to make stock.

Molluscs, Prawns and Crustacea

1 Squid: all year
Squid are often sold ready prepared, either as whole tubes or sliced into rings. Small squid can be sautéed, poached, grilled or deep-fried; larger ones require stewing.

2 Octopus: May–Dec
Octopus can grow to up to 3m (10ft). Small specimens are better for eating, as large ones are usually tough. All but the smallest need long, slow braising or stewing.

3 Crayfish: all year
Crayfish are sold both live and ready cooked. Use small crayfish to garnish fish dishes or in soups; larger ones are best served cold with a salad or hot with a creamy sauce.

4 Tiger prawn: all year
A translucent grey colour with dark stripes when raw, tiger prawns turn pink on cooking and have tender, juicy flesh. Sold either raw or cooked, peeled or unpeeled; sometimes partially shelled with just the tail left on. Raw prawns should be deveined, and can be peeled or cooked in the shell: grill, barbecue, stir-fry, pan-fry, braise, coat and deep-fry; add to fish stews and curries.

5 Shrimp: Feb–Oct
Greyish-brown when alive, shrimps become pink or brown when cooked. Fresh shrimps are invariably sold cooked, either peeled or whole, and have a delicate flavour; frozen and canned shrimps are also available.

6 Langoustine
Pink-shelled langoustines are a relative of the lobster. They are sometimes referred to as Norwegian lobster and Dublin Bay prawns. They have tender flesh that is sweet and succulent. They go well with Mediterranean flavours such as tomatoes, garlic, white wine and fresh herbs. Poach, grill or add to recipes such as paella and risotto.

7 (Common) Prawn: all year
Prawns are available in a variety of sizes and most are sold ready-cooked, but raw prawns – especially king prawns and tiger prawns – are increasingly available. Buy fresh ones if possible, as these tend to have a superior flavour and texture. Cook just until they turn pink and opaque: 3–8 minutes depending on size. Do not overcook or they will toughen. Heat ready-cooked prawns through for a few minutes only. Deep-sea and Mediterranean prawns are similar in appearance; treat in the same way.

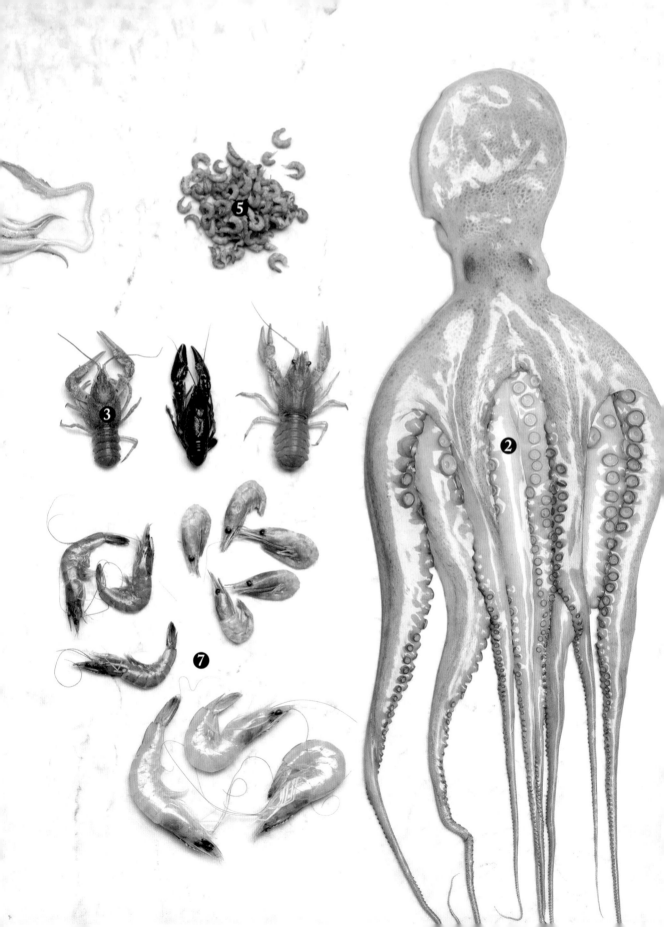

Crabs, Lobster and Other Crustacea

1 Common crab: all year
The common crab has firm, sweet and well-flavoured flesh. Boil raw crabs. Serve cooked crabmeat with mayonnaise in salads; toss into stir-fries, soups or crab cakes.

2 Soft-shell crab: all year
These crabs are caught after they have shed their hard shell and before they have grown a new one, so the whole crab can be eaten, shell and all. They are usually only available frozen in the UK. Flour and pan- or deep-fry; eat whole.

3 Lobster: April–Nov
Sold either live, ready-cooked or ready-dressed, lobsters have a fine, delicate flavour. Serve with a simple accompaniment, such as good mayonnaise or a warm butter sauce.

4 Mussel: Sept–March
With tender, smooth, sweet-tasting flesh, mussels can be steamed, stuffed and baked, or grilled.

5 Cockle: May–Dec
These molluscs are invariably sold cooked and shelled, and they are typically eaten plain or with vinegar.

6 Clam: all year, best in autumn
There are many varieties of this bivalve, varying considerably in size. Clams are sold live in their shells and smaller ones are eaten raw; larger ones are cooked before they are eaten. If eating raw, open as for oysters. Otherwise cook and shell clams as for mussels. Clams are available frozen, canned and smoked.

7 Razor clam: all year
Razor clams, a variety of the clam, have a long fragile shell with open ends.

8 Oyster: Sept–April
With the exception of the large varieties, oysters are considered at their best eaten raw. Frozen and smoked oysters are also available. Oysters can be used sparingly to enhance the flavour of some cooked dishes.

9 Scallop: Sept–March
Fresh scallops are sold both in the shell and ready-shelled; they are also available frozen. Scallops may be pan-fried, lightly poached or grilled, but care must be taken to avoid overcooking or their delicate texture will be ruined.

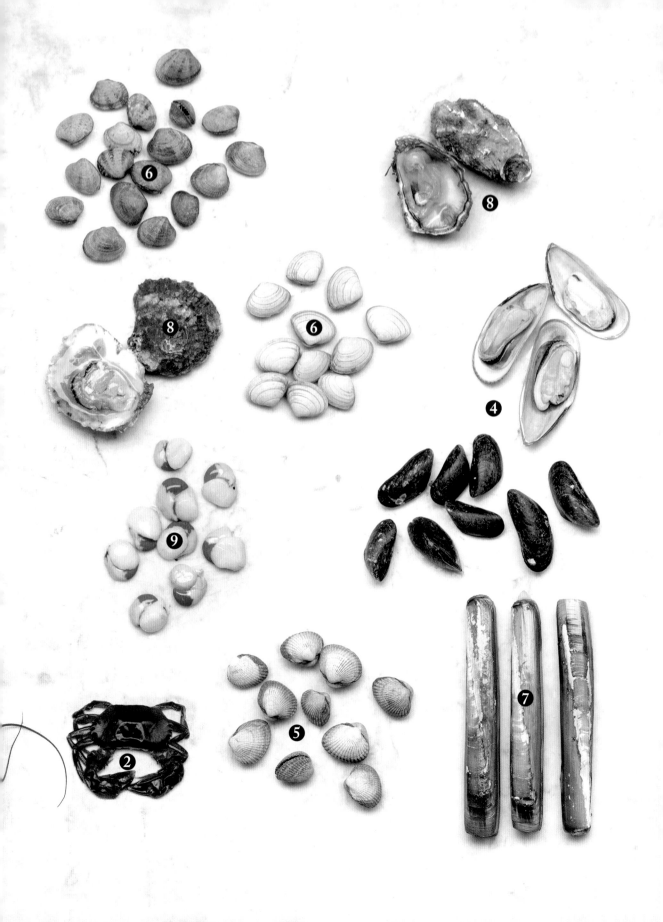

Grilled Lobster

Serves 2
Preparation time 20 minutes
Cooking time 15 minutes

1 killed fresh lobster, about 700g
  (1½lb) (see page 85)
25g (1oz) butter, softened, plus melted
  butter to brush and serve
salt and cayenne pepper

1 Split the lobster lengthways. Remove the head sac, which lies just behind the eyes, and discard. Remove the black coral (tomalley) and the green intestine, which lie inside the back of the shell just behind the head sac.
2 Brush the shell and flesh with melted butter and grill the flesh side for 8–10 minutes, then turn the lobster and grill the shell side for 5 minutes.
3 Dot the flesh with small pieces of softened butter, sprinkle with a little salt and cayenne pepper and serve immediately, with melted butter.

Cook's Tip
If you are able to buy a live lobster from your fishmonger, choose one that has all claws and legs intact. Prepare as page 85.

NUTRITION PER SERVING 186 cals | 120g fat (7g sats) | 0g carbs | 1.6g salt

Lobster Thermidor

Serves 4
Preparation time 30 minutes
Cooking time about 15 minutes

4 cooked lobsters, about 450g (1lb) each
25g (1oz) butter
1 shallot, finely chopped
150ml (¼ pint) dry white wine
300ml (½ pint) Béchamel Sauce (see page 16)
1½ tbsp freshly chopped parsley
2 tsp freshly chopped tarragon
6 tbsp freshly grated Parmesan
a pinch of mustard powder
salt
a pinch of paprika

1 Lay the lobsters, back upwards, on a board. Using a sharp knife, split each lobster lengthways cleanly in two, piercing through the cross at the centre of the head, then prepare them according to the instructions for raw lobster on page 85, steps 3–5. Cut the tail meat into thick slices. Scrub the body shell under cold running water and dry well.
2 Melt the butter in a pan, add the shallot and fry gently for 5 minutes to soften. Add the wine and let it bubble until reduced by half. Add the béchamel sauce and simmer until reduced to a creamy consistency.
3 Preheat the grill.
4 Add the lobster meat to the pan with the herbs, 4 tbsp of the Parmesan, and mustard, salt and paprika to taste.
5 Spoon the mixture into the cleaned shells, sprinkle with the remaining cheese and pop under the hot grill briefly, to brown the top. Serve at once.

Cook's Tip
To cook a lobster, once killed (see page 85), put into a pan of boiling water. Boil steadily, allowing 10 minutes for the first 450g (1lb) and a further 5 minutes for each additional 450g (1lb). Leave to cool in the liquid.

NUTRITION PER SERVING 400 cals | 19g fat (8g sats) | 8g carbs | 3g salt

Classic Dressed Crab

Serves 2
Preparation time 30 minutes

1 medium cooked crab, about
 900g (2lb), cleaned (see page 85)
1 tbsp lemon juice
2 tbsp fresh white breadcrumbs
1 medium egg, hard-boiled
1 tbsp freshly chopped parsley
salt and ground black pepper
salad leaves, and brown bread and butter to serve

1 Flake the white crab meat into a bowl, removing any shell or membrane, then add 1 tsp lemon juice and season with salt and pepper to taste. Mix lightly with a fork.
2 Pound the brown crab meat in another bowl and work in the breadcrumbs and remaining lemon juice. Season with salt and pepper to taste.
3 Using a small spoon, put the white crab meat into the cleaned crab shell, arranging it down either side and piling it up well. Spoon the brown meat into the middle between the sections of white meat.
4 Chop the egg white; press the yolk through a sieve. To garnish the crab, spoon lines of chopped parsley, sieved egg yolk and chopped egg white along the 'joins' between the white and brown crab meat. Serve on a bed of salad leaves, with brown bread and butter.

Cook's Tip
Crab is available cooked or live, but it is better to buy a live crab and cook it at home to ensure it is perfectly fresh (see page 85).

NUTRITION PER SERVING 180 cals | 8g fat (1g sats) | 5g carbs | 3g salt

Prawns Fried in Garlic

Serves 2
Preparation time 10 minutes
Cooking time 5 minutes

50g (2oz) unsalted butter
2 tbsp olive oil
12 raw Dublin Bay prawns in their
  shells
3 garlic cloves, crushed
4 tbsp brandy
salt and ground black pepper
fresh flat-leafed parsley to garnish
lemon wedges and crusty bread to
  serve

1 Heat the butter with the oil in a
large heavy-based frying pan.
2 Add the prawns and garlic and fry
over a high heat for about 5 minutes,
tossing the prawns constantly, until
the shells have turned pink.
3 Sprinkle the brandy over the
prawns and let it bubble rapidly to
reduce right down. Season with salt
and pepper.
4 Serve immediately, garnished with
parsley and with lemon wedges and
plenty of crusty bread. Remember to
provide everyone with finger bowls
and napkins.

NUTRITION PER SERVING 360 cals |
32g fat (15g sats) | 0.1g carbs | 1.4g salt

Oysters

Serves 2
Preparation time 20 minutes

12 oysters
salt and ground black pepper
lemon wedges and Tabasco sauce to
  serve

1 Scrub the oysters with a stiff
scrubbing brush, then prise open.
2 Remove the beard from each and
loosen the oysters, leaving them in the
deeper half-shell. Season lightly with
salt and pepper and serve with lemon
wedges and Tabasco sauce.

Cook's Tip
To open an oyster, hold firmly in a tea
towel with the pointed hinge sticking
out and the flat side up. Insert the
tip of an oyster knife near the hinge,
then slide it round the edge between
the shells, holding the oyster level to
avoid spilling the juice. Pull the shells
apart with your fingers, then detach
the oyster from the top shell.

NUTRITION PER SERVING 40 cals |
0.8g fat (0.2g sats) | 2g carbs | 2g salt

Moules Marinière

Serves 4
Preparation time 15 minutes
Cooking time 20 minutes

2kg (4½lb) fresh mussels, scrubbed, rinsed and beards
  removed (see Cook's Tips)
25g (1oz) butter
4 shallots, finely chopped
2 garlic cloves, crushed
200ml (7fl oz) dry white wine
2 tbsp freshly chopped flat-leafed parsley
100ml (3½fl oz) single cream
salt and ground black pepper
crusty bread to serve

1 Tap the mussels on the worksurface and discard any that
do not close or that have broken shells. Heat the butter in
a large non-stick lidded frying pan and sauté the shallots
over a medium-high heat for 10 minutes or until soft.
2 Add the garlic, wine and half the parsley to the pan and
bring to the boil. Tip in the mussels and reduce the heat a
little. Cover and cook for about 5 minutes or until all the
shells have opened; discard any mussels that are still closed.
3 Lift out the mussels with a slotted spoon and put into
serving bowls, then cover with foil to keep warm. Add the
cream to the pan, season with salt and pepper, and cook for
1–2 minutes to heat through.
4 Pour a little sauce over the mussels and sprinkle with the
rest of the parsley. Serve immediately with crusty bread.

Cook's Tips
• Mussels are sold either by weight or volume:
  1.1 litres (2 pints) of mussels is roughly equivalent
  to 900g (2lb).
• Do not buy mussels with cracked or open shells.
• To prepare fresh mussels, rinse them under cold running
  water to help rid them of any grit and sand. Scrub the
  mussel shells thoroughly, using a small stiff brush to
  remove any grit and barnacles.
• Pull away the hairy beard, which protrudes from one side
  of the shell. Tap any open mussels sharply with the back
  of the knife or on the surface. If they stay open, throw
  them away.
• Rinse the mussels again under cold running water before
  cooking them.

NUTRITION PER SERVING 262 cals | 13g fat (7g sats) | 2g carbs | 0.9g salt

Coquilles St Jacques

Serves 4
Preparation time 15 minutes
Cooking time 25 minutes

8 medium scallops, prepared (see Cook's Tips), shells
  put to one side
4 tbsp medium white wine
1 bay leaf
40g (1½oz) butter
3 tbsp plain flour
4 tbsp single cream
50g (2oz) Gruyère cheese, grated
450g (1lb) potatoes, boiled and creamed
salt and ground black pepper

1 Preheat the oven to 220°C (200°C fan oven) mark 7.
Scrub four of the round scallop shells under running water
and put to one side.
2 Put the scallops into a small pan and add 150ml (¼ pint)
water, the wine, bay leaf and a good pinch of salt. Bring
slowly to the boil, then cover and simmer gently for about
5 minutes or until the scallops are just tender when tested
with a sharp knife. Lift out with a slotted spoon. Strain and
keep the juices to one side.
3 Melt the butter in a pan. Stir in the flour and cook
gently for 1 minute, stirring. Remove the pan from the heat
and gradually stir in the reserved juices.
4 Bring to the boil slowly over a low heat, then continue
to cook, stirring, for a few minutes until the sauce thickens.
Season with salt and pepper, then simmer gently for
4–5 minutes. Lower the heat and stir in the cream and half
the grated cheese. Cut each scallop into two or three pieces
and stir in.
5 Pipe a border of mashed potato around the edges of
the round scallop shells. Spoon the sauce mixture into the
centre and sprinkle the remaining cheese over the top.
6 Cook in the oven for 15 minutes or until the sauce and
potato are golden.

Cook's Tips
• Two varieties of this pretty, ribbed-shelled mollusc are
  caught around the British coast: the larger great scallop
  and the small pink-shelled queen scallop.
• To prepare fresh scallops, scrub the shells under cold
  running water. Discard any scalllops that do not close
  when tapped sharply with the back of a knife.
• Hold, rounded-side down, in your palm and insert the
  point of a sturdy knife between the shells close to the
  hinge. Twist the knife to prise the shells apart. Cut round
  the top shell to sever the muscle. Push the top shell back
  until the hinge snaps. Rinse the scallop (still attached to
  the lower shell), under cold running water. Using a small
  knife, cut away and discard the soft grey, fringe-like
  membrane. Slide the knife under the black thread on the
  side of the scallop. Gently pull it off with the attached
  black intestinal bag. Ease the scallop free from the
  bottom shell. If required, separate the roe or 'coral' from
  the white scallop meat.

NUTRITION PER SERVING 465 cals | 18g fat (10g sats) | 36g carbs | 1.6g salt

Scampi Provençale

Serves 4
Preparation time 25 minutes
Cooking time 20 minutes

3 tbsp olive oil
4 shallots, finely chopped
3 garlic cloves, crushed
1 tbsp sun-dried tomato paste
150ml (¼ pint) dry white wine
700g (1½lb) ripe, flavourful tomatoes, skinned, seeded and
  roughly chopped (see page 277)
bouquet garni (1 bay leaf, a few fresh parsley and
  thyme sprigs)
700g (1½lb) peeled and deveined raw scampi or tiger prawns
  (see page 85)
salt and ground black pepper
freshly chopped parsley to garnish
rice and a leafy salad to serve

1 Heat the oil in a large frying pan, add the shallots
and cook for 1–2 minutes. Add the garlic and cook for
30 seconds, then stir in the tomato paste and cook for
1 minute. Pour in the wine, bring to the boil and let it
bubble for 10 minutes or until well reduced and syrupy.
2 Add the chopped tomatoes and bouquet garni, and
season with salt and pepper to taste. Bring to the boil and
simmer gently for 5 minutes or until pulpy.
3 Add the raw scampi or tiger prawns to the hot sauce and
simmer gently, stirring, for 2–3 minutes until the shellfish
are pink and just cooked through to the centre. Discard the
bouquet garni.
4 Scatter the parsley over and serve immediately, with rice
and a leafy salad.

NUTRITION PER SERVING 300 cals | 12g fat (1g sats) | 12g carbs | 4g salt

Prawn Gumbo

Serves 4
Preparation time 20 minutes
Cooking time 45 minutes

1 tbsp vegetable oil
1 onion, finely sliced
2 celery sticks, finely chopped
2 green peppers, seeded and roughly chopped
1–2 red chillies to taste, seeded and finely chopped (see
  Cook's Tip, page 69)
3 fresh thyme sprigs
2 garlic cloves, crushed
2 × 400g cans chopped tomatoes
1 litre (1¾ pints) vegetable stock
200g (7oz) okra, roughly chopped
150g (5oz) basmati rice, washed
300g (11oz) cooked peeled king prawns
a large handful of fresh flat-leafed parsley, roughly chopped
salt and ground black pepper

1 Heat the oil in a large pan and gently fry the onion,
celery and peppers for 5 minutes until beginning to soften.
Stir in the chillies, thyme, garlic, tomatoes, stock and okra.
Bring to the boil, then reduce the heat and simmer for
20 minutes or until everything is tender.
2 Stir in the rice, reduce the heat and simmer for a further
20 minutes, stirring occasionally or until the rice is cooked
and most of the liquid has been absorbed.
3 Stir in the prawns, heat through and season with salt and
pepper. Discard the thyme sprigs, garnish with the parsley
and serve at once.

NUTRITION PER SERVING 309 cals | 5g fat (1g sats)| 42g carbs | 0.6g salt

Fried Squid and Chorizo

Serves 4 as tapas
Preparation time 5 minutes
Cooking time 5 minutes

½ tbsp olive oil
250g (9oz) baby squid, sliced
1 garlic clove, crushed
75g (3oz) chorizo, skinned and sliced
420g can butter beans, drained and rinsed
a squeeze of lemon juice
a small handful of freshly chopped mint
salt and ground black pepper

1 Heat the oil in a frying pan and cook the squid and
garlic for 30 seconds or until the squid is cooked. Put into
a warmed serving dish.
2 Return the pan to the heat and cook the chorizo for
2 minutes or until golden. Toss through the butter beans
and add to the squid. Quickly stir in the lemon juice,
seasoning and mint, and then serve.

NUTRITION PER SERVING 205 cals | 8g fat (2g sats) | 15g carbs | 2.3g salt

Fish

Fish is classified into two main categories: white fish or demersal, which have their oil concentrated in the liver; and oily fish or pelagic, where the oil is dispersed throughout the flesh. There are two types of white fish: round species, such as cod, and flat species, such as plaice. White fish have a more delicate flavour and texture than oily fish.

Fish is tasty, satisfying and highly nutritious. It is high in protein and rich in B vitamins, minerals and natural oils. White fish are low in calories, while oil-rich fish are an important source of vitamins A and D, and omega-3 fatty acids that help to lower blood cholesterol levels.

Some fish are available fresh all year round, whereas others have a close period when they cannot be fished, which is usually the spawning time. General availability is given in the individual entries, but it can vary depending on the region and weather conditions. There is concern about the impact of over-fishing, in the North Sea in particular. Stocks of popular fish – including cod, haddock, skate and tuna – have become depleted and quotas have been established to prevent further deterioration. Consumers are being encouraged to buy farmed fish and less vulnerable species, such as hoki, witch and tilapia.

In addition to fresh fish, some varieties are sold preserved by salting, marinating or smoking. There are two methods of smoking fish: hot and cold. Most cold-smoked fish, like kippers, have a strong smoky flavour and must be cooked before they are eaten. The most notable exception is salmon, which is cold-smoked for a long time and eaten raw. Hot-smoked fish, such as trout, doesn't need further cooking. Both hot- and cold-smoked mackerel are available, although the former is more common.

Buying fish

Freshness is of prime importance when it comes to choosing and buying fish. Fresh fish should be evaluated with both your eyes and your nose. The smell of truly fresh fish is, somewhat surprisingly, not a fishy smell. It is a fresh sea smell or, in fact, hardly any smell at all – and you shouldn't be able to detect it until you get quite close to the fish. Whole fish must have bright eyes standing proud of the head rather than sunk into it, glossy, moist, firm skin, tight-fitting scales and vivid pink or red gills. The fish should feel stiff to the touch and smell like a whiff of sea air. Fillets, steaks and cutlets must have translucent flesh and show no signs of discoloration. Avoid any that look wet, shiny or slimy. Smoked fish should appear glossy with a fresh smoky aroma. Ideally, fish should be cooked on the day you purchase it, but it can be stored, well wrapped, in the fridge for up to 24 hours.

If you are buying frozen fish, make sure it is frozen hard with no sign of partial thawing, freezer burn or damaged packaging. Frozen fish is best thawed in the fridge overnight before cooking.

Preparing fish

Your supplier can gut and clean fish for you, if you don't want to do it. Ask for heads, bones and trimmings to make into stock, either for your chosen recipe, or to freeze for future use. Prepare and cook fish as soon as possible after purchase. Note that once fish has been cut into pieces it is liable to deteriorate more rapidly.

Storing fish

Fish is always best eaten fresh, so make it the last thing on your shopping list, then store it in the fridge as soon as you get home, and cook it that day.

Frozen fish is usually snap-frozen shortly after it is caught, and is generally of good quality. It is most often prepared as fillets, making it even easier to prepare and cook, and is also used in processed products, such as fish fingers and fish cakes. Many types of fish and processed foods can be cooked directly from frozen. Refer to the directions on the pack.

Other frozen fish should be thawed according to the pack instructions and cooked as for fresh fish.

Freezing and thawing fish

Fish can be frozen whole or in fillets, cutlets or steaks. Always prepare and freeze fish as soon as possible after purchase.

1 Gut and clean the fish. Pat dry on kitchen paper, then snip off any sharp fins or spikes.
2 Wrap fish or fillets individually in clingfilm or a freezer bag, making sure the wrapping is airtight. Label with the date and store in the freezer. Use within two to three months for the best flavour and texture.
3 To thaw, put the fish in the fridge until completely thawed. This may take 24 hours for a large fish.
4 Do not refreeze thawed raw fish. You can, however, freeze it again after you have cooked it.

Cooking fish

Fish is relatively quick to cook, whichever method you use. To check when fish is cooked, insert a thin skewer into the thickest part of the flesh. It should pass through easily and the flesh should begin to flake. White fish loses its translucency when it is cooked, turning white and opaque.

Bake This is suitable for most whole fish, steaks, cutlets and fillets. Put the fish into an ovenproof dish, season with salt and pepper, then add herbs, a knob of butter and a little stock or white wine. Or wrap the fish in greased foil with herbs, seasoning, lemon slices and a knob of butter or a little liquid. Bake at 180°C (160°C fan oven) mark 4, allowing 30–40 minutes for large whole fish, 15–25 minutes for steaks, cutlets and small fish.

Barbecue This is suitable for many types of fish, especially firm-textured varieties and oily fish including trout, red mullet and sardines. Special fish-shaped racks can be used to prevent whole fish from breaking up; or fish can be threaded on to long skewers.

Braise Cooking fish on a bed of sautéed vegetables in a sealed pan is another good method, especially suited to firm, meaty fish, such as monkfish or tuna. Lay the fish on top of the vegetables, add some stock, court bouillon or wine, cover and cook for 10–20 minutes over a low heat or in the oven at 180°C (160°C fan oven) mark 4.

Cook en papillote Small whole fish, cutlets and fillets cook well in a sealed paper or foil parcel with flavourings such as herbs, spices, a flavoured butter or citrus juice.

Deep-fry Small whole fish, such as whitebait and squid, as well as cutlets and fillets are suited to deep-frying. Normally the fish is first coated with seasoned flour, beaten egg and breadcrumbs, or batter, which forms a crisp, protective coating.

To make a suitable coating batter, sift 125g (4oz) plain flour with a large pinch of salt into a bowl, add 1 egg, then gradually beat in 150ml (¼ pint) milk, or milk and water mixed, until smooth.

Heat the oil in a deep-fryer to 190°C (test by frying a small cube of bread; it should brown in 20 seconds), dip the fish into the batter, or flour, egg and breadcrumbs, then lower into the oil in the basket and deep-fry for 4–5 minutes until the batter is crisp and golden brown and the fish is cooked. Drain on kitchen paper.

Griddle cook
Cooking fish on a ridged cast-iron or non-stick griddle pan is an excellent quick method. It's best applied to firmer fish, such as monkfish, tuna, swordfish and squid, which will hold together over the high heat. This method produces attractive criss-cross markings on the fish.

Grill This method is ideal for cooking small whole fish, thin fillets and thicker cuts. Make two or three slashes through the skin on each side of whole fish to allow the heat to penetrate through to the flesh. Brush with oil or melted butter and grill under a medium heat, basting frequently and turning thicker cuts halfway through. Allow 4–5 minutes for thin fillets; 8–10 minutes for thicker cuts and small whole fish.

Pan-fry A good technique for small oily fish, such as sardines, herring and red mullet, all need the merest lick of oil or butter. White fish should be coated in seasoned flour or egg and breadcrumbs before shallow-frying in a little hot oil, clarified butter, or oil and butter. Allow 3–4 minutes to pan-fry small whole fish, fillets and steaks, 8–10 minutes for larger cuts, which will need turning halfway through.

Poach This method is perfect for larger whole fish such as salmon and sea bass, as well as smaller whole fish, cutlets and fillets. The fish is gently cooked in a court bouillon, flavoured broth or milk. Heat the liquid in a shallow pan, or fish kettle if cooking large whole fish, then add the fish and simmer very gently until just cooked. Cooking times vary considerably, depending on size and thickness. The cooking liquor can be used to make a sauce.

To poach a whole salmon to serve cold: put the cleaned fish into a fish kettle, add sufficient court bouillon to cover, put on a tight-fitting lid and slowly bring to a simmer; simmer for about 2 minutes, then turn off the heat and leave the fish to cool completely; it will slowly cook in the residual heat.

Microwave cooking This is ideal for small whole fish, and fish fillets and steaks of uniform thickness. Cook in a covered container with a little butter or liquid and season after cooking. Cooking time is determined by the thickness of the fish and the quantity; for example, 450g (1lb) fish fillets would take about 4–5 minutes, plus 2 minutes standing time.

Steam This is a simple, healthy technique, suitable for whole fish, steaks and fillets. The fish cooks in its own juices, so much of the original flavour is retained. Season the fish, put in the steamer over boiling water and cover with a tight-fitting lid. Allow 5–10 minutes for fillets; 15–20 minutes for steaks and whole fish.

Round Sea Fish

1 Haddock: May–Feb
A grey-skinned fish with firm white flesh, usually sold as fillets or steaks. Suited to most cooking methods. Smoked haddock is pale yellow; a bright yellow-orange colour indicates it has been artificially dyed as well. Finnan haddock are split, lightly salted and smoked. Arbroath smokies are hot-smoked haddock, which don't need further cooking.

2 Bream (sea), red: June–Feb
With firm, delicately flavoured white flesh, whole bream may be stuffed and baked, poached or braised. Fry or grill fillets.

3 Coley (saithe): Aug–Feb
The pinkish-grey flesh of coley turns white when cooked. Sold as fillets. Cook as cod, with some liquid, as the flesh can be dry.

4 Hake: June–March
A member of the cod family and similar in shape, but with a closer-textured white flesh and a finer flavour. Hake is sold whole, and as steaks, cutlets and fillets. Cook as for cod.

5 Bass: Aug–March
Delicate white or pale pink flesh. Bass is sold whole (5a) – up to 4.5kg (10lb) – or as steaks or fillets (5b). Small whole fish can be grilled; steaks and fillets are usually poached or baked.

6 Cod: June–Feb
Popular for its close-textured white flesh, cod is usually sold as steaks or fillets; smaller fish may be sold whole. Suitable for most cooking methods. Smoked cod, salt cod and cod's roe are also available.

7 Mullet, red: May–Nov
Unrelated to the grey mullet, this small bright red fish has firm flesh with a unique, delicate flavour. Sold whole and suitable for pan-frying, grilling, barbecuing and baking.

8 Mullet, grey: Sept–Feb
Similar to sea bass but with an inferior flavour and texture, grey mullet is sold whole or as fillets. Suitable for baking, grilling, steaming or poaching.

9 Whiting: June–Feb
A fairly small fish with soft and white flesh with a delicate flavour. Sold whole or as fillets; it is best poached, steamed or pan-fried.

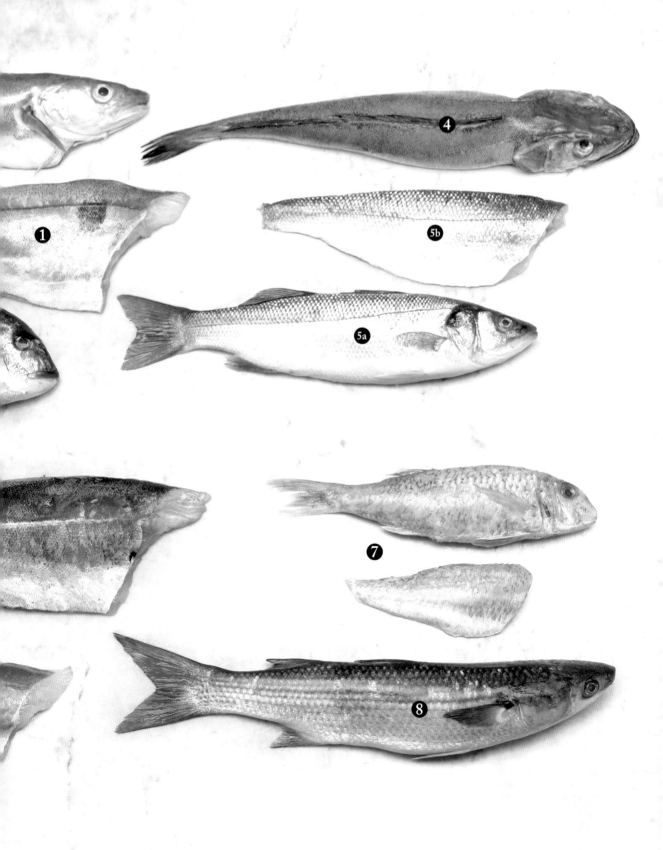

Flat Sea Fish

1 Sole: May–Feb
This name is applied to several species, including lemon sole (1a), Dover sole (1b) and witch, or Torbay sole. The Dover sole is one of the finest flat fish, with a delicate flavour. Lemon sole is lighter in colour, slightly longer and its head is more pointed than Dover sole. Witch is shaped like Dover sole, but it has slightly pinkish skin and its flesh tastes more like that of lemon sole. Sold whole or as fillets; sole can be grilled, fried, baked or steamed.

2 Halibut: June–March
A very large flat fish, halibut is prized for its fine-flavoured flesh. Sold as fillets or steaks; cook as for turbot or cod.

3 Turbot: April–Feb
A diamond-shaped fish with very small scales, turbot has tender, creamy-white flesh. It is considered to be the finest of all the flat fish. It is usually sold as steaks. Turbot is versatile and can be grilled, baked or poached.

4 Plaice: May–Feb
A popular variety with soft, white delicately flavoured flesh. Sold whole or as fillets; suitable for most cooking methods, including steaming, frying, baking and grilling.

5 Skate: May–Feb
This is a ray-shaped fish. Only the wings are sold for cooking. They may be fried, grilled or poached.

Oily and Migratory Fish

1 Sea trout: all year, best March–July
The flesh has a flavour and colour rather like salmon, but the texture is coarser and less succulent. Prepare and cook sea trout as for salmon.

2 Herring: May–Dec
A fairly small, round fish with creamy-coloured flesh that has a distinctive flavour. Usually grilled, fried or stuffed and baked. Cured herrings are also available.

3 Eel: all year, best Sept–Dec
With a dense, fatty flesh, eels must be eaten very fresh and are therefore often sold live. They are also sold as fillets and jellied. Fresh eels are best sautéed or stewed.

4 Sardine: Nov–Feb
These are immature pilchards. Most are sold canned in olive oil or tomato sauce, but fresh are increasingly available. They can be grilled, fried or baked.

5 Whitebait: all year, best Feb–June
Tiny silvery young of the sprat or herring, whitebait are eaten whole, typically coated in flour and deep-fried.

6 Salmon: all year
The deep pink flesh turns pale pink when cooked. Fresh wild Scottish salmon is the best; in season from February to August. Farmed and imported salmon are always available. Sold whole, and as steaks and fillets. Bake or poach whole salmon; grill, pan-fry, poach or bake steaks and cutlets.

7 Sprat: Oct; March
Small member of the herring family. Clean through the gills, then grill or fry.

8 Anchovy: all year
Small fish with a strong flavour, usually filleted and cured, by salting or brining. You can sometimes buy fresh anchovies.

9 Tuna: all year; fresh or frozen
The meaty flesh is deep reddish-pink and is sold in steaks or slices. Braise, poach, grill or pan-fry. Canned tuna is popular.

10 Mackerel: all year, best May–June
In plentiful supply and inexpensive. The average mackerel weighs about 450g (1lb). Its beige-pink flesh has a meaty texture and rich flavour. Whole fish and fillets can be grilled, baked, pan-fried or braised.

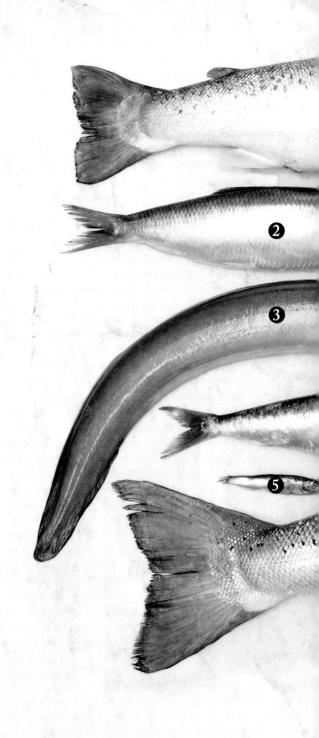

Navarin of Cod

Serves 6
Preparation time 15 minutes
Cooking time 25 minutes

175g (6oz) podded broad beans, skinned (see page 278)
25g (1oz) butter
2 tbsp sunflower oil
1 onion, sliced
225g (8oz) baby carrots, trimmed and halved
225g (8oz) courgettes, cut into 2cm (¾in) chunks
1 garlic clove, crushed
1.1kg (2½lb) thick cod fillet, skinned
4 tbsp plain flour
150ml (¼ pint) dry white wine
300ml (½ pint) fish stock
1 tbsp lemon juice
3 tbsp double cream
2 tbsp freshly chopped flat-leafed parsley, plus extra
 to garnish
salt and ground black pepper
baby new potatoes to serve (optional)

1 If the beans are large, blanch them in boiling water for
1–2 minutes, then drain and refresh in cold water.
2 Heat half the butter and half the oil in a large sauté
pan. Add the onion, carrots, courgettes and garlic, and
cook gently for about 3 minutes or until softened and just
beginning to brown. Remove from the pan and put
to one side.
3 Season the fish with salt and pepper, then dust lightly
with the flour. Heat the remaining butter and oil in the pan
over a medium heat, add the fish and brown on all sides.
Remove from the pan and put to one side.
4 Add the wine to the pan, scraping up any sediment from
the base. Simmer for 1–2 minutes, then put the carrot
mixture and fish back in the pan. Add the beans and stock.
Bring to the boil, then reduce the heat, cover the pan and
simmer gently for 10 minutes or until the fish is opaque
and flakes easily. Stir in the lemon juice, cream and parsley.
Divide among six bowls, garnish with parsley, and serve
with baby new potatoes, if you like.

Cook's Tip
With the depletion of North Sea cod stocks, try to buy
Icelandic or Norwegian cod instead. You can also cook this
recipe with other white fish.

NUTRITION PER SERVING 346 cals | 13g fat (5g sats) | 16g carbs | 0.4g salt

Cod Fillets with a Herby Cheese Crust

Serves 4
Preparation time 30 minutes, plus chilling
Cooking time 15 minutes

4 long skinless cod fillets, about 175g (6oz) each
plain flour, to coat
50g (2oz) fresh white breadcrumbs
50g (2oz) freshly grated Pecorino or Parmesan
2 tbsp freshly chopped parsley
2 tbsp freshly chopped chervil or dill
1 large egg, beaten
oil to grease
salt and ground black pepper
peas and grilled tomatoes to serve

1 Season the fish with salt and pepper and toss in flour to coat, shaking off the excess.
2 Mix the breadcrumbs with the grated cheese, herbs and salt and pepper.
3 Dip the floured cod fillets into the beaten egg, then immediately roll in the breadcrumb mixture to coat thoroughly. Put on a baking sheet, cover lightly and chill for 1 hour.
4 Preheat the grill to medium-hot.
5 Put the fish in a lightly oiled grill pan and grill for 12–14 minutes or until cooked through, turning halfway through. Serve with peas and tomatoes.

NUTRITION PER SERVING 260 cals | 7g fat (3g sats) | 11g carbs | 1.4g salt

Traditional Fish Pie

Serves 4
Preparation time 20 minutes
Cooking time 50 minutes

450g (1lb) haddock, cod or coley fillets
300ml (½ pint) milk
1 bay leaf
6 black peppercorns
2 onion slices for flavouring
65g (2½oz) butter
3 tbsp flour
150ml (¼ pint) single cream
2 medium eggs, hard-boiled, shelled and chopped
2 tbsp freshly chopped parsley
6 tbsp milk
900g (2lb) potatoes, cooked and mashed
1 medium egg
salt and ground black pepper

1 Put the fish in a frying pan, pour over the milk and add the bay leaf, peppercorns, onion slices and a good pinch of salt. Bring slowly to the boil, cover and simmer for 8–10 minutes until the fish flakes when tested with a fork.
2 Lift the fish out of the pan using a fish slice and put on a plate. Flake the fish, discarding the skin and bone. Strain and put the milk to one side. Preheat the oven to 200°C (180°C fan oven) mark 6.
3 Melt 40g (1½oz) butter in a pan, stir in the flour and cook gently for 1 minute, stirring. Remove the pan from the heat and gradually stir in the reserved milk. Bring to the boil slowly and continue to cook, stirring until the sauce thickens. Season with salt and pepper.
4 Stir in the cream and fish, together with any juices. Add the chopped eggs and parsley, and adjust the seasoning. Spoon the mixture into a 1.1 litre (2 pint) pie dish or similar ovenproof dish.
5 Heat the 6 tbsp milk and the remaining butter in a small pan, then beat the mixture into the potatoes. Season with salt and pepper and leave to cool slightly.
6 Spoon the cooled potato into a large piping bag fitted with a large star nozzle. Pipe shell-shaped lines of potato across the fish mixture. Alternatively, spoon the potato on top and roughen the surface with a fork.
7 Put the dish on a baking sheet and cook in the oven for 10–15 minutes until the potato is set.
8 Beat the egg with a good pinch of salt, then brush over the pie. Put back in the oven for about 15 minutes or until the top is golden brown.

TRY SOMETHING DIFFERENT
- Stir 125g (4oz) grated Cheddar into the sauce.
- Beat 125g (4oz) grated Cheddar or Red Leicester cheese into the mashed potatoes.
- Stir 175g (6oz) canned sweetcorn, drained, and ¼ tsp cayenne pepper into the fish mixture.
- Fry 125g (4oz) sliced button mushrooms in 25g (1oz) butter for 3 minutes. Stir into the fish mixture.
- Sprinkle the potato topping with 50g (2oz) mixed grated Parmesan and fresh breadcrumbs after the first 10–15 minutes.
- Cover the pie with puff pastry instead of the potatoes.

NUTRITION PER SERVING 610 cals | 28g fat (15g sats) | 56g carbs | 1.4g salt

Ceviche

Serves 4
Preparation time 20 minutes, plus overnight chilling
Cooking time 7 minutes, plus cooling and chilling

450g (1lb) haddock fillets, skinned and
 cut diagonally into thin strips
1 tsp coriander seeds
1 tsp black peppercorns
juice of 6 limes
1 tsp salt
2 tbsp olive oil
1 bunch of spring onions, sliced
4 tomatoes, peeled and chopped (see page 277)
a dash of Tabasco sauce, or to taste
2 tbsp freshly chopped coriander
1 avocado
lime slices (optional) and fresh coriander to garnish

1 Put the fish strips into a bowl. Using a pestle and mortar,
crush the coriander seeds and peppercorns to a fine powder,
mix with the lime juice and salt, then pour over the fish.
Cover and chill in the fridge for 24 hours, turning the fish
over occasionally.
2 The next day, heat the oil in a frying pan, add the spring
onions and fry gently for 5 minutes. Add the tomatoes and
Tabasco sauce to taste and toss together over brisk heat for
1–2 minutes. Remove from the heat and leave to cool for
20–30 minutes.
3 To serve, drain the fish from the marinade, discarding
the marinade, and mix with the spring onion and tomatoes
and the chopped coriander.
4 Halve the avocado, peel and remove the stone. Slice
the flesh crossways. Arrange the slices around the inside
of a serving bowl and pile the fish mixture in the centre.
Garnish with coriander and serve immediately with the
lime slices.

NUTRITION PER SERVING 227 cals | 14g fat (3g sats) | 4g carbs | 1.4g salt

Dover Sole with Parsley Butter

Serves 2
Preparation time 5 minutes
Cooking time 20 minutes

2 Dover soles, about 275g (10oz) each, gutted and descaled
3 tbsp plain flour
2 tbsp sunflower oil
25g (1oz) unsalted butter
2 tbsp freshly chopped flat-leafed parsley
juice of ½ lemon
salt and ground black pepper
lemon wedges to serve

1 Rinse the fish under cold water, then gently pat them
dry with kitchen paper. Put the flour on a large plate and
season with salt and pepper. Dip the fish into the seasoned
flour, to coat both sides, gently shaking off the excess.
2 Heat 1 tbsp oil in a large sauté pan or frying pan and fry
one fish for 4–5 minutes on each side until golden. Transfer
to a warmed plate and keep warm in a low oven. Add the
remaining oil to the pan and cook the other fish in the
same way; put on a plate in the oven to keep warm.
3 Add the butter to the pan and melt over a low heat. Turn
up the heat slightly and cook for a few minutes until it
turns golden, then take off the heat. Add the parsley and
lemon juice, then season well with salt and pepper.
4 Put one fish on each warmed dinner plate and pour over
the parsley butter. Serve with lemon wedges.

Cook's Tip

Descaling a fish can be messy, so hold the fish in the sink
or over a piece of clingfilm that you can then wrap up and
throw away. Hold the fish by the tail, using a cloth or a
piece of kitchen paper to help you grip, and scrape a short
knife away from you in short bursts against the grain of
the scales to scrape them off.

NUTRITION PER SERVING 450 cals | 25g fat (8g sats) | 16g carbs | 1.5g salt

Skate with Black Butter and Rocket Mash

Serves 6
Preparation time 40 minutes
Cooking time 40 minutes

6 skate wings, about 175g (6oz) each
125g (4oz) plain flour to dust
125g (4oz) butter
salt and ground black pepper
a handful of rocket leaves and lemon wedges to serve

For the rocket mash
1.8kg (4lb) floury potatoes, such as Maris Piper,
  cut into chunks
3 garlic cloves
200g carton crème fraîche
100g (3½oz) rocket leaves

For the black butter
175g (6oz) butter
30 capers, rinsed and drained
6 tbsp white wine vinegar

1 To make the rocket mash, put the potatoes and garlic into a large pan of cold salted water. Cover, bring to the boil and cook for 15 minutes or until tender.
2 Meanwhile, trim the skate wings, if necessary. Put the flour on a plate and season well with salt and pepper. Dip each skate wing in the seasoned flour to cover both sides evenly and shake off the excess.
3 Melt the 125g (4oz) butter in a large frying pan over a low heat, then fry the skate over a medium heat, in two or three batches, for 5 minutes on each side, taking care that the butter doesn't burn. Put the skate wings on a baking sheet and keep them warm in a low oven while you cook the rest. Don't throw away the butter in the frying pan when you have finished.
4 Drain the potatoes and garlic, then put them back in the pan. Add the crème fraîche and mash until smooth. Season well with salt and pepper. Chop the rocket leaves and stir them into the mash. Cover to keep the potatoes warm.
5 For the black butter, add the butter to the frying pan and melt over a low heat. Add the capers and wine vinegar, and stir until heated through. Season well with salt and pepper.
6 Transfer the skate wings to warmed plates, drizzle with the black butter and top with rocket leaves. Serve with lemon wedges and the rocket mash.

NUTRITION PER SERVING 830 cals | 56g fat (35g sats) | 6g carbs | 1.7g salt

Braised Monkfish in Parma Ham with Lentils

Serves 4
Preparation time 15 minutes, plus marinating
Cooking time 40 minutes

1kg (2¼lb) monkfish tail, filleted and skinned
1 tbsp freshly chopped marjoram
1 small lemon, peel and pith removed, thinly sliced
4–6 thin slices Parma ham (see Cook's Tip, page 76)
3 tbsp olive oil
1 small onion, finely diced
1 carrot, finely diced
1 celery stick, finely diced
1 garlic clove, finely chopped
350g (12oz) Puy lentils
150ml (¼ pint) red wine
2 tbsp freshly chopped coriander
salt and ground black pepper

1 Lay the fish, cut side up, on a board and sprinkle with the marjoram. Season with salt and pepper. Lay the lemon slices over one fillet, then sandwich together with the other monkfish fillet.
2 Wrap the fish in the Parma ham, making sure it is completely covered. Tie at 5cm (2in) intervals with fine cotton string. Cover and leave in a cool place for 1–2 hours to allow the flavours to develop.
3 Heat 2 tbsp oil in a medium pan, then add the onion, carrot, celery and garlic. Cook, stirring, for about 8 minutes or until golden. Stir in the lentils and wine. Add sufficient water to cover, bring to the boil and cook for 10 minutes.
4 Heat the remaining oil in a large frying pan. Add the monkfish parcel and fry, turning, until the Parma ham is browned all over. Carefully take out the fish parcel and transfer the lentils to the frying pan. Put the fish on top, partially burying it in the lentils. Cover and cook on a medium-low heat for 20 minutes or until the juices from the fish run clear when tested with a knife.
5 Remove the string and cut the fish into thick slices. Serve on a bed of lentils, sprinkled with the coriander.

NUTRITION PER SERVING 610 cals | 15g fat (2g sats) | 47g carbs | 1.1g salt

Roasted Salmon with Horseradish and Tarragon Dressing

Serves 20
Preparation time 20 minutes
Cooking time about 30 minutes, plus cooling and chilling

2 lemons, sliced, and the juice of ½ lemon, plus extra lemon
  slices to garnish
2 salmon sides, filleted, each 1.4kg (3lb), skin on, boned
  and trimmed
2 tbsp dry white wine
salt and ground black pepper
cucumber slices and 2 large bunches of watercress to garnish

For the dressing
500g (1lb) carton crème fraîche
500g (1lb) carton natural yogurt
2 tbsp horseradish sauce
3 tbsp freshly chopped tarragon
4 tbsp capers, roughly chopped, plus extra to garnish
¼ cucumber, seeded and finely chopped

1 Preheat the oven to 190°C (170°C fan oven) mark 5.
Take two pieces of foil, each large enough to wrap one side
of salmon, and put a piece of greaseproof paper on top.
Divide the lemon slices between each piece of greaseproof
paper and lay the salmon on top, skin side up. Season with
salt and pepper, then pour over the lemon juice and wine.
2 Score the skin of each salmon fillet at 4cm (1½in)
intervals to mark 10 portions. Scrunch the foil around
each fillet, keeping it loose so the fish doesn't stick. Cook
for 25 minutes or until the flesh is just opaque. Unwrap the
foil and cook for a further 5 minutes or until the
skin is crisp. Leave to cool quickly in a cold place.
Re-wrap and chill.
3 Put all the dressing ingredients in a bowl and season
with salt and pepper. Mix well, then cover and chill.
4 Serve the salmon on a serving plate garnished with
lemon, cucumber and watercress. Garnish the dressing with
chopped capers and cucumber.

GET AHEAD
Complete the recipe to the end of step 3, then keep the
salmon wrapped and chilled for up to one day.

Cook's Tips
• There will be a lot of hot liquid in the parcel of salmon,
  so ask someone to help you lift it out of the oven.
• To check the fish is cooked, ease a knife into one of the
  slashes in the skin. The flesh should look opaque and the
  knife should come out hot.

NUTRITION PER SERVING 347 cals | 25g fat (9g sats) | 3g carbs | 0.2g salt

Poached Salmon

Serves 8
Preparation time 15 minutes
Cooking time see below

1 salmon
dry white wine or court bouillon (see Try Something
  Different, page 11) (optional)
lemon slices and fresh chervil or parsley sprigs to garnish
ground black pepper

1 To prepare the salmon, slit the fish along the underside
between the head and rear gill opening. Cut out the
entrails and discard. Rinse the fish to remove all the blood.
2 Snip off the fins and trim the tail into a neat V shape.
Leave on the head, if you like. Pat dry with kitchen paper
and weigh the fish before cooking.
3 Fill a fish kettle or large pan with water, or a mixture of
water and wine or court bouillon. Bring to the boil, then
lower the fish into the kettle or pan. (A piece of muslin
wrapped round the salmon will make it easier to lift out.)
4 Bring the liquid back to the boil, then simmer for
7–8 minutes per 450g (1lb) if eating hot. If eating cold,
bring the liquid back to the boil, then cook for 5 minutes
for fish under 3.2kg (7lb), 10–15 minutes for fish over
3.2kg (7lb).
5 Leave to cool completely in the liquid, then lift out
the fish and remove the skin and bones. Garnish with
lemon slices and chervil or parsley sprigs and a sprinkling
of black pepper.

TRY SOMETHING DIFFERENT
Salmon can also be poached in the oven. Put the fish into
a deep roasting tin – it must fit snugly. Preheat the oven to
150°C (130°C fan oven) mark 2. Pour over enough water, or
water and wine or court bouillon to three-quarters cover it.
Cover tightly with buttered foil. Cook in a preheated oven,
allowing 10 minutes per 450g (1lb). If serving the fish hot,
allow an extra 10 minutes at the end of the cooking time.

NUTRITION PER SERVING 675 cals | 41g fat (7g sats) | 0g carbs | 0.4g salt

Teriyaki Tuna with Sesame Noodles

Serves 2
Preparation time 20 minutes, plus marinating
Cooking time 10 minutes

2 tuna steaks
2 nests medium egg noodles
75g (3oz) green beans, trimmed and halved
1 tsp toasted sesame oil
4 spring onions, sliced
1 tbsp freshly chopped coriander
2 tsp sesame seeds
lime wedges to serve

For the marinade
1 small garlic clove, crushed
2.5cm (1in) piece fresh root ginger, peeled and grated
3 tbsp teriyaki sauce
1 tbsp clear honey
1 tsp oil

1 Mix together the marinade ingredients in a non-metallic dish, add the tuna steaks and turn to coat in the marinade. Cover with clingfilm and leave to marinate in the fridge for at least 2 hours.
2 Preheat the grill to high. Cook the egg noodles according to the pack instructions with the green beans. Drain and cool under running water.
3 Meanwhile, put the tuna on a grill rack and cook for 3 minutes per side, brushing with the marinade, until firm but still moist.
4 Gently heat the sesame oil in a pan and toss in the noodles and green beans to reheat. Add the spring onions, coriander and sesame seeds.
5 To serve, divide the noodles between two plates, top with the tuna and garnish with lime wedges.

NUTRITION PER SERVING 508 cals | 17g fat (4g sats) | 48g carbs | 5.1g salt

Sea Bass with Saffron and Orange Sauce

Serves 6
Preparation time 25 minutes
Cooking time 40 minutes

75g (3oz) butter, plus extra to grease
1 large sea bass, about 1.4kg (3lb)
salt and ground black pepper
a handful of mixed fresh herb sprigs,
  such as tarragon, parsley and chervil,
  plus chopped herbs to garnish
orange wedges to garnish

For the saffron and orange sauce
½ tsp saffron
1 tsp cornflour
300ml (½ pint) double cream
finely grated zest of 1 orange

1 Preheat the oven to 220°C (200°C fan oven) mark 7. Line a roasting tin large enough to hold the fish with a lightly buttered sheet of foil. Rub the fish inside and out with salt and pepper and put in the foil-lined tin. Tuck the herbs into the cavity and dot the butter over the fish.
2 Cover the sea bass with foil and bake for 40 minutes or until the thickest part flakes easily when tested with a knife.
3 Meanwhile make the sauce. Crumble the saffron into a bowl, add 2 tbsp hot water and set aside. Blend the cornflour with a little cold water in a small pan, then stir in the cream, orange zest and a little salt and pepper. Add the saffron and liquid to the pan and cook, stirring, until slightly thickened. Simmer gently for 3 minutes.
4 Carefully lift the cooked sea bass on to a board and peel away the skin from the upper surface, then turn the bass on to a warmed serving plate. Remove the skin from the other side. Garnish the fish lavishly with herbs and with the orange wedges, and serve with the warm saffron and orange sauce.

TRY SOMETHING DIFFERENT
Use a sea trout instead of bass.

Cook's Tip
If the bass won't fit comfortably in the tin, cut off the head and bake it beside the fish. Reposition the head as you serve the fish.

NUTRITION PER SERVING 520 cals | 38g fat (24g sats) | 2g carbs | 1g salt

Red Mullet with Cherry Tomatoes and Basil Oil

Serves 6
Preparation time 10 minutes
Cooking time about 40 minutes

50g (1lb) cherry tomatoes, mixture of
  red and yellow
2 tbsp green peppercorns in brine,
  drained
8 garlic cloves, unpeeled, bruised
zest and juice of 1 small lemon
75ml (2½fl oz) basil oil
12 × 50g (2oz) red mullet fillets,
  descaled (see Cook's Tip, page 112)
a small handful of fresh basil leaves,
  sliced
salt and ground black pepper
new potatoes to serve

1 Preheat the oven to 180°C (160°C
fan oven) mark 4. Halve the larger
tomatoes, then put them all into
a shallow roasting tin. Add the
peppercorns, garlic and lemon zest,
drizzle with half the oil and cook in
the oven for 20 minutes.
2 Add the fish to the tin and drizzle
with the remaining oil. Cook for a
further 15–20 minutes until golden
and cooked through.
3 Pour the lemon juice over the fish
and sprinkle with basil leaves, salt and
pepper. Serve with the mullet with
steamed new potatoes.

NUTRITION PER SERVING 282 cals |
17g fat (2g sats) | 4g carbs | 0.4g salt

Fish and Chips

Serves 4
Preparation time 20 minutes
Cooking time 35 minutes

400g (14oz) new potatoes, quartered
2 tbsp olive oil
4 × 175g (6oz) skinless, boneless,
  undyed smoked haddock fillets
75g (3oz) fresh breadcrumbs
½ tbsp dried dill
grated zest and juice of 1 lemon, plus
  lemon wedges to serve
350g (12oz) frozen peas
4 fresh mint leaves
2 tbsp crème fraîche
salt and ground black pepper

1 Preheat the oven to 200°C (180°C
fan oven) mark 6. Put the potatoes
in a roasting tin, season well, then toss
with half the oil. Roast for 25 minutes.

2 Put the fish on a baking sheet. Mix
the breadcrumbs, dill, lemon zest and
juice and plenty of pepper. Top the
fish with the breadcrumb mixture.
3 Add the fish to the oven and bake
for 12–15 minutes until cooked.
4 Meanwhile, bring a pan of water
to the boil, add the peas and boil for
3–5 minutes until hot. Drain well,
then whiz in a food processor with
the mint and plenty of seasoning
until fairly smooth. Return to the pan,
stir in the crème fraîche and adjust
the seasoning to taste. Reheat gently
without allowing the peas to boil.
5 Serve the minted peas with the
fish, roast potatoes and extra lemon
wedges, if you like.

NUTRITION PER SERVING 409 cals |
8g fat (3g sats) | 37g carbs | 0.7g salt

Soused Herrings

Serves 4
Preparation time 10 minutes
Cooking time 45 minutes, plus cooling

4 large or 6–8 small herrings, cleaned, boned, and heads and tails removed
1 small onion, sliced into rings
6 black peppercorns
1–2 bay leaves
fresh parsley sprigs
150ml (¼ pint) malt vinegar
salt and ground black pepper
salad to serve (optional)

1 Preheat the oven to 180°C (160°C fan oven) mark 4. Season the fish and divide into fillets. Roll up and secure with a cocktail stick. Arrange in a shallow ovenproof dish with the onion rings, peppercorns and herbs.
2 Pour in the vinegar and enough water to almost cover the fish. Cover with greaseproof paper or foil and cook in the oven for 45 minutes or until tender.
3 Leave the herrings to cool in the cooking liquid before serving as an appetiser or with salad

NUTRITION PER SERVING 215 cals | 13g fat (3g sats) | trace carbs | 1.1g salt

Sardines with Herbs

Serves 4
Preparation time 10–30 minutes
Cooking time about 10 minutes

900g (2lb) sardines (at least 12), gutted
125ml (4fl oz) olive oil
3 tbsp lemon juice
2 tsp grated lemon zest
4 tbsp freshly chopped mixed herbs, such as parsley, chervil and thyme
salt and ground black pepper
crusty bread to serve

1 Preheat the grill to medium-high. If you like, bone the sardines (see Cook's Tip), leaving the heads and tails intact. Rinse the sardines and pat dry with kitchen paper.
2 In a non-metallic bowl, mix together the oil, lemon zest and juice, herbs, salt and pepper.

3 Lay the sardines on a grill rack, drizzle the herb dressing over them and grill for 5–7 minutes each side, basting frequently with the dressing. Serve hot or cold, with crusty bread.

Cook's Tip
To remove the backbones from small fish, like sardines, extend the cut along the belly to the tail. Open out the fish and press, slit side down, on a board. Press firmly with your thumbs along the backbone to loosen it from the flesh. Turn the fish over and pull out the backbone. Use scissors to snip the end of the backbone free inside the fish if needed.

NUTRITION PER SERVING 340 cals | 25g fat (7g sats) | 0g carbs | 1.3g salt

Trout with Almonds

Serves 4
Preparation time 5 minutes
Cooking time 10–15 minutes

4 trout, gutted, with heads and tails intact
2 tbsp plain flour
65g (2½oz) butter
50g (2oz) flaked almonds
juice of ½ lemon, or to taste
1–2 tbsp freshly chopped parsley
salt and ground black pepper

1 Rinse the trout and pat dry with kitchen paper. Put the flour on a plate and season with salt and pepper. Dust the fish with the seasoned flour to coat lightly. Melt 50g (2oz) of the butter in a large frying pan. Fry the trout, two at a time, for 5–7 minutes on each side, turning once, until golden on both sides and cooked through.
2 Remove the fish from the pan, drain on kitchen paper and put on a warmed serving plate; keep warm. Wipe out the pan.
3 Melt the remaining butter in the pan and fry the almonds over a medium-low heat for a few minutes until lightly browned. Add the lemon juice and spoon over the trout. Scatter with chopped parsley and serve immediately.

NUTRITION PER SERVING   450 cals | 28g fat (11g sats) | 6g carbs | 1.1g salt

Marinated Mackerel

Serves 4
Preparation time 20 minutes, plus marinating
Cooking time 25 minutes

4 mackerel, about 350g (12oz) each, cleaned
3 onions, 1 finely chopped, 2 finely sliced
3 garlic cloves, crushed and chopped
1 lemon, sliced, and the juice of 1 lemon
3 tbsp olive oil
1 red pepper, seeded and finely sliced into rings
5 black peppercorns
2 bay leaves
150ml (¼ pint) white wine vinegar
salt and ground black pepper

1 Rinse the mackerel and pat dry with kitchen paper. Put into a large shallow container and sprinkle inside and out with the chopped onion, a little salt and one-third of the garlic. Scatter over the lemon slices, pour over the lemon juice and season generously with pepper. Cover and leave to marinate in the fridge for at least 2 hours.
2 Heat 1 tbsp of the olive oil in a frying pan, add the sliced onions and fry over a low heat for 5 minutes to soften, stirring regularly. Add the remaining garlic and the red pepper, and cook for a further 3 minutes.
3 Add the peppercorns, bay leaves, wine vinegar and 150ml (¼ pint) water. Bring to the boil, then lower the heat and simmer for 10 minutes or until the liquid is reduced by one-third. Keep to one side.
4 Drain the mackerel. Heat the remaining 2 tbsp of oil in a large heavy-based frying pan. Add the mackerel and fry for 8–10 minutes, turning as needed, until the fish is tender and lightly browned.
5 Return the mackerel to a shallow dish and pour over the vinegar and pepper mixture. Serve warm, or cool and chill.

Cook's Tip
This dish is best prepared a day ahead to allow the flavours to mingle. To serve warm the next day, microwave on high for about 3 minutes.

NUTRITION PER SERVING 560 cals | 39g fat (13g sats) | 12g carbs | 1.2g salt

Traditional Kippers

Serves 2
Preparation time 5 minutes
Cooking time 5–15 minutes

2 kippers
butter, freshly chopped parsley and toast to serve

Three ways to cook kippers:

1 Grill the kippers for 5 minutes.
2 Alternatively, put into a jug of boiling water and leave in a warm place for 5–10 minutes.
3 Preheat the oven to 190°C (170°C fan oven) mark 5. Wrap the kippers in foil and cook them in the oven for 10–15 minutes.

Serve with butter, parsley and toast.

Cook's Tip
Kippers are whole herrings that have been split and opened out flat. They are lightly brined, then cold-smoked, which gives them a rich flavour.

NUTRITION PER SERVING 331 cals | 25g fat (4g sats) | 38g carbs | 3.1g salt

Smoked Haddock Kedgeree

Serves 4
Preparation time 10 minutes
Cooking time 20 minutes

175g (6oz) long-grain rice
450g (1lb) smoked haddock fillets
2 medium eggs, hard-boiled and shelled (see page 227)
75g (3oz) butter
salt and cayenne pepper
freshly chopped parsley to garnish
salad to serve

1 Cook the rice in a pan of fast-boiling salted water until tender. Drain well and rinse under cold water.
2 Meanwhile, put the haddock in a large frying pan with just enough water to cover. Bring to simmering point, then simmer for 10–15 minutes until tender. Drain, skin and flake the fish, discarding the skin and bones.
3 Chop one egg and slice the other into rings.
4 Melt the butter in a large pan, add the cooked rice, fish, chopped egg, salt and cayenne pepper, and stir over a medium heat for 5 minutes or until hot. Pile on to a warmed serving dish and garnish with parsley and the sliced egg. Serve with salad.

NUTRITION PER SERVING 429 cals | 20g fat (11g sats) | 38g carbs | 3.1g salt

Deep-fried Whitebait

Serves 4
Preparation time 5 minutes
Cooking time about 15 minutes

700g (1½lb) whitebait
4 tbsp plain flour
oil to deep-fry
lime or lemon wedges to serve (optional)
salt and ground black pepper

For the flavoured mayonnaise
150ml (¼ pint) mayonnaise (see Cook's Tip)
grated zest of 1 lime
1 tbsp chopped basil

1 Rinse the whitebait under cold running water, then pat
thoroughly dry with kitchen paper.
2 To make the flavoured mayonnaise, mix the ingredients
together in a bowl and season with salt and pepper.
3 Put the flour into a large plastic bag and season with salt
and pepper to taste. Add the whitebait and toss to coat in
the seasoned flour.
4 Heat the oil in a deep-fryer to 190°C (test by frying a
small cube of bread; it should brown in 20 seconds). Deep-
fry the whitebait in batches in the hot oil for 3 minutes or
until golden brown. Drain on crumpled kitchen paper and
keep hot in a low oven while cooking the rest of the fish.
5 Serve the hot whitebait with lime or lemon wedges, if
you like, and the flavoured mayonnaise.

Cook's Tip
Use either home-made Mayonnaise (see page 29) or a
good, thick ready-made alternative.

NUTRITION PER SERVING 800 cals | 77g fat (4g sats) | 5g carbs | 2g salt

Fritto Misto di Mare

Serves 6
Preparation time 20 minutes
Cooking time 10 minutes

450g (1lb) squid, cleaned
4 tbsp plain flour
225g (8oz) whitebait
4 small red mullet, boned, cleaned and heads and tails
  removed, sliced
225g (8oz) firm white fish fillets, such as cod, haddock or
  sole, skinned, and cut into long, thin strips
8–12 large raw prawns, peeled and deveined with tails intact
  (see page 85)
vegetable oil for deep-frying
salt and ground black pepper
fresh parsley sprigs and lemon wedges to garnish

1 Slice the body of the squid into rings 5mm (¼ in) thick
and the tentacles into 1cm (½ in) pieces. Put the flour in a
shallow dish and season with salt and pepper. Toss all the
fish in seasoned flour to coat shaking off the excess.
2 Heat the oil in a deep-fat fryer to 190°C (test by frying
a small cube of bread; it should brown in 20 seconds).
Add the fish pieces a few at a time and fry until crisp and
golden. Drain on absorbent kitchen paper and keep each
batch warm in a low oven while frying the rest.
3 Divide the fish between six warmed plates and garnish
with lemon wedges and sprigs of parsley.

TRY SOMETHING DIFFERENT
Fritter Batter Dip the fish in batter before frying. Sift 125g
(4oz) plain flour with a pinch of salt into a bowl and make
a well in the centre. Break in 1 egg and beat well with a
wooden spoon, then gradually beat in 150ml (¼ pint) milk,
or milk and water mixed, drawing in the flour from the sides
to make a smooth batter.

NUTRITION PER SERVING 512 cals | 33g fat (2g sats) | 11g carbs | 0.8g salt

Fish Goujons

Serves 4
Preparation time 15 minutes
Cooking time 10 minutes

450g (1lb) hake fillets, skinned, boned
  and cut into 20 even-sized pieces
1 medium egg, beaten
50g (2oz) fresh breadcrumbs
vegetable oil for deep-frying
lemon wedges to garnish
Tartare Sauce to serve (see page 22)

1 Coat the fish pieces in egg, then in
the breadcrumbs.
2 Heat the oil in a deep-fat fryer to
180°C (test by frying a small cube of
bread; it should brown in 40 seconds),
add the fish and fry until golden.
Drain on kitchen paper.
3 Garnish with lemon wedges and
serve the goujons on cocktail sticks
with the sauce handed separately.

TRY SOMETHING DIFFERENT
Other firm fish such as haddock, coley,
cod, monkfish and huss can be cooked
in the same way.

NUTRITION PER SERVING 267 cals |
15g fat (2g sats) |10g carbs | 0.6g salt

Salmon and Pea Fish Cakes

Serves 4
Preparation time 15 minutes
Cooking time 10 minutes

100g (3½oz) frozen peas
15 cream crackers, about 125g (4oz)
2 × 180g cans skinless and boneless
  salmon, drained
1 medium egg, separated
a few drops of Tabasco sauce to taste
1 tbsp freshly chopped dill
1 tbsp vegetable oil
3 tbsp Mayonnaise (see page 29)
2 tbsp sweet chilli sauce
salt and ground black pepper
green salad to serve

1 Cover the peas with boiling water
and leave for a few minutes. Whiz
5 cream crackers in a food processor
until finely ground. Tip on to a
shallow plate.
2 Whiz the remaining crackers until
finely ground. Add the salmon, egg
yolk, Tabasco, dill and seasoning and
whiz to mix. Drain the peas, add to
the salmon and pulse to combine.
3 Whisk the egg white in a shallow
bowl. Shape the fish mixture into
four patties, dip each one into the
egg white, then coat in the reserved
cracker crumbs.
4 Heat the oil in a large frying pan
and cook the fish cakes for 5 minutes
on each side or golden and piping hot.
5 Meanwhile, stir together the
mayonnaise and sweet chilli sauce in a
small bowl. Serve the fish cakes with
the dipping sauce and a green salad.

NUTRITION PER SERVING 396 cals |
22g fat (5g sats) | 24g carbs | 2.0g salt

Thai Green Curry

Serves 4
Preparation time 25 minutes
Cooking time 12 minutes

400ml can coconut milk
250ml (8fl oz) vegetable or chicken stock
250g (9oz) baby sweetcorn
300g (11oz) raw peeled and deveined king prawns
  (see page 85)
150g (5oz) mangetout
salt and ground black pepper
sticky jasmine rice and lime wedges to serve

For the curry paste
a large handful of fresh coriander (including stalks),
  roughly chopped
1 lemongrass stalk, trimmed and roughly chopped
2 spring onions, trimmed and roughly chopped
1–2 green chillies, seeded and roughly chopped to taste (see
  Cook's Tip, page 69)
2 garlic cloves
2.5cm (1in) piece of fresh root ginger, roughly chopped
2 freeze-dried kaffir lime leaves
2 tbsp soy sauce
½ tbsp Thai fish sauce

1 Start by making the curry paste. Reserve a little of the
coriander to garnish, then put all the remaining paste
ingredients into a food processor and blend until the paste
is as smooth as you can get it.
2 Bring the coconut milk to the boil in a large pan. Stir in
the curry paste and stock. Add the sweetcorn and simmer
for 5 minutes. Add the prawns and mangetout and cook
for a further 3 minutes or until the prawns are bright pink.
3 Check the seasoning, then garnish with the reserved
coriander. Serve with sticky jasmine rice and lime wedges.

NUTRITION PER SERVING 302 cals | 19g fat (15g sats) | 13g carbs | 2.4g salt

Poultry

Poultry

Domesticated birds that are bred for the table – including chicken, turkey, duckling, guinea fowl and goose – are classified as poultry (wild birds that are hunted for food, are referred to as game). Chicken, in particular, has become increasingly popular in recent years as a less expensive and healthier option to red meat. From a nutritional angle, it is an excellent food – high in protein and vitamins, yet low in fat (once the skin has been removed).

Choosing poultry

Whichever type of bird you are buying, freshness is of the utmost importance, so check the use-by date. Look for a bird with a good plump breast and firm, unblemished skin. If you are buying from a farm, refuse a bird that's been carelessly plucked and singed. A young chicken will have a pliable breastbone, and a young duckling a pliable beak.

Breeding and rearing

How poultry is bred and reared has a significant effect on its health and welfare, and on taste and texture. The issues arise mainly in connection with chickens and turkeys, as these are often intensively reared. Other birds, such as ducks and geese, are usually farmed in a more humane way because they do not adapt well to intensive rearing.

Selective breeding and intensive rearing methods have radically changed the way chicken and turkey are farmed, leading to a huge increase in production and a drop in the price paid by consumers. Whereas chicken was once a luxury, it is now one of the cheapest forms of animal protein, but with serious consequences for birds and for us.

The greatest changes are in maturation and in housing. Intensively reared chickens have been bred to take just six weeks to become fully grown (about 2kg/4½lb) and ready for slaughter. A naturally reared chicken will reach that weight in about 14 weeks. Intensively reared birds can suffer from health problems such as weak, under-developed legs that are not strong enough to carry the bird's ever-growing body. Because thousands of birds are packed into a single shed, antibiotics and other chemicals are routinely used to protect them from disease and infection. Traces of these chemicals will remain in the flesh after slaughter.

Dubious hygiene is a natural part of intensive rearing. Excrement-filled sheds containing dead birds cannot be cleaned adequately until the flock is removed for slaughter. Disease and bacterial infection such as salmonella spread quickly, and as these infections remain in the meat after slaughter, they pose risks for the consumer.

Categories for poultry

Organic chickens and other organic birds can roam freely and are reared without drugs. They can feed on organic pasture and are fed at least 80 per cent organic, non-GM (genetically modified) feed. Synthetic drugs and pesticides are avoided wherever possible. There's also a limit to the number of birds that can be reared in one space. All this helps to make a good, well-flavoured bird. Organic chickens cost about twice as much as intensively reared birds, but invariably have a superior flavour and texture.

Free-range birds are raised predominantly on a grain diet and allowed access to open-air runs, although they do not necessarily get as much exercise as organic chickens. Drugs may be used routinely. In the UK there are three categories of free-range bird: free range, traditional free range, and free range – total freedom. The last category is regarded as the best, and these birds are likely to cost more than the other two. Free-range birds are usually tastier than intensively reared chickens, but less so than organic birds.

Intensively reared poultry is raised in overcrowded huts. As the birds cannot move around easily, they end up fatter. The use of drugs and undesirable farming practices is routine.

Handling and storing poultry

All poultry contains low levels of salmonella and campylo-bacter, which can cause food poisoning if they multiply. Always get poultry home and into a fridge as soon as possible after buying. If the bird contains giblets, remove them and store in a separate container, since these will deteriorate most rapidly. To avoid spreading bacteria, never wash raw poultry (washing can spread germs and cooking will kill any bacteria present), but always wash your hands (and the tap) immediately after handling.
Never use the same utensils for preparing raw poultry and cooked foods. Thoroughly scrub chopping boards, knives and other utensils used for preparing raw poultry.

Freezing poultry

Fresh chicken and poultry can be frozen safely:
• Always freeze poultry before its use-by date, even better on the day of purchase.
• Follow any freezing or thawing instructions given.
• Wrap portions in individual freezer bags, seal tightly and label with the date of freezing. They can be stored in the freezer for up to three months.

- To thaw, put the poultry in a dish (to catch dripping juices) and leave overnight in the fridge until completely thawed, then cook within 24 hours.
- Do not refreeze thawed poultry. You can, however, freeze it again after you have cooked it.

Frozen poultry can be kept in the freezer for up to three months. Check that it is well wrapped to prevent the skin from being damaged by freezer burn. Thaw large birds at cool room temperature rather than in the fridge and make sure you allow sufficient time. A large turkey, weighing 6.8–9kg (15–20lb) for example, will take 24–30 hours to thaw thoroughly at cool room temperature. Even a 3.6–5kg (8–11lb) turkey will take 18–20 hours. Frozen poultry must be fully thawed before cooking. Check that there are no ice crystals in the body cavity. A fully thawed bird will be flexible, too – try moving the leg joints. Once fully thawed, poultry can be stored in the fridge for a short time but it should be cooked within 24 hours.

Trussing

1 Trussing poultry before roasting gives it a neater shape for serving at the table. Cut the wishbone out by pulling back the flap of skin at the neck end. Run a sharp knife along the inside of the bone on both sides. Use poultry shears to snip the tip of the bone from the breastbone, and pull away. Snip or pull out the two ends.
2 Put the wing tips under the breast and fold the neck flap on to the back. Use a trussing needle and fine string to secure the neck flap.

3 Push a metal skewer through the legs, at the joint between thigh and drumstick. Twist some string around both ends of the skewer and pull firmly to tighten. Turn the bird over. Bring the string over the ends of the drumsticks, pull tight and tie to secure the legs in place.

Jointing

1 Using a sharp meat knife with a curved blade, cut out the wishbone. Cut off the wings, then remove the wing tips.
2 With the tail pointing towards you and breast side up, pull one leg away and cut through the skin between leg and breast. Pull the leg down until you crack the joint between the thigh bone and ribcage. Cut through that joint, then cut through the remaining meat. Repeat on the other side.
3 To remove the breast without any bone, cut along the length of the breastbone. Gently teasing the flesh away from the ribs with the knife, work the blade down between the flesh and ribs and cut the breast off neatly. (Always cut in, towards the bone.) Repeat on the other side.
4 To remove the breast with bone in, cut down the length of the breastbone. Using poultry shears, cut through the breastbone, then cut through the ribcage, following the outline of the breast. Repeat on the other side. Trim off any flaps of skin or fat.

Cooking poultry

Make sure poultry is cooked thoroughly. To test, pierce the thickest part of the thigh with a skewer. The bird is cooked when the juices run clear, with no trace of pink. Chill leftover meat as soon as possible and eat within two days.

Roasting times for poultry

BIRD	OVEN TEMPERATURE	COOKING TIME	QUANTITIES FOR ROASTING
Poussin	200°C (180°C fan oven) mark 6	Allow 25–40 minutes total roasting time	Allow 1 bird per person
Chicken	200°C (180°C fan oven) mark 6	Allow 20 mins per 450g (1lb)	A 2kg (4½lb) bird will serve about 5 people
Capon	200°C (180°C fan oven) mark 6	Allow 20 mins per 450g (1lb)	A 3kg (6½lb) bird will serve 6–8 people
Duck	200°C (180°C fan oven) mark 6	Allow 20 mins per 450g (1lb)	Allow 450g (1lb) per person
Goose	220°C (200°C fan oven) mark 7	Allow 35 minutes per 1kg (2¼lb)	A 4.5kg (10lb) goose will serve 6–8 people
Guinea fowl	200°C (180°C fan oven) mark 6	Allow 35 minutes per 1kg (2¼lb), plus 15 minutes	1 bird will serve 2–4 people
Turkey	180°C (160°C fan oven) mark 4	Allow 45 minutes per 1kg (2¼lb), plus 20 minutes	A 3.5kg (7¾lb) turkey will serve about 10 people

Chicken and Other Birds

1 Duck
Domesticated duck has rich, dark, meaty flesh. It can also be very fatty. Roast whole birds; portions can be pan-fried, braised, casseroled or cut into strips and stir-fried. Wild duck has a stronger, more gamey flavour. Prepare and cook in the same way.

2 Capon
Strictly speaking, capons are cocks that were castrated when young, then fattened up. The practice is now illegal in the UK, but the term is used for larger birds. Cook as for chicken.

3 Guinea fowl
With darker flesh than chicken and a slightly gamey flavour, guinea fowl can be used in most chicken or pheasant recipes. Look for birds with a plump breast and smooth-skinned legs; one bird will feed 2–4 people. Bard with strips of bacon to roast or spatchcock.

4 Chicken
The breast is fine-textured, lean and white; leg meat is darker and more flavoursome. Chicken is available fresh and frozen. Whole birds can be roasted, casseroled or pot-roasted, or spatchcocked and grilled or barbecued. Portions can be pan-fried, coated and deep-fried, grilled, steamed, baked, braised, casseroled or cut into strips and stir-fried. Boiling chickens are usually older and are better suited to long, slow cooking. Corn-fed chickens have bright yellow flesh and, often, an improved flavour.

5 Poussin
These small, tender birds, 4–8 weeks old, weigh only about 450g (1lb) and have a mild flavour. They are usually sold whole, oven ready; one bird will feed one person. Cook in the same way as chicken, but for a shorter time.

6 Turkey
Oven-ready turkeys are available from 2.3kg (5lb) to 9kg (20lb). The flavour of a fresh turkey is superior to that of frozen. Also available are self-basting turkeys, turkey steaks, escalopes and mince. Similar cuts of chicken and turkey can be cooked in the same way.

7 Goose
Look for a young goose that is less than a year old (older geese have dark yellow fat.) A green goose is less than 3–4 months old; a gosling is less than 6 months old. The flesh is dark, rich, meaty and fatty, and suits a sharp, acidic sauce such as gooseberry.

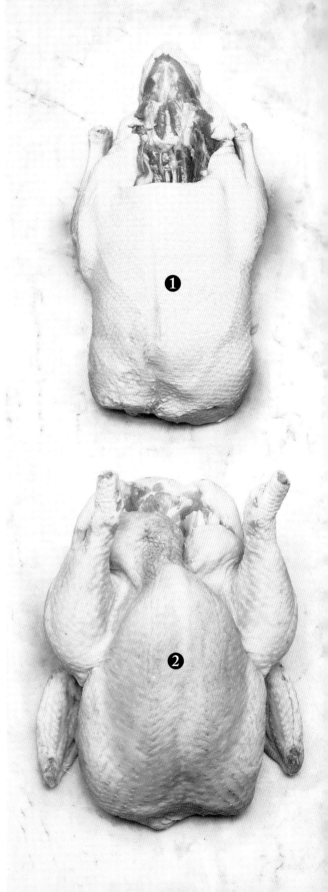

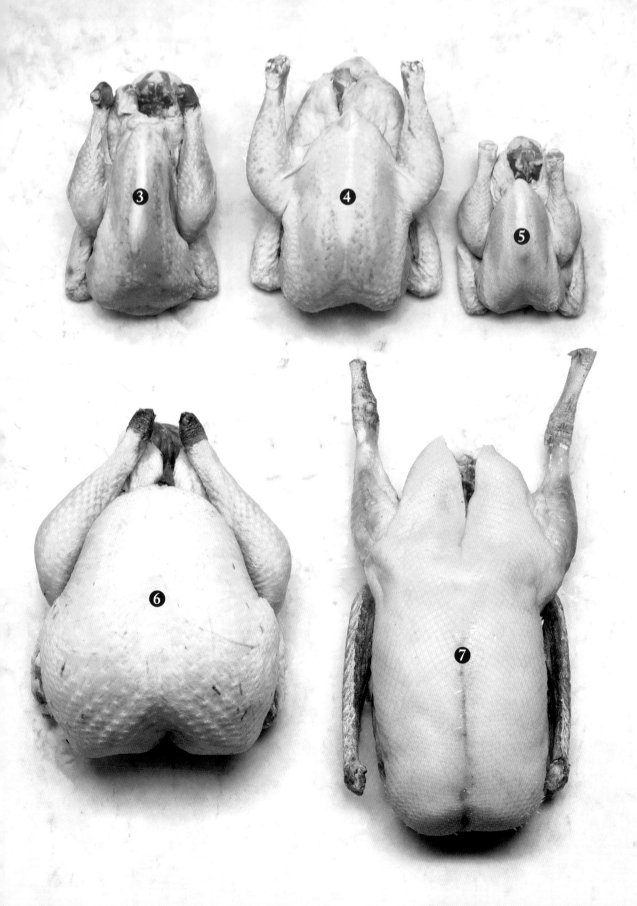

Classic Roast Chicken

Serves 5
Preparation time 30 minutes
Cooking time about 1 hour 20 minutes, plus resting

1.4kg (3lb) chicken
2 garlic cloves
1 onion, cut into wedges
2 tsp sea salt
2 tsp ground black pepper
4 fresh parsley sprigs
4 fresh tarragon sprigs
2 bay leaves
50g (2oz) butter, cut into cubes
salt and ground black pepper

For the stuffing
40g (1½oz) butter
1 small onion, chopped
1 garlic clove, crushed
75g (3oz) fresh white breadcrumbs
finely grated zest and juice of 1 small lemon, halves reserved
  for the chicken
2 tbsp freshly chopped flat-leafed parsley
2 tbsp freshly chopped tarragon
1 medium egg yolk

For the gravy
200ml (7fl oz) white wine
1 tbsp Dijon mustard
450ml (¾ pint) hot chicken stock
25g (1oz) butter, blended with 25g (1oz) plain flour (beurre
  manié, see Cook's Tip, page 140)

1 Preheat the oven to 190°C (170°C fan oven) mark 5.
To make the stuffing, melt the butter in a pan, and fry the
onion and garlic for 6 minutes or until soft. Cool, then
add the remaining ingredients, stirring in the egg yolk last.
Season well.
2 Put the chicken on a board, breast upwards, then put
the garlic, onion, reserved lemon halves and half the salt,
pepper and herb sprigs into the body cavity.
3 Lift the loose skin at the neck and fill the cavity with
stuffing. Turn the bird on to its breast and pull the neck
flap over the opening to cover the stuffing. Rest the wing
tips across it and truss the chicken (see page 133). Weigh
the stuffed bird to calculate the cooking time, and allow
20 minutes per 450g (1lb), plus an extra 20 minutes.

4 Put the chicken on a rack in a roasting tin. Season with
the remaining salt and pepper, then top with the remaining
herbs and the bay leaves. Dot with the butter and roast,
basting halfway through, until the juices run clear when the
thickest part of the thigh is pierced with a skewer.
5 Put the chicken on a serving dish and cover with foil.
Leave to rest while you make the gravy. Pour off all but
about 3 tbsp fat from the tin, put the tin over a high heat,
add the wine and boil for 2 minutes. Add the mustard
and hot stock and bring back to the boil. Gradually whisk
in knobs of the butter mixture until smooth, then season
with salt and pepper. Carve the chicken and serve with the
stuffing and gravy.

NUTRITION PER SERVING 682 cals | 49g fat (21g sats) | 17g carbs | 1g salt

Summer Roast Chicken

Serves 4
Preparation time 25 minutes
Cooking time 1½ hours, plus resting

100g (3½oz) feta, crumbled
50g (2oz) black olives, pitted and sliced
leaves from 2 fresh oregano sprigs, finely chopped
1 tbsp olive oil
1 chicken, about 1.6kg (3½lb)
1 lemon, halved
300g (11oz) cherry tomatoes
150g (5oz) couscous
a large handful of watercress
salt and ground black pepper

1 Preheat the oven to 190°C (170°C fan oven) mark 5.
In a small bowl, stir together half each of the feta, olives,
oregano and oil with plenty of black pepper. Set aside.
2 Lift up the neck flap of the chicken and use your fingers
to ease the skin gently away from the breast meat, working
all the way down the sides of the breasts and towards the
legs. Push the feta mixture between the skin and meat to
cover the whole breast area. Pull the neck flap down and
secure with a skewer or cocktail sticks. Put a lemon half in
the cavity of the chicken.
3 Put the chicken into a medium roasting tin, drizzle the
remaining oil over the top, season with salt and pepper and
roast for 1¼ hours. Add the tomatoes to the tin, shake to
coat in oil, then return to the oven for a further 15 minutes
or until the chicken is cooked through and the tomatoes
have burst.
4 Carefully transfer the chicken to a board and put the
tomatoes into a small serving bowl. Cover both with foil.
Spoon off as much fat as possible from the roasting tin,
leaving behind the darker juices. Add the couscous to the
roasting tin and stir to coat. Squeeze in the juice from the
remaining lemon half, then pour in just enough boiling
water to cover the couscous. Cover the tin well with
clingfilm and leave to soak for 10 minutes.
5 Fluff up the couscous with a fork and stir the watercress
and the remaining feta, olives and oregano through the
mixture. Season with salt and pepper to taste.
6 Leave the chicken to rest for at least 25 minutes before
serving with the couscous and tomatoes.

NUTRITION PER SERVING 653 cals | 38g fat (11g sats | 21g carbs | 2.1g salt

Spicy Pot Roast Chicken

Serves 6
Preparation time 25 minutes
Cooking time 1¾ hours

50g (2oz) butter, softened
1 garlic clove
½–1 red chilli, seeded and finely chopped to taste (see Cook's
  Tips, page 69)
finely grated zest and juice of 1 lime
a large handful of fresh coriander, finely chopped, plus extra
  to garnish
1 chicken, about 1.6kg (3½lb)
1 tbsp vegetable oil
4 shallots, finely sliced
500ml (17fl oz) chicken stock
600g (1lb 5oz) sweet potatoes, peeled and cut into
  2.5cm (1in) pieces
1 tsp cornflour
165ml can coconut milk
salt and ground black pepper

1 Preheat the oven to 180°C (160°C fan oven) mark 4. In a
small bowl, mix together the butter, garlic, chilli, lime zest,
coriander and plenty of seasoning. Lift up the neck flap
of the chicken and use your fingers to ease the skin gently
away from the breast meat – work all the way down the
sides of the breasts and towards the legs. Push most of the
butter mixture between the skin and the meat to cover the
whole breast area. Spread remaining butter over the outer
skin of the chicken. Set aside.
2 Heat the vegetable oil in a large flameproof casserole
dish (with a lid) over a medium heat and fry the shallots
for about 5 minutes until soft. Remove from the heat and
put the chicken in the dish. Pour in the stock, then season
and cover with a lid. Bake for 45 minutes.
3 Carefully remove the dish from the oven and take off
the lid. Add the sweet potatoes to the dish (try to get
them into the liquid) and roast, uncovered, for a further
45 minutes, turning the potatoes halfway through (to stop
them discolouring). Check the chicken is cooked through
– the juices should run clear when you pierce the thickest
part with a skewer or sharp knife.
4 Transfer the chicken to a board, cover well with foil to
keep it warm and leave to rest. Transfer the sweet potatoes
to a warmed serving bowl and cover.

5 To make the speedy gravy, spoon 1 tbsp of the pan juices
into a small bowl and blend with the cornflour. Put the
casserole over a medium heat and stir in the cornflour
mixture and the coconut milk. Bring the mixture to the
boil over a medium heat, then reduce the heat to low
and simmer for 5 minutes, stirring constantly or until
thickened. Check the seasoning and add salt, pepper and a
little lime juice to sharpen, if you like.
6 Serve the chicken with the sweet potatoes and coconut
gravy – all garnished with coriander.

NUTRITION PER SERVING 597 cals | 38g fat (15g sats) | 24g carbs | 0.5g salt

Chicken and Mushroom Pies

Serves 4
Preparation time 20 minutes, plus chilling
Cooking time about 1 hour

2 tbsp olive oil
1 trimmed leek, about 200g (7oz), finely sliced
2–3 garlic cloves, crushed
350g (12oz) boneless skinless chicken thighs, cut into
  2.5cm (1in) cubes
200g (7oz) chestnut mushrooms, sliced
150ml (¼ pint) double cream
2 tbsp freshly chopped thyme
500g pack puff pastry, thawed if frozen
plain flour to dust
1 medium egg, beaten
salt and ground black pepper

1 Heat the oil in a pan. Add the leek and fry over a
medium heat for 5 minutes, stirring occasionally. Add the
garlic and cook for 1 minute. Add the chicken pieces and
continue to cook for 8–10 minutes until just coloured. Add
the mushrooms and cook for 5 minutes or until all the
juices have disappeared.
2 Pour the cream into the pan and bring to the boil. Cook
for 5 minutes to make a thick sauce. Add the thyme, then
season well with salt and pepper. Tip into a bowl and
leave to cool.
3 Roll out the pastry on a lightly floured surface until it
measures 33cm (13in) square. Cut into four squares. Brush
the edges with water and spoon the chicken mixture into
the middle of each square. Bring each corner of the square
up to the middle to make a parcel. Crimp the edges to
seal, leaving a small hole in the centre. Brush the pies with
beaten egg, put on a baking sheet and chill for 20 minutes.
4 Preheat the oven to 200°C (180°C fan oven) mark 6.
Cook the pies for 30–40 minutes until golden.

TRY SOMETHING DIFFERENT

Leek and Mushroom Pie For a vegetarian alternative,
replace the chicken with 200g (7oz) cooked, peeled (or
vacuum-packed) chestnuts, roughly chopped. Add another
finely sliced leek and increase the quantity of mushrooms
to 300g (11oz).

NUTRITION PER SERVING 805 cals | 58g fat (14g sats) | 49g carbs | 1.2g salt

Coq au Vin

Serves 6
Preparation time 15 minutes
Cooking time 2 hours

2 tbsp plain flour
1 large chicken, jointed
  or 6–8 chicken joints
100g (3½oz) butter
125g (4oz) rindless lean bacon, diced
1 onion, quartered
1 carrot, quartered
4 tbsp brandy
600ml (1 pint) red wine
1 garlic clove, crushed
bouquet garni (1 bay leaf, a few
  fresh parsley and thyme sprigs)
1 sugar lump
2 tbsp vegetable oil
450g (1lb) button onions
a pinch of sugar
1 tsp wine vinegar
225g (8oz) button mushrooms
6 slices white bread, crusts removed
salt and ground black pepper

1 Season the flour with salt and pepper, then use half to coat the chicken pieces, shaking off any excess.
2 Melt 25g (1oz) butter in a flameproof casserole. Add the chicken and fry gently until golden brown on all sides. Add the bacon, onion and carrot and fry until softened.
3 Heat the brandy in a small pan, pour over the chicken and ignite, shaking the pan so that all the chicken pieces are covered in flames. Pour in the wine and stir to dislodge any sediment from the bottom of the casserole. Add the garlic, bouquet garni and sugar lumps and bring to the boil. Reduce the heat, cover and simmer for 1–1½ hours until the chicken is cooked through.
4 Meanwhile, melt 25g (1oz) butter with 1 tsp oil in a frying pan. Add the button onions and fry until they begin to brown. Add the pinch of sugar and the vinegar together with 1 tbsp water. Cover and simmer for 10–15 minutes until just tender. Keep warm.
5 Melt 25g (1oz) butter with 2 tsp oil in a pan. Add the mushrooms and cook for a few minutes, then turn off the heat and keep them warm.
6 Remove the chicken from the casserole and put in a dish. Surround with the onions and mushrooms and keep hot.
7 Discard the bouquet garni. Skim the excess fat from the cooking liquid, then boil the liquid in the casserole briskly for 3–5 minutes to reduce it.
8 Add the remaining oil to the fat in the frying pan and fry the pieces of bread until golden brown on both sides. Cut each slice into triangles.
9 Blend together the remaining butter and flour to make a beurre manié (see Cook's Tip). Remove the casserole from the heat and add small pieces of the beurre manié to the cooking liquid. Stir until smooth, then put back on to the heat and bring just to the boil. The sauce should be thick and shiny. Take off the heat and adjust the seasoning. Return the chicken, onions and mushrooms to the casserole and stir to combine. Garnish with the fried bread and serve.

Cook's Tip
A beurre manié is a mixture of equal parts of softened butter and flour that has been kneaded together to form a paste. It is used to thicken sauces and stews and is whisked in towards the end of cooking, then boiled briefly to allow it to thicken the sauce or gravy.

NUTRITION PER SERVING 740 cals | 44g fat (17g sats) | 26g carbs | 1.8g salt

Chicken Casserole

Serves 6
Preparation time 15 minutes
Cooking time 50 minutes

1 fresh rosemary sprig
2 bay leaves
1.4kg (3lb) chicken
1 red onion, cut into wedges
2 carrots, cut into chunks
2 leeks, trimmed and cut into chunks
2 celery sticks, cut into chunks
12 baby new potatoes
900ml (1½ pints) hot chicken stock
200g (7oz) green beans
salt and ground black pepper

1 Preheat the oven to 180°C (160°C fan oven) mark 4. Put the herbs and chicken into a large flameproof casserole. Add the onion, carrots, leeks, celery, potatoes, hot stock and seasoning. Bring to the boil, then cook in the oven for 45 minutes or until the chicken is cooked through. To test the chicken, pierce the thickest part of the leg with a knife; the juices should run clear.
2 Add the beans and cook for 5 minutes. Remove the chicken and spoon the vegetables into six bowls. Carve the chicken and divide among the bowls, then ladle the cooking liquid over the top.

TRY SOMETHING DIFFERENT
Omit the baby new potatoes and serve with mashed potatoes.

NUTRITION PER SERVING 323 cals | 18g fat (5g sats) | 17g carbs | 0.9g salt

Stuffed Chicken Breasts

Serves 4
Preparation time 5 minutes
Cooking time 20 minutes

vegetable oil to grease
150g (5oz) ball mozzarella
4 skinless chicken breasts, about
  125g (4oz) each
4 sage leaves
8 slices Parma ham (see Cook's Tip,
  page 76)
ground black pepper
new potatoes and spinach
  to serve

1 Preheat the oven to 200°C (180°C fan oven) mark 6. Lightly oil a baking tray. Slice the ball mozzarella into eight, then put two slices on top of each chicken breast. Top each one with a sage leaf.

2 Wrap each piece of chicken in two slices of Parma ham, covering the mozzarella. Season with pepper
3 Put on the prepared baking sheet and cook in the oven for 20 minutes or until the chicken is cooked through. Serve with new potatoes and spinach.

Cook's Tip
Sage has a strong, pungent taste, so you need only a little to flavour the chicken. Don't be tempted to add more than just one leaf to each chicken breast or it will overpower the finished dish.

NUTRITION PER SERVING 297 cals | 13g fat (7g sats) | trace carbs | 1.4g salt

Chicken Tarragon

Serves 4
Preparation time 15 minutes
Cooking time 15 minutes

4 × 125g (4oz) boneless chicken
  breasts, cut into bite-size pieces
25g (1oz) plain flour
2 tbsp olive oil
250g (9oz) chestnut mushrooms, sliced
150ml (¼ pint) white wine
300ml (½ pint) crème fraîche
½ tbsp Dijon mustard
2 tbsp freshly chopped tarragon
a large handful of spinach
salt and ground black pepper
crusty bread to serve

1 Toss the chicken with the flour, salt
and pepper.
2 Heat half the oil in a large frying
pan over medium-high heat. Add the
chicken and fry for 5 minutes or until
golden, in batches if necessary to stop
the chicken from sweating. Remove
from the pan and set aside.
3 Add the remaining oil and fry the
mushrooms for 3–5 minutes until
nearly cooked through.
4 Return the chicken and any juices
to the pan. Pour over the wine, bring
to the boil and simmer for 2 minutes.
Stir in the crème fraîche, mustard and
most of the tarragon and cook for 5
minutes, without allowing the sauce
to boil or until chicken is cooked.
5 Stir in the spinach, season and
sprinkle over the remaining tarragon.
Serve immediately with crusty bread
to mop up the juices.

NUTRITION PER SERVING 529 cals |
37g fat (21g sats) | 7g carbs | 0.5g salt

Lemon Chicken

Serves 4
Preparation time 2 minutes
Cooking time 6–8 minutes

4 small skinless chicken breasts, about
  125g (4oz) each
juice of 2 lemons
2 tbsp olive oil
4–6 tbsp demerara sugar
salt
watercress salad and lemon wedges to
  serve

1 Put the chicken into a large non-
metallic bowl and season with salt.
Add the lemon juice and oil and stir
to coat the chicken in the mixture.
2 Preheat the grill to medium.
Spread the chicken out on a
large baking sheet and sprinkle over
2–3 tbsp demerara sugar. Grill for
3–4 minutes or until caramelised,
then turn the chicken over, sprinkle
with the remaining sugar and grill
until the chicken is golden and
cooked through.
3 Divide the chicken among four
plates and serve with a watercress
salad and lemon wedges.

NUTRITION PER SERVING 231 cals |
7g fat (1g sats) | 13g carbs | 0.2g salt

Chicken Kiev

Serves 6
Preparation time 20 minutes, plus chilling
Cooking time 45 minutes

175g (6oz) butter, softened
grated zest of ½ lemon
1 tbsp lemon juice
1 tbsp freshly chopped parsley
1 garlic clove, crushed
6 large boneless skinless chicken breasts
25g (1oz) plain flour
1 medium egg, beaten
125g (4oz) fresh breadcrumbs
vegetable oil for deep-frying
salt and ground black pepper
potato wedges and peas to serve

1 Put the butter, lemon zest and juice, parsley, garlic
and salt and pepper to taste into a bowl and beat well to
combine. (Alternatively, whiz in a food processor.) Form
into a roll, wrap in clingfilm and chill for at least 1 hour.
2 Put the chicken breasts on a flat surface and, using
a meat mallet or rolling pin, pound them to an even
thickness. Cut the butter mixture into six pieces and put
one piece on the centre of each chicken breast. Roll up,
folding the ends in to enclose the butter completely. Secure
the rolls with wooden cocktail sticks.
3 Put the flour in a flat dish and season with salt and
pepper. Put the beaten egg and breadcrumbs in two more
flat dishes. Coat each chicken roll with the flour, then turn
them in the beaten egg and coat them with breadcrumbs,
patting the crumbs firmly on to the chicken.
4 Put the rolls on to a baking sheet, cover lightly with
non-stick or greaseproof paper and chill in the fridge for
2 hours or until required, to allow the coating to dry.
5 Heat the oil in a deep-fryer to 160°C (test by frying a
small cube of bread; it should brown in 60 seconds). Put
two chicken rolls into a frying basket and lower into the
oil. Fry for 15 minutes – the chicken is cooked when it is
browned and firm when pressed with a fork. Do not pierce.
6 Remove the rolls from the fryer, drain on kitchen paper
and keep them warm while you cook the remaining
chicken. Remove the cocktail sticks before serving.
7 Serve with potato wedges and peas.

TRY SOMETHING DIFFERENT
Spicy Chicken Kiev To make a spicy butter filling, sauté
1 finely chopped shallot with 2 tsp cayenne pepper in 1 tbsp
butter until soft but not brown. Cool. Stir in 1 tbsp freshly
chopped parsley. Combine with 175g (6oz) softened butter
and season. Form into a roll, cover and chill for at least
1 hour as step 1, then continue with the recipe.

NUTRITION PER SERVING 594 cals | 41g fat (19g sats) | 20g carbs | 1.2g salt

Classic Fried Chicken

Serves 4
Preparation time 5 minutes
Cooking time 35–45 minutes

4 chicken joints or pieces
3 tbsp plain flour
50g (2oz) butter or 3 tbsp
   vegetable oil
salt and ground black pepper
green salad to serve

1 Wipe the chicken joints and pat
dry with kitchen paper. Season with
salt and pepper.
2 Toss the chicken in the flour until
completely coated.
3 Heat the butter or oil in a large
frying pan or flameproof casserole
over a high heat. Add the chicken
and cook until golden brown on both
sides. Reduce the heat and cook for
30–40 minutes until tender. Drain
on kitchen paper. Serve with a fresh
green salad.

Cook's Tip
To ensure that the chicken pieces
remain moist, brown the surface at
a high temperature to seal in all the
juices and give a good colour, then
reduce the heat for the remaining
cooking time.

NUTRITION PER SERVING 565 cals |
41.7g fat (9.9g sats | 8.8g carbs | 0.5g salt

Sticky Chicken Thighs

Serves 4
Preparation time 5 minutes
Cooking time 20 minutes

1 garlic clove, crushed
1 tbsp clear honey
1 tbsp Thai sweet chilli sauce
4 chicken thighs
rice (optional) and green salad to serve

1 Preheat the oven to 200°C (180°C
fan oven) mark 6. Put the garlic into a
bowl with the honey and chilli sauce
and stir to mix. Add the chicken
thighs and toss to coat.
2 Put the chicken in a roasting tin
and roast for 15–20 minutes until
golden and the juices run clear when
the thighs are pierced with a skewer.
Serve with rice, if you like, and a crisp
green salad.

TRY SOMETHING DIFFERENT
- **Honey and Mustard Marinade** Mix
  2 tbsp wholegrain mustard, 3 tbsp
  honey, the zest and juice of 1 lemon.
- **Italian Marinade** Mix 1 crushed
  garlic clove, 4 tbsp olive oil, the juice
  of 1 lemon and 1 tsp dried oregano.
  If you like, leave to marinate for
  1–2 hours before cooking.
- **Oriental Marinade** Mix together
  2 tbsp soy sauce, 1 tsp demerara
  sugar, 2 tbsp dry sherry or apple
  juice, 1 tsp finely chopped fresh root
  ginger and 1 crushed garlic clove.
- **Sticky Sausages** Use sausages
  instead of chicken, if you like.

NUTRITION PER SERVING 218 cals |
12g fat (3g sats) | 5g carbs | 0.4g salt

Tandoori Chicken with Cucumber Raita

Serves 4
Preparation time 45 minutes, plus marinating
Cooking time 20 minutes

4 tbsp groundnut oil, plus extra to grease
3 × 150g cartons natural yogurt
juice of ½ lemon
4 boneless skinless chicken breasts, about 600g (1lb 5oz),
  cut into finger-width pieces
½ cucumber
salt and ground black pepper
fresh mint leaves to garnish

For the tandoori paste
24 garlic cloves, about 125g (4oz), crushed
5cm (2in) piece fresh root ginger, peeled and chopped
3 tbsp coriander seeds
3 tbsp cumin seeds
3 tbsp ground fenugreek
3 tbsp paprika
3 red chillies, seeded and chopped (see Cook's Tip, page 69)
1 tbsp English mustard
2 tbsp tomato purée
1 tsp salt

1 Put all the ingredients for the tandoori paste into a food
processor or blender with 8 tbsp water and blend to a paste.
Divide the paste into three equal portions, freeze two (see
Freezing Tip) and put the other in a large bowl.
2 To make the tandoori chicken, add 2 tbsp oil, 2 cartons
yogurt and the lemon juice to the tandoori paste. Add the
chicken and stir well to coat. Cover with clingfilm, chill
and leave to marinate in the fridge for at least 4 hours.
3 Preheat the oven to 220°C (200°C fan oven) mark 7. Oil
a roasting tin. Put the chicken in it, drizzle the remaining
oil over the chicken and roast in the oven for 20 minutes or
until cooked through.
4 Meanwhile, prepare the raita. Whisk the remaining
carton of yogurt. Using a vegetable peeler, scrape the
cucumber into very thin strips. Put the strips in a bowl
and pour the whisked yogurt over them. Season, then chill
until ready to serve. Garnish the cucumber raita with mint.
Sprinkle the chicken with mint and serve with the raita.

Freezing Tip
• To freeze the paste, at the end of step 1, put two of the
  portions of tandoori paste into separate freezer bags, seal,
  label and freeze. They will keep for up to three months.
• To use the frozen paste, put the paste in a microwave and
  cook on Defrost for 1 minute 20 seconds (based on
  a 900W oven), or thaw at a cool room temperature for
  about 1 hour.

NUTRITION PER SERVING 399 cals | 20g fat (4g sats) | 15g carbs | 2g salt

Chicken Tikka Masala

Serves 4
Preparation time 20 minutes
Cooking time 30 minutes

1 tbsp vegetable oil
1 large onion, finely sliced
2 tbsp tikka masala paste
2 tbsp tomato purée
500g (1lb 2oz) skinless chicken breasts,
  cut into bite-size pieces
400g can chopped tomatoes
2 tbsp mango chutney
100g (3½oz) natural yogurt
100ml (3½oz) double cream
salt and ground black pepper
a large handful of fresh coriander,
  roughly chopped to garnish
rice or garlic naan breads to serve

1 Heat the oil in a large pan that has a tightly fitting lid. Add the onion and a pinch of salt, cover and cook over a low heat for 20 minutes or until onions are completely softened.
2 Take off the lid and stir in the tikka masala paste, tomato purée and chicken pieces. Fry for a few minutes until blended, then add the tomatoes. Bring to the boil and simmer for 8–10 minutes until the chicken is cooked through.
3 Stir in the chutney, yogurt and cream and heat through gently. Season to taste with salt and pepper. Garnish with coriander and serve with rice or our garlic naan breads.

NUTRITION PER SERVING 361 cals | 19g fat (9g sats) | 13g carbs | 1.0g salt

Thai Green Chicken Curry

Serves 6
Preparation time 10 minutes
Cooking time 15 minutes

2 tsp vegetable oil
1 green chilli, seeded and chopped (see
  Cook's Tip, page 69)
4cm (1½in) piece fresh root ginger,
  peeled and finely grated
1 lemongrass stalk, trimmed and cut in 3
225g (8oz) brown or oyster mushrooms
1 tbsp Thai green curry paste
300ml (½ pint) coconut milk
150ml (¼ pint) chicken stock
1 tbsp Thai fish sauce
1 tsp light soy sauce
350g (12oz) boneless skinless chicken
  breasts, cut into bite-size pieces
350g (12oz) cooked peeled prawns
fresh coriander sprigs to garnish
boiled rice to serve

1 Heat the oil in a wok or large frying pan. Add the chilli, ginger, lemongrass and mushrooms and stir-fry for about 3 minutes or until the mushrooms begin to turn golden. Add the curry paste and fry for a further 1 minute.
2 Pour in the coconut milk, stock, fish sauce and soy sauce and bring to the boil. Stir in the chicken, then reduce the heat and simmer for about 8 minutes or until the chicken is cooked through.
3 Add the prawns and cook for a further 1 minute. Garnish with coriander sprigs and serve immediately with boiled rice.

NUTRITION PER SERVING 132 cals | 2g fat (0g sats) | 4g carbs | 1.4g salt

Coronation Chicken

Serves 6
Preparation time 20 minutes
Cooking time about 50 minutes, plus chilling

1 tbsp vegetable oil
1 onion, chopped
1 tbsp each ground coriander
1 tbsp ground cumin
1½ tsp ground turmeric
1½ tsp paprika
150ml (¼ pint) dry white wine
500ml (18fl oz) chicken stock
6 boneless skinless chicken breasts or thighs
2 bay leaves
2 fresh thyme sprigs
2 fresh parsley sprigs
salt and ground black pepper
3–4 tbsp freshly chopped flat-leafed parsley to garnish
mixed leaf salad and French bread to serve

For the dressing
150ml (¼ pint) Mayonnaise (see page 29)
5 tbsp natural yogurt
2 tbsp mango chutney
125g (4oz) ready-to-eat dried apricots, chopped
juice of ½ lemon

1 Heat the oil in a large, heavy-based pan, add the onion and fry for 5–10 minutes until softened and golden. Add the spices and cook, stirring, for 1–2 minutes.
2 Pour in the wine, bring to the boil and let it bubble for 5 minutes to reduce right down. Add the stock and bring to the boil again.
3 Season the chicken with salt and pepper, then add to the pan with the bay leaves and herb sprigs. Cover and bring to the boil. Reduce the heat to low and poach the chicken for 25 minutes or until cooked through. Cool quickly by plunging the base of the pan into a sink of cold water, replacing the water as it warms up. Drain the cooled stock from the chicken.
4 Meanwhile, to make the dressing, mix together the mayonnaise, yogurt and mango chutney in a bowl. Whisk in 200ml (7fl oz) of the cooled stock into the mayonnaise mixture. Add the apricots and lemon juice, and season well with salt and pepper.
5 Roughly chop the chicken into bite-size pieces, then stir it into the curried mayonnaise. Cover and chill until required. Garnish with chopped parsley and serve with a mixed leaf salad and French bread.

NUTRITION PER SERVING 425 cals | 26g fat (4g sats) | 14g carbs | 0.6g salt

Roast Turkey with Parsley, Sage and Thyme

Serves 16
Preparation time 40 minutes, plus chilling
Cooking time 3¾ hours

6.3kg (14lb) turkey
2 small red onions, cut into
 wedges
2 lemons, cut into wedges
6 whole garlic cloves
8 fresh thyme sprigs
8 fresh sage leaves
8 fresh flat-leafed parsley
 sprigs
250ml (9fl oz) olive oil
roast vegetables to serve

For the seasoning
1 tbsp pink peppercorns
2 tsp sea salt
2 tbsp paprika
2 tbsp celery salt

For the stuffing
4 tbsp olive oil
2 large onions, chopped
4 garlic cloves, crushed
150g (5oz) fresh white
 breadcrumbs
75g (3oz) medium cornmeal
 or polenta
100g (3½oz) hazelnuts,
 toasted and chopped
finely grated zest of 2 lemons
 and juice of 1 lemon
4 tbsp freshly chopped flat-
 leafed parsley
4 tbsp freshly chopped sage
2 medium eggs, beaten
salt and ground black pepper

1 To make the stuffing, heat the oil in a pan. Add the onions and garlic, and fry gently for 10 minutes to soften but not brown. Tip into a bowl to cool. Meanwhile, put the breadcrumbs, cornmeal or polenta, hazelnuts, lemon zest, parsley, sage and eggs into a large bowl and squeeze over the lemon juice. Add the cooled onion and garlic, and season with salt and pepper. Stir to bind together.
2 To make the seasoning, crush the peppercorns, sea salt, paprika and celery salt in a pestle and mortar, or whiz in a mini processor. Stand the turkey upright on a board, with the parson's nose (the rear end) facing upwards. Sprinkle the cavity with 1 tbsp of the peppercorn seasoning, then pack the cavity with half the onions and lemon wedges, garlic cloves, thyme and sage and all the parsley sprigs.
3 Sit the turkey with the parson's nose facing away from you. Lift up the loose skin at the neck end and fill the cavity with handfuls of cold stuffing. Turn the turkey on to its breast, then lift the neck flap up and over the stuffing to cover and bring the wing tips round on top.
4 Thread a trussing needle with 2m (6ft) fine string and sew the neck flap to the turkey. Push the skewer firmly through the wings, twist the string around the ends and pull to tighten both wings against the breast. Turn the

turkey over, tuck in the parson's nose, cross the legs, then bring the string up and over the legs and wrap around tightly, securing with a double knot. Cut off any excess.
5 Pour the olive oil into a large roasting tin. Immerse a muslin, about 60cm (24in), in it to coat completely, then stretch it out, with the edges overhanging the tin. Sit the turkey on top and sprinkle with the remaining peppercorn seasoning. Scatter with the remaining thyme and sage, then arrange the remaining lemon and onion wedges and the garlic cloves around the bird. Bring the muslin up and over to wrap the turkey completely, then turn it over breast side down in the tin. Over-wrap with clingfilm and leave to chill overnight in the bottom of the fridge.
6 Take the turkey out of the fridge 30 minutes before cooking to bring to room temperature. Preheat the oven to 180°C (160°C fan oven) mark 4. Remove the muslin and keep the turkey breast side down. Roast for 3¾ hours, basting occasionally to keep the flesh moist. Turn it over after cooking for 2 hours. To check that the turkey is cooked, pierce the thickest part of the thigh with a skewer; the juices should run clear. Serve with roasted vegetables.

NUTRITION PER SERVING 280 cals | 10g fat (2g sats) | 11g carbs | 2.2g salt

Turkey Curry

Serves 4
Preparation time 15 minutes
Cooking time 35 minutes

2 tbsp oil
1 large onion, chopped
2 garlic cloves, finely chopped
1 tsp ground turmeric
½ tsp chilli powder
1½ tsp ground cumin
1½ tsp ground coriander
400g can chopped tomatoes
½ tsp salt
600g (1lb 5oz) cooked turkey
1 tsp garam masala
150ml (¼ pint) thick yogurt
fresh coriander sprigs to garnish
boiled rice to serve

1 Heat the oil in a heavy-based pan, add the onion and garlic, and fry gently until softened and golden. Add the turmeric, chilli powder, cumin and ground coriander, and cook, stirring, for 1 minute.
2 Add the tomatoes and salt. Bring to the boil, then reduce the heat, cover and simmer for 20 minutes.
3 Remove any skin from the turkey, then cut into chunks. Add to the pan with the garam masala and 4 tbsp yogurt. Cover and cook gently for 10 minutes, without boiling, then stir in the remaining yogurt. Garnish with coriander and serve with rice.

TRY SOMETHING DIFFERENT
• For a more intense flavour, fry 1 tsp black mustard seeds with the spices.
• Scatter 2–3 tbsp freshly chopped coriander over the curry to serve.

Cook's Tip
This is an ideal recipe for using up turkey left over from your Christmas meal.

Roast Duck with Orange Sauce

Serves 4
Preparation time 50 minutes
Cooking time 1 hour 40 minutes, plus resting

2 large oranges
2 large fresh thyme sprigs
2.3kg (5lb) duck, with giblets if possible
4 tbsp vegetable oil
2 shallots, chopped
1 tsp plain flour
600ml (1 pint) chicken stock
25g (1oz) caster sugar
2 tbsp red wine vinegar
100ml (3½fl oz) fresh orange juice
100ml (3½fl oz) fruity German white wine
2 tbsp orange liqueur, such as Grand Marnier (optional)
1 tbsp lemon juice
salt and ground black pepper
glazed orange wedges (see Cook's Tip) to garnish
mangetouts and broccoli to serve

1 Preheat the oven to 200°C (180°C fan oven) mark 6. Using a zester, remove strips of zest from the oranges. Put half the zest into a pan of cold water, bring to the boil, then drain and put to one side. Remove the pith from both oranges and cut the flesh into segments.
2 Put the thyme and unblanched orange zest inside the duck and season. Rub the skin with 2 tbsp oil, sprinkle with salt and put, breast side up, on a rack over a roasting tin. Roast, basting every 20 minutes, for 1¼–1½ hours until just cooked and the juices run clear when the thickest part of the thigh is pierced with a skewer. After 30 minutes, turn breast side down, then breast side up for the last 10 minutes.
3 Meanwhile, cut the gizzard, heart and neck into pieces. Heat the remaining 2 tbsp oil in a heavy-based pan. Add the giblets and fry over a medium-high heat until dark brown. Add the chopped shallots and flour, and cook for 1 minute, stirring. Pour in the stock, bring to the boil and bubble until reduced by half, then strain.
4 Put the sugar and vinegar into a heavy-based pan over a low heat until the sugar dissolves. Turn up the heat and cook for a few minutes until it forms a dark caramel. Pour in the orange juice and stir. Cool, cover and put to one side.
5 Lift the duck off the rack and keep it warm. Skim all the fat off the juices to leave about 3 tbsp sediment. Stir the wine into the sediment, bring to the boil and bubble for

5 minutes or until syrupy. Add the stock and orange mixtures. Bring back to the boil and bubble until syrupy, skimming if necessary. Add the orange zest and segments, the Grand Marnier, if you like, and lemon juice to taste.
6 Carve the duck and garnish with the glazed orange wedges. Serve with the orange sauce, and steamed mangetouts and broccoli.

Cook's Tips

GLAZED ORANGES Preheat the grill. Quarter the oranges or cut into wedges. Dust with a little caster sugar and grill until caramelised.

- Some fat may be in the cavity of the duck, and should be pulled out before cooking. Most of the fat is under the skin and will melt out during cooking. Save it and use for roasting root vegetables.
- Whole ducks look large because they have a large cavity and carcass. They don't feed as many people as the size might suggest.

NUTRITION PER SERVING 561 cals | 38g fat (9g sats) | 20g carbs | 0.5g salt

Peking-style Duck

Serves 4
Preparation time 10 minutes, plus overnight drying
Cooking time about 1 hour

1.5–2kg (3lb 4oz–4½lb) duck
1 tsp palm sugar or dark soft brown sugar
2 tbsp dark soy sauce

To serve
ready-made Chinese pancakes (see Cook's Tip)
8 tbsp plum sauce
8 tbsp hoisin sauce
1 bunch spring onions, sliced into thin 5cm (2in) strips
½ cucumber, seeded and cut into thin 5cm (2in) sticks

1 Put the duck into a very large bowl. Pour a kettleful of boiling water over it, ensuring the whole bird is doused. Remove and dry inside and out with plenty of kitchen paper. Prick the skin all over with a fork, taking care not to pierce the flesh. Hang it up somewhere cool and airy to dry overnight, putting a bowl underneath to catch any drips.
2 Heat the oven to 190°C (170°C fan oven) mark 5. Mix the sugar with the soy sauce and rub over the duck. Leave to dry for 10 minutes. Put the duck on a wire rack set in a roasting tin and roast for 1 hour – do not baste.
3 Reheat the Chinese pancakes according to the pack instructions. Strip the skin and meat from the duck and put on a warmed serving plate. Put the remaining ingredients into separate bowls.
4 To assemble, spread a spoonful of plum or hoisin sauce on to a pancake, followed by strips of spring onion and cucumber and a layer of duck meat and skin. Roll the filling up in the pancake and enjoy.

Cook's Tip
Chinese pancakes can be found in the ready-meal chiller aisle or freezer aisles of major supermarkets or at specialist Asian stores.

NUTRITION PER SERVING 761 cals | 42g fat (11g sats) | 11g carbs | 1.2g salt

Roast Guinea Fowl

Serves 4
Preparation time 20 minutes, plus marinating
Cooking time 1 hour 10 minutes, plus resting

1 guinea fowl
grated zest and juice of 1 lemon, and
  1 lemon quartered lengthways
3 bay leaves
5 fresh thyme sprigs
1 tbsp black peppercorns, lightly crushed
25g (1oz) butter
150ml (¼ pint) hot chicken stock
roast potatoes and green beans to serve

For the gravy
2 tbsp redcurrant jelly
100ml (3½fl oz) dry white wine
salt and ground black pepper

1 Put the guinea fowl into a non-metallic bowl and add
the lemon zest and juice, bay leaves, thyme sprigs and
peppercorns. Cover, chill and leave to marinate for 1 hour.
2 Preheat the oven to 200°C (180°C fan oven) mark 6.
3 Put the bird into a roasting tin, breast side down, put the
lemon quarters and the butter into the cavity and pour the
hot stock over. Roast in the oven for 50 minutes.
4 Turn the guinea fowl breast side up and continue to roast
for about 20 minutes or until cooked and the juices run
clear when the thigh is pierced with a skewer.
5 Put the guinea fowl on a board, cover with foil and leave
to rest for 10 minutes.
6 To make the gravy, put the roasting tin on the hob and
scrape up the juices. Add the redcurrant jelly, wine and
50ml (2fl oz) water and bring to the boil. Reduce the heat
and simmer for 3–5 minutes. Season well with salt and
pepper. Carve the guinea fowl and serve with the gravy,
roast potatoes and green beans.

NUTRITION PER SERVING 585 cals | 27g fat (11g sats) | 5g carbs | 0.7g salt

Roast Goose with Wild Rice Stuffing

Serves 6
Preparation time 45 minutes
Cooking time about 3 hours, plus resting

5kg (11lb) goose (with giblets for stock)
Wild Rice Stuffing, thawed if frozen (see page 13)
25g (1oz) butter, plus extra to grease
3 red-skinned apples
4 fresh sage sprigs, plus extra to garnish
2 tbsp golden caster sugar
salt and ground black pepper

For the gravy
2 tbsp plain flour
150ml (¼ pint) red wine
600ml (1 pint) giblet stock (see Cook's Tip, page 11)
2 tbsp redcurrant jelly

1 To make the goose easier to carve, remove the wishbone from the neck by lifting the flap and cutting around the bone with a small knife. Remove the wishbone. Using your fingers, ease the skin away from the flesh to make room for the stuffing, then put the goose on a tray in the sink and pour a generous amount of freshly boiled water over, then pat dry with kitchen paper.
2 Preheat the oven to 230°C (210°C fan oven) mark 8. Pack the neck of the goose with half the stuffing and secure the neck shut with skewers or by using a trussing needle with fine string. Put the remaining stuffing on to a buttered sheet of foil and wrap it up. Season the cavity of the bird, then put 1 whole apple and the sage sprigs inside.
3 Put the goose on a rack in a roasting tin and season well with salt and pepper. Roast in the oven for 30 minutes, basting occasionally, then remove and drain off any excess fat. Reduce the oven temperature to 190°C (170°C fan oven) mark 5 and cook for a further 2½ hours, removing any excess fat every 20 minutes. Thirty minutes before the end of cooking, put the parcel of stuffing into the oven.
4 Test whether the goose is cooked by piercing the thigh with a skewer – the juices should run clear. Remove the goose from the oven and put it on a board. Cover with foil and leave to rest for at least 20 minutes.
5 Meanwhile, cut the remaining apples into thick wedges. Heat the butter in a heavy-based frying pan until it is no longer foaming. Add the apples and the sugar, and stir-fry over a high heat for 4–5 minutes until caramelised, then put to one side.
6 To make the gravy, drain all but 3 tbsp fat from the roasting tin. Add the flour and stir to make a smooth paste. Stir or whisk in the wine and boil for 5 minutes, stirring, then add the stock and redcurrant jelly, and mix well. Bring to the boil, then reduce the heat and simmer for 5 minutes. Strain before serving. Serve the goose, garnished with sage sprigs, with the stuffing and caramelised apples.

Cook's Tips
- Like ducks, geese have a large cavity and carcass, so will not feed as many people as a turkey of comparable size.
- Try to collect the fat and use it, as you would duck fat, for roasting potatoes. The best way to collect the fat is to spoon it out of the roasting tin regularly during cooking and put it to one side.

NUTRITION PER SERVING 820 cals | 51g fat (18g sats) | 32g carbs | 1.7g salt

Poussins with Pancetta, Artichoke and Potato Salad

Serves 6
Preparation time 20 minutes, plus overnight marinating
Cooking time 1 hour 40 minutes, plus resting

grated zest of 1 lemon
5 large fresh rosemary sprigs, leaves stripped
4 tbsp white wine vinegar
150ml (¼ pint) fruity white wine
4 garlic cloves, crushed
3 tbsp freshly chopped oregano or a pinch of dried oregano
290g jar marinated artichokes, drained, oil reserved
3 poussins, about 450g (1lb) each
½ tsp cayenne pepper
450g (1lb) new potatoes, quartered
225g (8oz) pancetta, prosciutto or streaky bacon, roughly chopped
350g (12oz) peppery salad leaves, such as watercress, mustard leaf and rocket
salt and ground black pepper

1 Put the lemon zest and rosemary leaves into a large bowl with the vinegar, wine, garlic, oregano and 4 tbsp oil from the artichokes. Stir well. Using a fork, pierce the skin of the poussins in five or six places, then season well with black pepper and the cayenne pepper. Put the birds, breast side down, in the bowl and spoon the marinade over them. Cover and chill overnight.
2 Cook the potatoes in lightly salted boiling water for 2 minutes. Drain. Preheat the oven to 200°C (180°C fan oven) mark 6.
3 Lift the poussins from the marinade and put, breast side up, into a large roasting tin. Scatter the potatoes, pancetta or bacon and artichokes around them and pour the marinade over. Cook for 1½ hours, basting occasionally or until golden and cooked through.
4 Cut each poussin in half lengthways and keep warm. Toss the salad leaves with about 5 tbsp warm cooking juices. Arrange the leaves on warmed plates, then top with the potatoes, pancetta, artichokes and poussins.

Cook's Tip
Use the oil drained from the artichokes to make a salad dressing for another meal.

NUTRITION PER SERVING 442 cals | 27g fat (8g sats) | 13g carbs | 1.5g salt

Game

Game

Wild animals or birds that are hunted for food are classified as game, although nowadays many types of game, including rabbit, pheasant, pigeon and quail, are farmed. Farmed game birds are available all year round, but true game birds are available only seasonally – usually in autumn and winter, and not during their breeding season in spring and early summer. Most game is protected by law and can only be hunted at certain times of the year; quail is now a protected species that cannot be hunted.

Fresh wild game meat is only available during the hunting season, but farmed varieties are obtainable year round from specialist suppliers and major supermarkets. Farmed game is usually milder in flavour than its hunted counterpart. Most game birds and meat need to be hung to develop the flavour and tenderise the flesh. Game meats include venison, wild boar, rabbit and hare, and there are also the more unusual 'new meats' such as ostrich, alligator and llama. All are good sources of protein but some can also be high in fats, particularly saturated fats, which everyone should aim to limit for health reasons.

Choosing game

Game birds are best eaten young. The feathers are a good guide, as young birds tend to have soft, even feathers. Young pheasants and partridges usually have long, V-shaped wing feathers, whereas in older birds the same feathers tend to be rounded. Also look for a plump breast, smooth legs and pliable spurs. For the best quality, choose birds that have not been extensively damaged by shot: telltale signs are red or black entrance wounds on the breast and/or broken legs. Game should be well cut and neatly trimmed.

You need smaller quantities when buying cuts of meat off the bone: allow 100–150g (3½–5oz) per person.

For meat on the bone, allow slightly more: 175–350g (6–12oz) per person depending on the cut.

Both wild and farmed rabbit are available. Farmed rabbit is often likened to chicken in flavour and texture while wild rabbit is much tougher.

Hare has darker, more strongly flavoured flesh and is not farmed. Young hare (leveret) is best and can be cooked quickly. Young animals have white fat, whereas that of older animals tends to be more yellow. Older hare requires long, slow cooking.

Boar is sold in various cuts, as well as minced and processed into products such as sausages. Meat from older deer has a better flavour than that from young but requires longer cooking.

Breeding and rearing

How farmed game is bred and reared has a significant effect on its health and welfare, and on taste and texture.

Categories for game meats

For game birds, see the details for poultry on page 132. Many game meats are now farmed, but as a general rule animals that have been allowed to grow naturally produce meat with a better flavour and texture.

The two main alternatives to intensively reared game are free-range and organic:

Free-range Different countries have their own guidelines as to what constitutes free-range rearing but, broadly speaking, the animals are allowed to roam and graze freely.

Organic Once again, different countries have their own guidelines but, generally, these animals are not intensively reared and are bred without artificial intervention. They are allowed to feed on organic pasture and are fed 80 per cent organic, non-GM (genetically modified) feed. Synthetic medicines and pesticides are avoided wherever possible. The organic label means that the animal should have been raised in accordance with the laws of the certifying body for the country of origin.

Handling and storing game

Game meats As for other meat (see page 172), game should be wrapped and stored in the fridge, placed in a dish so that if any juices escape they cannot drip and contaminate other foods. Do not allow the meat to touch any other foods.

Game birds are traditionally hung for several days to deepen their gamey flavour and tenderise the flesh – an unhung bird will be tough and tasteless. Most game from a butcher or supermarket will have been hung, but if you have a freshly shot bird, hang it yourself in a cool, airy place for the periods listed below.

Hanging times for game birds

Grouse	2–4 days
Partridge	3–5 days
Pheasant	3–10 days
Wood pigeon	Requires no hanging
Woodcock	3–5 days

A prepared bird can be stored in the fridge for one to two days. But birds that have been significantly damaged by shot will not keep as well, so cook as soon as possible.

Freezing game

• Freeze meat before its use-by date, even better on the day of purchase.
• Wrap portions in individual freezer bags, seal tightly and label with the date of freezing. To maintain the best flavour and texture, meat can be stored in the freezer for up to three months.
• To thaw, put the meat in a dish to catch any juices and put in the fridge until completely thawed. Use within two days.
• Do not refreeze raw meat that has thawed. You can, however, freeze dishes made from thawed meat that you have then cooked.

For game birds, check the advice given on page 132.

Food safety

Although raw meat does not carry the same food poisoning risks as poultry, it may still contain harmful bacteria so always follow the basic hygiene rules (see Food Storage, page 498).

Trussing and jointing

Prepare game birds as for poultry (see page 133).

Cooking game

When preparing game birds, follow the guidelines for poultry given on page 133 and consult the roasting chart below for cooking times and temperatures. Game birds become dry and tough if overcooked; there should still be a trace of pinkness in the flesh and juices.

Grill Best suited to cuts such as steaks, chops, cutlets, cubed meat made into kebabs, and burgers and sausages. Season or marinate, then cook under a preheated grill.

Griddle Best suited to cuts such as steaks, chops and cutlets. Preheat the griddle for about 3 minutes or until smoking hot, then brush the meat with oil and cook for a few minutes on each side until cooked to your liking.

Stir-fry Best suited to tender, lean cuts such as fillet. Slice the meat into strips no thicker than 5mm (¼in). Heat a wok or large heavy-based pan until hot, then add oil to coat the inside. Add the meat and stir-fry, moving the pan contents constantly. Remove, then cook the remaining ingredients. Return the meat to the pan to warm through.

Pan-fry Best suited to cuts such as steaks, chops and cutlets. Preheat a frying pan and season the meat. Add enough oil to coat the base of the pan, then add the meat and brown on one side, not moving it for at least 1 minute, before turning to cook on the other side.

Braise and pot-roast Suited to tougher cuts that require long, slow cooking. Preheat the oven to 170°C (150°C fan oven) mark 3. Heat some oil in a large flameproof casserole and brown the meat all over, working in batches if necessary. Remove from the pan and fry onions and garlic for a few minutes until beginning to colour, then return the meat to the pan with tomatoes or vegetables, and wine or stock. Stir well and season with salt and pepper, then cover and cook in the oven for 2 hours or until tender.

Roast Suited to larger and more tender joints of meat. Different cuts need different treatment, so follow the recipe and also see the general tips for roasting meat on page 173.

Roasting times for game birds

BIRD	OVEN TEMPERATURE	COOKING TIME	QUANTITIES FOR ROASTING
Grouse	200°C (180°C fan oven) mark 6	Allow about 40 minutes total roasting time	Allow 1 bird per person
Partridge	200°C (180°C fan oven) mark 6	Allow about 40 minutes total roasting time	Allow 1 bird per person
Pheasant	230°C (210°C fan oven) mark 8	Roast for 10 minutes, then reduce the temperature to 200°C (180°C fan oven) mark 6 and roast for a further 30–50 minutes	1 bird will serve 2–3 people
Pigeon	200°C (180°C fan oven) mark 6	Allow 20–30 minutes total roasting time	Allow 1 bird per person
Quail	220°C (200°C fan oven) mark 7	Allow about 25 minutes total roasting time	Allow 2 birds per person
Woodcock	190°C (170°C fan oven) mark 5	Allow 15–25 minutes total roasting time	Allow 1 bird per person

Game Meat and Birds

1 Grouse: 12 Aug –10 Dec
One of these small birds will serve 1–2 people. The young birds are best for eating; roast or grill. Braise or casserole older birds.

2 Quail: all year
Quail are tiny birds with a mild flavour; serve 2 per person. Roast whole or spatchcocked; or split and grill or pan-fry.

3 Partridge: all year
The pale flesh has a delicate flavour and fine texture. Young partridge, 2–4 months old, are best: wrap with bacon and roast; braise, pot-roast or stew older birds.

4 Pigeon: all year
Wild wood pigeon has very dark meat with a full flavour. Available fresh or frozen, usually plucked and oven ready. Cook as partridge.

5 Pheasant: 1 Oct–1 Feb
The hen pheasant is smaller than the cock pheasant and has more tender flesh. Roast only young pheasant; both young and older pheasants make good casseroles.

6 Rabbit: all year
Farmed rabbit has pale, tender meat; wild rabbit has darker, tougher flesh. Both can be bought whole or in pieces. The meat is lean: baste with oil, don't overcook. Wild: braise, casserole, stew or add to pie fillings. Farmed: grill, sauté, roast.

7 Boar: all year
A dark and strongly flavoured meat with lean flesh. Roast tender cuts; braise, stew or casserole tougher cuts or use in pie fillings, sauces, patties, meatballs and meat loaves.

8 Venison: all year
Has lean, dark, close-textured meat with a good flavour. Roast loin, saddle, fillet and leg; pan-fry escalopes and medallions; casserole neck and breast. Marinate before cooking.

9 Hare: all year
Hare has dark, strongly flavoured flesh. Roast young hare; braise, casserole or stew older hare, or add to pie fillings.

10 Goat: all year
The meat has a distinctive and pungent aroma. Braise, stew or casserole. Roast or barbecue young goat.

11 Woodcock: 1 Oct–31 Jan
These small birds are generally roasted whole (undrawn) and served on toast.

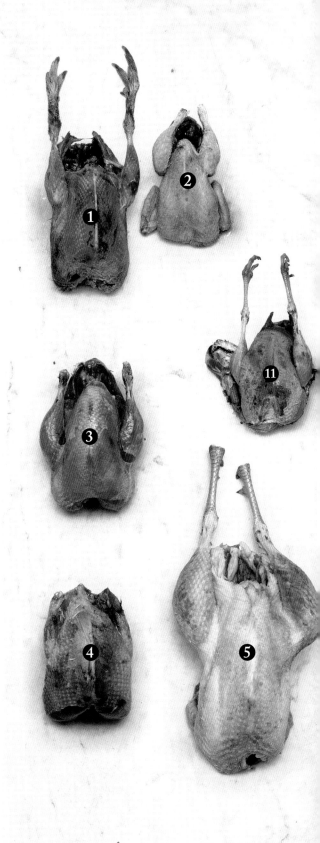

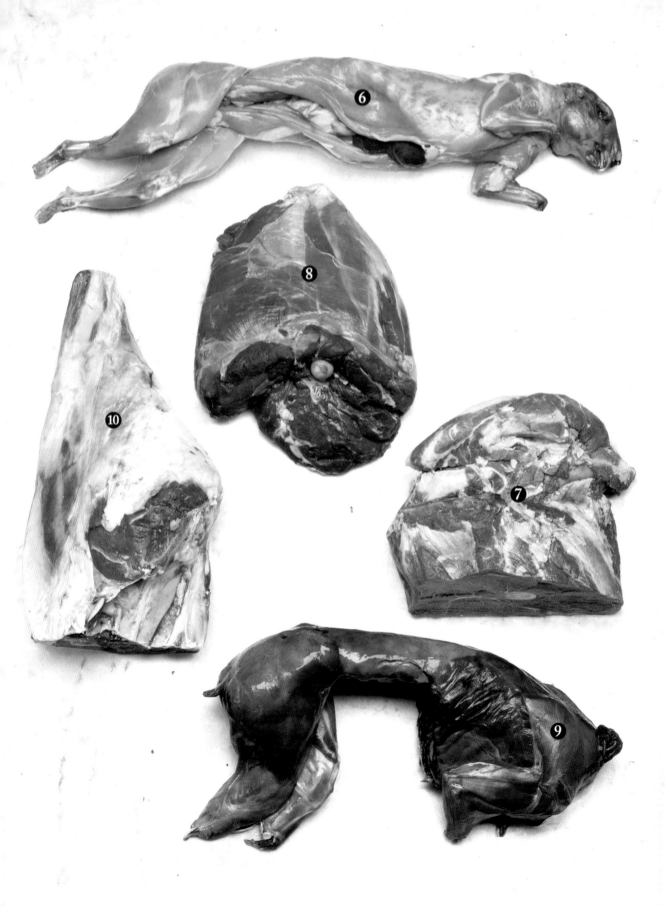

Roast Quail in Red Peppers

Serves 4
Preparation time 20 minutes
Cooking time 35–40 minutes

4 quails
4 tbsp olive oil
2 large red peppers, halved lengthways,
  cored and seeded
4 slices Parma ham (see Cook's Tip,
  page 76)
125ml (4fl oz) chicken stock
2 tbsp balsamic vinegar
salt and ground black pepper
Fried Herb Polenta to serve (see Try
  Something Different, page 266)

1 Preheat the oven to 200°C (180°C
fan oven) mark 6. Season the quails
inside and out, rubbing well into the
skin. Heat the oil in a heavy-based
frying pan and quickly fry the quails
over a high heat until browned on all
sides. Remove with a slotted spoon.
2 Fry the pepper halves in the oil left
in the pan until just softened. Line
each pepper cavity with a slice of ham
and sit a quail in each one. Put into
a flameproof casserole and sprinkle
with half the stock and vinegar.
3 Cook in the oven, basting regularly,
for 25–30 minutes until the quails are
cooked. Remove and keep warm.
4 Put the casserole over a high heat
and add the remaining stock and
vinegar, stirring to deglaze. Bubble
until reduced and slightly syrupy. Pour
over the quails and serve with piping
hot herb polenta.

NUTRITION PER SERVING (without
polenta) 480 cals | 35g fat (8g sats) |
3g carbs | 0.4g salt

Roast Grouse

Serves 4
Preparation time 10 minutes
Cooking time 40 minutes, plus resting

2 oven-ready grouse
6 streaky bacon rashers, rind removed
2 tbsp vegetable oil
2 tbsp freshly chopped rosemary or
  thyme (optional)
salt and ground black pepper
deep-fried thinly sliced potatoes and
  parsnips or hand-cooked salted crisps
  and watercress to serve

1 Preheat the oven to 200°C (180°C
fan oven) mark 6. Put the grouse into
a large roasting tin, with enough space
between them so that they can brown
evenly. Cover the breast of each with
bacon, then drizzle with 1 tbsp oil.
Season with salt and pepper and
sprinkle with herbs, if you like.
2 Roast in the oven for 40 minutes
or until the juices run clear when the
thigh is pierced with a skewer.
3 Leave to rest in a warm place for
10 minutes before serving.
4 Serve with crisp deep-fried slices
of potato and parsnip or ready-made
hand-cooked crisps, plus watercress to
contrast with the richness of the meat.

NUTRITION PER SERVING 320 cals |
18g fat (4g sats) | trace carbs | 0.3g salt

Pigeon on Crisp Polenta with Tomato Salsa

Serves 4
Preparation time 40 minutes
Cooking time 25 minutes

4 wood pigeons, plucked and drawn
25g (1oz) butter
1 garlic clove, crushed
4 chicken livers, trimmed
a pinch of powdered mace
oil to brush
salt and ground black pepper
freshly chopped herbs to garnish
Fried Herb Polenta to serve (see Try Something Different,
  page 266)

For the tomato salsa
4 large ripe tomatoes, skinned, seeded and diced
  (see page 277)
2 garlic cloves, finely chopped
4 tbsp freshly chopped mixed herbs, such as basil,
  oregano and parsley
5 tbsp olive oil

1 Mix together the ingredients for the tomato salsa in a
bowl and season with salt and pepper to taste.
2 Cut the legs from the pigeons and set aside. Using a
sharp knife, cut down the breastbone on each side and ease
off the pigeon breasts; cover and set aside.
3 Melt the butter in a frying pan, add the garlic and fry
gently for 2 minutes until golden. Add the chicken livers
and cook over a high heat for 5 minutes until browned and
cooked through. Season with the mace, salt and pepper.
Transfer to a bowl and set aside.
4 Lay the pigeon legs on the grill rack, brush with oil and
grill under a medium-high heat for 2 minutes. Turn the
legs over. Add the pigeon breasts to the rack, skin side up,
brush with oil and grill for 4 minutes. Turn the pigeon legs
and breasts and cook for a further 2 minutes.
5 Meanwhile, warm the tomato salsa in a small pan over
a low heat. Mash the chicken livers and spread on the hot
fried polenta slices, or serve on the side. Put the polenta
on warmed plates and top with the pigeon. Garnish with
herbs and serve with the tomato salsa.

NUTRITION PER SERVING 980 cals | 62g fat (12g sats) | 36g carbs | 0.7g salt

Roast Venison with Mustard and Mushrooms

Serves 4
Preparation time 15 minutes
Cooking time 30 minutes, plus resting

600g (1lb 5oz) piece loin of venison
1 tbsp wholegrain mustard
2 small onions, thinly sliced
350g (12oz) small shiitake or brown-
   cap mushrooms, halved
150ml (¼ pint) olive oil
1 tbsp freshly chopped thyme
1 tbsp freshly chopped parsley
5 tsp balsamic vinegar
lemon juice to taste
salt and ground black pepper

1 Preheat the oven to 230°C (210°C
fan oven) mark 8. Rub the meat with
the mustard and put in a roasting
tin. Surround with the onions and
mushrooms and drizzle with half
the oil. Roast for 30–35 minutes for
medium-rare or 40 for well-done.
2 Scatter the thyme and parsley
on a board. Roll the hot venison in
the chopped herbs to coat and put
on a warmed serving dish with the
mushrooms and onions. Cover with
foil and rest in a warm place.
3 Add the balsamic vinegar and the
remaining oil to the roasting tin and
warm on the hob, stirring. Season and
add lemon juice to taste.
4 Carve the venison into thick slices
and serve with the hot dressing.

NUTRITION PER SERVING 600 cals
| 42g fat (7g sats) | 6g carbs | 1g salt

Venison Sausages with Red Onion Marmalade

Serves 6
Preparation time 15 minutes
Cooking time 35 minutes

12 gluten-free (100% meat) venison
   sausages
6 tsp redcurrant jelly

For the red onion marmalade
400g (14oz) red onions, chopped
2 tbsp olive oil
4 tbsp red wine vinegar
2 tbsp demerara sugar
1 tsp juniper berries, crushed
a sprig of lovage, chopped, to garnish
mashed potatoes or Colcannon
   (see page 295) to serve

1 Preheat the oven to 220°C (200°C
fan oven) mark 7. Put the sausages
into a small roasting tin. Roast in the
oven for 25 minutes, turning once.
2 Spoon the redcurrant jelly over the
sausages and continue to cook for a
further 10 minutes until the sausages
are cooked through and glazed.
3 Meanwhile, gently fry the onions
in the oil for 15–20 minutes. Add the
vinegar, sugar and juniper berries, and
cook for a further 5 minutes or until
the onions are very tender. Serve the
sausages with the red onion marmalade
and mashed potatoes or Colcannon.
Garnish with lovage and serve.

NUTRITION PER SERVING 390 cals |
25g fat (10g sats) | 14g carbs | 0.3g salt

Warming Venison Casserole

Serves 6
Preparation time 20 minutes
Cooking time 2 hours 50 minutes

1.2kg (2lb 11oz) venison for casseroling, diced
2 tbsp vegetable oil
1 onion, sliced
250g (9oz) mixed mushrooms, such as chestnut and shiitake,
  sliced
1 garlic clove, crushed
150ml (¼ pint) dry cider
600ml (1 pint) beef stock
2 bay leaves
pared zest of 1 orange
1 tbsp cornflour
1 tbsp redcurrant jelly
a small handful of fresh parsley, chopped
salt and ground black pepper

1 Preheat the oven to 170°C (160°C fan oven) mark 3. Pat the venison dry with kitchen paper and season with salt and pepper. Heat 1½ tbsp of the oil in a large flameproof casserole that has a tight-fitting lid over a medium-high heat. Brown the venison in batches, then set the meat aside.
2 Heat the remaining oil and fry the onion for 5 minutes or until golden. Add the mushrooms and fry for 2–3 minutes until softened. Stir in the garlic.
3 Return the venison to the pan with any juices. Add the cider, stock, bay leaves and orange zest. Bring to the boil, then cover the surface of the casserole with greaseproof paper. Put on the lid and cook in the oven for 2¼ hours or until the venison is tender, adding a little extra stock if the pan looks too dry.
4 Strain the meat, reserving the venison mixture and the liquid. Return the liquid to the pan, then bring to the boil on the hob, then reduce the heat and simmer for about 10 minutes or until the flavour has intensified.
5 In a small bowl, mix together the cornflour with 2 tbsp water. Whisk into the simmering liquid, then boil the sauce for 4–5 minutes, stirring constantly, until the mixture thickens. Stir in the redcurrant jelly, then return the strained venison mixture to the pan and heat through gently, without allowing the sauce to boil or the meat will toughen. Discard the bay leaves, add the parsley and season with salt and pepper to taste. Serve immediately.

NUTRITION PER SERVING 286 cals | 7g fat (2g sats) | 6g carbs | 0.7g salt

Pot-roasted Pheasant with Red Cabbage

Serves 4
Preparation time 15 minutes
Cooking time about 1 hour

25g (1oz) butter
1 tbsp oil
2 oven-ready young pheasants, halved
2 onions, peeled and sliced
450g (1lb) red cabbage, cored and finely shredded
1 tsp cornflour
250ml (9fl oz) red wine
2 tbsp redcurrant jelly
1 tbsp balsamic vinegar
4 rindless smoked streaky bacon rashers, halved
salt and ground black pepper

1 Preheat the oven to 200°C (180°C fan oven) mark 6.
Melt the butter with the oil in a large flameproof casserole
over a medium heat. Add the pheasant halves and brown
on all sides, then remove and put to one side. Add the
onions and cabbage to the casserole and fry for
5 minutes, stirring frequently, until softened.
2 Blend the cornflour with a little water to make a paste.
Add to the casserole with the wine, redcurrant jelly and
vinegar. Season with salt and pepper, and bring to the
boil, stirring.
3 Arrange the pheasant halves, skin side up, on the
cabbage. Put the halved bacon rashers on top. Cover
the casserole and cook in the oven for 30 minutes or until
the birds are tender (older pheasants will take an extra
10–20 minutes).
4 Serve the pot-roasted pheasants and red cabbage with
the cooking juices spooned over them.

TRY SOMETHING DIFFERENT
Instead of the pheasants, use oven-ready poussins, small
corn-fed chickens or small guinea fowl; put an onion wedge
inside each bird before browning to impart extra flavour.

NUTRITION PER SERVING 659 cals | 21g fat (12g sats) | 11g carbs | 1.4g salt

Pheasant with Cider and Apples

Serves 8
Preparation time 1 hour
Cooking time 1–1½ hours

2 pheasants, each weighing about 700g (1½lb),
  each cut into four portions
2 tbsp plain flour, plus extra to dust
50g (2oz) butter
4 streaky bacon rashers, rind removed
225g (8oz) onions, roughly chopped
275g (10oz) celery, roughly chopped
4 eating apples, such as Granny Smith, cored,
  cut into large pieces and tossed in 1 tbsp lemon juice
1 tbsp dried juniper berries, lightly crushed
2.5cm (1in) piece fresh root ginger, peeled and
  finely chopped
300ml (½ pint) chicken stock
2 × 440ml cans dry cider
140ml (4½fl oz) double cream
salt and ground black pepper
fried apple wedges, thyme sprigs and juniper
  berries to garnish

1 Preheat the oven to 170°C (150°C fan oven) mark 3.
Season each pheasant portion and dust lightly with flour.
Melt the butter in a large flameproof casserole and brown
the pheasant pieces in batches until deep golden brown.
Remove and keep warm.
2 Put the bacon into the casserole and cook, stirring, for
2–3 minutes until golden. Add the onions, celery, apples,
lemon juice, juniper and ginger, and cook for 8–10 minutes.
Stir the flour into the vegetables and cook for 2 minutes,
then add the stock and cider and bring to the boil. Return
the pheasant to the casserole, cover and cook in the oven
for 45 minutes–1 hour until tender.
3 Lift the pheasant out of the sauce and keep it warm.
Strain the sauce through a sieve and return it to the
casserole with the cream. Bring to the boil and bubble for
10–15 minutes until syrupy. Return the pheasant to the
sauce and season.
4 To serve, garnish the pheasant with the fried apple
wedges, thyme sprigs and juniper berries.

GET AHEAD
- Complete the recipe to the end of step 3, cool quickly,
  cover and chill for up to two days.
- To use, bring the pheasant to the boil and reheat
  in the oven at 180°C (160°C fan oven) mark 4 for
  20–25 minutes.

NUTRITION PER SERVING 463 cals | 27g fat (13g sats) | 13g carbs | 0.7g salt

Rabbit Casserole with Grainy Mustard

Serves 4
Preparation time 15 minutes
Cooking time 1–1½ hours

4–6 rabbit joints, about 700–900g (1½–2lb) in total
2 tbsp plain flour, plus extra to dust
2 tbsp oil
15g (½oz) butter
2 garlic cloves, crushed
300g (11oz) shallots, halved if large
225g (8oz) carrots, thickly sliced
150ml (¼ pint) white wine
300ml (½ pint) chicken stock
3–4 tbsp wholegrain mustard
4 tbsp crème fraîche
salt and ground black pepper
chopped herbs to garnish

1 Preheat the oven to 170°C (150°C fan oven) mark 3.
Season the rabbit joints with salt and pepper, and toss in
flour to coat lightly, shaking off the excess.
2 Heat the oil and butter in a large flameproof casserole
and brown the rabbit joints on all sides over a high heat,
in batches if necessary. Remove and set aside.
3 Reduce the heat and add the garlic, shallots and carrots
to the casserole; cook for 5 minutes. Stir in the flour and
cook for 2 minutes.
4 Add the wine, stock and mustard, stir well and bring to
the boil. Return the rabbit to the casserole, then put the lid
on and cook in the oven for 1–1½ hours until the rabbit is
very tender.
5 Transfer the rabbit and vegetables to a warmed serving
dish, using a slotted spoon; keep warm.
6 If necessary, put the casserole over a high heat for a
few minutes to reduce the sauce a little. Stir in the crème
fraîche and check the seasoning. Pour the creamy mustard
sauce over the rabbit and garnish with herbs to serve.

Cook's Tip
Rabbit meat is low in fat and cholesterol, making
it a healthy option.

NUTRITION PER SERVING 410 cals | 24g fat (12g sats) | 16g carbs | 1.3g salt

Gamekeeper's Pie

Serves 8
Preparation 20 minutes
Cooking time 1¼ hours

2 tbsp sunflower oil
800g (1lb 12oz) minced venison
1 onion, finely chopped
1 celery stick, finely chopped
1 large carrot, grated
1 garlic clove, crushed
1½ tbsp plain flour
150ml (¼ pint) full-fat milk
2 tbsp port
150ml (¼ pint) red wine
350ml (12fl oz) hot beef or game stock
1 tbsp Worcestershire sauce
2 tsp dried juniper berries, roughly crushed
½ tbsp fresh thyme leaves
1 bay leaf
1.3kg (2lb 14oz) Desiree or similar waxy potatoes, cut into
  chunks
50g (2oz) butter
50–75ml (2–2½fl oz) double cream
salt and ground black pepper
seasonal vegetables to serve

1 Heat 1 tbsp oil in a large pan and brown the mince over a medium heat in batches. Remove from the pan using a slotted spoon and set aside.
2 Using the same pan, reduce the heat to low, add the remaining oil and gently fry the onion, celery and carrot for 15 minutes or until softened but not coloured. Add the garlic and fry for 1 minute. Sprinkle the flour over and cook, stirring, for 1 minute.
3 Reduce the heat to medium and add the milk, 2 tbsp at a time, stirring until it is absorbed. Stir in the port and wine and simmer until thickened. Add the hot stock, Worcestershire sauce, juniper berries, thyme and bay leaf and bring to the boil. Return the mince to the pan, cover and simmer for 45 minutes, stirring occasionally.
4 Meanwhile, bring a large pan of lightly salted water to the boil and cook the potatoes for about 15 minutes or until tender. Drain and leave to steam dry in the colander. Heat the butter and cream in a small pan. Push the potato through a potato ricer or sieve into the rinsed potato pan. Stir in enough cream and butter to make a smooth but not sloppy mash. Check the seasoning.

5 Preheat the grill to medium. Tip the hot venison into an ovenproof dish about 30.5 × 20.5cm (12 × 8in). Spread the mash on top and grill for 3–4 minutes until golden. Serve with seasonal vegetables.

GET AHEAD

• Assemble the pie up to two days ahead, wrap the dish in clingfilm and chill. Alternatively, wrap, label and freeze for up to three months.
• To use, if frozen, thaw overnight in the fridge. Reheat at 200°C (180°C fan oven) mark 6 for 25 minutes.

NUTRITION PER SERVING 403 cals | 17g fat (8g sats) | 34g carbs | 1g salt

Meat

Meat

Meat is a valuable source of high-quality protein, B vitamins and iron, and has an important role in a healthy balanced diet; however, it is also a source of saturated fatty acids, which are associated with raised blood cholesterol levels – a risk factor in coronary heart disease. For this reason, it is wise to avoid eating too much red meat, perhaps limiting it to a maximum of three main meals per week.

In the UK beef, lamb and pork are the most popular red meats, whereas veal is eaten to a much lesser extent. The flavour and texture of meat is determined by the breed of the animal, its environment and its feed. Meat from cattle raised on lush pastures will taste far superior to that from corn-fed animals. Organic meat is derived from animals that have been reared on a natural diet, and is therefore an endorsement of quality. With the exception of veal, meat is hung before it is sold to improve the texture and develop its flavour. The most expensive cuts – suitable for roasting, grilling and frying – are from those parts of the animal that are the least exercised – rump, tenderloin, and so on. Cheaper, tougher cuts from those parts of the animal that move the most need slow, gentle cooking with liquid to tenderise them. If you prefer to cut down on red meat, make it go further by serving it with lots of vegetables or by combining it with pulses in casseroles and stews.

Choosing meat

Always buy your meat from a reliable source. Quality butchers and supermarkets sell a wide range of cuts, and a helpful butcher should be able to offer you advice and also be willing to bone meat, cut steaks to a certain thickness and prepare meat in other ways to your specific requirements. For categories of meat see Game, page 158. Meat should look and smell fresh, but colour is not an obvious indicator. Bright red, for example, doesn't necessarily indicate quality. Instead, look for a good clear colour, which will darken naturally on exposure to the air. A greyish tinge is a bad sign.

A little fat is essential to prevent meat drying out during cooking, but look for relatively lean cuts without too much visible fat. Any fat should be creamy white. With the exception of some specialist breeds, such as Jersey and Guernsey beef, creamy yellow fat suggests that the meat is probably past its prime. Look for a smooth outer layer of fat, if appropriate to the cut, and a fine marbling of fat distributed throughout the meat; this will keep it moist during cooking and add flavour.

Always choose a neat, fairly well-trimmed piece of meat. Splinters of bone and ragged edges indicate poor butchery. Cuts should be trimmed of sinew. Joints and steaks should be of uniform thickness so that they cook evenly. Offal should look fresh and moist, and it should not smell.

Handling and storing meat

Once you've made your purchase, get the meat home and into the fridge as soon as possible. It should be stored in the coolest part of the fridge, loosely wrapped and well away from cooked foods to prevent cross-contamination.

If you've bought pre-packed meat from a supermarket, stick to the use-by date. Offal, minced meat and small cuts of veal are best eaten on the day of purchase. Larger joints, chops and steaks will keep in the fridge for two to three days. If meat is past its best, the fat will begin to turn rancid. Off or bad meat will have an unpleasant smell, a slimy surface and possibly a greenish tinge. Because of the danger of food poisoning, it's not worth taking risks – if you have any doubt about the freshness, don't eat it.

For freezing meat, see the advice given for Game on page 159. (See also Food Storage, page 498.)

Marinating meat

A good marinade tenderises tougher cuts of meat and lends a subtle aroma and flavour. Oil, fruit juice and wine-based marinades tend to permeate the meat, adding moisture to dry cuts, whereas yogurt will tenderise and form a soft crust on the food as it cooks. Aromatics – lemon zest, thyme, bay, garlic and onion – add fragrance and flavour.

Put the meat into a shallow non-metallic dish and pour over the marinade. Leave in a cool place for at least 1 hour or overnight. Remove the meat from the marinade and cook as the recipe, basting with marinade regularly if you are cooking on a barbecue or under the grill.

Cooking meat

Lean, fine-grained cuts can be cooked quickly whereas tougher cuts need long, slow cooking to make them tender.

Stew and casserole A stew is cooked on the hob whereas a casserole is cooked in the oven – both at a gentle simmer. Brown the meat before adding any liquid. Choose a heavy-based pan or casserole with a tight-fitting lid. Meat labelled 'stewing' will take longer to cook than meat labelled 'braising'. Skim off the excess fat before serving.

Braise involves less liquid than stewing or casseroling, and slightly more tender cuts are used. The browned meat is set on a bed of vegetables with sufficient liquid to create steam, covered tightly and cooked very gently.

Boil Meat for boiling is usually salted and must be soaked overnight in several changes of cold water before cooking. Cover the meat with fresh cold water and bring to a simmer. Cover with a tightly fitting lid and simmer gently for 25 minutes per 450g (1lb) plus 30 minutes for large joints; 1½ hours minimum for small joints; do not boil. Add aromatics if you intend using the liquid as stock.

Fry, grill and barbecue These methods are suitable for tender cuts. The pan, grill or barbecue must be hot before cooking so that the meat is sealed and browned. If cooking thicker pieces, or pork or sausages, reduce the heat once the meat has browned, or move it further from the heat source if barbecuing, so that it cooks right through.

Stir-fry Cut the meat into small even-sized pieces across the grain; marinate first if you like. Heat a little vegetable oil in a preheated wok until very hot. Add the meat and toss and stir continuously as it cooks.

Cooking steaks to perfection can be difficult. The most reliable way is to cut the steak open and look at it. Timing depends on the thickness of the meat. As a rough guide, a 2cm (¾in) thick steak will take about 2½ minutes' grilling or frying on each side for rare; 3–4 minutes each side for medium; 6 minutes for well-done.

Roast Only good-quality, tender joints are suitable for roasting. Roasting at a constant high temperature of 230°C (210°C fan oven) mark 8, is only suitable for prime cuts, such as beef fillet. Bring the meat to room temperature. Put it, fat side up, on a roasting rack and smear with mustard or stud with slivers of garlic. Pork should be rubbed with oil and salt to make crackling. Except for pork with crackling,

baste roasts during cooking to keep them moist; if the joint is very lean, add dripping or oil.

Use a meat thermometer to check that the joint is cooked. Or insert a skewer into the thickest part, press the surface and watch the colour of the juices: slightly red for rare meat; pink for medium; clear for well done.

Roasting times for meat
Roast meat at 230°C (210°C fan oven) mark 8 for the first 20 minutes, then reduce the temperature to 180°C (160°C fan oven) mark 4 and cook for the times as shown below.

Carving meat
Use a large, sharp knife and a carving fork. Rest the joint, loosely covered with foil, for 5–15 minutes before carving. Loosen the meat from any exposed bones. Cut across the grain of the meat (usually at right angles to the bone). Lay boned and rolled joints on their side and carve through.

Leg of lamb Cut a narrow wedge of meat from the top (middle) of the joint, cutting down to the bone. Carve slices from either side of the cut, then turn over and repeat.

Shoulder of lamb Hold the shank end with the crisp skin uppermost. Cut a wedge-shaped slice through the middle of the joint. Carve slices from the cut as before.

Pork loin Ask the butcher to chine the bone (see page 501). When you carve, sever the chined bone from the ribs. Cut off the crackling. Cut down between the rib bones to divide the joint into chops, or cut along the length between the meat and rib bones and carve off slices.

Leg of pork For a shank end, remove some crackling. Cut thin slices down to the bone. Carve at an angle over the top of the shank bone. Turn and cut down towards the thin end of the bone at an angle. For a fillet end, carve slices through to the bone on either side of it.

Roasting times for meat

MEAT		COOKING TIME	INTERNAL TEMPERATURE
Beef	Rare	20 minutes per 450g (1lb), plus 20 minutes	60°C
	Medium	25 minutes per 450g (1lb), plus 25 minutes	70°C
	Well done	30 minutes per 450g (1lb), plus 30 minutes	80°C
Veal	Well done	25 minutes per 450g (1lb), plus 25 minutes	70°C
Lamb	Medium	25 minutes per 450g (1lb), plus 25 minutes	70–75°C
	Well done	30 minutes per 450g (1lb), plus 30 minutes	75–80°C
Pork	Well done	35 minutes per 450g (1lb), plus 35 minutes	80–85°C

Beef Cuts

1 Topside
A very lean cut with little fat, topside is usually sold with a layer of fat tied around it. Roast, braise or use sliced for beef roulades.

2 Fillet or tenderloin
A lean tender cut. Cook in a large piece or as steaks. Filet mignon, chateaubriand and tournedos are also cut from the fillet.

3 Rump steak
A lean, tender cut from the hind quarter. Suitable for grilling and frying.

4 Silverside
A lean, boneless joint from the hind quarter, traditionally salted and boiled.

5 Sirloin
Sold boned and rolled for roasting, or cut into sirloin steaks. Porterhouse, bone-in T-bone steaks and minute steaks are also cut from the sirloin.

6 Rib
Forerib (6a) is sold both as a roasting joint on the bone, and boned and rolled (thin 6b and thick 6c); sometimes called rib eye. Rib has more fat than topside, but its flavour is superb. Entrecôte (not pictured) is the meat between the ribs.

7 Skirt
Cut from the belly, this is a well-flavoured, fairly tough cut that is lean but with quite a coarse texture. Stew, braise or pot-roast.

8 Thick flank (top rump)
A lean cut from the top of the leg for pot roasting and braising. Thin flank Braise or stew. Slice thinly and stir-fry.

9 Chuck and blade steak
Chuck (9a) and blade (9b) are both lean shoulder meat, usually sold sliced or cubed for braising, stewing and pie fillings. Look for some marbling of fat throughout.

10 Brisket
A shoulder joint. It has a good flavour but is inclined to be fatty. Sold boned and rolled, it may also be salted. Brisket is best braised or pot roasted, but it can be roasted.

11 Neck and clod
Economical cuts, used for stewing or mince.

12 Shin and leg
Quite lean cuts with lots of connective tissue; stew or casserole.

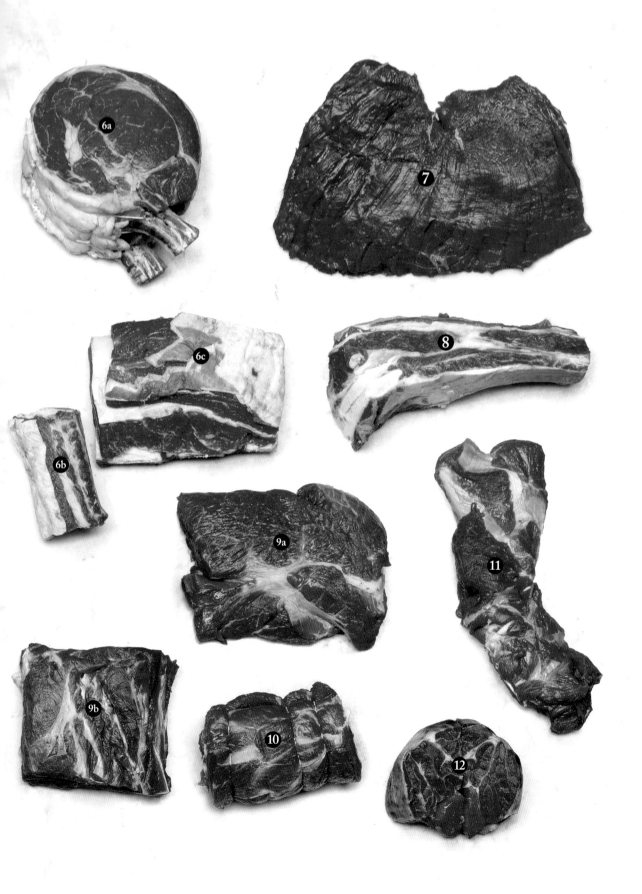

Classic Roast Beef with Yorkshire Puddings

Serves 8
Preparation time 20 minutes
Cooking time about 1½ hours, plus resting

1 boned and rolled rib, sirloin, rump or topside of beef, about
  1.8kg (4lb)
1 tbsp plain flour
1 tbsp mustard powder
salt and ground black pepper
fresh thyme sprigs to garnish
vegetables to serve

For the Yorkshire puddings
125g (4oz) plain flour
½ tsp salt
300ml (½ pint) milk
2 medium eggs

For the gravy
150ml (¼ pint) red wine
600ml (1 pint) beef stock

1 Preheat the oven to 230°C (210°C fan oven) mark 8. Put the beef in a roasting tin, thickest part of the fat uppermost. Mix the flour with the mustard powder and salt and pepper. Rub the mixture over the beef.
2 Roast the beef in the centre of the oven for 30 minutes.
3 Baste the beef and reduce the oven temperature to 190°C (170°C fan oven) mark 5. Cook for a further 1 hour, basting occasionally.
4 Meanwhile, prepare the Yorkshire pudding batter. Sift the flour and salt into a bowl. Mix in half the milk, then add the eggs and season with pepper. Beat until smooth, then whisk in the remaining milk.
5 Put the beef on a warmed carving dish, cover loosely with foil and leave to rest in a warm place. Increase the oven temperature to 220°C (200°C fan oven) mark 7.
6 Pour off about 3 tbsp fat from the roasting tin and use to grease 8–12 individual Yorkshire pudding tins. Heat in the oven for 5 minutes or until the fat is almost smoking. Pour the Yorkshire batter into the tins. Bake for 15–20 minutes until well risen, golden and crisp.

7 Meanwhile, make the gravy. Skim off any remaining fat from the roasting tin. Put the tin on the hob, add the wine and boil until syrupy. Pour in the stock and, again, boil until syrupy – there should be about 450ml (¾ pint) gravy. Taste and adjust the seasoning.
8 Carve the beef into slices. Garnish with thyme sprigs, and serve with the gravy, Yorkshire puddings and vegetables of your choice.

NUTRITION PER SERVING 510 cals | 24g fat (9g sats) | 16g carbs | 0.5g salt

Stuffed Topside of Beef

Serves 6
Preparation time 35 minutes, plus marinating
Cooking time 1–1¼ hours, plus resting

1.4kg (3lb) topside or top rump of beef
1 tbsp balsamic vinegar
2 tbsp white wine vinegar
3 tbsp olive oil
3 tbsp freshly chopped marjoram or thyme
2 red peppers, cored, seeded and quartered
75g (3oz) spinach, cooked and well drained
75g (3oz) pitted black olives, chopped
50g (2oz) smoked ham, chopped
75g (3oz) raisins or sultanas
salt and ground black pepper
roast potatoes and vegetables to serve

1 Make a deep cut along the beef to create a pocket
and put the joint into a dish. Combine the vinegars, oil,
marjoram or thyme and some black pepper. Pour over the
beef and into the pocket. Cover and marinate in a cool
place for 4–6 hours, or overnight.
2 Preheat the grill. Grill the peppers, skin side up, until
the skins are charred. Leave to cool in a covered bowl, then
remove the skins.
3 Squeeze the excess water from the spinach, then chop
and put into a bowl with the olives, ham and raisins or
sultanas. Mix well and season with salt and pepper.
4 Preheat the oven to 190°C (170°C fan oven) mark 5.
Line the pocket of the beef with the peppers, keeping
back two pepper quarters for the gravy. Spoon the spinach
mixture into the pocket and spread evenly. Reshape the
meat and tie at intervals with kitchen string. Put the beef
into a roasting tin just large enough to hold it and pour the
marinade over the top.
5 Roast for 1 hour for rare beef, or 1¼ hours for medium-
rare, basting from time to time. Put the beef on a board,
cover with foil and leave to rest in a warm place while you
make the gravy.
6 Skim off the excess fat from the roasting tin. Put the tin
on the hob and bring the pan juices to the boil. Add 125ml
(4fl oz) water and bubble for 2–3 minutes, stirring. Finely
chop the remaining pepper pieces and add to the gravy.
7 Carve the beef and serve with the gravy, roast potatoes
and vegetables of your choice.

NUTRITION PER SERVING 535 cals | 29g fat (10g sats) | 13g carbs | 1.4g salt

Fillet of Beef en Croûte

Serves 6

Preparation time 1 hour, plus soaking and
  chilling

Cooking time about 1 hour 20 minutes,
  plus resting

1–1.4kg (2¼–3lb) fillet of beef,
  trimmed
50g (2oz) butter
2 shallots, chopped
15g (½oz) dried porcini mushrooms,
  soaked in 100ml (3½fl oz) boiling
  water
2 garlic cloves, chopped
225g (8oz) flat mushrooms, finely
  chopped
2 tsp freshly chopped thyme, plus extra
  sprigs to garnish
175g (6oz) chicken liver pâté
175g (6oz) thinly sliced Parma ham
  (see Cook's Tip, page 76)
375g ready-rolled puff pastry
plain flour to dust
1 medium egg, beaten
salt and ground black pepper
Rich Red Wine Sauce (see Cook's Tip)
  to serve

1 Season the beef with salt and pepper. Melt 25g (1oz) butter in a large frying
pan and, when foaming, add the beef and cook for 4–5 minutes to brown all
over. Transfer to a plate and leave to cool.
2 Melt the remaining butter in a pan, add the shallots and cook for 1 minute.
Drain the porcini mushrooms, saving the liquid, and chop them. Add them to
the pan with the garlic and the fresh mushrooms, then strain in the reserved
liquid. Increase the heat and cook until the liquid has evaporated, then season
with salt and pepper and add the chopped thyme. Leave to cool.
3 Put the pâté into a bowl and beat until smooth. Add the mushroom mixture
and stir well until thoroughly combined. Season to taste with salt and pepper.
4 Lay half the Parma ham on a length of clingfilm, overlapping the slices.
Spread half the mushroom mixture evenly over one side of the beef. Invert
the mushroom-topped beef on to the ham. Spread the remaining mushroom
mixture on the other side of the beef, then lay the remaining Parma ham, also
overlapping, on top of the mushroom mixture. Wrap the beef in the clingfilm to
form a firm sausage shape and chill for 30 minutes.
5 Preheat the oven to 220°C (200°C fan oven) mark 7.
6 Cut off one-third of the pastry and roll out on a lightly floured surface to
3mm (⅛in) thick and 2.5cm (1in) larger all around than the beef. Prick all over
with a fork. Transfer to a baking sheet and bake for 12–15 minutes until brown
and crisp. Cool on a wire rack, then trim to the size of the beef and place on a
baking sheet. Remove the clingfilm from the beef, brush with the egg and place
on the cooked pastry.
7 Roll out the remaining pastry to a 25 × 30cm (10 × 12in) rectangle. Roll a
lattice pastry cutter over it and gently ease the lattice open. Cover the beef with
the lattice, tuck the ends under and seal the edges. Brush with the beaten egg,
then cook for 40 minutes for rare to medium-rare, 45 minutes for medium.
Leave to rest for 10 minutes before carving. Garnish with thyme and serve with
Red Wine Sauce.

Cook's Tip
RICH RED WINE SAUCE Soften 350g (12oz) finely chopped shallots in 2 tbsp olive
oil for 5 minutes. Add 3 chopped garlic cloves and 3 tbsp tomato purée and cook
for 1 minute, then add 2 tbsp balsamic vinegar. Simmer briskly until reduced
to almost nothing, then add 200ml (7fl oz) red wine and boil to reduce by half.
Pour in 600ml (1 pint) beef stock and simmer until reduced by one-third.

NUTRITION PER SERVING 802 cals | 53g fat (15g sats) | 27g carbs | 2.4g salt

Roast Rib

Serves 8
Preparation time 5 minutes
Cooking time 2½ hours, plus resting

2-bone rib of beef, about 2.5–2.7kg (5½–6lb)
1 tbsp plain flour
1 tbsp mustard powder
150ml (¼ pint) red wine
600ml (1 pint) beef stock
600ml (1 pint) water from parboiled potatoes
salt and ground black pepper
fresh thyme sprigs to garnish
Yorkshire Puddings (see page 176), roasted root vegetables
  and a green vegetable to serve

1 Preheat the oven to 230°C (210°C fan oven) mark 8.
Put the beef, fat side up, in a roasting tin just large enough
to hold the joint. Mix together the flour and mustard in a
small bowl and season with salt and pepper, then rub the
mixture over the beef. Roast in the centre of the oven for
30 minutes.
2 Move the beef to a lower shelf, near the bottom of the
oven. Turn the oven down to 220°C (200°C fan oven)
mark 7 and continue to roast the beef for a further 2 hours,
basting occasionally.
3 Put the beef on a carving dish, cover loosely with foil and
leave to rest while you make the gravy. Skim off most of the
fat from the roasting tin. Put the roasting tin on the hob,
pour in the wine and boil vigorously until very syrupy. Pour
in the stock and, again, boil until syrupy. Add the vegetable
water and boil until syrupy. There should be about 450ml
(¾ pint) gravy. Taste and adjust the seasoning.
4 Remove the rib bone and carve the beef. Garnish with
thyme. Serve with gravy, Yorkshire puddings, roasted root
vegetables and a green vegetable.

NUTRITION PER SERVING 807 cals | 53g fat (24g sats) | 2g carbs | 0.5g salt

Steak au Poivre

Serves 4
Preparation time 10 minutes
Cooking time 4–12 minutes

2 tbsp black or green peppercorns
4 rump or sirloin steaks, 200g (7oz) each
25g (1oz) butter
1 tbsp oil
2 tbsp brandy
150ml (¼ pint) double cream or crème fraîche
salt
herbed roast potatoes and green beans to serve

1 Crush the peppercorns coarsely using a pestle and
mortar or a rolling pin. Scatter the peppercorns on a board,
lay the steaks on top and press hard to encrust the surface
of the meat; repeat with the other side.
2 Heat the butter and oil in a frying pan and quickly sear
the steaks over a high heat. Lower the heat to medium and
cook for a further 3–12 minutes, according to taste, turning
every 2 minutes (see Cook's Tip). Season with salt.
3 Remove the steaks from the pan; keep warm. Add the
brandy to the pan, take off the heat and set alight. When
the flame dies, stir in the cream or crème fraîche, season
and reheat gently. Pour the sauce over the steaks to serve.

TRY SOMETHING DIFFERENT
Steak Diane Trim 4 pieces fillet steak, 5mm (¼in) thick,
of excess fat. Fry the steaks in 25g (1oz) butter and 2 tbsp
vegetable oil for 1–2 minutes on each side. Remove with
a slotted spoon and keep warm. Stir 2 tbsp Worcestershire
sauce and 1 tbsp lemon juice into the pan juices. Warm
through, then add 1 small onion, skinned and grated and
2 tsp freshly chopped parsley, and cook gently for 1 minute.
Serve the sauce spooned over the steaks.

Cook's Tip
Allow 4 minutes (one turn) for rare steaks; 8 minutes
(three turns) for medium. For well-done, 12 minutes,
increasing the time between turns to 3 minutes.

NUTRITION PER SERVING 480 cals | 35g fat (19g sats) | 1g carbs | 1g salt

Sesame Beef

Serves 4
Preparation time 20 minutes
Cooking time 10 minutes

2 tbsp soy sauce
2 tbsp Worcestershire sauce
2 tsp tomato purée
juice of ½ lemon
1 tbsp sesame seeds
1 garlic clove, crushed
400g (14oz) rump steak, sliced
1 tbsp vegetable oil
3 small pak choi, chopped
1 bunch of spring onions, thickly sliced
egg noodles or tagliatelle to serve

1 Put the soy and Worcestershire sauces, tomato purée,
lemon juice, sesame seeds and garlic into a non-metallic
bowl and mix well. Add the steak and toss to coat.
2 Heat the oil in a large wok or non-stick frying pan over
a high heat until hot. Add the steak and sear well. Remove
from the wok and put to one side.
3 Add any sauce from the bowl to the wok and heat for
1 minute. Add the pak choi, spring onions and steak and
stir-fry for 5 minutes. Add freshly cooked and drained
noodles or tagliatelle, toss and serve immediately.

TRY SOMETHING DIFFERENT
Use 400g (14oz) pork escalope cut into strips instead of beef.
Cook for 5 minutes before removing from the pan at step 2.

NUTRITION PER SERVING 207 cals | 10g fat (3g sats) | 4g carbs | 2g salt

Beef Stroganoff

Serves 4
Preparation time 10 minutes
Cooking time about 20 minutes

700g (1½lb) rump or fillet steak, trimmed
50g (2oz) unsalted butter or 4 tbsp olive oil
1 onion, thinly sliced
225g (8oz) brown-cap mushrooms, sliced
3 tbsp brandy
1 tsp French mustard
200ml (7fl oz) crème fraîche
100ml (3½fl oz) double cream
3 tbsp freshly chopped flat-leafed parsley
salt and ground black pepper
rice or noodles to serve

1 Cut the steak into strips about 5mm (¼in) wide and 5cm (2in) long.
2 Heat half the butter or oil in a large heavy-based frying pan over a medium heat. Add the onion and cook gently for 10 minutes or until soft and golden. Remove with a slotted spoon and put to one side. Add the mushrooms to the pan and cook, stirring, for 2–3 minutes until golden brown; remove and put to one side.
3 Increase the heat and add the remaining butter or oil to the pan. Quickly fry the meat, in two or three batches, for 2–3 minutes, stirring constantly to ensure even browning. Remove from the pan. Add the brandy to the pan and allow it to bubble to reduce until syrupy.
4 Put all the meat, onion and mushrooms back into the pan. Reduce the heat and stir in the mustard, crème fraîche and cream. Heat through, but do not allow the liquid to boil. Stir in most of the parsley and season with salt and pepper to taste. Serve with rice or noodles, with the remaining parsley scattered over the top.

Freezing Tip
• To freeze, complete the recipe, transfer to a freezerproof container, cool, label and freeze for up to three months.
• To use, thaw overnight in the fridge. Put in a pan, cover and bring to the boil; reduce the heat to low and simmer until piping hot.

NUTRITION PER SERVING 750 cals | 60g fat (35g sats) | 3g carbs | 0.5g salt

Smoky Pimento Goulash

Serves 8
Preparation time 20 minutes
Cooking time about 3 hours

1.1kg (2½lb) braising steak
3 tbsp olive oil
16 shallots or button onions
225g (8oz) piece chorizo sausage, roughly chopped
1 red chilli, seeded and finely chopped (see Cook's Tips, page 69)
3 bay leaves
3 garlic cloves, crushed
2 tbsp plain flour
2 tbsp smoked paprika
700g jar tomato passata
100ml (3½fl oz) hot beef stock
salt and ground black pepper
mashed potatoes and green vegetables to serve

For the minted soured cream
284ml carton soured cream
1 tbsp finely chopped fresh mint
1 tbsp extra virgin olive oil, plus extra to drizzle

1 Mix together all the ingredients for the minted soured cream and season with a little salt and plenty of coarsely ground black pepper. Cover and chill until needed.
2 Preheat the oven to 170°C (150°C fan oven) mark 3. Cut the braising steak into large cubes, slightly larger than bite-size.
3 Heat the olive oil in a 4 litre (7 pint) flameproof casserole until really hot. Brown the beef, a few cubes at a time, over a high heat until it is deep brown all over. Remove with a slotted spoon and set aside. Repeat with the remaining beef until all the pieces have been browned.
4 Reduce the heat under the casserole, then add the onions, chorizo, chilli, bay leaves and garlic. Fry for 7–10 minutes until the onions are golden brown and beginning to soften. Return the meat to the casserole and stir in the flour and paprika. Cook, stirring, for 1–2 minutes, then add the passata. Season, cover and cook in the oven for 2½ hours or until the beef is meltingly tender. Check halfway through cooking – if the beef looks dry, add the hot beef stock. Serve with the minted soured cream, drizzled with a little olive oil and a grinding of black pepper, and some creamy mashed potatoes and green vegetables.

GET AHEAD
• To prepare ahead, complete the recipe. Cool and chill (it will keep for up to three days) or freeze (it will keep for up to one month).
• To use, if frozen, thaw overnight at a cool room temperature. Return the goulash to the casserole, bring to the boil and simmer gently for 15–20 minutes until piping hot, adding 100ml (3½fl oz) hot beef stock if it looks dry.

NUTRITION PER SERVING 515 cals | 35g fat (14g sats) | 13g carbs | 1.3g salt

Cottage Pie

Serves 4
Preparation time 15 minutes
Cooking time about 1 hour

1 tbsp olive oil
1 onion, finely chopped
2 garlic cloves, crushed
450g (1lb) minced beef
1 tbsp plain flour
450ml (¾ pint) beef stock
2 tbsp Worcestershire sauce
1 medium carrot, peeled and diced
125g (4oz) button mushrooms, sliced
1kg (2¼lb) potatoes, roughly chopped
25g (1oz) butter
75ml (3fl oz) milk
salt and ground black pepper

1 Heat the oil in a large pan, add the onion and fry over a medium heat for 15 minutes or until softened and golden, stirring occasionally. Add the garlic and cook for 1 minute.
2 Preheat the oven to 200°C (180°C fan oven) mark 6. Add the minced beef to the onion and garlic and, as it browns, use a wooden spoon to break up the pieces. Once it has browned, stir in the flour. Stir in the stock to the browned mince, cover the pan and bring to the boil. Add the Worcestershire sauce, carrot and mushrooms and season well with salt and pepper. Reduce the heat, cover and cook for 15 minutes.
3 Meanwhile, put the potatoes into a large pan of salted water. Bring to the boil and cook for about 20–25 minutes until very soft. Drain and put back into the pan for 1 minute over a low heat to dry off. Mash until smooth, and then beat in the butter and milk. Season with salt and pepper to taste.
4 Spoon the sauce into a 1.7 litre (3 pint) ovenproof dish, cover with the mashed potato and rough the top with a fork. Cook in the oven for 20–25 minutes or until the filling is piping hot and the topping is golden brown.

TRY SOMETHING DIFFERENT
To make individual pies, use four 450ml (¾ pint) shallow ovenproof dishes.

NUTRITION PER SERVING 581 cals | 28g fat (12g sats) | 55g carbs | 1.8g salt

Beef Bourguignon

Serves 6
Preparation time 30 minutes
Cooking time 3 hours

1kg (2¼lb) topside, rump or lean
  braising steak
50g (2oz) butter
2 tbsp oil
125g (4oz) bacon lardons
1 garlic clove, crushed
3 tbsp plain flour
bouquet garni (1 bay leaf, a few fresh
  parsley and thyme sprigs)
150ml (¼ pint) beef stock
300ml (½ pint) Burgundy or other
  full-bodied red wine
12 baby onions, peeled
175g (6oz) button mushrooms
salt and ground black pepper
freshly chopped parsley to garnish

1 Cut the meat into 3cm (1¼in) cubes.
2 Melt half the butter with 1 tbsp oil in a large flameproof casserole. Add the bacon and brown quickly over a high heat, then remove with a slotted spoon.
3 Reheat the fat in the casserole and brown the meat in batches. Return the bacon to the casserole and add the garlic. Sprinkle in the flour and stir well.
4 Add salt and pepper, the bouquet garni, stock and wine. Bring to the boil, stirring, then cover and cook in the oven at 170°C (150°C fan oven) mark 3 for about 2½ hours.
5 Meanwhile, heat the remaining butter and oil in a frying pan and fry the onions until glazed and golden brown. Remove with a slotted spoon and keep to one side. Sauté the mushrooms in the pan over a medium heat for 2–3 minutes until slightly softened.
6 Add the sautéed mushrooms and onions to the casserole and cook for a further 30 minutes. Discard the bouquet garni, check the seasoning and serve sprinkled with chopped parsley.

Meat Loaf

Serves 4
Preparation time 10 minutes
Cooking time 1 hour 40 minutes

25g (1oz) butter, plus extra to grease
1 onion, finely chopped
1 tsp paprika
450g (1lb) minced beef
50g (2oz) fresh breadcrumbs
3 tbsp natural wheatgerm
1 garlic clove, crushed
1 tbsp freshly chopped herbs or 1 tsp dried mixed herbs, plus
  fresh herbs to garnish
4 tbsp tomato purée
1 medium egg, beaten
salt and ground black pepper
Fresh Tomato Sauce to serve (see page 20)

1 Preheat the oven to 180°C (160°C fan oven) mark 4.
Grease and base line a 450g (1lb), capacity 900ml
(1½ pint), loaf tin.
2 Melt the butter in a frying pan, add the onion and cook
until softened. Add the paprika and cook for 1 minute,
stirring, then turn the mixture into a large bowl.
3 Add all the remaining ingredients and stir thoroughly
until evenly mixed. Spoon the mixture into the loaf tin,
level the surface and cover tightly with foil.
4 Stand the loaf tin in a roasting tin and pour in water to a
depth of 2.5cm (1in). Cook in the oven for 1½ hours. Turn
out, garnish with herb sprigs and serve with the sauce.

NUTRITION PER SERVING 406 cals | 26g fat (12g sats) | 17g carbs | 1.4g salt

Chilli con Carne

Serves 4
Preparation time 5 minutes
Cooking time about 1 hour

2 tbsp olive oil
450g (1lb) minced beef
1 large onion, finely chopped
1 tsp hot chilli powder
1 tsp ground cumin
3 tbsp tomato purée
300ml (½ pint) hot vegetable stock
400g can chopped tomatoes with garlic (see Cook's Tips)
25g (1oz) plain chocolate (at least 70% cocoa solids) (see
  Cook's Tips)
400g can red kidney beans, drained and rinsed
40g (1½oz) fresh coriander, chopped
salt and ground black pepper
guacamole, salsa, soured cream, grated cheese, tortilla chips
  and pickled chillies to serve

1 Heat 1 tbsp oil in a large non-stick pan and fry the beef
for 10 minutes or until well browned, stirring to break up
any lumps. Remove from the pan with a slotted spoon and
leave to one side.
2 Add the remaining oil to the pan, then fry the onion,
stirring, for 10 minutes or until soft and golden.
3 Add the spices and fry for 1 minute, then return the beef
to the pan. Add the tomato purée, hot stock and tomatoes.
Bring to the boil, then reduce to a simmer. Continue to
bubble gently, uncovered, for 35–40 minutes or until the
sauce is well reduced and the mixture is quite thick.
4 Stir in the chocolate, kidney beans and coriander, season
with salt and pepper, then simmer for 5 minutes.
5 Serve with guacamole, salsa, soured cream, grated cheese,
tortilla chips and pickled chillies.

Cook's Tips
• Instead of a can of tomatoes with garlic, use a can of
  chopped tomatoes and 1 crushed garlic clove.
• Adding a little plain chocolate to chilli con carne brings
  out the flavours of this tasty dish.

NUTRITION PER SERVING 408 cals | 19g fat (7g sats) | 28g carbs | 1.1g salt

Hamburgers

Serves 6
Preparation time 20 minutes, plus chilling
Cooking time 10 minutes

1kg (2¼lb) extra-lean minced beef
2 tsp salt
2 tbsp steak seasoning
sunflower oil to brush
6 large soft rolls, halved
6 thin-cut slices havarti or raclette cheese
4 small cocktail gherkins, sliced lengthways
6 tbsp Mustard Mayonnaise (see page 29)
6 lettuce leaves, such as frisée
4 large vine-ripened tomatoes, thickly sliced
2 large shallots, sliced into thin rings
ground black pepper

1 Put the minced beef into a large bowl and add the salt, steak seasoning and plenty of pepper. Use your hands to mix the ingredients together thoroughly. Lightly oil the inside of six 10cm (4in) rosti rings and put on a foil-lined baking sheet. Press the meat firmly into the rings, or use your hands to shape the mixture into six even-sized patties. Cover with clingfilm and chill for at least 1 hour.
2 Heat a large griddle pan until it is really hot. Put the rolls, cut sides down, on the griddle and toast.
3 Lightly oil the griddle, ease the burgers out of the moulds and brush with oil. Griddle over a medium heat for about 3 minutes, then carefully turn the burgers over. Put a slice of cheese and a few slices of gherkin on top of each one and cook for a further 3 minutes.
4 While the burgers are cooking, spread the Mustard Mayonnaise on the toasted side of the rolls. Add the lettuce, tomatoes and shallots. Put the burgers on top and sandwich with the other half-rolls.

TRY SOMETHING DIFFERENT
For a more sophisticated burger, replace the cheese and gherkins with thick slices of ripe avocado and use a generous handful of fresh rocket instead of the lettuce.

NUTRITION PER SERVING 645 cals | 45g fat (17g sats) | 19g carbs | 2.3g salt

Lentil and Beef Burgers

Serves 4
Preparation time 15 minutes
Cooking time 15 minutes

175g (6oz) canned lentils
40g (1½oz) brown bread
1 small onion, roughly chopped
a large handful of fresh parsley
200g (7oz) extra-lean beef mince (5% fat)
1 tbsp dried mixed herbs
1 medium egg
½–1 tbsp wholegrain mustard to taste
1 tbsp olive oil
4 slices brown bread
salt and ground black pepper
lettuce, tomato slices and watercress, to serve

1 Drain the lentils, rinse well under cold water, then leave
to drain again.
2 Put the bread into a food processor and whiz to make
crumbs. Empty into a large bowl. Put the onion and
parsley in the processor and whiz until finely chopped. Add
the lentils, beef, dried herbs and plenty of seasoning and
whiz again until well combined, but still retaining texture.
3 Scrape the beef mixture into the bowl of breadcrumbs
and mix in the egg and mustard (with hands is easiest).
Shape into four equal patties.
4 Heat the oil in a large non-stick frying pan and fry the
burgers for 15 minutes, turning midway, or until golden on
both sides and cooked through.
5 When the burgers are nearly ready, toast the bread.
Divide the toast among four plates, top with lettuce and
tomato, add the burgers and watercress and serve.

NUTRITION PER SERVING 289 cals | 11g fat (3g sats) | 25g carbs | 0.7g salt

Veal Schnitzel with Salsa Verde

Serves 4
Preparation time 30 minutes
Cooking time 15 minutes

4 veal escalopes, about 100g (3½oz) each
175g (6oz) dried breadcrumbs
125g (4oz) ground almonds
plain flour to coat
1 medium egg, beaten
6 tbsp sunflower oil
salt and ground black pepper
Salsa Verde (see page 23) and lemon wedges to serve

1 Lay the veal escalopes between two pieces of greaseproof paper and beat with a rolling pin to flatten. If too large for the frying pan, cut in half.
2 Mix together the dried breadcrumbs and ground almonds on a plate. Season the veal, then coat lightly with flour. Dip each piece in beaten egg, then into the breadcrumb mixture to coat, patting to make sure it is evenly covered.
3 Heat 2 tbsp oil in a large heavy-based frying pan, add one-third of the veal and fry for 1–2 minutes on each side until deep golden brown. Transfer to a heatproof plate and keep warm in a low oven. Wipe out the frying pan with kitchen paper and cook the remaining veal in the same way, using fresh oil for each batch.
4 Serve the schnitzel as soon as it is all cooked, with the Salsa Verde and lemon wedges.

NUTRITION PER SERVING (without salsa verde) 650 cals | 41g fat (22g sats) | 39g carbs | 1.4g salt

Saltimbocca alla Romana

Serves 8
Preparation time 10 minutes
Cooking time about 10 minutes

8 veal escalopes, about 125g (4oz) each
1–2 tbsp lemon juice
8 thin slices Parma ham (see Cook's
  Tip, page 76)
8 fresh sage leaves
50g (2oz) butter
1 tbsp oil
2 tbsp Marsala
ground black pepper
fried sage leaves to garnish
bread to serve

1 Put the veal escalopes between two sheets of greaseproof paper and pound with a rolling pin to flatten. Sprinkle with lemon juice and pepper.
2 Wrap each escalope in a slice of Parma ham. Place a sage leaf on top of the ham and secure with a wooden cocktail stick.
3 Heat the butter and oil in a frying pan, then add the veal and fry gently until golden brown. Stir in the Marsala, bring to simmering point, then cover the pan and simmer gently for 8–10 minutes.
4 Serve the veal with the pan juices poured over, and garnished with fried sage leaves. Serve with bread.

NUTRITION PER SERVING 220 cals | 11g fat (5g sats) | trace carbs | 1.3g salt

Osso Buco

Serves 4
Preparation time 15 minutes
Cooking time 1 hour 50 minutes–2 hours
  20 minutes

50g (2oz) butter
1 tbsp olive oil
1 onion, finely chopped
4 large or 8 small ossi buchi (veal shin,
  hind cut), weighing about 1.7kg
  (3¾lb), sawn into 5cm (2in) lengths
3 tbsp seasoned flour
300ml (½ pint) dry white wine
300ml (½ pint) veal or chicken stock
finely grated zest of 1 lemon
1 garlic clove, finely chopped
3 tbsp freshly chopped parsley
Risotto Milanese (see page 263)
  to serve

1 Melt the butter with the oil in a flameproof casserole, add the onion and fry gently for 5 minutes or until soft but not coloured.
2 Coat the veal in the flour, add it to the casserole and fry for about 10 minutes or until browned.
3 Pour over the wine and boil rapidly for 5 minutes, then add the stock.
4 Cover the pan tightly and simmer for 1½–2 hours, basting and turning the meat occasionally.
5 Transfer the meat to a warmed serving dish, cover and keep warm. If necessary, boil the sauce rapidly to thicken, then pour it over the meat.
6 Sprinkle with the lemon zest, garlic and parsley, and serve with the risotto.

NUTRITION PER SERVING 559 cals | 26g fat (8g sats) | 22g carbs | 1.3g salt

Lamb Cuts

1 Loin

The loin comprises both chump and loin chops. Chump chops (1b) have a small round bone in the centre, and loin chops (1a) a small T-bone. Loin steaks are boneless loin chops. The whole loin can also be roasted.

2 Neck fillet

A lean cut from the middle neck; roast, fry or cook en croûte.

3 Scrag (3a) and middle neck (3b)

Cuts on the bone for stewing and braising.

4 Saddle or double loin

The whole loin. It is sometimes sold sliced into butterfly or Barnsley chops.

5 Leg

A lean cut, good for roasting. Traditionally sold with the bone in (5a), either whole or as a half leg – fillet end or knuckle/shank end. Boned and rolled leg is also available. Boned, it can also be 'butterflied' – flattened for grilling or barbecuing. Leg steaks (5b) are prime cuts for grilling and pan-frying.

6 Rack

Also known as best end of neck, this is a whole roasting joint of 6–8 chops or cutlets. Usually chined to make serving easier, the tips of the cutlet bones are then scraped of all fat and meat to look neat, known as 'French-trimmed'. This cut is used for 'crown roast' and 'guard of honour'.

7 Shoulder

Sold whole or as a half shoulder – knuckle or blade end – for roasting, or as chops or steaks for grilling or braising.

8 Cutlets

Boned and rolled cutlets are called noisettes; these neat lean portions are excellent grilled or pan-fried.

9 Breast

Sold ready boned and rolled, this is best cooked slowly and thoroughly. If braised, it must be well trimmed, as it is a fatty cut.

10 Shank

Taken from the lower part of the hind leg, the shank is usually cooked on the bone. Braise, casserole or pot-roast.

11 Mince

Look for mince with a low proportion of fat. Use in stuffings, sauces, burgers, meat loaf, kebabs, and so on.

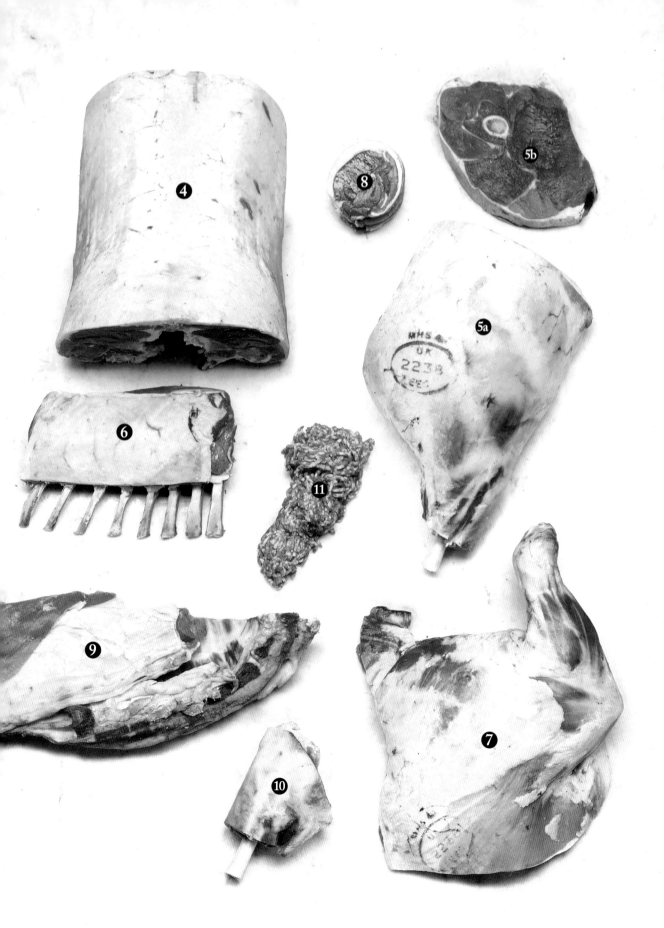

Roast Leg of Lamb with Rosemary

Serves 8
Preparation time 15 minutes
Cooking time 1½ hours, plus resting

2.5kg (5½lb) leg of lamb
4 rosemary sprigs
½ tbsp oil
4 garlic cloves, cut into slivers
4 anchovy fillets, roughly chopped
4 oregano sprigs
1 large onion, thickly sliced
1 lemon, cut into 6 wedges
salt and ground black pepper
seasonal vegetables and a side salad to serve (optional)

1 Take the lamb out of the fridge an hour before roasting. Pat the skin dry with kitchen paper.
2 Preheat the oven to 220°C (200°C fan oven) mark 7. Cut the rosemary into smaller sprigs. Rub the oil over the lamb. Cut small slits all over the meat and insert the garlic slivers, rosemary sprigs, anchovy pieces and the leaves from two oregano sprigs into the gaps. Season well.
3 Put the onion slices into the base of a roasting tin just large enough to hold the lamb. Top with the remaining oregano, then put in the meat, fat side up (the onions must be covered to prevent them burning). Tuck lemon wedges around the meat.
4 Put the lamb into the oven and reduce the oven temperature to 190°C (170°C fan oven) mark 5. Roast for 15 minutes per 450g (1lb) for pink meat, or longer if you like it more cooked.
5 Transfer the lamb to a board and cover with foil, reserving the roasting tin and its contents to make gravy (see page 11). Leave to rest for 30 minutes before carving (see page 173). Serve with vegetables and salad, if you like.

GET AHEAD
• Prepare the lamb to the end of step 3 up to 2 hours ahead.
• To use, complete the recipe.

Cook's Tip
Buy the best meat you can to ensure great flavour and texture. The lamb is served pink here, but allow an extra 20–30 minutes if you prefer your meat more cooked.

NUTRITION PER SERVING 601 cals | 39g fat (17g sats) | 1g carbs | 1.3g salt

Guard of Honour with Hazelnut and Herb Crust

Serves 6
Preparation time 30 minutes
Cooking time 25–35 minutes, plus resting

2 trimmed racks of lamb
ground black pepper
roasted root vegetables to serve

For the hazelnut and herb crust
75g (3oz) fresh breadcrumbs made from Italian bread, such
  as ciabatta
2 tbsp freshly chopped flat-leafed parsley
2 tbsp freshly chopped thyme
1 tbsp freshly chopped rosemary
2 garlic cloves, crushed
2 tbsp olive oil
50g (2oz) hazelnuts, toasted and roughly chopped
4 tbsp Dijon mustard
salt and ground black pepper

1 Preheat the oven to 200°C (180°C fan oven) mark 6.
Trim off and put aside as much of the fat from the lamb as
possible. Season the lamb well with pepper.
2 Heat the reserved fat in a large heavy-based frying pan,
add the lamb and sear on both sides. Remove the lamb
from the pan and leave to one side until cool enough to
handle. Put the racks together so that the ribs interlock.
Put the lamb in a roasting tin, rib bones uppermost, with
the lamb fat. Roast for 10 minutes.
3 Meanwhile, make the hazelnut and herb crust. Combine
the breadcrumbs, herbs, garlic, oil and seasoning for
30 seconds in a food processor, then add the hazelnuts
and pulse for a further 30 seconds.
4 Remove the lamb from the oven and spread the fatty
side with the mustard. Press the hazelnut crust firmly on to
the mustard.
5 Baste the lamb with the fat in the roasting tin and put
back in the oven for 15–20 minutes for rare, 20–25 minutes
for medium-rare and 25–30 minutes for well done. When
cooked, remove the lamb from the oven, cover with foil
and leave in a warm place for 10 minutes before carving.
Arrange the lamb on a serving dish and serve with roasted
root vegetables.

GET AHEAD
- Complete the recipe to the end of step 4. Cool quickly
  and chill for up to 24 hours.
- To use, bring the lamb to room temperature. Complete
  the recipe.

NUTRITION PER SERVING 488 cals | 39g fat (15g sats) | 11g carbs | 1.2g salt

Mustard Lamb Chops

Serves 4
Preparation time 10 minutes, plus marinating (optional)
Cooking time 15 minutes

3 tbsp redcurrant jelly
1 tbsp Dijon mustard
8 lamb loin chops, excess fat trimmed for the sauce
3 tbsp Mayonnaise (see page 29)
3 tbsp crème fraîche
1 tsp wholegrain mustard
salt and ground black pepper
boiled or roasted new potatoes and a green salad to serve

1 In a non-metallic bowl, mix together the redcurrant jelly, mustard, salt and pepper. Add the lamb chops and make sure they are well coated. If you have time, marinate the chops in the fridge for 1 hour.
2 Preheat the grill to medium. Arrange the chops on a non-stick baking tray and grill for 15 minutes, turning occasionally, or until the chops are golden and cooked to your liking (watch them carefully as the sugar in the jelly can make them burn a little faster than usual).
3 Carefully take the tray from under the grill and cover with foil. Leave to rest while you make the sauce.
4 In a small serving bowl, mix together the mayonnaise, crème fraîche and mustard. Serve the chops with the sauce, some boiled or roasted new potatoes and a green salad.

NUTRITION PER SERVING 521 cals | 32 fat (13g sats) | 8g carbs | 0.9g salt

Crisp Crumbed Lamb Cutlets

Serves 4
Preparation time 20 minutes
Cooking time 10 minutes

75g (3oz) breadcrumbs, made from one-day-old bread
40g (1½oz) Parma ham (see Cook's Tip, page 76), finely
  chopped
3 tbsp freshly grated Parmesan
8 lamb cutlets, well trimmed, or 2 French-trimmed racks of
  lamb, about 350g (12oz) each, divided into cutlets
2 medium eggs, beaten
3 tbsp oil
3 large garlic cloves, peeled but left whole
salt and ground black pepper
Tomato Relish (see page 484), new potatoes and a salad or
  green vegetable to serve

1 Mix together the breadcrumbs, Parma ham and
Parmesan, then spread them out on a large plate and leave
to one side.
2 Season the lamb with salt and pepper, and brush lightly
with beaten egg. Press the lamb into the breadcrumbs to
coat evenly but lightly.
3 Heat the oil in a large non-stick frying pan, add the
peeled garlic cloves and heat gently until golden brown,
then discard the garlic.
4 Fry the lamb in the garlic-infused oil over a low-medium
heat for 4–5 minutes on each side until deep golden brown
and crisp. Turn and fry the fat edge for 1–2 minutes.
5 Serve the cutlets with Tomato Relish, new potatoes and
a salad or green vegetable.

NUTRITION PER SERVING 639 cals | 51g fat (21g sats) | 15g carbs | 1.9g salt

Irish Stew

Serves 4
Preparation time 15 minutes
Cooking time 2 hours

700g (1½lb) middle neck lamb cutlets,
  fat trimmed
2 onions, thinly sliced
450g (1lb) potatoes, thinly sliced
1 tbsp freshly chopped parsley, plus
  extra to garnish
1 tbsp dried thyme
300ml (½ pint) lamb stock
salt and ground black pepper

1 Preheat the oven to 170°C (150°C
fan oven) mark 3. Layer the meat,
onions and potatoes in a deep
flameproof casserole, sprinkling some
herbs and seasoning between each
layer. Finish with a layer of potato,
overlapping the slices neatly.
2 Pour the stock over the potatoes,
then cover with greaseproof paper and
a lid. Cook for about 2 hours or until
the meat is tender.
3 Preheat the grill. Take the lid off
the casserole and remove the paper.
Put under the grill and brown the top
of the potatoes. Sprinkle with parsley
and serve immediately.

NUTRITION PER SERVING 419 cals |
20g fat (9g sats) | 24g carbs | 0.6g salt

Braised Lamb Shanks with Cannellini Beans

Serves 6
Preparation time 15 minutes
Cooking time 3 hours

3 tbsp olive oil
6 lamb shanks
1 large onion, chopped
3 carrots, sliced
3 celery sticks, sliced
2 garlic cloves, crushed
2 × 400g cans chopped tomatoes
125ml (4fl oz) balsamic vinegar
2 bay leaves
2 × 400g cans cannellini beans, drained
  and rinsed
salt and ground black pepper
steamed spinach to serve

1 Preheat the oven to 170°C (150°C
fan oven) mark 3. Heat the oil in a
flameproof casserole and brown the

lamb shanks. Remove and set aside.
2 Add the onion, carrots, celery
and garlic and cook gently until the
vegetables are soft and just coloured.
3 Return the lamb to the casserole,
add the tomatoes and vinegar, and stir
well. Season with salt and pepper and
add the bay leaves. Bring to a simmer,
then cover, reduce the heat and cook
on the hob for 5 minutes.
4 Transfer to the oven and cook for
1½–2 hours until the lamb shanks are
nearly tender.
5 Remove the casserole from the
oven and add the cannellini beans.
Cover and return to the oven for a
further 30 minutes. Serve the lamb
shanks with steamed spinach.

NUTRITION PER SERVING 382 cals |
18g fat (6g sats) | 29g carbs | 1.2g salt

Lancashire Hotpot

Serves 4
Preparation time 20 minutes
Cooking time 2½ hours

12 lamb cutlets
2 medium onions, sliced
2 large carrots, sliced
leaves from 2 sprigs of thyme
750ml (1¼ pints) hot lamb stock
450g (1lb) potatoes, sliced
25g (1oz) butter
salt and ground black pepper
Pickled Red Cabbage (see page 483)
  to serve

1 Heat the oven to 180°C (160°C fan oven) mark 4. Put a layer of cutlets into a large lidded casserole. Cover with a layer of onions and carrots and a sprinkling of thyme. Season well with salt and ground black pepper.

Repeat with the remaining lamb, onions, carrots and thyme.
2 Pour in enough hot stock to almost cover the meat. Top with an overlapping layer of potatoes. Season, cover and cook in the oven for 2 hours.
3 Increase the oven temperature to 230°C (210°C fan oven) mark 8. Remove the lid and dot the top of the casserole with knobs of butter. Continue cooking for 30 minutes, uncovered, until the potatoes are golden brown. Serve with Pickled Red Cabbage.

NUTRITION PER SERVING 653 cals | 48g fat (24g sats) | 29g carbs | 1.4g salt

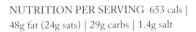

Lamb Noisettes with Tarragon Sauce

Serves 4
Preparation time 25 minutes
Cooking time 25 minutes

2 tbsp olive oil
8 lamb noisettes, about
  125g (4oz) each
175g (6oz) onion, finely chopped
1 tbsp tarragon vinegar
150ml (¼ pint) white wine
150ml (¼ pint) double cream
300ml (½ pint) lamb or chicken stock
1 tbsp freshly chopped tarragon, plus
  extra sprigs to garnish
salt and ground black pepper
vegetables to serve

1 Heat 1 tbsp oil in a frying pan and brown the lamb in batches for 2 minutes each side until the fat is crisp and golden.

2 Preheat the oven to 200°C (180°C fan oven) mark 6. Roast the lamb for 10 minutes for medium-rare; 15 minutes for well done.
3 Meanwhile, heat the remaining oil in the frying pan and fry the onion for 5–7 minutes until softened but not coloured. Add the tarragon vinegar and wine, bring to the boil and bubble for 2 minutes. Add the cream and stock; let it bubble for 10 minutes or until syrupy. Check the seasoning.
4 Remove the string from the lamb. Add the chopped tarragon and roasting juices to the sauce and warm through. Pour the sauce over the lamb, garnish with tarragon sprigs and serve with fresh vegetables.

NUTRITION PER SERVING 743 cals | 60g fat (29g sats) | 1g carbs | 1g salt

Lamb Moussaka

Serves 4
Preparation time 30 minutes
Cooking time 1 hour

2 aubergines, cut lengthways into 1cm (½in) wide strips
4 tbsp olive oil
1 onion, finely chopped
500g (1lb 2oz) lean lamb mince
½ tsp ground cinnamon
100ml (3½fl oz) white wine
2 × 400g cans chopped tomatoes
300ml (½ pint) chicken stock
a small handful of fresh parsley, chopped
200g (7oz) Greek yogurt
1 large egg, beaten
25g (1oz) Parmesan, grated
salt and ground black pepper
green salad to serve

1 Preheat the grill to medium. Arrange the aubergine slices on two large baking sheets and brush with half the oil. Sprinkle a little salt over the top and grill each tray separately for 12 minutes, turning the slices halfway through. Set aside.
2 Meanwhile, heat the remaining oil in a large frying pan and gently fry the onion for 8 minutes or until softened. Add the lamb mince and fry until golden, stirring to break up the mince. Stir in the cinnamon and wine and fry for a further 1 minute. Add the tomatoes and stock, bring the mixture to the boil, then reduce the heat and simmer for 15 minutes or until thick and pulpy. Stir in the parsley and season with salt and pepper to taste.
3 Preheat the oven to 220°C (200°C fan oven) mark 7. Stir together the yogurt, egg and cheese.
4 Spoon half the mince mixture into a 1.8 litre (3¼ pint) ovenproof dish and cover with half the aubergine slices. Spoon the remaining mince over the top, then finish with the remaining grilled aubergines. Pour the yogurt mixture over the top and spread evenly to cover.
5 Cook in the oven for 25–30 minutes until bubbling and golden. Serve with a green salad.

NUTRITION PER SERVING 549 cals | 35g fat (3g sats) | 15g carbs | 0.8g salt

Lamb, Prune and Almond Tagine

Serves 6
Preparation time 20 minutes, plus marinating
Cooking time 2½ hours

2 tsp coriander seeds
2 tsp cumin seeds
2 tsp chilli powder
1 tbsp paprika
1 tbsp ground turmeric
5 garlic cloves, chopped
6 tbsp olive oil
1.4kg (3lb) lamb leg steaks
75g (3oz) ghee or clarified butter (see Cook's Tip)
2 large onions, finely chopped
1 carrot, roughly chopped
900ml (1½ pints) lamb stock
300g (11oz) ready-to-eat prunes
4 cinnamon sticks
4 bay leaves
50g (2oz) ground almonds
12 shallots
1 tbsp honey
salt and ground black pepper
toasted blanched almonds and freshly chopped
  flat-leafed parsley to garnish
couscous to serve

1 Using a pestle and mortar or a blender, combine the coriander and cumin seeds, chilli powder, paprika, turmeric, garlic and 4 tbsp oil. Coat the lamb with the paste, then cover and chill for at least 5 hours.
2 Preheat the oven to 170°C (150°C fan oven) mark 3. Melt 25g (1oz) ghee or butter in a large flameproof casserole. Add the onions and carrot, and cook until soft. Remove and put to one side. Fry the paste-coated lamb on both sides in the remaining ghee or butter. Add a little of the stock and bring to the boil, scraping up the sediment from the base. Put the onions and carrot back in the casserole and add 100g (3½oz) prunes. Add the remaining stock with the cinnamon sticks, bay leaves and ground almonds. Season, cover and cook in the oven for 2 hours or until the meat is really tender.
3 Meanwhile, fry the shallots in the remaining oil and the honey until they turn a deep golden brown. Add to the casserole 30–40 minutes before the end of the cooking time.
4 Take the lamb out of the sauce and put to one side. Put the casserole over the heat and bring the sauce to the boil, then boil to reduce to a thick consistency. Put the lamb back in the casserole, add the remaining prunes and simmer for 3–4 minutes. Garnish with the almonds and parsley. Serve hot with couscous.

Cook's Tip
CLARIFIED BUTTER Heat butter in a pan without allowing it to colour. Skim off the foam; the solids will sink. Pour the clear butter into a bowl through a lined sieve. Leave for 10 minutes. Pour into a bowl, leaving any sediment behind. Cool. Store in a jar in the fridge for up to six months.

NUTRITION PER SERVING 652 cals | 44g fat (16g sats) | 31g carbs | 0.6g salt

Pork Cuts

1 Chump

A roasting cut from the hindquarters. Cook the joint whole to feed 2–4 people.

2 Chump chop

A cut from between the loin and leg. Grill, pan-fry, braise or use in a casserole.

3 Loin chop

This cut from the hind loin, gives tender, well-flavoured chops. Grill, pan-fry, braise or casserole; slice into strips and stir-fry.

4 Loin

Consists of the hind loin, for roasting, and the foreloin, which is the rib end. Roast, either on the bone or boned, stuffed and rolled. Loin steaks are boned loin chops.

5 Shoulder steak

These steaks are sweet and succulent. Remove the rind before cooking. Grill, pan-fry or braise; cut into strips and stir-fry.

6 Blade bone

A fatty joint, cut from the neck end of the shoulder and sold off the bone. Whole: roast, pot-roast or braise; cut into cubes, thread on to skewers and grill, or casserole.

7 Leg

Comprises fillet end (7a) and knuckle or shank end (7b); both good for roasting. The fillet end is sometimes cut into leg steaks. Roast, or split, stuff and roll. Grill, pan-fry or braise steaks or escalopes.

8 Tenderloin or pork fillet

A versatile, lean cut from the hind loin. Split, stuff and roast; pan-fry or grill medallions or escalopes; pan-fry or braise cubes; stir-fry strips.

9 Belly and spare ribs

Belly (9a) is long, thin cut streaked with fat. Roast whole or boned as a rolled joint. Grill or fry slices; add pieces to casseroles and stews; mince for sausages. Spare ribs (9a) are cut from the belly or the ribs. Spare rib chops can be casseroled or braised; trimmed American or Chinese spare ribs are typically cooked in a spicy barbecue sauce.

10 Hand and spring

Cut from the lower part of the forequarter; often divided into two: the hand (10a) and shank. Pot-roast, casserole or braise; cut into cubes and stew; roast. Knuckle (10b): bone, stuff, roll and roast; pot-roast, braise or casserole; cut into cubes and stew.

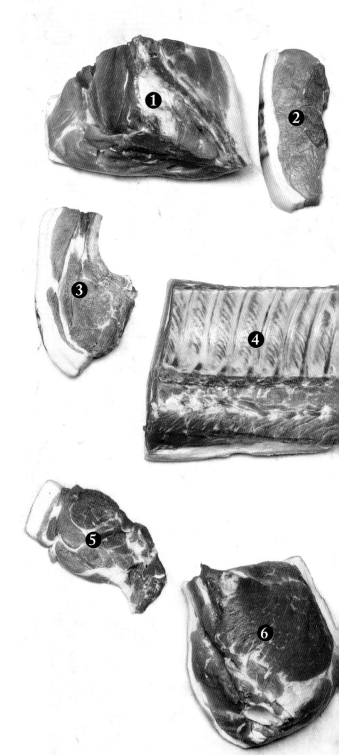

Crisp Roast Pork with Apple Sauce

Serves 6
Preparation time 30 minutes, plus standing
Cooking time 2 hours, plus resting

1.6kg (3½lb) boned rolled loin of pork
olive oil
1kg (2¼lb) cooking apples
1–2 tbsp granulated sugar
1 tbsp plain flour
600ml (1 pint) chicken stock or dry cider
salt and ground black pepper
roast potatoes and green vegetables to serve (optional)

1 Score the pork skin, sprinkle generously with salt and leave at room temperature for 1–2 hours.
2 Preheat the oven to 220°C (200°C fan oven) mark 7. Wipe the salt off the skin, rub with oil and sprinkle again with salt. Core and roughly chop the apples, then put half in a small roasting tin, sit the pork on top and roast for 30 minutes. Turn the oven down to 190°C (170°C fan oven) mark 5 and roast for a further 1½ hours or until cooked.
3 Meanwhile, put the remaining apples in a pan with the sugar and 2 tbsp water, cover with a tight-fitting lid and cook until just soft. Put this sauce into a small serving dish.
4 Remove the pork from the tin and leave to rest. Skim off most of the fat, leaving about 1 tbsp and the apples in the tin. Stir in the flour until smooth, stir in the stock and bring to the boil. Simmer gently for 2–3 minutes, skimming if necessary. Strain the sauce through a sieve into a jug, pushing through as much of the apple as possible.
5 Slice the pork and serve with the sauce, gravy, roast potatoes and green vegetables, if you like.

NUTRITION PER SERVING 769 cals | 50g fat (18g sats) | 22g carbs | 0.4g salt

Stuffed Pork Tenderloins

Serves 6
Preparation time 25 minutes, plus cooling
Cooking time 1 hour, plus resting

25g (1oz) butter
1 onion, finely chopped
1 tbsp freshly chopped thyme
grated zest of ½ orange
50g (2oz) fresh white breadcrumbs
2 pork fillets (tenderloins)
2 tbsp olive oil
200ml (7fl oz) hot chicken stock
50ml (2fl oz) red wine
salt and ground black pepper
herby mashed potato and carrots to serve

1 Melt the butter in a pan, add the onion and cook for
3–4 minutes until softened. Add the thyme and
orange zest, and cook for a further 1 minute. Add the
breadcrumbs, stir and season with salt and pepper. Allow
to cool.
2 Preheat the oven to 190°C (170°C fan oven) mark 5.
Trim any fat from the pork, then cut each fillet lengthways
down the middle, almost but not quite through. Season
well, then open out and spoon half the breadcrumb mixture
along each fillet. Bring the sides over the filling to enclose
and carefully tie with string at intervals to secure.
3 Heat the olive oil in a heavy-based roasting tin on the
hob, add the pork fillets and brown all over, then transfer
to the oven and roast for 40–45 minutes until the meat is
cooked through.
4 Lift the pork on to a warmed plate, cover with foil
and leave to rest. Add the hot stock and red wine to the
roasting tin and bring to the boil, scraping up the sediment
from the base. Season with salt and pepper to taste and
simmer for 5–6 minutes until syrupy. Slice the pork and
serve with the sauce, mashed potato and carrots.

NUTRITION PER SERVING 280 cals | 16g fat (3g sats) | 7g carbs | 0.3g salt

Perfect Roast Belly Pork

Serves 6
Preparation time 15 minutes, plus drying
Cooking time 3½ hours, plus resting

1.5kg (3¼lb) piece pork belly
salt

1 Using a small, sharp knife, score lines into the pork skin
(cutting into the fat) about 1cm (½in) apart, but not so
deep that you cut into the meat. Pat the pork completely
dry, then leave uncovered at room temperature to air dry
for about 45 minutes.
2 Preheat the oven to 220°C (200°C fan oven) mark
7. Rub lots of salt over the pork skin. Rest a wire rack
above a deep roasting tin and put the pork, skin side up,
on the rack. Roast for 30 minutes, then reduce the oven
temperature to 170°C (150°C fan oven) mark 3 and
continue cooking for 3 hours. By this stage, the crackling
should be crisp and golden.
3 Transfer the pork to a board and use a sharp knife
to slice off the crackling in one piece (about the outer
2cm/¾in). Cover the pork meat loosely with foil and leave
to rest for 30–40 minutes.
4 Cut the crackling into six long strips, then cut the pork
belly into six neat squares. Serve each square topped with a
strip of crackling.

Italian Pork Chops

Serves 4
Preparation time 15 minutes
Cooking time 20 minutes

25g (1oz) pinenuts
1tbsp extra virgin olive oil, plus extra
  to garnish
4 x 200g (7oz) pork chops, excess
  fat trimmed
200g (7oz) cherry tomatoes on
  the vine, snipped into bunches
100g (3½oz) rocket
25g (1oz) Parmesan shavings
2 tbsp balsamic vinegar, plus extra
  to drizzle
a large handful of fresh basil,
  roughly chopped
salt and ground black pepper

1 Heat a large frying pan over medium heat and toast the pinenuts, stirring frequently, until golden brown (watch them carefully, as they catch easily). Tip on to a plate and set aside.
2 Heat the oil in the empty pan and fry the pork until golden and cooked through, about 15 minutes, turning occasionally. Add the tomato bunches to the pan for the final 5 minutes of cooking time.
3 Meanwhile, in a large serving bowl, toss together the rocket, Parmesan shavings, balsamic vinegar and some seasoning.
4 Divide the chops and tomatoes among four plates. Scatter the basil and pinenuts over them and drizzle with extra balsamic, if you like. Serve with the salad.

NUTRITION PER SERVING 483 cals | 22g fat (6g sats) | 4g carbs | 0.5g salt

Barbecued Spare Ribs

Serves 4
Preparation time 10 minutes
Cooking time 1¾–2 hours

2 tbsp vegetable oil
2 onions, chopped
1 garlic clove, crushed
2 tbsp tomato purée
4 tbsp malt vinegar
¼ tsp dried thyme
¼ tsp chilli seasoning
3 tbsp honey
150ml (¼ pint) beef stock
1kg (2¼lb) spare ribs (American cut)
coleslaw, orange wedges and deep-
  fried red onion rings to serve

1 Preheat the oven to 190°C (170°C fan oven) mark 5. Heat the oil in a pan, add the onions and cook for 5 minutes or until softened. Add all the remaining ingredients, except the spare ribs, and simmer gently for 10 minutes.
2 Put the spare ribs in a roasting tin in a single layer and brush with a little of the sauce.
3 Roast in the oven for 30 minutes, then pour off the fat and spoon the remaining sauce over the meat. Cook for a further 1–1¼ hours, basting occasionally. Serve with coleslaw, orange wedges and deep-fried red onion rings.

NUTRITION PER SERVING 615 cals | 39g fat (14g sats) | 19g carbs | 1g salt

Cassoulet

Serves 12
Preparation time 30 minutes
Cooking time 2½–3½ hours

225g (8oz) salt pork or bacon, in one piece
2 tbsp vegetable oil or fat from preserved goose
2 onions, thinly sliced
3 garlic cloves, finely chopped
450g (1lb) loin or shoulder of pork, boned, rinded and cubed
1.4kg (3lb) shoulder of lamb (or ½ large shoulder),
  boned and cubed
1 piece preserved goose
450g (1lb) piece coarse pork and garlic sausage,
  cut into large cubes
4 tbsp tomato purée
750g (1lb 10oz) dried haricot beans, soaked overnight
bouquet garni (1 bay leaf, a few fresh parsley and
  thyme sprigs)
125g (4oz) fresh breadcrumbs
salt and ground black pepper
parsley sprig to garnish

1 Preheat the oven to 150°C (130°C fan oven) mark 2.
Remove the rind from the salt pork or bacon and set aside.
2 Heat the oil or goose fat in a large frying pan and fry the
onions and garlic for 5 minutes or until softened. Add the
pieces of pork rind and fry gently for 5 minutes. Using a
slotted spoon, remove the onion and rind, and set aside.
3 Turn up the heat and add, in turn, the pork and salt pork,
the shoulder of lamb, the piece of goose and the sausage,
and fry until browned on all sides. Remove each from the
pan and leave to one side.
4 Add the tomato purée to the pan with 300ml (½ pint)
cold water, stir well to amalgamate any sediment and bring
quickly to the boil.
5 Drain the beans, rinse them under cold running water
and put them into a flameproof casserole with 1.4 litres
(2½ pints) cold water. Bring to the boil, then add the
contents of the frying pan with salt and pepper to taste and
stir well. Bury the salt pork or bacon, the pork, shoulder of
lamb, preserved goose and sausage among the beans, add
the bouquet garni and bring to simmering point.

6 Sprinkle over a thick layer of breadcrumbs (about one-
third of the crumbs). Cook in the oven for 2–3 hours until
the meat and beans are tender.
7 From time to time, press down the crust that will have
formed on top and sprinkle on two further layers of
breadcrumbs. Cut up larger pieces of meat before serving.
Garnish with a parsley sprig.

NUTRITION PER SERVING 811 cals | 49g fat (19g sats) | 45g carbs | 2.5g salt

Sweet and Spicy Pork with Pineapple

Serves 4
Preparation time 5 minutes
Cooking time 35 minutes

425g can pineapple pieces in natural
 juice
4 pork shoulder steaks
2 garlic cloves, crushed
1 tbsp mild curry paste
2 tbsp lemon juice
2 tbsp mango chutney
freshly chopped parsley to garnish
boiled rice to serve

1 Preheat the oven to 200°C (180°C
fan oven) mark 6. Drain and roughly
chop the pineapple pieces, putting the
juice to one side.
2 Heat a non-stick frying pan and
dry-fry the pork steaks over a high
heat for 2 minutes each side until
golden brown. Transfer to a small
ovenproof dish just large enough to
hold the pork steaks in one layer.
3 Add the garlic and curry paste to
the pan and fry gently for 30 seconds.
Stir in the pineapple and juice, lemon
juice and mango chutney. Bring to
the boil and bubble to reduce slightly,
then pour over the pork.
4 Bake for 25 minutes, basting the
pork steaks occasionally. Scatter with
parsley and serve with rice.

TRY SOMETHING DIFFERENT
Use 700g (1½lb) pork tenderloin. Fry
in 1 tbsp oil at step 2, turning to brown
all over. Slice to serve.

NUTRITION PER SERVING 420 cals |
25g fat (7g sats) | 21g carbs | 1g salt

Sausage Rolls

Makes 28
Preparation time 25 minutes
Cooking time 30 minutes

450g (1lb) puff pastry, thawed if frozen
flour to dust and milk to brush
450g (1lb) pork sausage meat
beaten egg to glaze

1 Preheat the oven to 220°C (200°C
fan oven) mark 7. Roll out half
the puff pastry on a lightly floured
surface to a 40.5 × 20.5cm (16 × 8in)
rectangle; cut in half lengthways.
2 Divide the sausage meat into four,
dust with flour and form two portions
into rolls, the length of the pastry. Lay
a sausage-meat roll on each strip of
pastry. Brush the pastry edges with a
little milk, fold one side of the pastry
over and press the long edges together
to seal. Repeat with the remaining
pastry and sausage. Trim the ends.
3 Brush the pastry with beaten egg to
glaze and cut each roll into 5cm (2in)
lengths. Make three slits in each one.
4 Transfer to a baking sheet and
cook for 15 minutes. Reduce the oven
temperature to 180°C (160°C fan
oven) mark 4 and cook for a further
15 minutes. Serve hot or cold.

TRY SOMETHING DIFFERENT
Add 1 hot red chilli, seeded and finely
chopped (see Cook's Tips, page 69),
1 tbsp freshly grated ginger and a
handful of freshly chopped coriander
leaves to the pork sausage meat.

NUTRITION PER SERVING 119 cals |
9g fat (2g sats) | 8g carbs | 0.4g salt

Toad in the Hole

Serves 2
Preparation time 10 minutes
Cooking time 25–30 minutes

125g (4oz) plain flour, sifted
2 large eggs, lightly beaten
150ml (¼ pint) semi-skimmed milk
2 tbsp oil
4 pork sausages
salt and ground black pepper
steamed carrots and broccoli or green beans to serve

1 Preheat the oven to 220°C (200°C fan oven) mark 7.
Put the flour into a bowl, make a well in the centre and
pour in the eggs and milk. Whisk the batter thoroughly
and season it well with salt and pepper.
2 Divide the oil and sausages between two 600ml
(1 pint) shallow ovenproof dishes and cook in the oven
for 10 minutes, turning once or twice.
3 Divide the batter between the dishes and continue to
cook for 15–20 minutes or until the batter is puffy and
a rich golden colour all over. Serve immediately, with
steamed carrots and broccoli or green beans.

Sausages

As well as ground meat, sausages also contain some type
of fat, as well as a variety of herbs, spices, seasoning
and cereal. The meat-to-fat ratio varies hugely between
varieties of sausage, and from region to region, but a pork
sausage should contain a minimum of 42 per cent pork
meat. Sausages are usually sold twisted into links. There
are endless varieties of sausage, but the following are some
of the most famous of the pork-based types:
CHIPOLATAS Slender sausages which are usually
grilled or oven-roasted rather than pan-fried. In the UK,
they are traditionally wrapped in bacon and served with
the Christmas turkey.
CHORIZO A distinctive red Spanish sausage, strongly
flavoured with paprika, chorizo has a coarse texture and
a hot, spicy flavour. It is available both raw and cooked,
smoked and unsmoked. It is used on pizza, in fried and
oven-baked dishes.

CUMBERLAND Traditionally sold in a coil, rather than twisted
into links, with a chunky texture and peppery flavour, they
are a great all-round sausage.
FRANKFURTERS Lightly smoked German sausages with a fine
texture, these are the classic hot dog sausage.
LINCOLNSHIRE These have a chunky and open texture and are
flavoured with thyme and sage.
TOULOUSE A pungent, coarse sausage flavoured with wine,
garlic and seasoning. Great in hot-pots or cassoulets.

NUTRITION PER SERVING 571 cals | 31g fat (8g sats) | 57g carbs | 2.6g salt

Italian Meatballs

Serves 4
Preparation time 15 minutes
Cooking time 50 minutes

50g (2oz) fresh breadcrumbs
450g (1lb) lean minced pork
1 tsp fennel seeds, crushed
¼ tsp dried chilli flakes, or to taste
3 garlic cloves, crushed
4 tbsp freshly chopped flat-leafed parsley
3 tbsp red wine
oil–water spray (see Cook's Tip)
freshly chopped oregano to garnish
spaghetti to serve

For the tomato sauce
oil–water spray
2 large shallots, finely chopped
3 pitted black olives, shredded
2 garlic cloves, crushed
2 pinches of dried chilli flakes
250ml (9fl oz) vegetable or chicken stock
500g carton passata
2 tbsp freshly chopped flat-leafed parsley
2 tbsp freshly chopped basil
2 tbsp freshly chopped oregano
salt and ground black pepper

1 To make the tomato sauce, spray a pan with the oil–water spray and add the shallots. Cook gently for 5 minutes. Add the olives, garlic, chilli flakes and stock, and bring to the boil, then reduce the heat, cover and simmer for 3–4 minutes.
2 Uncover and simmer for 10 minutes or until the shallots and garlic are soft and the liquid syrupy. Stir in the passata and season with salt and pepper. Bring to the boil, then reduce the heat and simmer for 10–15 minutes. Stir in the herbs. Preheat the grill.
3 Put the breadcrumbs into a large bowl and mix in the pork, fennel seeds, chilli flakes, garlic, parsley, wine, salt and pepper, using your hands, until combined. (To check the seasoning, fry a little, taste and adjust if necessary.)
4 With wet hands, roll the mixture into balls. Line a grill pan with foil, shiny side up, and spray with the oil–water spray. Cook the meatballs under the grill for 3–4 minutes on each side. Serve with the tomato sauce and spaghetti, garnished with oregano.

Cook's Tip
Oil–water spray is far lower in calories than oil alone and, as it sprays on thinly and evenly, you'll use less. Fill one-eighth of a travel-sized spray bottle with oil such as sunflower, light olive or vegetable (rapeseed) oil, then top up with water. To use, shake well before spraying. Store the bottle in the fridge.

NUTRITION PER SERVING 275 cals | 12g fat (4g sats) | 16g carbs | 1.8g salt

Stuffed Rack of Pork with Cider Gravy

Serves 8
Preparation time 30 minutes, plus resting
Cooking time 2½ hours

6 pork and apple sausages, about 400g (14oz)
a large handful of fresh parsley, finely chopped
finely grated zest of 1 lemon
2 tbsp wholegrain mustard
2kg (4½lb) pork rack
2 onions, sliced in thick rings
2 tbsp plain flour
200ml (7fl oz) cider
500ml (17fl oz) chicken stock
1 tbsp clear honey or redcurrant jelly
½ tbsp wholegrain mustard
salt and ground black pepper

1 Preheat the oven to 220°C (200°C fan oven) mark 7.
Peel off and discard the sausage skins. Put the meat into a
medium bowl and mix in the parsley, lemon zest, mustard
and some freshly ground black pepper (the sausage meat
should provide enough salt).
2 Make a flap along the length of the joint by partially
cutting the skin and fat away from the meat. Press the
sausage mixture into this space, then tie the skin flap
in place with string around the joint, along its length.
Weigh the joint and calculate the cooking time, allowing
25 minutes per 450g (1lb).
3 Keeping the onion rings intact, arrange in the base of
a roasting tin just large enough to hold the meat. Rest the
pork on top, skin side up.
4 Season the skin with salt and roast for the calculated
time, reducing the oven temperature to 180°C (160°C fan
oven) mark 4 after the first 40 minutes. Continue cooking
for the calculated time or until the juices run clear when
the meat is pierced deeply with a knife. If using a meat
thermometer, the temperature should reach 70°C in the
thickest part of the joint.
5 Transfer the pork to a board and cover loosely with foil.
Leave to rest in a warm place for at least 30 minutes while
you make the gravy.
6 Spoon off all but 1 tbsp of the fat from the roasting tin
and put the tin on the hob over a medium heat. Sprinkle
in the flour and stir, scraping up all the meaty bits stuck
to the bottom.

7 Take the tin off the heat and gradually mix in the
cider. Return to the heat, bring to the boil and bubble for
2 minutes, stirring often. Add the stock, bring back to
the boil, then reduce the heat and simmer for 15 minutes,
stirring frequently or until the gravy reaches the desired
consistency.
8 Strain the gravy into a warmed gravy boat and stir in the
honey or jelly, the mustard and any juices that have leaked
from the pork. Check the seasoning and add salt and
pepper to taste. Serve immediately with the meat, or pour
into a pan to reheat later.

NUTRITION PER SERVING 750 cals | 53g fat (19g sats) | 11g carbs | 1.7g salt

Cumberland Glazed Baked Gammon

Serves 16
Preparation time 30 minutes
Cooking time 3½–4¼ hours

4.5kg (10lb) smoked gammon joint, on the bone
2 celery sticks, roughly chopped
1 onion, quartered
1 carrot, roughly chopped
1 tsp black peppercorns
1 tbsp cloves
75g (3oz) redcurrant sprigs

For the Cumberland glaze
grated zest and juice of ½ lemon
grated zest and juice of ½ orange
4 tbsp redcurrant jelly
1 tsp Dijon mustard
2 tbsp port
salt and ground black pepper

1 Put the gammon into a large pan. Add the celery,
onion, carrot and peppercorns. Cover the meat and
vegetables with cold water and bring to the boil. Cover
the pan and simmer for 2¾–3½ hours, or allowing
15–20 minutes per 450g (1lb) plus 15 minutes. Lift
the gammon out of the pan.
2 Preheat the oven to 200°C (180°C fan oven) mark 6.
3 Meanwhile, make the glaze. Heat the lemon and orange
zests and juices, redcurrant jelly, mustard and port in a pan
to dissolve the jelly. Bring to the boil, then let it bubble for
5 minutes or so until syrupy. Season with salt and pepper
to taste.
4 Cut off the gammon rind and score the fat in a neat
diamond pattern. Put the gammon into a roasting tin, then
stud the fat with cloves. Spoon the glaze evenly over the
gammon joint.
5 Roast the gammon for 40 minutes, basting the meat
with any juices. Add the redcurrant sprigs 10 minutes
before the end of the cooking time. Serve the gammon
hot or cold, carved into thin slices and garnished with the
redcurrant sprigs.

NUTRITION PER SERVING 406 cals | 21g fat (7g sats) | 4g carbs | 6.3g salt

Raised Pork Pie

Serves 8
Preparation time 45 minutes, plus cooling
  and chilling
Cooking time about 3½ hours, plus
  cooling and chilling

3 or 4 small veal bones
1 small onion, peeled
1 bay leaf
4 black peppercorns
900g (2lb) boneless leg or shoulder of
  pork, cubed
¼ tsp cayenne pepper
¼ tsp ground ginger
¼ tsp ground mace
¼ tsp dried sage
¼ tsp dried marjoram
1 tbsp salt
½ tsp pepper
450g (1lb) plain flour
300ml (½ pint) milk and water mixed
150g (5oz) lard
1 medium egg, beaten
salad to serve

1 Put the bones, onion, bay leaf and peppercorns in a pan and cover with water. Bring to the boil, then reduce the heat and simmer for 20 minutes. Turn up the heat and boil to reduce the liquid to 150ml (¼ pint). Strain and cool. Base-line a 20.5cm (8in) springform cake tin.
2 Mix the pork with the spices and herbs, 1 tsp salt and the pepper.
3 Put the flour and remaining salt in a bowl. Bring the milk, water and lard to the boil in a pan, then gradually beat it into the flour to form a soft dough. Knead the dough for 3–4 minutes.
4 Roll out two-thirds of the pastry on a lightly floured surface and mould into the prepared tin. Cover and chill for 30 minutes. Keep the remaining pastry covered. Preheat the oven to 220°C (200°C fan oven) mark 7.
5 Spoon the meat mixture and 4 tbsp cold stock into the pastry case. Roll out the remaining pastry to make a lid and put on top of the meat mixture, sealing the pastry edges well. Decorate with pastry trimmings and make a hole in the centre. Brush with the beaten egg to glaze.
6 Bake for 30 minutes. Cover loosely with foil, reduce the oven temperature to 180°C (160°C fan oven) mark 4 and bake for a further 2½ hours. Cool.
7 Warm the remaining jellied stock until liquid, then pour through a funnel into the centre hole of the pie. Chill and serve with salad.

TRY SOMETHING DIFFERENT
Raised Veal and Ham Pie Mix together 700g (1½lb) diced pie veal and 225g (8oz) diced cooked ham, 1 tbsp freshly chopped parsley, grated zest and juice of 1 lemon and salt and pepper, and use to half-fill the pie. Put one hard-boiled egg in the centre and cover with the remaining veal mixture. Proceed as above.

Cook's Tip
If you have no bones available to make a jellied stock, use 2 tsp gelatine to 300ml (½ pint) stock to achieve the right consistency.

NUTRITION PER SERVING 617 cals | 37g fat (14g sats) | 45g carbs | 2g salt

Offal

1, 2, 3, 4, 5 Liver

Chicken (1), duck and turkey livers are similar in taste. Make into pâtés, or sauté in butter and/or oil. Goose liver (2) in the form of foie gras is produced by intensive feeding of geese to enlarge their livers (also comes from ducks fed in the same way). Calf's liver (3) has a delicate flavour and is usually pan-fried. Lamb's liver (4) is slightly stronger in flavour than calf's. Pig's (5) and ox liver are strongly flavoured, with a coarser texture.

6   Oxtail

A tough but flavourful cut, usually sold jointed. Casserole larger pieces; smaller pieces are better for making stocks and soups. Braise, stew or casserole.

7   Lamb's heart

Hearts have a tender texture and mild flavour. Pig's and ox hearts are larger and coarser. All suit long, slow cooking. Soak in salted water for 1 hour, then rinse and slice or stuff. Braise, casserole or stew.

8   Kidney

Veal kidneys (8a) are mild. Lamb's kidneys (8b) have a similar flavour to the meat. Pig's and ox kidneys (8c) have a stronger flavour and suit long, slow cooking. Grill, pan-fry, or add to casseroles, stews, pies and savoury puddings.

9   Lamb sweetbreads

Sweetbreads require precooking in stock or water and can then be pan-fried, roasted or braised. Soak in lightly salted water, rinse, blanch and remove the outer membrane.

10 Tripe

The stomach lining of the cow, tripe is sold bleached, and par-boiled to varying degrees. Casserole or stew.

11 Ox tongue

Sold fresh or brined, tongue is cooked, then pressed and served cold, cut into thin slices, or hot. Soak fresh tongue for about 2 hours, and brined ox tongue overnight. Boil with spices until tender; drain and peel.

12 Pig's trotter

Pig's feet release gelatine when cooked. Boil for stock; boil to pickle; or boil, then grill or bake, with or without a filling.

13 Brain

Usually taken from the heads of lambs and calves, brains need soaking and par-boiling before pan-frying or braising.

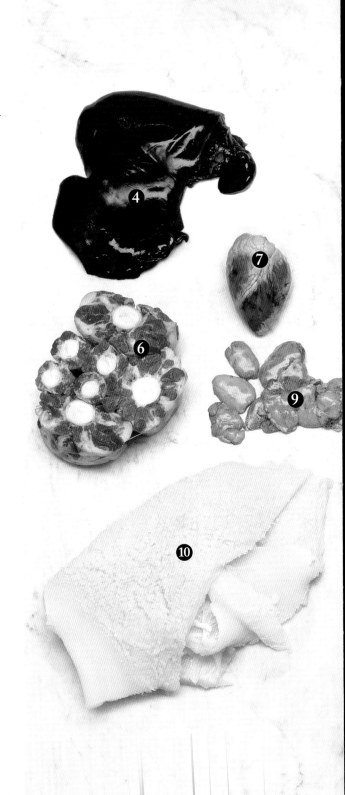

Bovine Spongiform Encephalopathy
More commonly known as BSE, or mad cow disease, bovine spongiform encephalopathy is a fatal neurodegenerative disease found in cattle. It is thought to have arisen as a result of feeding ground-up sheep carcasses infected with a similar disease that affects sheep – scrapie – to cattle. Cattle in the UK have been the most widely affected and any animals suspected of having the disease are slaughtered. It is widely believed that the disease can be transferred to humans who eat the brain and spinal cords of infected carcasses; it presents itself in the form of new variant Creuzfeldt-Jacob disease (vCJD). As a result, high-risk products are banned from sale in the UK.

Braised Oxtail

Serves 6
Preparation time 20 minutes
Cooking time about 4 hours

2 oxtails, about 1.6kg (3½lb) in total, trimmed
2 tbsp plain flour
4 tbsp oil
2 large onions, sliced
900ml (1½ pints) beef stock
150ml (¼ pint) red wine
1 tbsp tomato purée
finely grated zest of ½ lemon
2 bay leaves
2 medium carrots, chopped
450g (1lb) parsnips, chopped
salt and ground black pepper
freshly chopped parsley to garnish

1 Cut the oxtails into large pieces. Season the flour with salt and pepper, then toss the pieces in the flour.
2 Heat the oil in a large flameproof casserole and brown the oxtail pieces, a few at a time. Remove from the casserole with a slotted spoon and leave to one side.
3 Add the onions to the casserole and fry over a medium heat for about 10 minutes or until softened and lightly browned. Stir in any remaining flour.
4 Stir in the stock, red wine, tomato purée, lemon zest and bay leaves. Season with salt and pepper. Bring to the boil, then return the oxtail to the casserole and reduce the heat. Cover and simmer very gently for 2 hours.
5 Skim off the fat from the surface, then stir in the carrots and parsnips. Re-cover the casserole and simmer very gently for a further 2 hours or until the oxtail is very tender.
6 Skim off all the fat from the surface, then check the seasoning. Serve scattered with chopped parsley.

Cook's Tip
Oxtail contains a modest amount of meat and often plenty of firm white fat, although the fat can be trimmed before cooking. It also releases generous amounts of gelatine, which helps to enrich dishes.

NUTRITION PER SERVING 616 cals | 35g fat (12g sats) | 16g carbs | 1.2g salt

Lancashire Tripe and Onions

Serves 4
Preparation time 20 minutes
Cooking time about 2¼ hours

450g (1lb) dressed tripe
225g (8oz) shallots, peeled
600ml (1 pint) milk
a pinch of freshly grated nutmeg
1 bay leaf
25g (1oz) butter
3 tbsp plain flour
salt and ground black pepper
freshly chopped parsley to garnish
crusty bread to serve

1 Put the tripe into a pan and cover with cold water. Bring to the boil, then drain and rinse under cold running water. Cut into 2.5cm (1in) pieces.
2 Put the tripe, shallots, milk, seasoning, nutmeg and bay leaf into the rinsed-out pan. Bring to the boil, cover and simmer for about 2 hours or until tender. Strain and keep to one side 600ml (1 pint) of the liquid. Remove and discard the bay leaf.
3 Melt the butter in a pan, stir in the flour and cook gently for 1 minute, stirring. Remove the pan from the heat and gradually stir in the reserved cooking liquid. Bring to the boil and continue to cook, stirring, until the sauce thickens.
4 Add the tripe and shallots and reheat thoroughly. Check the seasoning and sprinkle with chopped parsley. Serve with bread.

NUTRITION PER SERVING 240 cals | 10g fat (5g sats) | 20g carbs | 1g salt

Liver and Onions

Serves 4
Preparation time 10 minutes
Cooking time 20–25 minutes

25g (1oz) butter
450g (1lb) onions, sliced or chopped
½ tsp freshly chopped sage (optional)
450g (1lb) calf's or lamb's liver, cut into
   thin strips
salt and ground black pepper
bread to serve

1 Melt the butter in a frying pan, add the onions and fry gently until they begin to colour, then add the seasoning and the sage, if you like. Cover the frying pan and simmer very gently for 10 minutes or until the onions are soft.
2 Add the liver strips to the onions, increase the heat slightly and continue cooking for 5–10 minutes, stirring all the time, until the liver is just cooked. Transfer to a warmed serving dish and serve with bread.

NUTRITION PER SERVING 204 cals | 9g fat (4g sats) | 9g carbs | 0.9g salt

Calf's Liver with Sage and Balsamic

Serves 4
Preparation time 5 minutes
Cooking time 5 minutes

15g (½oz) butter
1 tbsp olive oil
12 sage leaves
4 thin slices calf's liver
1–2 tbsp balsamic vinegar
rice, with freshly chopped parsley
   stirred through, or grilled polenta
   to serve

1 Preheat the oven to 110°C (90°C fan oven) mark ¼. Melt the butter with the oil in a heavy-based frying pan and when it is foaming, add the sage leaves. Cook for 1–2 minutes until crisp. Put in a single layer in a shallow dish and keep hot in the oven.
2 Add a little extra oil to the pan, put in two slices of calf's liver and cook quickly for 30 seconds on each side over a high heat. Remove and place on a plate while you quickly cook the remaining two slices.
3 Return all four slices to the pan, splash the balsamic vinegar over the top and cook for another minute or so. Serve immediately with the sage leaves, rice or grilled polenta.

NUTRITION PER SERVING 88 cals | 6g fat (3g sats) | trace carbs | 0.1g salt

Sautéed Lamb's Kidneys and Baby Onions

Serves 4
Preparation time 10 minutes
Cooking time 30 minutes

8 lamb's kidneys, membrane removed
225g (8oz) baby onions, peeled
25g (1oz) unsalted butter
3 tbsp balsamic vinegar
1 tbsp plain flour
300ml (½ pint) well-flavoured lamb stock
3 tbsp Madeira
salt and ground black pepper
freshly chopped parsley, to garnish
boiled rice to serve

1 Halve the lamb's kidneys lengthways and snip out the white cores with kitchen scissors. Add the baby onions to a pan of boiling water and blanch for 3–5 minutes, then drain well.
2 Melt the butter in a sauté pan, add the onions and cook gently for 10–15 minutes until soft and browned. Increase the heat and add the lamb's kidneys, stirring and turning them for about 2 minutes or until browned. Lift out the kidneys and onions and put on to a plate.
3 Deglaze the pan with the balsamic vinegar, scraping up any sediment from the base of the pan, and allow almost all of the liquid to evaporate. Sprinkle in the flour and cook, stirring, over a medium heat until it begins to colour. Whisk in the stock and Madeira. Bring the sauce to the boil, then reduce the heat to low and simmer until reduced and slightly syrupy. Check the seasoning.
4 Return the kidneys and baby onions to the sauce and reheat gently for 5 minutes. Scatter with plenty of chopped parsley and serve with rice.

NUTRITION PER SERVING 180 cals | 8g fat (4g sats) | 8g carbs | 1.6g salt

Eggs and Cheese

Eggs

Eggs are a concentrated source of protein and vitamins, including A, B$_{12}$, D, E and K; they also contain iron. Although not high in calories, eggs are relatively high in cholesterol; however, this dietary cholesterol does not have a marked affect on the cholesterol in our blood. Providing you are eating a healthy, balanced diet there should be no reason to limit the number of eggs you eat in week. Eggs are a wonderfully useful fast food and have special culinary properties: they are invaluable for thickening, binding, emulsifying, raising and glazing.

Buying and storing eggs

Most supermarkets stock a range of eggs produced by different farming methods, including organic, free-range, eggs from hens fed only with grain, and barn eggs. Eggs labelled as 'organic' are strictly controlled and come from hens that have easy access to open pasture and are fed a natural cereal diet. Free-range hens also have access to open foraging. The majority of eggs sold in the UK, however, are still produced by 'battery hens', which are raised entirely indoors using intensive farming methods.

Never buy cracked or damaged eggs; open the box before buying and check that all the eggs are sound. Always refer to the use-by date on the pack.

Store eggs in the fridge, pointed-end down, to centre the yolk in the white. Bring to room temperature before use.

There is no intrinsic difference in flavour or value between white and brown eggs – the colour relates to the hens' diet. However, studies suggest that the nutritional qualities of free-range, and particularly organic, eggs are superior because of the greens and insects in the hens' diet.

Eggs are now graded into four weight categories: very large, large, medium and small. It is important to use the correct size of egg for a recipe. Unless otherwise stated, medium eggs should be used for the recipes in this book.

Egg safety

Eggs are susceptible to salmonella, one of the bacteria responsible for food poisoning, because their porous shells can absorb the bacteria if they come into contact with it. However, the implementation of the internationally recognised lion symbol on eggs and boxes, which indicates that the produce conforms to a strict code of practice throughout the entire chain of production, has helped almost to eliminate salmonella from eggs in the UK.

Thorough cooking will destroy any salmonella that may be present, so it isn't generally a problem. However, raw or lightly cooked eggs are used in many classic recipes, including mayonnaise, cold soufflés, meringues, ice creams and sorbets, lemon curd and scrambled eggs. Although the risk is small, those who are particularly vulnerable – including the young, the elderly, pregnant women and anyone with an immune-deficiency disease – should avoid eating raw or lightly cooked eggs.

Types of egg

Hen's eggs are the most frequently used and any general culinary reference to eggs implies these, although other types are available.

Duck's eggs are larger and richer (higher in fat) than hen's eggs, and they have a smooth shell, which is stronger and less porous. The yolk is a deep yellow and the white is more gelatinous.

Quail's eggs are tiny and attractively speckled; they are usually soft-boiled for 1–2 minutes and often used as a garnish or as or canapé. They have a light-textured pale yolk and very thin shells, which are laborious to peel.

A goose egg weighs about the same as three hen's eggs. They have a slightly stronger taste and make excellent scrambled egg and omelettes. Allow about 7 minutes for a soft-boiled egg.

Because duck and goose eggs are often sold loose rather than in labelled cartons, you may have to ask what the use-by date is. Duck and goose eggs are particularly vulnerable to salmonella and, therefore, should always be cooked thoroughly.

Cooking eggs

In addition to being poached, fried, baked, boiled, scrambled or turned into omelettes, eggs are used to lighten soufflés and cakes; thicken mousses; bind stuffings; set baked custards; glaze pastry and breads; and emulsify sauces and dressings, such as hollandaise and mayonnaise.

Whisked egg whites incorporate air and dramatically increase their volume, giving soufflés, meringues and whisked cakes their characteristic light, airy texture.

To separate an egg

Crack the egg against the rim of a clean, dry bowl and open the two halves, allowing some of the white to run into the bowl. Carefully pass the egg yolk back and forth between the two half-shells without breaking it, allowing the egg white to fall into the bowl. Put the yolk into another bowl. Don't let the yolk break and mingle with the white, because egg whites will not whisk satisfactorily if a trace of yolk is present.

To whisk egg whites

Use a large balloon whisk or a hand-held electric whisk. Make sure the bowl and whisk are scrupulously clean and dry with no trace of grease, water or egg yolk, which will adversely affect the whisking.

Whisk the egg whites until they stand in soft or stiff peaks (as specified in the recipe). Do not over-whisk or you will have dry powdery whites, which will be impossible to fold into a mixture evenly.

Fold in egg whites as soon as you have whisked them or they will collapse. Make sure the mixture you are folding into is neither too hot nor too cold, otherwise much of the volume will be lost. To lighten the mixture, quickly fold in a spoonful of whisked egg white, then lightly fold in the remaining whites, using a large metal spoon and a cutting and folding action in a figure-of-eight motion.

Cooking methods

Baked Put a knob of butter into individual ramekins and heat in the oven until melted. Break a large egg into each ramekin and bake at 170°C (150°C fan oven) mark 3 for 10 minutes.

Boiled Lower the egg(s) into a small pan of simmering water, using a spoon, making sure there is sufficient water to cover. If the egg cracks, add a little salt or vinegar to coagulate the white. For soft-boiled eggs, allow 3½–5 minutes, according to size and whether you prefer a very soft or slightly firmer set.

Eggs mollet are soft-boiled eggs with firm whites. Simmer for about 6 minutes, then plunge into cold water and peel.
For lightly set coddled eggs, put into a pan of boiling water, cover with a lid, take off the heat and leave to stand in a warm place for 8–10 minutes.
For hard-boiled eggs, allow 10–12 minutes. Once cooked, drain and cool quickly under cold running water, then crack the shell to prevent a black rim round the yolk.

Fried Heat a little butter or oil in a frying pan. Break an egg into a cup and add to the hot fat. Fry over a medium heat until lightly set, spooning the hot fat on top of the yolk as it cooks. The eggs can also be fried on both sides.

Omelette You will need a good heavy-based non-stick omelette pan or frying pan. Use an 18–20.5cm (7–8in) pan for a two- or three-egg omelette, or a 23–25.5cm (9–10in) pan for a six-egg omelette. Lightly beat the eggs in a bowl with 1–2 tbsp water, using a fork or balloon whisk. Heat a large knob of butter in the pan, then pour in the eggs. Stir with a fork or wooden spatula until the mixture is three-quarters set to ensure an even, creamy texture, then cook without stirring for a further 30 seconds or until set; do not overcook. Serve immediately.

Poached Take a wide shallow pan and two-thirds fill it with boiling water, adding 1 tbsp vinegar to each 600ml (1 pint) water. Carefully break an egg into a saucer, make a whirlpool in the water using a spoon and lower in the egg. Reduce the heat and cook for 3 minutes or until the white is just set and the yolk soft. Using a slotted spoon, lift the egg out of the pan. (Alternatively, cook the eggs in a poacher. Half-fill the lower container with water and boil. Put a small knob of butter into each cup. Break an egg into each cup and cook gently for 3 minutes or until set.)

Scrambled Beat the eggs well with a little salt and pepper. Melt a knob of butter in a heavy non-stick pan and add the eggs. Stir over a very gentle heat until just beginning to thicken. Add another knob of butter and continue stirring over the heat until the eggs start to scramble. Take off the heat and continue to stir; the eggs will continue to cook in the residual heat. They should still be moist.

Cheese

For culinary purposes, most cheeses can be categorised as follows: hard cheeses, such as Parmesan and Pecorino; semi-hard cheeses, such as Cheddar, Gruyère and Stilton; soft ripened cheeses, such as Brie and Camembert; and fresh soft cheeses, such as mozzarella, mascarpone and soft goat's cheeses. Most cheeses have a high fat content and should be consumed in moderate quantities, although low-fat varieties are available. In the cheese-making process, rennet (or a vegetarian alternative) is used to curdle milk and separate it into firm curds and liquid whey. The curds are then processed, shaped and matured as necessary to create a wide range of cheeses. The method varies according to the type of cheese. Very hard cheeses, such as Parmesan, take up to three years to develop their full flavour, whereas soft cheeses, such as Brie, are ready to eat within a month or two. Fresh soft goat's cheeses, mozzarella and cream cheeses are not matured in this way and most can be eaten within a few days of being made.

Buying and storing cheese

Probably the best place to buy cheese is from a specialist cheese shop if you are lucky enough to have access to one, otherwise many supermarkets have a fresh cheese counter offering a good variety of farmhouse and factory-made cheeses.

Try to taste first before you commit to buying a cheese, as artisan cheeses will vary within, as well as across, varieties – some cheeses differ according to the time of year, and certain varieties are seasonal. Once you have made your choice, make sure the cheese is freshly sliced to your requirements. Buy only as much or as little as you think you need – central heating and refrigeration will dry out the cheese once you get it home.

The best way to store cheese is to wrap it in waxed paper then to put it into an unsealed plastic food bag or cheese box. Keep in the fridge in the least cold area away from the freezer compartment. If you have a whole, rinded cheese, cover the cut surface with clingfilm.

To enjoy cheese at its best, you should always remove it from the fridge at least 2 hours before serving to bring it to room temperature. Loosen the wrapping and remove it just before serving. If you are serving more than one cheese, provide separate knives, so that there is always a separate one for blue cheese, at least.

Vegetarian cheeses

Some vegetarians prefer to avoid cheeses that have been produced by the traditional method, because this uses animal-derived rennet (see opposite); however, most supermarkets and cheese shops now stock an excellent range of vegetarian cheeses, produced using vegetarian rennet. The recipes marked as vegetarian in this book assume that you will choose a suitable cheese if cooking for vegetarians. Always check the label when buying.

Selecting for a cheeseboard

Choosing cheeses for a cheeseboard is a matter of satisfying everyone's taste, so a range of flavours from mild to strong, and a variety of textures, is important. Think about shapes and colours, too. If you are serving four cheeses, choose one hard, one soft, one blue and one goat's cheese. If you are buying from a specialist cheese shop or a supermarket cheese counter, ask to try a piece first so that you know what you are getting and can balance the flavours. It is a question of quality rather than quantity, as serving a few excellent cheeses is more appealing than offering five or six with competing flavours.

To accompany your cheeses, choose crisp apples, juicy pears, grapes or figs. Very mild, soft goat's cheeses can be eaten with strawberries; slightly harder ones go well with cherry tomatoes or olives. Salad leaves should be bitter – try some chicory, frisée or rocket. Walnuts and celery are excellent with blue cheese. Oatcakes, wheat wafers and digestive biscuits go well with most cheeses, and if you want to serve bread, make sure it is fresh and crusty. Butter should be unsalted.

As for when you serve cheese, rounding off the meal with the cheeseboard is the norm in the UK, but the French custom of moving from main course to cheese course, before the dessert, is worth considering. It enables you to savour the cheeses before you are too full to enjoy them, and you can carry on with the same wine.

Cream cheese is a fresh, bland cheese made from pasteurised milk. Its fat content varies depending on the type. Cream cheese has many uses, including dips, nibbles and cheesecakes.

Cottage cheese is made from the curds of skimmed milk, which are heated to make them firm and dense. The resulting curd cheese is then broken up and finished with a little cream. Cottage cheese is low in fat.

Curd cheese has a clean, acidic flavour and a soft, slightly granular texture. It is made solely by the action of lactic acid; rennet is not used. There are several varieties of this soft, fresh cheese, including quark, which has a very low fat content.

Fresh cheeses are soft and light, with a refreshing tang. There are many different types of fresh cheese, with different fat content, depending on whether they are made from whole or skimmed milk. These cheeses have a relatively short shelf life.

Fromage frais is a soft cheese produced from skimmed milk and rennet. The curd is stirred and the whey drained off. Fromage frais can be used as an alternative to cream.

Goat's cheeses are increasingly popular, as reflected in the infinite variety now available, most of which are just termed chèvres. British-made goat's cheeses are now widely produced, in response to the demand. Young, soft goat's cheese is rindless with a mild, clean flavour – ideal for recipes using soft cheeses. Harder, rinded varieties are often sliced and grilled, then served on salads or bread.

Hard and semi-hard cheeses are produced by removing as much of the whey as possible from the curds, then moulding and ripening the cheese. Hard cheeses undergo a further process which involves heating the curd so that it shrinks and hardens. Semi-hard cheeses include Cheddar and Edam, and the most familiar hard cheeses are Parmesan and Pecorino.

Soft ripened cheeses Soft ripened cheeses are generally made by coagulating milk with rennet; the addition of a starter ensures a clean, acidic flavour. Some varieties of soft cheese, such as Brie, Camembert and the blue-veined cheeses are mould-ripened. It is these cheeses that are susceptible to listeria contamination.

Vegetarian cheeses, produced using vegetarian rennet, are becoming increasingly available from supermarkets as well as specialist cheese shops. If you are cooking for vegetarians always check that the cheese you are using for your recipe is suitable.

Classic Omelette

Serves 1
Preparation time 5 minutes
Cooking time 5 minutes

2–3 medium eggs
1 tbsp milk or water
25g (1oz) unsalted butter
salt and ground black pepper
sliced tomatoes and freshly chopped
  flat-leafed parsley to serve

1 Whisk the eggs in a bowl, just enough to break them down – over-beating spoils the texture of the omelette. Season with salt and pepper, and add the milk or water.
2 Heat the butter in an 18cm (7in) omelette pan or non-stick frying pan until it is foaming, but not brown. Add the eggs and stir gently with a fork or wooden spatula, drawing the mixture from the sides to the centre as it sets and letting the liquid egg in the centre run to the sides. When set, stop stirring and cook for 30 seconds or until the omelette is golden brown underneath and still creamy on top: don't overcook. If you are making a filled omelette, add the filling (see Cook's Tip, page 231).
3 Tilt the pan away from you slightly and use a palette knife to fold over one-third of the omelette to the centre, then fold over the opposite third. Slide the omelette out on to a warmed plate, letting it flip over so that the folded sides are underneath. Serve immediately, with tomatoes sprinkled with parsley.

NUTRITION PER SERVING 449 cals | 40g fat (19g sats) | 1g carbs | 1g salt Ⓥ

Omelette Arnold Bennett

Serves 2
Preparation time 15 minutes
Cooking time about 20 minutes

125g (4oz) smoked haddock
50g (2oz) butter
150ml (¼ pint) double or single cream
3 medium eggs, separated
50g (2oz) Cheddar, grated
salt and ground black pepper
rocket salad to serve

1 Put the fish in a pan and cover with water. Bring to the boil and simmer gently for 10 minutes. Drain and flake the fish, discarding the skin and bones.
2 Put the fish in a pan with half the butter and 2 tbsp cream. Toss over a high heat until the butter melts. Leave to cool.
3 Beat the egg yolks in a bowl with 1 tbsp cream and season with salt and pepper. Stir in the fish mixture.
4 Put the egg whites into a clean, grease-free bowl and whisk until they form stiff peaks; fold into the yolks.
5 Preheat the grill to hot.
6 Heat the remaining butter in an omelette pan. Fry the egg mixture, but make sure it remains fairly fluid. Do not fold over. Slide it on to a flameproof serving dish.
7 Blend together the cheese and remaining fresh cream, then spread on top of the omelette and brown under the grill. Serve with a rocket salad.

NUTRITION PER SERVING 835 cals | 79g fat (46g sats) | 1g carbs | 2.8g salt

Spanish Omelette

Serves 4
Preparation time 15 minutes
Cooking time 30–45 minutes

900g (2lb) potatoes, peeled and left whole
3–4 tbsp vegetable oil
1 onion, finely sliced
8 medium eggs
3 tbsp freshly chopped flat-leafed parsley
3 streaky bacon rashers
salt and ground black pepper
green salad to serve

1 Put the potatoes into a pan and cover with cold lightly salted water. Bring to the boil, then reduce the heat and simmer for 15–20 minutes or until almost cooked. Drain and leave until cool enough to handle, then slice thickly.
2 Heat 1 tbsp oil in an 18cm (7in) non-stick frying pan (suitable for use under the grill). Add the onion and fry gently for 7–10 minutes until softened but not coloured; remove and set aside. Preheat the grill.
3 Lightly beat the eggs in a bowl and season well with salt and pepper.
4 Heat the remaining oil in the frying pan, then layer the potato slices, onion and 2 tbsp chopped parsley in the pan. Pour in the beaten eggs and cook for 5–10 minutes until the omelette is firm underneath.
5 Meanwhile, grill the bacon until golden and crisp, then break into pieces.
6 Put the omelette in the pan under the hot grill for 2–3 minutes until the top is just set. Scatter the bacon and remaining chopped parsley over the surface. Serve cut into wedges, with a green salad.

Cook's Tips
Try some of these fillings for a folded omelette but make sure the flavour does not overpower that of the omelette.
• Freshly chopped herbs and grated cheese.
• Chopped ham.
• Fried mushrooms.
• Cooked seafood.
• Chopped chorizo.
• Chunks of cooked sausage.
• Diced and fried red, yellow or green pepper.

NUTRITION PER SERVING 453 cals | 25g fat (6g sats) | 38g carbs | 1.6g salt

Eggs Benedict

Serves 4
Preparation time 15 minutes
Cooking time 10 minutes

4 slices bread
4 medium eggs
150ml (¼ pint) Hollandaise Sauce (see page 17)
4 thin slices lean ham
fresh parsley sprigs to garnish

1 Toast the bread on both sides. Poach the eggs (see page 227). Gently warm the hollandaise sauce.
2 Top each slice of toast with a folded slice of ham, then with a poached egg. Finally, coat with hollandaise sauce.
3 Garnish each one with a sprig of parsley and serve.

TRY SOMETHING DIFFERENT
Eggs Florentine Cook 900g (2lb) washed spinach in a pan with a little salt until tender. Drain well, chop and reheat with 15g (½oz) butter. Melt 25g (1oz) butter, stir in 3 tbsp plain flour and cook gently for 1 minute, stirring. Remove from the heat and gradually stir in 300ml (½ pint) milk. Bring to the boil and cook, stirring, until thickened. Add 50g (2oz) grated Gruyère or Cheddar cheese and season. Do not allow to boil. Poach the eggs. Put the spinach in an ovenproof dish, arrange the eggs on top and pour the cheese sauce over them. Sprinkle with 25g (1oz) grated cheese and brown under the grill.

NUTRITION PER SERVING 402 cals | 33g fat (18g sats) | 14g carbs | 1.6g salt

Piperade

Serves 4
Preparation time 20 minutes
Cooking time 20 minutes

2 tbsp olive oil
1 medium onion, finely chopped
1 garlic clove, finely chopped
1 red pepper, seeded and chopped
375g (13oz) tomatoes, peeled, seeded
  and chopped (see page 277)
a pinch of cayenne pepper
8 large eggs
salt and ground black pepper
freshly chopped flat-leafed parsley
  to garnish
fresh bread to serve (optional)

1 Heat the oil in a heavy-based frying pan. Add the onion and garlic, and cook gently for 5 minutes. Add the red pepper and cook for 10 minutes or until softened.
2 Add the tomatoes, increase the heat and cook for about 8 minutes or until they are reduced to a thick pulp. Season well with cayenne pepper, salt and pepper.
3 Lightly whisk the eggs and add to the frying pan. Using a wooden spoon, stir gently until they've just begun to set but are still creamy. Garnish with parsley and serve with bread, if you like.

NUTRITION PER SERVING 232 cals |
17g fat (4g sats) | 7g carbs | 0.4g salt Ⓥ

Spicy Baked Eggs

Serves 4
Preparation time 20 minutes
Cooking time 30 minutes

1 tbsp oil
1 red onion, finely sliced
1 red chilli, seeded and finely chopped
  see Cook's Tips, page 69)
1 garlic clove, crushed
2 × 400g cans chopped tomatoes
1 tsp caster sugar
400g can kidney beans, drained and
  rinsed
a large handful of fresh coriander,
  roughly chopped, plus extra to garnish
8 medium eggs
salt and ground black pepper
soured cream and crusty bread to serve

1 Preheat the oven to 200°C (180°C fan oven) mark 6. Heat the oil in a frying pan and gently cook the onion for 10 minutes or until soft. Add the chilli and garlic and cook for 1 minute.
2 Add the tomatoes, sugar and kidney beans and simmer for 5 minutes. Stir in the coriander and seasoning.
3 Tip the mixture into a large shallow, ovenproof serving dish. Make a small well in the mixture and crack an egg into it. Repeat with the remaining eggs, spacing them apart.
4 Cook in oven for 15–20 minutes until the egg whites are set. Garnish with the coriander and serve with soured cream and some crusty bread.

NUTRITION PER SERVING 317 cals |
14g fat (3g sats) | 21g carbs | 1.3g salt

Cheese Soufflé

Serves 4
Preparation time 20 minutes, plus infusing
Cooking time 30 minutes

25g (1oz) butter, plus extra to grease
1 tbsp freshly grated Parmesan
200ml (7fl oz) milk
a few onion and carrot slices
1 bay leaf
6 black peppercorns
2 tbsp plain flour
2 tsp Dijon mustard
a large pinch of cayenne pepper
4 large eggs, separated, plus 1 large egg white
75g (3oz) Gruyère or mature Cheddar, finely grated (see Vegetarian Cheeses, page 228)
salt and ground black pepper

1 Butter a 1.3 litre (2¼ pint) soufflé dish and sprinkle the Parmesan over the base and sides to coat evenly. Put the milk into a pan with the onion and carrot slices, bay leaf and peppercorns. Bring slowly to the boil, then remove from the heat, cover and leave to infuse for 30 minutes. Strain the milk into a jug.
2 Preheat the oven to 180°C (160°C fan oven) mark 4. Melt the butter in a pan and stir in the flour and mustard. Season with salt, pepper and cayenne, and cook for about 1 minute, stirring. Remove from the heat and gradually stir in the milk. Bring to the boil slowly and cook, stirring constantly, until the sauce thickens. Leave to cool slightly, then beat in the egg yolks, one at a time. Stir in all but 1 tbsp of the cheese.
3 Put the 5 egg whites into a clean, grease-free bowl and whisk until they form soft peaks. Mix one large spoonful of egg white into the sauce to lighten it. Gently pour the sauce over the remaining egg whites and carefully fold the ingredients together, using a metal spoon; do not over-mix.
4 Pour the soufflé mixture gently into the prepared dish; it should come about three-quarters of the way up the side of the dish. Sprinkle with the reserved cheese and run a knife around the edge of the mixture. Stand the dish on a baking sheet and bake for 30 minutes or until golden brown, well risen and just firm to the touch. Serve at once. There should be a hint of softness in the centre of the soufflé.

TRY SOMETHING DIFFERENT
Blue Cheese Soufflé Use a semi-hard blue cheese, such as Stilton or Wensleydale, instead of Cheddar.
Mushroom Soufflé Replace the cheese with 125g (4oz) field, wild or button mushrooms, chopped and sautéed in butter.
Smoked Haddock Soufflé Replace the cheese with 75g (3oz) cooked smoked haddock, finely flaked.

Cook's Tips
• Use a straight-sided soufflé dish to obtain the best rise.
• Running a knife around the edge before baking helps to achieve the classic 'hat' effect.
• If necessary, the soufflé can be prepared ahead to the end of step 2, then left to stand for several hours before completing the recipe.

NUTRITION PER SERVING 280 cals | 20g fat (13g sats) | 8g carbs | 1.1g salt Ⓥ

Egg Mayonnaise

Serves 2
Preparation time 10 minutes
Cooking time 10 minutes

4 medium eggs, hard-boiled and
 shelled (see Cook's Tip)
a few lettuce leaves
150ml (¼ pint) Mayonnaise
 (see page 29)
freshly chopped parsley or paprika
 to garnish
rocket and tomato salad to serve

1 Halve the eggs lengthways. Wash
and drain the lettuce and arrange in
a shallow dish.
2 Put the eggs on the lettuce, cut side
down and coat with the mayonnaise.
Garnish with parsley or paprika and
serve with salad.

Cook's Tip
HARD-BOILING EGGS Use eggs at room
temperature for perfect boiled eggs.
Cook in boiling water as explained
on page 227 or cover with cold water
plus 2.5cm (1in). Cover with a lid and
bring to the boil. Remove the lid and
cook for 7 minutes.

NUTRITION PER SERVING 681 cals |
69g fat (12g sats) | trace carbs | 1.3g salt Ⓥ

Scotch Eggs

Serves 4
Preparation time 15 minutes
Cooking time 17 minutes

2 tsp plain flour
4 medium eggs, hard-boiled (see
 Cook's Tip above) and shelled
a few drops of Worcestershire sauce
225g (8oz) sausage meat
1 medium egg, beaten
125g (4oz) fresh breadcrumbs
vegetable oil for deep-frying
salt and ground black pepper
tomato sauce or green salad and
 chutney to serve

1 Season the flour with salt and
pepper, then use to dust the eggs.
2 Add the Worcestershire sauce to
the sausage meat, then quarter it and
form into flat cakes. Shape each one

evenly around an egg, making sure
there are no cracks in the meat.
3 Brush with beaten egg and roll in
the breadcrumbs.
4 Heat the oil in a deep-fat fryer to a
temperature of 160°C (test by frying
a small cube of bread; it should brown
in 60 seconds). Gently lower the
Scotch eggs into the oil and fry for
7–8 minutes until golden brown and
cooked through. (The fat must not
be too hot as the raw meat must have
time to cook.)
5 Remove the eggs from the pan and
drain on kitchen paper.
6 Cut the eggs in half lengthways and
serve either hot with tomato sauce or
cold with a green salad and chutney.

NUTRITION PER SERVING 444 cals |
28g fat (8g sats) | 32g carbs | 2g salt

Welsh Rarebit

Serves 4
Preparation time 5 minutes
Cooking time 6–8 minutes

225g (8oz) Cheddar, grated (see
  Vegetarian Cheeses, page 228)
25g (1oz) butter
1 tsp English mustard
4 tbsp brown ale
4 slices white bread, crusts removed
salt and ground black pepper
fresh parsley sprig to garnish
tomato quarters to serve

1 Preheat the grill.
2 Put the cheese, butter, mustard and beer into a heavy-based pan over a low heat and stir occasionally until the cheese is melted and the mixture is smooth and creamy. Season with salt and pepper to taste.
3 Toast the bread under the grill on one side only. Turn the slices over and spread the cheese mixture on the untoasted side. Put under the grill for 1 minute or until golden and bubbling, then serve with tomato quarters and a parsley garnish.

NUTRITION PER SERVING 380 cals | 25g fat (15g sats) | 21g carbs |1.9g salt Ⓥ

Croque Monsieur

Serves 2
Preparation time 5 minutes
Cooking time 8 minutes

4 slices white bread
butter, softened, to spread, plus extra
  for frying
Dijon mustard to taste
125g (4oz) Gruyère cheese
4 slices ham

1 Spread each slice of bread on both sides with the butter. Then spread one side of two slices of bread with a little Dijon mustard.
2 Divide the cheese and ham between the two mustard-spread bread slices. Top each with the remaining bread and press down.
3 Heat a griddle with a little butter until hot, then fry the sandwiches for 2–3 minutes on each side until they are golden and crispy and the cheese begins to melt. Slice each one in half and serve immediately.

NUTRITION PER SERVING 551 cals | 35g fat (22g sats) | 27g carbs | 3.6g salt

Cheese Fondue

Serves 4
Preparation time 10 minutes
Cooking time about 10 minutes

1 large garlic clove, halved
2 tsp cornflour
3 tbsp Kirsch
200ml (7fl oz) dry white wine
1 tbsp lemon juice
200g (7oz) Gruyère cheese, grated
200g (7oz) Emmental cheese, grated
  (see Vegetarian Cheeses, page 228)
ground black pepper
bite-sized chunks of crusty bread
  to serve

1 Rub the halved garlic clove around the inside of a fondue pan (or heavy-based pan). Blend the cornflour to a smooth paste with the Kirsch.
2 Put the wine, lemon juice and cheeses in the pan with the blended cornflour and slowly bring to the boil over a very low heat, stirring all the time. Simmer gently for 3–4 minutes, stirring frequently. Season with pepper to taste.
3 Set the pan over the fondue burner (or over a heated serving tray) at the table. Serve with plenty of chunks of crusty bread for dipping into the fondue using long-handled forks.

NUTRITION PER SERVING (without bread) 460 cals | 32g fat (20g sats) | 6g carbs | 1.4g salt Ⓥ

Cauliflower Cheese

Serves 2
Preparation time 5 minutes
Cooking time 20 minutes

1 cauliflower
1 quantity cheese (mornay) sauce (see
  Béchamel Sauce, page 16)
extra grated cheese to sprinkle
salt
jacket potato to serve (optional)

1 Preheat the grill. Remove the coarse outer leaves from the cauliflower, cut a cross in the stalk end and wash the whole cauliflower under the tap.
2 Put the cauliflower into a medium pan, with the stem side down, then pour over enough boiling water to come halfway up it. Add a pinch of salt and cover the pan. Bring to the boil and cook for 10–15 minutes.

Stick a sharp knife into the florets – they should be tender but not mushy.
3 Drain the cauliflower and put it into an ovenproof dish. Pour the cheese sauce over it, sprinkle with cheese, then grill for 2–3 minutes until golden. Serve on its own or with a jacket potato, if you like.

TRY SOMETHING DIFFERENT
Make this with ½ head of cauliflower and ½ head of broccoli (pictured). Cut the stems off the florets, then peel and chop them into pieces the same size as the cauliflower and broccoli florets. They will take only about 4 minutes to cook until just tender. Make as above.

NUTRITION PER SERVING 383 cals | 24g fat (14g sats) | 20g carbs | 2.2g salt Ⓥ

Pasta and Gnocchi

Pasta

Endlessly versatile, inexpensive and quick to cook, pasta is incredibly popular. It is primarily a carbohydrate food, but it also provides protein, useful vitamins and some minerals. Certain types of pasta, notably those made with eggs, may contain as much as 13 per cent protein. Contrary to popular belief, pasta isn't particularly high in calories – it's the rich, creamy accompanying sauces that give some pasta dishes a high calorie value.

Fresh pasta

Pasta is surprisingly easy and very satisfying to make. Good home-made pasta has an excellent light texture and incomparable flavour – almost melting in the mouth. You need very little basic equipment – a rolling pin, metal pastry cutters, a sharp knife and a pastry wheel will suffice – but, if you intend to make pasta regularly, it is worth buying a pasta machine to take the hard work out of rolling and cutting the dough.

Pasta dough can be made either by hand, in a food processor with a dough attachment, or in a large mixer with a dough hook. Initially, it is probably best to make it by hand to learn how the dough should feel at each stage. The more you make fresh pasta, the easier it will be to judge the correct texture of the dough – it should be soft, not at all sticky, and with a good elasticity.

The best type of flour to use for making pasta is 00 or farino tipo 00. This very fine-textured soft wheat flour is available from larger supermarkets and delicatessens. Once you have mastered the basic pasta recipe, try making flavoured pastas; these are just as easy to make and taste especially good.

If you want to buy fresh pasta rather than making your own, find a good Italian delicatessen where it is freshly prepared on the premises. Commercially produced fresh pasta can be stodgy and disappointing – quite unlike home-made pasta.

Dried pasta

There is an extensive range of shapes, sizes and flavours available for dried pasta. The best are made from 100 per cent durum wheat (pasta di semola grano duro); some varieties include eggs (all'uova). Dried pasta is suitable for using with all the recipes in this chapter.

The choice of pasta is largely a matter of personal taste, but you will find that some shapes are more suited to particular sauces than others. Smooth-textured, slippery sauces are generally better served with long, fine pastas, such as spaghetti or linguine, whereas chunky sauces are better with short-shaped varieties. Shapes such as conchiglie (shells) and penne are ideal because they hold the sauce. Larger pasta shapes can be stuffed.

The names of pasta shapes often vary from one region of Italy to another, and new ones are constantly being introduced. Note that the suffix gives an indication of the size of the pasta: -oni suggests large, as in conchiglioni (large shells); -ette or -etti denotes small, as in spaghetti and cappelletti (small hats); while -ine or -ini means tiny, as in pastina (tiny soup pasta) and spaghettini, the finer version of spaghetti.

Storing pasta

Pasta is arguably the world's greatest industrial food product, and one of the few manufactured ingredients that is often better when made commercially than at home. Furthermore, fresh pasta is not 'better' than dried. It is just different. And most commercial fresh pasta is vastly inferior to dried. Many Italian cooks choose dried pasta over fresh – and the best dried pasta still comes from Italy.

Dried pasta has a long shelf life. Stored in an airtight container in a cool, dry place, it will keep for many months (or even years). Fresh pasta should be stored in the fridge and used within a few days.

Cooking pasta

All pasta should be cooked until al dente – tender yet firm to the bite, definitely not soft, and without a hard, uncooked centre. It is essential to cook pasta in plenty of fast-boiling water. If there is too little water, the pasta will cook unevenly and become stodgy. Allow 4 litres (7 pints) water and 1 tbsp salt to 500g (1lb 2oz) pasta. There's no need to add any oil. Bring the salted water to the boil in a large pan. Add the pasta to the fast-boiling water and stir once to prevent sticking. Cook until al dente.

Fresh pasta needs only the briefest of cooking, so watch it carefully. Fresh tagliatelle or spaghetti will take only about 1–2 minutes to cook. Stuffed pasta shapes, such as ravioli or tortelloni, need about 3 minutes to cook the filling through. Most dried pasta takes about 8–12 minutes. Use the pack instructions as a guideline, but the only way to determine when pasta is cooked is by tasting. Avoid overcooking at all costs.

As soon as the pasta is cooked, drain it in a colander or large strainer, then immediately add to the sauce, or it may start to stick together. When combining pasta with an oily sauce, hold back a few tablespoons of the cooking water; this helps to make a glossy coating sauce.

Quantities

It is difficult to give specific quantity guidelines for pasta, because there are so many factors, including the nature of the sauce and whether you are serving the pasta as a starter, lunch or main meal. Individual appetites for pasta seem to vary enormously too. As a very approximate guide, allow about 100–125g (3½–4oz) uncooked weight per person when cooking pasta.

It's not easy to weigh spaghetti to calculate the correct quantity to cook, but a spaghetti tool is a handy way of measuring it. Made of wood, plastic or metal it is a gauge with holes that correspond to different portion sizes. You line up the tool with the open end of the spaghetti pack and drop the spaghetti through the relevant hole. Alternatively, you can use the spaghetti gauge on this page by holding a small or large handful of strands against the portion circle. Once you have an idea of how much you need for the portions you regularly use, you'll soon be able to estimate the quantity just by holding the spaghetti in your hand.

Serving pasta

Pasta quickly loses its heat once drained, so have warmed serving plates or bowls ready. Toss the pasta with the sauce, butter or olive oil as soon as it is cooked, then transfer to the serving bowls. If Parmesan is the finishing touch, either grate it over the finished dish or shave off thin flakes, using a swivel potato peeler.

Gnocchi

Not actually a type of pasta, but often grouped with it, these little Italian potato dumplings are usually boiled for a few minutes, then served with butter or a sauce, or they can be coated in sauce and baked. Gnocchi are usually made from mashed potato and flour, rolled into ridged ovals. Other varieties include spinach and ricotta or Parmesan, semolina and pumpkin. Store in a plastic bag in the fridge. Use within a few days.

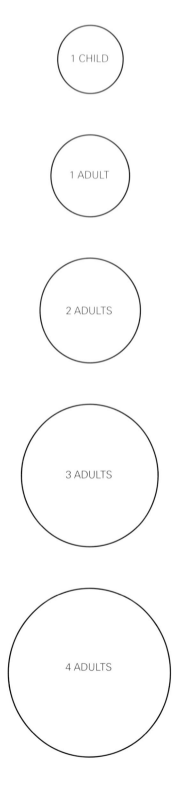

Basic Pasta Dough

Serves 4
Preparation time 5 minutes, plus resting
Cooking time 1–2 minutes

225g (8oz) 00 pasta flour, plus extra to dust
1 tsp salt
2 medium eggs, plus 1 medium egg yolk, beaten
1 tbsp extra virgin olive oil

1 Sift the flour and salt into a mound on a clean surface. Make a well in the centre and add the eggs, egg yolk, olive oil and 1 tbsp water.
2 Gently beat the eggs together with a fork, then gradually work in the flour, adding a little extra water if needed to form a soft but not sticky dough.
3 Transfer to a lightly floured surface and knead for about 5 minutes or until firm, smooth and elastic.
4 Form the dough into a flattish ball, wrap in clingfilm and leave to rest for at least 30 minutes.

TRY SOMETHING DIFFERENT

Flavoured pastas are easy to make and taste wonderful. Vegetable purées and flavoured pastes, such as sun-dried tomato and olive, make vibrant coloured pastas – note that some of the colour will be lost during cooking, without detriment to the flavour. Adapt the recipe above.
Herb Pasta Sift the flour and salt into a bowl and stir in 3 tbsp freshly chopped mixed herbs, such as basil, marjoram and parsley. Continue as for the basic pasta dough.
Olive Pasta Beat the eggs with 2 tbsp black olive paste before adding to the flour. Reduce the water to about 2 tsp.
Sun-dried Tomato Pasta Beat the eggs with 2 tbsp sun-dried tomato paste before adding to the flour. Reduce the water to about 2 tsp.
Spinach Pasta Blanch 50g (2oz) spinach leaves in a little boiling water until just wilted. Refresh under cold running water, then drain thoroughly and squeeze out all the excess water. Finely chop the spinach and add to the flour and salt, together with the remaining ingredients. Continue as for the basic pasta dough.

Rolling and shaping pasta

To use a pasta machine, feed small pieces of dough through the rollers two or three times, narrowing the space until the pasta is the correct thickness, then cut as required. If you do not have a pasta machine you can roll the dough out very thinly by hand on a clean surface. Keep lifting and rotating the dough as you roll to prevent it from sticking. For lasagne, trim the pasta sheets to neaten and cut into lengths. For tagliatelle, fold the sheet of dough to make a cigar shape, then cut into strips. For stuffed pastas, roll out the dough to form a long thin sheet. Lay it on a clean surface dusted with semolina flour, cut in half and cover with a damp cloth. Dust the surface with semolina flour. Brush one sheet of pasta with beaten egg. Top with heaped teaspoons of filling, set 1cm (½in) apart. Cover this with a second pasta sheet. Starting at the middle, press down gently around the mounds of filling to expel any air trapped inside. Cut around each mound with a pastry wheel. Lay them on trays dusted with semolina flour and leave for 30 minutes to dry. Don't chill or the pasta will become sticky.

Cook's Tip

To make pasta in a food processor, sift the flour and salt into the bowl and add the eggs, egg yolk, olive oil and 1 tbsp water (together with any flavourings). Whiz until the dough just begins to come together, adding the extra water if necessary to form a soft but not sticky dough. Wrap in clingfilm and rest (as above).

NUTRITION PER SERVING 280 cals | 9g fat (2g sats) | 42g carbs | 1.3g salt Ⓥ

Spaghetti alla Carbonara

Serves 4
Preparation time 10 minutes
Cooking time 10 minutes

2 tbsp olive oil
25g (1oz) butter
125–150g (4–5oz) smoked pancetta (see Cook's Tips),
 rind removed, cut into strips
1 garlic clove, halved
3 medium eggs
2 tbsp dry white wine
40g (1½oz) freshly grated Parmesan
40g (1½oz) freshly grated Pecorino
400g (14oz) dried spaghetti
salt and ground black pepper
2 tbsp freshly chopped parsley to garnish

1 Heat the olive oil and butter in a heavy-based pan.
Add the pancetta and garlic, and cook over a medium heat
for 3–4 minutes until the pancetta begins to crisp. Turn off
the heat; discard the garlic.
2 Meanwhile beat the eggs in a bowl with the wine and
half of each of the cheeses. Season with salt and pepper.
3 Cook the spaghetti in a large pan of boiling salted water,
according to the pack instructions, until al dente.
4 When the spaghetti is almost cooked, gently reheat the
pancetta in the pan.
5 Drain the spaghetti thoroughly, then return it to the
pan. Immediately add the egg mixture together with the
pancetta. Take the pan off the heat and toss well; the eggs
will cook in the residual heat to form a light creamy sauce.
Add the remaining cheeses, toss lightly and serve garnished
with parsley.

Cook's Tips
• If smoked pancetta is unobtainable, use smoked bacon
 instead, increasing the quantity to 175–225g (6–8oz).
• If Pecorino is unobtainable, simply double the quantity
 of Parmesan.

NUTRITION PER SERVING 750 cals | 38g fat (12g sats) | 74g carbs | 2.2g salt

Spaghetti Bolognese

Serves 6
Preparation time 15 minutes
Cooking time 40 minutes

500g (1lb 2oz) dried spaghetti
50g (2oz) Parmesan, freshly grated

For the Bolognese sauce
2 tbsp olive oil
1 onion, finely chopped
2 garlic cloves, crushed
450g (1lb) extra-lean minced beef
2 tbsp sun-dried tomato paste
300ml (½ pint) red wine
400g can chopped tomatoes
125g (4oz) chestnut mushrooms, sliced
2 tbsp Worcestershire sauce
salt and ground black pepper

1 To make the Bolognese sauce, heat the oil in a large pan, add the onion and fry over a medium heat for 10 minutes or until softened and golden. Add the garlic and cook for 1 minute.
2 Add the minced beef and brown evenly, using a wooden spoon to break up the pieces. Stir in the tomato paste and the red wine, cover and bring to the boil. Add the tomatoes, mushrooms and Worcestershire sauce, and season with pepper. Bring back to the boil, reduce the heat and simmer for 20 minutes.
3 Cook the spaghetti in a large pan of boiling salted water, according to the pack instructions, until al dente. Drain well, then return it to the pan. Add the Bolognese sauce and toss to mix together. Season with salt and pepper to taste.
4 Divide among warmed plates and sprinkle with the Parmesan to serve.

TRY SOMETHING DIFFERENT
Add 125g (4oz) chopped rinded smoked streaky bacon with the mince, brown, then stir in 200g (7oz) chopped chicken livers. Cook for 3 minutes before adding the tomato paste, then continue as above.

NUTRITION PER SERVING 510 cals | 12g fat (4g sats) | 67g carbs | 1.5g salt

Spaghetti with Clams

Serves 4
Preparation time 10 mins
Cooking time 25 minutes

2 tbsp olive oil
2 shallots, finely sliced
3 garlic cloves, thinly sliced
150ml (¼ pint) dry white wine
400g can chopped tomatoes
350g (12oz) spaghetti
1kg (2¼lb) fresh clams, scrubbed
salt and ground black pepper
1 tbsp freshly chopped parsley to garnish

1 Heat the oil in a very large pan and gently fry the
shallots for 5 minutes or until soft. Add the garlic and cook
for 1 minute.
2 Add the wine and bubble until reduced by half, then add
the tomatoes along with half a can of water. Season with
salt and pepper. Bring to the boil, then reduce the heat and
simmer for 15 minutes or until reduced slightly.
3 Meanwhile, cook the spaghetti in a large pan of
boiling salted water, according to the pack instructions,
until al dente.
4 Add the clams to the tomato sauce, cover and simmer
for 1–2 minutes until they have opened – discard any that
stay closed. Season with salt and pepper to taste.
5 Drain the pasta and toss into the clam sauce. Serve
garnished with parsley.

NUTRITION PER SERVING 488 cals | 8g fat (1g sats) | 71g carbs | 4.4g salt

Pasta with Anchovies, Tomatoes and Olives

Serves 4
Preparation time 15 minutes
Cooking time 20–25 minutes

50g can anchovy fillets in oil
2 garlic cloves, crushed
4 sun-dried tomatoes, drained and roughly chopped
400g can chopped tomatoes
500g (1lb 2oz) dried spaghetti
200g (7oz) pitted black olives, roughly chopped
2 tbsp capers, drained
2–3 tbsp freshly chopped flat-leafed parsley
ground black pepper

1 Drain the oil from the anchovies into a large pan. Heat
the oil, then add the garlic and cook for 1 minute. Add the
anchovies and sun-dried tomatoes and cook, stirring, for a
further 1 minute. Add the canned tomatoes and bring to
the boil. Season well with salt and pepper and simmer for
10–15 minutes.
2 Meanwhile, cook the spaghetti in a large pan of
boiling salted water, according to the pack instructions,
until al dente.
3 Stir the olives and capers into the tomato sauce. Drain
the spaghetti thoroughly, reserving about 4 tbsp of the
cooking water, then return it to the pan.
4 Add the tomato sauce and chopped parsley to the pasta
and toss well to mix, thinning the sauce with the reserved
cooking water, if necessary. Serve at once.

Cook's Tip
Spaghetti takes its name from the Italian word *spago,*
meaning string.

NUTRITION PER SERVING   620 cals | 12g fat (2g sats) | 96g carbs | 4.5g salt

Tuna Pasta

Serves 4
Preparation time 10 minutes
Cooking time 30 minutes

225g can tuna steak in olive oil
1 onion, finely sliced
1 garlic clove, chopped
2 × 400g cans chopped tomatoes
500g (1lb 2oz) dried penne pasta
50g can anchovy fillets in oil, drained
  and chopped
2 tbsp small capers
2 tbsp basil leaves, roughly torn
salt and ground black pepper

1 Drain the oil from the tuna into a
pan and put the tuna to one side.
2 Heat the tuna oil, then add the
sliced onion and fry over a low heat
for 10 minutes or until softened but
not browned. Add the chopped garlic

and cook for 1 minute.
3 Add the tomatoes and stir well.
Season generously with salt and
pepper, then simmer over a medium
heat for 15 minutes to reduce and
thicken the sauce.
4 Meanwhile, cook the pasta in a
large pan of boiling salted water,
according to the pack instructions,
until al dente.
5 Flake the tuna and add to the
tomato sauce with the anchovies,
capers and basil leaves. Mix well.
6 Drain the pasta well, return to the
pan and add the tuna sauce. Toss
everything together to mix and serve
immediately in warmed bowls.

NUTRITION PER SERVING 650 cals |
16g fat (2g sats) | 102g carbs | 2.3g salt

Penne with Smoked Salmon

Serves 4
Preparation time 5 minutes
Cooking time 10–15 minutes

350g (12oz) penne or other short
  tubular pasta
200ml (7fl oz) half-fat crème fraîche
150g (5oz) smoked salmon, roughly
  chopped
20g (¾oz) fresh dill, finely chopped
salt and ground black pepper
lemon wedges to serve (optional)

1 Cook the pasta in a large pan of
boiling salted water, according to
the pack instructions, until al dente.
Drain well.
2 Put the crème fraîche into a large
bowl. Add the smoked salmon and
chopped dill, season well with salt
and pepper and mix together. Gently
stir into the drained penne and serve
immediately with lemon wedges, if
you like, to squeeze over the top.

Cook's Tip
Penne means quill, and reflects the
shape of this pasta. Varieties include
smooth, ridged and flavoured.

NUTRITION PER SERVING 432 cals |
11g fat (6g sats) | 67g carbs | 1.7g salt

Macaroni Cheese

Serves 4
Preparation time 10 minutes
Cooking time 15 minutes

225g (8oz) short-cut macaroni
50g (2oz) butter
50g (2oz) plain flour
900ml (1½ pints) milk
½ tsp freshly grated nutmeg or mustard powder
225g (8oz) mature Cheddar, grated (see Vegetarian Cheeses,
  page 228)
3 tbsp fresh white or wholemeal breadcrumbs
salt and ground black pepper

1 Cook the macaroni in a large pan of boiling salted water, according to the pack instructions, until al dente.
2 Meanwhile, melt the butter in a pan, stir in the flour and cook, stirring, for 1 minute. Remove from the heat and gradually stir in the milk. Bring to the boil and cook, stirring, until the sauce thickens. Remove from the heat. Season with salt and pepper to taste, and add the nutmeg or mustard.
3 Drain the macaroni and add to the sauce, together with three-quarters of the cheese. Mix well, then turn into an ovenproof dish.
4 Preheat the grill to high. Mix together the breadcrumbs and remaining cheese and sprinkle over the macaroni. Put under the grill for 2–3 minutes until golden brown on top and bubbling. Serve hot.

NUTRITION PER SERVING 680 cals | 34g fat (21g sats) | 67g carbs | 2g salt Ⓥ

Spinach and Ricotta Cannelloni

Serves 4
Preparation time 25 minutes
Cooking time 1 hour 10 minutes

1 tbsp olive oil
1 small onion, chopped
1 bay leaf
1 garlic clove, crushed
400g can chopped tomatoes
300g (11oz) spinach, coarse stalks removed
2 × 250g cartons ricotta cheese (see Vegetarian Cheeses
  on page 228)
1 large egg
25g (1oz) freshly grated Parmesan
freshly grated nutmeg
15 cannelloni tubes
125g mozzarella ball, roughly torn
salt and ground black pepper
fresh basil leaves to garnish (optional)

1 Heat the oil in a pan and gently fry the onion with the
bay leaf for 10 minutes or until softened but not coloured.
Add the garlic and fry for 1 minute. Pour in the tomatoes
along with half a can of cold water, bring to the boil, then
simmer for 20 minutes or until slightly thickened.
2 Meanwhile, wash the spinach and put into a large pan
set over a low heat. Cover the pan and cook the spinach
for 2 minutes or until just wilted. Drain and cool under
running water. When cool enough to handle, squeeze out
the excess moisture and roughly chop.
3 Preheat the oven to 180°C (160°C fan oven) mark 4
and lightly oil a baking dish. Mix together the ricotta, egg,
Parmesan and spinach with a grating of nutmeg and season
with plenty of salt and ground black pepper. Spoon or pipe
into the cannelloni tubes and put into the dish in one layer.
4 Pour the tomato sauce over the pasta, then dot with
the mozzarella. Bake for 30–40 minutes until golden and
bubbling. Scatter with the basil, if you like, and serve.

Cook's Tip
Usually made from egg pasta, cannelloni are large, broad
tubes designed to be stuffed, coated in sauce and baked.

NUTRITION PER SERVING 409 cals | 14g fat (7g sats) | 53g carbs | 1.5g salt Ⓥ

Classic Lasagne

Serves 6
Preparation 40 minutes
Cooking time 45 minutes (without the Bolognese Sauce)

1 quantity Bolognese Sauce (see page 244)
butter to grease
350g (12oz) fresh lasagne, or 225g (8oz) 'no need to pre-
   cook' lasagne sheets, about 12–15 sheets (see Cook's Tip)
1 quantity of Béchamel Sauce (see page 16)
3 tbsp freshly grated Parmesan
salad leaves to serve

1 Preheat the oven to 180°C (160°C fan oven) mark 4.
Spoon one-third of the Bolognese Sauce over the base of a
greased 2.3 litre (4 pint) ovenproof dish. Cover with a layer
of lasagne sheets, then a layer of béchamel sauce. Repeat
these layers twice more, finishing with a layer of béchamel.
2 Sprinkle the Parmesan over the top and stand the dish
on a baking sheet. Cook in the oven for 45 minutes or until
well browned and bubbling. Serve with salad leaves.

Cook's Tip
If using 'no need to pre-cook' dried lasagne, add a little
extra stock or water to the sauce.

NUTRITION PER SERVING 320 cals | 17g fat (8g sats) | 30g carbs | 1g salt (V)

Gnocchi with Zesty Ricotta

Serves 4
Preparation 30 minutes
Cooking time 30 minutes

600g (1lb 5oz) floury potatoes,
  peeled and halved
1 medium egg
125g (4oz) plain flour, plus extra to dust
1 tbsp olive oil, plus extra to drizzle
50g–75g (2–3oz) ham slices, torn
about 40g (1½oz) rocket
125g (4oz) ricotta cheese, crumbled
1 red chilli, seeded and finely chopped
finely pared zest and juice of 1 lemon
salt and ground black pepper

1 Put the potatoes in a large pan,
cover with cold water and add a little
salt. Bring to the boil, then cook for
15 minutes or until tender. Drain,
then return to the pan and cook over
a low heat for a few minutes to dry off.

2 While still warm, mash the potatoes
until completely smooth, then tip into
a bowl and leave to cool for 5 minutes.
Stir in the egg and some seasoning,
then gradually knead in the flour until
just combined. Divide the dough into
four pieces. On a lightly floured
surface, roll each section into a long
sausage about 1.5cm (⅔in) wide.
Cut each into 2.5cm (1in) pieces.
3 Heat the oil in a large frying pan.
Fry the ham for 2–3 minutes until
crisp, then lift out and set aside.
4 Fry the gnocchi in batches for 5
minutes until golden, then season and
toss the rocket and ham through it.
Crumble the ricotta over, then scatter
on the chilli and lemon zest. Drizzle
with lemon juice and olive oil and serve.

NUTRITION PER SERVING 334 cals |
9g fat (3g sats) | 49g carbs | 0.5g salt

Quick Creamy Gnocchi

Serves 4
Preparation time 15 minutes
Cooking time 15 minutes

2 tbsp olive oil
700g (1½lb) fresh gnocchi
200g (7oz) cream cheese
200g (7oz) frozen peas
finely grated zest of ½ lemon
2 tbsp freshly chopped chives
100–200ml (3½–7fl oz) milk,
  depending on consistency of the sauce
40g (1½oz) Cheddar, grated (see
  Vegetarian Cheeses, page 228)
40g (1½oz) fresh white breadcrumbs
salt and ground black pepper
crisp green salad to serve

1 Preheat the grill to medium. Heat
the oil in a large deep frying pan over
a high heat and add the gnocchi.
Fry for about 10 minutes, stirring
occasionally, until the gnocchi are
turning golden and softening.
2 Stir in the cream cheese, peas,
lemon zest, most of the chives, the
milk and some salt and pepper,
adding a little more milk if you prefer
a looser mixture. Heat through, then
transfer to a flameproof serving dish.
Sprinkle the cheese, breadcrumbs and
remaining chives on top.
3 Grill until golden and bubbling.
Serve immediately with a crisp
green salad.

NUTRITION PER SERVING 793 cals |
35g fat (18g sats) | 98g carbs | 2.2g salt Ⓥ

Rice, Grains, Pulses and Seeds

Rice and Grains

In many countries, rice and grains are staple foods. They provide energy and useful amounts of protein, fibre, B vitamins, calcium and iron. There are many varieties of rice and grain, each with its own characteristics, and it is important to choose the correct type for any specific dish. Most grains can be stored for several years, making them the perfect standby storecupboard ingredients. Keep them in a cool, dry place.

Rice

Some rice varieties cook to a separate firm texture, some to a creamy consistency, others to a sticky mass. Brown rice is the whole rice grain with only the tough outer husk removed. Like other unrefined grains, it is richer in fibre, protein and B vitamins than refined rice. Because the bran is retained, brown rice has a good chewy texture and nutty flavour, and it takes longer to cook than white rice.

Long-grain white rice is the most common general-purpose rice and there are many varieties, including Patna and Carolina. The cooked rice grains are separate, dry and fluffy and suitable as an accompaniment to many dishes.

Other rices are used for their special qualities, such as Arborio, a short-grained rice that is used to make creamy risottos, and glutinous rice, which is cooked to make sticky rice used in Chinese and South-east Asian cuisines.

Cooking rice

Some of the speciality rices are cooked in specific ways: hot liquid is added gradually to Arborio when making a risotto, for example; pudding rice is usually baked slowly in the oven; glutinous rice is steamed; but in general all long-grain varieties can be cooked in the same way – by boiling in plenty of water or by the absorption method. In general, the absorption method works better. Check the pack instructions for suggested cooking times and methods.

Most rice is bought pre-packed and does not require washing, but if you do buy it loose, wash thoroughly. With some varieties, such as basmati, rinsing is advisable to remove the excess starch. To rinse rice, put it into a sieve and hold under cold running water until the water runs clear, picking out any tiny bits of grit. Don't wash risotto rice before cooking, as it is the starch that lends its essential creamy texture.

To cook rice by the absorption method, measure it in a measuring jug and note the volume. Tip the rice into a heavy-based pan and add twice its volume of cold water. Add salt, bring to the boil, cover with a tight-fitting lid and reduce the heat to low. Cook until the water is absorbed and the rice is tender – allow 15–20 minutes for white rice, 40–45 minutes for brown rice. Don't lift the pan lid during cooking. (Alternatively, just add rice to a large pan of fast-boiling salted water, bring back to the boil, stir once and cook, uncovered, until tender. White rice generally takes 10–12 minutes; brown rice usually cooks in 35–40 minutes. Drain the rice in a sieve and rinse with a kettleful of boiling water.)

To impart extra flavour, cook rice with herbs or spices. For saffron rice, add a large pinch of saffron to the cooking water. For spiced rice, add a cinnamon stick, 1 clove, a blade of mace and a bay leaf to the pan; discard the spices once the rice is cooked. For herb-flavoured rice, add 1–2 tbsp freshly chopped parsley, coriander, thyme or mixed herbs to the cooking liquid. Rice can also be cooked in stock rather than water for extra flavour.

Grains

Wheat, barley, corn, oats and rye are the edible seeds of different grasses. Probably the most familiar grains are those from wheat, corn and rye that are ground into flours, but other grains are becoming popular to cook as wholesome and sustaining side dishes, such as barley, wheat berries and quinoa (a seed-like grain with a high protein content). Buckwheat is sold as a grain, although it is actually the seed of a plant related to rhubarb. Oats are one of the more commonly eaten grains used in breakfast cereals such as muesli and cooked into porridge. Some grains are high in the protein gluten, and a significant number of the population is sensitive to this so need to avoid foods that contains it. Wheat is especially high in gluten and lower levels are found in barley and rye; very low levels are also present in oats.

Storing rice and grains

Direct sunlight and high temperatures can cause grains to become stale, losing their flavour and nutritional value. Keep grains in a cool, dark, dry cupboard in a sealed packet or airtight container and use within the use-by date.

Flour

There are numerous types of flour, all made by finely grinding grains to make a fine or medium-fine powder. Flours may be white or brown, depending on whether the husk and germ have been removed before grinding.

Pulses and Seeds

The term 'pulse' is used to describe all of the various beans, peas and lentils that have been preserved by drying. They are highly nutritious, especially when eaten with grains, such as couscous, pasta, rice or bread. Pulses and seeds are rich in nutrients and are a good source of vegetarian protein. However, most do not constitute a whole protein (containing all eight amino acids) and need to be combined with grains or cereals to make up full protein. Pulses and seeds are also a good source of fibre, B vitamins, potassium and iron.

Storing pulses

Pulses should be stored in airtight containers in a cool, dry cupboard. They keep well, but after about six months their skins start to toughen, and they take progressively longer to cook the longer they are stored.

Preparing and cooking pulses

The weight of dried beans approximately doubles during soaking and cooking, so if a recipe calls for 225g (8oz) cooked beans, you would need to start with 125g (4oz) dried weight. Once cooked, pulses keep well in the fridge for two to three days.

With the exception of lentils and split peas, pulses need to be soaked overnight in plenty of cold water. The following day, drain off the water before cooking. Cooking dried pulses is quite a lengthy process. For some pulses, notably red kidney beans, aduki beans, black-eyed beans, black beans, soy beans and borlotti beans, it is essential to pre-boil the beans before cooking to destroy any toxins present on the skins. Put the beans in a pan, cover with plenty of fresh cold water, bring to the boil over a high heat and boil vigorously for 10 minutes. Although pre-boiling isn't essential for other dried pulses, it does no harm and saves the need to remember which ones require it.

After the initial fast-boiling, lower the heat, then cover and simmer until tender. To enhance the flavour, a bouquet garni (1 bay leaf, a few fresh parsley and thyme sprigs) and/ or 1 or 2 garlic cloves can be added to the cooking water. Salt should only be added 10–15 minutes before the end of the cooking time; if it is added at the start, it will toughen the skins.

The cooking time is determined by the type of pulse, the soaking time and, above all, by the length of time the pulses have been stored, so you need to watch and assess when the pulses are ready. As an approximate guide: red lentils cook in about 20 minutes; green lentils take 30–45 minutes; split peas require 45–60 minutes; aduki, black-eyed, borlotti, butter, pinto, flageolet and haricot beans need 1–1½ hours; black beans and red kidney beans take 1½–2 hours; chickpeas require 2–3 hours; while soya beans need 3–4 hours.

(Note that soya beans must always be pre-boiled for 1 hour, to destroy a substance they contain that prevents the body from absorbing protein.)

Using canned pulses

Canned pulses are a convenient, quick alternative to cooking your own, and most supermarkets stock a wide range. A 400g can is roughly equivalent to 75g (3oz) dried beans and contains about 150ml (¼ pint) liquid. Always drain canned pulses, then rinse and drain thoroughly again before using.

Seeds

Seeds are an excellent, highly nutritious vegetarian ingredient, adding texture, flavour and interest to a variety of foods, including breads, cakes and salads. Sunflower seeds, poppy seeds, sesame seeds and pumpkin seeds are especially popular. To enhance their flavour, toast in a dry frying pan for a few minutes, shaking the pan constantly.

Sprouted beans and seeds

These are rich in nutrients and lend a nutty taste and crunchy texture to salads and stir-fries. Fresh bean sprouts are available from most supermarkets. Many beans and seeds can be sprouted at home, though it is important to buy ones that are specifically produced for sprouting – from a healthfood shop or other reliable source. Mung beans, aduki beans, alfalfa seeds and fenugreek are all suitable. (See also Bean Sprout, page 278.)

Rice and Corn

Basmati rice
Slender and fragrant, this long-grain rice has a good flavour and texture and is available as white and brown. Serve as an accompaniment to curries and other dishes or in pilaus. Rinse the grains well in cold water, then add two-and-a-half times its volume of boiling water and a pinch of salt. Cover the pan tightly and simmer for 12 minutes for white rice or 20–25 minutes for brown until all the water has been absorbed, then leave to stand for 5 minutes.

Glutinous rice
Used in Chinese and South-east Asian dishes, this glutinous, short, fat rice is often called sticky or sweet rice because the cooked grains are sticky. It may be black or white and can be sweetened and served with fruit as a dessert. In Japan, glutinous rice is often served with savoury dishes as it can be eaten easily with chopsticks. Wash in cold water, then leave to stand for 1 hour. Simmer, covered, in an equal volume of boiling water until the liquid is absorbed.

Long-grain rice
These long, narrow grains may be white or brown. Brown rice contains the husk and bran and has a nutty flavour and chewy texture. White rice has been milled to remove the husk. It is tender and delicately flavoured, but lacks the fibre and nutritional benefits of brown rice. Serve with curries and stews, in pilaus or salads, and in stuffings for vegetables and meat. Easy-cook rice is long-grain rice that has been steam-treated to harden the grain so they don't stick together.

Paella rice
Sometimes referred to as Valencia rice, paella rice is fat and starchy. There are three main varieties: bomba, bahia and grano largo. It is usually cooked gently in a large, flat paella pan with ingredients including onions, garlic, saffron, tomatoes, stock, sausage, chicken and rabbit and/or shellfish. A traditional paella is not stirred during cooking but shaken occasionally. It is ready when the grains have plumped up and are slightly sticky and all the liquid has been absorbed.

Risotto rice
There are three main varieties of the fat, high-starch rice used to make Italian risotto: Arborio, carnaroli and vialone nano. The grains are simmered and stirred frequently during cooking to release their starches into the cooking liquid and to produce a rich, creamy-textured risotto. It is often cooked with garlic, onions, white wine and stock, then flavoured with Parmesan or a variety of other additions.

Thai fragrant rice
Also called jasmine rice, this white rice is prized in Thailand for its fragrance, flavour and tender, slightly sticky texture. It is cooked in water or coconut milk, and served with South-east Asian dishes, and can also be cooked in milk or coconut milk with spices and sugar to make a rice pudding. Cook with double the volume of boiling water; cover the pan tightly and simmer for 12 minutes or until all the water has been absorbed. Leave to stand for 5 minutes.

Wild rice
Not actually a rice, but the grain of a wild marsh grass, wild rice is dark brown-black with a rich, complex, nutty flavour and firm texture. It is costly to buy and is often sold in mixes with long-grain or basmati rice. Most wild rice is now farmed and makes a delightful and luxurious treat. Red rice is a natural hybrid of wild rice and has a red-brown colour and nutty flavour. Boil wild or red rice in salted water for 30 minutes or until tender.

Cornmeal
The white or yellow colour of cornmeal depends on the colour of the corn (maize) from which it is ground but there is no other difference. Most cornmeal is ground to remove all the bran and germ, and it can be fine, medium or coarse. It is used to make a quick yeast-free bread, sometimes for cakes, muffins and biscuits, and with flour to make bread. Mexican tortillas can be made solely with cornmeal. It is also used to coat foods for deep-frying, to give a crunchy crust.

Polenta
Italian cooks prepare polenta by boiling cornmeal (usually fine) in water with salt to make a thick purée. It is served both as a staple and a side dish, either plain or with cheese stirred through it. It may also be left to cool until firm, then sliced and pan-fried, griddled or baked. Traditional polenta should be added to boiling salted water, then stirred constantly for 45 minutes or until thick and tender. Quick-cook varieties can be cooked in only a few minutes.

Corn and Wheat

Bulgur wheat
Although sometimes referred to as cracked wheat, bulgur is a completely different product. It has a pleasantly chewy texture and nutty taste, and is available in various grades, from fine to coarse. Popular in Middle Eastern cooking, bulgur wheat is used in tabbouleh and several other herby salads. It can also be used in pilaus or as an accompaniment. Soak in boiling, salted water for 20 minutes or until tender, then drain and use as required.

Couscous
These tiny, pasta-like pellets are made from moistened, rolled grains of semolina. Available as fine, medium and giant, it is served with spicy stews and to make salads. The giant variety is known as Israeli couscous, pearl couscous and *moghrabieh*. You may also find barley and maize varieties, and flavoured brands. Traditionally, the grains are soaked, then steamed over a pan of stew. Quick-cook varieties can just be soaked in boiling water for 5 minutes.

Cracked wheat
Uncooked wheat berries are crushed to produce cracked wheat. It has a nutty flavour and chewy texture similar to whole wheat and can be served as an accompaniment or used in salads and added to soups, stews and casseroles. Boil cracked wheat in salted water until tender.

Grits
Popular in the southern states of the US, hominy grits, or grits, are the American version of polenta. They are made from coarsely ground white or yellow maize, boiled in water to make a thin, pale porridge. Grits is usually served as a savoury breakfast food, often with eggs and sausage. They can also be flavoured with cheese and baked to make the dish, cheese grits. Boil grits in water with a pinch of salt.

Popcorn
Golden popcorn is a type of specially bred corn kernel. When heated, the starch inside expands rapidly, creating a white, fluffy ball. Popcorn is eaten as a snack food, sprinkled with salt, tossed in butter or drizzled with honey, syrup or caramel. The unpopped kernels are also referred to as popping corn. Heat a little oil in a pan with enough popcorn to cover the base in a single layer. Cover tightly and cook at medium-high heat until it stops popping.

Semolina
Pale yellow semolina is made from durum wheat, ground either coarsely or finely. It is used to make sweet milk puddings and is added to cake and biscuit mixtures and some breads.

Wheat bran
Bran is the thin, brown, papery outer layer of the wheat grain. Wheat bran is not nutritious, but it provides a valuable source of fibre. Added in small quantities to breads, cereals and some cakes and biscuits, it adds a rich brown colour and wholesome, slightly nutty flavour. Bran contains phytates, which can prevent minerals, such as calcium and iron, being absorbed into the body, so should not be consumed in excess or routinely added to food. Use sparingly.

Wheat flakes
Whole grains are steamed to soften them and then flattened by rollers to produce wheat flakes. They are added to breakfast cereals, such as muesli, and can be sprinkled over loaves before baking or added to fruit crumble mixtures. Malted wheat flakes, made from grains that have briefly germinated, have a darker colour and richer, slightly sweeter, fruitier flavour. Also known as rolled wheat.

Whole wheat
Also called wheat berries, these small, golden-brown grains of husked wheat are chewy and have a nutty taste when cooked. They are good in soups, stews, casseroles, pilaus and can be sprinkled over bread before baking. Soak overnight in cold water, then boil in salted water for 1 hour until tender. The processed form requires no pre-soaking and cooks more quickly. Wheat germ is the highly nutritious tiny embryo of a wholewheat grain from which the grain will sprout.

Flour

Wheat flour

The most widely used type of flour, wheat flour has a high gluten content – the substance that gives bread its structure and elasticity – making it ideal for baking breads, cakes and biscuits. It is also used for pastry, pasta, crumbles and batters, to thicken sauces and soups and to coat meat and fish before frying.

Plain white flour By far the most versatile of all wheat flours, white flour can be used for most cooking purposes (apart from bread-making or pasta). It is generally called plain or all-purpose flour.

Wholemeal flour Made from wholewheat grains, this flour is pale brown with a slightly coarse texture and a nutty flavour. It is denser than white flour.

Self-raising flour Usually made from white flour with the addition of baking powder. Self-raising flour is used primarily for cakes and biscuits.

Strong bread flour Specifically produced for making bread. Strong flour contains high levels of gluten, which improve the elasticity of the dough so that air is trapped inside as it rises. The flour may be white, brown (a mixture of white and wholemeal), wholemeal or Granary (with malted wheat flakes).

Chapati flour Also known as ata, this fine wholemeal wheat flour is used to make Indian flatbreads.

Tipo 00 Also known as farina bianca, this fine white Italian flour is used to make pasta.

Other flours

Arrowroot A white starch powder from the maranta plant, arrowroot becomes clear when dissolved in liquid. It is used as a thickener for desserts and fruit sauces.

Barley flour A pale, mildly flavoured flour, barley flour has a low gluten content and is usually combined with wheat flour to make soft-textured breads.

Buckwheat flour This grey-brown flour has a distinctively earthy taste and is traditionally used to make blini and pancakes, especially traditional Breton crêpes.

Chestnut flour Made from ground sweet chestnuts, this pale, sweet and nutty flour is used in cakes, such as Italian castagnaccio, biscuits and bread.

Chickpea flour Also known as gram flour and besan, chickpea flour is a pale, creamy yellow flour with a nutty and slightly bitter flavour. It is used to make batter for Indian-style fritters such as pakora, or to thicken savoury sauces.

Cornflour Pure white, and much finer than wheat flour, cornflour is ground from the white part of the corn kernel. It is used to thicken soups, sauces and gravies, and added in small quantities to desserts such as pavlova to give the meringue a slightly chewy consistency. As a thickener, cornflour is blended with a small amount of cold liquid, then added towards the end of cooking. It is wheat- and gluten-free (although gluten-intolerant people should always check the packaging to ensure there are no traces).

Millet flour Pale yellow millet flour has a mild, slightly sweet flavour. Low in gluten, it is best combined with wheat flour to make crumbly breads and cakes.

Rice flour This flour is gluten-free and can be used as a thickener. Finely ground rice flour is used in Asia to make doughs, dumpling wrappers, cakes and sweets.

Potato flour This fine, white, soft flour is gluten-free and favoured by those on a gluten-free diet for making cakes. It gives a spongy result. Potato flour is best used in conjunction with other flours.

Rye flour This greyish-brown flour has a distinctive, slightly sharp flavour. It is widely used in Russia, Scandinavia and Germany to make dense, dark, rye breads.

Spelt flour Ground from a type of wheat that has been cultivated since the Bronze Age, spelt flour has a slightly nuttier flavour than ordinary wheat flour. Use alone or blend with wheat flour in cakes and breads.

Soya flour This fine white flour, ground from partially cooked soya beans, is gluten-free with a high protein content. It can be used with other flours to make cakes, biscuits and bread.

Other Grains

Barley
The grains of pearl barley, the most common, have been husked, steamed and polished. They have a delicate, sweet flavour and a slightly chewy texture. Add to soups, salads and stews, or serve as a side dish. Barley can also be cooked like risotto. Pot barley is used in the same way but it needs longer cooking as it has less of the husk removed. Add pearl barley to soups and stews, or boil in salted water for 50 minutes until tender. Soak pot barley overnight, then cook for 1–2 hours.

Buckwheat
Not in fact a cereal or grass, buckwheat has triangular seeds and is widely used in Eastern European and Ashkenazi Jewish cooking. Sold toasted or plain and has a nutty, flavour and soft texture. It is traditionally cooked into a porridge known as kasha, and served as an accompaniment to lamb and beef pot roasts and stews. Toast plain buckwheat in a dry frying pan for a few minutes, then simmer in stock or salted water for 10–20 minutes, until tender.

Millet
This small, round, mildly flavoured pale-brown grain is widely eaten in some European countries. Millet can be cooked with milk and sugar into a sweet 'porridge' rather like rice pudding, or added to soups, stews and pilaus. Millet flakes can be used in place of millet, or added to muesli or multigrain breads. Toast millet grains in a dry frying pan for a few minutes before simmering in liquid until tender.

Oats
Sold mainly as rolled oats and oatmeal, pinhead oatmeal is the coarsest grade and is used in haggis and for making Scottish porridge, although many people now use rolled oats. Finer grades of oatmeal are often combined with wheat flour to make breads, cakes such as parkin, and biscuits, or for coating herring and other oily fish before frying. Rolled oats are the main ingredient in flapjacks and can be added to breads, cakes, biscuits and cereals such as muesli.

Quinoa
This South American grain is the only grain to contain all eight amino acids and can therefore be considered a complete protein. The tiny round grains swell up when cooked and have a mildly nutty taste with a firm, slightly slippery texture. Quinoa can be used in pilaus, salads and baked dishes, as well as in stuffings for vegetables. Rinse before using. Simmer in boiling water for 20 minutes or until tender.

Spelt
A type of wheat that has been cultivated since the Bronze Age, spelt has slender golden grains. It is often more readily tolerated by those who cannot eat wheat or gluten due to a food intolerance. With a slightly chewy and firm texture, spelt can be cooked and used in the same way as whole wheat, in soups, stews and pilaus.

Tapioca
Derived from the vegetable root cassava, this starchy product consists of small, round, pearly white granules. Tapioca is used in South-east Asia, India and Brazil to make sweet desserts, cooked with milk and sugar rather like rice pudding. The pearls become extremely soft with cooking. Some recipes recommend soaking the grains first, but others simmer tapioca in milk with sugar, and often spices, until tender.

Pulses

Aduki bean
Popular in Japanese cooking, these have a smooth texture and distinctive, slightly sweet flavour. They are most often used to make sweet dishes, such as cooked to a purée with sugar and used as a filling for pancakes, or wrapped around rice balls to make the Japanese sweet rice cakes, *ohagi*. They can also be used in savoury dishes, added to stews, stir-fries and salads. Soak beans overnight in cold water. Drain, then boil in fresh, unsalted water for 1½ hours or until tender.

Black bean
Black beans have a distinctive, slightly sweet, earthy flavour. They are good added to soups, stews and salads, and can be cooked with spices to make purées. Soak dried black beans overnight in cold water. Drain, then boil rapidly in fresh, unsalted water for 15 minutes. Drain, then boil in fresh, unsalted water for 1 hour or until tender. Note: black beans contain toxic substances (see Kidney Bean, opposite).

Black-eyed bean
Also known as black-eyed peas and cow peas, these creamy white beans have a distinctive black mark where the bean was once attached to the pod. With a tender texture and mild flavour, they are good added to soups, stews, curries and salads, and go particularly well with pork and ham. Soak dried black-eyed beans overnight in cold water. Drain, then boil in fresh, unsalted water for 1½ hours or until tender.

Borlotti bean
Borlotti beans have a pale, tender and buttery flesh with a sweetish, earthy flavour. They are good in soups, stews and salads, and feature in the classic, *pasta e fagioli*. They lose some colour when cooked, but retain enough to remain attractive. Soak dried borlotti beans overnight in cold water. Drain, then boil rapidly in fresh, unsalted water for 10 minutes. Simmer for 1½ hours or until tender. Note: borlotti beans contain toxic substances (see Kidney Beans, opposite).

Broad bean
Dried broad beans are pale brown and flat. When whole, the skins can be tough, but they are also sold skinned, when they are off-white, thin and 'split'. Popular in Middle Eastern cooking, they are used to make falafel and for spiced bean purées. The distinctive flavour and tender texture also benefit meat and vegetable stews. Soak overnight in cold water. Drain, then boil in fresh, unsalted water for 30–50 minutes until tender.

Butter bean
One of the largest dried beans, these flat, kidney-shaped beans are mild and creamy with a floury texture. Add them to vegetable and meat stews, and they go well with strong flavours such as tomatoes and spices. Often used in traditional Greek and Mediterranean dishes, they are good in soups, mixed bean and couscous salads. Soak overnight in cold water. Drain, then boil in fresh, unsalted water for 1 hour or until tender.

Cannellini bean
A tender, buttery texture and mild flavour make these a good addition to tomato-based and meat stews with robust flavours and plenty of herbs and aromatics. Toss in a little dressing with salad vegetables or in the Italian bean and tuna salad, *tonno e fagioli*. Soissons is a dried haricot bean used in France, particularly in cassoulet. Soak dried cannellini beans overnight in cold water. Drain, then boil in fresh, unsalted water for 1½ hours or until tender.

Chickpea
These hazelnut-sized peas are also known as chana and garbanzo beans. They have a slightly knobbly surface, a rich, nutty flavour and a firm but tender texture. The cooked beans can be puréed to make hummus, and the raw, soaked beans can be ground to make falafel. They make a good addition to mixed bean and couscous salads. Soak dried chickpeas overnight in cold water. Drain, then boil in fresh, unsalted water for 2 hours or until tender.

Flageolet bean
These small haricot beans are harvested and dried before they are fully ripe. Their subtle, fresh flavour and smooth, buttery texture tastes good on it own, with other beans or in robust, tomato-based and meat stews; also with fresh herbs and olive oil, or tossed with garlic and olive oil and served with lamb. Soak dried beans overnight in cold water. Drain, then boil in fresh, unsalted water for 1–1½ hours until tender.

Haricot bean
Known as navy beans in the US, these are small, oval and creamy white, and are the classic ingredient in Boston baked beans (with cured pork, tomato and spices). With a mild flavour and smooth, buttery texture, they are good in robust, well-flavoured soups and stews, such as cassoulet, or made into purées with spices, herbs and aromatics. Soak overnight in cold water. Drain, then boil in fresh, unsalted water for 1–1½ hours until tender.

Kidney bean
With a pale flesh, a smooth, firm texture and sweetish, earthy flavour, these beans are good in any spicy stew or soup, and in mixed bean salads. Soak dried beans overnight in cold water. Drain, boil rapidly in fresh, unsalted water for 10 minutes, then simmer for 1–1½ hours until just tender. Note: kidney beans contain toxic substances that can only be removed by boiling rapidly for 10 minutes. They should be added to stews only if they have been pre-boiled.

Lentil, green (photo), brown
Grey-green lentils have a mild flavour and soft texture. They retain their shape well (unless overcooked) and are a good addition to soups and stews, but can also be used to stuff vegetables or added to salads. Cook without soaking in boiling unsalted water for 30 minutes or until tender. Brown lentils are similar and can be used in the same way in soups, stews and rice dishes. The colour is dull, but they have good flavour and a skin that holds up well.

Lentil, Puy
These are highly prized for their excellent taste and texture. Grown in France, they are often boiled until tender, then cooked briefly with a little stock, fried onion or garlic and herbs, and served with meats and fish, or tossed in salads. They are also used in soups and stews in the same way as green lentils. They hold their shape better than any other lentil, even when cooked. Cook without soaking in boiling unsalted water for 30 minutes or until tender.

Lentil, red split (photo), yellow
These tiny lentils both disintegrate as they cook, producing a thick purée. As they have a mild flavour, they benefit from the addition of spices and strong flavours. They are used to make spicy Indian dhal but they can also be used to thicken soups and casseroles. Cook without soaking in boiling unsalted water for 20 minutes (red lentils), 30 minutes (yellow lentils) or until tender. Split peas are similar – cook as above for 45 minutes or until tender.

Lima bean
As lima beans are similar in appearance, taste and texture to butter beans, they can be used in the same way. The pale, flat bean is found in the US, where it is often added to soups, stews and salads. Cook as for butter beans. Soak dried lima beans overnight in cold water. Drain, then boil in fresh, unsalted water for 1–1½ hours until tender.

Mung bean
Also known as green gram and moong dal, these small beans are widely used in India to make curries. They are available both whole and split. With a tender texture and fresh, slightly sweet flavour, mung beans are also good added to soups, stews and salads and are the most popular bean for sprouting. Mung beans require no soaking and can be boiled in unsalted water for 40 minutes or until tender. If soaked overnight, the cooking time can be reduced to 25 minutes.

Pinto bean
A type of kidney bean that is popular in both Spain and Mexico, pinto beans have a pinky-beige skin with dark orange-red streaks and a tender pale flesh with a nutty flavour. Good used in soups, stews and salads, they were the original bean used in Mexican refried beans. Pinto beans are also a popular addition to Spanish stews. Soak dried pinto beans overnight in cold water. Drain, then boil in fresh, unsalted water for 1–1½ hours or until tender.

Soya bean
As well as being rich in nutrients, soya beans are an excellent source of protein. They are rather bland and are best added to spicy soups and stews where they will absorb the flavours. Soak dried soya beans overnight in cold water. Drain, then boil rapidly in fresh, unsalted water for 1 hour. Drain, then boil in fresh, unsalted water for 2 hours or until tender. Kidney beans contain toxic substance (Kidney bean (above). Tofu is made from pressed soya beans.

Basic Pilau Rice

Serves 4
Preparation time 5 minutes
Cooking time 20 minutes, plus standing

50g (2oz) butter
225g (8oz) long-grain white rice
750ml (1¼ pints) chicken stock
salt and ground black pepper
generous knob of butter to serve

1 Melt the butter in a pan, add the rice and fry gently for 3–4 minutes until translucent.
2 Slowly pour in the stock, season with salt and pepper, stir and cover with a tight-fitting lid. Leave undisturbed over a very low heat for about 15 minutes or until all the water has been absorbed and the rice is just tender.
3 Remove the lid and cover the surface of the rice with a clean cloth. Replace the lid and leave to stand in a warm place for about 15 minutes to dry the rice before serving.
4 Fork through and add a knob of butter to serve.

NUTRITION PER SERVING 320 cals | 13g fat (8g sats) | 45g carbs | 0.8g salt

Special Fried Rice

Preparation time 5 minutes
Cooking time 10–15 minutes
Serves 4

200g (7oz) long-grain rice
1 tbsp sesame oil
6 tbsp nasi goreng paste (see Cook's Tip)
200g (7oz) green cabbage, shredded
250g (9oz) large cooked peeled prawns
2 tbsp light soy sauce
1 tbsp sunflower oil
2 medium eggs, beaten
2 spring onions, thinly sliced
1 lime, cut into wedges to serve

1 Cook the rice according to the pack instructions.
2 Heat the sesame oil in a large pan and fry the nasi goreng paste for 2 minutes. Add the cabbage and stir-fry for 2–3 minutes. Stir in the prawns, rice and soy sauce and cook for 5 minutes, stirring occasionally.
3 Heat the sunflower oil in a non-stick frying pan and add the eggs. Swirl to cover the base in a thin layer and cook for 3 minutes or until set.
4 Roll up the omelette and cut it into strips. Serve the rice scattered with strips of omelette and spring onions, with the lime wedges to squeeze over.

Cook's Tip
You can buy nasi goreng paste at large supermarkets and Asian stores.

NUTRITION PER SERVING 412 cals | 18g fat (3g sats) | 46g carbs | 1.9g salt

Risotto Milanese

Serves 4
Preparation time 15 minutes
Cooking time about 30 minutes

50g (2oz) butter
1 onion, finely chopped
150ml (¼ pint) dry white wine
300g (11oz) Arborio rice
1 litre (1¾ pints) chicken stock
a large pinch of saffron
50g (2oz) Parmesan, freshly grated,
 plus shavings to serve
salt and ground black pepper

1 Melt half the butter in a heavy-based pan. Add the onion and cook gently for 5 minutes to soften, then add the wine and boil rapidly until almost totally reduced. Add the rice and cook, stirring continuously, for 1 minute or until the grains are coated with the butter and glossy.
2 Meanwhile, heat the stock in a separate pan to a steady, low simmer.
3 Add the saffron and a ladleful of the stock to the rice and simmer, stirring, until absorbed. Continue adding the stock, a ladleful at a time, until the rice is tender but still has some bite to it. This will take about 25 minutes and you may not need to add all the stock.
4 Add the remaining butter and the grated Parmesan. Season with salt and pepper to taste, garnish with shavings of Parmesan and serve.

NUTRITION PER SERVING 461 cals | 15g fat (9g sats) | 64g carbs | 0.6g salt

---

Mushroom and Two-grain Risotto

Serves 4
Preparation time 20 minutes
Cooking time 25 minutes

200g (7oz) risotto rice, such as Arborio
 or Carnaroli
100g (3½oz) quinoa
1.1 litres (2 pints) vegetable stock
25g (1oz) butter
1 onion, finely chopped
250g pack chestnut mushrooms, sliced
leaves from 4 thyme sprigs
2 garlic cloves, crushed
a large handful of rocket
Parmesan shavings to serve (optional)
 (see Vegetarian Cheeses, page 228)
salt and ground black pepper

1 Put the rice, quinoa and stock in a large pan, bring to the boil, then reduce the heat and simmer, stirring often, for 20 minutes or until tender.
2 Meanwhile, heat the butter in a separate pan and gently cook the onion for 10 minutes or until soft. Turn up the heat to high and add the mushrooms. Cook, stirring frequently, for 5 minutes or until tender and any moisture has evaporated. Add the thyme leaves, garlic, salt and pepper. Cook for a further 1 minute. Take off the heat and set aside.
3 Stir the cooked rice into the mushroom mixture with most of the rocket. Adjust the seasoning. Spoon into individual bowls and garnish with the remaining rocket. Top with Parmesan shavings, if you like, and serve immediately.

NUTRITION PER SERVING 353 cals | 8g fat (3g sats) | 59g carbs | 0.2g salt Ⓥ

Paella

Serves 4
Preparation time 15 minutes
Cooking time 30 minutes

1 tbsp vegetable oil
1 large onion, thinly sliced
4 boneless skinless chicken thighs, roughly chopped
2 garlic cloves, finely chopped
a pinch of saffron
¼ tsp smoked paprika
1 red pepper, seeded and finely diced
300g (11oz) paella rice
1.2 litres (2 pints) chicken stock
180g tub mussel meat, drained if in brine
a large handful of curly parsley, roughly chopped
salt and ground black pepper

1 Gently heat the oil in a large paella pan or frying pan
and cook the onion for 5 minutes or until soft. Add the
chicken and cook for 3 minutes. Stir in the garlic, saffron
and paprika and cook for 1 minute to release the flavours.
2 Stir in the diced pepper and paella rice. Pour in the
stock, bring to the boil, then reduce the heat and simmer
gently for 20 minutes, stirring occasionally, or until the rice
is cooked through.
3 Stir in the mussels and parsley and season with salt and
pepper. Serve immediately.

NUTRITION PER SERVING 494 cals | 10g fat (2g sats) | 68g carbs | 0.56g salt

Jambalaya

Serves 6
Preparation time 15 minutes, plus standing
Cooking time 50 minutes

1 tbsp olive oil
6 boneless skinless chicken thighs, cut into bite-size chunks
3 rashers smoked streaky bacon, rind removed and roughly
  chopped
1 large onion, finely chopped
2 celery sticks, finely chopped
2 green peppers, seeded and cut into chunks
½ tsp cayenne pepper
1 heaped tsp smoked paprika
225g (8oz) long-grain rice
400g can chopped tomatoes
200g (7oz) raw king prawns, deveined (see page 85)
a small handful of fresh flat-leafed parsley, chopped
salt and ground black pepper
lemon wedges to serve

1 Heat half the oil in a large pan, add the chicken and
fry for 5 minutes or until just browned. Remove with
a slotted spoon and set aside. Fry the bacon in the pan
juices for 3–4 minutes until golden, then set aside.
2 Reduce the heat and add the remaining oil to the pan.
Gently fry the onion and celery for 8–10 minutes until
soft. Add the peppers and fry for 2–3 minutes. Stir in the
spices and rice, then fry for 1 minute.
3 Return the chicken and bacon to the pan with the
tomatoes and 450ml (¾ pint) hot water. Season with
salt and pepper. Bring to the boil, then reduce the heat,
cover and simmer for 20 minutes, stirring occasionally, or
until the rice is just cooked. Stir in the prawns for the last
5 minutes.
4 Remove from the heat, cover and leave to stand for
5 minutes. Garnish with parsley and serve with lemon
wedges.

NUTRITION PER SERVING 328 cals | 11g fat (3g sats) | 36g carbs | 0.7g salt

Cheese Polenta with Tomato Sauce

Serves 6
Preparation time 15 minutes, plus cooling
Cooking time 45 minutes

oil to grease
225g (8oz) polenta
4 tbsp freshly chopped herbs, such as oregano, chives and
  flat-leafed parsley
100g (3½oz) freshly grated Parmesan, plus fresh Parmesan
  shavings to serve (see Vegetarian Cheeses, page 228)
salt and ground black pepper

For the tomato and basil sauce
1 tbsp vegetable oil
3 garlic cloves, crushed
500g carton creamed tomatoes or passata
1 bay leaf
1 fresh thyme sprig
a large pinch of caster sugar
3 tbsp freshly chopped basil, plus extra to garnish

1 Lightly oil a 25.5 × 18cm (10 × 7in) dish. Bring
1.1 litres (2 pints) water and ¼ tsp salt to the boil in a large
pan. Sprinkle in the polenta, whisking constantly. Reduce
the heat and simmer, stirring, for 10–15 minutes until
the mixture leaves the sides of the pan. Stir in the herbs,
Parmesan, salt and pepper. Turn into the dish and cool.
2 To make the sauce, heat the oil in a pan and fry the
garlic for 30 seconds (do not brown). Add the creamed
tomatoes or passata, the bay leaf, thyme and sugar. Season
with salt and pepper and bring to the boil, then reduce the
heat and simmer, uncovered, for 5–10 minutes. Remove the
bay leaf and thyme sprig and add the chopped basil.
3 To serve, cut the polenta into pieces and lightly brush
with oil. Preheat a griddle and fry for 3–4 minutes on
each side, or grill under a preheated grill for 7–8 minutes
on each side. Serve with the tomato and basil sauce, fresh
Parmesan shavings and chopped basil.

GET AHEAD
Complete the recipe to the end of step 2. Cover and chill
separately for up to two days. To use, complete the recipe.

TRY SOMETHING DIFFERENT
Fried Herb Polenta Bring 900ml (1½ pints) salted water to
the boil in a large pan. Sprinkle in 175g (6oz) coarse polenta,
whisking constantly. Lower the heat and simmer, stirring
frequently, for 20 minutes or until the polenta leaves the
sides of the pan; it will be very thick. Stir in 2 tbsp freshly
chopped sage and 1 tbsp freshly chopped rosemary and
plenty of salt and pepper. Turn out on to a board and shape
into a thick rectangular mound. Leave for about 1 hour
until set, then cut into slices. Melt the butter in a frying pan.
When foaming, fry the polenta slices on both sides until
golden. Serve with meat, poultry or vegetarian dishes.
Soft Herb Polenta Serve Fried Herb Polenta after stirring in
the sage and rosemary, as you would mashed potato.

NUTRITION PER SERVING 249 cals | 9g fat (4g sats) | 31g carbs | 0.9g salt Ⓥ

Mediterranean Vegetable Couscous with Feta

Serves 4
Preparation time 20 minutes, plus soaking
Cooking time 1 hour

2 red onions, roughly chopped
2 courgettes, roughly chopped
1 aubergine, roughly chopped
2 red peppers, seeded and roughly chopped
2 garlic cloves, sliced
4 tbsp olive oil
350g (12oz) tomatoes, quartered
225g (8oz) couscous
300ml (½ pint) hot vegetable stock
4 tbsp roughly chopped fresh flat-leafed parsley
2 tbsp balsamic vinegar
200g (7oz) feta cheese, cubed (see Vegetarian Cheeses
  on page 228)
salt and ground black pepper

1 Preheat the oven to 200°C (180°C fan oven) mark 6. Put the red onions, courgettes, aubergine, peppers and garlic into a roasting tin and drizzle with the oil. Season with salt and pepper, then toss together and roast for 30 minutes.
2 Add the tomatoes to the tin. Toss together and roast for a further 30 minutes.
3 Meanwhile, put the couscous into a large bowl. Pour in the hot stock, stir and cover. Leave to one side to soak for 10 minutes.
4 Fluff up the warm couscous with a fork, then add the chopped parsley, balsamic vinegar and roasted vegetables. Toss together, then spoon into warmed bowls, scatter over the feta cheese and serve.

NUTRITION PER SERVING 580 cals | 25g fat (8g sats) | 73g carbs | 2.3g salt Ⓥ

Lentil Chilli

Serves 4
Preparation time 10 minutes
Cooking time 25 minutes

1 tbsp vegetable oil
1 red onion, finely chopped
1 tsp ground cumin
1 tsp ground coriander
1 tsp chilli powder
2 × 400g cans chopped tomatoes
1 vegetable stock cube, crumbled
2 × 400g cans lentils, drained and
  rinsed
400g can kidney beans, drained and
  rinsed
a handful of fresh coriander, chopped
salt and ground black pepper
crisp flatbreads or brown rice to serve

1 Heat the oil in a large pan and fry the onion for 10 minutes or until soft. Add the ground spices and cook for a further 1 minute. Stir in the tomatoes, stock cube and lentils, bring to the boil, then reduce the heat and simmer for 10 minutes or until thickened.
2 Add the kidney beans and heat through. Stir through most of the coriander and check the seasoning. Garnish with the remaining coriander and serve with crisp flatbreads or cooked brown rice.

NUTRITION PER SERVING 299 cals | 5g fat (0.5g sats) | 39g carbs | 1.6g salt Ⓥ

Chickpeas with Spinach

Serves 6
Preparation time 10 minutes
Cooking time 12–15 minutes

3 tbsp olive oil
2.5cm (1in) piece fresh root ginger,
  finely chopped
3 garlic cloves, chopped
2 tsp ground coriander
2 tsp paprika
1 tsp ground cumin
2 × 400g cans chickpeas, drained and
  rinsed
4 tomatoes, roughly chopped
a handful of fresh coriander leaves
450g (1lb) fresh spinach
salt and ground black pepper
rice and grated carrots with lemon
  juice to serve

1 Heat the oil in a large heavy-based pan, add the ginger, garlic and spices, and cook for 2 minutes, stirring. Stir in the chickpeas.
2 Add the tomatoes to the pan with the coriander leaves and spinach, and cook gently for 10 minutes. Season to taste with salt and pepper, and serve immediately, with rice and a salad of grated carrots tossed in a little lemon juice to taste.

NUTRITION PER SERVING 204 cals | 10g fat (1g sats) | 21g carbs | 0.8g salt Ⓥ

Sweet Chilli Tofu Stir-fry

Serves 4
Preparation time 5 minutes, plus marinating
Cooking time 12 minutes

200g (7oz) firm tofu (see Cook's Tips)
4 tbsp sweet chilli sauce
2 tbsp light soy sauce
1 tbsp sesame seeds
2 tbsp toasted sesame oil
600g (1lb 5oz) ready-prepared mixed stir-fry vegetables, such
   as carrots, broccoli, mangetouts and bean sprouts
a handful of pea shoots or young salad leaves to garnish

1 Drain the tofu, pat it dry and cut it into large cubes. Put
the tofu in a shallow container and pour over 1 tbsp sweet
chilli sauce and 1 tbsp light soy sauce. Cover and marinate
for 10 minutes.
2 Meanwhile, toast the sesame seeds in a hot wok or large
frying pan until golden. Tip on to a plate.
3 Return the wok or frying pan to the heat and add
1 tbsp sesame oil. Add the marinated tofu and stir-fry for
5 minutes or until golden. Remove and leave to one side.
4 Heat the remaining 1 tbsp oil in the pan, add the
vegetables and stir-fry for 3–4 minutes until just tender.
Stir in the cooked tofu.
5 Pour the remaining sweet chilli sauce and soy sauce into
the pan, toss well and cook for a further 1 minute until
heated through. Sprinkle with the toasted sesame seeds
and pea shoots or salad leaves and serve immediately.

Cook's Tips
• Tofu is highly nutritious and readily absorbs other
  flavours when marinating. It is sold as a chilled product
  and should be stored in the fridge. Once the packet is
  opened, the tofu should be kept immersed in a bowl of
  water in the fridge and eaten within four days.
• Firm tofu is usually cut into chunks, then immersed in
  tasty marinades and dressings prior to grilling, stir-
  frying, deep-frying, adding to stews, or tossing raw into
  salads. It can also be chopped and made into burgers and
  nut roasts.
• Smoked tofu has more flavour than firm tofu; it is used
  in the same way.
• Silken tofu is softer and creamier than firm tofu and is
  useful for sauces and dressings.

NUTRITION PER SERVING 290 cals | 26g fat (6g sats) | 8g carbs | 1.5g salt ⓥ

Mushroom and Bean Hotpot

Serves 6
Preparation time 15 minutes
Cooking time 45 minutes

3 tbsp olive oil
700g (1½lb) chestnut mushrooms, roughly chopped
1 large onion, finely chopped
2 tbsp plain flour
2 tbsp mild curry paste (see Cook's Tip)
150ml (¼ pint) dry white wine (see Alcoholic Drinks and
   Vegetarians, page 489)
400g can chopped tomatoes
2 tbsp sun-dried tomato paste
2 × 400g cans mixed beans, drained and rinsed
3 tbsp Sweet Mango Chutney (see page 485)
3 tbsp roughly chopped coriander and mint

1 Heat the oil in a large pan over a low heat, then fry the
mushrooms and onion until the onion is soft and dark
golden. Stir in the flour and curry paste, and cook for
1–2 minutes.
2 Add the wine, tomatoes, sun-dried tomato paste and
beans. Bring to the boil, then reduce the heat and simmer
gently for 30 minutes or until most of the liquid has
reduced. Stir in the chutney and herbs before serving.

Cook's Tip
If cooking for vegetarians, check the ingredients in the
curry paste: some brands may not be suitable.

NUTRITION PER SERVING 280 cals | 10g fat (1g sats) | 34g carbs | 1.3g salt Ⓥ

Boston Baked Beans

Serves 4
Preparation time 10 minutes, plus overnight soaking
Cooking time 2–2½ hours

225g (8oz) dried black-eyed beans, soaked overnight
 in cold water
2 tbsp olive oil
1 large onion, chopped
1 large garlic clove, finely chopped
600ml (1 pint) dry cider (see Alcoholic Drinks and
 Vegetarians, page 489)
150g (5oz) passata
2 tbsp sun-dried tomato paste or tomato purée
1 tbsp black treacle
1 tbsp demerara sugar
1 tsp French mustard
sea salt and ground black pepper
freshly chopped parsley to garnish
garlic bread or jacket potatoes and salad to serve

1 Drain the beans, rinse under cold running water, then
put into a large pan. Cover with plenty of fresh cold water,
bring to the boil and boil steadily for 10 minutes. Remove
any scum from the surface with a slotted spoon. Lower the
heat, cover and simmer for a further 20 minutes. Preheat
the oven to 170°C (150°C fan oven) mark 3.
2 Heat the olive oil in another pan, add the onion and
garlic, and fry gently until tender. Add the cider, passata,
tomato paste, black treacle, demerara sugar and mustard.
Bring to the boil.
3 Drain the beans and transfer to a casserole. Stir in
the tomato mixture. Cover and cook in the oven for
1½ –2 hours or until the beans are tender. Check and stir
the beans occasionally during cooking and add a little extra
cider or water if necessary to prevent them drying out; the
finished sauce should be thick and syrupy.
4 Season with salt and pepper to taste. Serve garnished
with parsley and with hot crusty garlic bread or jacket
potatoes and a salad.

TRY SOMETHING DIFFERENT
Use haricot beans instead of black-eyed beans, adjusting
the cooking time accordingly.

NUTRITION PER SERVING 310 cals | 8g fat (1g sats) | 45g carbs | 0.9g salt Ⓥ

Tex-Mex Veggie Burgers

Serves 4
Preparation time 20 minutes
Cooking time 10 minutes

410g can black-eyed beans, drained and rinsed
410g can kidney beans, drained and rinsed
150g (5oz) sweetcorn
2 tbsp sliced jalapeño peppers
 a small handful of fresh coriander, plus extra to garnish
2 medium eggs
75g (3oz) fresh or dried white breadcrumbs
1 tbsp olive oil
4 burger buns, toasted
1 avocado, peeled, stoned and thinly sliced
4 tsp soured cream
4 tsp tomato salsa
salt and ground black pepper

1 Put the black-eyed and kidney beans, sweetcorn, peppers
and coriander and plenty of salt and pepper into a food
processor and pulse briefly until combined but still with a
chunky texture. Empty into a large bowl and stir the eggs
and breadcrumbs into the mixture. Shape into four patties.
2 Heat the oil in a large non-stick frying pan and gently
fry the patties for 8–10 minutes, carefully turning once,
until golden and piping hot.
3 Serve the burgers on toasted burger buns, topped with
a few avocado slices, a small dollop of soured cream and
some tomato salsa.

Skinny Bean Tacos

Serves 4
Preparation time 15 minutes
Cooking time 10 minutes

2 × 400g cans chopped tomatoes
2 tsp clear honey
410g can cannellini beans, drained and rinsed
400g can kidney beans, drained and rinsed
198g can sweetcorn, drained
1 red onion, finely chopped
8 corn tacos
salt and ground black pepper
a large handful of fresh parsley, chopped
reduced-fat guacamole to serve

1 Put the tomatoes in a medium pan with the honey and
plenty of seasoning. Bring to the boil, then reduce the heat
and simmer for about 8 minutes until thickened.
2 Stir in both types of beans, the sweetcorn, red onion and
some seasoning. Heat through, then season with salt and
pepper to taste.
3 Warm the taco shells according to the pack instructions.
4 Put the hot bean mixture, tacos, guacamole and chopped
parsley into separate bowls, take to the table and let
everyone serve themselves.

NUTRITION PER SERVING 371 cals | 8g fat (1g sats) | 54g carbs | 1.8g salt Ⓥ

Vegetables

Vegetables

Low in fat and cholesterol, yet high in fibre, vegetables are an important source of roughage and are highly nutritious. In particular, they are an excellent source of vitamins and minerals. Starchy varieties, such as potatoes, are also a good source of energy, but most vegetables are low in calories. Many varieties provide some protein too. Frozen vegetables are as nutritious as fresh, because they will have been snap frozen soon after picking.

Most supermarkets now stock a wide range of organic vegetables – produce that is grown without the use of chemical pesticides and artificial fertilisers – although they do tend to be more expensive.

Vegetables can be classified into various categories:

Brassicas, otherwise known as the cabbage family, include broccoli, Brussels sprouts, cauliflower and curly kale, as well as the many different types of cabbage.

Leafy vegetables include the array of salad leaves – baby spinach, rocket, lamb's lettuce, frisée, radicchio, chicory and all kinds of lettuces.

Mushrooms are a type of fungus. A number of cultivated varieties are available, and seasonal fresh wild mushrooms, such as chanterelles and ceps, are now easier to obtain.

The onion family comprises red, white and brown-skinned onions, as well as leeks, garlic, shallots and spring onions.

Pods, peas and beans take in the many varieties of fresh beans, along with peas, mangetouts, okra and sweetcorn.

Roots and tubers are vegetables that grow underground, such as carrots, potatoes, parsnips, turnips, swede, celeriac, Jerusalem artichokes, beetroot and the lesser-known salsify and eddoes.

Stalks and shoots encompass such prized delicacies as asparagus, globe artichokes and fennel, along with celery.

Vegetable fruits is a diverse category in which the vegetables are more correctly the fruits of their plants. Aubergines, avocado, peppers, tomatoes, cucumbers, courgettes and the other varieties of squash are all included.

Buying and storing vegetables

Look for bright, firm vegetables. Avoid any that look shrivelled or bruised. Resist buying the largest specimens, particularly when choosing roots. In general, the younger and smaller the vegetable, the sweeter and more tender it will be, although some of the baby vegetables may lack flavour because they are so immature.

To enjoy them at their best and most nutritious, vegetables should be eaten as soon as possible after picking or buying, but most will keep for a few days in a cool, dark place. Store green vegetables and salad ingredients in the salad drawer of the fridge. Root vegetables can be stored in a cool, dark place, such as a wire rack in a cool larder, for up to one week. Exposure to light turns potatoes green, so they must be kept in the dark.

Preparing and cooking vegetables

Clean all vegetables thoroughly before cooking. Brush or shake off any loose dirt, then wash thoroughly (except mushrooms, which are best wiped).

If the produce is organic and the skins are edible, there is no need to peel. Non-organic produce is better peeled as washing alone is not necessarily enough to remove all traces of residual chemicals. As soon as vegetables are peeled they begin to lose vitamins so, where possible, prepare at the last minute. Never prepare vegetables hours in advance and leave them immersed in cold water, as water-soluble vitamins will be lost.

Vegetables can be cooked by a variety of methods, including steaming, boiling, sautéeing, stir-frying, roasting, braising and grilling.

If you are boiling vegetables, minimise the loss of water-soluble vitamins by cooking in the minimum amount of water, and by reserving the cooking water when you strain the vegetables to use as vegetable stock or to make a gravy or sauce.

Whichever method you are using to cook the vegetables, avoid overcooking. In general, vegetables are at their best cooked until al dente – tender but still retaining some bite.

Potatoes

Most of the nutrients in a potato are stored just beneath the skin so, where possible, leave the skin on. New potatoes can be scrubbed, or scraped with a knife, although you may need to peel maincrop potatoes if you are planning to boil and mash or roast them. Use a vegetable peeler that removes the skin in a thin, even layer.

Bake Scrub large potatoes well and pat dry. Prick with a fork, then bake at 200°C (180°C fan oven) mark 6 for 1–1½ hours until tender.

Boil Cut peeled maincrop potatoes into large chunks. Put in cold salted water, bring to the boil, then cook for 10–20 minutes until tender. To mash, drain and allow to steam dry. Mash with plenty of butter and milk until smooth, then season with salt and pepper.

New potatoes can be put into a pan of boiling water and cooked for 15–20 minutes until tender. To crush boiled new potatoes, drain and leave to steam dry in the pan for 2 minutes. Crush gently with a potato masher, then drizzle with olive oil and sprinkle with fresh herbs and pepper.

Deep-fry For chips, peel and cut into thick slices, then into sticks. Leave in a bowl of cold water for 30 minutes to remove excess starch, then drain and dry using a tea towel or kitchen paper. Heat the oil in a deep frying pan or deep-fryer to 190°C or until one chip dropped in rises to the surface immediately, surrounded by bubbles. Quarter-fill the frying basket with chips, lower into the oil and cook for 6–7 minutes, until beginning to colour. Raise the basket to drain; repeat with the remaining potatoes. Fry all the chips for a second time, for 3 minutes or until golden and crisp.

Roast Parboil prepared maincrop potatoes for 10 minutes, then drain and leave to steam dry for 2 minutes. Shake to roughen the surface. Heat oil, goose fat or lard in a roasting tin at 220°C (200°C fan oven) mark 7 until very hot, add the potatoes, turn to coat, then roast, turning once or twice and basting with fat, for 45–60 minutes until golden.

Sauté Parboil prepared maincrop potatoes for 10 minutes, then drain and leave to steam dry for 2 minutes. Cut into thick slices. Coat the base of a heavy-based frying pan with oil and heat until medium-hot. Add the potatoes, and turn to coat with the oil. Season. cover the pan and cook for 5–8 minutes until they start to soften. Remove the lid and stir every minute or so while the potatoes cook.

Onions

Peel away the papery skin and any discoloured layers underneath and trim the top. Cut the onion in half from tip to base and put it cut side down on a chopping board. To slice an onion, hold it firmly and cut it across into vertical slices, discarding the root. To chop an onion, make three horizontal cuts from the pointed end almost to the root, then make vertical cuts lengthways, cutting almost to the root. Finally, chop across the width to make dice. Throw away the root.

Tomatoes

To skin tomatoes, plunge them into boiling water for 30 seconds, then refresh in cold water. Cut lightly into the skin, then peel it away. To remove the seeds, halve the tomato and scoop out the seeds with a spoon or cut out with a small sharp knife.

For other vegetable preparation see the following pages.

Vegetables

Artichoke, Globe
Choose heavy heads with tight leaves. Baby artichokes can be eaten whole, allowing 1 per person. If serving only the hearts, allow 2–3 each. Cut off the stalks and leaf spikes. Cook in boiling salted water with a slice of lemon for 40 minutes or until you can pull out a leaf easily. Serve warm with melted butter or hollandaise, or cold with dressing. Pull off each leaf, dip in the dressing, then suck off the fleshy part. Discard the hairy choke and eat the delicate heart.

Artichoke, Jerusalem
Unrelated to the globe artichoke, this is a knobbly tuber with a nutty flavour. Choose the smoothest as these will be easier to peel, allowing 175g (6oz) per person. Scrub well and peel thinly. If they are very difficult to peel, cook first. They can be cubed, diced, sliced or cut into julienne. Cook in boiling salted water, with 1 tbsp lemon juice to prevent discoloration, for 10–15 minutes. Serve as a side dish, a purée or make into a creamy soup.

Asparagus
Varieties include thick or thin green, fine sprue and white. Choose fresh bundles with tight buds and smooth stems; avoid wilted or woody stems. Allow 6–8 spears each. Snap off the lower stem, where it begins to toughen, and peel, if thick. Stand the spears upright in a deep pan of simmering salted water, so the tips steam while the stems boil. Simmer for 5 minutes until tender. Serve hot with hollandaise or butter or cold with mayonnaise or French dressing.

Aubergine
Available in various varieties, choose firm and shiny aubergines, allowing 175g (6oz) per person. Cut off the stem, trim the ends and halve or slice. It isn't usually necessary to soak them in salt, then rinse them. Sauté or grill slices for 5–8 minutes, or bake in a moussaka. Bake aubergine halves, with or without stuffing, as a starter or main dish. Serve slices as an accompaniment; stuffed halves as a main dish or starter.

Avocado pear
Buy undamaged fruits that give when gently squeezed; avoid soft fruits; ripen hard fruits at room temperature. To use, cut lengthways around the large stone and twist apart. Tap a knife into the stone, then twist the blade to lift it out. Ripe flesh is mild, buttery and smooth but browns on exposure to air, so prepare just before use. Slice or chop in salsas and salads, fill with prawn cocktail, or blend into soups or smoothies.

Bamboo shoot
Native to Asia, bamboo shoots are the conical-shaped shoots of the bamboo plant. They are sometimes obtainable fresh from Asian food stores but you can easily buy canned ready-cooked bamboo shoots from supermarkets. Allow 50–75g (2–3oz) per person. Peel fresh bamboo shoots, then cook in boiling water for 40 minutes or until tender. Or parboil the shoots and use in stir-fries.

Bean, broad
Choose small pods and allow about 250g (9oz) whole beans in pods per person. Very young broad beans, less than 7.5cm (3in) long, can be cooked in their pods and eaten whole. Pod older beans and, after blanching, slip the beans out of their outer skin, which toughens with age. Cook in boiling salted water for 8–10 minutes until tender. Serve with melted butter and herbs. Older beans can also be made into soup or puréed.

Bean, French (green bean), runner
Choose young, tender beans. Allow 150g (5oz) per person. Trim the ends. Most varieties are stringless, otherwise remove the strings from the seams of the pods. Cut runner beans lengthways into fine slices using a bean slicer, or cut young beans into short lengths. Cook in boiling salted water or steam for 5–7 minutes until tender. Serve hot as a side dish or serve French beans cold as a salad tossed in a herb vinaigrette.

Bean sprout
These are the crunchy shoots of germinated dried beans, such as mung or aduki beans. Choose crisp, small, fresh shoots, or sprout your own, but be sure to buy beans or seeds specifically produced for sprouting – from a health-food shop or other reliable source. Mung beans take only five to six days to sprout. Allow about 125g (4oz) per person. Rinse bean sprouts thoroughly, then drain. Cook in boiling salted water or steam for 30 seconds, or stir-fry for 1–2 minutes.

Beetroot

Baby beetroot have a wonderful earthy flavour. Maincrop are sold fresh or cooked, vacuum packed or preserved in vinegar. Choose firm, smallish beetroot with crisp tops and intact skin. Allow 150g (5oz) per person. Cut off the stalks 2.5cm (1in) above the bulb and wash well. Cook in lightly salted boiling water for 40 minutes or until soft. Or roast at 180°C (160°C fan oven) mark 4 until tender (20 minutes for small, up to 1 hour for large), then peel, slice or dice.

Broccoli (calabrese)

There are two types of broccoli: the compact, dark-green headed calabrese and sprouting broccoli (see right). Choose firm, tightly packed heads with strong stalks. Allow 125–150g (4–5oz) per person. Trim the stalks. Halve the shoots if large. Cook upright in boiling salted water (to allow the heads to steam) for 5–6 minutes, or steam for about 10–15 minutes. Alternatively you can stir-fry small broccoli florets in a wok over a high heat for 4–5 minutes.

Broccoli, purple sprouting

This purple-green variety grows on shooting, fleshy stems rather than in a head. It is most often served as a side dish with butter or oil and lemon, or as an appetiser drizzled with hollandaise. Look for firm stems and fresh-looking heads and eat within a few days of purchase. To use, wash, trim the stalks, stripping away any thick skin; halve if large. Stand the stems upright in water so the stems are boiled and the heads steamed, until just tender.

Brussels sprout

Choose small round sprouts with tightly packed heads and no wilted leaves. Allow 125–175g (4–6oz) sprouts per person. Remove damaged or wilted leaves and cut off the stem. Cut a cross on the stump to help the thick part cook quickly. Cook in boiling salted water for 7–10 minutes or steam for 10–15 minutes. Serve hot as an accompaniment. Very young, tender sprouts are also good shredded and served raw in salads.

Butternut squash

These range in size from around 15–30cm (6–12in) and may be pear- or club-shaped. The flesh is an intense orange colour with a firm texture. Look for firm squash with smooth, unblemished skin. Butternut squash is good halved, seeded and baked in its skin, with or without stuffing. To stuff, leave unpeeled, halve and scoop out the seeds. The flesh can also be chopped, sliced or diced and steamed, stir-fried, braised and added to stews and soups.

Cabbage

You can buy spring, summer and winter cabbages. Savoy is considered one of the finest winter crops. Choose fresh-looking cabbage with firm leaves. Allow 175–225g (6–8oz) per person. Remove the coarse outer leaves, cut in half and remove the stalk. Serve raw white or red cabbage shredded in salads. Cook wedges for 10 minutes or shredded cabbage for 3–5 minutes in boiling salted water or steam; braise or stir-fry; or stuff cabbage leaves.

Carrot

Choose brightly coloured, firm carrots with smooth skins. Allow 125–175g (4–6oz) per person. Scrub small new carrots, leaving them whole with a tuft of green stalk. Peel older carrots and quarter lengthways or slice. Cook them in boiling salted water for 10–15 minutes or steam them for 12–18 minutes. Serve hot as a side dish or make into a purée or soup. Raw carrots, either grated or cut into julienne, are excellent in salads.

Cauliflower

Choose a cauliflower with a firm, compact creamy white head and fresh-looking green leaves. They are usually cooked, but can be eaten raw in salads. A medium cauliflower serves four to six people. Cut off the outer leaves and stem, and cut the head into florets. To cook whole, cut a cross on the stump to help it cook quickly. Cook whole in boiling salted water for 15 minutes, keeping the heads out of the water, so the florets steam. Boil or steam florets for about 6 minutes.

Celeriac

Celeriac has a strong celery flavour. Allow 175g (6oz) per person. Choose small, firm, unblemished bulbs, scrub well, cut off the roots and peel thickly. Grate or cut into julienne for salads; cut into slices or strips for cooking. Immerse in cold water with a little lemon juice to prevent discoloration before cooking. Cook in boiling salted water for 15–20 minutes, or steam for 25 minutes. Serve hot with butter, or mash with seasoning and butter or cream.

Vegetables

Celery
The intense flavour of celery makes it excellent for flavouring soups and stews, but it is also delicious served as a vegetable. Pale green celery is available all year; white (blanched) winter celery from October to January. Choose firm, crisp sticks and fresh leafy tops. Allow 3–4 sticks per person. Trim off the base, separate and scrub the stalks. Leave whole or slice. Braise in stock for 20 minutes, or stir-fry or steam until tender. Serve raw in salads or with cheese.

Chard, Swiss
Swiss chard is related to seakale beet and is grown mainly for its leaves, which resemble spinach. The prominent white central ribs are also eaten. Choose fresh-looking chard, with clean, unblemished ribs and crisp leaves. Allow 225g (8oz) leaves and 175g (6oz) ribs per person. Prepare and cook the leaves as for spinach (see page 282). Cook the ribs a minute or two longer, or they can be cooked for 20 minutes or more to reach a luxuriously melting softness.

Chicory
This compact, spear-shaped vegetable is grown in darkness to produce crisp white leaves. Choose chicory heads with crisp white leaves – too much green indicates a bitter flavour. Red-leafed chicory is also available. Allow ½ head per person in salads; one head if serving cooked. Trim off the root base and remove any damaged outer leaves. Leave whole, halve lengthways or slice. Blanch in boiling salted water for 3–4 minutes; or grill, braise or bake. Serve raw in salads.

Courgette
Green or yellow, tender baby courgettes are subtly flavoured. The flowers can also be eaten. Choose small, firm courgettes with smooth, shiny skins. Large ones often lack flavour and are best halved, stuffed and baked. Allow 150g (5oz) per person. Trim, slice or dice, or cook baby courgettes whole. Cook in a little boiling salted water for 5 minutes, or steam, microwave or sauté in butter. Serve raw in salads or with dips.

Cucumber
Although usually a salad vegetable, cucumber can also be served hot. Choose small ones with blemish-free skins. Slice or dice. If required, seed by halving lengthways and scooping out the seeds using a teaspoon. Cook by steaming or sautéeing in butter. Toss with chervil, dill or fennel or serve raw in salads.

Fennel
Known as Florence or sweet fennel to distinguish it from the herb, this looks like a bulbous celery heart. It has a distinctive aniseed flavour. Choose well-rounded, white or pale green bulbs – dark green indicates bitterness. Allow 125–150g (4–5oz) per person. Trim root and stalk ends, reserving the feathery leaves for garnish or to add to salads. Halve, quarter, slice or chop. Boil in salted water for 15 minutes, or steam, sauté in butter, braise or bake. Serve raw in salads.

Kale
From the same family as cabbage, kale has a more intense flavour, coarse-textured curly or flat dark green or purple leaves. Curly kale is the most common. Avoid kale that shows signs of wilting or yellowing. Allow 125–150g (4–5oz) per person. Trim tough stalks and shred or tear leaves into pieces. Wash well. Boil in salted water, or steam, for 6–8 minutes until crisp-tender, then top with a knob of butter. Or stir-fry finely sliced kale for 3 minutes.

Kohlrabi
An unusual white or purple-skinned vegetable, similar in size and flavour to a turnip, kohlrabi is a swollen stalk with protruding leaves. Choose small fresh-looking kohlrabi, no more than 5cm (2in) in diameter, as larger ones can be tough. Allow 150g (5oz) per person. Trim the base, cut off the leaves and stalks, peel thinly, quarter or slice. Boil in salted water for 20–30 minutes, or steam for a little longer. Toss in butter or with a sauce. Or grate or slice thinly and eat raw.

Leek
Choose small, young firm leeks with white stalks and blemish-free leaves. Trim both ends and discard tough outer leaves. Slit lengthways and rinse under cold running water to remove any grit. (If serving whole, slit the top only.) Allow 1–2 leeks per person. Boil in salted water for 8–10 minutes; steam for 12–15 minutes; braise in stock or sauté in butter. Serve topped with herbs or a sauce. Or cool and serve with a herb dressing, or raw in salads. Good in soups.

Lettuce

Look for fresh, springy leaves and avoid any that look limp, yellowing, bruised or slimy. Store in the fridge and use within three days. Trim, then tear the leaves into pieces. Rinse in cold water and pat dry. Dress just before serving. Normally served raw in salads, but lettuce can be cooked as a vegetable. Allow 1 small lettuce per person if cooked, less in salads. Cut in quarters, and braise in stock for 10 minutes, or stir-fry. Lettuce also makes a good soup.

Marrow

Choose young, firm marrow, less than 30.5cm (12in) or 900g (2lb). Allow 175g (6oz) per person. Trim, then cut into pieces. Larger ones can lack flavour. so peel, halve lengthways, discard the seeds and fibres, then cut into pieces or rings. Sprinkle with salt in a colander and leave for 30 minutes to extract the bitter juices; rinse and dry. Boil in salted water for 5–10 minutes; steam for a little longer, sauté for 5 minutes or stuff and bake halves for 45 minutes.

Mushroom

Try cultivated, dried, oriental and wild mushrooms. Gather wild mushrooms only if you are sure you can identify them; use them soon after purchase as they deteriorate quickly. Soak dried mushrooms in warm water for 20 minutes before use; 25g (1oz) dried is equivalent to 150g (5oz) fresh. Fresh mushrooms have firm caps and fresh stalks. Allow 125g (4oz) per person. Wipe with a damp cloth. Leave whole, halve, quarter or slice. Sauté, stir-fry, grill or bake.

Okra

Also known as ladies' fingers, these green tapering pods are used in Caribbean and Indian dishes. Choose firm, bright green pods, about 7.5cm (3in) long. Allow 125g (4oz) per person. Trim okra carefully, removing a tiny piece from each end without cutting into the seed pod, otherwise a sticky juice is released which lends a gelatinous texture. Boil in salted water for 5 minutes, or steam, sauté or stew with spices.

Onion

There are several varieties of onion. Brown-skinned are most common. Spanish onions are larger and milder. Italian red onions are mild, almost sweet. White onions are mildly flavoured. Pickling onions are also referred to as button, pearl or silverskin onions. Allow 1 onion per person if serving as a vegetable. Trim root and top, then peel. Slice, chop or leave whole, then sauté, fry, bake, braise or grill. To reduce pungency, blanch for 2–3 minutes before cooking.

Pak choi

Also known as bok choy, the broad, thick, fleshy white stems gather in a bulbous base and are topped with firm, dark green leaves. A fresh taste, like spinach, with a mildly peppery finish. Look for firm, unblemished stalks and fresh leaves. Store in the fridge and use within a few days. To use, wash, trim the bases, then halve or quarter, and steam or quickly braise; slice the stems and leaves and stir-fry or add to Asian-style soups at the last minute.

Palm heart

The edible inner part of the palm tree shoot is the palm heart, which has firm, creamy-coloured flesh with a delicate flavour like artichoke or asparagus. They are rarely found fresh in the UK, but are sold pre-cooked and canned. Serve hot as a vegetable or add to salads.

Parsnip

The nutty, sweet flavour of parsnips improves if it is harvested after frosts. Choose firm, small or medium parsnips with no side shoots or brown marks. Allow 175g (6oz) per person. Scrub, trim the top and base, and peel thinly. Leave whole or slice, quarter or core larger ones. Steam, or boil in salted water for 10–15 minutes, then sprinkle with herbs, or mash with butter and seasoning. Par-boil for 2 minutes, then roast round a joint of meat or sauté in butter or oil.

Pea

Fresh peas have a delicious sweet flavour. Tiny petits pois are particularly sweet and tender. Choose crisp, well-filled pods with some air space between the peas; very full pods are likely to contain tough peas. Allow 225g (8oz) in the pod, or 125g (4oz) shelled weight per person. Shell the peas and discard any that are discoloured; rinse and cook immediately in the minimum boiling salted water for 5–7 minutes. Toss with butter and mint. Popular frozen.

Vegetables

Pepper, chilli
The many types of chilli vary in appearance and potency, but are all hot and spicy. Most start green and ripen to red, but there are yellow and black ones. Choose those free from wrinkles and brown spots. The volatile oils can cause skin irritation so avoid touching your eyes and wash hands after touching (see also Cook's Tips, page 69). Use whole, sliced or diced, discarding the seeds for a less hot flavour. Use sparingly to spice up in curries, stews and stir-fries.

Pepper, sweet
The young fruit is green, turning yellow, then orange and red as it matures. Red peppers are the sweetest and softest. Choose firm, shiny peppers to eat raw or cooked. Cut off the stalk end. If serving whole, scoop out the core and seeds; otherwise halve lengthways, core and seed. To skin peppers, grill skin side up, until charred, then cover with an upturned bowl; the steam will help to lift the skins ready to peel. Slice or dice. Grill, stir-fry or blanch, or stuff and bake whole.

Plantain
They taste slightly of banana, but much less sweet. When cooked, the flesh is much firmer and more starchy than a banana, and similar to potato in texture. Don't substitute plantains for bananas; the two are quite different. They can be baked, boiled, grilled, steamed, mashed, or dried and ground into flour. Plantains are always cooked as a savoury ingredient, usually sliced, fried and served either as a snack, appetiser or accompaniment in place of rice or potatoes.

Potato
Varying in size, colour and texture, they fall into two categories: firm, waxy new potatoes, and floury old potatoes that soften on cooking. Refer to the pack or ask your supplier for advice on which variety suits which cooking method. Choose potatoes with smooth, firm skins and no green tinge, as these are unfit for eating. Buy new potatoes in small quantities and use them quickly. Allow 175–225g (6–8oz) per person. Bake, roast, boil, steam, mash or fry.

Pumpkin
Large pumpkins are often sold by the wedge. They should be firm and, if visible, the flesh should not be fibrous. Allow 175–225g (6–8oz) per person. Peel and halve, scoop out the seeds and cut into wedges or chop evenly. Steam rather than boil, which turns them mushy. Or drizzle with olive oil and roast at 200°C (180°C fan oven) mark 6 for 30 minutes or until tender. Top with melted butter and herbs. Can be stuffed and baked or used in soups or stews.

Radish
The small, round red and white radish varieties are sold all year, and typically eaten raw in salads. The white Japanese radish (mooli or daikon) is larger and elongated. It is milder than others and is usually peeled, grated and used as a garnish, or pickled. The black-skinned round Spanish radish has a stronger flavour; peel and eat raw or cooked. Choose radishes with fresh green tops or look for ones with firm bright skins. Allow 75–125g (3–4oz) per person.

Salsify and scorzonera
Salsify has a white skin and a flavour like oysters – it is known as vegetable oyster. Scorzonera – or black salsify – has a brownish-black skin and a stronger flavour. Choose smooth, firm specimens. Allow 125–175g (4–6oz) per person. Top and tail, then scrub well. Boil in salted water with a little lemon juice for 25–30 minutes until crisp-tender. Serve hot with lemon juice, melted butter and chopped herbs, purée for soups, or use in casseroles or salads.

Shallot
There are various varieties of these small onions. Brown: use in dressings and sauces; roasted whole or caramelised. Pink: slice or finely chop and sauté; cook whole and use in tarts and salads. Red Thai: use raw in spice pastes and salads; slice and fry until brown and crisp for a garnish; pickle whole. Banana: slice or finely chop and use raw in salads and dressings; sauté in butter or olive oil.

Spinach
Choose bright green leaves; avoid any that are wilting or yellow. Allow at least 225g (8oz) spinach per person. Wash thoroughly using several changes of water. Remove the tough stalks and central ribs, if necessary. Young, tender leaves are excellent raw in salads. Cook larger leaves in a covered pan with just the water that clings to the leaves after washing until just wilted. Drain well and press out the excess water from the leaves with the back of a wooden spoon.

Spring greens

An early variety of cabbage with tender, loose-packed leaves; it is harvested before it forms a heart. Originally available only in spring, they are now on sale most of the year. Look for fresh-looking heads and avoid any with wilting or flabby leaves. Store in the fridge and use within a few days. To use, wash well and shred. Boil or steam spring greens briefly to retain their sweet, fresh flavour and serve as an accompaniment topped with a knob of butter.

Spring onion

Also called salad onions, green onions or scallions, they vary in size from slender to bulbous. They have a mild, sweet flavour. Buy fresh-looking spring onions, store in a cool place or the fridge and use within a few days. Usually the green part is discarded (except in some Chinese dishes), but there is no reason not to use it as long as it is clean and in good condition. Trim off the root and any coarse leaves, then slice or use whole in salads, stir-fries and as a garnish.

Swede

Heavy, coarse root with orange flesh and a strong flavour. Choose small swede, as large ones can be tough. Avoid those with damaged skins. Allow about 175g (6oz) per person. Peel thickly, then cut into chunks. Steam or boil in cold salted water for 15–20 minutes, drain, then return to the pan to dry. Mash or purée with butter and seasoning. Or, parboil, then sauté in butter, or roast in hot fat round the meat at 200°C (180°C fan oven) mark 6 for 1–1½ hours.

Sweetcorn

At its best freshly picked, choose cobs with a tightly fitting husk and plump, cream kernels. Baby corn is eaten whole. Allow one cob per person, or 75–125g (3–4oz) loose or baby corn. Remove the stem, leaves and fibres. Hold the cob upright on a board and slice down with a sharp knife to cut off the kernels. Cook whole cobs in boiling water (without salt) for 5–15 minutes until a kernel comes away easily. Cook loose corn kernels in boiling water for 5–10 minutes.

Sweet potato

The sweet potato is not related to the common potato. Sweet potatoes are mostly elongated in shape, although some are round. The outer skin colour varies from tan to red, and the sweet flesh may be white or yellow. The red-skinned variety is most common in the UK. Choose small, firm sweet potatoes; large ones tend to be fibrous. Allow 225g (8oz) per person. Scrub well. If boiling, peel afterwards. Cook as for potatoes – boil, bake, fry or roast.

Tomato

The many varieties are a fruit but used as a vegetable. Baby plum and cherry tomatoes (see below) are sweet and tasty. Beef tomatoes can weigh up to 450g (1lb) – stuff or use raw. Choose firm, unblemished tomatoes with a hint of fragrance. Allow 1–2 raw tomatoes per person, sliced or quartered in salads. Allow 1 large tomato for stuffing. Cut a sliver from the base, then cut off the top and scoop out seeds and flesh. Serve hot or cold. Use overripe tomatoes in sauces.

Tomato, cherry

These have a much sweeter, more intense flavour than salad tomatoes. Their appealing size makes them good for salads, garnishes and canapés, but they are also good for quickly cooked pasta sauces, because they do not require much cooking to achieve a sweet, rich flavour. They can also be threaded on to skewers and briefly barbecued, or stir-fried quickly with some crushed garlic to serve as an accompaniment.

Turnip

Young turnips are sweet and usually tender. Maincrop turnips have thicker skins and coarser flesh. Choose smooth, unblemished turnips. Allow 175g (6oz) per person. Peel young turnips thinly but older ones thickly, then slice or cut into chunks. Young ones can be served raw, sliced thinly or grated into salads. Cook small young turnips whole; cut up older ones. Steam or boil in salted water for 20–30 minutes until tender. Serve in chunks or mashed.

Yam

A member of the tuber family, originating from Africa. Yams have a brownish-pink skin and white flesh. Allow 175g (6oz) per person. Wash and peel, then dice. Boil in salted water, with a little lemon juice, for 20 minutes or until tender; or steam. Yams can also be roasted, baked or fried.

Spring Vegetable Stew

Serves 4
Preparation time 20 minutes
Cooking time 30–35 minutes

225g (8oz) new potatoes, scrubbed and halved
75g (3oz) unsalted butter
4 shallots, blanched in boiling water, drained and thinly
   sliced
1 garlic clove, crushed
2 tsp freshly chopped thyme
1 tsp grated lime zest
6 baby leeks, trimmed and sliced into 5cm (2in) lengths
125g (4oz) baby carrots, scrubbed
125g (4oz) podded peas
125g (4oz) podded broad beans, skinned (see page 278)
300ml (½ pint) vegetable stock
1 Little Gem lettuce, shredded
4 tbsp freshly chopped herbs, such as chervil, chives,
mint and parsley, plus extra chives to garnish
salt and ground black pepper

1 Put the potatoes into a pan of lightly salted water. Bring
to the boil, cover the pan and parboil for 5 minutes. Drain
and refresh under cold water.
2 Meanwhile, melt half the butter in a large sauté pan, add
the shallots, garlic, thyme and lime zest and fry gently for
5 minutes or until softened and lightly golden. Add the
leeks and carrots, and sauté for a further 5 minutes. Stir in
the potatoes, peas and broad beans, then pour in the stock
and bring to the boil. Reduce the heat, cover the pan and
simmer gently for 10 minutes.
3 Remove the lid and cook, uncovered, for a further
5–8 minutes until all the vegetables are tender.
4 Add the shredded lettuce to the stew with the chopped
herbs and remaining butter. Heat through until the butter
is melted. Season to taste with salt and pepper and serve at
once garnished with chives.

NUTRITION PER SERVING 270 cals | 17g fat (10g sats) | 23g carbs | 0.6g salt Ⓥ

Veggie Paneer Curry

Serves 4
Preparation time 20 minutes
Cooking time 20 minutes

1 tbsp vegetable oil
1 onion, finely sliced
1 garlic clove, crushed
2 tbsp mild curry paste
165ml can coconut milk
300ml (½ pint) vegetable stock
300g (11oz) mix of broccoli and
  cauliflower florets
200g (7oz) frozen peas
150g (5oz) paneer cheese, cubed
a large handful of spinach
salt and ground black pepper
wholegrain rice to serve

1 Heat the oil in a large pan over a low heat and gently cook the onion for about 10 minutes until soft. Add the garlic and curry paste and cook for 1 minute.
2 Stir in the coconut milk and stock. Bring to the boil, then reduce the heat to low, add the florets and simmer for 5 minutes or until nearly cooked through.
3 Add the peas and paneer, season with salt and pepper and heat through. Fold the spinach through until wilted and serve with wholegrain rice.

NUTRITION PER SERVING 272 cals | 16g fat (9g sats) | 14g carbs | 0.8g salt

Ratatouille

Serves 6
Preparation time 20 minutes
Cooking time about 45 minutes

4 tbsp olive oil
2 onions, thinly sliced
1 large garlic clove, crushed
350g (12oz) small aubergine,
  thinly sliced
450g (1lb) small courgettes,
  thinly sliced
450g (1lb) tomatoes, skinned, seeded
  and roughly chopped (see page 277)
1 green pepper, cored, seeded and sliced
1 red pepper, cored, seeded and sliced
1 tbsp freshly chopped basil
2 tsp freshly chopped thyme
2 tbsp freshly chopped flat-leafed
  parsley
2 tbsp sun-dried tomato paste
salt and ground black pepper

1 Heat the olive oil in a large pan, add the onions and garlic and fry gently for 10 minutes or until softened and golden.
2 Add the aubergine, courgettes, tomatoes, sliced peppers, herbs, tomato paste and salt and pepper. Fry, stirring, for 2–3 minutes.
3 Cover the pan tightly and simmer for 30 minutes or until all the vegetables are just tender. If necessary, uncover towards the end of the cooking time to evaporate some of the liquid.
4 Season to taste with salt and pepper. Serve the ratatouille either hot or cold.

NUTRITION PER SERVING 200 cals | 10g fat (2g sats) | 19g carbs | 0.7g salt Ⓥ

Green Beans and Flaked Almonds

Serves 4
Preparation time 5 minutes
Cooking time 5–7 minutes

200g (7oz) green beans
1 tsp olive oil
25g (1oz) flaked almonds
½ lemon

1 Bring a large pan of water to the boil. Add the green beans and cook for 4–5 minutes. Drain.
2 Meanwhile, heat the oil in a large frying pan. Add the almonds and cook for 1–2 minutes until golden. Turn off the heat, add the drained beans to the frying pan and toss. Squeeze a little lemon juice over the top just before serving.

TRY SOMETHING DIFFERENT
• Use basil-infused oil and increase the amount of oil to 2 tbsp.
• Use pinenuts instead of almonds, drizzle with balsamic vinegar and scatter with basil leaves to serve.

NUTRITION PER SERVING 57 cals | 5g fat (trace sats) | 2g carbs | 0g salt Ⓥ

Braised Chicory in White Wine

Serves 6
Preparation time 5 minutes
Cooking time about 1 hour

50g (2oz) butter, softened
6 heads of chicory, trimmed
100ml (3½fl oz) white wine
  (see Alcoholic Drinks and
  Vegetarians, page 489)
salt and ground black pepper
freshly snipped chives to serve

1 Preheat the oven to 190°C (170°C fan oven) mark 5. Grease a 1.7 litre (3 pint) ovenproof dish with 15g (½oz) butter and put the chicory in the dish.
2 Season to taste with salt and pepper, add the wine and dot the remaining butter over the top. Cover with foil and cook in the oven for 1 hour or until soft. Scatter with chives to serve.

NUTRITION PER SERVING 80 cals | 7g fat (5g sats) | 3g carbs | 0.1g salt Ⓥ

Honey-glazed Shallots

Serves 4
Preparation time 15 minutes, plus soaking
Cooking time 25 minutes

450g (1lb) shallots, halved
25g (1oz) butter
1 tbsp clear honey
juice of ½ lemon
1 tbsp Worcestershire sauce
1 tbsp balsamic vinegar
salt and ground black pepper

1 Put the shallots into a bowl, add cold water to cover and leave to soak for 20 minutes. Drain and peel away the skins.
2 Tip the shallots into a pan and add just enough cold water to cover. Bring to the boil, lower the heat and simmer for 5 minutes. Drain well, then return the shallots to the pan.
3 Add all the remaining ingredients and stir until the shallots are well coated with the glaze. Cover the pan and cook gently, stirring occasionally, until the shallots are tender. Remove the lid and bubble for 2–3 minutes until the liquid is reduced and syrupy. Serve the shallots hot.

NUTRITION PER SERVING 100 cals |
5g fat (3g sats) | 14g carbs | 0.5g salt

Creamed Spinach

Serves 6
Preparation time 15 minutes
Cooking time 5 minutes

900g (2lb) spinach leaves, tough stalks
  removed
4 tbsp crème fraîche
salt and ground black pepper

1 Cook the spinach with just the water clinging to the leaves in a covered pan for 3–4 minutes until just wilted.
2 Stir in the crème fraîche and season with salt and pepper to taste. Serve at once.

NUTRITION PER SERVING 80 cals |
5g fat (3g sats) | 3g carbs | 0.2g salt Ⓥ

Mediterranean Stuffed Peppers

Serves 4
Preparation time 15 minutes
Cooking time 35 minutes

2 Romero peppers, halved and seeded
75g (3oz) couscous
hot vegetable stock
50g (2oz) chopped dried apricots
finely grated zest and juice of ½ lemon
15g (½oz) chopped roasted hazelnuts (see Cook's Tip,
  page 312
25g (1oz) pitted black olives, chopped
4 tbsp chopped mixed soft herbs
25g (1oz) vegetarian feta cheese (see Vegetarian Cheeses
  on page 228)
salt and ground black pepper

1 Preheat the oven to 200°C (180°C fan oven) mark 6. Put
the peppers into an ovenproof serving dish and roast
for 25 minutes or until just tender.
2 Meanwhile put the couscous into a heatproof bowl, pour
over just enough hot vegetable stock to cover, stir, then
leave to stand for 10 minutes. Fluff up with a fork, then stir
in the apricots, lemon zest and juice, chopped hazelnuts,
olives and herbs. Season with salt and pepper.
3 Spoon the mixture into the peppers, then crumble
the feta over them. Return to the oven for 10 minutes until
the cheese has melted and browned on top. Serve warm or
at room temperature.

NUTRITION PER SERVING 140 cals | 5g fat (1g sats) | 18g carbs | 0.6g salt Ⓥ

Petits Pois à la Française

Serves 4
Preparation time 5 minutes
Cooking time 15 minutes

1 firm-hearted lettuce
50g (2oz) butter
900g (2lb) young peas, shelled
12 spring onions, sliced
1 tsp sugar
150ml (¼ pint) chicken stock
salt and ground black pepper

1 Remove the outer leaves of the lettuce and cut the heart into quarters.
2 Melt the butter in a large pan, add the peas, spring onions, lettuce, sugar, stock and salt and pepper. Bring to the boil, then lower the heat, cover and simmer for 15–20 minutes until all the vegetables are tender.

NUTRITION PER SERVING 297cals | 14g fat (7g sats) | 28g carbs | 0.7g salt

Jersey Royals with Mint and Petits Pois

Serves 6
Preparation time 15 minutes
Cooking time 30 minutes

3 tbsp olive oil
900g (2lb) new potatoes, preferably Jersey Royals, thickly sliced
175g (6oz) frozen petits pois
3 tbsp chopped mint
salt and ground black pepper

1 Cooking in batches, if necessary, heat the oil in a large non-stick frying pan, add the potatoes and cook for 5 minutes, turning, until browned on both sides.
2 When all the potatoes are browned, partially cover the pan and cook for a further 10–15 minutes until tender.

3 Meanwhile, cook the petits pois in a pan of boiling water for 2 minutes, then drain well. Add them to the potatoes and cook through for 2–3 minutes.
4 Add the chopped mint, and salt and pepper to taste, then serve.

Cook's Tip
Jersey Royals are highly regarded for their distinctively nutty flavour, waxy texture, yellow flesh and papery skin and also for their true seasonality: they are at their best between April and June. When not in season, use other new potatoes for this recipe.

NUTRITION PER SERVING 180 cals | 7g fat (1g sats) | 27g carbs | 0.2g salt Ⓥ

Crispy Roast Potatoes

Serves 8
Preparation time 20 minutes
Cooking time 1 hour 50 minutes

1.8kg (4lb) potatoes, preferably King
  Edward, cut into two-bite pieces
2 tsp paprika
2–3 tbsp goose or white vegetable fat
salt

1 Put the potatoes in a pan of salted
cold water. Cover the pan and bring
to the boil, then reduce the heat and
simmer for 7 minutes. Drain in a
colander.
2 Sprinkle the paprika over the
potatoes in the colander, then cover
and shake the potatoes roughly, so
they become fluffy around the edges.
3 Preheat the oven to 220°C (200°C
fan oven) mark 7. Heat the fat in a
large roasting tin on the hob. When
it sizzles, add the potatoes. Tilt the
pan to coat, taking care as the fat will
splutter. Roast in the oven for 1 hour.
4 Reduce the oven temperature to
200°C (180°C fan oven) mark 6
and roast for a further 40 minutes
until golden and crisp. Shake them
only once or twice during cooking,
otherwise the edges won't crisp.
Season with salt before serving.

Freezing Tip
• To freeze, complete the recipe to the end
  of step 2, then cool, seal in freezer bags
  and freeze for up to one month.
• To use, cook from frozen, allowing
  an additional 15–20 minutes total
  cooking time.

NUTRITION PER SERVING 211 cals |
6g fat (3g sats) | 37g carbs | 0.1g salt

Oven Chips

Serves 4
Preparation time 10 minutes
Cooking time 40 minutes

900g (2lb) floury potatoes, preferably
  Desirée
2–3 tbsp olive oil
salt and sea salt flakes

1 Preheat the oven to 240°C (220°C
fan oven) mark 9. Peel the potatoes
and cut into chips. Add to a pan of
boiling salted water, cover the pan
and bring to the boil, then boil for 2
minutes. Drain well, then carefully pat
dry with kitchen paper.
2 Tip the parboiled potatoes into a
large non-stick roasting tin, toss with
the oil and season with sea salt. Roast
for 40 minutes or until golden and
cooked, turning from time to time.
Drain on kitchen paper and serve.

NUTRITION PER SERVING 220 cals |
6g fat (1g sats) | 39g carbs | 0.3g salt Ⓥ

Potato Croquettes

Serves 6
Preparation time 30 minutes, plus chilling
Cooking time 45 minutes

1kg (2¼lb) potatoes, preferably Desirée, scrubbed
50g (2oz) butter, softened, plus extra to grease
150g (5oz) fresh white breadcrumbs
100g (3½oz) Parmesan, freshly grated
2 tbsp freshly chopped flat-leafed parsley
freshly grated nutmeg to taste
2 medium eggs, beaten
olive oil to drizzle
salt and ground black pepper

1 Put the potatoes into a pan of cold salted water. Bring to
the boil, then reduce the heat and simmer for about
20 minutes or until tender.
2 Preheat the oven to 230°C (210°C fan oven) mark 8 and
grease two roasting tins.
3 Meanwhile, spread the breadcrumbs on to a baking sheet
and bake for 15 minutes or until golden. Tip on to a plate.
Turn off the oven.
4 Drain the potatoes well, leave to cool for 5 minutes, then
peel. Mash until smooth. Add the butter, Parmesan and
parsley. Season well with nutmeg, salt and pepper, and mix
together thoroughly.
5 Put the beaten eggs into a shallow bowl. Take about
2 tbsp of the potato mixture and shape into a small sausage.
Roll the croquette first in the beaten egg and then in the
breadcrumbs to coat. Put into the prepared roasting tin.
6 Repeat to use up all the potato mixture. Cover with
clingfilm and chill for 30 minutes.
7 Preheat the oven to 230°C (210°C fan oven) mark 8.
8 Uncover the croquettes, drizzle with a little olive oil and
bake for 25 minutes or until golden. Serve at once.

Cook's Tip
Using a potato ricer insead of a masher gives them a lovely
fluffy texture – make sure the potatoes are still hot when
you begin to mash them.

NUTRITION PER SERVING 370 cals | 17g fat (8g sats) | 41g carbs | 1.4g salt Ⓥ

Gratin Dauphinois

Serves 4–6
Preparation time 10 minutes
Cooking time 50 minutes

oil to grease
900g (2lb) floury potatoes, cut into
  slices
1 garlic clove, crushed
a pinch of freshly grated nutmeg
150ml (¼ pint) single cream
75g (3oz) Gruyère, grated (see
  Vegetarian Cheeses, page 228)
salt and ground black pepper

1 Preheat the oven to 180°C (160°C
fan oven) mark 4 and grease a 1.1 litre
(2 pint) ovenproof dish.
2 Cook the potatoes in boiling salted
water for 5 minutes, then drain well.
Turn into the prepared dish.
3 Stir the garlic, nutmeg, salt and
pepper into the cream and pour over
the potatoes.
4 Sprinkle with cheese, cover and
cook in the oven for 45 minutes or
until the potatoes are tender.
5 Preheat the grill. Uncover the dish
and brown under the hot grill.

NUTRITION PER SERVING 444 cals |
24g fat (11g sats) | 38g carbs | 1g salt Ⓥ

Rösti Potatoes with Fried Eggs

Serves 4
Preparation time 20 minutes, plus cooling
Cooking time 20–25 minutes

900g (2lb) red potatoes, scrubbed
  and left whole
40g (1½oz) butter
4 large eggs
salt and ground black pepper
fresh flat-leafed parsley sprigs to
  garnish

1 Put the potatoes into a pan of cold
water. Cover, bring to the boil and
parboil for 5–8 minutes. Drain and
leave to cool for 15 minutes.
2 Preheat the oven to 150°C (130°C
fan oven) mark 2. Put a baking tray
inside to warm. Peel the potatoes and
coarsely grate lengthways into long
strands. Divide into eight portions
and shape into mounds. Season.
3 Melt half the butter in a large non-
stick frying pan. When it is beginning
to brown, add four of the potato
mounds, spacing them well apart, and
flatten them a little. Fry gently for
6–7 minutes until golden brown, then
turn them and brown the other side
for 6–7 minutes. Transfer to a warmed
baking tray and keep them warm in
the oven while you fry the rest.
4 Just before serving, carefully break
the eggs into the hot pan and fry for
about 2 minutes or until the white is
set and the yolk is still soft. Season
with salt and pepper and serve at
once, with the rösti. Garnish with
sprigs of parsley.

NUTRITION PER SERVING 324 cals |
16g fat (7g sats) | 36g carbs | 0.4g salt Ⓥ

Hasselback Potatoes

Serves 4
Preparation time 10 minutes
Cooking time 45 minutes

8 potatoes, weighing about 75g (3oz) each
vegetable oil for brushing
coarse salt and ground black pepper

1 Preheat the oven to 220°C (200°C fan oven) mark 7
and oil a baking tin. Cut the potatoes across their width at
5mm (¼in) intervals three-quarters of the way through.
2 Put in a single layer in the prepared tin. Brush with oil
and season with salt and pepper. Roast, uncovered, for
45 minutes until tender and golden brown.

Cook's Tip
To stop you from slicing all the way through the potatoes,
place them in the bowl of a wooden spoon on a cutting
board while you cut them.

NUTRITION PER SERVING   162 cals | 6g fat (1g sats) | 26g carbs | 0.3g salt Ⓥ

Bubble and Squeak Cake

Makes 8
Preparation time 10 minutes
Cooking time 15 minutes

a small knob of butter
225g (8oz) savoy cabbage, shredded
400g (14oz) mashed potato (or about
 500g (1lb 2oz) raw potatoes, boiled
 and mashed)
75g (3oz) chopped ham
25g (1oz) Cheddar, grated
1 tbsp wholegrain mustard
a splash of milk
a splash of vegetable oil
salt and ground black pepper
chutney to serve

1 Heat the butter in a large frying pan over a medium heat and fry the cabbage for 5 minutes or until wilted.
2 Transfer to a large bowl and stir in the mashed potato, ham, cheese, mustard and a splash of milk and blend well. Season with salt and pepper.
3 Divide the mixture equally into eight and shape each portion into a flattened patty.
4 Return the pan to the heat with a thin layer of oil. Fry the patties over a medium heat for 8–10 minutes, turning once or until golden and piping hot. Serve immediately with plenty of your favourite chutney.

NUTRITION PER SERVING 114 cals | 5g fat (2g sats) |11g carbs | 0.4g salt Ⓥ

Savoy Cabbage with Crème Fraîche

Serves 6
Preparation time 8 minutes
Cooking time 5 minutes

1 large Savoy cabbage, about 900g (2lb)
25g (1oz) butter
200ml crème fraîche
2 tbsp freshly chopped flat-leafed
 parsley
salt and ground black pepper

1 Cut the Savoy cabbage into large wedges. Bring a pan of salted water to the boil. Add the cabbage wedges, bring back to the boil and boil for 1–2 minutes only. Drain thoroughly.
2 Heat the butter in a large frying pan, add the cabbage and stir-fry for 3–4 minutes until it is just beginning to colour.
3 Add the crème fraîche and chopped parsley, toss briefly and season with pepper to taste. Do not allow the sauce to boil. Serve straight away.

NUTRITION PER SERVING 200 cals | 17g fat (11g sats) | 6g carbs | 0.3g salt Ⓥ

Colcannon

Serves 4
Preparation time 10 minutes
Cooking time 20 minutes

900g (2lb) floury potatoes, cut into
  even-sized chunks
50g (2oz) butter
¼ Savoy cabbage, shredded
100ml (3½fl oz) semi-skimmed milk
salt and ground black pepper

1 Put the potatoes into a pan of cold
salted water. Bring to the boil, then
lower the heat and simmer, partially
covered, for 15–20 minutes until the
potatoes are tender.
2 Meanwhile, melt the butter in a
large frying pan. Add the cabbage and
stir-fry for 3 minutes.
3 Drain the potatoes well, then tip
back into the pan and put over a
medium heat for 1 minute to drive
off the excess moisture. Turn into a
colander and cover to keep warm.
4 Pour the milk into the potato pan
and bring to the boil, then take off the
heat. Add the potatoes and mash well
until smooth.
5 Add the cabbage and any butter
from the pan and mix together.
Season with salt and pepper to taste
and serve.

NUTRITION PER SERVING 310 cals |
12g fat (7g sats) | 45g carbs | 0.5g salt Ⓥ

Neeps and Tatties

Serves 4
Preparation time 15 minutes
Cooking time 25 minutes

250g (9oz) swede, cut into chunks
450g (1lb) floury potatoes, cut into
  chunks
50–100g (2–3½oz) butter
1 tbsp double cream (optional)
freshly grated nutmeg
salt and ground black pepper
haggis to serve

1 Bring a large pan of lightly salted
water to the boil, add the swede and
cook for 20–25 minutes until tender.
Drain and steam dry for 2 minutes.
2 Meanwhile, bring another large
pan of lightly salted water to the
boil, add the potatoes and cook for
15–20 minutes until tender. Drain
and steam dry for 2 minutes.
3 Mash each vegetable with half the
butter until smooth, adding a splash
of cream, if you like. Season with
nutmeg, salt and pepper to taste.
Serve with haggis.

NUTRITION PER SERVING 276 cals |
20g fat (12g sats) | 23g carbs | 0.3g salt Ⓥ

Mushroom and Cranberry Nut Roast

Serves 8
Preparation time 30 minutes, plus soaking
Cooking time 1 hour 20 minutes

15g (½oz) dried wild mushrooms
50g (2oz) butter, plus extra to grease
1 medium onion, finely chopped
2 celery sticks, diced
1 garlic clove, crushed
125g (4oz) mixed mushrooms, such as chestnut or
 Portobello, finely chopped
100g (3½oz) risotto rice, such as Arborio
100ml (3½fl oz) dry vermouth or dry white wine
500–600ml (17–20fl oz) hot vegetable stock
75g (3oz) fresh breadcrumbs
50g (2oz) blanched almonds, toasted and
 roughly chopped (see Cook's Tip, page 312)
50g (2oz) pistachios, toasted and roughly chopped
125g (4oz) mature Cheddar, grated (see Vegetarian Cheeses,
 page 228)
2 medium eggs, beaten
1 tbsp freshly chopped thyme leaves
1 tbsp freshly chopped curly parsley
200g (7oz) fresh cranberries
1 tbsp cranberry sauce
a few fresh bay leaves
salt and ground black pepper

1 Put the dried mushrooms into a small bowl and cover
with boiling water. Leave to stand for 20 minutes.
2 Melt the butter in a large pan and gently fry the onion
and celery for 10 minutes or until softened. Add the garlic
and cook for 1 minute.
3 Drain the mushrooms, reserving 150ml (¼ pint) of the
soaking liquid. Chop the mushrooms and add them to
the pan with the fresh mushrooms. Cook for 5 minutes,
stirring often. Strain the reserved soaking liquid.
4 Stir in the rice and cook for 1 minute. Slowly add the
vermouth or wine and bubble until almost evaporated, then
add the mushroom liquid and simmer until it has almost
disappeared.
5 Add a ladleful of hot stock and simmer until absorbed.
Keep adding a ladleful at a time, stirring and keeping the
rice at a gentle simmer, for about 20 minutes or until the
rice is tender. Season with salt and pepper. Put in a bowl to
allow it to cool.

6 Preheat the oven to 180°C (160°C fan oven) mark 4 and
grease an 18 × 12.5 × 7.5cm (7 × 5 × 3in) ovenproof dish
or loaf tin. Stir the remaining ingredients, except the fresh
cranberries and sauce, into the mushroom mixture and
season with salt and pepper. Put the fresh cranberries into
the bottom of the prepared dish, then tip in the mushroom
mixture and pack down firmly. Cover with foil and bake for
1 hour, removing the foil for the last 10 minutes. Leave to
stand for 10 minutes.
7 Meanwhile, heat the cranberry sauce with 1 tbsp water,
then push through a sieve. Carefully turn out the nut roast
on to a platter and brush with the cranberry glaze. Garnish
with fresh bay leaves.

NUTRITION PER SERVING 332 cals | 219g fat (8g sats) | 23g carbs | 0.7g salt Ⓥ

Mushroom Roulade

Serves 6
Preparation time 20 minutes
Cooking time 15 minutes

250g (9oz) frozen spinach, thawed
4 large eggs, separated
freshly grated nutmeg
3½ tbsp cornflour
15g (½oz) butter
2 shallots, finely sliced
350g (12oz) mushrooms, sliced
400ml (14fl oz) skimmed milk
25g (1oz) mature vegetarian Cheddar, grated (see Vegetarian
  Cheeses, page 228)
1 tsp English mustard
salt and ground black pepper
green salad to serve

1 Preheat the oven to 190°C (170°C fan oven) mark 5.
Line a 30.5 × 23cm (12 × 9in) baking tin with baking
parchment. Squeeze out as much moisture as you can from
the thawed spinach and put it in a large bowl. Stir in the
egg yolks, nutmeg and plenty of salt and pepper.
2 Put the egg whites into a separate bowl and whisk
until they hold stiff peaks. Quickly beat in 1½ tbsp of
the cornflour, then fold the mixture into the spinach
bowl. Empty on to the prepared tin, spreading it to the
corners, then cook for 12–15 minutes until golden and
firm to the touch.
3 Meanwhile, heat the butter in a large frying pan and
cook the shallots for 5 minutes or until softened. Turn up
the heat and add the mushrooms. Cook for 8–10 minutes
until softened and any water in the pan has evaporated.
Stir in the remaining cornflour, then the milk. Heat,
stirring, until thickened. Stir in the cheese and mustard
and check the seasoning.
4 Take the spinach base out of the oven and transfer with
the paper to a board. Slide a palette knife underneath the
roulade to loosen, if necessary, then spread the mushroom
mixture over the top. Roll up lengthways as neatly as you
can (don't worry if there's some spillage) and serve warm in
slices with a green salad.

NUTRITION PER SERVING 177 cals | 9g fat (4g sats) | 12g carbs | 0.5g salt ⓥ

Braised Red Cabbage

Serves 6
Preparation time 15 minutes
Cooking time 50 minutes

1 tbsp olive oil
1 red onion, halved and sliced
2 garlic cloves, crushed
1 large red cabbage, about 1kg (2¼lb), shredded
2 tbsp light muscovado sugar
2 tbsp red wine vinegar
8 juniper berries
¼ tsp ground allspice
300ml (½ pint) vegetable stock
2 pears, cored and sliced
salt and ground black pepper
fresh thyme sprigs to garnish

1 Heat the oil in a large pan, add the onion and fry for 5 minutes or until soft. Add the remaining ingredients, except the pears, and season with salt and pepper. Bring to the boil, then reduce the heat, cover the pan and simmer for 30 minutes.
2 Add the pears and cook for a further 15 minutes or until nearly all the liquid has evaporated and the cabbage is tender. Serve hot, garnished with thyme.

NUTRITION PER SERVING 63 cals | 1g fat (0g sats) | 12g carbs | 0.9g salt Ⓥ

Slow-roasted Tomatoes

Serves 4
Preparation time 10 minutes, plus cooling
Cooking time 2½–3 hours

12 large ripe tomatoes
2 garlic cloves, roughly chopped
2 fresh thyme sprigs, bruised
a pinch of sugar
4 tbsp extra virgin olive oil
squeeze of lemon juice
basil leaves to garnish
salt and ground black pepper

1 Preheat the oven to 150°C (130°C fan oven) mark 2. Halve the tomatoes and scoop out most of the seeds. Put the tomato halves into a baking dish in which they fit closely together and scatter over the garlic, thyme, sugar, salt and pepper.
2 Drizzle the olive oil over the tomatoes and add a good squeeze of lemon juice. Roast for 2½–3 hours until the tomatoes are shrivelled (but not as dried as sun-dried tomatoes). Leave to cool.
3 Scatter the basil leaves over the tomatoes and serve, as a side dish to cold meats and cheese.

NUTRITION PER SERVING 170 cals | 14g fat (2g sats) | 9g carbs | 0.3g salt Ⓥ

Roasted Root Vegetables

Serves 4
Preparation time 15 minutes
Cooking time 1 hour

1 large potato, cut into large chunks
1 large sweet potato, cut into large
  chunks
3 carrots, cut into large chunks
4 small parsnips, halved
1 small swede, cut into large chunks
3 tbsp olive oil
2 fresh rosemary sprigs
2 fresh thyme sprigs
salt and ground black pepper

1 Preheat the oven to 200°C
(180°C fan oven) mark 6. Put all the
vegetables into a large roasting tin.
Add the oil.
2 Use scissors to snip the herbs over
the vegetables, then season with
salt and and black pepper and toss
everything together. Roast for 1 hour
or until tender.

TRY SOMETHING DIFFERENT

Use other combinations of vegetables:
try celeriac instead of parsnips, fennel
instead of swede, peeled shallots
instead of carrots.

NUTRITION PER SERVING 251 cals |
10g fat (1g sats) | 39g carbs | 0.2g salt Ⓥ

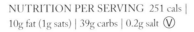

Baked Beetroot

Serves 6
Preparation time 15 minutes
Cooking time 1¼–1½ hours

1.25kg (2lb 12oz) beetroot
15g (½oz) butter
salt and ground black pepper
freshly chopped parsley or chives to
  garnish

1 Preheat the oven to 200°C (180°C
fan oven) mark 6. Trim the beetroot
and carefully rinse in cold water,
making sure you do not tear the skins.
2 Rub the butter over the middle of a
large piece of foil. Put the beetroot on
the buttered foil and season with salt
and pepper. Bring the edges of the foil
up over the beetroot and fold together
to seal and form a parcel. Put on a
baking sheet.

3 Bake for 1¼–1½ hours until the
beetroot are soft and the skin comes
away easily.
4 Leave for a minute or two until
cool enough to handle, then rub off
the skins. Roughly chop the beetroot,
then scatter chopped parsley or chives
over the beetroot to serve.

TRY SOMETHING DIFFERENT

Use baby beetroot. Roast them whole
as per the method, then in step 4 rub
off the skins and halve or leave whole.

NUTRITION PER SERVING 90 cals |
2g fat (1g sats) | 15g carbs | 0.2g salt Ⓥ

Crunchy Parsnips

Serves 8
Preparation time 10 minutes
Cooking time 1 hour 10 minutes

4 tbsp goose fat or sunflower oil
8 parsnips, halved lengthways
2 tbsp semolina

1 Preheat the oven to 200°C (180°C fan oven) mark 6. Put the fat or oil into a roasting tin large enough for the parsnips to sit in one layer without touching each other. Heat up while the parsnips are parboiling.
2 Put the parsnips in a pan of cold, salted water and bring to the boil. Cook for 5 minutes. Drain and leave in the colander to steam for 2 minutes.

3 Put the semolina on a plate and coat the parsnips evenly all over, shaking off any excess semolina.
4 Tip the parsnips into the roasting tin, tossing to coat in the hot fat. Roast for 45 minutes–1 hour, turning twice during cooking to re-coat, until the parsnips are crisp.

GET AHEAD

Prepare the parsnips up to step 2, up to 24 hours ahead. Chill in a sealed plastic bag. To use, complete the recipe.

NUTRITION PER SERVING 145 cals | 8g fat (2g sats) | 15g carbs | 1g salt

---

Creamy Leeks

Serves 8
Preparation time 15 minutes, plus cooling
Cooking time 20 minutes

900g (2lb) trimmed leeks, cut into chunks
25g (1oz) butter
150ml (¼ pint) crème fraîche
freshly grated nutmeg to taste
salt and ground black pepper

1 Cook the leeks in a pan of boiling salted water for 7–10 minutes until just tender. Drain and immediately plunge into a bowl of icy cold water to refresh. When cool, drain and pat dry with kitchen paper.
2 Roughly chop the leeks in a food processor. Take out half and set aside. Whiz the remainder until smooth.
3 Melt the butter in a frying pan, add the chopped and puréed leeks, and stir over a high heat for a minute or two.
4 Add the crème fraîche and season with salt and pepper. Stir over a low heat until hot through but not boiling (or the crème fraîche may separate). Sprinkle with grated nutmeg to serve.

NUTRITION PER SERVING 120 cals | 11g fat (7 sats) | 3g carbs | 0.7g salt Ⓥ

Fennel Gratin

Serves 6
Preparation time 10 minutes
Cooking time 15–20 minutes

3 fennel bulbs, trimmed
300ml (½ pint) vegetable stock
25g (1oz) butter
1 garlic clove, crushed
1 bunch of spring onions, trimmed and
  finely chopped
2 tbsp chopped fennel fronds or dill
300ml (½ pint) double cream
50g (2oz) Cheddar, grated (see
  Vegetarian Cheeses, page 228)
ground black pepper

1 Cut the fennel lengthways into
5mm (¼in) thick slices and put into
a large shallow pan with the stock
and half the butter. Bring to the boil,
lower the heat, cover and simmer for
10–15 minutes until just tender.
2 Meanwhile, melt the remaining
butter in another pan, add the garlic
and spring onions and fry gently for
5 minutes or until softened. Stir in
the chopped fennel fronds or dill.
3 Lift out the poached fennel with
a slotted spoon and put into a gratin
dish. Add 150ml (¼ pint) of the
cooking liquid to the spring onions.
Pour in the cream, bring to the boil
and simmer gently for 1 minute. Take
off the heat, stir in the cheese and
season with pepper to taste.
4 Pour the sauce over the fennel
and grill under a high heat for
1–2 minutes until bubbling and
golden brown.

NUTRITION PER SERVING 310 cals |
31g fat (21g sats) | 4g carbs | 0.8g salt Ⓥ

Caramelised Carrots

Serves 8
Preparation time 15 minutes
Cooking time 10–15 minutes

700g (1½ lb) baby carrots, scraped
50g (2oz) butter
50g (2oz) light muscovado sugar
300ml (½ pint) vegetable or chicken
  stock
2 tbsp balsamic vinegar
2 tbsp freshly chopped parsley
salt and ground black pepper

1 Thinly slice the carrots lengthways,
then put into a pan with the butter,
sugar and stock. Season with salt
and pepper, then cover the pan and
bring to the boil. Reduce the heat and
simmer for 5 minutes.
2 Remove the lid, sprinkle in
the balsamic vinegar and cook for
5–10 minutes or until the carrots are
tender and the liquid has reduced
to form a glaze. Scatter with the
chopped parsley to serve.

NUTRITION PER SERVING 100 cals |
5g fat (3g sats) | 13g carbs | 0.8g salt Ⓥ

Grilled Mushrooms with Herb and Garlic Butter

Serves 4
Preparation time 10 minutes, plus chilling
Cooking time 10 minutes

125g (4oz) butter, softened
2 garlic cloves, crushed
2–3 tsp freshly snipped chives
2–3 tsp freshly chopped parsley
1 tsp grated lemon zest
12 field mushrooms, trimmed
1 tbsp olive oil
salt and ground black pepper

1 Cream the butter, garlic, herbs, lemon zest and a little
salt and pepper together in a bowl. Cover and chill in the
fridge for at least 30 minutes.
2 Preheat the grill.
3 Brush the mushrooms with oil, lay gill side down on
a grill pan and grill under a high heat for 5 minutes.
Meanwhile, cut the flavoured butter into pieces.
4 Turn the mushrooms gill side up. Dot with the butter
and grill for a further 4–5 minutes until tender and
sizzling. Serve at once, as a starter or as an accompaniment
to grilled meat or vegetables.

TRY SOMETHING DIFFERENT
Flavour the butter with chopped basil, garlic and chopped
sun-dried tomatoes.

NUTRITION PER SERVING 300 cals | 30g fat (17g sats) | 0.8g carbs | 0.5g salt Ⓥ

Spiced Okra with Onion and Tomato

Serves 4
Preparation time 20 minutes
Cooking time 25 minutes

450g (1lb) okra
2.5cm (1in) piece fresh root ginger, peeled
1 onion, quartered
2 garlic cloves, roughly chopped
2 tsp ground coriander
½ tsp ground cinnamon
½ tsp ground turmeric
3 tbsp oil
3 tomatoes, skinned and chopped (see page 277)
2 tbsp thick yogurt
2 tbsp freshly chopped coriander
salt and ground black pepper

1 Trim the okra, removing a small piece from each end; don't cut into the flesh or the dish will acquire an unpleasant glutinous texture during cooking.
2 Roughly chop the ginger and put into a blender with the onion, garlic and 1 tbsp water. Process until smooth. Add the spices and process again.
3 Heat the oil in a large frying pan, add the spicy onion paste and stir-fry over a high heat for 2 minutes. Lower the heat and cook for 5 minutes or until the onion paste is golden brown and loses its raw aroma.
4 Add the chopped tomatoes and season with salt and pepper. Cook for 5 minutes or until the tomato has reduced, then add the okra and stir to coat in the mixture. Cover the pan and simmer gently for 5 minutes or until the okra is just tender.
5 Stir in the yogurt, then add the chopped coriander and heat through gently. Serve straight away.

NUTRITION PER SERVING 150 cals | 12g fat (2g sats) | 8g carbs | 0.4g salt Ⓥ

Brussels Sprouts with Chestnuts and Shallots

Serves 8
Preparation time 15 minutes
Cooking time 12 minutes

900g (2lb) small Brussels sprouts, trimmed
1 tbsp olive oil
8 shallots, finely chopped
200g pack peeled cooked chestnuts
15g (½oz) butter
a pinch of freshly grated nutmeg
salt and ground black pepper

1 Add the sprouts to a large pan of boiling salted water, bring back to the boil and blanch for 2 minutes. Drain the sprouts and refresh with cold water.
2 Heat the olive oil in a wok or sauté pan. Add the shallots and stir-fry for 5 minutes or until almost tender.
3 Add the sprouts to the pan with the chestnuts and stir-fry for about 4 minutes to heat through.
4 Add the butter and nutmeg, and season generously with salt and pepper. Serve immediately.

NUTRITION PER SERVING140 cals | 5g fat (1g sats) | 8g carbs | 0.3g salt Ⓥ

Peperonata

Serves 6
Preparation time 15 minutes
Cooking time about 45 minutes

4 red peppers
3 orange peppers
1 green pepper
100ml (3½fl oz) olive oil
2 garlic cloves, crushed
2 tbsp capers, drained and rinsed
18 black olives
1 tbsp freshly chopped flat-leafed parsley
salt and ground black pepper
crusty bread to serve

1 Halve the peppers through the core and remove the seeds. Heat the oil in a large pan, add the garlic and stir-fry over a medium heat for 1 minute.
2 Add the peppers, season well and toss to coat in the oil. Cover the pan and continue to cook over a low heat for 40 minutes, stirring occasionally.
3 Add the capers, olives and chopped parsley, and stir to mix. Either serve straightaway or cool and chill until required. Serve with warm crusty bread.

Cook's Tip
This Italian sweet pepper stew is best made two to three days ahead to allow time for the flavours to develop. Cover and chill, but bring to room temperature to serve.

NUTRITION PER SERVING 180 cals | 16g fat (2g sats) | 0.8g carbs | 1.2g salt Ⓥ

Salads

Salads

Endlessly versatile, quick and easy to prepare, as well as mouthwatering, salads can be served as starters, accompaniments, main courses, snacks, lunches or light suppers. A side salad needs to be carefully composed so that the colours, flavours and textures complement the main dish and don't overpower it. Substantial salads – served with some good bread – are excellent, healthy main dishes, especially in the summer. A satisfying complete-meal salad is generally based around one or two high-protein foods with complementary flavouring ingredients, which offer a contrast in texture as well as taste. A tempting salad, served in moderate portions, is an ideal starter to stimulate the taste buds without taking the edge off the appetite. Warm salads, which are either tossed in a warm dressing or feature warm ingredients, also make perfect starters.

Salad leaves
The wonderful array of lettuces and other salad leaves on sale in most supermarkets, quality greengrocers and markets is inspiring. There are soft delicate leaves, such as the familiar round lettuce, lamb's lettuce (also known as corn salad and mâche), russet-coloured oak leaf and frilly-leafed lollo rosso. Crisper lettuces include cos, iceberg and little gem or, for a crunchy texture, buy Chinese leaves. In addition, there are deliciously bitter leaves such as dark red radicchio, peppery rocket, crisp chicory, watercress, frisée (curly endive) and tender baby spinach.

Ready-prepared bags of mixed salad leaves are a convenient way of buying salad leaves if you want a selection but only require a small quantity. Leaf salads are simple, refreshing and easily enhanced by the addition of fresh herbs or edible flowers.

When you are choosing lettuces, look for fresh, crisp leaves and a tightly packed head if appropriate. Avoid any with wilted or bruised leaves. Store loosely wrapped in the salad drawer of the fridge.

Preparing salad leaves
Pull off and discard any coarse or damaged outer leaves. Tear the leaves into pieces, if necessary. Rinse in a bowl of cold water and pat or spin dry. Assemble and dress just before serving.

Other salad vegetables
Beetroot, carrots, celery, courgettes, cucumber, fennel, mushrooms, peppers, radishes and salad onions are just a few of the many vegetables that are eaten raw in salads. Beans and peas, such as broad beans, French beans and mangetouts, are best blanched for a minute or so in boiling water, then refreshed in cold water first. Tomatoes and avocados are ideal in salads, but they must be at their peak of ripeness and flavour for optimum results. New potatoes are another excellent salad option, especially if they are combined with the dressing while still warm.

Salad herbs
Fresh herbs will enhance most salads and it is well worth growing your own supply in the garden or in tubs or window boxes. The flowers from herbs such as borage, chives, fennel and thyme can also be added to salads. Not all herbs are good in raw salads, but most work well.

Basil is almost indispensable in tomato salads, and it complements leafy salads too. Chervil, chives and flat-leafed parsley will flatter most salads. Coriander is excellent with robust green leaves, bulgur wheat and couscous. Dill and fennel are particularly good in fish salads, while mint combines well with oranges and peas. Oregano is a classic ingredient in traditional Greek salads and, like marjoram and thyme, it works well in cooked salads too. Strongly flavoured tarragon is great with chicken salads; it also enhances creamy salad dressings, particularly those containing mustard.

Salad dressings
See pages 28–29.

Tomato and Spring Onion Salad

Serves 4
Preparation time 15 minutes, plus standing

500g (1lb 2oz) baby plum tomatoes, halved
1 bunch of spring onions, sliced
500g (1lb 2oz) plum tomatoes, sliced lengthways
a handful of fresh basil leaves, roughly torn, plus fresh sprigs
  to garnish
2 beef tomatoes, about 450g (1lb) in total, sliced
100g (3½oz) pinenuts, toasted (see Cook's Tip, page 312)
250g (9oz) medium tomatoes, cut into wedges
salt and ground black pepper

For the dressing
100ml (3½fl oz) extra virgin olive oil
50ml (2fl oz) balsamic vinegar
a pinch of golden caster sugar

1 First make the dressing. Put the olive oil, balsamic
vinegar and sugar into a screw-topped jar and season
generously with salt and pepper. Shake well to combine.
2 Layer the baby plum tomatoes, spring onions, plum
tomatoes, basil, beef tomatoes, pinenuts and finally the
medium tomatoes in a shallow serving bowl, seasoning
each layer with salt and pepper.
3 Drizzle the dressing over the salad and leave to one side
for 1 hour to allow the flavours to mingle. Garnish with
basil sprigs to serve.

TRY SOMETHING DIFFERENT
Simple Tomato and Basil Salad To make this salad, simply
omit the spring onions and pinenuts, and reduce the quantity
of dressing by one-third.

NUTRITION PER SERVING 450 cals | 40g fat (4g sats) | 16g carbs | 0.3g salt Ⓥ

Mixed Leaf Salad

Serves 8
Preparation time 10 minutes

3 round lettuce hearts, roughly
  shredded
100g (3½oz) watercress
2 ripe avocados, roughly chopped
1 box salad cress, chopped
100g (3½oz) sugarsnap peas,
roughly sliced
4 tbsp French Dressing (see page 29)

1 Put the lettuce hearts into a bowl
and add the watercress, avocados,
salad cress and sugarsnap peas.
2 Pour the dressing over the salad
and toss to mix. Serve immediately.

Cook's Tip
Vary the salad leaves according
to taste and availability. Try using
treviso, red chicory and baby spinach
leaves, for example.

NUTRITION PER SERVING 90 cals |
9g fat (1g sats) | 1g carbs | 0.5g salt Ⓥ

Broad Bean and Feta Salad

Serves 2
Preparation time 10 minutes
Cooking time 5 minutes

225g (8oz) podded broad beans (see
  Cook's Tip)
100g (3½oz) feta cheese, chopped (see
  Vegetarian Cheeses, page 228)
2 tbsp freshly chopped mint
2 tbsp extra virgin olive oil
a squeeze of lemon juice
salt and ground black pepper
lemon wedges to serve (optional)

1 Cook the beans in boiling salted
water for 3–5 minutes until tender.
Drain, then plunge into cold water
and drain again. Remove their skins if
you like (see page 278).
2 Tip the beans into a bowl, add the
feta, mint, olive oil and a squeeze of
lemon juice. Season well with salt and
pepper and toss together. Serve with
lemon wedges, if you like.

Cook's Tip
For this quantity of broad beans, you
will need to buy about 750g (1½lb)
beans in pods. Choose small pods, as
the beans will be young and more
flavourful than bigger, older beans.

NUTRITION PER SERVING 197 cals |
16g fat (4g sats) | 5g carbs | 1.3g salt Ⓥ

Classic Coleslaw

Serves 6
Preparation time 15 minutes

¼ medium red cabbage, shredded
¼ medium white cabbage, shredded
1 carrot, grated
20g (¾oz) fresh flat-leafed parsley, finely chopped

For the dressing
1½ tbsp red wine vinegar
4 tbsp olive oil
½ tsp Dijon mustard
salt and ground black pepper

1 To make the dressing, put the vinegar into a small bowl, add the oil and mustard, season well with salt and pepper and mix well.
2 Put the cabbage and carrot into a large bowl and toss to mix well. Add the parsley.
3 Mix the dressing again, then pour it over the cabbage mixture and toss well to coat.

TRY SOMETHING DIFFERENT
Thai-style Coleslaw Replace the red cabbage with a good handful of fresh bean sprouts, the parsley with freshly chopped coriander, and add 1 seeded and finely chopped red chilli (see Cook's Tips, page 69). For the dressing, replace the vinegar with lime juice, the olive oil with toasted sesame oil and the mustard with soy sauce.

NUTRITION PER SERVING   92 cals | 8g fat (1g sats) | 5g carbs | 0.1g salt Ⓥ

Red Cabbage and Beetroot Salad

Serves 8
Preparation time 15 minutes

½ red cabbage, finely sliced
500g (1lb 2oz) cooked beetroot
  (see Cook's Tips)
8 cornichons (baby gherkins), sliced
2 tbsp baby capers in vinegar, rinsed

For the dressing
6 tbsp extra virgin olive oil
2 tbsp sherry vinegar
3 tbsp freshly chopped dill
salt and ground black pepper

1 Put the red cabbage into a large bowl. Cut the beetroot into matchstick strips or grate coarsely and add to the cabbage with the cornichons and capers. Toss together well to mix.

2 To make the dressing, put the oil, sherry vinegar and chopped dill into a small bowl. Season well with salt and pepper, then add a splash of cold water to help emulsify the dressing. Whisk together thoroughly.
3 Pour the dressing over the salad and toss everything together well.

Cook's Tips
• Buy vacuum-packed cooked beetroot or cook it yourself. Beetroot pickled in vinegar is not suitable.
• This salad is particularly good with baked ham.

NUTRITION PER SERVING 150 cals | 10g fat (1g sats) | 11g carbs | 0.3g salt Ⓥ

Chicory, Fennel and Orange Salad

Serves 4
Preparation time 15 minutes
Cooking time 2–3 minutes

1 small fennel bulb, with fronds
2 chicory heads, divided into leaves,
  or ½ head Chinese leaf, shredded
2 oranges, peeled and cut into rounds,
  plus juice of ½ orange
25g (1oz) hazelnuts, chopped and
  toasted (see Cook's Tip)
2 tbsp hazelnut or walnut oil
salt and ground black pepper

1 Trim the fronds from the fennel, roughly chop them and put to one side. Finely slice the fennel bulb lengthways and put into a serving bowl with the chicory or Chinese leaves, the orange slices and the toasted hazelnuts.

2 Put the orange juice, hazelnut or walnut oil and the reserved fennel fronds into a small bowl, season well with salt and pepper, and mix thoroughly. Pour over the salad and toss everything together.

Cook's Tip
Put the nuts into a dry frying pan and toast over a medium heat, shaking the pan, until evenly toasted.

NUTRITION PER SERVING 127 cals | 10g fat (1g sats) | 9g carbs | trace salt Ⓥ

Roasted Tomato Bulgur Salad

Serves 6

Preparation time 10 minutes, plus soaking and standing

Cooking time 10–15 minutes

175g (6oz) bulgur wheat
700g (1½lb) cherry tomatoes or baby plum tomatoes
8 tbsp extra virgin olive oil
a handful of fresh mint, roughly chopped
3–4 tbsp balsamic vinegar
a handful of fresh basil, roughly chopped, plus fresh basil sprigs to garnish
1 bunch of spring onions, sliced
salt and ground black pepper

1 Put the bulgur wheat into a bowl and add boiling water to cover by 1cm (½ in). Leave to soak for 30 minutes.

2 Preheat the oven to 220°C (200°C fan oven) mark 7. Put the tomatoes into a small roasting tin, drizzle with half the oil and add half the mint. Season with salt and pepper and roast for 10–15 minutes or until beginning to soften.

3 Put the remaining oil and the vinegar into a large bowl. Add the warm pan juices from the tomatoes and the soaked bulgur wheat.

4 Stir in the remaining chopped herbs and the spring onions and season with salt and pepper. You may need a little more vinegar depending on the sweetness of the tomatoes.

5 Add the tomatoes and toss gently to mix, then serve garnished with basil.

NUTRITION PER SERVING 225 cals | 15g fat (2g sats) | 19g carbs | 0g salt Ⓥ

Potato Salad with Basil

Serves 4

Preparation time 10 minutes

Cooking time 15 minutes, plus cooling

700g (1½lb) firm waxy potatoes, scrubbed and cut into bite-sized pieces
90ml (3fl oz) extra virgin olive oil
1 garlic clove, crushed
grated zest of 1 lemon
2–3 tbsp freshly chopped basil
1 tbsp sherry vinegar
4 spring onions, finely chopped
25g (1oz) pinenuts, toasted (see Cook's Tip, page 312)
salt and ground black pepper

1 Put the potatoes into a pan, add cold salted water to cover, bring to the boil and cook for about 12–15 minutes until just tender.

2 Meanwhile, heat 2 tbsp of the oil in a large frying pan, add the garlic and lemon zest, and fry gently for 5 minutes or until soft but not golden.

3 In a bowl, whisk the remaining oil with the chopped basil, sherry vinegar and seasoning.

4 Drain the potatoes and shake off the excess water. Add to the frying pan and stir-fry for 1 minute. Stir in the basil mixture and remove from the heat. Set aside to cool to room temperature.

5 Just before serving, add the spring onions and pinenuts, toss lightly together and season to taste with salt and pepper.

NUTRITION PER SERVING 350 cals | 24g fat (3g sats) | 31g carbs | 0.3g salt Ⓥ

Chicken Caesar Salad

Serves 4
Preparation time 15–20 minutes
Cooking time 12 minutes

2 tbsp olive oil
1 garlic clove, crushed
2 thick slices country-style bread,
  cubed
6 tbsp freshly grated Parmesan
1 cos lettuce, washed, chilled and cut
  into bite-size pieces
700g (1½ lb) cooked chicken breast,
  sliced

For the dressing
4 tbsp Mayonnaise (see page 29)
2 tbsp lemon juice
1 tsp Dijon mustard
2 anchovy fillets, very finely chopped
salt and ground black pepper

1 Preheat the oven to 180°C (160°C fan oven) mark 4. Put the olive oil, garlic and bread cubes in a bowl and toss well. Tip on to a baking sheet and bake in the oven for 10 minutes, turning halfway through.
2 Sprinkle the Parmesan over the croûtons and bake for 2 minutes or until the cheese has melted and the bread is golden.
3 Put all the ingredients for the dressing in a bowl, season with salt and pepper and mix together.
4 Put the lettuce and sliced chicken in a bowl, pour the dressing over and toss. Top with the cheese croûtons.

NUTRITION PER SERVING 482 cals |
27g fat (8g sats) | 8g carbs | 1.4g salt

Traditional Greek Salad

Serves 4
Preparation time 15 minutes, plus standing

1 red onion, thinly sliced
½ cucumber, peeled and cut into
  chunks
1 green pepper, seeded and finely sliced
3 beef tomatoes, sliced
10 Kalamata olives packed in olive oil
  with oregano, drained
200g pack feta cheese, chopped (see
  Vegetarian Cheeses, page 228)
juice of ½ lemon
4 tbsp extra virgin olive oil
salt and ground black pepper

1 Put the red onion, cucumber, green pepper, tomatoes, olives and feta cheese into a large bowl and toss to mix. Season very lightly with salt (as feta is quite salty) and generously with pepper.
2 Drizzle the lemon juice and olive oil over the salad and toss everything together. Leave to stand for about 10 minutes before serving to allow the flavours to mingle. Serve as a starter or light lunch.

TRY SOMETHING DIFFERENT
Use plain black olives and add 1–2 tbsp chopped oregano to the salad dressing.

NUTRITION PER SERVING 280 cals |
24g fat (9g sats) | 6g carbs | 2.3g salt Ⓥ

Roasted Vegetable Salad with Mustard Mayonnaise

Serves 4
Preparation time 15 minutes
Cooking time 40 minutes

900g (2lb) mixed vegetables, such as fennel,
  courgettes, leeks, aubergines, baby turnips,
  new potatoes and red onions
2 garlic cloves, unpeeled
4–5 fresh marjoram or rosemary sprigs
5 tbsp olive oil
1 tsp flaked sea salt
mixed crushed peppercorns to taste
4 tsp balsamic vinegar
warm crusty bread to serve

For the mustard mayonnaise
150ml (¼ pint) Mayonnaise (see page 29)
2 tbsp Dijon mustard
salt and ground black pepper

1 Preheat the oven to 220°C (200°C fan oven) mark 7.
For the vegetables, quarter the fennel, chop the courgettes,
leeks and aubergines, trim the turnips and cut the onions
into wedges. Place the vegetables, garlic, marjoram or
rosemary, the olive oil, salt and peppercorns in a roasting
tin and toss well (see Cook's Tip).
2 Cook in the oven for 30–35 minutes until the vegetables
are golden, tossing frequently. Sprinkle the balsamic
vinegar over the vegetables and return to the oven for a
further 5 minutes.
3 To make the mustard mayonnaise, mix together the
mayonnaise and mustard, then season with salt and pepper
and put to one side.
4 Arrange the vegetable salad on a serving dish and serve
with the mustard mayonnaise and crusty bread.

Cook's Tip
It's best to roast vegetables in a single layer as otherwise
they will steam and become soggy. Use two baking tins if
necessary so you can spread them out.

NUTRITION PER SERVING 420 cals | 43g fat (6g sats) | 5g carbs | 1g salt Ⓥ

Halloumi and Avocado Salad

Serves 4
Preparation time 10 minutes
Cooking time 2 minutes

250g (9oz) halloumi, sliced into eight (see Cook's Tip
  below and Vegetarian Cheeses, page 228)
1 tbsp plain flour
2 tbsp olive oil
200g (7oz) mixed leaf salad
2 avocados, halved, stoned, peeled and sliced
fresh rocket leaves to garnish
lemon halves to serve

For the mint dressing
3 tbsp lemon juice
8 tbsp olive oil
3 tbsp freshly chopped mint
salt and ground black pepper

1 To make the dressing, whisk the lemon juice with the
olive oil and mint, then season with salt and pepper.
2 Season the flour with salt and pepper, then coat the
halloumi with the flour. Heat the oil in a large frying pan
and fry the cheese for 1 minute on each side or until it
forms a golden crust.
3 Meanwhile, in a large bowl, add half the dressing to the
salad leaves and avocado, and toss together. Arrange the
hot cheese on top and drizzle the remaining dressing over.
Garnish with rocket leaves and serve with lemon halves to
squeeze over.

Cook's Tip
Halloumi is a firm cheese made from ewe's milk.
It is best used sliced and cooked.

NUTRITION PER SERVING 397 cals | 34g fat (13g sats) | 11g carbs | 2.3g salt Ⓥ

Salade Niçoise

Serves 4
Preparation time 40 minutes, plus marinating
Cooking time 30 minutes

450g (1lb) fresh tuna steaks
1 garlic clove, crushed
grated zest of ½ lemon
2 tbsp olive oil, plus extra to cook
1 fresh thyme sprig
2 small red peppers, halved and seeded
350g (12oz) vine-ripened tomatoes, peeled (see page 277)
2 large eggs
250g (9oz) podded broad beans
2 large fresh basil sprigs, leaves only
½ cucumber, seeded and cut into chunks
50g (2oz) small pitted black olives
6 spring onions, trimmed and chopped
50g can anchovy fillets, drained and chopped
50g (2oz) rocket or other salad leaves
salt and ground black pepper

For the dressing
2 tbsp lemon juice
1 tsp Dijon mustard
6 tbsp extra virgin olive oil

1 Rub the tuna steaks with the garlic, lemon zest and a twist of black pepper. Put into a dish, spoon over the oil, cover and leave to marinate in a cool place for 3–4 hours.
2 Transfer the tuna to a small pan, add the thyme and enough oil to barely cover the tuna. Bring slowly to the boil, turn the tuna over and remove the pan from the heat. Leave to stand for 5 minutes, then remove the fish with a slotted spoon and leave to cool. Preheat the grill.
3 Grill the peppers, skin side up, until charred. Put in a bowl, cover with clingfilm and leave until cool. Thickly slice or quarter the tomatoes. Skin the peppers, cut into thick strips and put to one side.
4 Bring a small pan of water to the boil, add the eggs (making sure they're covered with water) and simmer for 8 minutes. Cool under cold running water, shell and quarter. Add the broad beans to a pan of boiling water and cook for 2–3 minutes. Drain and refresh in cold water, then slip off the skins.
5 To make the dressing, put all the ingredients into a screw-topped jar, season and shake well until combined.

6 Pound the basil leaves with 1 tsp salt in a wide salad bowl to release their flavour. Flake the tuna and add it to the bowl with the other salad ingredients except the leaves. Season with salt and pepper and add just enough dressing to moisten the salad and toss gently.
7 Serve on a bed of rocket or other leaves as a main course. Hand the remaining dressing separately.

TRY SOMETHING DIFFERENT
- Instead of fresh tuna, use 2 × 200g cans tuna steak in olive oil. Drain well and add at step 6.
- Add about 12 cooked small new potatoes at step 6.

NUTRITION PER SERVING 570 cals | 41g fat (6g sats) | 11g carbs | 2.8g salt

Salad Caprese

Serves 4
Preparation time 10 minutes

3 × 150g balls mozzarella di bufala,
 drained (see Vegetarian Cheeses,
 page 228)
1kg (2¼lb) very ripe tomatoes, sliced
 into rounds
extra virgin olive oil to drizzle
a small handful of fresh basil leaves,
 roughly shredded
sea salt and ground black pepper

1 Slice the mozzarella into rounds
and layer on a serving plate with the
tomato slices.
2 Drizzle with the oil, season with
sea salt and ground black pepper and
scatter the basil over.

NUTRITION PER SERVING 381 cals |
29g fat (17g sats) | 8g carbs | 1.5g salt Ⓥ

Mixed Bean Salad with Lemon Vinaigrette

Serves 6
Preparation time 15 minutes

400g can mixed beans, drained and
 rinsed
400g can chickpeas, drained and rinsed
2 shallots, finely sliced
fresh mint sprigs and lemon zest to
 garnish

For the lemon vinaigrette
juice of 1 lemon
2 tsp clear honey
8 tbsp extra virgin olive oil
3 tbsp freshly chopped mint
4 tbsp roughly chopped flat-leafed
 parsley
salt and ground black pepper

1 Put the beans, chickpeas and
shallots in a large bowl.
2 To make the lemon vinaigrette,
whisk together the lemon juice, honey
and seasoning. Gradually whisk in the
oil and stir in the chopped herbs.
3 Pour the vinaigrette over the beans,
toss well, then garnish with the mint
sprigs and lemon zest to serve.

GET AHEAD
• Complete the recipe (but don't add
 the herbs or garnish), then cover
 and chill for up to two days.
• To use, remove from the fridge up
 to 1 hour before serving and add the
 herbs. Garnish just before serving.

NUTRITION PER SERVING 265 cals |
16g fat (2g sats) | 22g carbs | 0.9g salt Ⓥ

Waldorf Salad

Serves 4

Preparation time 15 minutes, plus standing

450g (1lb) eating apples
juice of ½ lemon
1 tsp sugar
150ml (¼ pint) Mayonnaise
  (see page 29)
1 small crisp lettuce
½ head of celery, sliced
50g (2oz) walnut pieces, chopped
a few walnut halves to garnish
  (optional)

1 Peel and core the apples, slice one and dice the rest. Dip the slices into lemon juice to prevent discoloration, then put to one side. Add the diced apples to the lemon juice with the sugar and 1 tbsp mayonnaise, stir well, then leave to stand for about 30 minutes.
2 Just before serving, line a salad bowl with lettuce leaves.
3 Add the celery, walnuts and remaining mayonnaise to the diced apples and toss together. Spoon into the salad bowl and garnish with the apple slices and a few walnut halves, if you like.

NUTRITION PER SERVING 413 cals | 38g fat (5g sats) | 16g carbs | 0.1g salt Ⓥ

Asparagus, Pea and Mint Rice Salad

Serves 6
Preparation time 10 minutes
Cooking time 20 minutes

175g (6oz) mixed basmati and
  wild rice
grated zest and juice of 1 small lemon
1 large shallot, finely sliced
2 tbsp sunflower oil
12 fresh mint leaves, roughly chopped,
  plus extra fresh sprigs to garnish
150g (5oz) asparagus tips
75g (3oz) fresh or frozen peas
salt and ground black pepper
lemon zest to garnish

1 Put the rice in a pan with twice its volume of water and a pinch of salt. Cover the pan and bring to the boil. Reduce the heat to very low and cook according to the pack instructions. Once cooked, tip the rice on to a baking sheet and spread out to cool quickly. When cool, spoon into a large bowl.
2 Reserve a little of the lemon zest to garnish. In a small bowl, mix the remaining zest with the lemon juice, shallot, oil and chopped mint, then stir into the rice.
3 Bring a large pan of lightly salted water to the boil. Add the asparagus and peas, and cook for 3–4 minutes until tender. Drain and refresh in a bowl of cold water. Drain well, then stir into the rice. Put into a serving dish and garnish with mint sprigs and reserved lemon zest.

NUTRITION PER SERVING 157 cals | 4g fat (trace sats) | 26g carbs | trace salt Ⓥ

Warm Goat's Cheese Salad

Serves 4
Preparation time 20 minutes
Cooking time 1–2 minutes

1 bunch of watercress
4 slices goat's cheese log (with rind)
  (see Vegetarian Cheeses, page 228)
1 quantity Rocket Pesto (see page 22)
50g (2oz) rocket leaves
40g (1½oz) walnut halves, toasted
  (see Cook's Tip, page 312)

For the dressing
1 tbsp walnut oil
1 tbsp sunflower oil
1 tsp balsamic or sherry vinegar
salt and ground black pepper

1 Whisk the dressing ingredients
together in a bowl, seasoning with salt
and pepper to taste. Preheat the grill.

2 Trim the watercress and discard the
coarse stalks. Lay the goat's cheese
slices on a foil-lined baking sheet and
grill, as close to the heat as possible,
for 1–2 minutes until browned.
3 Put a slice of goat's cheese on
each plate and top with a spoonful
of rocket pesto. Toss the rocket and
watercress leaves with the dressing
and then arrange around the goat's
cheese. Scatter the walnuts over the
salad and serve immediately.

TRY SOMETHING DIFFERENT
Use halved crottins de Chavignol
(small hard goat's cheese) instead of
the log chèvre.

NUTRITION PER SERVING 520 cals |
46g fat (12g sats) | 2g carbs | 1.5g salt Ⓥ

Asparagus and Quail Egg Salad

Serves 8
Preparation time 30 minutes
Cooking time 2 minutes

100g (3½oz) watercress
24 quail's eggs
24 asparagus spears, trimmed
juice of ½ lemon
5 tbsp olive oil
4 large spring onions, finely sliced
a few fresh dill and tarragon sprigs
salt and ground black pepper

1 Trim the watercress and discard the
coarse stalks, then chop roughly. Add
the quail's eggs to a pan of boiling
water and cook for 2 minutes, then
drain and plunge into cold water.
Cook the asparagus in lightly salted
boiling water for 2 minutes or until
just tender. Drain, plunge into cold
water and leave to cool.
2 Whisk together the lemon juice,
oil and seasoning. Stir in the spring
onions and put to one side.
3 Peel the quail's eggs and cut in
half. Put into a large bowl with
the asparagus, watercress, dill and
tarragon. Pour the dressing over and
lightly toss all the ingredients together.
Adjust the seasoning and serve.

NUTRITION PER SERVING 127 cals |
11g fat (2g sats) | 1g carbs | 0.1g salt Ⓥ

Bacon, Avocado and Pinenut Salad

Serves 4
Preparation time 5 minutes
Cooking time 7 minutes

125g (4oz) streaky bacon rashers,
  rinded and cut into small, neat pieces
  (lardons)
1 shallot, finely chopped
120g bag mixed baby salad leaves
1 ripe avocado
50g (2oz) pinenuts
4 tbsp olive oil
4 tbsp red wine vinegar
salt and ground black pepper

1 Put the lardons into a frying pan
over a medium heat for 1–2 minutes
until the fat runs. Add the shallot and
fry for 5 minutes until golden.
2 Meanwhile, divide the salad leaves
among four serving plates. Halve,
stone and peel the avocado, then slice
the flesh. Arrange on the salad leaves.
3 Add the pinenuts, oil and vinegar to
the frying pan and let it bubble for
1 minute. Season with salt and pepper.
4 Tip the bacon, pinenuts and
dressing over the salad and serve at
once, while still warm.

TRY SOMETHING DIFFERENT
Replace the pinenuts with walnuts.

NUTRITION PER SERVING 352 cals |
34g fat (6g sats) | 3g carbs | 1g salt

Smoked Mackerel Salad

Serves 4
Preparation time 15 minutes

250g (9oz) cooked (vacuum-packed
  without vinegar) beetroot, diced
1 tbsp olive oil
2 tsp white wine vinegar
350g (12oz) potato salad
1–2 tbsp lemon juice
4 peppered smoked mackerel fillets,
  skinned and flaked
2 tbsp freshly snipped chives, plus extra
  to garnish
salt and ground black pepper

1 Put the beetroot in a bowl.
Sprinkle with the olive oil and
vinegar. Season with salt and
pepper, and toss together.
2 In a large bowl, mix the potato
salad with the lemon juice to taste.
Season with salt and pepper. Add the
flaked mackerel and chopped chives,
and toss together.
3 Just before serving, pile the
mackerel mixture into four serving
bowls. Sprinkle the beetroot over
the top of the salad and garnish with
freshly snipped chives.

NUTRITION PER SERVING 656 cals |
56g fat (10g sats) | 16g carbs | 2.4g salt

Pastry

Pastry

The art of successful pastry-making lies in measuring the ingredients accurately, using the correct proportion of fat to flour and light, careful handling. With the exceptions of choux pastry and hot water crust pastry, everything needs to be kept cool when making pastry – the worksurface, equipment, ingredients and your hands. It is also important to 'rest' pastry before baking, otherwise it is liable to shrink during cooking. Pastries that are handled a great deal, such as puff, must be rested before and after shaping. Most pastries are rested in the fridge and need to be well wrapped in clingfilm to prevent them from drying out.

The main types of pastry are short pastries, such as shortcrust, and flaked pastries, such as puff. Other pastries include hot water crust, suet crust, choux pastry and filo

pastry. Sweetened short pastries can be used for sweet tarts. If you haven't the time or inclination to make your own pastry, buy a pack of ready-made chilled fresh or frozen pastry from the supermarket. Sweet shortcrust pastry is available as well as standard shortcrust. Ready-made puff pastry is so quick to use and successful that you may well prefer to buy it, as the alternative of making your own is very time-consuming.

Packets of ready-made filo sheets are widely available and give excellent results. Note that the size of filo sheets varies considerably between brands – check whether the recipe states a specific size before buying. It is essential to keep filo sheets covered as you work to prevent them from drying out and becoming brittle.

Pastry ingredients

Flours For most pastries, plain flour works best, as it gives a light, crisp result. Self-raising flour would produce a soft, spongy pastry, although it can be used for suet crust, which needs a raising agent (see right). Wholemeal flour gives a heavier dough, which is more difficult to roll. For wholemeal pastry, it is therefore better to use half wholemeal and half white flour. Puff pastry is usually made with strong plain (bread) flour as this contains extra gluten to strengthen the dough, enabling it to withstand intensive rolling and folding. A little lemon juice is usually added to puff pastry to soften the gluten and make the dough more elastic. Strong plain flour is also used for making filo (strudel) pastry to allow it to be stretched out very thinly, although this is rarely made at home.

Fats Traditionally, shortcrust pastry is made with a mixture of lard (for shortness) and either butter or margarine (for flavour); however, it is now more often made with a mixture of white vegetable fat and butter or margarine, or all butter for a rich flavour. If you prefer to use margarine, it should be the hard, block type rather than soft tub margarine.

Suet crust, as the name suggests is made using suet, which is the fat around the kidneys, heart and liver of beef and mutton, and is sold shredded, although vegetarian suet is also available.

Liquids Care must be taken when adding the liquid to a pastry dough: too much will create a tough end result; too little will produce a crumbly pastry that is difficult to handle. Use chilled water and add just enough to bind the dough. Egg yolks are often used to enrich pastry.

Raising agents Steam acts as the raising agent in flaked pastries in combination with the air enclosed in the layers of dough. In choux pastry the raising agents are eggs and steam. Unlike other pastries, suet crust needs a raising agent to lighten the dough. You can use either plain flour sifted with 2½ tsp baking powder to each 225g (8oz) or self-raising flour can be used instead.

Salt The quantity of salt varies according to the type of pastry. Only a pinch is added to shortcrust pastry for flavour, but a measured quantity is added to flaked pastries and hot water crust to strengthen the gluten in the flour and, in the case of hot water crust, to allow for the amount of handling during shaping.

Mixing pastry by hand

Shortcrust and similar pastries involve rubbing the fat into the flour. To do this, cut the fat into small pieces, then add to the flour and salt, and mix briefly, using a round-bladed knife, to coat the pieces with flour. Then, using your fingertips, pick up a small amount of the mixture at a time and rub the fat and flour together to break the fat down into tiny pieces. Do this as lightly and quickly as possible until the mixture resembles fine crumbs; avoid using the palm of your hands.

When you are ready to add the liquid, sprinkle this evenly over the surface; uneven addition may cause blistering once the pastry is cooked. Use a round-bladed knife to mix in the liquid. You may need a little more or less than the quantity stated in the recipe because the absorbency of flours varies. For this reason, don't add it all at once. Collect the dough with your hands and knead lightly for a few seconds until you have a smooth ball.

Mixing pastry in a food processor

Short pastries can be made very successfully and quickly in a food processor. To ensure that the dough is not over-worked, use the pulse button or operate the processor in short bursts. Avoid making too large a quantity at one time or the result will be disappointing.

Rolling out pastry

To reduce the risk of shrinkage during baking, wrap the pastry in clingfilm to prevent it drying out and rest in the fridge for 20 minutes before rolling out. Lightly dust the worksurface and rolling pin – never the pastry – with flour to prevent sticking. Roll the dough lightly and evenly in one direction only – until thin. Always roll away from you, using light, firm strokes, and rotate the pastry frequently to keep an even shape and thickness.

Avoid over-rolling, pulling or stretching the dough as you roll it, otherwise it will shrink badly during cooking. The usual thickness for rolling out pastries is 3mm (⅛in), although puff pastry is sometimes rolled out to a 5mm (¼in) thickness, depending on the use.

Shaping and glazing

Pastry is most often used to line tart tins and cover pies. It can also be folded around fillings to form pasties, or wrapped around whole boned fish or meat, as in salmon or beef en croûte.

To line a flan case, roll out the pastry thinly to a circle about 5cm (2in) wider than the flan ring. With a rolling pin, lift the pastry and lower it into the ring. Lift the edges and ease the pastry into the flan shape, lightly pressing the pastry against the edges. Turn any surplus pastry outwards over the rim and roll across the top with the rolling pin or use a knife to trim the edges.

To cover a pie dish, roll out the pastry to the required thickness and 5cm (2in) wider than the pie dish, using the inverted dish as a guide. Cut a 2.5cm (1in) wide strip from the outer edge and put it on the dampened rim of the dish. Seal the join and brush the strip with water. Lift the remaining pastry on the rolling pin and lay it over the pie dish. Press the lid lightly on to the pastry-lined rim to seal. Trim off any excess pastry.

Seal the edges firmly so that they do not open up during cooking, pressing a fork along the edge or pinching it between your thumb and finger. Cut a slit in the centre of the pie crust for the steam to escape.

For a double-crust pie, divide the pastry in two, one piece slightly larger. Shape the larger piece into a ball, then roll it out to 2.5cm (1in) wider than the inverted pie plate. Lift the pastry using a rolling pin, unroll it over the dish and press into shape. Add the cold filling, then the lid as above.

To shape a large raised pie in a mould, make up 450g (1lb) Hot Water Crust Pastry (see page 329) and keep it warm. Grease a 1.7 litre (3 pint) hinged pie mould or use a loose-based round cake tin or loaf tin. Put the mould on a baking sheet. Roll out two-thirds of the pastry to 5mm (¼in) thick and use to line the tin. Fill and put on the lid as for a pie above.

To line a bowl with suet crust pastry, roll out a scant three-quarters of the dough (see page 329) on a lightly floured surface and use to line the pudding basin. Fill with the mixture. Brush the top edge of the pastry with water. Roll out the remainder to make a lid and lay it over the pudding, pressing the edges together to seal. Cover the basin with a pleated, double layer of greaseproof paper, securing under the rim with string. Cover with foil.

Glazing

As well as giving pies an attractive sheen, glazing pastry seals the surface. Brush the pastry with egg glaze (egg yolk beaten with a little water), or with beaten whole egg. Alternatively, for a less shiny finish, brush with milk. Part-baked pastry cases are sometimes glazed, then baked for a little longer to seal before filling. When adding cut-out decorations, use some glaze to position the decorations and then brush the whole surface of the pie.

Ready-made Pastry

When buying chilled or frozen ready-made pastry, it is important to note that the weight specified on the pack is the combined weight of the ingredients, not the flour weight. As a guide, a 375g (13oz) pack of ready-made shortcrust pastry is roughly equivalent to home-made pastry made with 225g (8oz) flour.

Pastry Quantities

Where a recipe specifies a weight of pastry, this generally refers to the weight of flour in the recipe rather than the combined weight of the ingredients; for example, if a pie or tart recipe calls for 225g (8oz) shortcrust pastry, you will need this amount of flour and 125g (4oz) fat, as the correct proportion of flour to fat is 2:1.

Recipes for the basic pastries are provided on the following pages. If your pie or tart requires more (or less) than the basic recipe quantity, just increase (or decrease) the pastry ingredients in proportion, remembering to adjust the liquid quantity accordingly.

Quantity guide for tarts

Tart tins, including individual ones, vary in depth and this obviously affects the quantity of pastry needed to line them. Therefore the following chart is an approximate guide only. For a deep tart tin, allow extra pastry. Pastry quantity refers to the quantity of flour used to make the dough.

TART TIN SIZE	PASTRY
18cm (7in)	125g (4oz)
20.5cm (8in)	175g (6oz)
23cm (9in)	200g (7oz)
25.5cm (10in)	225g (8oz)

Baking blind

If a recipe instructs you to 'bake blind', you need to bake or part-bake the pastry case without its filling. The pastry may be partially cooked before filling, or completely cooked if the filling does not require baking. Cooking the pastry before you add the filling gives a crisp result.

Preheat the oven according to the recipe. Prick the pastry base with a fork to prevent air bubbles forming. Cover with foil or baking paper 8cm (3¼in) larger than the tin. Spread baking beans or dried pulses on top to weight the dough. Bake for 15 minutes or until the pastry looks set. Remove the foil or paper and beans and bake for 5–10 minutes until the base is firm to the touch and light golden; or a further 15 minutes until crisp and golden brown if the pastry case requires complete baking.

Shortcrust Pastry

Makes a 225g (8oz) quantity
Preparation time 10 minutes, plus chilling

225g (8oz) plain flour, plus extra to dust
a pinch of salt
125g (4oz) butter, or half white vegetable fat and half butter,
  cut into pieces

1 Sift the flour and salt into a bowl, add the fat and mix
lightly. Using your fingertips, rub the fat into the flour until
the mixture resembles fine breadcrumbs.
2 Sprinkle 3–4 tbsp cold water evenly over the surface and
stir with a round-bladed knife until the mixture begins
to stick together in large lumps. If the dough seems dry,
add a little extra water. With one hand, collect the dough
together to form a ball.
3 Knead lightly on a lightly floured surface for a few
seconds to form a smooth, firm dough; do not over-work.
Wrap in clingfilm and leave to rest in the fridge for
30 minutes before rolling out.

TRY SOMETHING DIFFERENT

Wholemeal Pastry Replace half the white flour with
wholemeal and add little extra water if necessary.
Nut Pastry Replace 50g (2oz) flour with finely chopped or
ground walnuts, hazelnuts or almonds. Add before the water.
Cheese Pastry Stir in 3–4 tbsp freshly grated Parmesan
or 75g (3oz) finely grated Cheddar and a small pinch of
mustard powder before adding the water.
Herb Pastry Stir in 3 tbsp finely chopped fresh herbs, such as
parsley, sage, thyme or rosemary, before adding the water.
Olive Pastry Stir in 4 tbsp chopped pitted olives at step 2.
Poppy Seed Pastry Add 15g (½oz) poppy seeds before the water.

Cook's Tips

• To use a food processor, put the flour, salt and butter in
  the processor bowl and whiz until the mixture resembles
  fine crumbs, then add the water. Pulse briefly until it just
  comes together in a ball. Continue from step 3.
• Store in the fridge for up to three days, or freeze.

NUTRITION PER 25g (1oz)
110 cals | 6g fat (3g sats) | 12g carbs | 0.6g salt Ⓥ

Sweet Pastry

Makes a 125g (4oz) quantity
Preparation time 10 minutes, plus resting

125g (4oz) plain flour, plus extra to dust
a pinch of salt
50g (2oz) unsalted butter, at room temperature, cut
  into pieces
2 egg yolks
50g (2oz) caster sugar

1 Sift the flour and salt into a mound on a clean surface.
Make a large well in the centre and add the butter, egg
yolks and sugar.
2 Using the fingertips of one hand, work the sugar, butter
and egg yolks together until well blended.
3 Gradually work in all the flour to bind the mixture
together to a smooth dough.
4 Knead the dough gently on a lightly floured clean
surface until smooth, then wrap in clingfilm and leave to
rest in the fridge for at least 30 minutes before rolling out.

NUTRITION PER 25g (1oz)
120 cals | 5g fat (2g sats) | 13g carbs | 0.5g salt Ⓥ

Rich Shortcrust Pastry

Makes a 125g (4oz) quantity
Preparation time 10 minutes, plus chilling

125g (4oz) flour, plus extra to dust
a pinch of salt
75g (3oz) butter, diced
1 tsp caster sugar
1 medium egg, beaten

1 Put the flour and salt into a bowl. Rub in the fat until
the mixture resembles fine breadcrumbs. Stir in the sugar.
2 Add the egg, stirring with a round-bladed knife until the
ingredients begin to stick together in large lumps.
3 Using one hand, collect the mixture together and knead
lightly for a few seconds to a smooth dough. Wrap in
clingfilm and chill for at least 30 minutes before using.

NUTRITION PER 25g (1oz)
110 cals | 6g fat (4g sats) | 14g carbs | 0.5g salt Ⓥ

Flaky (Rough Puff) Pastry

Makes a 225g (8oz) quantity
Preparation time 25 minutes, plus resting

225g (8oz) plain flour, plus extra to dust
a pinch of salt
175g (6oz) butter, chilled and diced into 2cm (¾in) cubes
1 tsp lemon juice

1 Sift the flour and salt together into a bowl, add the butter and mix lightly to coat the pieces of butter with flour.
2 Using a round-bladed knife, stir in 100ml (3½fl oz) chilled water together with the lemon juice to make a soft elastic dough. If the mixture is too dry, add a little extra water, a drop at a time.
3 Turn out on to a lightly floured worksurface and lightly knead the dough until smooth.
4 Roll the pastry out to a neat rectangle, measuring 30.5 × 10cm (12 × 4in) with the short edge facing you. Fold the bottom third up and the top third down, then give the pastry a quarter turn, so that the folded edges are at the sides. Press the edges with a rolling pin to seal. Wrap in clingfilm and leave to rest in the fridge for 15 minutes.
5 Put the pastry back on the floured worksurface with the folded edges to the sides. Repeat the rolling, folding and turning sequence four more times, then wrap in clingfilm and leave to rest in the fridge for a further 30 minutes before rolling out.
6 Shape the rough puff pastry as required, then rest in the fridge for 30 minutes before baking.

Cook's Tip
Rough puff pastry has the buttery flakiness of puff pastry, although it won't rise as much.

NUTRITION PER 25g (1oz)
100 cals | 7g fat (4g sats) | 9g carbs | 0.6g salt Ⓥ

Puff Pastry

Makes a 450g (1lb) quantity
Preparation time 40 minutes, plus resting

450g (1lb) strong plain (bread) flour, plus extra to dust
a pinch of salt
450g (1lb) butter, chilled
1 tbsp lemon juice

1 Sift the flour and salt together into a bowl. Cut off 50g (2oz) of the butter and flatten the remaining large block with a rolling pin to a slab about 2cm (¾in) thick; leave to one side.
2 Cut the 50g (2oz) butter into small pieces and rub into the flour, using your fingertips.
3 Using a round-bladed knife, stir in the lemon juice and enough chilled water to make a soft elastic dough; you will need about 300ml (½ pint).
4 Turn out on to a lightly floured surface and quickly knead the dough until smooth. Cut a cross through half the depth, then open out to form a star.
5 Roll out, keeping the centre four times as thick as the flaps. Put the slab of butter in the centre of the dough. Fold the flaps over the dough, envelope-style.
6 Press gently with a rolling pin and roll out to a rectangle, measuring 40.5 × 20.5cm (16 × 8in) with the short side facing you.
7 Fold the bottom third up and the top third down, keeping the edges straight. Wrap in clingfilm and leave to rest in the fridge for 30 minutes.
8 Put the pastry on a lightly floured surface with the folded edges to the sides. Repeat the rolling, folding, resting and turning sequence five times.
9 Shape the puff pastry as required, then rest in the fridge for about 30 minutes before baking.

Cook's Tips
• If possible, the pastry should be made the day before it is to be used. It is not practical to make less than a 450g (1lb) flour weight quantity.
• Ready-made puff pastry is available fresh and frozen, so use this for convenience if you prefer. Two 375g (13oz) packs would be roughly equivalent to this quantity.

NUTRITION PER 25g (1oz)
100 cals | 8g fat (4g sats) | 7g carbs | 0.6g salt Ⓥ

Hot Water Crust Pastry

Makes a 300g (11oz) quantity
Preparation time 10 minutes

300g (11oz) plain flour
¼ tsp salt
65g (2½oz) white vegetable fat

1 Sift the flour and salt in a bowl and make a well in the centre.
2 Put the fat and 150ml (¼ pint) water in a small pan and heat slowly until the fat melts, then increase the heat and bring to the boil.
3 Pour the hot liquid into the flour well. Gradually stir the flour into the liquid, then beat together.
4 Lightly knead against the side of the bowl until smooth. Wrap the dough in a tea towel and leave to rest in a warm place for 20 minutes. Use the pastry while it is still warm.

Cook's Tip
This firm-textured pastry is used for raised pies. It must be shaped soon after making, while still pliable.

NUTRITION PER 25g (1oz)
80 cals | 3g fat (1g sats) | 10g carbs | 0.5g salt ⓥ

Suet Crust Pastry

Makes a 300g (11oz) quantity
Preparation time 10 minutes

300g (11oz) self-raising flour
½ tsp salt
150g (5oz) shredded suet

1 Sift the flour and salt into a bowl, add the shredded suet and stir to mix.
2 Using a round-bladed knife, mix in enough cold water to make a soft dough; you will need about 175ml (6fl oz). If the dough seems too dry, add a little extra liquid.
3 Knead very lightly until smooth. Use as required.

Cook's Tip
Suet is derived from animal fat so is not suitable for vegetarians, but you can buy vegetarian suet in most major supermarkets.

NUTRITION PER 25g (1oz)
110 cals | 6g fat (3g sats) | 12g carbs | 0.6g salt ⓥ

Choux Pastry

Makes a 2-egg quantity
Preparation time 10 minutes

65g (2½oz) plain flour
a pinch of salt
50g (2oz) butter
2 medium eggs, lightly beaten

1 Sift the flour and salt on to a generous sheet of greaseproof paper.
2 Pour 150ml (¼ pint) cold water into a medium pan, add the butter and melt over a low heat. Increase the heat and bring to a rolling boil.
3 Take off the heat, immediately tip in all of the flour and beat vigorously, using a wooden spoon. Continue beating until the mixture is smooth and leaves the side of the pan to form a ball; do not over-beat. Leave to cool slightly, for 1–2 minutes.

4 Gradually add the eggs, beating well between each addition, adding just enough to give a smooth dropping consistency. The choux pastry should be smooth and shiny.

Cook's Tip
This light, airy, crisp pastry is used for sweet and savoury choux puffs, eclairs, profiteroles and gougères. It can either be spooned or piped into shape, usually directly on to a dampened baking sheet.

NUTRITION PER 25g (1oz)
50 cals | 4g fat (2g sats) | 3g carbs | 0.4g salt ⓥ

Caramelised Onion and Goat's Cheese Tart

Serves 6
Preparation time 10 minutes
Cooking time 1 hour, plus cooling

230g ready-made shortcrust pastry case
275g jar onion confit
300g (11oz) mild soft goat's cheese
1 medium egg, beaten
25g (1oz) freshly grated Parmesan (see Vegetarian Cheeses,
 page 228)
50g (2oz) wild rocket
balsamic vinegar and extra virgin olive oil to drizzle
salt and ground black pepper

1 Preheat the oven to 200°C (180°C fan oven) mark
6. Line the pastry case with greaseproof paper, fill with
baking beans and bake blind (see page 326) for 10 minutes.
Remove the paper and beans, prick the pastry base all over
with a fork and cook for a further 15–20 minutes until the
pastry is golden.
2 Spoon the onion confit into the pastry case. Beat the
goat's cheese and egg together in a bowl until smooth,
season with salt and pepper, then spoon on top of the
onions. Level the surface with a knife, and sprinkle over
the Parmesan.
3 Cook the tart for 25–30 minutes until the filling is set
and just beginning to turn golden.
4 Leave to cool in the tin for 15 minutes, then cut away
the sides of the foil case and carefully slide the tart on to
a plate. Just before serving, arrange the rocket on top of the
tart and drizzle with balsamic vinegar and olive oil. Serve
the tart warm.

NUTRITION PER SERVING 480 cals | 28g fat (14g sats) | 44g carbs | 1.5g salt ⓥ

Crispy Spinach Pie

Serves 6
Preparation time 30 minutes
Cooking time 40 minutes

500g bag spinach
300g (11oz) lean lamb mince
¼–½tsp freshly grated nutmeg
1½ tsp dried oregano
1 medium egg
50g (2oz) feta cheese
4 filo pastry sheets, each measuring about 32 × 38cm
 (12½ × 15in)
1 tsp vegetable oil
salt and ground black pepper
green salad to serve

1 Bring a little water in a large pan to a simmer, then
add the spinach (a little at a time, if necessary). Stir,
then cook for a few minutes until wilted. Tip into a
colander and set aside.
2 Return the empty pan to the heat, add the lamb and fry
until golden. Drain, discarding the excess fat. Set aside to
cool slightly.
3 Preheat the oven to 200°C (180°C fan oven) mark 6.
When cool enough to handle, squeeze out as much water
as you can from the spinach, chop it roughly and put it in
a large bowl. Stir through the lamb, nutmeg, oregano, egg
and plenty of seasoning. Crumble the feta over the top and
gently stir everything together.
4 Brush one side of each filo sheet with a little oil, then
arrange, oil side down, in a 20.5cm (8in) round springform
cake tin, leaving the excess filo hanging over the edges and
making sure there are no gaps at the base or sides.
5 Spoon the filling into the pastry case and level the
surface. Fold the excess pastry over the filling, scrunching
up the filo.
6 Bake the pie in the oven for 20 minutes, then unclip
and remove the metal rim. Bake for a further 10 minutes
or until the sides are golden. Serve warm or at room
temperature with a green salad.

NUTRITION PER SERVING 228 cals | 11g fat (5g sats) | 17g carbs | 0.7g salt

Pissaladière

Serves 6
Preparation time 10 minutes
Cooking time 1 hour 5 minutes

4 tbsp olive oil, plus extra to grease
3 large Spanish onions, very finely sliced
1 garlic clove, crushed
375g pack ready-rolled puff pastry
125g (4oz) roasted red peppers in oil, drained and cut into
  thin strips
50g can anchovies in olive oil, drained
12 pitted black olives, halved
1 tsp mixed dried herbs
salt and ground black pepper

1 Preheat the oven to 220°C (200°C fan oven) mark 7 and
grease two small baking sheets.
2 Heat the oil in a deep frying pan and stir in the onions
and garlic. Season with salt and pepper. Cook, uncovered,
over a gentle heat for 30–40 minutes, stirring occasionally
to make sure the vegetables don't stick, until the onions are
meltingly soft and pale golden.
3 While the onions are cooking, unroll the pastry, cut
into six equal rectangles, then arrange on the prepared
baking sheets.
4 Divide the cooked onion among the pastry bases and
spread out evenly, leaving a 1cm (½in) gap around the
edges. Arrange the red peppers in a diamond-shaped lattice
pattern over the onions.
5 Cut the anchovies in half lengthways and arrange on
top of the onions in swirls. Dot the olives over the top.
Sprinkle over the dried herbs, then cook for 20–25 minutes
until the pastry is golden and crisp.

NUTRITION PER SERVING 411 cals | 28g fat (2g sats) | 3.5g carbs | 1.8g salt

Leek and Ham Galette

Serves 4
Preparation time 30 minutes, plus cooling and chilling
Cooking time 40 minutes

350g (12oz) medium leeks, trimmed and cut into
 2cm (¾in) thick slices
25g (1oz) butter, plus extra to grease
25g (1oz) plain flour, plus extra to dust
50ml (2fl oz) milk
1 tbsp freshly chopped marjoram
50g (2oz) Gruyère cheese, cubed, plus 2 tbsp, grated
150g (5oz) cooked sliced ham, thickly shredded
225g (8oz) Puff Pastry (see page 328), thawed if frozen
½ medium egg, beaten with a pinch of salt
salt and ground black pepper

1 Cook the leeks in boiling salted water for 2–3 minutes
until just beginning to soften. Drain, keeping the cooking
liquid to one side. Plunge the leeks into cold water, drain
and dry well on kitchen paper.
2 Melt the butter in a pan, remove from the heat and mix
in the flour to form a smooth paste. Mix in 225ml (8fl oz)
leek water and the milk, stirring until smooth. Bring to the
boil, simmer for 1–2 minutes, then remove from the heat,
cover and cool for 20 minutes or until cold.
3 Preheat the oven to 220°C (200°C fan oven) mark 7 and
grease a baking sheet.
4 Add the marjoram, leeks, cubed cheese and ham to the
leeks and season with salt and pepper.
5 Roll out the pastry on a lightly floured surface to a
30.5 × 33cm (12 × 13in) rectangle. Cut into two rectangles,
one 15 × 30.5cm (6 × 12in) and the other 18 × 30.5cm
(7 × 12in). Put the smaller piece on to the prepared baking
sheet. Spoon on the ham mixture, leaving a 2cm (¾in)
border all the way around. Brush the border with beaten
egg. Cover the filling with the larger pastry rectangle and
press the edges together. Cut slashes in the top of the
pastry to prevent the filling seeping out. Crimp the edges
to seal, then cover and freeze for 20 minutes or until firm.
6 Remove from the freezer, brush again with the
beaten egg and sprinkle with the grated cheese. Bake
for 20–30 minutes until brown and crisp. Serve hot.

Freezing Tip
• To freeze, cover the uncooked galette in clingfilm
 and freeze on the baking sheet. When firm, remove
 from the baking sheet. Wrap in baking paper, and then
 in clingfilm.
• To use, thaw for 3 hours at cool room temperature on
 baking paper. Preheat the oven to 220°C (200°C fan
 oven) mark 7 and put a baking tray in the oven to heat.
 Brush the galette with beaten egg and sprinkle with
 cheese. Put the galette on the hot tray (this will keep the
 pastry base crisp) and bake for 40 minutes until piping
 hot and golden.

NUTRITION PER SERVING 395 cals | 25g fat (6g sats) | 29g carbs | 2g salt

Chicken and Artichoke Filo Pie

Serves 4
Preparation time 20 minutes
Cooking time 45 minutes

3 boneless, skinless chicken breasts, about 350g (12oz)
150ml (¼ pint) dry white wine
225g (8oz) reduced-fat soft cheese with garlic and herbs
400g can artichoke hearts, drained and quartered
4 sheets filo pastry, thawed if frozen
olive oil
1 tsp sesame seeds
salt and ground black pepper

1 Preheat the oven to 200°C (180°C fan oven) mark 6. Put
the chicken and wine in a pan and bring to the boil, then
cover the pan and simmer for 10 minutes. Remove the
chicken with a slotted spoon and set aside. Add the cheese
to the wine and mix until smooth. Bring to the boil, then
simmer the sauce until thickened.
2 Cut the chicken into bite-size pieces, then add to the
sauce with the artichokes. Season with salt and pepper and
mix together well.
3 Put the mixture in an ovenproof dish. Brush the pastry
lightly with oil, scrunch slightly and put on top of the
chicken. Sprinkle with sesame seeds, then cook for
30–35 minutes until crisp. Serve hot.

TRY SOMETHING DIFFERENT
Replace the artichoke hearts with 225g (8oz) brown-cap
mushrooms, cooked in a little water with a sprinkling of
lemon juice and a little salt and pepper.

NUTRITION PER SERVING 241 cals | 9g fat (5g sats) | 7g carbs | 0.2g salt

Chicken and Bacon Pie

Serves 4
Preparation time 30 minutes, plus cooling
Cooking time about 55 minutes

1 tbsp olive oil
4 chicken breasts, cut into 2.5cm (1in) cubes
1 medium onion, peeled and sliced
1 carrot, peeled and roughly chopped
50g (2oz) smoked streaky bacon, chopped
1 tbsp flour
200ml (7fl oz) chicken stock
100ml (3½fl oz) double cream
25g (1oz) frozen peas
1½ tsp wholegrain mustard
1 tbsp freshly chopped tarragon
175g (6oz) Puff Pastry (see page 328), thawed if frozen
plain flour to dust
1 medium egg, beaten
salt and ground black pepper

1 Heat half the oil in a large pan, then brown the chicken in batches. Remove from the pan and put to one side. Add the remaining oil and fry the onion and carrot for 10 minutes. Add the bacon and cook for 3 minutes.
2 Stir in the flour and cook for 1 minute. Gradually add the stock, stirring well. Add the cream and return the chicken and any juices to the pan. Simmer for 5 minutes or until the chicken is cooked.
3 Add the peas, mustard and tarragon, then season to taste with salt and pepper. Leave to cool a little.
4 Preheat the oven to 200°C (180°C fan oven) mark 6. Put a pie funnel, if you have one, in the centre of a 1 litre (1¾ pint) pie dish or casserole and tip in the filling.
5 Roll out the pastry on a lightly floured surface to make a lid (make a slit for the pie funnel). Brush the pastry edges with the egg, then lay the pastry over the dish and trim with a sharp knife. Seal and brush with beaten egg to glaze. Cook for 25–30 minutes until golden.

GET AHEAD
Assemble the pie, then cover and chill for up to two days. To use, brush with beaten egg and complete the recipe.

Cook's Tip
If you don't have a pie funnel, use an upturned egg cup.

NUTRITION PER SERVING 554 cals | 34g fat (6g sats) | 24g carbs | 1.3g salt

Steak and Kidney Pie

Serves 6
Preparation time 40 minutes, plus cooling
Cooking time about 1½ hours

2 tbsp plain flour, plus extra to dust
700g (1½lb) stewing steak, cubed
3 tbsp vegetable oil
25g (1oz) butter
1 small onion, peeled and finely chopped
175g (6oz) ox kidney, cut into small pieces
150g (5oz) flat mushrooms, cut into large chunks
a small pinch of cayenne pepper
1 tsp anchovy essence
350g (12oz) Puff Pastry (see page 328), thawed if frozen
1 large egg, beaten with a pinch of salt to glaze
salt and ground black pepper

1 Preheat the oven to 170°C (150°C fan oven) mark 3.
2 Season the flour with salt and pepper, then toss half the steak with half the flour. Heat the oil in a flameproof non-stick casserole and add the butter. Fry the steak in batches until brown, remove and put to one side. Repeat with the remaining steak.
3 Add the onion to the pan and cook gently until soft. Return the steak to the casserole with 200ml (7fl oz) water, the kidney, mushrooms, cayenne and anchovy essence. Bring to the boil, then reduce the heat, cover the pan and simmer for 5 minutes.
4 Transfer to the oven and cook for 1 hour or until tender. The sauce should be syrupy. If not, transfer the casserole to the hob, remove the lid, bring to the boil and bubble for 5 minutes to reduce and thicken the liquid. Leave the steak mixture to cool.
5 Preheat the oven to 200°C (180°C fan oven) mark 6. Put the steak and kidney mixture into a 900ml (1½ pint) pie dish. Pile it high to support the pastry.
6 Roll out the pastry on a lightly floured surface to 5mm (¼in) thick. Cut off four to six strips, 1cm (½in) wide. Dampen the edge of the dish with cold water, then press the pastry strips on to the edge. Dampen the pastry rim and lay the sheet of pastry on top. Press the surfaces together, trim the edge and press down with the back of a knife to seal. Brush the pastry with the glaze and score with the back of a knife. Put the pie dish on a baking sheet and cook for 30 minutes or until the pastry is golden brown and the filling is hot to the centre.

Freezing Tip
- To freeze, complete the recipe but do not glaze or bake. Wrap the uncooked pie and freeze.
- To use, thaw at cool room temperature overnight. Glaze the pastry and add 5–10 minutes to the cooking time, covering the pie with foil if the top starts to turn brown too quickly.

NUTRITION PER SERVING 565 cals | 36g fat (8g sats) | 26g carbs | 0.9g salt

Red Onion Tarte Tatin

Serves 12
Preparation time 15 minutes
Cooking time 35–40 minutes

50g (2oz) butter
2 tbsp olive oil
1.1kg (2½lb) red onions, sliced into rounds
1 tbsp light muscovado sugar
175ml (6fl oz) white wine (see Alcoholic Drinks and
  Vegetarians, page 489)
4 tsp white wine vinegar
1 tbsp freshly chopped thyme, plus extra to garnish
  (optional)
450g (1lb) Puff Pastry (see page 328), thawed if frozen
plain flour to dust
salt and ground black pepper

1 Lightly grease two 23cm (9in) non-stick sandwich tins
with a little of the butter and put to one side.
2 Melt the remaining butter with the oil in a large non-
stick frying pan. Add the sliced onions and sugar, and fry
for 10–15 minutes or until golden, keeping the onions in
their rounds.
3 Add the wine, vinegar and thyme to the pan. Bring to
the boil, and let it bubble until the liquid has evaporated.
Season with salt and pepper, then divide the mixture
between the tins and leave to cool.
4 Preheat the oven to 220°C (200°C fan oven) mark 7.
5 Halve the pastry. On a lightly floured surface, roll out
each piece thinly into a round shape just larger than the
sandwich tin. Put one pastry round over the onion mixture
in each tin and tuck in the edges. Prick the pastry dough
all over with a fork.
6 Cook the tarts for 15–20 minutes or until the pastry
is risen and golden. Take out of the oven and put a large
warm plate over the pastry. Turn over and shake gently to
release the tart, then remove the tin. Scatter with thyme, if
you like, and cut into wedges to serve.

GET AHEAD
Complete the recipe to the end of step 4 up to one day in
advance. Cover and keep in the fridge for up to 24 hours. To
use, complete the recipe.

NUTRITION PER SERVING 235 cals | 15g fat (3g sats) | 23g carbs | 0.4g salt Ⓥ

Wild Mushroom Pithiviers

Serves 8
Preparation time 1 hour, plus cooling and chilling
Cooking time about 1 hour

450g (1lb) wild mushrooms
300ml (½ pint) milk
200ml (7fl oz) double cream
2 garlic cloves, crushed
450g (1lb) floury potatoes, peeled and thinly sliced
freshly grated nutmeg
50g (2oz) butter, plus extra to grease
2 tsp freshly chopped thyme, plus fresh sprigs to garnish
2 × 500g packs puff pastry, thawed if frozen
plain flour to dust
1 large egg, beaten
salt and ground black pepper

1 Rinse the mushrooms in cold running water to remove any grit, then pat dry with kitchen paper. Roughly slice.
2 Pour the milk and cream into a large heavy-based pan and add the garlic. Bring to the boil, then add the potatoes. Bring back to the boil, then reduce the heat and simmer gently, stirring occasionally, for 15–20 minutes until the potatoes are tender. Season with salt, pepper and nutmeg. Leave to cool.
3 Melt the butter in a large frying pan. When it is sizzling, add the mushrooms and cook over a high heat, stirring all the time, for 5–10 minutes until the mushrooms are cooked and the juices have evaporated completely. Season with salt and pepper, stir in the chopped thyme, then put to one side to cool. Grease two baking sheets.
4 Roll out the pastry thinly on a lightly floured surface. Cut into eight rounds, approximately 12.5cm (5in) in diameter, for the tops, and eight rounds, approximately 11.5cm (4½in) in diameter, for the bases. Put the smaller pastry rounds on baking sheets and brush the edges with beaten egg. Put a large spoonful of the cooled potato mixture in the centre of each round, leaving a 1cm (½in) border around the edge. Top with a spoonful of the mushroom mixture, then cover with the pastry tops. Press the edges together well to seal. Chill in the fridge for 30 minutes–1 hour.
5 Meanwhile, preheat the oven to 220°C (200°C fan oven) mark 7 and put two baking sheets in the oven to heat up. Use the back of a knife to scallop the edges of the pastry

and brush the top with the remaining beaten egg. If you like, use a knife to decorate the tops of the pithiviers.
6 Put the pithiviers, on their baking sheets, on the preheated baking trays. Cook for 15–20 minutes until deep golden brown, swapping the trays around in the oven halfway through cooking. Serve immediately, garnished with thyme sprigs.

GET AHEAD
For convenience, complete the recipe to the end of step 4, then cover and chill overnight until ready to cook.

NUTRITION PER SERVING 710 cals | 51g fat (12g sats) | 58g carbs | 1.2g salt Ⓥ

Cornish Pasties

Serves 6
Preparation time 30 minutes
Cooking time 1¼ hours

25g (1oz) butter, plus extra to grease
450g (1lb) stewing steak, trimmed and cut into very small
  pieces
175g (6oz) potato, peeled and diced
175g (6oz) swede, peeled and diced
1 onion, peeled and chopped
1 tbsp freshly chopped thyme
1 tbsp freshly chopped parsley
1 tbsp Worcestershire sauce
Shortcrust Pastry (see page 327), made with
  500g (1lb 2oz) plain flour
plain flour to dust
1 medium egg, beaten, to glaze
salt and ground black pepper
salad to serve (optional)

1 Preheat the oven to 220°C (200°C fan oven) mark 7 and
grease a baking sheet.
2 Put the meat into a bowl with the potato, swede and
onion. Add the chopped herbs, Worcestershire sauce and
seasoning, then mix well.
3 Divide the pastry into six and roll out each piece thinly
on a lightly floured surface to a 20.5cm (8in) round. Spoon
the filling on to one half of each round and top with a
small knob of butter.
4 Brush the edges of the pastry with water, then fold the
uncovered side over to make pasties. Press the edges firmly
together to seal and crimp them. Make a slit in the top of
each pasty. Put on the prepared baking sheet.
5 Brush the pastry with beaten egg to glaze and bake the
pasties for 15 minutes. Reduce the oven temperature to
170°C (150°C fan oven) mark 3 and bake for a further 1
hour to cook the filling. Serve the pasties warm or cold
with salad, if you like.

NUTRITION PER SERVING 756 cals | 42g fat (25g sats) | 74g carbs | 1.1g salt

Quiche Lorraine

Serves 8
Preparation time 35 minutes, plus chilling
Cooking time 1 hour

butter to grease
Shortcrust Pastry (see page 327), made with 200g (7oz) plain
  flour, a pinch of salt, 100g (3½oz) chilled butter and
  1 large egg
plain flour to dust

For the filling
5 large eggs
225g (8oz) unsmoked streaky bacon, rind removed
40g (1½oz) butter
125g (4oz) shallots, onions or spring onions, peeled and
  finely chopped
400g (14oz) crème fraîche
100g (3½oz) Gruyère cheese, grated
salt and ground black pepper
crispy bacon and fried spring onions to garnish

1 Preheat the oven to 200°C (180°C fan oven) mark 6 and
grease a 23cm (9in), round 3cm (1¼in) deep, loose-based
tart tin.
2 Roll out the pastry thinly on a lightly floured surface and
use to line the prepared tart tin. Bake the pastry case blind
(see page 326).
3 Meanwhile, lightly whisk the eggs for the filling. Brush
a little on the inside of the pastry case and return it to the
oven for 5 minutes to seal any cracks. Reduce the oven
temperature to 190°C (170°C fan oven) mark 5.
4 Cut the bacon into 5mm (¼in) strips. Put the bacon in
a pan of cold water and bring to the boil. Drain, refresh
under cold water and dry on kitchen paper.
5 Melt the butter in a frying pan, add the shallots or
onions and cook for 1 minute. Add the bacon and cook,
stirring, until brown.
6 Mix the eggs with the crème fraîche and cheese, and
season with salt and pepper. Put the bacon mixture in the
pastry case and spoon the crème fraîche mixture on top
(see Cook's Tip). Cook for 30–35 minutes until golden and
just set. Cool for 10 minutes before serving. Garnish with
bacon and fried spring onions.

Cook's Tip
Fill the pastry case as full as possible. You may find you
have a little mixture left, as flan tins vary in size.

NUTRITION PER SERVING 595 cals | 50g fat (29g sats) | 22g carbs | 1.5g salt

Broccoli, Gorgonzola and Walnut Quiche

Serves 6
Preparation time 15 minutes, plus chilling
Cooking time about 1 hour

butter to grease
400g (14oz) Shortcrust Pastry (see page 327)
plain flour to dust
150g (5oz) broccoli florets
100g (3½oz) gorgonzola, crumbled (see Vegetarian Cheeses, page 228)
2 medium eggs, plus 1 medium egg yolk
300ml (½ pint) double cream
25g (1oz) walnut halves, roughly chopped
salt and freshly ground black pepper

1 Preheat the oven to 200°C (180°C fan oven) mark 6 and grease a 23cm (9in) × 2.5cm (1in) deep fluted tart tin.
2 Roll out the pastry on a lightly floured surface to about 3mm (⅛in) thick, then use to line the prepared tin. Prick the base all over and chill for 15 minutes.
3 Bake blind (see page 326) for 20 minutes with the paper and beans, then for 5 minutes without. Reduce the oven temperature to 150°C (130°C fan oven) mark 2.
4 Cook the broccoli in boiling water for 3 minutes, then drain and dry on kitchen paper. Arrange the broccoli in the pastry case and dot with the gorgonzola. Whisk together the eggs, egg yolk and cream and season with salt and pepper. Pour into the case. Scatter the walnuts over the surface.
5 Cook the quiche for 40 minutes or until the filling is set. Serve warm or at room temperature.

Freezing Tip
• To freeze, complete the recipe up to one month in advance. Leave to cool in the tin, then wrap in clingfilm and freeze.
• To use, thaw completely, then serve at room temperature, or gently reheat for 20 minutes in an oven preheated to 150°C (130°C fan oven) mark 2.

NUTRITION PER SERVING 683 cals | 57g fat (27g sats) | 33g carbs | 1g salt Ⓥ

Puddings

Baked Apples

Serves 6
Preparation time 5 minutes, plus soaking
Cooking time 15–20 minutes

125g (4oz) hazelnuts
125g (4oz) sultanas
2 tbsp brandy
6 large cooking apples, such as
  Bramley, cored
4 tbsp light or dark soft brown sugar
100ml (3½fl oz) apple juice
thick cream to serve

1 Preheat the oven to 190°C (170°C
fan oven) mark 5 and preheat the grill
to hot.
2 Spread the hazelnuts over a baking
sheet and toast under the hot grill for
a few minutes until golden brown,
turning them frequently. Put the
hazelnuts in a clean tea towel and rub
off the skins, then chop the nuts. Put
to one side.
3 Meanwhile, soak the sultanas in the
brandy for 10 minutes.
4 Using a small sharp knife, score
around the middle of the apples to
stop them from bursting, then stuff
each apple with equal amounts of
brandy-soaked sultanas. Put the
apples in a roasting tin and sprinkle
with the brown sugar and apple juice.
5 Bake for 15–20 minutes until soft.
Serve the apples with the toasted
hazelnuts and a dollop of cream.

NUTRITION PER SERVING 280 cals |
13g fat (1g sats) | 36g carbs | 0g salt Ⓥ

Spiced Pears

Serves 4
Preparation time 15 minutes
Cooking time 50 minutes

4 Williams or Comice pears
150g (5oz) granulated sugar
300ml (½ pint) red wine (see Alcoholic
  Drinks and Vegetarians, page 489)
150ml (¼ pint) sloe gin
1 cinnamon stick
zest of 1 orange
6 star anise
Greek yogurt or whipped cream to
  serve (optional)

1 Peel the pears, cut out the calyx and
core at the base of each one and leave
the stalks intact. If necessary, cut a thin
slice off the base so they stand upright.
2 Put the sugar, wine, sloe gin and
300ml (½ pint) water in a pan and
heat gently until the sugar dissolves.
3 Bring to the boil and add the
cinnamon stick, orange zest and star
anise. Add the pears, then cover the
pan and poach over a low heat for
30 minutes or until tender.
4 Remove the pears with a slotted
spoon, then continue to heat the
liquid until it has reduced to about
200ml (7fl oz) or until syrupy. Pour
the syrup over the pears. Serve warm
or chilled with Greek yogurt or
whipped cream, if you like.

GET AHEAD
Complete the recipe, cool, cover and
chill for up to three days.

NUTRITION PER SERVING 305 cals |
trace fat (0g sats) | 52g carbs | 0g salt Ⓥ

Apple Crumble

Serves 4
Preparation time 15 minutes
Cooking time 45 minutes

125g (4oz) plain flour
50g (2oz) unsalted butter, cubed
50g (2oz) golden caster sugar
450g (1lb) apples, peeled, cored and
  sliced
custard or double cream to serve

1 Preheat the oven to 180°C (160°C fan oven) mark 4.
2 Put the flour into a bowl, add the butter and rub in with your fingertips until the mixture resembles fine breadcrumbs. Stir in half the sugar. Put to one side.
3 Arrange half the apples in a 1.1 litre (2 pint) pie dish and sprinkle with the rest of the sugar. Add the remaining apple slices to the dish. Spoon the crumble mixture over the fruit.
4 Bake for 45 minutes or until the fruit is soft. Serve hot with custard or a drizzle of double cream.

NUTRITION PER SERVING 425 cals |
18g fat (7g sats) | 74g carbs | 0.3g salt ⓥ

Cherry Clafoutis

Serves 6
Preparation time 20 minutes, plus 1 hour
  soaking
Cooking time about 1 hour

350g (12oz) cherries, pitted
3 tbsp Kirsch
125g (4oz) golden caster sugar
4 large eggs
25g (1oz) plain flour
150ml (¼ pint) milk
150ml (¼ pint) double cream
1 tsp vanilla extract
a little butter to grease

1 Soak the cherries in the Kirsch and 1 tbsp sugar for 1 hour.
2 Meanwhile, whisk together the eggs, 100g (3½oz) of the sugar and the flour. Bring the milk and cream to the boil, then pour on to the egg mixture, add the vanilla and whisk until combined. Strain into a bowl, cover and set aside for 30 minutes.
3 Preheat the oven to 180°C (160°C fan oven) mark 4. Butter a 1.7 litre (3 pint) shallow ovenproof dish and sprinkle with the remaining sugar.
4 Spoon the cherries into the dish. Whisk the batter again, then pour it over the cherries. Bake for 1 hour or until golden and just set. Serve warm.

TRY SOMETHING DIFFERENT
Autumnal Clafoutis Replace the cherries with blackberries, the Kirsch with blackberry or liqueur and the vanilla with ¼ tsp ground cinnamon.

NUTRITION PER SERVING 326 cals |
18g fat (10g sats) | 33g carbs | 0.2g salt ⓥ

Blackberry and Apple Crumble

Serves 6
Preparation time 45 minutes
Cooking time 25 minutes

50g (2oz) plain white flour
25g (1oz) plain wholemeal flour
75g (3oz) light muscovado sugar
50g (2oz) ground almonds
50g (2oz) unsalted butter
custard, cream or ice cream to serve

For the filling
700g (1½lb) eating apples
50g (2oz) unsalted butter
50g (2oz) golden caster sugar
225g (8oz) blackberries

1 Preheat the oven to 190°C (170°C fan oven) mark 5.
Sift the flours into a bowl, then tip in any bran from the
sieve. Stir in the sugar and ground almonds, then work
in the butter, using your fingertips, to make a very
crumbly mixture.
2 To make the filling, quarter the apples, then peel, core
and cut into 2.5cm (1in) chunks. Melt the butter in a
large frying pan. Add the apples with the sugar, and cook,
stirring, over a high heat for 3–5 minutes until golden
brown and tender. Transfer to a 1.7 litre (3 pint) pie dish.
Scatter the blackberries on top.
3 Spoon over the crumble topping and bake for about
25 minutes or until the topping is golden brown. Serve
warm, with custard, cream or ice cream.

TRY SOMETHING DIFFERENT
Red Fruit Crumble Replace the blackberries with
225g (8oz) mixed summer fruits, such as red and
blackcurrants, raspberries and pitted cherries.

NUTRITION PER SERVING 0 cals | g fat (9g s) | 4 g carbs | .3 salt Ⓥ

Summer Pudding

Serves 8
Preparation time 10 minutes, plus overnight chilling
Cooking time 10 minutes

800g (1lb 12oz) mixed summer berries, such as 250g (9oz) each redcurrants and blackcurrants and 300g (11oz) raspberries
125g (4oz) golden caster sugar
3 tbsp crème de cassis
9 thick slices slightly stale white bread, crusts removed
crème fraîche or clotted cream to serve

1 Put the redcurrants and blackcurrants into a medium pan. Add the sugar and cassis. Bring to the boil, then reduce the heat and simmer for 3–5 minutes until the sugar has dissolved. Add the raspberries and cook for 2 minutes. Once the fruit is cooked, taste it – there should be a good balance between tart and sweet.
2 Meanwhile, line a 1 litre (1¾ pint) bowl with clingfilm. Put the base of the bowl on one piece of bread and cut around it. Put the circle of bread in the base of the bowl. Line the inside of the bowl with more slices of bread, slightly overlapping them to prevent any gaps. Spoon in the fruit, making sure the juice soaks into the bread. Keep back a few spoonfuls of juice in case the bread is unevenly soaked when you turn out the pudding.
4 Cut the remaining bread to fit the top of the pudding neatly, using a sharp knife to trim any excess bread from around the edges. Wrap in clingfilm, weigh down with a saucer and a can, and chill overnight.
5 To serve, unwrap the outer clingfilm, upturn the pudding on to a plate and remove the inner clingfilm. Drizzle with the reserved juice and serve with crème fraîche or clotted cream.

NUTRITION PER SERVING 173 cals | 1g fat (trace sats) | 38g carbs | 0.4g salt Ⓥ

Syrup Sponge Pudding

Serves 4
Preparation time 15 minutes
Cooking time 1½ hours

125g (4oz) butter, plus extra to grease
2 tbsp golden syrup
125g (4oz) caster sugar
2 medium eggs, beaten
a few drops of vanilla extract
175g (6oz) self-raising flour, sifted
a little milk to mix
Fresh Vanilla Custard (see page 24) to serve

1 Half-fill a steamer or large pan with water and put it on
to boil. Grease a 900ml (1½ pint) pudding basin and spoon
the syrup into the base.
2 Cream together the butter and sugar until pale and
fluffy. Add the beaten eggs and the vanilla, a little at a time,
beating well after each addition.
3 Using a metal spoon, fold in half the sifted flour,
then fold in the remainder, with enough milk to give a
dropping consistency.
4 Pour the mixture into the prepared basin, cover with
greased greaseproof paper or foil and secure with string.
Steam for 1½ hours, topping up with boiling water as
necessary. Serve with custard.

TRY SOMETHING DIFFERENT
Steamed Jam Sponge Pudding Put 4 tbsp raspberry or
blackberry jam into the base of the basin instead of the syrup.
Steamed Chocolate Sponge Pudding Omit the golden syrup.
Blend 4 tbsp cocoa powder with 2 tbsp hot water, then
gradually beat into the creamed mixture in step 2 before
adding the eggs.

NUTRITION PER SERVING 582 cals | 29 fat (17g sat) | 77g carbs | 1.1g salt Ⓥ

Spotted Dick

Serves 4
Preparation time 20 minutes
Cooking time 2 hours

125g (4oz) fresh breadcrumbs
75g (3oz) self-raising flour, plus extra to dust
75g (3oz) shredded suet
50g (2oz) caster sugar
175g (6oz) currants
finely grated zest of 1 lemon
5 tbsp milk
butter to grease
Fresh Vanilla Custard (see page 24) to serve

1 Half-fill a preserving pan or large pan with water and put on to boil.
2 Put the breadcrumbs, flour, suet, sugar, currants and lemon zest in a bowl and stir well until thoroughly mixed.
3 Pour in the milk and stir until well blended. Using one hand, bring the ingredients together to form a soft, slightly sticky dough.
4 Turn the dough on to a floured surface and knead gently until just smooth. Shape into a neat roll about 15cm (6in) in length.
5 Make a 5cm (2in) pleat across a clean tea towel or pudding cloth, or pleat together sheets of greased greaseproof paper and strong foil. Encase the roll in the cloth or foil, pleating the open edges tightly together.
6 Tie the ends securely with string to form a cracker shape. Make a string handle across the top. Lower the suet roll into the pan of boiling water and boil for 2 hours.
7 Using the string handle, lift the Spotted Dick out of the water. Put on a wire rack standing over a plate and allow the excess moisture to drain off.
8 Snip the string and gently roll the pudding out of the cloth or foil on to a warmed serving plate. Serve sliced with vanilla custard.

NUTRITION PER SERVING 502 cals | 18g fat (10g sats) | 84g carbs | 0.8g salt

Jam Roly-poly

Serves 4
Preparation time 15 minutes
Cooking time 1½–2 hours

butter to grease
175g (6oz) Suet Crust Pastry
  (see page 329)
flour to dust
4–6 tbsp jam
a little milk
Fresh Vanilla Custard (see page 24)
  to serve

1 Half-fill a steamer with water and put on to boil. Grease a piece of kitchen foil 23 × 33cm (9 × 13in).
2 Roll out the suet crust pastry on a lightly floured surface to a rectangle about 23 × 28cm (9 × 11in). Spread the jam on the pastry, leaving 5mm (¼in) clear along each edge. Brush the edges with milk and roll up the pastry evenly, starting from one short side.
3 Put the roll on the greased foil and wrap the foil around it loosely, to allow room for expansion, but seal the edges well.
4 Steam for 1½–2 hours. Remove from the foil and serve with custard.

NUTRITION PER SERVING 345 cals | 16g fat (9g sats) | 50g carbs | 0.6g salt

Sticky Toffee Pudding

Serves 4
Preparation time 20 minutes, plus 5
  minutes resting
Cooking time 25–30 minutes

1 tbsp golden syrup
1 tbsp black treacle
150g (5oz) butter, softened
25g (1oz) pecan nuts or walnuts, finely
  ground
75g (3oz) self-raising flour
125g (4oz) caster sugar
2 large eggs, beaten
cream or custard to serve

1 Preheat the oven to 180°C (160°C fan oven) mark 4. Put the syrup, treacle and 25g (1oz) butter into a bowl and beat until smooth. Divide the mixture among four 150ml (¼ pint) timbales or ramekins and set aside.

2 Put the nuts into a bowl, sift in the flour and mix together well.
3 Put the remaining butter and the sugar into a food processor and blend briefly. (Alternatively, use a hand-held electric whisk.) Add the eggs and the flour mixture and blend or mix again for 30 seconds. Spoon the mixture into the timbales or ramekins, covering the syrup mixture on the base. Bake for 25–30 minutes until risen and golden.
4 Remove the puddings from the oven and leave to rest for 5 minutes, then unmould on to warmed plates. Serve immediately with cream or custard.

NUTRITION PER SERVING 715 cals | 38g fat (21g sats) | 83g carbs | 0.9g salt

Cranberry Christmas Pudding

Serves 12
Preparation time 20 minutes, plus soaking
Cooking time 6 hours

200g (7oz) currants
200g (7oz) sultanas
200g (7oz) raisins
75g (3oz) dried cranberries or cherries
grated zest and juice of 1 orange
50ml (2fl oz) rum
50ml (2fl oz) brandy
1–2 tsp Angostura bitters
1 small apple, peeled, cored and grated
1 carrot, grated
175g (6oz) fresh breadcrumbs
100g (3½oz) plain flour, sifted
1 tsp mixed spice
175g (6oz) light vegetarian suet
100g (3½oz) dark muscovado sugar
50g (2oz) blanched almonds, roughly chopped
2 medium eggs
butter to grease
frosted cranberries and bay leaves (see Cook's Tip),
  and icing sugar to decorate
Brandy Butter (see page 27) to serve

1 Put the fruit, orange zest and juice, rum, brandy and
Angostura bitters in a large bowl. Cover and leave to soak
in a cool place for at least 1 hour or preferably overnight.
2 Add the apple, carrot, breadcrumbs, flour, mixed spice,
suet, sugar, almonds and eggs to the bowl of soaked fruit.
Use a wooden spoon to mix everything together well.
Now's the time to make a wish!
3 Grease a 1.8 litre (3¼ pint) pudding basin and line with
a 60cm (24in) square piece of muslin. Spoon the mixture
into the pudding basin and flatten the top. Gather the
muslin over the top, then twist and secure with string.
4 Put the basin on an upturned heatproof saucer or trivet
in the base of a large pan. Pour in enough boiling water to
come halfway up the side of the basin. Cover with a tight-
fitting lid and simmer for 6 hours, topping up with boiling
water as necessary. Remove the basin from the pan and
leave to cool. When cold, remove the pudding from the
basin and muslin, then wrap it in clingfilm and a double
layer of foil. Store in a cool, dry place for up to six months.
5 To reheat, steam for 2½ hours; check the water level
every 40 minutes and top up if necessary. Keep the

pudding warm in the covered pan until needed. Decorate
with cranberries and bay leaves, and dust with icing sugar.
Serve with Brandy Butter.

Cook's Tip

FROSTED BERRIES AND LEAVES Lightly beat 1 medium egg
white and spread 25g (1oz) caster sugar out on a tray,
making sure there are no lumps. Brush a few fresh
cranberries and bay leaves with the beaten egg white. Dip
the berries and leaves into the sugar, shake off any excess,
then leave to dry on a tray lined with baking parchment
for about 1 hour.

NUTRITION PER SERVING 448 cals | 17g fat (7g sats) | 68g carbs | 0.3g salt Ⓥ

Bread and Butter Pudding

Serves 4
Preparation time 10 minutes, plus soaking
Cooking time 30–40 minutes

50g (2oz) butter, softened, plus extra to grease
275g (10oz) white farmhouse bread, cut into 1cm (½in) slices, crusts removed
50g (2oz) raisins or sultanas
3 medium eggs
450ml (¾ pint) milk
3 tbsp golden icing sugar, sifted, plus extra to dust

1 Lightly butter four 300ml (½ pint) gratin dishes or one 1.1 litre (2 pint) ovenproof dish.
2 Butter the bread, then cut into quarters to make triangles. Arrange the bread in the dish(es), sprinkling with the raisins or sultanas as you layer the bread.
3 Beat the eggs, milk and sugar in a bowl. Pour the mixture over the bread and leave to soak for 10 minutes. Preheat the oven to 180°C (160°C fan oven) mark 4.
4 Put the pudding(s) in the oven and bake for 20–30 minutes for individual puddings or 30–40 minutes for one large pudding. Dust with icing sugar to serve.

NUTRITION PER SERVING 450 cals | 13g fat (5g sats) | 70g carbs | 1.1g salt Ⓥ

Rice Pudding

Serves 6
Preparation time 5 minutes
Cooking time 1½ hours

butter to grease
125g (4oz) short-grain pudding rice
1.1 litres (2 pints) milk
50g (2oz) golden caster sugar
1 tsp vanilla extract
grated zest of 1 orange (optional)
freshly grated nutmeg to taste

1 Preheat the oven to 170°C (150°C fan oven) mark 3 and lightly butter a 1.7 litre (3 pint) ovenproof dish.
2 Put the rice, milk, sugar, vanilla extract and orange zest, if you like, into the dish and stir everything together. well. Grate the nutmeg over the top of the mixture.
3 Bake the pudding in the middle of the oven for 1½ hours or until the top is golden brown.

NUTRITION PER SERVING 239 cals | 8g fat (5g sats) | 34g carbs | 0.2g salt Ⓥ

Warm Chocolate Fondants

Serves 6
Preparation time 25 minutes
Cooking time 10–12 minutes

150g (5oz) unsalted butter, plus extra
  to grease
3 medium eggs, plus 3 medium egg
  yolks
50g (2oz) golden caster sugar
175g (6oz) plain chocolate (at least
  70% cocoa solids), broken into pieces
50g (2oz) plain flour, sifted
6 chocolate truffles

1 Preheat the oven to 200°C (180°C
fan oven) mark 6. Lightly grease six
200ml (7fl oz) ramekins. Put the
whole eggs, egg yolks and sugar into a
large bowl and beat with a hand-held
electric whisk for 8–10 minutes until
pale and fluffy.

2 Meanwhile, melt the chocolate
and butter in a heatproof bowl set
over a pan of gently simmering
water, stirring the chocolate mixture
occasionally.
3 Stir a spoonful of the melted
chocolate into the egg mixture,
then gently fold in the remaining
chocolate. Fold in the flour.
4 Put a large spoonful of mixture into
each ramekin. Put a chocolate truffle
in the centre of each, taking care not
to push it down. Divide the remainder
of the mixture among the ramekins to
cover the truffle; they should be about
three-quarters full. Bake for 10–12
minutes until the top is firm and
starting to rise and crack. Serve warm.

NUTRITION PER SERVING 502 cals |
37g fat (21g sats) | 39g carbs | 0.5g salt Ⓥ

Queen of Puddings

Serves 4
Preparation time 20 minutes, plus
  standing
Cooking time about 1¼ hours

4 medium eggs
600ml (1 pint) milk
125g (4oz) fresh breadcrumbs
3–4 tbsp raspberry jam
75g (3oz) caster sugar

1 Separate 3 eggs and beat together
the 3 egg yolks and 1 whole egg.
Add to the milk and mix well. Stir
in the breadcrumbs.
2 Spread the jam on the base of a pie
dish. Pour in the milk mixture and
leave for 30 minutes.
3 Preheat the oven to 150°C (130°C
fan oven) mark 2.
4 Bake in the oven for 1 hour or until
set. When almost ready, put the egg
whites into a clean, grease-free bowl
and whisk until they form stiff peaks.
Fold in the sugar, then pile on top of
the custard and return it to the oven
for a further 15–20 minutes until the
meringue is set and lightly golden.

NUTRITION PER SERVING 387 cals |
9g fat (3g sats) | 65g carbs | 1g salt Ⓥ

Banoffee Pie

Serves 14
Preparation time 15 minutes, plus chilling
Cooking time 2–3 minutes

100g (3½oz) butter, melted, plus extra to grease
200g (7oz) digestive biscuits, roughly broken
2 small bananas, peeled and sliced
8 tbsp dulce de leche toffee sauce
284ml carton double cream
1 tbsp cocoa powder to dust

1 Grease the base and sides of a 23cm (9in) loose-based
tart tin. Whiz the biscuits in a food processor until they
resemble breadcrumbs. Pour in the melted butter and whiz
to combine. Press the mixture evenly into the prepared tart
tin, using the back of a metal spoon, and chill for 2 hours.
2 Arrange the banana slices evenly over the biscuit base
and spoon the dulce de leche on top. Whip the cream until
thick and spread it over the top. Dust with a sprinkling of
cocoa powder and serve.

TRY SOMETHING DIFFERENT
• Top with a handful of toasted flaked almonds instead of
  the cocoa powder.
• Whiz 25g (1oz) chopped pecan nuts into the biscuits with
  the butter.
• Scatter grated plain chocolate over the cream.

NUTRITION PER SERVING 250 cals | 19g fat (10g sats) | 18g carbs | 0.4g salt Ⓥ

Sugar-crusted Fruit Pie

Serves 4
Preparation time 30 minutes, plus chilling
Cooking time about 40 minutes, plus cooling

75g (3oz) hazelnuts
350g (12oz) cherries, stoned
75g (3oz) caster sugar, plus 2 tbsp
175g (6oz) plain flour, plus extra to dust
125g (4oz) butter
275g (10oz) cooking apples, peeled, cored and quartered

1 Spread the hazelnuts over a baking sheet. Toast under a hot grill until golden brown, turning them frequently. Put the hazelnuts in a clean tea towel and rub off the skins. Leave to cool. Put the cherries into a bowl with 25g (1oz) caster sugar. Cover and leave to one side.
2 For the hazelnut pastry, put 50g (2oz) hazelnuts into a food processor with the flour and pulse to a powder. Remove and leave to one side. In the food processor, whiz the butter with 50g (2oz) sugar. Add the flour mixture and pulse until it forms a dough. Turn out on to a lightly floured surface and knead lightly, then wrap in clingfilm and chill for 30 minutes. If the pastry cracks, just work it together.
3 Preheat the oven to 180°C (160°C fan oven) mark 4. Cut the apples into small chunks and put into a 900ml (1½ pint) oval pie dish. Spoon the cherries on top.
4 Roll out the pastry on a lightly floured surface to about 5mm (¼in) thick. Cut into 1cm (½in) strips. Dampen the edge of the pie dish with a little water and press a few of the strips on to the rim to cover it. Dampen the pastry rim. Put the remaining strips over the cherries to create a lattice pattern. Brush the pastry with water and sprinkle with the extra sugar.
5 Bake for 30–35 minutes until the pastry is golden. Leave to cool for 15 minutes. Chop the remaining toasted hazelnuts and sprinkle over the tart. Serve warm.

NUTRITION PER SERVING 673 cals | 38g fat (17g sats) | 79g carbs | 0.5g salt Ⓥ

Lemon Meringue Pie

Serves 8
Preparation time 30 minutes, plus 1 hour chilling
Cooking time about 1 hour, plus standing

Sweet Pastry (see page 327), made with 225g (8oz) plain
  flour, a pinch of salt, 150g (5oz) butter, cut into pieces,
  1 medium egg yolk, 2 tbsp caster sugar and 3 tbsp cold
  water
plain flour to dust
a little beaten egg

For the filling and topping
7 medium eggs, 4 separated, at room temperature
finely grated zest of 3 lemons
175ml (6fl oz) freshly squeezed lemon juice
  (about 4 lemons), strained
400g can condensed milk
150ml (¼ pint) double cream
225g (8oz) golden icing sugar, sifted

1 Roll out the pastry on a lightly floured surface and use
to line a 23cm (9in) round, 4cm (1½in) deep, loose-based
fluted tart tin. Prick the base with a fork and chill for 30
minutes. Meanwhile, preheat the oven to 190°C (170°C fan
oven) mark 5.
2 Bake the pastry case blind (see page 326) for 10 minutes
at each stage. Brush the inside with beaten egg and put
back in the oven for 1 minute to seal. Increase the oven
temperature to 180°C (160°C fan oven) mark 4.
3 To make the filling, put 4 egg yolks into a bowl with the
3 whole eggs. Add the lemon zest and juice, and whisk
lightly. Mix in the condensed milk and cream.
4 Pour the filling into the pastry case and bake for
30 minutes or until just set in the centre. Leave to one side
to cool while you prepare the meringue. Decrease the oven
temperature to 200°C (180°C fan oven) mark 6.
5 For the meringue, whisk the egg whites and icing sugar
together in a heatproof bowl set over a pan of gently
simmering water, using a hand-held electric whisk, for
10 minutes or until shiny and thick. Take off the heat and
continue to whisk at low speed for 5–10 minutes until the
bowl is cool. Pile the meringue on to the filling and swirl
to form peaks. Bake for 5–10 minutes until the meringue is
tinged brown. Leave to stand for about 1 hour, then serve.

TRY SOMETHING DIFFERENT
Use lime zest and juice instead of lemon.

NUTRITION PER SERVING 173 cals | 1g fat (trace sats) | 38g carbs | 0.4g salt Ⓥ

Proper Apple Pie

Serves 8
Preparation time 30 minutes, plus chilling
Cooking time 50 minutes

300g (11oz) plain flour, plus extra to dust
200g (7oz) unsalted butter, chilled and diced, plus extra to
  grease
1.4kg (3lb) Bramley apples, peeled, cored and cut into 2cm
  (¾in) pieces
100g (3½oz) caster sugar, plus extra to sprinkle
1 tsp ground cinnamon
75g (3oz) sultanas
1 medium egg, beaten
salt
double cream to serve

1 Put the flour, 175g (6oz) of the butter and a pinch of salt
into a food processor and pulse until the mixture resembles
fine breadcrumbs. If you don't have a food processor, rub
the butter into the flour using your fingers. Add 3–4 tbsp
icy cold water and whiz again (or mix with a blunt-ended
cutlery knife) until the pastry just comes together. Tip on
to a worksurface, bring together and wrap in clingfilm.
Chill for 30 minutes.
2 Meanwhile, put the apple pieces into a large frying
pan with the remaining butter, the sugar and cinnamon.
Cook gently for about 10 minutes until the apples are just
tender and there's barely any moisture in the pan. Add the
sultanas and leave to cool completely.
3 Preheat the oven to 200°C (180°C fan oven) mark 6,
grease a 20.5cm (8in) round, 7cm (2¾in) deep springform
cake tin and put a baking sheet in the oven to heat up.
4 Lightly dust a worksurface with flour, roll out two-thirds
of the pastry and use to line the prepared tin.
5 Spoon the cooled apple mixture into the tin, level the
surface, then fold the excess pastry over the apples. Roll out
remaining pastry as before until it is larger than the base
of the tin. Put the tin on the pastry and cut round the base.
Lay the pastry circle on top of the apple mixture and press
the edges down. If you like, cut apple and letter shapes
from pastry trimmings, moisten and stick on to the pie.

6 Cut a small cross in the middle of the lid to allow steam
to escape. Brush the top of the pie with beaten egg and
sprinkle with a little sugar. Stand the tin on the heated
baking sheet and bake for 35–40 minutes until golden.
7 Leave the pie to cool for 10 minutes in the tin, then take
it out of the tin and serve warm or at room temperature
with lashings of cream.

NUTRITION PER SERVING 457 cals | 22g fat (13g sats) | 57g carbs | 0.4g salt Ⓥ

Mince Pies

Makes 24
Preparation time 15 minutes, plus chilling
Cooking time 12–15 minutes

225g (8oz) plain flour, plus extra to dust
125g (4oz) unsalted butter, chilled and diced, plus extra to
 grease
100g (3½oz) cream cheese (see Vegetarian Cheeses,
 page 270)
1 medium egg yolk
finely grated zest of 1 orange
400g jar mincemeat (see below)
1 medium egg, beaten
icing sugar, sifted, to dust

1 Put the flour in a food processor. Add the butter, cream
cheese, egg yolk and orange zest, and whiz until the mixture
just comes together. Tip the mixture into a large bowl and
bring the dough together with your hands. Shape into a
ball, wrap in clingfilm and put in the freezer for 5 minutes.
2 Preheat the oven to 220°C (200°C fan oven) mark 7 and
lightly grease two 12-hole patty tins.
3 Cut off about one-third of the pastry dough and leave to
one side. Roll out the remainder on a lightly floured surface
to 5mm (¼in) thick. Stamp out circles with a 6.5cm (2½in)
cutter to make 24 rounds, re-rolling the dough as necessary.
Use the pastry circles to line the prepared tins. Roll out the
reserved pastry and use a star cutter to stamp out the stars.
4 Put 1 tsp mincemeat into each pastry case, then top with
pastry stars. Brush the tops with beaten egg, then bake for
12–15 minutes until golden.
5 Remove from the tins and leave to cool on a wire rack.
Serve warm or cold, dusted with icing sugar. Store in an
airtight container for up to four days.

TRY SOMETHING DIFFERENT

Jars of mincemeat Improve the flavour of jars of bought
mincemeat by adding 2 tbsp brandy, the grated zest of
1 lemon and 25g (1oz) pecan nuts, chopped. Or, instead of
the nuts, try a piece of preserved stem ginger, finely chopped.
Luxury Mincemeat Put the following into a large mixing
bowl and mix thoroughly to combine: 350g (12oz) each
seedless raisins, currants, sultanas; 150g (5oz) candied peel,
finely chopped; 250g pack shredded vegetable suet; 100g
(3½oz) blanched almonds, finely chopped; 350g (12oz)
demerara sugar; 125g (4oz) natural glacé cherries, chopped;
2 medium cooking apples, such as Bramley, peeled, cored and
grated; 3 tsp ground mixed spice; grated zest and juice of
1 lemon and 1 orange; 150ml (¼ pint) each brandy and
Drambuie. Cover and set aside in a cool place for 24 hours,
stirring from time to time. Either use the mincemeat
immediately or spoon into sterilised jars, cover and seal.
Store in a cool, dark place and use within three months.
Makes 2.6kg (5¾lb).

Cook's Tip
For vegetarians, make sure you use mincemeat made
with vegetable suet rather than beef suet and a vegetarian
cheese.

NUTRITION PER SERVING 150 cals | 8g fat (4g sats) | 17g carbs | 0.2g salt Ⓥ

Treacle Tart

Serves 8
Preparation time 35 minutes, plus chilling
Cooking time 45 minutes

175g (6oz) plain flour, plus extra to dust
125g (4oz) butter, cold and cubed
40g (1½oz) caster sugar
1 medium egg yolk
575g (1lb 5oz) golden syrup
½–1 tsp ground ginger to taste
finely grated zest and juice of 1 lemon
175g (6oz) fine fresh white breadcrumbs
double cream or crème fraîche to serve

1 To make the pastry, put the flour and butter into a
food processor and pulse until the mixture resembles fine
breadcrumbs. Alternatively, rub the butter into the flour
using your fingers. Add the sugar and briefly whiz (or stir)
to combine. Next, add the egg yolk and 2 tsp water and
pulse (or stir with a blunt-ended cutlery knife) until the
pastry comes together. Bring the pastry together into
a disc with your hands, wrap in clingfilm and chill for
30 minutes.
2 Grease a 20.5cm (8in) round, roughly 4cm (1½in) deep
cake tin. Lightly dust a worksurface with flour, roll out the
pastry and use to line the prepared tin. Prick the base with
a fork and chill for 20 minutes.
3 Preheat the oven to 200°C (180°C fan oven) mark
6. Line the pastry case with a large square of baking
parchment, then fill with ceramic baking beans or
uncooked rice. Put the tin on a baking sheet, then bake for
15 minutes. Carefully remove the parchment and baking
beans or rice, return the tin to the oven and bake for a
further 8 minutes or until the pastry is cooked through and
feels sandy to the touch. Remove from the oven but leave
in the tin.
4 Gently warm the syrup, ground ginger and lemon zest
and juice in a pan until the mixture is loose and runny.
Take off the heat and stir in the breadcrumbs. Pour into
the pastry case.
5 Return the tart to the oven and cook for 15–20 minutes
until the filling looks lightly firm. Lift the tart out of the
tin and serve just warm or at room temperature with cream
or crème fraîche.

NUTRITION PER SERVING (without cream or crème fraîche) 520 cals| 14g fat (8g sats) | 92g carbs | 1.2g salt Ⓥ

Almond Bakewell Tarts

Makes 6
Preparation time 25 minutes, plus chilling
Cooking time 50 minutes, plus cooling

Sweet Pastry (see page 327), made with 200g (7oz) plain
  flour, 100g (3½oz) unsalted butter, 3 large egg yolks,
  75g (3oz) caster sugar and ½ tsp vanilla extract
plain flour to dust
Plum Sauce (see Cook's Tip) to serve

For the filling
125g (4oz) unsalted butter, softened
125g (4oz) caster sugar
3 large eggs
125g (4oz) ground almonds
2–3 drops almond essence
6 tbsp redcurrant jelly

For the crumble topping
25g (1oz) unsalted butter
75g (3oz) plain flour
25g (1oz) caster sugar

1 Roll out the pastry thinly on a lightly floured surface
and line six 10cm (4in), 3cm (1¼in) deep tartlet tins.
Chill for 30 minutes. Preheat the oven to 190°C (170°C
fan oven) mark 5.
2 Bake the tartlet cases blind (see page 326) for 10 minutes
plus 10 minutes. Remove from the oven and leave to cool.
3 To make the filling, beat the butter and sugar together
until light and fluffy. Gradually beat in 2 eggs, then beat in
the remaining egg with one-third of the ground almonds.
Fold in the remaining almonds and the almond essence.
4 Melt the redcurrant jelly in a small pan and brush over
the inside of each pastry case. Carefully spoon in the
almond filling. Put the tarts on a large baking sheet and
bake for 20–25 minutes until golden and just firm. Leave
in the tins for 10 minutes, then unmould on to a wire rack
and leave to cool completely.
5 To make the crumble topping, rub the butter into the
flour until the mixture resembles breadcrumbs. Stir in
the sugar. Spread evenly on a baking sheet and grill until
golden. Cool, then sprinkle over the tarts. Decorate with
plums (see right) and serve with Plum Sauce.

Cook's Tip
PLUM SAUCE Put 450g (1lb) halved and stoned ripe plums,
50–75g (2–3oz) soft brown sugar and 150ml (¼ pint) sweet
white wine into a pan with 150ml (¼ pint) water. Bring
to the boil, then simmer for bout 10 minutes until tender
but still holding their shape. Remove 3 plums to decorate;
thickly slice or quarter and put to one side. Cook the
remaining plums for about 15 minutes or until very soft.
Put into a food processor and whiz until smooth. Sieve, if
you like, adding more sugar to taste. Leave to cool.

NUTRITION PER SERVING 931 cals | 52g fat (24g sats) | 104g carbs | 0.8g salt Ⓥ

Tarte Tatin

Cuts into 6 slices
Preparation time 30 minutes, plus chilling
Cooking time about 1 hour, plus cooling

Sweet Pastry (see page 327), made with 225g (8oz) plain
  flour, ¼ tsp salt, 150g (5oz) unsalted butter, 1 medium egg,
  50g (2oz) golden icing sugar in addition to the caster sugar,
  2–3 drops vanilla extract
plain flour to dust

For the filling
200g (7oz) golden caster sugar
125g (4oz) chilled unsalted butter
1.4–1.6kg (3–3½lb) crisp dessert apples, peeled and cored
juice of ½ lemon

1 To make the filling, sprinkle the sugar over the base
of a 20.5cm (8in) tarte tatin tin or ovenproof frying
pan. Cut the butter into slivers and dot over the sugar.
Halve the apples and pack them tightly, cut side up,
on top of the butter.
2 Put the tin or pan on the hob and cook over a medium
heat for 30 minutes (making sure it doesn't bubble over
or catch on the base) or until the butter and sugar turn
a dark golden brown (see Cook's Tip). Sprinkle with the
lemon juice, then allow to cool for 15 minutes. Meanwhile,
preheat the oven to 220°C (200°C fan oven) mark 7.
3 Put the pastry on a large sheet of lightly floured baking
parchment. Roll out the pastry to make a round 2.5cm
(1in) larger than the tin or pan. Prick several times with
a fork. Lay the pastry over the apples, tucking the edges
down the side of the tin.
4 Bake for 25–30 minutes until golden brown. Leave
in the tin for 10 minutes, then carefully upturn on to a
serving plate. Serve warm.

Cook's Tip

When caramelising the apples in step 2, be patient and
do not turn the heat up too high. Allow the sauce to turn
a dark golden brown – any paler and it will be too sickly.
Don't let it burn, though, as this will make the caramel
taste bitter.

NUTRITION PER SERVING 727 cals | 39g fat (24g sats) | 94g carbs | 0.7g salt Ⓥ

Maple Pecan Tart

Serves 10
Preparation time 40 minutes, plus chilling
Cooking time 1¼ hours

250g (9oz) plain flour, sifted
a large pinch of salt
225g (8oz) unsalted butter, cubed and chilled
100g (3½oz) light muscovado sugar
125g (4oz) dates, stoned and roughly chopped
grated zest and juice of ½ lemon
100ml (3½fl oz) maple syrup, plus 6 tbsp extra
1 tsp vanilla extract
4 medium eggs
300g (11oz) pecan nut halves
300ml (½ pint) double cream
2 tbsp bourbon whiskey

1 Put the flour and salt into a food processor. Add 125g
(4oz) of the butter and whiz to fine crumbs. (Alternatively,
rub the butter into the flour in a large bowl by hand or
using a pastry cutter.) Add 2 tbsp water and whiz, or stir,
until the mixture just comes together. Wrap in clingfilm
and chill for 30 minutes. Use to line a 28 × 4cm (11 ×
1½in) loose-based tart tin, then cover and chill for
30 minutes. Preheat the oven to 200°C (180°C fan oven)
mark 6.
2 Bake blind (see page 326) for 25 minutes, then for a
further 5 minutes or until the base is dry and light golden.
3 Meanwhile, whiz, or beat, the rest of the butter until
soft. Add the sugar and dates and whiz, or beat, to cream
together. Add the lemon zest and juice, 100ml (3½fl oz)
maple syrup, the vanilla extract, eggs and 200g (7oz) nuts.
Whiz until the nuts are finely chopped – the mixture will
look curdled. Pour into the pastry case and top with the
rest of the nuts.
4 Bake for 40–45 minutes until almost set in the middle.
Cover with greaseproof paper for the last 10 minutes if the
nuts turn very dark. Cool slightly before removing from the
tin, then brush with 4 tbsp maple syrup. Lightly whip the
cream with the whiskey and 2 tbsp maple syrup, then serve
with the pie.

TRY SOMETHING DIFFERENT
Replace the lemon with orange, the pecans with walnut
halves and the whiskey with Cointreau.

NUTRITION PER SERVING 748 cals | 57g fat (24g sats) | 51g carbs | 0.6g salt Ⓥ

Deep Custard Tart

Serves 8
Preparation time 25 minutes, plus chilling
Cooking time 1 hour 10 minutes

125g (4oz) unsalted butter, chilled and cut into cubes, plus
  extra to grease
75g (3oz) icing sugar, sifted
225g (8oz) plain flour, plus extra to dust
1 medium egg
5 medium egg yolks
100g (3½oz) caster sugar
600ml carton double cream, at room temperature
2 tsp vanilla extract or vanilla bean paste
a few good pinches of ground cinnamon to sprinkle

1 Lightly grease a 20.5cm (8in) springform cake tin.
2 Put the icing sugar, flour and butter into a food processor
and whiz until the mixture resembles fine breadcrumbs.
Alternatively, rub the butter into the icing sugar mixture
using your fingers. Add 2½ tbsp ice-cold water and whiz
again (or mix with a blunt-ended cutlery knife) until the
dough just comes together. Tip on to a worksurface, bring
together and wrap in clingfilm. Chill for 30 minutes.
3 Lightly dust a worksurface with flour. Roll out the pastry
to 3mm (⅛in) thick and use to line the prepared tin. Prick
the base all over with a fork, then chill for 10 minutes.
4 Preheat the oven to 200°C (180°C fan oven) mark 6.
Line the pastry case with baking parchment and fill with
baking beans. Bake for 15 minutes or until pastry sides are
set. Remove the beans and paper and return the pastry to
the oven for 5 minutes or until the base is cooked through.
Reduce the oven temperature to 160°C (140°C fan oven)
mark 3.
5 In a large bowl, whisk together the whole egg, yolks,
caster sugar, cream and vanilla until combined. Strain
through a fine sieve into the pastry case. Sprinkle the
cinnamon over the top and return to the oven for
45–50 minutes until just set. Serve warm, at room
temperature or lightly chilled.

NUTRITION PER SERVING 719 cals | 58g fat (34g sats) | 44g carbs | 0.3g salt Ⓥ

Chocolate Orange Tart

Serves 8
Preparation time 30 minutes, plus chilling
Cooking time about 1 hour, plus cooling

Sweet Pastry (see page 327), made with 150g (5oz) plain
 flour, a pinch of salt, 75g (3oz) unsalted butter, grated zest
 of 1 orange, 2 large egg yolks and 25g (1oz) golden icing
 sugar in addition to the caster sugar
flour to dust
icing sugar to dust

For the filling
175g (6oz) plain chocolate (at least 50% cocoa solids),
 chopped
175ml (6fl oz) double cream
75g (3oz) light muscovado sugar
2 medium eggs
1 tbsp Grand Marnier or Cointreau

1 Roll out the pastry on a lightly floured worksurface and
use to line a 20.5cm (8in) loose-based tart tin. Prick the
base all over with a fork, put the tin on a baking sheet and
chill for 30 minutes. Preheat the oven to 190°C (170°C fan
oven) mark 5.
2 Bake the pastry case blind for 15 minutes, then for a
further 5 minutes (see page 326). Remove from the oven
and put to one side. Reduce the oven temperature to 170°C
(150°C fan oven) mark 3.
3 To make the filling, melt the chocolate in a heatproof
bowl set over a pan of gently simmering water, making sure
the base of the bowl doesn't touch the water. Remove the
bowl from the pan and leave to cool for 10 minutes.
4 Put the cream, muscovado sugar, eggs and liqueur into
a bowl and stir, using a wooden spoon to mix thoroughly.
Gradually stir in the chocolate, then pour into the pastry
case and bake for 20 minutes or until just set.
5 Serve warm or cold, dusted liberally with icing sugar.

TRY SOMETHING DIFFERENT
Omit the orange zest and replace the Grand Marnier with
crème de menthe.

NUTRITION PER SERVING 441 cals | 28g fat (17g sats) | 42g carbs | 0.2g salt Ⓥ

Lemon Tart

Serves 8
Preparation time 30 minutes, plus chilling
Cooking time 40–50 minutes

butter to grease
plain flour to dust
Sweet Pastry (see page 327), made with 150g (5oz) plain
  flour, 75g (3oz) unsalted butter, 2 large egg yolks and
  50g (2oz) icing sugar
peach slices and fresh or frozen raspberries, thawed to
  decorate
icing sugar to dust

For the filling
1 large egg, plus 4 large egg yolks
150g (5oz) caster sugar
grated zest of 4 lemons
150ml (¼ pint) freshly squeezed lemon juice (about
  4 medium lemons)
150ml (¼ pint) double cream

1 Grease and flour a 23cm (9in) round, 2.5cm (1in) deep,
loose-based flan tin. Roll out the pastry on a lightly floured
worksurface into a round – if the pastry sticks to the
surface, gently ease a palette knife under it to loosen. Line
the tin with the pastry and trim the excess. Prick the base
all over with a fork. Chill for 30 minutes.
2 Preheat the oven to 190°C (170°C fan oven) mark 5.
3 Put the tin on a baking sheet and bake the pastry case
blind for 15 minutes, then for a further 5 minutes (see
page 326). Remove from the oven, leaving the flan tin on
the baking sheet. Reduce the oven temperature to 170°C
(150°C fan oven) mark 3.
4 Meanwhile, to make the filling, put the whole egg, egg
yolks and caster sugar into a bowl and beat together with
a wooden spoon or balloon whisk until smooth. Carefully
stir in the lemon zest, lemon juice and cream. Leave to
stand for 5 minutes.
5 Spoon three-quarters of the filling into the pastry case,
position the baking sheet on the oven shelf and ladle in
the remainder. Bake for 25–30 minutes until the filling
bounces back when touched lightly in the centre. Cool for
15 minutes to serve warm, or cool completely and chill.
Decorate with peaches and raspberries and dust with
icing sugar.

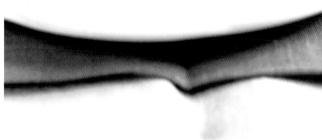

Cook's Tip
Remember that ovens vary, so check the tart after
15 minutes of cooking. Turn it round if it is cooking
unevenly, otherwise the eggs might curdle.

NUTRITION PER SERVING 385 cals | 23g fat (13g sats) | 42g carbs | 0.2g salt

Raspberry Milles-feuilles

Serves 8
Preparation time 40 minutes, plus chilling and standing
Cooking time 40 minutes, plus cooling

550g (1¼lb) Puff Pastry (see page 328), thawed if frozen
plain flour to dust
25g (1oz) caster sugar, plus 3 tbsp
50g (2oz) hazelnuts, toasted and chopped (see Cook's Tip,
  page 312)
225g (8oz) raspberries
1 tbsp lemon juice
1 × quantity Confectioner's Custard (see Cook's Tip)
300ml (½ pint) double cream
50g (2oz) icing sugar, sifted

1 Cut the pastry into three and roll out each piece on
a lightly floured surface into an 18 × 35.5cm (7 × 14in)
rectangle. Put each on a dampened baking sheet, prick and
chill for 30 minutes.
2 Preheat the oven to 220°C (200°C fan oven) mark 7.
3 Bake the pastry for 10 minutes, then turn the pieces over
and cook for another 3 minutes. Sprinkle each sheet with
1 tbsp caster sugar and one-third of the nuts. Return to
the oven for 8 minutes or until the sugar dissolves. Cool
slightly, then transfer to wire racks to cool.
4 Sprinkle the raspberries with 25g (1oz) caster sugar and
the lemon juice. Beat the custard until smooth and whip
the cream until thick, then fold the cream into the custard
with the raspberries and juices. Cover and chill.
5 Put the icing sugar into a bowl, then stir in 2 tbsp water.
Trim each pastry sheet to 15 × 30.5cm (6 × 12in), then
drizzle with the icing. Leave for 15 minutes.
6 Spoon half the custard over a sheet of pastry. Put another
sheet on top and spoon on the remaining custard. Top with
the final sheet and press down lightly. Leave for 30 minutes
before slicing.

Cook's Tip

CONFECTIONER'S CUSTARD Scrape the vanilla seeds from
1 vanilla pod into a pan. Add the pod and 450ml (¾ pint)
milk, bring to the boil, then set aside for 30 minutes.
Remove the vanilla pod. Whisk 4 large egg yolks and 75g
(3oz) caster sugar until pale. Mix in 50g (2oz) plain flour.
Strain in a quarter of the infused milk, mix, then stir in
the remainder. Return to the pan and bring to the boil over
a low heat, stirring. Pour into a bowl, cover with clingfilm,
cool and chill for 3–4 hours.

NUTRITION PER SERVING 828 cals | 57g fat (23g sats) | 65g carbs | 1.4g salt Ⓥ

Pear and Cranberry Strudel

Serves 8
Preparation time 20 minutes
Cooking time 40–45 minutes

75g (3oz) butter, melted, plus extra to grease
125g (4oz) fresh cranberries
550g (1¼lb) firm pears, such as Williams or Comice, cored
  and sliced
50g (2oz) Brazil nuts, chopped and toasted (see Cook's Tip,
  page 312)
grated zest and juice of 1 lemon
25g (1oz) golden caster sugar
1 tbsp fresh white breadcrumbs
1 tsp ground cinnamon
7 sheets filo pastry, thawed if frozen
icing sugar to dust

1 Preheat the oven to 190°C (170°C fan oven) mark 5 and
grease a large baking sheet.
2 Toss the cranberries with the pears, nuts and lemon
juice. Mix the lemon zest with 1 tbsp caster sugar, the
breadcrumbs and cinnamon, then combine with the
cranberry mixture.
3 Lay a clean tea towel on a board and put three sheets of
filo pastry on to it, each overlapping the other by 2.5cm
(1in) to make a 56 × 48cm (22 × 19in) rectangle. Brush
with melted butter, then put three more sheets on top and
brush again.
4 Spoon the pear mixture on to the pastry and roll up from
a long edge. Carefully lift on to the baking sheet, placing it
seam side down. Cut the remaining filo pastry into strips,
crumple and place on the strudel, brush with melted butter
and sprinkle the strudel with the remaining caster sugar.
5 Bake for 40–45 minutes, covering with foil if the top
browns too quickly. Dust the strudel with icing sugar and
serve warm.

TRY SOMETHING DIFFERENT
Replace the lemon zest and juice with orange, the cranberries
with blueberries and the Brazil nuts with hazelnuts.

NUTRITION PER SERVING 190 cals | 12g fat (6g sats) | 9g carbs | 0.2g salt Ⓥ

Profiteroles

Serves 6
Preparation time 25 minutes
Cooking time 30 minutes, plus cooling and chilling

65g (2½oz) plain flour
a pinch of salt
50g (2oz) butter, diced
2 large eggs, lightly beaten
300ml (½ pint) double cream
a few drops of vanilla extract
1 tsp caster sugar

For the chocolate sauce
225g (8oz) plain chocolate (at least 70% cocoa solids),
 broken into pieces
140ml (4½fl oz) double cream
1–2 tbsp Grand Marnier to taste (optional)
1–2 tsp golden caster sugar to taste (optional)

1 Preheat the oven to 220°C (200°C fan oven) mark 7.
2 Sift the flour with the salt on to a sheet of greaseproof paper. Put the butter into a medium heavy-based pan with 150ml (¼ pint) water. Heat gently until the butter melts, then bring to a rapid boil. Take off the heat and immediately tip in all the flour and beat thoroughly with a wooden spoon until the mixture is smooth and forms a ball. Turn into a bowl and leave to cool for about 10 minutes.
3 Add the eggs a little at a time, beating well after each addition until thick and shiny. If added too quickly, the paste will become runny and the buns will be flat.
4 Sprinkle a large baking sheet with a little water. Using two damp teaspoons, spoon about 18 small mounds of the choux paste on to the baking sheet, spacing well apart to allow them to expand. (Or spoon the paste into a piping bag with a 1cm (½in) plain nozzle and pipe little mounds.)
5 Bake for 25 minutes or until well risen, crisp and golden brown. Make a small hole in the side of each bun to allow the steam to escape and then put back in the oven for a further 5 minutes or until thoroughly dried out. Slide on to a large wire rack and put to one side to cool.
6 To make the sauce, put the chocolate and cream in a medium pan with 4 tbsp water. Heat gently, stirring occasionally, until the chocolate melts to a smooth sauce; do not boil. Remove from the heat.
7 To assemble, lightly whip the cream with the vanilla extract and sugar until it just holds its shape. Pipe into the hole in each choux bun, or split the buns open and spoon in the cream. Chill for up to 2 hours.

8 Just before serving, gently reheat the chocolate sauce. Add Grand Marnier and sugar to taste, if you like. Divide the choux buns among serving bowls and pour the warm chocolate sauce over them. Serve immediately.

TRY SOMETHING DIFFERENT
Eclairs Put the choux pastry into a piping bag fitted with a medium plain nozzle and pipe twelve 9cm (3½in) long fingers on to the baking sheet. Trim with a wet knife. Bake at 200°C (180°C fan oven) mark 6 for about 35 minutes until crisp and golden. Using a sharp, pointed knife, make a slit down the side of each bun to release the steam, then transfer to a wire rack and leave for 20–30 minutes to cool completely. Just before serving, whip 300ml (½ pint) double cream until stiff and use it to fill the eclairs. Break 125g (4oz) plain chocolate (at least 70% cocoa solids) into a bowl set over a pan of simmering water, making sure the base of the bowl doesn't touch the water. Stir until melted. Pour into a wide shallow bowl and dip the top of each filled eclair into it, drawing each one across the surface of the chocolate. Leave to set.

NUTRITION PER SERVING 652 cals | 59g fat (33g sats) | 35g carbs | 0.3g salt Ⓥ

Warm Ginger Ricotta Cake

Serves 8
Preparation time 25 minutes
Cooking time 1¼ hours, plus cooling

75g (3oz) unsalted butter, melted, plus extra to grease
225g (8oz) digestive biscuits
200g (7oz) cream cheese
225g (8oz) ricotta cheese (see Vegetarian Cheeses
  on page 228)
4 tbsp double cream
3 medium eggs, separated
1 tbsp cornflour
1 piece of preserved stem ginger in syrup, finely chopped,
  plus 1 tbsp syrup
125g (4oz) icing sugar
Ginger and Whisky Sauce to serve (optional, see
  Cook's Tips)

1 Preheat the oven to 200°C (180°C fan oven) mark 6 and
grease a 20.5cm (8in) springform cake tin.
2 Whiz the biscuits in a food processor until they resemble
breadcrumbs. (Alternatively, put them in a plastic bag and
crush with a rolling pin.) Put the biscuits into a bowl, add
the melted butter and mix to combine. Tip just over half
the crumb mixture into the prepared tin and press evenly
into the base and up the side. Put to one side while you
make the filling.
3 Beat together, or whiz in a food processor, the
cheeses, cream, egg yolks, cornflour, ginger and syrup.
Transfer to a bowl.
4 Put the egg whites into a clean, grease-free bowl and
whisk until soft peaks form. Gradually whisk in the icing
sugar, keeping the mixture stiff and shiny. Fold into the
ginger mixture. Spoon on to the biscuit base and smooth
the surface. Sprinkle the top with the remaining crumbs.
5 Bake for 30 minutes. Reduce the oven temperature to
180°C (160°C fan oven) mark 4, cover the cake loosely
with foil and bake for a further 45 minutes. The cake
should be just set in the centre. Cool for 15 minutes
on a wire rack.
6 Serve warm, with Ginger and Whisky Sauce, if you like.

Cook's Tips
- GINGER AND WHISKY SAUCE Gently heat 300ml (½ pint)
  single cream with 2 tsp preserved stem ginger syrup and
  1 tsp whisky. Serve just warm, with the cake.
- GINGER, ORANGE AND COINTREAU RICOTTA CAKE The cake
  can also be served with sliced oranges soaked in ginger
  syrup and Cointreau.

NUTRITION PER SERVING 494 cals | 36g fat (21g sats) | 38g carbs | 0.8g salt Ⓥ

Classic Baked Cheesecake

Serves 12
Preparation time 30 minutes, plus chilling
Cooking time 55 minutes, plus cooling
  and chilling

125g (4oz) unsalted butter, melted,
  plus extra to grease
250g pack digestive biscuits

For the filling
2 large lemons
2 × 250g cartons curd cheese (see
  Vegetarian cheeses, page 228)
142ml carton soured cream
2 medium eggs
175g (6oz) golden caster sugar
1½ tsp vanilla extract
1 tbsp cornflour
50g (2oz) sultanas

1 Grease a 20.5cm (8in) springform cake tin. Whiz the biscuits in a food processor until they resemble breadcrumbs. (Alternatively, put them in a plastic bag and crush with a rolling pin.) Put the biscuit crumbs into a bowl, add the melted butter and mix until well combined. Tip the crumb mixture into the prepared tin and press evenly on to the base, using the back of a metal spoon to level the surface. Chill for 1 hour or until firm.
2 Preheat the oven to 180°C (160°C fan oven) mark 4. To make the filling, grate the zest from 1 of the lemons and set aside. Halve the same lemon and squeeze out the juice. Halve the other lemon and cut into very thin slices.
3 Put the lemon zest, lemon juice, curd cheese, soured cream, eggs, sugar, vanilla extract and cornflour into a large bowl. Using a hand-held electric whisk, beat together until thick and smooth, then fold in the sultanas. Pour the mixture into the tin and shake gently to level the surface.
4 Bake for 30 minutes. Put the lemon slices, overlapping, on top. Bake for a further 20–25 minutes until the cheesecake is just set and golden brown. Turn off the oven and leave the cheesecake inside, with the door ajar, until it is cool, then chill for at least 2 hours or overnight.
5 Remove the cheesecake from the fridge about 30 minutes before serving. Run a knife around the edge, release the clasp on the tin and remove the cake. Cut the cheesecake into slices to serve.

NUTRITION PER SLICE 340 cals | 19g fat (11g sats) | 36g carbs | 1g salt ⓥ

Plain Crêpes

Makes 8
Preparation time 10 minutes, plus optional standing
Cooking time about 15 minutes

125g (4oz) plain flour
a pinch of salt
1 medium egg
300ml (½ pint) milk
a little sunflower oil to fry
golden caster sugar and lemon juice to serve

1 Sift the flour and salt into a bowl and make a well in the centre. Add the egg and whisk well with a balloon whisk. Gradually beat in the milk, drawing in the flour from the sides to make a smooth batter. Cover and leave to stand, if possible, for 20 minutes.
2 Heat a few drops of oil in an 18cm (7in) heavy-based crêpe pan or non-stick frying pan. Pour in just enough batter to thinly coat the bottom of the pan. Cook over a medium-high heat for about 1 minute or until golden brown. Turn or toss and cook the second side for ½ –1 minute until golden.
3 Transfer the crêpe to a plate and keep hot. Repeat to cook the remaining batter, stacking the cooked crêpes on top of each other with greaseproof paper in between; keep warm in the oven while cooking the remaining crêpes.
4 Serve as soon as the crêpes are all cooked, sprinkled with sugar and lemon juice.

TRY SOMETHING DIFFERENT
Buckwheat Crêpes Replace half the flour with buckwheat flour and add an extra egg white
Lemon, Orange or Lime Crêpes Add the finely grated zest of 1 lemon, ½ orange or 1 lime, with the milk.
Chocolate Crêpes Replace 15g (½oz) of the flour with sifted cocoa powder.

NUTRITION PER CRÊPE 100 cals | 3g fat (1g sats) | 16g carbs | 0.2g salt Ⓥ

Crêpes Suzette

Serves 4
Preparation time 20 minutes, plus standing
Cooking time 15 minutes

1 quantity crêpe batter (see opposite)
1 tsp golden icing sugar
grated zest of ½ orange
a knob of butter, plus extra to fry
2 tbsp brandy

For the orange sauce
50g (2oz) golden caster sugar
50g (2oz) butter
juice of 2 oranges
grated zest of 1 lemon
3 tbsp Cointreau

1 Flavour the crêpe batter with the icing sugar and orange zest, then leave to stand for 30 minutes. Just before cooking the crêpes, melt the knob of butter and stir it into the batter.
2 To cook the crêpes, heat a small amount of butter in a 15–18cm (6–7in) heavy-based frying pan. Pour in just enough batter to cover the base, swirling it to coat. Cook over a medium heat for about 1 minute or until the crêpe is golden underneath. Using a palette knife, flip it over and cook briefly on the other side. Lift on to a plate, cover with greaseproof paper and keep warm while you cook the others in the same way, interleaving each with a square of greaseproof paper to keep them separated.
3 To make the orange sauce, put the sugar into a large heavy-based frying pan and heat gently, shaking the pan occasionally, until the sugar has melted and turned golden brown. Remove from the heat and add the butter, orange juice and lemon zest. Return the pan to the heat, and stir the sauce until it begins to simmer. Add the Cointreau.
4 Fold each crêpe in half and then in half again. Put all the crêpes back into the pan and simmer for a few minutes to reheat, spooning the sauce over them.
5 To flambé, warm the brandy and pour it over the crêpes. Using a taper and standing well clear, ignite the brandy. When the flame dies down, serve at once.

NUTRITION PER SERVING 392 cals | 16g fat (9g sats) | 48g carbs | 0.7g salt Ⓥ

Waffles

Serves 4
Preparation time 5 minutes
Cooking time 16 minutes

125g (4oz) self-raising flour
a pinch of salt
1 tbsp caster sugar
1 medium egg, separated
25g (1oz) butter, melted
150ml (¼ pint) milk
½ tsp vanilla flavouring (optional)
butter and golden or maple syrup to serve

1 Heat the waffle iron according to the manufacturer's instructions.
2 Mix the flour, salt and sugar together in a bowl. Add the egg yolk, melted butter, milk and flavouring, if you like, and beat to give a smooth coating batter.
3 Put the egg white into a clean, grease-free bowl and whisk until it forms stiff peaks; fold into the batter. Pour just enough batter into the iron to run over the surface.
4 Close the iron and cook for 2–3 minutes, turning the iron if using a non-electric type. When the waffle is cooked, it should be golden brown and crisp and easily removed from the iron – if it sticks, cook for a minute longer. Cook the remainder in the same way.
5 Serve immediately with butter and golden or maple syrup. Alternatively, layer the waffles with whipped cream or vanilla ice cream and fresh fruit.

NUTRITION PER SERVING 207 cals | 8g fat (4g sats) | 31g carbs | 0.8g salt Ⓥ

Lemon and Blueberry Pancakes

Serves 4
Preparation time 5 minutes
Cooking time 15 minutes

125g (4oz) wholemeal plain flour
1 tsp baking powder
¼ tsp bicarbonate of soda
2 tbsp golden caster sugar
finely grated zest of 1 lemon
125g (4oz) natural yogurt
2 tbsp milk
2 medium eggs
40g (1½oz) butter
100g (3½oz) blueberries
1 tsp sunflower oil
natural yogurt and fruit compôte to serve

1 Sift the flour, baking powder and bicarbonate of soda into a bowl. Add the sugar and lemon zest. Pour in the yogurt and milk. Break the eggs into the mixture and whisk together until smooth.
2 Melt 25g (1oz) butter in a pan, add to the bowl with the blueberries and stir everything together.
3 Heat a dot of butter with the oil in a frying pan over a medium heat until hot. Add four large spoonfuls of the mixture to the pan to make four pancakes. Fry for about 2 minutes until golden underneath, then flip them over and cook for 1–2 minutes. Repeat with the remaining mixture, adding a dot more butter each time.
4 Serve with natural yogurt and some fruit compôte.

TRY SOMETHING DIFFERENT
Instead of fresh blueberries and lemon, use 100g (3½oz) chopped ready-to-eat dried apricots and 2 tsp grated fresh root ginger.

NUTRITION PER SERVING 290 cals | 13g fat (6g sats) | 39g carbs | 0.6g salt Ⓥ

Crème Brûlée

Serves 6
Preparation time 15 minutes, plus infusing and chilling
Cooking time 30–35 minutes, plus cooling

600ml (1 pint) double cream
1 vanilla pod, split lengthways
4 large egg yolks
125g (4oz) golden caster sugar

1 Preheat the oven to 150°C (130°C fan oven) mark 2.
2 Pour the cream into a pan, add the vanilla pod and bring
slowly to the boil. Remove from the heat, cover and set
aside to infuse for at least 30 minutes. Stand six ramekins
in a roasting tin.
3 Beat the egg yolks with 1 tbsp caster sugar in a
large bowl. Pour in the vanilla-infused cream, stirring
constantly. Strain into a jug, then pour into the ramekins.
Surround with hand-hot water to come halfway up the
sides of the ramekins.
4 Bake for 30–35 minutes until just set. Cool, then chill for
at least 4 hours or, even better, overnight.
5 Preheat the grill to maximum. Sprinkle the remaining
sugar evenly on top of the custards to form a thin layer.
Put under the very hot grill for 2–3 minutes until the sugar
caramelises. (Alternatively, you can wave a cook's blowtorch
over the surface to caramelise the sugar.) Allow to cool for
1 hour, but do not chill – the caramel will form a crisp layer
on the surface. Serve within 2–3 hours.

Crème Caramel

Serves 6
Preparation time 15 minutes
Cooking time 20–30 minutes, plus cooling

175g (6oz) granulated sugar
600ml (1 pint) whole or semi-skimmed milk
1 vanilla pod, split lengthways, or a few drops of
  vanilla extract
4 large eggs, plus 4 egg yolks
50–65g (2–2½oz) golden caster sugar to taste

1 Warm six ramekins. To make the caramel, put the granulated sugar into a heavy-based pan and heat gently until melted, brushing any sugar down from the side of the pan. Increase the heat and boil rapidly for a few minutes until the syrup turns to a rich golden brown caramel, gently swirling the pan to ensure even browning. Immediately, dip the base of the pan into a bowl of cool water to prevent further cooking.

2 Pour a little caramel into each of the warmed ramekins and quickly rotate to coat the base and part way up the sides. Leave to cool.

3 Preheat the oven to 170°C (150°C fan oven) mark 3 and stand the ramekins in a roasting tin containing enough hot water to come halfway up the sides.

4 To make the custard, put the milk and vanilla pod in a pan and heat until almost boiling; if using vanilla extract, add after heating the milk.

5 Meanwhile, beat the eggs, egg yolks and caster sugar in a bowl until well mixed. Stir in the hot milk. Strain, then pour into the prepared ramekins.

6 Bake for 20–30 minutes until just set and a knife inserted into the centre comes out clean. Remove from the tin. Leave to cool.

7 To turn out, free the edges by pressing with the fingertips then run a knife around the edge of each custard. Put a serving dish over the top, invert and lift off the ramekin; the caramel will have formed a sauce around the custard.

TRY SOMETHING DIFFERENT

Make one large crème caramel in a 15cm (6in) soufflé dish; bake as above for 1 hour or until just set. After cooling, chill for several hours. Transfer to room temperature 30 minutes before serving.

NUTRITION PER SERVING 300 cals | 10g fat (3g sats) | 45g carbs | 0.3g salt ⓥ

Coffee Bavarois

Serves 6
Preparation time 30 minutes, plus infusing
Cooking time 20 minutes, plus cooling and chilling

125g (4oz) well-roasted coffee beans
900ml (1½ pints) milk
6 egg yolks
75g (3oz) caster sugar
4 tsp powdered gelatine
300ml (½ pint) double cream
2 tbsp coffee-flavoured liqueur, such as Tia Maria (optional)
coffee dragées and grated chocolate to decorate

1 Put the coffee beans in a pan and warm very gently over
a low heat for 2–3 minutes, shaking the pan frequently.
Remove from the heat, pour the milk into the pan, return
to the heat and bring to the boil. Remove from the heat,
cover and leave to infuse for 30 minutes.
2 Put the egg yolks and caster sugar in a deep mixing
bowl and beat until the mixture is thick and light in colour.
Strain the coffee infusion on to the egg yolks, then stir well.
Return the custard mixture to the rinsed-out pan and cook
very gently, stirring, until the custard thickens very slightly.
Do not boil. Strain into a large bowl and leave to cool.
3 In a small bowl, sprinkle the gelatine over 4 tbsp water.
Place over a pan of hot water and stir until dissolved. Stir
the gelatine into the cool custard. Stand the custard in a
roasting tin of water and surround with ice cubes. Stir the
custard frequently while it cools to setting point.
4 Meanwhile, lightly whip half the cream and grease a
1.4 litre (2½ pint) soufflé dish or mould.
5 When the custard is well chilled and beginning to
thicken, fold in the whipped cream. Pour into the dish and
chill until completely set.
6 With a dampened finger, gently ease the edges of the
cream away from the dish. Invert on to a plate and shake
gently. Ease off the dish and slide the cream into the centre
of the plate.
7 Whisk the remaining cream until it holds its shape, then
gradually whisk in the liqueur, if you like. Serve the coffee
cream separately, or spoon into a piping bag fitted with
a 1cm (½in) star nozzle and pipe around the top edge in
a shell pattern. Decorate with coffee dragées and grated
chocolate.

TRY SOMETHING DIFFERENT
Chocolate Bavarois Omit the coffee beans, liqueur and
coffee dragées. Melt 75g (3oz) plain chocolate (at least 70%
cocoa solids) in a little milk, whisk in the remaining milk.
Complete as above.

NUTRITION PER SERVING 440 cals | 35g fat (20g sats) | 23g carbs | 0.2g salt

Panna Cotta

Serves 6
Preparation time 15 minutes
Cooking time 12 minutes, plus chilling

2 sheets of leaf gelatine
vegetable oil to grease
568ml carton double cream
125ml (4fl oz) milk
1 tsp vanilla extract
150g (5oz) golden caster sugar
2 oranges
2 tbsp Cointreau or orange liqueur

1 Put the gelatine sheets in a shallow dish, cover with 600ml (1 pint) cold water and leave to soak for 5 minutes. Lightly oil six 150ml (¼ pint) dariole moulds and leave to one side.
2 Put the cream, milk, vanilla extract and 100g (3½oz) sugar in a pan and slowly bring to the boil, then take off the heat. Squeeze the the excess liquid out of the gelatine sheets. Add the sheets to the cream mixture and stir well to dissolve. Pour the mixture into the dariole moulds, then cool and chill in the fridge for 4–6 hours.
3 Using a swivel vegetable peeler, pare the zest from the oranges and cut into fine strips. Squeeze the juice from the oranges and strain into a pan. Add the remaining sugar, the Cointreau and orange zest. Bring to the boil and simmer for 10 minutes. Leave to cool.
4 To serve, run a palette knife around the edge of each panna cotta and invert on to a dessert plate. Spoon some of the orange sauce and zest over the panna cotta and serve.

NUTRITION PER SERVING 570 cals | 47g fat (31g sats) | 35g carbs | 0.1g salt

Luscious Chocolate Pots

Serves 4
Preparation time 10 minutes
Cooking time 3 minutes

175g (6oz) condensed milk
75g (3oz) plain chocolate (at least 70% cocoa solids), finely chopped
1–2 tsp almond liqueur, plus extra for drizzling (optional)
150ml (¼ pint) double cream
Chocolate Curls to decorate (see Cook's Tip)
almond biscuits to serve

1 Heat the condensed milk in a small pan over a low heat until bubbling at the edges. Take off the heat and stir in the chocolate. Add the liqueur, if you like, and mix until smooth and shiny. Empty into a bowl and stir until cool.
2 In a separate bowl, whip the cream until it just holds its shape – don't overwhip or it will turn grainy. Fold into the chocolate mixture using a metal spoon.
3 Divide the mixture among four small glasses and sprinkle chocolate shavings and liqueur, if you like, over each one. Serve with almond biscuits.

Cook's Tip
CHOCOLATE CURLS Melt some chocolate, spread it in a thin layer on the worksurface and leave to firm up. Use a sharp flat-ended knife or metal spatula to shave off thin slices, holding the blade at a 45° angle. The shavings will curl up as you cut.

NUTRITION PER SERVING 434 cals | 30g fat (18g sats) | 35 g carbs | 0.2g salt

Lemon Syllabub

Serves 4
Preparation time 15 minutes, plus cooling
and chilling

grated zest and juice of 1 lemon
150ml (¼ pint) medium dry
   white wine (see Alcoholic Drinks and
   Vegetarians, page 489)
75g (3oz) golden caster sugar
284ml carton double cream
2 medium egg whites

1 Put the lemon zest and juice into
a pan with the white wine and sugar.
Warm over a low heat until the sugar
dissolves, then remove the pan from
the heat. Strain the liquid, reserving
the lemon zest, and set aside to cool.

2 In a large bowl, whip the cream
until just holding its shape, then
slowly add the cooled wine syrup,
whisking continuously.
3 Put the egg whites into a clean,
grease-free bowl and whisk until they
form soft peaks. Fold them gently
into the cream mixture.
4 Divide the syllabub among serving
glasses and sprinkle the reserved
lemon zest on top to decorate. Chill
for 1 hour before serving.

NUTRITION PER SERVING 420 cals |
34g fat (23g sats) | 22g carbs | trace salt Ⓥ

Zabaglione

Serves 6
Preparation time 5 minutes
Cooking time 20 minutes

8 medium egg yolks
200g (7oz) golden caster sugar
225ml (8fl oz) sweet Marsala (see
   Alcoholic Drinks and Vegetarians,
   page 489)
savoiardi or sponge fingers to serve
   (optional)

1 Put the egg yolks and sugar into a
large heatproof bowl set over a pan of
gently simmering water, making sure
the base of the bowl doesn't touch the
water (or put in the top of a double
boiler). Using a hand-held electric
whisk, whisk for 15 minutes or until
pale, thick and foaming.
2 With the bowl or pan still over the
heat, gradually pour in the Marsala,
whisking all the time.
3 Pour the zabaglione into warmed
glasses or small coffee cups. Serve
immediately, with savoiardi or sponge
fingers, if you like.

NUTRITION PER SERVING 193 cals |
6g fat (2g sats) | 37g carbs | 0g salt Ⓥ

Gooseberry Fool

Serves 4
Preparation time 20 minutes, plus chilling
Cooking time 10 minutes

450g (1lb) gooseberries, topped and tailed
125g (4oz) golden caster sugar
1 tbsp custard powder
150ml (¼ pint) milk
a few drops of green food colouring (optional)
150ml (¼ pint) whipping cream
chopped toasted nuts to decorate

1 Put the gooseberries, sugar and 2 tbsp water into a pan, cover and cook for 10 minutes or until the fruit is soft. Leave to cool slightly.
2 Purée the fruit in a blender or food processor. Pass through a nylon sieve to remove the pips.
3 Blend the custard powder with a little of the milk; heat the remaining milk in a pan. Pour the hot milk on to the blended custard powder, stirring constantly, then return to the pan and stir over a gentle heat until the custard has thickened.
4 Beat the custard into the fruit pulp and allow to cool. Add the food colouring, if you like.
5 Whip the cream until soft peaks form, then fold into the gooseberry purée. Spoon into individual glasses and chill in the fridge until required. Decorate with toasted nuts to serve.

TRY SOMETHING DIFFERENT
Use raspberries, strawberries or blackberries instead of gooseberries. Omit step 1. Sweeten the fruit purée with golden caster sugar to taste at step 2.

NUTRITION PER SERVING 370 cals | 19g fat (10g sats) | 50g carbs | 0.1g salt Ⓥ

Old-English Trifle

Serves 6
Preparation time 20 minutes, plus soaking
Cooking time 15 minutes

600ml (1 pint) milk
½ vanilla pod
2 medium eggs, plus 2 egg yolks
2 tbsp caster sugar, plus extra to sprinkle
8 trifle sponges
175g (6oz) raspberry or strawberry jam
125g (4oz) macaroons, lightly crushed
100ml (3½fl oz) medium sherry
300ml (½ pint) double cream
40g (1½oz) flaked almonds, toasted, and 50g (2oz) glacé
  cherries to decorate

1 Bring the milk to the boil with the vanilla pod. Remove
from the heat, cover and leave to infuse for 20 minutes.
2 Beat together the eggs, egg yolks and sugar, and strain on
to the milk. Cook gently without boiling, stirring, until the
custard thickens slightly. Pour into a bowl; lightly sprinkle
the surface with sugar, then leave to cool.
3 Spread the trifle sponges with jam, cut into pieces and
put in a 2 litre (3½ pint) shallow serving dish with the
macaroons. Spoon over the sherry and leave for 2 hours.
Pour over the cold custard.
4 Lightly whip the cream. Top the custard with half the
cream. Pipe the remaining cream on top and decorate with
almonds and cherries.

NUTRITION PER SERVING 532 cals | 24g fat (9g sats) | 66g carbs | 0.3g salt

Tiramisu

Serves 10
Preparation time 20 minutes, plus chilling

200g carton mascarpone cheese (see Vegetarian Cheeses,
  page 228)
1 vanilla pod, split lengthways and seeds scraped out
450ml (¾ pint) warm strong black coffee
4 medium egg yolks
75g (3oz) golden caster sugar
284ml carton double cream
100ml (3½fl oz) grappa
200g pack savoiardi or sponge fingers
cocoa powder to dust

1 Put the mascarpone into a bowl with the seeds from the
vanilla pod.
2 Pour the coffee into a shallow dish, add the empty
vanilla pod and set aside to infuse.
3 In a large bowl, whisk the egg yolks and sugar together
until pale and thick, then gently whisk in the mascarpone
until smooth.
4 Whip the cream in another bowl to soft peaks, then fold
into the mascarpone mixture with the grappa.
5 Take half of the sponge fingers and dip each in turn
into the coffee mixture, then arrange over the base of
a 2.4 litre (4¼ pint) shallow dish. Spread a layer of
mascarpone mixture over the sponge fingers, then dip the
remaining sponge fingers into the coffee and arrange on
top. Finish with a top layer of mascarpone. Cover and chill
for at least 2 hours.
6 Dust with cocoa and cut into portions with a sharp
knife. Use a spatula to lift them neatly on to plates.

Cook's Tip
For optimum flavour, prepare a day ahead. Cover and keep
in the fridge.

NUTRITION PER SERVING 380 cals | 27g fat (16g sats) | 27g carbs | 0.1g salt Ⓥ

Iles Flottantes

Serves 4
Preparation time 30 minutes
Cooking time 18–20 minutes, plus cooling and chilling

2 large eggs, separated
150g (5oz) golden caster sugar
300ml (½ pint) single cream
300ml (½ pint) milk

For the praline
vegetable oil to grease
50g (2oz) unskinned pistachio nuts
50g (2oz) golden caster sugar

1 To make the praline, first oil a baking sheet. Put the pistachio nuts and sugar into a small heavy-based pan over a low heat and stir until the sugar melts and begins to caramelise. Cook for a few minutes to a deep brown colour, then immediately pour on to the oiled baking sheet. Leave to cool completely, then whiz to a coarse powder in a food processor.
2 Put the egg whites into a clean, grease-free bowl and whisk until they form soft peaks. Gradually whisk in 75g (3oz) caster sugar until the mixture is very stiff and shiny. Quickly and lightly fold in all but 2 tbsp of the praline.
3 Put the cream, milk and remaining sugar into a medium pan and bring to a gentle simmer. Spoon 5–6 small rounds of meringue mixture into the pan and cook gently for 2–3 minutes or until doubled in size and firm to the touch. Carefully remove with a slotted spoon and drain on kitchen paper. Repeat with the remaining mixture to make 12–18 poached meringues, depending on size.
4 Whisk the egg yolks into the poaching liquid. Heat gently, stirring all the time, until the custard thickens slightly to the consistency of double cream; do not boil.
5 Strain the custard into a serving dish, or individual dishes, and position the meringues on top. Cool, then chill for 30 minutes, or up to 2–3 hours.
6 Serve sprinkled with the reserved pistachio praline.

NUTRITION PER SERVING 500 cals | 25g fat (17g sats) | 61g carbs | 0.4g salt Ⓥ

Hot Orange Soufflés

Serves 6
Preparation time 20 minutes
Cooking time 25–30 minutes

65g (2½oz) unsalted butter, melted
2 tbsp dried breadcrumbs
40g (1½oz) plain flour
grated zest and juice of 1 small
   or ½ large orange
grated zest and juice of ½ lemon
75ml (2½fl oz) milk
60g (2oz) golden caster sugar
2 tbsp Grand Marnier
2 egg yolks and 8 egg whites
icing sugar, sifted, to dust

1 Preheat the oven to 190°C (170°C
fan oven) mark 5. Grease six ramekins
with a little of the butter, then coat
with the breadcrumbs; put to one side.

2 Cook the remaining butter, the
flour, orange and lemon zest in a pan
for 30 seconds. Off the heat, gradually
beat in the milk and cook, stirring,
over a low heat until the sauce is thick
and smooth, then for 2 more minutes.
3 Remove from the heat. Stir in the
sugar, orange and lemon juices and
Grand Marnier. Beat in the egg yolks.
4 Put the egg whites into a clean,
grease-free bowl and whisk until they
form stiff peaks, then fold into the
sauce until evenly blended. Spoon
into the soufflé dishes and run a knife
around the outside of the mixture.
5 Bake for 12–15 minutes until the
soufflés are risen and golden. Dust
with icing sugar and serve at once.

NUTRITION PER SERVING 310 cals |
14g fat (7g sats) | 38g carbs | 0.3g salt Ⓥ

Chocolate Mousse

Serves 8
Preparation time 20 minutes, plus chilling

350g (12oz) plain chocolate (at least
   70% cocoa solids), broken into
   pieces
6 tbsp rum, brandy or cold black coffee
6 large eggs, separated
a pinch of salt
Chocolate Curls to decorate (see
   Cook's Tip, page 379)

1 Put the chocolate with the
rum, brandy or black coffee into a
heatproof bowl set over a pan of
gently simmering water, making sure
the base of the bowl doesn't touch
the water. Leave to melt, stirring
occasionally. Take the bowl off the pan
and leave to cool slightly for
3–4 minutes, stirring frequently.

2 Beat the egg yolks with 2 tbsp
water, then beat into the chocolate
mixture until evenly blended.
3 Put the egg whites and salt into
a clean, grease-free bowl and whisk
until they form firm peaks, then fold
into the chocolate mixture.
4 Carefully pour the mixture into
a 1.4–1.7 litre (2½ –3 pint) soufflé
dish or divide among eight 150ml
(¼ pint) cups or ramekins. Chill for
at least 4 hours, or overnight, until
set. Decorate with Chocolate Curls.

NUTRITION PER SERVING 309 cals |
17g fat (9g sats) | 28g carbs | 0.1g salt Ⓥ

Chilled Cranberry Soufflé

Serves 8
Preparation time 30 minutes
Cooking time 10 minutes, plus chilling

300g (11oz) fresh cranberries, plus
  extra to decorate
finely grated zest and juice of 1 large
  orange
225g (8oz) caster sugar
5 tsp powdered gelatine
4 large eggs, separated
300ml carton double cream

1 You will need a straight-sided 1.3 litre (2¼ pint) serving dish. Tightly wrap a double-thickness collar of baking parchment around the outside of the serving dish, so it comes at least 7.5cm (3in) above the rim. Secure with tape.
2 Put the cranberries, orange zest, juice and 75g (3oz) of the caster sugar into a pan and heat gently until the cranberries start bursting. Blend until smooth, then push through a fine sieve and discard the pips. Set aside to cool completely.
3 Meanwhile, put the gelatine into a small pan and add 100ml (3½fl oz) cold water. Leave for 10 minutes (the mixture will become almost solid), then heat gently until the gelatine dissolves and the mixture becomes clear. Set aside.
4 Using a hand-held electric whisk, beat the egg yolks and 50g (2oz) of the remaining sugar for about 3 minutes until thick and creamy (when you lift out the beaters, they should leave a visible trail in the mix for at least 4 seconds). Whisk in the gelatine mixture, followed by the cooled cranberry purée.
5 Pour the cream into the empty cranberry bowl and lightly whip until it holds soft peaks. Using a large metal spoon, fold the cream into the cranberry mixture.
6 In a large clean bowl (and using clean, dry beaters), whisk the egg whites until stiff, then gradually whisk in the remaining sugar. Fold the whites into the cranberry mixture. Pour the mixture into the prepared dish and chill overnight.
7 Peel off the paper and serve decorated with crystallised cranberries.

NUTRITION PER SERVING 356 cals | 23g fat (13g sats) | 30g carbs | 0.1g salt

Tangerine Jellies

Makes 12
Preparation time 10 minutes
Cooking time about 3 minutes, plus chilling

5 gelatine leaves
12 tangerines, about 1kg (2¼lb)
150g (5oz) caster sugar
double cream to serve (optional)

1 Put the gelatine in a bowl and cover with cold water. Leave the gelatine to soak for 5 minutes. Meanwhile, zest two tangerines and put the zest into a large pan. Squeeze the juice from the zested and whole tangerines and add to the pan with the sugar.
2 Lift the gelatine out of the water and discard the water. Add the gelatine to the pan. Heat gently until the sugar dissolves. Strain the mixture into a large jug with a good pouring spout and make up to 1 litre (1¾ pints) with cold water. Pour the mixture into 12 small glasses and chill for at least 5 hours or, better still, overnight.
3 To serve, take out of the fridge 5 minutes before serving to allow them to soften slightly. Serve topped with double cream, if you like.

GET AHEAD
Make the jellies up to two days ahead.

NUTRITION PER JELLY (without cream) 73 cals | 0g fat | 18g carbs | 0g salt

Knickerbocker Glory

Serves 6
Preparation time 15 minutes, plus chilling

¼ × 140g (4½oz) pack raspberry or strawberry jelly
¼ × 140g (4½oz) pack lemon jelly
200g can peach slices, drained and chopped
200g can pineapple chunks, drained
500ml block vanilla ice cream
150ml (¼ pint) double cream
6 glacé cherries
chocolate vermicelli to decorate
wafers to serve

1 Make up the jellies as directed on the pack, allow to set and then chop them roughly.
2 Put small portions of the fruit into the base of six tall sundae glasses. Cover with a layer of red jelly. Put a scoop of ice cream on top and add a layer of yellow jelly.
3 Repeat the layering, finishing with a layer of cream and a cherry. Decorate with chocolate vermicelli and serve with a wafer.

NUTRITION PER SERVING 331 cals | 22g fat (13g sats) | 32g carbs | 0.2g salt

Classic Meringues

Serves 6
Preparation time 20 minutes
Cooking time 2–3 hours, plus cooling

3 medium egg whites, at room
  temperature
175g (6oz) golden caster sugar

To serve
200ml (7fl oz) double cream, whipped
icing sugar, sifted, to dust (optional)

1 Preheat the oven to 110°C (90°C
fan oven) mark ¼. Line two baking
sheets with baking parchment or a
Teflon non-stick liner.
2 Put the egg whites into a clean,
grease-free bowl and whisk, using an
electric whisk, until they form stiff
peaks. Gradually add the caster sugar,
a tablespoonful at a time, whisking
well after each addition. Whisk until
the meringue is very stiff and shiny.
3 Using two large spoons, shape the
meringue into 12–15 ovals or rounds,
spacing them well apart on the
prepared baking sheets.
4 Bake for 2–3 hours until the
meringues are crisp and well dried
out, but still pale; switch the baking
sheets around halfway through
cooking. Carefully peel the meringues
off the paper and transfer to a wire
rack to cool.
5 Sandwich the meringues together
in pairs with cream and serve, dusted
with icing sugar, if you like.

NUTRITION PER SERVING 270 cals |
16g fat (11g sats) | 32g carbs | trace salt Ⓥ

Boozy Eton Mess

Serves 4
Preparation time 10 minutes

½ tsp arrowroot
125ml (4fl oz) crème de cassis
300ml (½ pint) double cream
2–3tbsp icing sugar, sifted
½ tsp vanilla extract
25g (1oz) meringue nests,
  broken up
150g (5oz) blueberries
15g (½oz) flaked almonds

1 Put the arrowroot into a small pan
and gradually whisk in the crème de
cassis. Put the pan over a high heat,
bring to the boil, then simmer for
1–2 minutes, whisking constantly,
until the syrup thickens. Take off
the heat, empty into a small jug
and leave to cool.
2 Pour the cream into a large bowl.
Add the icing sugar and vanilla, then
whisk until the cream just holds it
shape – don't overwhip or it will
turn grainy.
3 Divide the meringues among four
large glasses. Spoon a few blueberries
into each glass, then drizzle a little of
the cassis syrup over the top. Next,
divide the cream equally among
the glasses and top each one with a
quarter of the remaining blueberries
and cassis syrup. Sprinkle the almonds
and serve at once.

NUTRITION PER SERVING 558 cals |
43g fat (25g sats) | 30g carbs | 0.1g salt Ⓥ

Strawberry Pavlova with Rosewater Syrup

Serves 10
Preparation time 20 minutes, plus cooling
Cooking time about 40 minutes

10 medium egg whites
600g (1lb 5oz) caster sugar
1¾ tbsp cornflour
1kg (2¼lb) strawberries, hulled
150ml (¼ pint) dessert wine, such as Muscat de Beaumes
  de Venise (see Alcoholic Drinks and Vegetarians, page 489)
1 tsp rosewater
600ml (1 pint) double cream
3 tbsp icing sugar, sifted

1 Preheat the oven to 150°C (130°C fan oven) mark 2.
Line a large baking sheet with baking parchment.
Use a pencil to draw a 28cm (11in) diameter circle on
the parchment, then flip it over so the pencil mark is
underneath.
2 Using electric beaters, whisk the egg whites in a large,
grease-free bowl until stiff but not dry. Gradually add 550g
(1¼lb) caster sugar, whisking all the time, until the mixture
is stiff and glossy. Quickly beat in 1 tbsp cornflour.
3 Spoon the mixture on to the prepared baking tray within
the marked circle, pushing it into peaks at the edges of the
circle. Bake for 40 minutes or until the meringue is firm to
the touch and peels away from the parchment. Transfer to a
rack and leave to cool.
4 Meanwhile, put 200g (7oz) strawberries with the wine,
remaining caster sugar and the rosewater into a pan. Heat
and simmer gently for 5 minutes. Blend until smooth, then
push through a fine sieve, discarding the pips. Return the
mixture to the pan and whisk in the remaining cornflour.
Heat gently for 3–4 minutes until the syrup thickens,
whisking constantly to remove any lumps. Take off the heat
and leave to cool.
5 Transfer the cooled meringue to a serving plate. Gently
whip the cream with the icing sugar until it just holds its
shape. Dollop on top of the meringue, then pile on the
remaining strawberries. Drizzle the cooled syrup over
and serve.

GET AHEAD
Cook the meringue, make the strawberry syrup and hull the
strawberries up to one day ahead. Cool the meringue on the
baking sheet, then cover with clingfilm and store at room
temperature. Cool the syrup, then cover and chill. Keep the
hulled strawberries covered in the fridge. Whip the cream
mixture up to 2 hours ahead, then chill. To serve, bring the
syrup, strawberries and cream up to room temperature, then
complete the recipe.

NUTRITION PER SERVING 614 cals | 32g fat (20g sats) | 78g carbs | trace salt ⓥ

Baked Alaska

Serves 8
Preparation time 30 minutes, plus freezing
Cooking time 3–4 minutes

1 large sponge flan case, 25.5cm (10in) diameter
5 tbsp orange juice
7 tbsp jam – any kind
1.5 litre tub vanilla ice cream
6 large egg whites
a pinch of cream of tartar
a pinch of salt
275g (10oz) golden caster sugar

1 Put the flan case on an ovenproof plate. Spoon the
orange juice over the sponge, then spread with the jam.
Scoop the ice cream on top of the jam, then put in the
freezer for at least 30 minutes.
2 Put the egg whites into a large, clean, grease-free bowl
and whisk until stiff. Beat in the cream of tartar and salt.
Using a large spoon, fold in the sugar, 1 tbsp at a time, then
whisk until very thick and shiny.
3 Spoon the meringue over the ice cream to cover, making
sure that the meringue is sealed to the flan case edge all the
way round. Freeze for at least 1 hour or overnight.
4 Preheat the oven to 230°C (210°C fan oven) mark 8.
Bake for 3–4 minutes until the meringue is tinged golden
brown. Serve immediately. If the Baked Alaska has been
in the freezer overnight, bake and leave to stand for about
15 minutes before serving.

NUTRITION PER SERVING 659 cals | 30g fat (17g sats) | 91g carbs | 0.5g salt Ⓥ

Vanilla Ice Cream

Serves 4
Preparation time 20 minutes, plus infusing
    and freezing
Cooking time 15 minutes

300ml (½ pint) milk
1 vanilla pod, split lengthways and
    seeds scraped out
3 medium egg yolks
50–75g (2–3oz) golden caster sugar
300ml (½ pint) double cream

1 Pour the milk into a heavy-based pan, add the vanilla seeds and pod and heat slowly until almost boiling. Take off the heat and leave to infuse for about 20 minutes. Remove the vanilla pod.
2 Whisk the egg yolks and sugar together in a bowl until thick and creamy. Gradually whisk in the hot milk, then strain back into the pan. Cook over a low heat, stirring constantly, until the custard has thickened enough to coat the back of the wooden spoon; do not boil. Pour into a chilled bowl and allow to cool.
3 Whisk the double cream into the cold custard until evenly blended.
4 Pour the mixture into an ice-cream maker and churn until frozen. (Alternatively, freeze in a shallow container, whisking two or three times during freezing to break down the ice crystals and ensure an even-textured result.)
5 Allow the ice cream to soften slightly at cool room temperature before serving.

TRY SOMETHING DIFFERENT

Strawberry Ice Cream Omit the vanilla pod. Sweeten 300ml (½ pint) strawberry purée with sugar to taste, then add the cooled custard. (Other fruit ice creams can be made in the same way.)
Chocolate Ice Cream Omit the vanilla pod. Add 125g (4oz) plain chocolate (at least 70% cocoa solids) to the milk and heat gently until melted, then bring almost to the boil and continue as above.
Coffee Ice Cream Omit the vanilla pod. Add 150ml (¼ pint) freshly made strong cooled coffee to the cooled custard, or 2 tsp instant coffee granules to the hot milk, stirring to dissolve.
Rum and Raisin Ice Cream Put 250g (9oz) large raisins into a pan, add 100ml (3½fl oz) dark rum and bring to the boil. Turn off the heat and leave to soak. Whip 600ml (1 pint) double cream until it just holds its shape. Put 4 large egg yolks, 3 tbsp golden syrup and 1 tbsp black treacle into another bowl. Whisk for 2–3 minutes until mousselike. Pour into the cream and whisk for a further 3–4 minutes until thick. Set the freezer to fast freeze. Pour the ice cream mixture into a 2 litre (3½ pint) roasting tin and freeze for 45 minutes–1 hour until it begins to harden around the edges. Add the soaked fruit and any liquid to the ice cream and mix well. Freeze for 45 minutes. Spoon into a 1.7 litre (3 pint) sealable container and freeze for at least 2 hours.
Instant Banana Ice Cream Peel 6 ripe bananas, about 700g (1½lb), slice and spread on a large non-stick baking tray. Put into the freezer for 30 minutes or until frozen. Let the frozen banana slices stand at room temperature for 2–3 minutes. Put the still frozen pieces in a food processor or blender with 1 tbsp fromage frais, 1 tbsp orange juice, 1 tsp vanilla extract and a splash of rum or Cointreau, if you like. Whiz until smooth, scraping down the sides of the bowl and adding more fromage frais and orange juice as necessary to give a creamy consistency. Add lime juice to taste and serve or turn into a freezerproof container and freeze for up to one month.

Lemon Sorbet

Serves 4
Preparation time 10 minutes, plus chilling and freezing
Cooking time 15 minutes

finely pared zest and juice of 3 large lemons
125g (4oz) golden caster sugar
1 large egg white

1 Put the lemon zest into a pan with the sugar and
350ml (12fl oz) water and heat gently until the sugar has
dissolved. Increase the heat and boil for 10 minutes. Leave
to cool.
2 Stir the lemon juice into the cooled sugar syrup. Cover
and chill in the fridge for 30 minutes.
3 Strain the syrup through a fine sieve into a bowl.
4 In another bowl, beat the egg white until just frothy, then
whisk into the lemon mixture.
5 For best results, freeze in an ice-cream maker. Otherwise,
pour into a shallow freezerproof container and freeze until
almost frozen; mash well with a fork and freeze until solid.
Transfer the sorbet to the fridge 30 minutes before serving
to soften slightly.

TRY SOMETHING DIFFERENT
Orange Sorbet Replace two of the lemons with oranges.
Lime Sorbet Replace two of the lemons with four limes.
Mango Sorbet Make the sugar syrup as directed, but using
the zest of 1 lime instead of the lemons. Blend the flesh
of two ripe mangos with the juice of the lime until smooth
and then stir in the cooled sugar syrup. Complete the recipe
from step 4.

NUTRITION PER SERVING 130 cals | 0g fat | 33g carbs | trace salt Ⓥ

Chocolate Ginger Refrigerator Cake

Makes 36 squares
Preparation time 15 minutes
Cooking time 10 minutes, plus chilling

a little oil to grease
350g (12oz) plain chocolate (at least 70% cocoa solids,
  broken into pieces
150g (5oz) unsalted butter
75g (3oz) golden syrup
300g (11oz) crunchy ginger biscuits, roughly crushed
75g (3oz) flaked almonds
75g (3oz) dried cranberries
50g (2oz) white chocolate, roughly chopped

1 Lightly oil a deep 23cm (9in) square tin and line the
base and sides with greaseproof paper.
2 Put the plain chocolate, butter and syrup into a
heatproof bowl set over a pan of gently simmering water,
making sure the base of the bowl doesn't touch the water.
Leave for 5–10 minutes, without stirring, until melted,
then stir everything to combine. Set aside to cool slightly.
3 Put the ginger biscuits into a large bowl with the
almonds and cranberries. Pour the chocolate mixture into
the bowl and stir well. Spoon into the prepared tin and
level the surface.
4 Melt the white chocolate in a small heatproof bowl set
over a pan of gently simmering water, making sure the
base of the bowl doesn't touch the water, then drizzle over
the top of the chocolate and biscuit mixture. Use a skewer
to swirl the chocolate and create a marbled effect. Cover
the tin with clingfilm, making sure it doesn't touch the
chocolate. Chill for at least 4 hours or overnight.
5 Cut into squares to serve.

TO STORE
Cover and store in the fridge. The cake will keep for up to
three weeks.

NUTRITION PER SQUARE 152 cals | 9g fat (5g sats) | 17g carbs | 0.2g salt Ⓥ

Cakes and Bakes

Madeleines

Makes 24
Preparation time 20 minutes, plus chilling
Cooking time 10–12 minutes, plus cooling

125g (4oz) unsalted butter, melted and cooled until tepid
125g (4oz) plain flour, plus extra to dust
4 medium eggs
125g (4oz) golden caster sugar
finely grated zest of 1 lemon
1 tsp baking powder
a pinch of salt
icing sugar, sifted, to dust

1 Brush two Madeleine trays with a little of the melted
butter. Allow to set, then dust with flour, shaking out
any excess.
2 Whisk the eggs, sugar and lemon zest together in a bowl,
using an electric whisk, until the mixture is pale, creamy
and thick enough to leave a trail when the whisk is lifted.
3 Sift in half the flour, together with the baking powder
and salt. Carefully pour in half the melted butter around
the edge of the bowl and gently fold in until evenly
incorporated. Repeat with the remaining flour and butter.
Cover and chill the mixture in the fridge for 45 minutes.
4 Preheat the oven to 220°C (200°C fan oven) mark 7.
5 Two-thirds fill the Madeleine moulds with the mixture
and bake for 10–12 minutes or until well risen and golden.
Ease out of the tins and cool on a wire rack. Serve dusted
with icing sugar.

Cook's Tips
• Resting the sponge mixture before baking gives the
  Madeleines their characteristic dense texture.
• If you have only one Madeleine tray, bake the cakes in
  two batches.

NUTRITION PER CAKE 90 cals | 5g fat (3g sats) | 10g carbs | 0.2g salt Ⓥ

Fairy Cakes

Makes 18
Preparation time 20 minutes
Cooking time 10–15 minutes, plus cooling and setting

125g (4oz) self-raising flour, sifted
1 tsp baking powder
125g (4oz) caster sugar
125g (4oz) unsalted butter, very soft
2 medium eggs
1 tbsp milk

For the icing and decoration
225g (8oz) icing sugar, sifted
assorted food colourings (optional)
sweets, sprinkles or coloured sugar

1 Preheat the oven to 200°C (180°C fan oven) mark 6. Put
paper cases into 18 of the cups in two bun tins.
2 Put the flour, baking powder, sugar, butter, eggs and
milk into a mixing bowl and beat with a hand-held electric
whisk for 2 minutes or until the mixture is pale and very
soft. Half-fill each paper case with the mixture.
3 Bake for 10–15 minutes until golden brown. Transfer to
a wire rack and leave to cool completely.
4 Put the icing sugar into a bowl and gradually blend
in 2–3 tbsp warm water until the icing is fairly stiff, but
spreadable. Add a couple of drops of food colouring, if
you like.
5 When the cakes are cold, spread the tops with the icing
and decorate with sweets, sprinkles or sugar.

TO STORE
Store in an airtight container. The cakes will keep for
three to five days.

TRY SOMETHING DIFFERENT
Chocolate Fairy Cakes Replace 2 tbsp of the flour with the
same amount of cocoa powder. Stir 50g (2oz) chocolate
drops, sultanas or chopped dried apricots into the mixture at
the end of step 2. Complete the recipe.

Freezing Tip
• To freeze, complete the recipe to the end of step 3. Open-
freeze, then wrap and freeze.
• To use, thaw for about 1 hour, then complete the recipe.

NUTRITION PER CAKE 160 cals | 6g fat (4g sats) | 26g carbs | 0.2g salt

Raspberry Ripple Cupcakes

Makes 9
Preparation time 30 minutes
Cooking time 20 minutes, plus cooling

50g (2oz) seedless raspberry jam
50g (2oz) fresh raspberries
125g (4oz) unsalted butter, softened
100g (3½oz) caster sugar
2 medium eggs
1 tbsp milk
150g (5oz) self-raising flour, sifted

For the topping and decoration
150g (5oz) fresh raspberries
300ml (½ pint) whipping cream
50g (2oz) icing sugar, sifted

1 Preheat the oven to 190°C (170°C fan oven), mark 5. Line 9 cups of a bun tin or muffin pan with paper muffin cases.
2 Mix the raspberry jam with the raspberries, lightly crushing the raspberries. Leave to one side.
3 Using a hand-held electric whisk, whisk the butter and caster sugar in a bowl, or beat with a wooden spoon, until pale and creamy. Gradually whisk in the eggs and milk until just combined. Using a metal spoon, fold in the flour until just combined, then carefully fold in the raspberry jam mixture until just marbled, being careful not to over-mix. Divide the mixture equally among the paper cases.
4 Bake for 20 minutes or until golden and risen. Leave to cool in the tin for 5 minutes, then transfer to a wire rack to cool completely.
5 For the decoration, keep 9 raspberries to one side. Mash the remaining raspberries in a bowl with a fork. Pass through a sieve into a bowl to remove the seeds. Using a hand-held electric whisk, whisk the cream and icing sugar together until stiff peaks form. Gently mix the raspberry purée into the cream until combined.
6 Insert a star nozzle into a piping bag, then fill the bag with the cream and pipe a swirl on to the top of each cake. Decorate each one with a raspberry.

TO STORE
Store in an airtight container in the fridge. They will keep for up to two days.

TRY SOMETHING DIFFERENT
Chocolate Cupcakes Whisk 125g (4oz) softened unsalted butter with 125g (4oz) light muscovado sugar. Beat in 2 medium eggs. Sift 15g (½oz) cocoa powder with 100g (3½oz) self-raising flour and fold into the mixture with 100g (3½oz) chopped plain chocolate (at least 70% cocoa solids). Divide among 18 paper cases. Bake and cool. Topping: put 150ml (¼ pint) double cream and 100g (3½oz) plain chocolate into a heavy-based pan over a low heat and heat until melted, then allow to cool and thicken slightly. Spoon on to the cakes, then leave to set.
Orange and Poppy Seed Cupcakes Whisk 175g (6oz) softened unsalted butter and 175g (6oz) caster sugar until pale and creamy. Gradually whisk in 3 medium eggs until just combined. Fold in 175g (6oz) self-raising flour, grated zest and juice of 1 large orange, 2 tbsp poppy seeds and 1 tsp baking powder. Divide among 12 paper cases. Bake as above. Cool. Topping: whisk 125g (4oz) softened unsalted butter until fluffy. Gradually whisk in 250g (9oz) icing sugar and 1 tbsp orange flower water until light and fluffy. Pipe a swirl of the topping on to each cake.

Freezing Tip
• To freeze, complete the recipe to the end of step 4. Open-freeze, then wrap and freeze.
• To use, thaw for about 1 hour, then complete the recipe.

NUTRITION PER CUPCAKE 385 cals | 26g fat (16g sats) | 36g carbs | 0.5g salt

Blueberry Muffins

Makes 12
Preparation time 10 minutes
Cooking time 20–25 minutes, plus cooling

2 medium eggs
250ml (9fl oz) semi-skimmed milk
250g (9oz) golden granulated sugar
2 tsp vanilla extract
350g (12oz) plain flour
4 tsp baking powder
250g (9oz) blueberries, frozen
finely grated zest of 2 lemons

1 Preheat the oven to 200°C (180°C fan oven) mark 6.
Line a 12-cup bun tin or muffin pan with paper
muffin cases.
2 Put the eggs, milk, sugar and vanilla extract into a bowl
and mix well.
3 In another bowl, sift the flour and baking powder
together, then add the blueberries and lemon zest. Toss
together, then make a well in the centre.
4 Pour the egg mixture into the flour and blueberries, and
mix in gently – over-beating will make the muffins tough.
Divide the mixture equally among the paper cases.
5 Bake for 20–25 minutes until risen and just firm.
Transfer to a wire rack and leave to cool completely. These
are best eaten on the day they are made.

Freezing Tip
• To freeze, complete the recipe. Once the muffins are cold,
  pack, seal and freeze.
• To use, thaw at cool room temperature.

TRY SOMETHING DIFFERENT
Cranberry Muffins Sift 300g (11oz) plain flour and 2 tsp
baking powder into a bowl. Stir in 150g (5oz) caster sugar,
the finely grated zest of 1 lemon and 125g (4oz) dried
cranberries. Put 1 medium egg, 1 tsp vanilla extract, 225ml
(8fl oz) milk and 50g (2oz) melted butter into a jug and
mix with a fork. Pour into the dry ingredients and lightly
fold together – don't over-mix. Spoon into 10 muffin cases
to three-quarters fill them. Bake as main recipe. Cool
slightly, then dust with icing sugar.
Double Chocolate Chip Muffins Follow the method for the
main recipe but omit the blueberries and lemon zest, replace
the flour with 300g (11oz) plain flour and 50g (1¾oz) cocoa
powder, then add 150g (5oz) chopped plain chocolate to the
dry ingredients in step 3.
Honey and Yogurt Muffins Sift 225g (8oz) plain flour,
1½ tsp baking powder, 1 tsp bicarbonate of soda, ½ tsp each
ground mixed spice and grated nutmeg and a pinch of salt
into a bowl. Stir in 50g (2oz) ground oatmeal and 50g (2oz)
light muscovado sugar. Mix 225g (8oz) Greek yogurt with
125ml (4fl oz) milk in a bowl, then beat in 1 medium egg,
50g (2oz) butter, melted and cooled, and 4 tbsp clear
honey. Pour on to the dry ingredients and stir in quickly
until just blended. Divide among 12 paper cases. Bake for
17–20 minutes until the muffins are well risen and just firm.
Cool in the tin for 5 minutes, then transfer to a wire rack.

NUTRITION PER MUFFIN 218 cals | 2g fat (trace sats) | 49g carbs | 0.5g salt Ⓥ

Eccles Cakes

Makes 8
Preparation time 10 minutes, plus resting
Cooking time 15 minutes, plus cooling

212g (7½oz) pack frozen puff pastry,
  thawed
plain flour to dust
25g (1oz) butter, softened
25g (1oz) dark brown soft sugar
25g (1oz) finely chopped mixed peel
50g (2oz) currants
caster sugar to sprinkle

1 Roll out the pastry on a lightly
floured surface and cut into 9cm
(3½in) rounds.
2 For the filling, mix the butter, sugar,
mixed peel and currants in a bowl.
3 Put 1 tsp of the fruit and butter
mixture in the centre of each pastry
round. Draw up the edges of each

pastry round to enclose the filling and
then reshape. Turn each round over
and roll lightly until the currants just
show through. Prick the top of each
with a fork. Leave to rest for about
10 minutes in a cool place. Preheat
the oven to 230°C (210°C fan oven)
mark 8.
4 Put the pastry rounds on a damp
baking sheet and bake for about
15 minutes until golden. Transfer
to a wire rack and leave to cool for
30 minutes. Sprinkle with caster sugar
while still warm.

NUTRITION PER CAKE 158 cals |
9g fat (2g sats) | 19g carbs | 0.3g salt Ⓥ

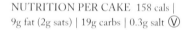

Rock Buns

Makes 12
Preparation time 5 minutes
Cooking time 20 minutes, plus cooling

125g (4oz) butter or margarine, plus
  extra to grease
225g (8oz) plain flour
a pinch of salt
2 tsp baking powder
75g (3oz) demerara sugar
75g (3oz) mixed dried fruit
zest of ½ lemon
1 medium egg, lightly beaten
milk

1 Preheat the oven to 200°C (180°C
fan oven) mark 6. Lightly grease two
baking sheets.
2 Sift together the flour, salt and
baking powder. Rub in the butter
until the mixture resembles fine
breadcrumbs. Add the sugar, fruit
and lemon zest, and mix everything
together thoroughly.
3 Using a fork, mix to a moist but
stiff dough with the beaten egg and a
little milk, if necessary.
4 Using two forks, shape into really
rocky heaps on the baking sheets.
Bake for about 20 minutes or until
golden brown. Transfer to a wire rack
and leave to cool. Rock buns are best
eaten on the day they are made.

NUTRITION PER BUN 192 cals |
9g fat (6g sats) | 26g carbs | 0.5g salt Ⓥ

Sultana Scones

Makes 12
Preparation time 20 minutes
Cooking time 15 minutes, plus cooling

450g (1lb) self-raising flour, plus extra to dust
100g (3½oz) butter, chilled and cubed
50g (2oz) caster sugar
100g (3½oz) sultanas
200ml (7fl oz) semi-skimmed milk
3 medium eggs
clotted cream and jam to serve

1 Preheat the oven to 220°C (200°C fan oven) mark 7.
Lightly flour a large baking tray.
2 In a food processor, whiz the flour, butter and sugar until
the mixture resembles fine breadcrumbs. Tip into a bowl
and stir in the sultanas.
3 In a large jug, whisk the milk with 2 of the eggs, then stir
into the dry ingredients, using a blunt-ended cutlery knife,
to make a soft dough.
4 Turn the mixture on to a lightly floured surface, bring
together and pat down until 2.5cm (1in) thick, working
the dough as little as possible. Cut out rounds with a 5cm
(2in) fluted cutter and transfer to the floured baking tray.
Beat the remaining egg and brush a little over the tops of
the scones.
5 Bake in the oven for 10–12 minutes until golden brown
and risen. Cool on a wire rack before serving with cream
and jam.

NUTRITION PER SERVING (served plain) 258 cals | 9g fat (5g sats) | 38g carbs | 0.5g salt

Drop Scones (Scotch Pancakes)

Makes 15
Preparation time 10 minutes
Cooking time 12–18 minutes

125g (4oz) self-raising flour
2 tbsp caster sugar
1 medium egg, beaten
150ml (½ pint) milk
vegetable oil to grease
butter, or whipped cream and jam,
 to serve

1 Mix the flour and sugar together in a bowl. Make a well in the centre and mix in the egg, with enough of the milk to make a batter the consistency of thick cream – working as quickly and lightly as possible.
2 Cook the mixture in batches: drop spoonfuls on to an oiled hot griddle or heavy-based frying pan. Keep the griddle at a steady heat and when bubbles rise to the surface of the scone and burst, after 2–3 minutes, turn over with a palette knife.
3 Cook for a further 2–3 minutes until golden brown on the other side.
4 Put the cooked drop scones on a clean tea towel and cover with another tea towel to keep them moist. Serve warm, with butter, or cream and jam.

NUTRITION PER SCONE 50 cals | 1g fat (0.2g sats) | 9g carbs | 0.1g salt Ⓥ

Welsh Cakes

Makes about 16
Preparation time 10 minutes
Cooking time 3 minutes per batch

50g (2oz) butter, plus extra to grease
225g (8oz) plain flour, plus extra to dust
1 tsp baking powder
a pinch of salt
50g (2oz) lard
75g (3oz) caster sugar
50g (2oz) currants
1 medium egg, beaten
about 2 tbsp milk

1 Grease a griddle or heavy frying pan. Rub the fats into the flour, baking powder and salt until it resembles fine breadcrumbs. Add the sugar and currants and make a well in the centre.
2 Mix in the egg and enough milk to make a stiff paste like pastry.
3 Roll out on a lightly floured surface until 5mm (¼in) thick and cut into rounds using a 7.5cm (3in) cutter.
4 Cook on the medium-hot griddle for 3 minutes on each side or until golden. Cool. Eat on the same day.

TRY SOMETHING DIFFERENT

Griddle Scones Use self-raising flour instead of plain, with 1 tsp baking powder, a pinch of salt and ½ tsp grated nutmeg. Omit the lard and currants. Use 50g (2oz) caster sugar. You may need 3–4 tbsp milk. Roll out to 1cm (½in) thick and cut into triangles. Cook for 5 minutes on each side. Serve warm, split and buttered.

NUTRITION PER CAKE 123 cals | 6g fat (3g sats) | 18g carbs | 0.2g salt Ⓥ

Banana and Butterscotch Loaf

Cuts into 15 slices
Preparation time 20 minutes
Cooking time 1 hour, plus cooling

a little butter to grease
175g (6oz) plain flour, sifted
2 tsp baking powder
½ tsp bicarbonate of soda
½ tsp salt
175g (6oz) light muscovado sugar
2 large eggs
3 medium-size ripe bananas, mashed
150g carton natural yogurt
150g bar butterscotch chocolate, roughly chopped
100g (3½oz) pecan nuts, chopped
1–2 tbsp demerara sugar

1 Preheat the oven to 170°C (150°C fan oven) mark 3.
Grease a 1.4kg (3lb) loaf tin and line it with
greaseproof paper.
2 Put the flour, baking powder, bicarbonate of soda and
salt into a large bowl and mix together.
3 In a separate bowl, beat the muscovado sugar and eggs
together, using a hand-held electric whisk, until pale and
fluffy. Carefully stir in the bananas, yogurt, chocolate and
50g (2oz) pecan nuts, followed by the flour mixture.
4 Spoon the mixture into the prepared tin and level the
surface. Sprinkle with the remaining chopped pecan nuts
and the demerara sugar. Bake for 1 hour or until a skewer
inserted into the centre comes out clean. Leave to cool in
the tin on a wire rack, then turn out and slice.

TO STORE
Store in an airtight container. It will keep for up to two days.

TRY SOMETHING DIFFERENT
If you can't find butterscotch chocolate, use a bar of plain
chocolate (at least 70% cocoa solids) instead.

NUTRITION PER SLICE 221 cals | 9g fat (2g sats) | 34g carbs | 0.2g salt Ⓥ

Ginger and Fruit Teabread

Cuts into 12 slices
Preparation time 15 minutes, plus soaking
Cooking time 1 hour, plus cooling

125g (4oz) dried apricots, chopped
125g (4oz) dried apples, chopped
125g (4oz) pitted prunes, chopped
300ml (½ pint) strong fruit tea
a little butter to grease
25g (1oz) preserved stem ginger in syrup, chopped
225g (8oz) wholemeal flour
2 tsp baking powder
125g (4oz) dark muscovado sugar
1 medium egg, beaten

1 Put the dried fruit into a large bowl, add the tea and
leave to soak for 2 hours.
2 Preheat the oven to 180°C (160°C fan oven) mark 4.
Grease a 900g (2lb) loaf tin and line the base with
baking parchment.
3 Add the remaining ingredients to the soaked fruit and
mix thoroughly. Spoon into the prepared tin and brush
with 2 tbsp cold water. Bake for 1 hour or until a skewer
inserted into the centre comes out clean.
4 Cool in the tin for 10–15 minutes, then turn out on to a
wire rack and leave to cool completely.

TO STORE
Wrap the teabread in clingfilm and store in an airtight
container. It will keep for up to three days.

NUTRITION PER SLICE 145 cals | 1g fat (trace sats) | 33g carbs | 0g salt Ⓥ

Chocolate Fudge Brownies

Makes 12 brownies
Preparation time 20 minutes
Cooking time 1 hour, plus cooling

a little butter to grease
125g (4oz) milk chocolate, broken into pieces
9 ready-to-eat pitted prunes
200g (7oz) light muscovado sugar
3 large egg whites
1 tsp vanilla extract
75g (3oz) plain flour
50g (2oz) white chocolate, chopped
icing sugar, sifted, to dust

1 Preheat the oven to 180°C (160°C fan oven) mark 4.
Grease and base-line a 15cm (6in) square shallow cake tin.
2 Melt the milk chocolate in a large heatproof bowl over a
pan of gently simmering water, making sure the base of the
bowl doesn't touch the water. Remove from the heat and
leave to cool slightly.
3 Put the prunes in a food processor or blender with
100ml (3½fl oz) water and whiz for 2–3 minutes to make a
purée. Add the muscovado sugar and whiz briefly to mix.
4 In a clean, grease-free bowl, whisk the egg whites until
they form soft peaks.
5 Add the vanilla extract, prune mixture, flour, white
chocolate and egg whites to the bowl of melted chocolate.
Fold everything together gently. Pour the mixture into the
prepared tin and bake for 1 hour or until firm to the touch.
6 Leave to cool in the tin. Turn out, cut into 12 squares
and dust with icing sugar.

TO STORE
Store in an airtight container. They will keep for up to
two days.

NUTRITION PER BROWNIE 174 cals | 5g fat (3g sats) | 33g carbs | 0.1g salt Ⓥ

Sticky Gingerbread Ⓑ

Cuts into 10 slices
Preparation time 15 minutes, plus cooling
Cooking time 1 hour 10 minutes, plus cooling

125g (4oz) unsalted butter, plus extra to grease
125g (4oz) light muscovado sugar
75g (3oz) black treacle
200g (7oz) golden syrup
250g (9oz) plain flour
2 tsp ground mixed spice
65g (2½oz) preserved stem ginger, finely chopped
2 large eggs
100ml (3½fl oz) milk
1 tsp bicarbonate of soda
extra treacle or golden syrup to glaze (optional)

1 Grease and line a bread maker bucket with baking
parchment, if specified in the manual.
2 Put the butter, sugar, treacle and golden syrup in a pan
and heat gently until the butter has melted. Leave to cool
for 5 minutes.
3 Sift the flour and mixed spice together into a bowl. Add
the syrup mixture, chopped ginger, eggs and milk, and stir
well until combined.
4 In a cup, mix the bicarbonate of soda with 2 tbsp hot
water, then add to the bowl. Stir the mixture well and pour
into the bread maker bucket.
5 Fit the bucket into the bread maker and set to the Cake
or Bake-only program. Select 1 hour 10 minutes on the
timer and choose a light crust. Press start.
6 To check whether the cake is done, pierce the centre
with a skewer; it should come out fairly clean. If necessary,
re-set the timer for a little longer.
7 Remove the bucket from the machine, leave the cake in
the bucket for 5 minutes, then turn out on to a wire rack.
8 Brush the top of the cake with the treacle or syrup to
glaze, if you like, and leave to cool.

TO MAKE CONVENTIONALLY

Preheat the oven to 180°C (160°C fan oven) mark 4 and
grease and line a 900g (2lb) loaf tin. Follow steps 2 to 4
of the main recipe, pouring the mixture into the prepared
tin. Bake for 1 hour or until a skewer inserted into the
centre comes out fairly clean. Leave to cool in the tin
for 5 minutes, then turn out on to a wire rack. Brush the
top of the cake with the treacle or syrup to glaze, if you like,
and leave to cool.

TO STORE

Wrap and store in an airtight container. It will keep for up to
one week.

NUTRITION PER SLICE 341 cals | 12g fat (7g sats) | 58g carbs | 0.7g salt Ⓥ

Apricot and Almond Traybake

Cuts into 18 bars
Preparation time 20 minutes
Cooking time 30–40 minutes, plus cooling

250g (9oz) unsalted butter, softened, plus extra to grease
225g (8oz) golden caster sugar
275g (10oz) self-raising flour, sifted
2 tsp baking powder
finely grated zest of 1 orange and 2 tbsp orange juice
75g (3oz) ground almonds
5 medium eggs, lightly beaten
225g (8oz) ready-to-eat dried apricots, roughly chopped
25g (1oz) flaked almonds
icing sugar, sifted, to dust (optional)

1 Preheat the oven to 180°C (160°C fan oven) mark 4.
Grease a 33 × 20.5cm (13 × 8in) baking tin and base-line
with baking parchment.
2 Put the butter, caster sugar, flour, baking powder, orange
zest and juice, ground almonds and eggs into the bowl
of a large freestanding mixer. Mix on a low setting for
30 seconds, then increase the speed and mix for 1 minute
or until thoroughly combined. (Alternatively, mix well,
using a wooden spoon.)
3 Remove the bowl from the mixer. Using a large metal
spoon, fold in the apricots. Spoon the mixture into the
prepared tin, level the surface and sprinkle the flaked
almonds over the top.
4 Bake for 30–40 minutes until risen and golden brown
and a skewer inserted into the centre comes out clean.
Leave to cool in the tin.
5 Cut into 18 bars. Dust with icing sugar, if you like.

TO STORE
Wrap in clingfilm and store in an airtight container. They
will keep for up to three days.

Blackberry Traybake

Cuts into 24 squares
Preparation time 20 minutes
Cooking time about 45 minutes, plus cooling and setting

275g (10oz) unsalted butter, softened, plus extra to grease
275g (10oz) golden caster sugar
400g (14oz) self-raising flour
1½ tsp baking powder
5 medium eggs, beaten
finely grated zest of 1 large orange
1 tbsp vanilla extract
4–5 tbsp milk
250g (9oz) blackberries
40g (1½oz) flaked almonds

For the icing
150g (5oz) icing sugar, sifted
1 tsp vanilla extract
about 2 tbsp orange juice

1 Preheat the oven to 190°C (170°C fan oven) mark 5.
Grease a shallow 30.5 × 20.5cm (12 × 8in) baking tin and
line with greaseproof paper.
2 Put the butter and caster sugar into a large bowl. Sift
in the flour and baking powder, then add the eggs, orange
zest, vanilla extract and milk, and beat together until light
and fluffy.
3 Using a metal spoon, fold in the blackberries. Spoon into
the prepared tin and dot with the almonds.
4 Bake for 40–45 minutes until springy to the touch. Cool
in the tin for 5 minutes, then turn out on to a wire rack and
leave to cool completely.
5 When the cake is cool, make the icing. Sift the icing
sugar into a bowl, then add the vanilla extract and orange
juice, mixing as you go, until smooth and runny. Drizzle
over the cake and leave for 30 minutes to set. Cut into
24 squares to serve.

TO STORE
Wrap in clingfilm and store in an airtight container. It will
keep for up to four days.

Freezing Tip
- To freeze, complete the recipe to the end of step 4. Cool
  completely, keeping the cake in its greaseproof paper,
  then wrap in clingfilm. Freeze for up to one month.
- To use, thaw overnight at cool room temperature.
  Complete the recipe.

NUTRITION PER SQUARE 239 cals | 12g fat (7g sats) | 32g carbs | 0.4g salt ⓥ

Victoria Sponge

Cuts into 10 slices
Preparation time 30 minutes
Cooking time about 25 minutes, plus cooling

175g (6oz) unsalted butter at room temperature, plus
   extra to grease
175g (6oz) golden caster sugar
3 medium eggs
175g (6oz) self-raising flour, sifted
3–4 tbsp jam
a little icing sugar to dust

1 Grease two 18cm (7in) sandwich tins and base-line with
parchment paper. Preheat the oven to 190°C (170°C fan
oven) mark 5.
2 Put the butter and caster sugar into a large bowl and,
using a hand-held electric whisk, beat together until pale
and fluffy. Add the eggs, one at a time, beating well after
each addition and adding a spoonful of flour to the mixture
if it looks as if it's about to curdle. Using a large metal
spoon, fold in the remaining flour.
3 Divide the mixture evenly between the prepared tins and
level the surface with a palette knife. Bake in the centre of
the oven for 20–25 minutes until the cakes are well risen
and spring back when lightly pressed in the centre. Loosen
the edges with a palette knife and leave in the tins for
5 minutes.
4 Turn out, remove the lining paper and leave to cool on a
wire rack. Sandwich the two cakes together with jam and
dust icing sugar over the top. Slice and serve.

TO STORE
Store in an airtight container. It will keep for up to three
days. If stored in the fridge it will keep for up to one week.

NUTRITION PER SLICE 445 cals | 21g fat (11g sats) | 30g carbs | 0.8g salt Ⓥ

Best-ever Carrot Cake

Serves 12
Preparation time 40 minutes
Cooking time 1¼ hours, plus cooling

For the cake
225ml (8fl oz) sunflower oil, plus extra to grease
225g (8oz) light muscovado sugar
4 medium eggs
225g (8oz) self-raising flour
1 tsp bicarbonate of soda
1½ tsp each mixed spice, ground cinnamon and ground
 ginger
150g (5oz) sultanas
200g (7oz) carrots, coarsely grated
50–75g (2–3oz) walnuts or pecans, roughly chopped

For the icing
250g (9oz) unsalted butter, very soft
1 tsp vanilla extract
400g (14oz) full-fat cream cheese at room temperature
300g (11oz) icing sugar
carrot decorations (optional) (see Cook's Tip)

1 Preheat the oven to 170°C (150°C fan oven) mark 3.
Grease the base and sides of a round 20.5cm (8in) cake
tin and line with parchment paper. Put the oil, muscovado
sugar and eggs into a large bowl and whisk together until
smooth.
2 Add the flour, soda and spices to the bowl and mix to
combine. Stir in the sultanas, carrots and nuts. Scrape the
mixture into the prepared tin, level the surface and bake for
1–1¼ hours until a skewer inserted into the centre comes
out clean. Leave to cool in the tin for 5 minutes, then turn
out on to a wire rack and leave to cool completely.
3 To make the icing, in a large bowl, beat the butter and
vanilla until completely smooth, then add the cream cheese
and mix to combine. Sift the icing sugar into the bowl and
mix (carefully at first, as otherwise there will be clouds of
icing sugar) until smooth and fluffy.
4 Cut the cooled cake in half horizontally through the
middle. Use half the icing to sandwich the halves back
together, then place the cake on a cake stand or plate.
Spread the remaining icing over the top of the cake, and
place the carrot decorations on top, if you like. Slice and
serve.

TO STORE
Place the iced cake in a container in the fridge. It will keep
for up to five days.

Cook's Tip
Make the marzipan carrots by colouring 75g (3oz)
marzipan with orange colouring and 15g (½oz) with green
colouring. Divide the orange marzipan into 12, shape into
cones and mark ridges with a cocktail stick. Divide the
green marzipan into 12, shape into fronds and stick on to
the carrots. Use to decorate the cake.

NUTRITION PER SLICE 757 cals | 52g fat (23g sats) | 66g carbs | 1.1g salt

Black Forest Gâteau

Cuts into 12 slices
Preparation time 30 minutes, plus cooling
Cooking time about 50 minutes

125g (4oz) unsalted butter, melted
200g (7oz) plain flour
50g (2oz) cornflour
50g (2oz) cocoa powder, plus extra to dust
2 tsp espresso instant coffee powder
1 tsp baking powder
4 large eggs, separated
300g (11oz) golden caster sugar
2 × 300g jars morello cherries in syrup
2 tbsp Kirsch
200ml (7fl oz) double cream
2 tbsp icing sugar, sifted
fresh cherries and Chocolate Curls (see Cook's Tip, page
  379) to decorate

1 Preheat the oven to 180°C (160°C fan oven) mark 4.
Brush a little of the melted butter over the base and sides
of a 20.5cm (8in) round × 9cm (3½in) deep cake tin. Line
the base and sides with baking parchment.
2 Sift the flour, cornflour, cocoa powder, coffee powder and
baking powder together three times – this helps to add air
and makes sure the ingredients are well mixed.
3 Put the egg yolks, caster sugar and 100ml (3½fl oz) cold
water into a freestanding mixer and whisk for 8 minutes
until the mixture leaves a trail for 3 seconds when the
whisk is lifted.
4 Add the rest of the melted butter, pouring it around the
edge of the bowl so that the mixture doesn't lose any air,
then quickly fold it in, followed by the sifted flour mixture
in two batches.
5 In another bowl, whisk the egg whites until stiff peaks
form, then fold a spoonful into the cake mixture to loosen.
Carefully fold in the rest of the egg whites, making sure
there are no white blobs left. Pour into the prepared tin
and bake in the oven for 45–50 minutes until a skewer
inserted into the centre comes out clean. Leave in the
tin for 10 minutes, then turn out on to a wire rack to
cool completely.
6 When the cake is cold, trim the top to make a flat
surface. Turn the cake over so that the top becomes the
base. Using a long serrated bread knife, carefully cut
horizontally into three. Drain the cherries, reserving 250ml
(9fl oz) of the syrup. Put the syrup into a pan and simmer

to reduce by half. Stir in the Kirsch. Brush all the hot syrup
on to each layer of the cake – including the top.
7 Lightly whip the cream with the icing sugar. Spread
one-third over the bottom layer of cake and cover with half
the cherries. Top with the next cake layer and repeat with
another third of the cream and the remaining cherries. Top
with the final cake layer and spread the remaining cream
over. Decorate with fresh cherries, Chocolate Curls and a
dusting of cocoa powder.

GET AHEAD
Make the gateau up to 2 hours ahead to allow the flavours to
mingle and the syrup to moisten the cake.

NUTRITION PER SLICE 440 cals | 22g fat (12g sats) | 59g carbs | 0.8g salt Ⓥ

One-stage Fruit Cake

Cuts into 12 slices
Preparation time 10 minutes
Cooking time 1¾ hours, plus cooling

125g (4oz) soft tub margarine, plus
  extra to grease
225g (8oz) self-raising flour
2 tsp mixed spice
1 tsp baking powder
125g (4oz) soft brown sugar
225g (8oz) mixed dried fruit
2 medium eggs, beaten
2 tbsp milk

1 Preheat the oven to 170°C (150°C fan oven) mark 3. Grease and base-line an 18cm (7in) round cake tin with greaseproof paper. Sift the flour, spice and baking powder into a large bowl, add the remaining ingredients and beat until thoroughly combined.
2 Turn the mixture into the tin and bake for 1¾ hours or until a fine warmed skewer inserted into the centre comes out clean. Turn out and cool on a wire rack.

NUTRITION PER SLICE 245 cals | 10g fat (2g sats) | 38g carbs | 0.3g salt Ⓥ

Madeira Cake

Cuts into 12 slices
Preparation time 20 minutes
Cooking time 50 minutes, plus cooling

175g (6oz) butter, softened, plus extra
  to grease
175g (6oz) golden caster sugar
1 tsp vanilla extract
3 large eggs, beaten
125g (4oz) plain flour, sifted
125g (4oz) self-raising flour, sifted
1–2 tbsp milk (optional)
2–3 thin slices citron peel

1 Preheat the oven to 180°C (160°C fan oven) mark 4. Grease and line a deep 18cm (7in) round cake tin.
2 Cream the butter and sugar in a bowl until pale and fluffy, then beat in the vanilla. Add the eggs, a little at a time, beating well after each addition.

3 Using a metal spoon, fold in the sifted flours, adding a little milk, if necessary, to give a light dropping consistency.
4 Spoon the mixture into the prepared tin and level the surface. Bake for 20 minutes. Lay the citron peel on the cake and bake for a further 30 minutes or until a skewer inserted into the centre comes out clean. Turn out on to a wire rack and leave to cool.

TRY SOMETHING DIFFERENT
Add the grated zest of 1 lemon at step 2. Add the juice of the lemon instead of the milk at step 3.

NUTRITION PER SLICE 260 cals | 14g fat (8g sats) | 31g carbs | 0.4g salt Ⓥ

Battenburg Cake

Makes about 10 slices
Preparation time 40 minutes
Cooking time 40 minutes, plus cooling

350g (12oz) butter or margarine, plus extra for greasing
350g (12oz) caster sugar
a few drop of vanilla flavouring
6 medium eggs, beaten
350g (12oz) self-raising flour
a few drops of pink food colouring (note that not all food
  colourings are vegetarian)
milk
apricot jam
400g (14oz) white marzipan or Almond Paste (see page 436)
icing sugar, sifted, to dust

1 Preheat the oven to 190°C (170°C fan oven) mark 5.
Grease and line a Swiss roll tin measuring 30.5 × 20.5 ×
4cm (12 × 8 × 1½ in) and divide it lengthways with a 'wall'
of folded greaseproof paper or kitchen foil.
2 Cream the butter and sugar together until light and
fluffy. Add a few drops of vanilla flavouring, then gradually
add the eggs a little at a time, beating well after each
addition. When all the egg has been added, lightly fold in
the flour, using a metal spoon.
3 Turn half the mixture into one side of the tin. Fold two
drops of pink food colouring into the other half with a
little milk and spoon this mixture into the second side of
the tin.
4 Bake for 40–45 minutes until well risen and firm to the
touch. Turn out and cool on a wire rack.
5 When the cake is cold, cut each half in half lengthways
and then carefully cut away all the brown surfaces. Spread
all the sides of the strips with jam and stick each yellow
strip to a pink strip. Then stick one double strip on top
of the other, so that the colours alternate. Press the pieces
well together.
6 Roll out the marzipan thinly on a worksurface dusted
with a little icing sugar, into a rectangle measuring about
35.5 × 25.5cm (14 × 10in). Wrap completely around the
cake. Press firmly against the sides and trim the edges.
Crimp along the outer edges and score the top of the cake
with a sharp knife to give a criss-cross pattern.

TRY SOMETHING DIFFERENT
To make a chocolate Battenburg, omit the pink food
colouring and add 15g (½oz) cocoa powder to the coloured
half of the cake mixture.

NUTRITION PER SLICE 450 cals | 26g fat (11g sats) | 42g carbs | 0.5g salt Ⓥ

Lemon Drizzle Loaf

Cuts into 10 slices
Preparation time 20 minutes
Cooking time 50 minutes, plus cooling

175g (6oz) unsalted butter, softened, plus extra to grease
175g (6oz) caster sugar
4 medium eggs, lightly beaten
3 lemons
125g (4oz) self-raising flour
50g (2oz) ground almonds
75g (3oz) sugar cubes

1 Preheat the oven to 180°C (160°C fan oven) mark 4.
Grease and line a 900g (2lb) loaf tin with baking
parchment.
2 In a large bowl, beat together the butter and caster sugar
with a hand-held electric whisk until pale and fluffy, about
5 minutes. Gradually beat in the eggs, followed by the
finely grated zest of 2 of the lemons and the juice of
½ lemon.
3 Fold the flour and ground almonds into the butter
mixture, then spoon into the prepared tin and bake for
40–50 minutes until a skewer inserted into the centre
comes out clean. Cool in the tin for 10 minutes, then invert
on to a wire rack and leave to cool until warm.
4 Meanwhile, put the sugar cubes into a small bowl with
the juice of 1½ lemons and the pared zest of 1 lemon
(you should have 1 un-juiced lemon left over). Soak for
5 minutes, then use the back of a spoon to roughly crush
the sugar cubes. Spoon over the warm cake and leave to
cool completely before serving in slices.

TO STORE
Store in an airtight container. It will keep for up to four days.

TRY SOMETHING DIFFERENT
Use gluten-free self-raising flour instead of the ordinary flour
to make this suitable for those with a gluten-intolerance.

NUTRITION PER SLICE 424 cals | 25g fat (13g sats) | 46g carbs | 0.6g salt Ⓥ

Swiss Roll

Cuts into 8 slices
Preparation time 25 minutes
Cooking time 10–12 minutes, plus cooling

a little butter to grease
125g (4oz) golden caster sugar, plus extra to dust
125g (4oz) plain flour, plus extra to dust
3 large eggs

To assemble
caster sugar to sprinkle
125g (4oz) jam, warmed

1 Lightly grease a 33 × 23cm (13 × 9in) Swiss roll tin with butter. Cut a piece of baking parchment into a rectangle 7.5cm (3in) wider and longer than the tin. Press it into the tin and cut at the corners, then fold to fit neatly. Grease the paper, then dust with caster sugar and flour. Preheat the oven to 200°C (180°C fan oven) mark 6.
2 Put the eggs and sugar into a large heatproof bowl and, using a hand-held electric whisk, whisk until well blended. Put the bowl over a pan of hot water and whisk until the mixture is pale and creamy and thick enough to leave a trail on the surface when the whisk is lifted. Remove the bowl from the pan and whisk until cool and thick.
3 Sift half the flour over the mixture and fold it in very lightly, using a large metal spoon or spatula. Sift in the remaining flour and gently fold in until evenly incorporated. Carefully fold in 1 tbsp hot water.
4 Pour into the prepared tin and tilt the tin backwards and forwards to spread the mixture evenly. Bake for 10–12 minutes until pale golden, risen and springy to the touch.
5 Meanwhile, put a sheet of greaseproof paper on a damp teatowel. Dredge the paper with caster sugar.
6 Quickly turn out the cake on to the paper and remove the lining paper. Trim off the crusty edges and spread the cake with jam.
7 Using the greaseproof paper to help, roll up the cake from a short side. Make the first turn firmly so that the cake will roll evenly and have a good shape when finished, but roll more lightly after this turn. Put seam-side down on a wire rack and sprinkle with sugar to serve.

TRY SOMETHING DIFFERENT
Chocolate Swiss Roll Replace 1 tbsp flour with cocoa powder and make and bake as the main recipe. Turn out and trim the sponge as above, then cover with a sheet of greaseproof paper and roll with the paper inside. When cold, unroll and remove the paper. Spread with whipped cream or Buttercream (see page 434) and re-roll. Dust with icing sugar to serve.

NUTRITION PER SLICE 200 cals | 3g fat (0.7g sats) | 41g carbs | 0.9g salt Ⓥ

Chocolate Roulade

Cuts into 8 slices
Preparation time 25 minutes
Cooking time 15 minutes, plus cooling

150g (5oz) plain chocolate (at least 70% cocoa solids),
  broken into pieces
5 large eggs, separated
150g (5oz) caster sugar
1 tbsp cornflour
cocoa powder to dust

For the topping
125ml (4fl oz) double cream
75g (3oz) plain chocolate (at least 70% cocoa solids),
  finely chopped
2 tbsp golden syrup
silver and gold balls, plus edible glitter to decorate

For the filling
150ml (¼ pint) double cream
1 tbsp icing sugar, sifted (optional), plus extra to dust

1 Preheat the oven to 180°C (160°C fan oven) mark 4.
Line a 33 × 23cm (13 × 9in) Swiss roll tin with baking
parchment. Melt the chocolate in a heatproof bowl over
a pan of gently simmering water, making sure the base of
the bowl doesn't touch the water. Leave to cool.
2 Beat together the egg yolks and caster sugar in a large
bowl, using an electric hand whisk, for about 5 minutes or
until pale and thick. Fold in the cooled chocolate.
3 Put the egg whites and cornflour into a clean, grease-free
bowl and whisk (using clean beaters) until they form soft
peaks. Use a large metal spoon to fold the whites into the
chocolate mixture – be careful not to knock out too much air.
4 Spoon the mixture into the prepared tin and level the
surface. Bake for 12–15 minutes, then take out of the oven
and cover with a damp tea towel. Leave to cool.
5 Meanwhile, to make the topping, put the cream into a
pan and bring just to the boil, then take off the heat and
stir in the 75g (3oz) chocolate until melted. Stir in the
golden syrup and leave to cool.

6 Make the filling by lightly whipping the cream and icing
sugar in a bowl until the cream just holds its shape. Dust
a rectangle of greaseproof paper, a little larger than the
baking tin, with cocoa powder, then invert the cake on to
the paper.
7 Remove the tin and peel off the paper. Spread the
cream mixture over the cooled cake. Roll up the cake
from the short edge, using the paper underneath it to help
you. Transfer to a serving plate. Dust with icing sugar or
decorate with silver balls, if you like.

NUTRITION PER SLICE 480 cals | 31g (18g sats) | 45g carbs | 0.5g salt Ⓥ

Almond and Orange Torte

Cuts into 12 slices
Preparation time 30 minutes
Cooking time 1 hour 50 minutes, plus cooling

sunflower oil to grease
plain flour to dust
1 medium orange
3 medium eggs
225g (8oz) golden caster sugar
250g (9oz) ground almonds
½ tsp baking powder
icing sugar, sifted, to dust
crème fraîche to serve

1 Grease and line with greaseproof paper, then oil and
flour a 20.5cm (8in) springform cake tin. Put the whole
orange into a small pan and cover with water. Bring to the
boil, then cover the pan and simmer for at least 1 hour or
until tender (see Cook's Tip). Remove from the water and
leave to cool.
2 Cut the orange in half and remove the pips. Whiz in a
food processor or blender to make a smooth purée.
3 Preheat the oven to 180°C (160°C fan oven) mark 4. Put
the eggs and caster sugar into a bowl and whisk together
until thick and pale. Fold in the almonds, baking powder
and orange purée. Pour the mixture into the prepared tin.
4 Bake for 40–50 minutes until a skewer inserted into the
centre comes out clean. Leave to cool in the tin.
5 Release the clasp on the tin and remove the cake.
Carefully peel off the lining paper and put the cake on
a serving plate. Dust with icing sugar, then cut into 12
wedges. Serve with crème fraîche.

TO STORE
Store in an airtight container. The cake will keep for up to
three days.

Cook's Tip
To save time, you can microwave the orange. Put it into
a small heatproof bowl, cover with 100ml (3½fl oz) water
and cook in a 900W microwave oven on full power for
10–12 minutes until soft.

NUTRITION PER SLICE 223 cals | 13g fat (1g sats) | 22g carbs | 0.1g salt Ⓥ

White Chocolate Torte

Cuts into 16 slices
Preparation time about 50 minutes, plus chilling and freezing
Cooking time about 30 minutes, plus cooling

125g (4oz) unsalted butter
225g (8oz) ginger snaps or digestive biscuits, roughly broken
750g (1lb 11oz) white chocolate
568ml carton double cream
white Maltesers to decorate

1 Line the base and sides of a 20.5 × 6.5cm (8 × 2½in)
springform cake tin with non-stick baking parchment
or greaseproof paper. Melt the butter in a pan. Whiz the
biscuits in a food processor until finely crushed. Tip the
crumbs into a bowl and stir in the melted butter. Spread
evenly over the base of the prepared tin and press down.
Chill for 15 minutes to set.
2 Chop 700g (1½lb) chocolate and combine with half
the cream in a bowl set over a pan of barely simmering
water, making sure the base of the bowl doesn't touch the
water. Leave the chocolate to melt, but don't stir it – this
might take as long as 30 minutes. Once melted, remove
from the heat and stir until smooth, then leave to cool
for 15 minutes or until just beginning to thicken, stirring
occasionally. Don't allow it to cool completely or the cream
won't fold in evenly.
3 In a separate bowl, whip the remaining cream until soft
peaks form, then fold into the chocolate mixture. Pour over
the biscuit base and chill for 3 hours.
4 Pull a vegetable peeler across the remaining white
chocolate to make rough curls and scatter them over the
torte, then arrange the Maltesers on top. Freeze for 15
minutes, then remove from the tin and serve.

Freezing Tip
To freeze, complete the recipe up to one month ahead,
then freeze the torte in its tin. When frozen, remove the
torte from the tin and carefully wrap in clingfilm before
returning to the freezer. To use, thaw overnight in the
fridge, then put back in the freezer for 15 minutes before
serving to make sure it's chilled.

NUTRITION PER SLICE 563 cals | 44g fat (26g sats) | 40g carbs | 0.5g salt Ⓥ

Dundee Cake

Cuts into 16 slices
Preparation time 20 minutes
Cooking time about 2 hours, plus cooling

225g (8oz) butter or margarine, softened, plus extra to grease
125g (4oz) currants
125g (4oz) raisins
50g (2oz) blanched almonds, chopped
125g (4oz) chopped mixed peel
300g (11oz) plain flour
225g (8oz) light muscovado sugar
finely grated zest of 1 lemon
4 large eggs, beaten
75g (3oz) split almonds

1 Preheat the oven to 170°C (150°C fan oven) mark 3.
Grease and line a deep 20cm (8in) round cake tin. Wrap
a double thickness of brown paper around the outside and
secure with string.
2 Combine the dried fruit, chopped nuts and peel in a
bowl. Sift in a little flour and stir to coat the fruit.
3 Cream the butter and sugar together in a bowl until pale
and fluffy, then beat in the lemon zest. Add the eggs a little
at a time, beating well after each addition.
4 Sift in the remaining flour and fold in lightly, using a
metal spoon, then fold in the fruit and nut mixture.
5 Turn the mixture into the prepared tin and, using the
back of a metal spoon, make a slight hollow in the centre.
Arrange the split almonds on top.
6 Bake on the centre shelf of the oven for 2 hours or until
a skewer inserted into the centre comes out clean. Loosely
cover the top of the cake with foil if it appears to be
browning too quickly. Leave in the tin for 15 minutes, then
turn out on to a wire rack and leave to cool completely.
7 Wrap in greaseproof paper and foil and leave to mature
for at least a week before cutting.

NUTRITION PER SLICE 350 cals | 18g fat (8g sats) | 45g carbs | 0.4g salt ⓥ

Sachertorte

Cuts into 8 slices
Preparation time 25 minutes
Cooking time 40 minutes, plus cooling and setting

125g (4oz) unsalted butter, softened, plus extra to grease
300g (11oz) plain chocolate (at least 70% cocoa solids),
 broken into pieces
125g (4oz) caster sugar
a pinch of salt
4 large eggs, separated
125g (4oz) plain flour
6 tbsp apricot jam

For the icing:
225g (8oz) plain chocolate (at least 70% cocoa solids),
 broken into pieces
40ml (1½fl oz) strong black coffee
2 tbsp golden syrup
150g (5oz) icing sugar, sifted
edible star decorations (optional)

1 Preheat the oven to 180°C (160°C fan oven) mark 4.
Grease a 20.5cm (8in) round cake tin and line with baking
parchment.
2 Melt the chocolate in a heatproof bowl set over a pan of
simmering water, making sure the base of the bowl does
not touch the water. Set aside to cool.
3 Put the butter, 100g (3½oz) of the caster sugar and
salt into a large bowl and beat together with a hand-held
electric whisk for about 3 minutes until pale and fluffy.
Gradually add the egg yolks, beating well after each
addition. Next, beat in the cooled chocolate, then fold in
the flour, using a large metal spoon, to give a stiff mixture.
4 In a separate bowl (and using clean, dry beaters),
whisk the egg whites until they hold stiff peaks. Add the
remaining sugar and beat again. Stir a spoonful of the egg
whites into the chocolate mixture to loosen it, then fold
in the remaining egg whites. Scrape the mixture into the
prepared tin, then bake for 30 minutes or until a skewer
inserted into the centre comes out clean. Leave to cool in
the tin for 10 minutes, then take the cake out of the tin
and leave to cool completely on a wire rack.
5 Peel off the parchment paper, then cut the cake in half

horizontally. Melt the jam in a small pan, then spread some
on top of the bottom half of the cake. Top with the other
half of the cake, then brush the remaining jam over the top
and sides. Leave to set for 10 minutes.
6 For the icing, put the chocolate, coffee and syrup into
a large pan and heat gently until melted. Mix in the icing
sugar to make a smooth icing. Immediately spread over
cake. Scatter the star decorations over the cake, if you like,
and allow to set for 2 hours before serving.

NUTRITION PER SLICE 737 cals | 35g fat (20g sats) | 96g carbs | 0.7g salt Ⓥ

Simnel Cake

Cuts into 12 slices
Preparation time 30 minutes
Cooking time 1½ hours, plus cooling

225g (8oz) butter, softened, plus extra
 to grease
225g (8oz) self-raising flour
2 tsp ground mixed spice
400g (14oz) mixed dried fruit
150g (5oz) light muscovado sugar
50g (2oz) golden syrup
finely grated zest of 2 lemons
4 medium eggs, lightly beaten
icing sugar, sifted, to dust
500g (1lb 2oz) Almond Paste
 (see page 436)
2 tbsp apricot jam

1 Preheat the oven to 170°C (150°C fan oven) mark 3. Grease a 20.5cm (8in) round cake tin with butter and line with baking parchment.
2 In a large bowl, stir together the flour, mixed spice and dried fruit until combined.
3 Put the butter, muscovado sugar, syrup and lemon zest into a separate large bowl and beat together, using a hand-held electric whisk, for about 3 minutes until pale and fluffy. Gradually beat in the eggs, whisking well after each addition. Add the flour mixture and fold everything together using a large metal spoon.
4 Spoon the mixture into the prepared tin and bake for 1 hour, then cover the cake with foil and cook for a further 25 minutes or until cake is risen and springy to the touch. A skewer inserted into the centre should come out clean, but don't be tempted to test too early or the cake may sink.
5 Leave to cool completely in the tin. Take the cake out of the tin, peel off the parchment and transfer to a serving plate.
6 To decorate, dust the worksurface with icing sugar and roll out two-thirds of the marzipan until large enough for a 20.5cm (8in) circle (cut round the base of the cake tin). Heat the jam with 1 tsp water in a small pan over a medium heat until runny. Brush the top of the cake with some jam, then lay the almond paste circle on top and gently press down to stick. Using a small knife, score lines on top of the cake to make a diamond pattern. Crimp the edge of the marzipan using the thumb and forefinger of one hand, and the index finger of the other.
7 Roll the remaining marzipan into 11 equal-sized balls. Brush the underside of each with a little jam or water and stick around the edge of the cake. If you like, use a blowtorch to lightly brown the marzipan.

NUTRITION PER SLICE 555 cals | 23g fat (11g sats) | 79g carbs | 0.6g salt

Rich Fruit Cake

Cuts into 24 slices
Preparation time 30 minutes, plus soaking
Cooking time about 4 hours, plus cooling

500g (1lb 2oz) sultanas
400g (14oz) raisins
150g (5oz) each Agen prunes and
  dried figs, roughly chopped
200g (7oz) dried apricots, roughly
  chopped
zest and juice of 2 oranges
200ml (7fl oz) hazelnut liqueur,
  plus extra to drizzle
250g (9oz) unsalted butter, softened,
  plus extra to grease
150g (5oz) each dark muscovado
  and light brown soft sugar
200g plain flour, sifted
1 tsp ground cinnamon
1 tsp mixed spice
¼ tsp ground cloves
¼ tsp freshly grated nutmeg
pinch of salt
4 large eggs, beaten
100g (3½oz toasted, blanched
  hazelnuts, roughly chopped
40g (1½oz) toasted pinenuts
1 tbsp brandy (optional)

Makes enough to cover a 23cm (9in) cake
Preparation time about 30 minutes

4 tbsp apricot jam
1 fruit cake (see above)
icing sugar, sifted, to dust
450g (1lb) Almond Paste (see page 436)
vegetable oil to grease
150g (5oz) glacier mint sweets
500g pack royal icing sugar
silver ribbon

TO STORE

Once cut, store in a container in a cool,
dark place for up to two weeks.

1 Put the fruit into a non-metallic bowl and stir in the orange zest and juice and the hazelnut liqueur. Cover and leave to soak overnight, or up to three days.
2 Preheat the oven to 140°C (120°C fan oven) mark 1. Grease a 23cm (9in) cake tin and double-line with greaseproof paper, making sure the paper comes at least 5cm (2in) above the top of the tin. Grease the paper lightly. Then wrap a double layer of greaseproof paper around the outside of the tin, securing with string.
3 Using a hand-held electric mixer, beat together the butter and sugars in a large bowl until light and fluffy – this should take about 5 minutes.
4 In a separate bowl, sift together the flour, spices and salt. Beat 2 tbsp of the flour mix into the butter and sugar, then gradually add the eggs. If it looks as if the mixture might be about to curdle, add a little more flour.
5 Using a large metal spoon, fold the remaining flour into the mixture, followed by the soaked fruit and the nuts. Tip into the prepared tin and level the surface. Using the end of the spoon, make a hole in the centre of the mix, going right down to the base of the tin – this will stop the top of the cake rising into a dome shape as it cooks. Bake for 4 hours or until a skewer inserted into the centre comes out clean. Cover with foil if it is browning too quickly. Leave to cool in the tin for 10 minutes, then turn out on to a wire rack, keeping the greaseproof paper wrapped around the outside of the cake, and leave to cool completely.
6 To store, leave the cold cake in its greaseproof paper. Wrap a few layers of clingfilm around it, then cover with foil. Store in a cool place in an airtight container. After two weeks, unwrap the cake, prick all over and pour over 1 tbsp of hazelnut liqueur, or brandy if you prefer. Rewrap and store as before. Ice up to three days before serving.

ICING THE CAKE

1 Gently heat the jam in a pan with 1 tbsp water until softened, then press through a sieve. Put the cake on a board and brush with the jam glaze.
2 Dust a rolling pin and worksurface with icing sugar and roll out the almond paste to a circle 15cm (6in) larger than the cake. Position on the cake and ease to fit around the sides. Press out creases, trim, then leave to dry for 24 hours.
3 Preheat the oven to 180°C (160°C fan oven) mark 4. Line a baking sheet with foil and brush lightly with oil. Unwrap the mints and put pairs of sweets on the baking sheet about 1cm (½in) apart, leaving 5cm (2in) of space between each pair. Cook for 3–4 minutes until the sweets have melted and are just starting to bubble around the edges. Leave to cool for 3–4 minutes until firm enough to be lifted off the foil. Snip the pieces into large slivers and shards.
4 Wrap the ribbon around the edge of the cake. Make up the icing sugar with water according to the pack instructions. Using a small palette knife, spread the icing over the top of the cake, flicking it into small peaks, then tease down the sides of the cake to form icicles.
5 Push the mint shards into the top of the icing and insert the silver candles. Leave to dry. Light the candles and serve.

NUTRITION PER SLICE (cake and icing) 569 cals | 17g fat (6g sats) | 100g carbs | 0.2g salt

Quantities and sizes for rich fruit cake

To make a formal cake for a birthday, wedding or anniversary, this chart will show you the quantity of ingredients needed for the recipe on the previous page to fill the cake tin or tins, round or square.

Note: When baking large cakes, over 25.5cm (10in), reduce the oven temperature to 130°C (110°C fan oven)

mark ½ after two-thirds of the cooking time.

The amounts of almond paste quoted will give a thin covering. The quantities of royal icing should be enough for two coats. If you are using ready-to-roll fondant icing, follow the quantities suggested here for royal icing as a rough guide.

SIZE	SQUARE TIN	ROUND TIN	COOKING TIME	WEIGHT WHEN COOKED	INGREDIENTS
1	12.5cm (5in)	15cm (6in)	2½–3 hours	1.1kg (2½lb)	225g (8oz) currants, 125g (4oz) each sultanas and raisins, 50g (2oz) glacé cherries, 25g (1oz) each mixed peel and flaked almonds, 175g (6oz) plain flour, 4 tsp each mixed spice and cinnamon, 150g (5oz) each softened butter and soft brown sugar, a little lemon zest, 2½ medium eggs, beaten, 2–3 tbsp brandy. **Almond paste:** 350g (12oz) **Royal icing:** 450g (1lb)
2	15cm (6in)	18cm (7in)	3 hours	1.6kg (3½lb)	350g (12oz) currants, 125g (4oz) each sultanas and raisins, 75g (3oz) glacé cherries, 50g (2oz) each mixed peel and flaked almonds, 200g (7oz) plain flour, ½ tsp each mixed spice and cinnamon, 175g (6oz) each softened butter and soft brown sugar, a little lemon zest, 3 medium eggs, beaten, 2–3 tbsp brandy. **Almond paste:** 450g (1lb) **Royal icing:** 550g (1¼lb)
3	20.5cm (8in)	23cm (9in)	4 hours	2.7kg (6lb)	625g (1lb 6oz) currants, 225g (8oz) each sultanas and raisins, 175g (6oz) glacé cherries, 125g (4oz) each mixed peel and flaked almonds, 400g (14oz) plain flour, 1 tsp each cinnamon and mixed spice, 350g (12oz) each softened butter and soft brown sugar, zest of ¼ lemon, 6 medium eggs, beaten, 4–5 tbsp brandy. **Almond paste:** 800g (1¾lb) **Royal icing:** 900g (2lb)
4	23cm (9in)	25.5cm (10in)	6 hours	4kg (8lb 13oz)	800g (1¾lb) currants, 375g (13oz) each sultanas and raisins, 250g (9oz) glacé cherries, 150g (5oz) each mixed peel and flaked almonds, 600g (1lb 5oz) plain flour, 1 tsp each mixed spice and cinnamon, 500g (1lb 2oz) each softened butter and soft brown sugar, zest of ¼–½ lemon, 9 medium eggs, beaten, 5–6 tbsp brandy. **Almond paste:** 900g (2lb) **Royal icing:** 1kg (2¼lb)
5	28cm (11in)	30.5cm (12in)	8 hours	6.7kg (14¾lb)	1.5kg (3lb 4oz) currants, 525g (1lb 3oz) each sultanas and raisins, 350g (12oz) glacé cherries, 250g (9oz) each mixed peel and flaked almonds, zest of ½ lemon, 825g (1lb 13oz) plain flour, 2½ tsp each mixed spice and cinnamon, 800g (1¾lb) each softened butter and soft brown sugar, 14 medium eggs, beaten, 7–8 tbsp brandy. **Almond paste:** 1.1kg (2½lb) **Royal icing:** 1.4kg (3lb)
6	30.5cm (12in)	33cm (13in)	8½ hours	7.7kg (17lb)	1.7kg (3lb 12oz) currants, 625g (1lb 6oz) each sultanas and raisins, 425g (15oz) glacé cherries, 275g (10oz) each mixed peel and flaked almonds, 1kg (2¼lb) plain flour, 2½ tsp each mixed spice and cinnamon, 950g (2lb 2oz) each softened butter and soft brown sugar, zest of 1 lemon, 17 medium eggs, beaten, 8–9 tbsp brandy. **Almond paste:** 1.4kg (3lb) **Royal icing:** 1.6kg (3½lb)

Easter Fudge Chocolate Cake

Cuts into 12 slices
Preparation time 30 minutes, plus cooling
Cooking time about 50 minutes

175g (6oz) unsalted butter, softened, plus extra to grease
150g (5oz) plain flour
50g (2oz) cocoa powder
1 tsp baking powder
a pinch of salt
150g (5oz) light muscovado sugar
3 medium eggs, beaten
250ml (9fl oz) soured cream
1 tsp vanilla extract

For the icing and decoration
100g (3½oz) plain chocolate (at least 70% cocoa solids),
  finely chopped
150g (5oz) unsalted butter, softened
125g (4oz) cream cheese
175g (6oz) icing sugar, sifted
50g (2oz) Chocolate Curls (see page 379), lightly crushed
foil-covered chocolate eggs to decorate

1 Preheat the oven to 180°C (160°C fan oven) mark 4.
Grease and line a 20.5cm (8in) round springform tin.
2 Sift the flour, cocoa powder, baking powder and salt into
a large bowl.
3 Using an electric mixer or electric beaters, beat together
the butter and muscovado sugar in a separate bowl until
pale and fluffy. This will take about 5 minutes.
4 Gradually add the beaten eggs, mixing well after each
addition. Add a little of the flour mixture if the butter
mixture looks like curdling. In one go, add the remaining
flour mixture, the soured cream and vanilla extract, then
fold everything together gently with a metal spoon.
5 Spoon into the prepared tin and bake for 40–50 minutes
until a skewer inserted into centre comes out clean. Cool
in the tin.
6 To make the icing, melt the chocolate in a heatproof
bowl set over a pan of barely simmering water, making
sure the base of the bowl doesn't touch the water. Stir
occasionally, then remove the bowl from the heat and leave
to cool for 15 minutes.

7 In a separate bowl, beat the butter and cream cheese
with a wooden spoon until combined. Beat in the icing
sugar, then the cooled chocolate. Take care not to over-beat
the mixture – it should be fudgey, not stiff.
8 Remove the cake from the tin, cut in half horizontally
and use some icing to sandwich the layers together.
Transfer to a cake stand, then ice the top and sides,
smoothing with a palette knife. Decorate with crushed
curls and chocolate eggs.

NUTRITION PER SLICE 590 cals | 42g fat (25g sats) | 0g carbs | 0.1g salt Ⓥ

Celebration Cake

Serves 40

Preparation time 25 minutes, plus cooling, plus about
1 hour for filling and decoration

Cooking time 2 hours, plus cooling

350g (12oz) butter, chopped, plus extra to grease
350g (12oz) plain chocolate (at least 70% cocoa
  solids), broken into pieces
275ml (9fl oz) milk
375g (13oz) plain flour
3 tsp baking powder
60g (2½oz) cocoa powder
750g (1lb 11oz) caster sugar
6 medium eggs
250ml (8fl oz) soured cream

For the white chocolate buttercream filling
175g (6oz) white chocolate, chopped
250g (9oz) unsalted butter, softened
500g (1lb 2oz) icing sugar
3 tbsp milk

For the chocolate and fruit decoration
350g (12oz) plain chocolate (at least 70% cocoa
  solids), broken into pieces
mixed berries such as raspberries, strawberries,
  blackberries and blueberries
icing sugar to dust

1 Preheat the oven to 170°C (160°C fan oven) mark 3.
Grease a 25.5cm (10in) round cake tin and line with
baking parchment. Put the butter, chocolate and milk into
a pan and heat gently until melted, smooth and glossy. Set
aside to cool slightly.
2 Meanwhile, sift the flour, baking and cocoa powders into
a large bowl, then stir in the sugar. In a separate large jug,
mix together the eggs and soured cream. Pour both the
chocolate and egg mixtures into the flour bowl and whisk
well until combined.
3 Pour the cake mixture into the prepared tin and level
the surface, then bake in the centre of the oven for about
2 hours until a skewer inserted into the centre comes out
clean. Allow to cool completely in the tin before icing with
buttercream, and decorating.

4 While the cake is cooling, make the chocolate and fruit
decoration. Cover two large baking sheets or trays with
baking parchment and secure in place with tape.
5 Melt the chocolate in a bowl set over a pan of simmering
water, making sure the base of the bowl doesn't touch the
water. When smooth, take off the heat and pour half on to
each baking sheet. Spread the chocolate so it's just shorter
than the baking sheet in length, and twice the height of the
cake plus 7.5cm (3in) in width. Chill for 10 minutes.
6 Using a large, non-serrated knife, trim the edges of
chocolate to neaten, then cut in half lengthways. Now cut
across rectangles in parallel lines, about 4cm (1½in) apart,
to make shards. If you like, trim one end of each small
rectangle at an angle, then chill until solid.
7 When you are ready to decorate the cake, make the
buttercream filling. Melt the white chocolate in a heatproof
bowl set over a pan of gently simmering water, making sure
the base of the bowl doesn't touch the water. When melted
and smooth, remove from the heat and set aside to cool for
15 minutes.
8 Put the softened butter into a separate large bowl and
sift in the icing sugar. Using a hand-held electric whisk
and starting slowly (otherwise there will be clouds of icing
sugar), beat together until fluffy and combined. Beat in the
cooled white chocolate and the milk.
9 Take the cooled cake out of the tin and peel off the
parchment paper. Use a bread knife to level the top of the
cake, if necessary. Slice the cake in half horizontally.
10 Spread about half the buttercream over the bottom
half of the cake, then sandwich back together. Next, smear
a little buttercream on a cake board the same size as the
cake and stick the cake to the board. Spread the remaining
buttercream sparingly over the cake. Working quickly
before the buttercream sets, stick chocolate shards to the
side of the cake. Arrange the berries to cover the surface of
the cake, then lightly dust with icing sugar.

PREPARE AHEAD

Make the cake up to three days ahead, remove from the tin,
cool, then wrap first in baking parchment, then kitchen foil.
Alternatively, freeze the wrapped cake for up to two months.
Defrost at room temperature, then ice and decorate.

NUTRITION PER SLICE 418 cals | 21g fat (13g sats) | 52g carbs | 0.4g salt

Rosebud Wedding Cake

Cuts into 180–200 slices
Preparation time at least 1 day, plus drying
Cooking time see chart page 428

250g (9oz) sugar flower paste (available
from cake decorating suppliers as are
the other supplies)
pink food colouring (note that many
food colourings are not vegetarian)
30.5cm (12in) round Rich Fruit Cake
(see page 428), covered in Almond
Paste set on a 40.5cm (16in) cake
board (drum)
5kg (11lb) white ready-to-roll icing
23cm (9in) round Rich Fruit Cake,
covered in Almond Paste set on a
23cm (9in) cake board (double thick)
15cm (6in) round Rich Fruit Cake,
covered in Almond Paste set on a
15cm (6in) cake board (double thick)
no. 2 and no. 3 piping nozzles
white Royal Icing (see page 437) made
with 225g (8oz) icing sugar
6 plastic cake dowels
pink ribbon

1 To make sugar roses, colour the flower paste different shades of pale pink.
Roll the flower paste out thinly, using only small amounts at a time, and cut out
a 5-petal rose shape with a petal cutter. Each petal should be about 2cm (¾in)
wide and 1cm (½in) long. Thin the edges of the petals slightly with a bone tool,
or roll them over a cocktail stick. Make a cone shape a bit smaller than the size
of the petals.
2 Dampen the lower part of each petal with a little water and wrap the petals
around the cone one at a time, slightly overlapping each petal as you go.
Repeat with a second set of 5 petals. Using your fingers, curl the outer edges
of the petals to give a natural rose shape. Repeat to make at least 12 roses.
Use a smaller cutter to make at least 24 roses for the sides of the cakes. Leave
overnight to harden.
3 Take the largest cake on its cake board. Roll out some of the ready-to-roll
icing so that it is 5mm (¼in) thick and large enough to cover the cake. Dampen
the cake with a little boiled water. Lift the icing on to the cake and smooth over
the top and sides, trimming the excess icing away around the base. Dampen the
surrounding cake board. Roll out a long thin strip of icing to cover the board
and trim away the excess. Ice the two smaller tiers in the same way.
4 Cut a circle of greaseproof paper to the size of the top of each cake. Fold the
largest two into eight segments, the smallest into six segments. Using a compass
or the bottom of a glass with the correct diameter, pencil a scallop on the
rounded edge between the folds about 5cm (2in) deep for the larger cakes and
2.5cm (1in) deep for the top tier. Cut out the scallops.
5 Open out the paper and place the smallest piece in the centre of the smallest
cake and the two larger pieces in the centre of the two larger cakes. Hold the
paper with one hand and prick the scalloped outline on to the icing with a pin.
6 For the side scallops, cut a strip of greaseproof paper the circumference of
the cake. As before, fold into eight segments and mark the scallops in the same
way. Remove the paper and, using an icing bag fitted with the plain no. 3 icing
nozzle and filled with white royal icing, pipe a line of icing along the line of the
scallops. Leave to dry for about 1 hour before piping a second, thinner line on
top of the first using the no. 2 nozzle.
7 Using a pin, mark the diameter of the middle cake on top of the first (largest)
cake. Measure a square within the diameter and push a dowel into each corner
until it reaches the bottom of the cake. Using a pencil, mark on each dowel
where it emerges from the surface of the cake. Remove. Cut the dowels at the
pencil mark with a craft knife or hacksaw, making sure they are all the same
length. Push back into the holes. Spread a little royal icing over the centre. Put
the next cake layer on top, then repeat the previous steps.
8 Secure a piece of ribbon around each cake with a small dot of royal icing.
9 Complete the decoration by piling up the large icing roses on the centre of
the top cake and placing a smaller rose at each of the points where the scallops
meet. Surround with fresh roses and petals, if you like.

NUTRITION PER SLICE 555 cals | 16g fat (5g sats) | 92g carbs | 0.2g salt Ⓥ

Icings and Frostings

Icings and frostings are used to fill, cover and decorate cakes. Some are poured smoothly over the cake, others need to be spread or swirled to give a textured finish. Sometimes the same mixture is used to fill and cover the cake, or it may be different – a jam-filled sponge, for example, can be topped with buttercream or glacé icing.

The filling must have the right consistency for spreading: if too firm it will pull the crumbs from the cake, making an untidy layer; if too soft it will cause the cake layers to slip and move around, and ooze out of the side of the cake.

To cover a cake with buttercream icing, use a small palette knife dipped in hot water to spread the icing smoothly and evenly. For a textured effect, paddle the palette knife backwards and forwards, or swirl the icing decoratively. For a more formal finish, pipe a design directly on to the surface of the cake, such as a piped scroll, shell or swirl edging. Jam for a filling should be warmed gently until thinned to a spreading consistency.

If you are covering a cake with frosting, it should be thick enough to coat the back of a spoon. Frostings are often warm at this stage; if too thick, the bowl will need to be placed over hot water, or the frosting may be thinned with a little water. If the frosting is too slack, leave it to cool and thicken slightly. Pour all the frosting over the top of the cake and allow it to fall over the sides, gently tapping the cake to encourage it to flow; don't be tempted to use a knife, which would leave marks. When the frosting has stopped falling, neaten the bottom edge and allow to dry. Once a cake has been covered with icing or frosting, the sides may be coated with crushed praline, grated chocolate or toasted chopped or flaked nuts.

Glacé Icing

Makes 225g (8oz), enough to cover the top of one large sandwich cake, or about 18 fairy cakes
Preparation time 5 minutes

225g (8oz) icing sugar
few drops of vanilla extract (optional)
few drops of food colouring (optional)

1 Sift the icing sugar into a bowl. Add a few drops of vanilla extract, if you like.
2 Using a wooden spoon, gradually stir in 2–3 tbsp hot water until the mixture is the consistency of thick cream. Beat until white and smooth and the icing is thick enough to coat the back of the spoon. Add colouring if you like, and use straight away.

TRY SOMETHING DIFFERENT
Orange or Lemon Glacé Icing Replace the water with strained orange or lemon juice.
Chocolate Glacé Icing Sift 2 tsp cocoa powder with the icing sugar.
Coffee Glacé Icing Flavour the icing with 1 tsp coffee essence or 2 tsp instant coffee granules dissolved in 1 tbsp of the hot water.

NUTRITION PER 25g (1oz) 100 cals | 0g fat | 26g carbs | trace salt (V)

Buttercream

Makes 250g (9oz), enough to cover the top of a 20.5cm (8in) cake; increase by one-third to make enough to cover the top and sides
Preparation time 5 minutes

75g (3oz) unsalted butter, softened
175g (6oz) icing sugar, sifted
few drops of vanilla extract
1–2 tbsp milk or water

1 Put the butter into a bowl and beat with a wooden spoon until it is light and fluffy.
2 Gradually stir in the icing sugar, vanilla extract and milk. Beat well until light and smooth.

TRY SOMETHING DIFFERENT
Orange, Lime or Lemon Buttercream Replace the vanilla extract with a little finely grated orange, lime or lemon zest. Add 1–2 tbsp juice from the fruit instead of the milk, beating well to avoid curdling the mixture. If the mixture is to be piped, omit the zest.
Chocolate Buttercream Blend 1 tbsp cocoa powder with 2 tbsp boiling water and cool before adding to the mixture.
Coffee Buttercream Replace the vanilla extract with 2 tsp instant coffee granules dissolved in 1 tbsp boiling water; cool before adding to the mixture.

NUTRITION PER 25g (1oz) 118 cals | 6g fat (4g sats) | 17g carbs | 0.1g salt (V)

Coffee Fudge Frosting

Makes 400g (14oz), enough to cover the top and sides of a 20.5cm (8in) cake
Preparation time 5 minutes
Cooking time 5 minutes

50g (2oz) butter
125g (4oz) light muscovado sugar
2 tbsp single cream or milk
1 tbsp coffee granules dissolved in 2 tbsp boiling water
200g (7oz) golden icing sugar, sifted

1 Put the butter, muscovado sugar, cream or milk and coffee into a pan. Heat gently until the sugar dissolves, then bring to the boil and boil briskly for 3 minutes.
2 Remove from the heat and gradually stir in the icing sugar. Beat with a wooden spoon for 1 minute until smooth.
3 Use the frosting immediately. Spread over the cake with a wet palette knife, or dilute with water for a smooth coating.

TRY SOMETHING DIFFERENT
Chocolate Fudge Frosting Omit the coffee. Add 75g (3oz) plain chocolate (at least 70% cocoa solids), broken into pieces, to the pan with the butter at the start of step 1.

NUTRITION PER 25g (1oz) 110 cals | 3g fat (2g sats) | 21g carbs | 0.1g salt Ⓥ

American Frosting

Makes 225g (8oz), enough to cover the top and sides of a 20.5cm (8in) cake
Preparation time 15 minutes
Cooking time 5 minutes

1 large egg white
225g (8oz) golden caster or granulated sugar
a pinch of cream of tartar

1 Put the egg white into a clean, grease-free bowl and whisk until it forms stiff peaks. Put the sugar, 4 tbsp water and the cream of tartar into a heavy-based pan. Heat gently, stirring, until the sugar has dissolved. Bring to the boil, without stirring, and boil until the syrup registers 115°C on a sugar thermometer. (Alternatively, in cold water, the mixture will form a soft ball which you can easily squash between your finger and thumb.)
2 Remove from the heat and, as the bubbles subside, pour the syrup on to the egg white in a thin stream, whisking constantly until thick and white. Leave to cool slightly.
3 When the frosting begins to turn dull around the edges and is almost cold, pour quickly over the cake and spread evenly with a palette knife.

NUTRITION PER 25g (1oz) 100 cals | 0g fat | 6g carbs | trace salt Ⓥ

Vanilla Frosting

Makes about 175g (6oz), enough to cover the top and sides of an 18cm (7in) cake
Preparation time 5 minutes

150g (5oz) icing sugar, sifted
5 tsp vegetable oil
1 tbsp milk
a few drops of vanilla extract

1 Put the icing sugar into a bowl and beat in the oil, milk and vanilla extract until smooth.

NUTRITION PER 25g (1oz) 102 cals | 2g fat (0.3g sats) | 22g carbs | trace salt Ⓥ

7-minute Frosting

Makes about 175g (6oz), enough to cover the top and sides of an 18cm (7in) cake
Preparation time 15 minutes
Cooking time 5 minutes

1 medium egg white
175g (6oz) caster sugar
2 tbsp water
a pinch of salt
a pinch of cream of tartar

1 Put all the ingredients into a heatproof bowl and whisk lightly, using an electric or hand whisk.
2 Put over a pan of hot water. Heat, whisking, for about 7 minutes until the mixture thickens enough to stand in peaks. Pour over the cake and spread with a palette knife.

NUTRITION PER 25g (1oz) 74 cals | 0g fat | 19g carbs | 0.1g salt Ⓥ

Chocolate Ganache

Makes 475g (1lb 1oz), enough to cover an 18cm (7in) round cake
Preparation time 10 minutes
Cooking time 1 minute, plus cooling

225g (8oz) plain chocolate (at least 70% cocoa solids),
  broken into small pieces
250ml (9fl oz) double cream

1 Put the chocolate into a medium heatproof bowl. Pour
the cream into a small heavy-based pan and bring to the
boil over a low heat.
2 Immediately pour the cream on to the chocolate and stir
gently in one direction until the chocolate has melted and
the mixture is smooth. Set aside to cool for 5 minutes.
3 Whisk the ganache until it begins to hold its shape.
Used at room temperature, the mixture should be the
consistency of softened butter.

TRY SOMETHING DIFFERENT
These are all suitable for a sauce made with 225g (8oz)
chocolate:
Milk or single cream Substitute in whole or in part
for the water.
Coffee Stir in 1 tsp instant coffee or a shot of espresso when
melting the chocolate.
Spices Add a pinch of ground cinnamon, crushed cardamom
seeds or freshly grated nutmeg to the melting chocolate.
Vanilla extract Stir in ¼ tsp vanilla extract when melting
the chocolate.
Rum, whisky or cognac Stir in about 1 tsp alcohol when
melting the chocolate.
Butter Stir in 25g (1oz) towards the end of heating.

NUTRITION PER 50g (2oz) 298 cals | 25g fat (15g sats) |
18g carbs | trace salt Ⓥ

Apricot Glaze

Makes 450g (1lb)
Preparation time 5 minutes
Cooking time 2 minutes

450g (1lb) apricot jam

1 Put the jam and 2 tbsp water into a pan and heat gently,
stirring occasionally, until melted. Boil the jam rapidly for
1 minute, then strain through a sieve.
2 Using a wooden spoon, rub through as much fruit as
possible. Discard the skins left in the sieve.
3 Pour the glaze into a clean, hot jar, then seal with a clean
lid and cool. Store in the fridge for up to two months.
To use, brush over cakes before icing or applying almond
paste, or use to glaze fruit finishes. If the consistency is a
little stiff, then stir in a few drops of boiled water. You only
need 3–4 tbsp apricot glaze for a 23cm (9in) cake, so this
quantity will glaze six to seven cakes.

NUTRITION PER 25g (1oz) 60 cals | 0g fat |
16g carbs | trace salt Ⓥ

Almond Paste

Makes 450g (1lb), enough to cover the top and sides of an 18cm
  (7in) round cake or 15cm (6in) square cake
Preparation time 10 minutes

225g (8oz) ground almonds
125g (4oz) golden caster sugar
125g (4oz) golden icing sugar
1 large egg
1 tsp lemon juice
1 tsp sherry (see Alcoholic Drinks and Vegetarians, page 489)
1–2 drops of vanilla extract

1 Put the ground almonds, caster sugar and icing sugar
into a bowl and mix together. In a separate bowl, whisk the
egg with the remaining ingredients and add to the
dry mixture.
2 Stir well to mix, pounding gently to release some of the
oil from the almonds. Knead with your hands until smooth.
Cover until ready to use.

Cook's Tip
If you wish to avoid using raw egg to bind the almond paste,
mix the other liquid ingredients with a little water instead.

NUTRITION PER 25g (1oz) 130 cals | 7g fat (1g sats) |
15g carbs | trace salt Ⓥ

Royal Icing

Makes 450g (1lb), enough to cover the top and sides of a 20.5cm (8in) cake

Preparation time 20 minutes

2 large egg whites, or 1 tbsp egg albumen powder
2 tsp liquid glycerine
450g (1lb) icing sugar, sifted

1 If using the egg whites and the glycerine, put them in a bowl and stir just enough to break up the egg whites. If you are using albumen powder, mix according to the pack instructions.
2 Add a little icing sugar and mix gently with a wooden spoon to incorporate as little air as possible.
3 Add a little more icing sugar as the mixture becomes lighter. Continue to add the icing sugar, stirring gently but thoroughly until the mixture is stiff and stands in soft peaks. For coating it should form soft peaks; for piping it should be a little stiffer.
4 Transfer to an airtight container, cover the surface closely with clingfilm to prevent it drying out, then seal. When required, stir the icing slowly.

NUTRITION PER 25g (1oz) 100 cals | 0g fat |
26g carbs | trace salt Ⓥ

Easiest Icing

Makes 675g (1lb 7oz), enough to cover a 20.5cm (8in) almond paste-covered cake

Preparation time 20 minutes, plus drying

3 medium egg whites
2 tbsp lemon juice
2 tsp glycerine
675g (1lb 7oz) icing sugar, sifted

1 Put the egg whites into a large bowl and whisk until frothy. There should be just a layer of bubbles across the top. Add the lemon juice, glycerine and 2 tbsp icing sugar, and whisk until smooth.
2 Whisk in the rest of the sugar, a little at a time, until the mixture is smooth, thick and forming soft peaks.
3 Using a palette knife, smooth half the icing over the top and sides of the cake, then repeat using the remaining icing to cover. Run the knife around the sides to neaten, then use the tip to make peaks all over the top. Leave to dry in a cool place for at least 48 hours.

NUTRITION PER 25g (1oz) 84 cals | 0g fat |
22g carbs | trace salt Ⓥ

Ready-to-roll Fondant Icing

Ready-to-roll icing is pliable and can be used to cover cakes or moulded into decorative shapes. Blocks of ready-to-roll icing (fondant or sugar paste) are available in a variety of colours from supermarkets and specialist cake decorating shops. A 450g (1lb) pack will cover an 18cm (7in) cake. Wrap any unused icing in clingfilm to stop it drying out and store in a cool, dry place.

Biscuits

Shortbread

Makes 18 biscuits
Preparation time 20 minutes, plus chilling
Cooking time 15–20 minutes, plus cooling

225g (8oz) butter, at room temperature
125g (4oz) golden caster sugar
225g (8oz) plain flour
125g (4oz) rice flour
a pinch of salt
golden or coloured granulated sugar to coat
caster sugar to sprinkle

1 Cream the butter and sugar together in a bowl until pale and fluffy. Sift the flours and salt together on to the creamed mixture and stir in, using a wooden spoon, until the mixture resembles breadcrumbs.
2 Gather the dough together with your hand and turn on to a clean surface. Knead very lightly until it forms a ball, then lightly roll into a sausage, about 5cm (2in) thick. Wrap in clingfilm and chill in the fridge until firm.
3 Preheat the oven to 190°C (170°C fan oven) mark 5. Line two baking sheets with greaseproof paper. Remove the clingfilm and slice the dough into discs, 7–10mm (⅓–½in) thick. Pour some granulated sugar on to a plate and roll the edge of each disc in the sugar. Put the shortbread, cut side up, on the baking sheets.
4 Bake the shortbread for 15–20 minutes, depending on thickness, until very pale golden. Remove from the oven and sprinkle with caster sugar. Leave on the baking sheets for 10 minutes to cool slightly, then transfer to a wire rack and leave to finish cooling.

TO STORE
Store in an airtight container. They will keep for up to two weeks.

NUTRITION PER BISCUIT 190 cals | 10g fat (7g sats) | 23g carbs | 0.3 g salt Ⓥ

Ultimate Chocolate Chip Cookies

Makes about 25 cookies
Preparation time 15 minutes
Cooking time about 12 minutes

225g (8oz) unsalted butter, very soft
125g (4oz) caster sugar
150g (5oz) light muscovado sugar
1½ tbsp golden syrup
1 tsp vanilla extract
2 large eggs, beaten
375g (13oz) plain flour
1 tsp bicarbonate of soda
¼ tsp salt
350g (12oz) milk chocolate, cut into large chunks

1 Preheat the oven to 200°C (180°C fan oven) mark 6.
Line three baking sheets with baking parchment.
2 Put the butter, caster and muscovado sugars, golden
syrup and vanilla extract into a bowl and, using a hand-
held electric whisk or freestanding mixer, beat until pale
and fluffy – this should take about 5 minutes.
3 Gradually beat in the eggs, adding 2 tbsp flour if
the mixture looks as if it's about to curdle. Sift in the
remaining flour, the bicarbonate of soda and salt all at once
and beat in quickly for a few seconds. Using a large metal
spoon, mix in the milk chocolate chunks.
4 Spoon heaped teaspoonfuls of the mixture on to the
baking sheets, spacing them well apart. Don't press the
mixture down – the mounds will spread during baking. For
a chewy biscuit, bake for 10 minutes until pale and golden;
for a crisper version, bake for 12 minutes. Transfer from the
trays on to wire racks and leave to cool.

TO STORE
Store in an airtight container. They will keep for up to
one week.

NUTRITION PER COOKIE 223 cals | 11g fat (7g sats) | 28g carbs | 0.9g salt Ⓥ

Sultana and Pecan Cookies

Makes 20
Preparation time 15 minutes
Cooking time 12–15 minutes, plus cooling

225g (8oz) unsalted butter, at room temperature,
 plus extra to grease
175g (6oz) light muscovado sugar
2 medium eggs, lightly beaten
225g (8oz) pecan nut halves
300g (11oz) self-raising flour, sifted
¼ tsp baking powder
125g (4oz) sultanas
2 tbsp maple syrup

1 Preheat the oven to 190°C (170°C fan oven) mark 5.
Lightly grease four baking sheets.
2 Cream the butter and sugar together until the mixture is
pale and fluffy. Gradually beat in the eggs until thoroughly
combined.
3 Put 20 pecan nut halves to one side, then roughly chop
the rest and fold into the mixture with the flour, baking
powder, sultanas and syrup.
4 Roll the mixture into 20 balls and place them, spaced
well apart, on the prepared baking sheets. Using a
dampened palette knife, flatten the cookies and top each
with a piece of pecan nut.
5 Bake for 12–15 minutes until pale golden. Leave on the
baking sheets for 5 minutes, then transfer to a wire rack
and leave to cool completely.

TO STORE
Store in an airtight container. They will keep for up to
one week.

Freezing Tip
• To freeze, complete the recipe to the end of step 4, then
 open-freeze a tray of unbaked cookies. When frozen, pack
 into bags or containers.
• To use, cook from frozen for 18–20 minutes.

NUTRITION PER COOKIE 276 cals | 18g fat (7g sats) | 27g carbs | 0.2g salt Ⓥ

Christmas Cookies

Makes about 22 cookies
Preparation time 25 minutes, plus chilling
Cooking time about 15 minutes, plus cooling

75g (3oz) unsalted butter, softened
100g (3½oz) caster sugar
1 medium egg
½ tsp vanilla extract
250g (9oz) plain flour, plus extra to dust
½ tsp baking powder
a selection of coloured ready-to-roll fondant icings,
  Royal Icing (see page 437), food colourings and edible
  decorations

1 Using a wooden spoon, cream the butter and sugar
together in a large bowl until smooth. Beat in the egg
and vanilla extract. Sift the flour and baking powder into
the bowl and stir until combined. Tip out on to a lightly
floured surface and knead gently to make a soft dough.
Shape into a disc and wrap in clingfilm, then chill for
1 hour until firm.
2 Preheat the oven to 180°C (160°C fan oven) mark 4.
Roll out the dough on a lightly floured surface until 5mm
(¼in) thick. Using Christmas cookie cutters, stamp out
shapes, re-rolling the trimmings if necessary. If the cookies
are to be hung as decorations, use a skewer to make a 5mm
(¼in) hole in each one. Place on two non-stick baking trays
and bake for 10–15 minutes until pale golden and risen.
Leave to cool on the trays for 3 minutes to harden, then
transfer to a wire rack to cool completely.
3 When the cookies are completely cool, decorate
with coloured fondant icings or royal icing and edible
decorations.

TO STORE
Store in an airtight container. They will keep for up to
two weeks.

NUTRITION PER COOKIE 94 cals | 3g fat (2g sats) | 16.5g carbs | 0.1g salt Ⓥ

Ginger Biscuits

Makes 24 biscuits
Preparation time 15 minutes
Cooking time about 12 minutes, plus
cooling

50g (2oz) butter, plus extra to
grease
125g (4oz) golden syrup
50g (2oz) dark muscovado sugar
finely grated zest of 1 orange
2 tbsp orange juice
175g (6oz) self-raising flour
1 tsp ground ginger

1 Preheat the oven to 180°C (160°C
fan oven) mark 4. Lightly grease two
large baking sheets.
2 Put the butter, golden syrup, sugar,
orange zest and juice into a heavy-
based pan and heat very gently until
melted and evenly blended.

3 Leave the mixture to cool slightly,
then sift in the flour with the ginger.
Mix thoroughly until smooth. Put
small spoonfuls of the mixture on the
baking sheets, spacing them well apart
to allow room for spreading.
4 Bake for 12 minutes or until the
biscuits are golden brown. Leave on
the baking sheets for 1 minute, then
carefully transfer to a wire rack and
leave to cool.

TO STORE
Store in an airtight container. They will
keep for up to five days.

NUTRITION PER BISCUIT 55 cals |
2g fat (1g sats) | 10g carbs | 0.1g salt Ⓥ

Almond Macaroons

Makes 22 biscuits
Preparation time 10 minutes
Cooking time 12–15 minutes, plus cooling

2 medium egg whites
125g (4oz) caster sugar
125g (4oz) ground almonds
¼ tsp almond extract
22 blanched almonds

1 Preheat the oven to 180°C (fan
oven 160°C) mark 4. Line two baking
sheets with baking parchment.
2 Whisk the egg whites in a clean,
grease-free bowl until stiff peaks
form. Gradually whisk in the sugar, a
little at a time, until thick and glossy.
Gently stir in the ground almonds and
almond extract.
3 Spoon teaspoonfuls of the mixture
on to the prepared baking sheets,

spacing them slightly apart. Press
an almond into the centre of
each one and bake in the oven for
12–15 minutes until just golden and
firm to the touch.
4 Leave on the baking sheets for
10 minutes, then transfer to a wire
rack and leave to cool completely. On
cooling, these biscuits have a soft,
chewy centre; they harden up after a
few days.

TO STORE
Store in airtight containers. They will
keep for up to one week.

NUTRITION PER MACAROON 86
cals | 6g fat (1g sats) | 7g carbs | 0g salt Ⓥ

Florentines

Makes 18
Preparation time 15 minutes
Cooking time 16–20 minutes, plus cooling

65g (2½oz) unsalted butter, plus extra to grease
50g (2oz) golden caster sugar
2 tbsp double cream
25g (1oz) sunflower seeds
20g (¾oz) chopped mixed candied peel
20g (¾oz) sultanas
25g (1oz) natural glacé cherries, roughly chopped
40g (1½oz) flaked almonds, lightly crushed
15g (½oz) plain flour
125g (4oz) plain chocolate (at least 70% cocoa solids),
  broken into pieces

1 Preheat the oven to 180°C (160°C fan oven) mark 4.
Lightly grease two large baking sheets.
2 Melt the butter in a small heavy-based pan. Add the
sugar and heat gently until dissolved, then bring to the boil.
Take off the heat and stir in the cream, seeds, peel, sultanas,
cherries, almonds and flour. Mix until evenly combined.
Put heaped teaspoonfuls on to the prepared baking sheets,
spaced well apart to allow for spreading.
3 Bake one sheet at a time, for 6–8 minutes, until the
biscuits have spread considerably and the edges are golden
brown. Using a large plain metal biscuit cutter, push the
edges into the centre to create neat rounds. Bake for a
further 2 minutes or until deep golden. Leave on the
baking sheet for 2 minutes, then transfer to a wire rack and
leave to cool completely.
4 Melt the chocolate in a heatproof bowl set over a pan
of gently simmering water, making sure the base of the
bowl doesn't touch the water, stirring occasionally. Spread
on the underside of each Florentine and mark wavy lines
with a fork. Put, chocolate side up, on a sheet of baking
parchment and leave to set.

TO STORE
Store in an airtight container. They will keep for up to two
weeks.

NUTRITION PER BISCUIT 115 cals | 8g fat (4g sats) | 11g carbs | 0.1g salt Ⓥ

Chocolate Viennese Fingers

Makes 20 fingers
Preparation time 15 minutes
Cooking time 15–20 minutes, plus cooling

125g (4oz) butter, softened, plus extra to grease
25g (1oz) icing sugar, sifted
125g (4oz) plain flour
¼ tsp baking powder
a few drops of vanilla extract
50g (2oz) plain chocolate or plain chocolate-flavour cake
  covering, broken into pieces
icing sugar, sifted to decorate (optional)

1 Preheat the oven to 190°C (170°C fan oven) mark 5 and
grease two baking sheets.
2 Beat the butter until smooth, then beat in the icing sugar
until pale and fluffy.
3 Sift in the flour and baking powder. Beat well, adding
the vanilla extract.
4 Put into a piping bag fitted with a medium star nozzle.
Pipe out finger shapes, about 7.5cm (3in) long, on to the
baking sheets, spacing them well apart.
5 Bake for 15–20 minutes until dry and golden. Cool on a
wire rack.
6 Melt the chocolate in a heatproof bowl over a pan of
gently simmering water. Dip the ends of each Viennese
Finger into the melted chocolate. Leave to set on the wire
rack. Dredge with icing sugar, if you like.

TO STORE
Store in an airtight container. They will keep for up to
one week.

NUTRITION PER BISCUIT 86 cals | 6g fat (4g sats) | 8g carbs | 0.1g salt Ⓥ

Hazelnut and Chocolate Biscotti

Makes about 28 biscotti
Preparation time 10 minutes
Cooking time 35–40 minutes, plus cooling

125g (4oz) plain flour, sifted, plus extra to dust
75g (3oz) golden caster sugar
¼ tsp baking powder
a pinch of cinnamon
a pinch of salt
1 large egg, beaten
1 tbsp milk
¼ tsp vanilla extract
25g (1oz) hazelnuts
25g (1oz) plain chocolate chips

1 Preheat the oven to 200°C (180°C fan oven) mark 6.
2 Put the flour into a large bowl. Stir in the sugar, baking powder, cinnamon and salt. Make a well in the centre and, using a fork, stir in the beaten egg, milk, vanilla extract, hazelnuts and chocolate chips to form a sticky dough.
3 Turn out the dough on to a lightly floured surface and gently knead into a ball. Roll into a 28cm (11in) log shape. Put on a non-stick baking sheet and flatten slightly. Bake for 20–25 minutes until pale golden.
4 Reduce the oven temperature to 150°C (130°C fan oven) mark 2. Transfer the biscotti log on to a chopping board and slice diagonally with a bread knife at 1cm (½in) intervals. Arrange the slices on the baking sheet and put back into the oven for 15 minutes or until golden and dry. Transfer to a wire rack and leave to cool completely.

TO STORE
Store in an airtight container. They will keep for up to one month.

Cook's Tips
• To enjoy Italian-style, dunk in coffee or dessert wine.
• To make as gifts, divide the biscuits among four large squares of cellophane, then draw up the edges and tie with ribbon. Label the packages with storage information and an eat-by date.

NUTRITION PER BISCOTTI 50 cals | 1g fat (trace sats) | 9g carbs | 0g salt Ⓥ

Millionaire's Shortbread

Makes 20 squares
Preparation time 30 minutes
Cooking time 20 minutes, plus cooling

175g (6oz) unsalted butter, at room temperature, diced,
  plus extra to grease
250g (9oz) plain flour, plus extra to dust
75g (3oz) golden caster sugar

For the topping
2 × 397g cans sweetened condensed milk
100g (3½ oz) light muscovado sugar
100g (3½ oz) butter
250g (9oz) plain chocolate (at least 70% cocoa solids),
  broken into pieces

1 Preheat the oven to 180°C (160°C fan oven) mark 4.
Grease a 33 × 23cm (13 × 9in) Swiss roll tin and line
with baking parchment. Put the flour, caster sugar and
butter into a food processor and blend until the mixture
forms crumbs, then pulse a little more until it forms a
ball. (Alternatively, rub the butter into the flour and sugar
in a large bowl by hand, or using a pastry cutter, until it
resembles fine crumbs. Gather together into a ball.) Turn
out on to a lightly floured surface and knead lightly to
combine.
2 Press the mixture into the prepared tin and bake for 20
minutes or until firm to the touch and a very pale brown.
3 To make the topping, put the condensed milk,
muscovado sugar and butter into a non-stick pan and cook
over a medium heat, stirring continuously until a fudge-
like consistency. (Alternatively, put into a heatproof bowl
and microwave on full power for 12 minutes – based on
a 900W oven – or until the mixture is thick and fudgy,
beating with a whisk every 2–3 minutes.) Spoon the
caramel on to the shortbread, smooth over and allow to
cool.
4 To finish, melt the chocolate in a heatproof bowl set
over a pan of gently simmering water, making sure the base
of the bowl doesn't touch the water, then pour over the
caramel layer. Leave to set at room temperature, then cut
into 20 squares to serve.

TO STORE
Store in an airtight container. They will keep for up to
one week.

NUTRITION PER SQUARE 369 cals | 19g fat (12g sats) | 48g carbs | 0.4g salt Ⓥ

Traditional Flapjacks

Makes 12 squares
Preparation time 10 minutes
Cooking time 17 minutes, plus cooling

200g (7oz) butter, plus extra to grease
150g (5oz) demerara sugar
4 tbsp golden syrup
1 tsp ground cinnamon
finely grated zest of ½–1 orange to taste
400g (14oz) jumbo oats
100g (3½oz) raisins or sultanas

1 Preheat the oven to 190°C (170°C fan oven) mark 5.
Grease a 20.5cm (8in) square baking tin and line with
baking parchment.
2 Melt the butter in a large pan and add the sugar,
syrup, cinnamon and orange zest. Heat gently until the
sugar dissolves.
3 Remove the pan from the heat and stir in the oats and
raisins or sultanas. Press the mixture into the prepared
tin and bake for 17–20 minutes until lightly golden. Cool
before cutting into squares.

TO STORE
Store the flapjacks in an airtight container for up to
three days.

NUTRITION PER SQUARE 354 cals | 17g fat (9g sats) | 50g carbs | 0.4g salt Ⓥ

Breads, Pizzas and Pastries

White Farmhouse Loaf ⓑ

Cuts into about 12 slices
Preparation time 10 minutes, plus machine dough-making and
  rising
Cooking time 30–35 minutes, plus cooling

1 tsp easy-blend dried yeast
500g (1lb 2oz) strong white bread flour, plus extra
  to sprinkle
1 tbsp caster sugar
2 tbsp milk powder
1½ tsp salt
25g (1oz) butter
350ml (12fl oz) water

1 Put the ingredients into the bread maker bucket,
following the order and method specified in the manual.
2 Fit the bucket into the bread maker and set to the Basic
program with a crust of your choice. Press start.
3 Just before baking starts, brush the top of the dough
with water and sprinkle with flour. If preferred, slash the
top of the bread lengthways with a sharp knife, taking care
not to scratch the bucket.
4 After baking, remove the bread from the machine and
shake out on to a wire rack to cool.

Cook's Tip
To make conventionally, follow the method for the
Wholemeal Loaf opposite.

NUTRITION PER SLICE 180 cals | 3g fat (1g sats) | 34g carbs | 0.9g salt ⓥ

Wholemeal Loaf

Cuts into 16 slices
Preparation time 15 minutes, plus rising
Cooking time 30–35 minutes, plus cooling

225g (8oz) strong white bread flour, plus extra to dust
450g (1lb) strong wholemeal bread flour
2 tsp salt
1 tsp golden caster sugar
2 tsp easy-blend dried yeast (see Cook's Tip)
vegetable oil to grease

1 Sift the white flour into a large bowl and stir in the
wholemeal flour, salt, sugar and yeast. Make a well in
the centre and add about 450ml (¾ pint) warm water.
Work to a smooth, soft dough, adding a little extra
water if necessary.
2 Knead for 10 minutes or until smooth, then shape the
dough into a ball and put into an oiled bowl. Cover and
leave to rise in a warm place for 2 hours or until doubled
in size.
3 Knock back the dough on a lightly floured surface and
shape into a rectangle. Press into an oiled 900g (2lb) loaf
tin, cover and leave to rise for a further 30 minutes.
4 Preheat the oven to 230°C (210°C fan oven) mark 8.
Bake the loaf for 15 minutes. Reduce the oven temperature
to 200°C (180°C fan oven) mark 6 and bake for a further
15–20 minutes until the bread is risen and sounds hollow
when tapped underneath. Leave in the tin for 10 minutes,
then turn out on to a wire rack and leave to cool.

Cook's Tip
If available, use 40g (1½oz) fresh yeast instead of dried.
Blend the yeast and sugar and leave for 15 minutes to
froth, then add to the flour and salt.

NUTRITION PER SLICE 140 cals | 1g fat (0.1g sats) | 29g carbs | 0.6g salt Ⓥ

Granary Bread

Cuts into 16 slices
Preparation time 20 minutes, plus rising
Cooking time 30–35 minutes, plus cooling

125g (4oz) strong wholemeal bread
  flour, plus extra to dust
450g (1lb) malted strong Granary flour
2 tsp salt
15g (½oz) butter, diced
125g (4oz) rolled oats, plus extra to dust
2 tsp easy-blend dried yeast
150ml (¼ pint) warm milk
1 tbsp malt extract
vegetable oil to grease

1 Put the flours and salt in a bowl, rub in the butter, then stir in the oats and yeast. Make a well in the centre and add the warm milk and malt extract. Work to a smooth dough with about 300ml (½ pint) warm water.

2 Knead for 10 minutes until smooth. Shape into a ball, put in an oiled bowl, cover and leave to rise in a warm place for 1–2 hours until doubled.
3 Knock back and shape into a round. Put on a baking sheet, cover and leave to rise for a further 30 minutes.
4 Preheat the oven to 230°C (210°C fan oven) mark 8. Cut a cross on the top of the loaf and sprinkle a few more oats over. Bake for 15 minutes. Reduce the oven temperature to 200°C (180°C fan oven) mark 6 and bake for a further 15–20 minutes until the bread is risen and sounds hollow when tapped underneath. Transfer to a wire rack and leave to cool.

NUTRITION PER SLICE 160 cals |
2g fat (0.7g sats) | 30g carbs | 0.6g salt Ⓥ

Floury Baps Ⓑ

Makes 8 rolls
Preparation time 10 minutes, plus
  machine dough-making and rising
Cooking time 18–20 minutes, plus cooling

1 tsp easy-blend dried yeast
450g (1lb) strong white bread flour,
  plus extra to dust
1 tsp salt
1 tsp golden caster sugar
15g (½oz) butter
150ml (¼ pint) milk, plus extra to brush
125ml (4fl oz) water

1 Put the ingredients into the bread maker bucket, following the order and method specified in the manual.
2 Fit the bucket into the bread maker and set to the Dough program. Lightly grease a large baking sheet.
3 Once the dough is ready, turn it out on to a lightly floured surface and punch it down to deflate. Divide into eight even-sized pieces. Shape each piece into a round and flatten with the palm of your hand until about 10cm (4in) in diameter. Space slightly apart on a baking sheet and brush lightly with milk. Sprinkle generously with flour, cover loosely with a cloth and leave to rise for 30–40 minutes until doubled in size.
4 Preheat the oven to 200°C (180°C fan oven) mark 6. Make a deep impression in the centre of each bap with your thumb. Dust with flour and bake for 18–20 minutes until risen and pale golden. Eat warm or transfer to a wire rack to cool.

NUTRITION PER ROLL 220 cals |
3g fat (1g sats) | 45g carbs | 0.7g salt Ⓥ

Dark Rye Bread

Cuts into 16 slices
Preparation time 20 minutes, plus rising
Cooking time about 50 minutes, plus cooling

350g (12oz) rye flour, plus extra to dust
50g (2oz) strong wholemeal bread flour
zest of 1 lemon
1 tsp salt
25g (1oz) butter
1 tsp caraway seeds, lightly crushed (optional)
125g (4oz) cool mashed potato
15g (½oz) fresh yeast or 1½ tsp dried yeast and 1 tsp sugar
1 tsp sugar
50g (2oz) molasses or black treacle
oil to grease

1 Mix together the flours, lemon zest and salt. Rub in the
butter, caraway seeds, if you like, and mashed potato.
2 Blend the fresh yeast with 150ml (¼ pint) tepid water. If
using dried yeast, sprinkle it into the water with 1 tsp sugar
and leave in a warm place for 15 minutes or until frothy.
Heat the other 1 tsp sugar, the molasses and 2 tbsp water
together. Cool until tepid.
3 Pour the yeast liquid and molasses mixture on to the dry
ingredients and beat well to form a firm dough. Knead
on a lightly floured surface for 10 minutes or until smooth
and no longer sticky. Place in an oiled bowl, cover with
oiled clingfilm and leave to rise in a warm place for about
1½ hours or until doubled in size.
4 Knead again for 5 minutes, then shape into a large
round, about 18cm (7in) in diameter. Place on a baking
sheet. Cut a criss-cross pattern on the surface of the loaf to
a depth of 5mm (¼in). Dust with a little more flour. Leave
to rise in a warm place for 10–15 minutes. Preheat the
oven to 200°C (180°C fan oven) mark 6.
5 Bake the loaf in the oven for about 50 minutes. Turn on
to a wire rack and leave to cool completely.

NUTRITION PER SLICE 112 cals | 2g fat (1g sats) | 22g carbs | 0.4g salt Ⓥ

Cornbread

Serves 8
Preparation time 5 minutes
Cooking time 25–30 minutes, plus resting

vegetable oil to grease
125g (4oz) plain flour
175g (6oz) dried polenta or cornmeal
1 tbsp baking powder
1 tbsp caster sugar
½ tsp salt
300ml (½ pint) buttermilk, or equal
  quantities of natural yogurt and milk,
  mixed together
2 medium eggs
4 tbsp extra virgin olive oil
butter to serve

1 Preheat the oven to 200°C (180°C fan oven) mark 6. Generously grease a 20.5cm (8in) square shallow tin.
2 Put the flour into a large bowl, then add the polenta or cornmeal, the baking powder, sugar and salt. Make a well in the centre and pour in the buttermilk or yogurt and milk mixture. Add the eggs and olive oil, and stir together until evenly mixed.
3 Pour the mixure into the tin and bake for 25–30 minutes until firm to the touch. Insert a skewer into the centre – if should come out clean.
4 Leave the cornbread to rest in the tin for 5 minutes, then turn out and cut into chunky triangles. Serve warm with butter.

NUTRITION PER SERVING 229 cals |
8g fat (1g sats) | 33g carbs | 1.3g salt Ⓥ

Oatmeal Soda Bread

Cuts into about 10 slices
Preparation time 10 minutes
Cooking time 25 minutes

25g (1oz) butter, plus extra to grease
275g (10oz) plain wholemeal flour
175g (6oz) coarse oatmeal
2 tsp cream of tartar
1 tsp salt
about 300ml (½ pint) milk and water,
  mixed
butter to serve

1 Preheat the oven to 220°C (200°C fan oven) mark 7. Grease and base-line a 900g (2lb) loaf tin.
2 Mix together all the dry ingredients in a bowl. Rub in the butter, then add the milk and water to bind to a soft dough. Spoon into the prepared tin.
3 Bake in the oven for 25 minutes or until golden brown and well risen. Turn out on to a wire rack and leave to cool slightly. The bread is best eaten on the day it is made. Serve with butter.

NUTRITION PER SLICE 183 cals |
4g fat (2g sats) | 31g carbs | 0.6g salt Ⓥ

Focaccia ⓑ

Serves 8
Preparation time 5 minutes, plus machine dough-making and
   rising
Cooking time 20 minutes, plus cooling

1 tsp easy-blend dried yeast
475g (1lb 1oz) strong white bread flour, plus extra to dust
1½ tsp salt
3 tbsp olive oil, plus extra to grease
300ml (½ pint) water

For the topping
fresh rosemary sprigs
2 tbsp olive oil
sea salt flakes

1 Put the dough ingredients into the bread maker bucket,
following the order and method specified in the manual.
2 Fit the bucket into the bread maker and set to the
Dough program. Press start. Grease a 28cm (11in) metal
flan ring and place on a greased baking sheet.
3 Once the dough is ready, turn it out on to a floured
surface and punch it down to deflate. Roll out to a 25.5cm
(10in) round and lay inside the flan ring, pushing the
dough to the edges with your fingertips. (Don't worry if
it shrinks back, the dough will expand to fill the ring as it
proves.) Cover loosely with oiled clingfilm and leave to rise
in a warm place for 30 minutes.
4 Using fingertips dipped in flour, make deep dimples all
over the dough. Scatter with small rosemary sprigs, drizzle
with the olive oil and sprinkle generously with sea salt
flakes. Re-cover with oiled clingfilm and leave for a further
10 minutes, as the dough might have shrunk back when
dimpled. Meanwhile, preheat the oven to 200°C (fan oven
180°C) mark 6.
5 Drizzle the dough with water. (This is not essential
but helps the crust to stay soft during baking.) Bake for
20–25 minutes until just firm and pale golden. Transfer to
a wire rack and leave to cool.

TO MAKE CONVENTIONALLY
Put the dry ingredients into a bowl and gradually stir in the
oil and enough water to work to a smooth dough. Knead for
10 minutes until smooth, then shape into a ball, put in an
oiled bowl, cover and leave to rise in a warm place for
1–2 hours until doubled. Continue at step 3.

Cook's Tip
The flan ring helps the bread to rise and bake in a perfect
round, but don't worry if you haven't got one, just lay the
dough, pizza style, on the baking sheet.

NUTRITION PER SERVING 264 cals | 8g fat (1g sats) | 45g carbs | 1.2g salt Ⓥ

Crumpets

Makes about 24
Preparation 20 minutes, plus rising
Cooking time about 35 minutes

350g (12oz) strong plain white flour
½ tsp salt
½ tsp bicarbonate of soda
1½ tsp easy-blend dried yeast
250ml (9fl oz) warm milk
a little vegetable oil to fry
butter to serve

1 Sift the flour, salt and bicarbonate of soda into a large
bowl and stir in the yeast. Make a well in the centre, then
pour in 300ml (½ pint) warm water and the milk. Mix to
a thick batter.
2 Using a wooden spoon, beat the batter vigorously for
about 5 minutes. Cover and leave in a warm place for about
1 hour until sponge-like in texture. Beat the batter for a
further 2 minutes, then transfer to a jug.
3 Put a large non-stick frying pan over a high heat and
brush a little oil over the surface. Oil the insides of four
crumpet rings or 7.5cm (3in) plain metal cutters. Put the
rings, blunt-edge down, on to the hot pan surface and leave
for about 2 minutes until very hot.
4 Pour a little batter into each ring to a depth of 1cm
(½ in). Cook the crumpets for 5–7 minutes until the
surface is set and appears honeycombed with holes.
5 Carefully remove each metal ring. Flip the crumpets over
and cook the other side for 1 minute only. Transfer to a
wire rack. Repeat to use all of the batter.
6 To serve, toast the crumpets on both sides and serve
with butter.

Cook's Tip
The pan and metal rings must be well oiled each time, and
heated between frying each batch.

NUTRITION PER CRUMPET 60 cals | 1g fat (0.1g sats) | 12g carbs | 0.2g salt (V)

Pistachio and Rosewater Stollen Ⓑ

Makes 10 thick slices
Preparation time 20 minutes, plus machine dough-making
and rising
Cooking time 20 minutes, plus cooling

1¼ tsp easy-blend dried yeast
350g (12oz) strong white bread flour
½ tsp salt
1 tsp ground mixed spice
25g (1oz) golden caster sugar
50g (2oz) butter, melted
150ml (¼ pint) milk
3 tbsp rosewater
75g (3oz) sultanas
50g (2oz) pistachio nuts
50g (2oz) candied peel, chopped
icing sugar to dust

For the marzipan
150g (5oz) pistachio nuts, skinned (see Cook's Tip)
40g (1½oz) golden caster sugar
40g (1½oz) golden icing sugar
2 medium egg yolks
oil to grease

1 Put all the dough ingredients except the sultanas,
pistachio nuts, candied peel and icing sugar into the bread
maker bucket, following the order and method specified in
the manual.
2 Fit the bucket into the bread maker and set to the
Dough programme with Raisin setting, if applicable. Press
start. Add the sultanas, pistachio nuts and candied peel
when the machine beeps, or halfway through the kneading
cycle.
3 Meanwhile, make the marzipan. Put the pistachio nuts
into a food processor and blend until finely ground. Add
the sugars and egg yolks and blend to a paste. Turn out on
to a worksurface and shape into a log, 24cm (9½in) long.
Grease a large baking sheet.
4 Once the dough is ready, turn out on to a floured surface
and punch it down to deflate. Roll out to a rectangle, 28cm
(11in) long and 15cm (6in) wide. Lay the marzipan on the
dough, slightly to one side of the centre. Brush the long
edges of the dough with water, then fold the wider piece of
dough over the paste, sealing well.
5 Transfer to the baking sheet, cover loosely with oiled
clingfilm and leave in a warm place for 40 minutes or until

doubled in size. Preheat the oven to 200°C (180°C fan
oven) mark 6.
6 Bake for 20–25 minutes until risen and golden. Transfer
to a wire rack to cool. Serve generously dusted with icing
sugar.

Cook's Tip
For a vibrantly coloured marzipan it's best to skin the
pistachio nuts first. Soak them in boiling water for a couple
of minutes, then rub them between pieces of kitchen paper
to remove the skins.

NUTRITION PER SLICE 380 cals | 17g fat (5g sats) | 51g carbs | 0.7g salt Ⓥ

Hot Cross Buns

Makes 12
Preparation time 45 minutes, plus rising
Cooking time 15 minutes

50g (2oz) cold unsalted butter, cut into cubes, plus extra to
  grease
600g (1lb 5oz) strong white bread flour, plus extra
  to dust
2 tsp mixed spice
½ tsp salt
75g (3oz) caster sugar
finely grated zest of 1 lemon
1 × 7g sachet fast-action dried yeast
325ml (11fl oz) semi-skimmed milk
1 medium egg
150g (5oz) sultanas
2 tbsp plain flour
1–2 tbsp golden syrup to glaze

1 Lightly grease a large bowl and a baking sheet. Put
the strong flour, mixed spice, butter and salt into a food
processor and pulse until the mixture resembles fine
breadcrumbs (alternatively, rub the butter into the flour
mixture using your fingers).
2 Add the sugar, lemon zest and yeast and pulse again (or
stir) to combine. Empty the mixture into a large bowl and
make a well in the centre.
3 Gently heat the milk until it is just warm, then add the
milk and egg to the flour bowl and stir quickly to make a
soft dough (add a little more cold milk if the mixture feels
too dry).
4 Dust a worksurface with flour, then knead the dough
for 5 minutes or until elastic. Transfer the dough to the
prepared bowl, cover with clingfilm and leave in a warm
place to rise for 1 hour.
5 Transfer the dough to a worksurface and knead in the
sultanas (you may need to flour the worksurface again).
Return the dough to the bowl, cover with clingfilm and
leave to rise again for 30 minutes.
6 Turn the dough out again on to a floured worksurface
and divide it into 12 equal pieces. Shape each piece into a
ball, then flatten slightly. Arrange the balls on the prepared
baking sheet, spacing a little apart. Cover with a clean tea
towel and leave to rise for 45 minutes.

7 Preheat the oven to 220°C (200°C fan oven) mark 7.
To make the cross topping, put the plain flour into a small
bowl and mix in just enough cold water to reach a smooth,
pipeable consistency (about 2 tbsp). Transfer the flour
mixture to a piping bag (no need for a nozzle), then snip
the tip and, working quickly, pipe a cross on top of each
bun.
8 Bake the buns for 12–15 minutes or until golden and
risen. As soon as the they come out of the oven, brush with
golden syrup. Then allow to cool completely on a wire rack
– or eat warm with lashings of butter.

NUTRITION PER BUN 302 cals | 5g fat (3g sats) | 54g carbs | 0.3g salt Ⓥ

Brioche

Serves 10
Preparation time 20 minutes, plus rising
Cooking time 15–20 minutes, plus cooling

15g (½oz) fresh yeast or 1½ tsp easy-blend dried yeast
225g (8oz) strong plain white flour, plus extra to dust
a pinch of salt
1 tbsp golden caster sugar
2 extra-large eggs, beaten
50g (2oz) butter, melted and cooled until tepid
vegetable oil to grease
beaten egg to glaze

1 If using fresh yeast, blend with 2 tbsp tepid water. Mix the flour, salt and sugar together in a large bowl. (Stir in easy-blend dried yeast if using.)
2 Make a well in the centre and pour in the yeast liquid (or 2 tbsp tepid water if using easy-blend dried yeast) plus the eggs and melted butter. Work the ingredients together to a soft dough.
3 Turn out on to a lightly floured surface and knead for about 5 minutes until smooth and elastic. Put the dough into a large oiled bowl, cover and leave in a warm place for about 1 hour until doubled in size.
4 Knock back the dough on a lightly floured surface. Shape three-quarters of it into a ball and put into an oiled 1.1 litre (2 pint) brioche mould. Press a hole through the centre. Shape the remaining dough into a round, put on top of the brioche and press down lightly. Cover and leave in a warm place until the dough is puffy and nearly risen to the top of the mould.
5 Preheat the oven to 230°C (210°C fan oven) mark 8. Brush the brioche dough lightly with beaten egg and bake for 15–20 minutes until golden.
6 Turn out on to a wire rack and leave to cool. Serve warm or cold.

Cook's Tip
For individual brioches, divide the dough into 10 pieces. Shape as above. Bake in individual tins, for 10 minutes..

NUTRITION PER SERVING 140 cals | 6g fat (3g sats) | 19g carbs | 0.2g salt Ⓥ

Danish Pastries

Makes 16
Preparation time 1 hour, plus rising and
   resting
Cooking time 15 minutes

25g (1oz) fresh yeast or 1 tbsp dried
  yeast and 1 tsp sugar
450g (1lb) plain white flour, plus extra
  to dust
1 tsp salt
50g (2oz) lard
2 tbsp sugar
2 medium eggs, beaten
275g (10oz) butter, softened
1 medium egg, beaten, to glaze
Glacé Icing (see page 434) and flaked
  almonds to decorate

For the almond paste
15g (½oz) butter
75g (3oz) caster sugar
75g (3oz) ground almonds
1 medium egg, beaten

For the cinnamon butter
50g (2oz) butter
50g (2oz) caster sugar
2 tsp ground cinnamon

1 Blend the fresh yeast with the water. If using dried yeast, sprinkle it into 150ml (¼ pint) tepid water with the 1 tsp sugar and leave in a warm place for 15 minutes or until frothy.

2 Mix the flour and salt, rub in the lard and stir in the 2 tbsp sugar. Add the yeast liquid and beaten eggs and mix to an elastic dough, adding a little more water if necessary. Knead well for 5 minutes on a lightly floured surface, until smooth. Return the dough to the rinsed-out bowl, cover with a clean tea towel and leave to rest in the fridge for 10 minutes.

3 Shape the butter into a rectangle. Roll out the dough on a floured board to a rectangle about three times as wide as the butter. Put the butter in the centre of the dough and fold the sides of the dough over the butter. Press the edges to seal.

4 With the folds at the sides, roll the dough into a strip three times as long as it is wide; fold the bottom third up, and the top third down, cover and leave to rest in the fridge for 10 minutes. Turn and repeat the rolling, folding and resting twice more.

5 To make the almond paste, cream the butter and sugar, stir in the almonds and add enough egg to make a soft and pliable consistency. Make the cinnamon butter by creaming the butter and sugar and beating in the cinnamon.

6 Roll out the dough into the required shapes (see below) and fill with almond paste or cinnamon butter. Cover the pastries with a clean tea towel and leave to rise in a warm place for 20–30 minutes until doubled in size. Preheat the oven to 220°C (200°C fan oven) mark 7. Brush the pastries with beaten egg. Bake for 15 minutes or until golden. While hot, brush with thin glacé icing and sprinkle with flaked almonds.

TO SHAPE THE PASTRIES

Foldovers and Cushions Cut into 7.5cm (3in) squares and put a little almond paste in the centre. Fold over two opposite corners to the centre. Make a cushion by folding over all four corners, securing the tips with beaten egg.

Imperial Stars Cut into 7.5cm (3in) squares. Make diagonal cuts from each corner to within 1cm (½in) of the centre. Put a piece of almond paste in the centre. Fold one corner of each cut section down to the centre, secure the tips with beaten egg.

Twists Cut into 25.5 × 10cm (10 × 4in) rectangles. Cut each rectangle lengthways into four pieces. Spread each one with cinnamon butter and fold the bottom third of each up and the top third down; seal and cut each across into thin slices. Form into twists.

NUTRITION PER DANISH 376 cals | 25g fat (14g sats) | 35g carbs | 0.7g salt

Pizza Base Dough

Makes 1 large or 2 small pizza bases
Preparation time 15 minutes, plus rising

225g (8oz) strong white bread flour, plus extra to dust
½ tsp sea salt
½ tsp easy-blend dried yeast
1 tbsp extra virgin olive oil, plus extra to grease

1 Sift the flour and salt into a bowl and stir in the dried yeast. Make a well in the centre and gradually work in 150ml (¼ pint) warm water and the olive oil to form a soft dough.
2 Turn the pizza dough on to a lightly floured worksurface and knead well for 8–10 minutes until smooth and elastic. (Alternatively, knead the dough in a large food mixer fitted with a dough hook.)
3 Put into an oiled bowl, turn the dough once to coat the surface with oil and cover the bowl with clingfilm. Leave to rise in a warm place for 1 hour or until doubled in size.
4 Knock back the dough, divide in half, if you like, then roll out on a lightly floured surface.

TOPPINGS

Top the pizza with a thin layer of tomato purée, then scatter one or two of the following on top and finish with grated cheese or slices of mozzarella:
- Bacon or pancetta bits, or slices of prosciutto
- Rocket leaves
- Dried chilli flakes
- Capers
- Sliced sun-dried tomatoes
- Pepperoni slices
- Roasted peppers
- Artichoke hearts, drained and quartered
- Sliced mushrooms

Cook the topped pizzas on baking sheets in an oven preheated to 200°C (180°C fan oven) mark 6 for 15–18 minutes until golden.

Cook's Tip
If you like, use 15g (½oz) fresh yeast instead of easy-blend dried yeast. Mix with 2 tbsp of the flour, a pinch of sugar and the warm water. Leave in a warm place for 10 minutes or until frothy, then add to the rest of the flour and salt. Mix to a dough and continue as main recipe.

NUTRITION PER 25g (1oz) 60 cals | 1g fat (0.1g sats) | 11g carbs | 0.2g salt Ⓥ

Pepperoni Pizza

Makes 1 × 30.5cm (12in) pizza
Preparation time: 10 minutes, plus making
   the dough
Cooking time: 40 minutes

a little flour to dust
1 recipe quantity Pizza Base Dough
   (see opposite)
½ onion, finely chopped
1 tsp olive oil
1 garlic clove, finely chopped
1–2 tsp dried oregano to taste
2 tbsp tomato purée
400g can chopped tomatoes
1 tsp caster sugar
125g (4oz) mozzarella cheese, diced
70g pack small pepperoni slices

1 Lightly flour a large baking sheet.
Make the dough and leave it to rise.
2 Fry the onion in the oil until soft.

Add the garlic, oregano and tomato
purée, then the tomatoes and sugar
and simmer for 15 minutes, stirring,
or until thick. Season.
3 Preheat the grill to high with the
rack 9cm (3½in) away from the heat.
4 On a lightly floured surface, roll
the dough into a 30.5cm (12in) circle.
Transfer to the prepared baking sheet.
5 Grill the pizza for 1–2 minutes
until browning (it will blister). Flip
and grill for a further 1–2 minutes.
6 Spread the tomato sauce over the
base, leaving a thin border. Scatter
the mozzarella and pepperoni over
and return to grill for 8-10 minutes,
checking frequently, until golden and
bubbling. Serve immediately.

NUTRITION PER ½ PIZZA 700 cals |
38g fat (17g sats) | 57g carbs | 2.6g salt

Family-favourite Pizza

Makes 1 × 30.5cm (12in) pizza
Preparation time: 10 minutes, plus making
   the dough
Cooking time: 15 minutes

1 tbsp extra virgin olive oil, plus extra
   for greasing
1 recipe quantity Pizza Base Dough
   (see opposite)
a little flour to dust
6 tbsp home-made pizza sauce or
   good-quality ready-made sauce
125g ball buffalo mozzarella, drained
   and torn into pieces
2 heaped tbsp ready-made pesto
basil and/or oregano leaves to garnish
ground black pepper

1 Lightly oil a large baking sheet.
Make the dough and leave it to rise.
2 Preheat the oven to 230°C (210°C

fan oven) mark 8. Turn the dough out
on to a lightly floured surface, knock
the air out of the dough and roll it
into a 30.5cm (12in) circle. Transfer
to the prepared baking sheet.
3 Spread the base with the pizza
sauce, then top with mozzarella and
dollops of pesto. Drizzle with the oil.
4 Bake for 10–15 minutes until crisp
and golden. Garnish with herbs and
plenty of freshly ground black pepper.

NUTRITION PER ¼ PIZZA 387 cals |
167 fat (5g sats) | 41g carbs | 1.5g salt

Sweets

Peppermint Creams

Makes 50
Preparation time 45 minutes

450g (1lb) icing sugar, sifted, plus extra to dust
½ tsp cream of tartar
4–5 tbsp evaporated milk
2 tsp peppermint essence
a few drops of red food colouring

1 Put the icing sugar and cream of tartar into a bowl.
Add the evaporated milk and peppermint essence, and stir
together until evenly combined. Use your hands to bring
the mixture together into a ball.
2 Knead on a surface dusted with icing sugar to make a
smooth fondant. Cut the fondant in half; wrap one piece in
clingfilm and leave to one aside.
3 Dust the surface with more icing sugar. Roll out the
other half of the fondant to a round, about 5mm (¼in)
thick. Stamp out 4cm (1½in) rounds, with a plain cutter,
re-rolling and cutting the trimmings. Transfer the fondant
discs to a tray lined with baking parchment.
4 Unwrap the other portion of fondant. Dip a skewer
into the food colouring, press on to the fondant to apply a
little colouring, then knead until it is evenly pink in colour.
Roll out to a 5mm (¼in) thickness, stamp out 4cm (1½in)
rounds and then put on a lined tray, as above. Cover
the mints loosely with baking parchment and leave to
dry overnight.
5 Store in airtight containers for up to three weeks and
serve as after-dinner mints, or put into paper sweet cases
and pack into boxes to offer as a gift.

Cook's Tip
Because they contain uncooked egg white, peppermint
creams are not recommended for children, the
elderly, pregnant women or other susceptible groups
(see page 226).

NUTRITION PER PEPPERMINT CREAM 40 cals | trace fat (0g sats) | 12g carbs | trace salt

Butterscotch

Makes about 450g (1lb)
Preparation time 15 minutes
Cooking time about 15 minutes, plus cooling

sunflower oil to grease
450g (1lb) demerara sugar
50–75g (2–3oz) unsalted butter, diced

1 Lightly oil a 15cm (6in) shallow square tin.
2 Put the sugar and 150ml (¼ pint) water in a heavy-based pan and heat gently until the sugar has dissolved. Bring to the boil and boil steadily until the syrup registers 138°C on a sugar thermometer (the medium crack stage – when a little of the mixture dropped into a cup of cold water separates into hard, but not brittle, threads). While the syrup is boiling, brush down the sides of the pan occasionally with a damp pastry brush.
3 Add the butter, a little at a time, stirring until each piece is incorporated before adding more. Pour the mixture into the prepared tin. When almost set, mark into pieces.
4 Leave until completely cold, then break into pieces. Store in an airtight container.

NUTRITION PER 25g (1oz) 120 cals | 3g fat (2g sats) | 26g carbs | trace salt ⓥ

Clotted Cream Vanilla Fudge

Makes 700g (1½lb)
Preparation time 15 minutes, plus overnight chilling
Cooking time 20–30 minutes, plus cooling

50g (2oz) butter, plus extra to grease
450g (1lb) granulated sugar
170g can evaporated milk
113g carton clotted cream
1 tsp vanilla extract

1 Lightly grease a shallow 18cm (7in) square tin.
2 Put the sugar, evaporated milk, clotted cream and butter into a large heavy-based pan and heat gently until the sugar has dissolved.
3 Bring to the boil and boil steadily, stirring frequently to prevent sticking. The mixture is ready when it registers 115°C on a sugar thermometer (the soft ball stage: in cold water it forms a soft ball which you can easily squash between your finger and thumb). Immediately plunge the base of the pan into a sink of cold water to stop the cooking process, then remove.

4 Add the vanilla extract and beat with a hand-held electric whisk, scraping down the sides from time to time, until the mixture is thick, paste-like and no longer glossy; this will take about 5 minutes.
5 Pour the fudge into the prepared tin, patting it into the corners with the back of a spoon. Cover and chill overnight until completely set.
6 Cut into squares and pack into boxes, or store in an airtight container in the fridge for up to two weeks.

TRY SOMETHING DIFFERENT
Ginger Fudge Add 75g (3oz) chopped stem ginger (drained of syrup) at the end of step 4.
Coffee and Pecan Fudge Add 3–4 tbsp coffee essence in step 2 and 75g (3oz) chopped pecan nuts at the end of step 4. Omit the vanilla extract.

NUTRITION PER 25g (1oz) 120 cals | 4g fat (2g sats) | 20g carbs | 0.1g salt ⓥ

Chocolate Fudge

Makes 675g (1lb 7oz)
Preparation time 15 minutes
Cooking time 6–8 minutes, plus cooling

50g (2oz) unsalted butter, plus extra to grease
225g (8oz) granulated sugar
397g can sweetened condensed milk
1 tbsp clear honey
1 tsp vanilla extract
100g (3½oz) plain chocolate (at least 70% cocoa
  solids), grated

1 Grease a 20.5cm (8in) square cake tin and line the base
and 2.5cm (1in) up the sides with baking parchment.
2 Put the sugar in a medium heavy-based pan and add the
butter, condensed milk, honey and vanilla extract. Heat
gently until the sugar dissolves. Bring to the boil, stirring,
and boil for 6–8 minutes, stirring frequently to prevent
sticking. The mixture is ready when it reaches 115°C on
a sugar thermometer (the soft ball stage: in cold water it
forms a soft ball which you can easily squash between your
finger and thumb).
3 Remove the pan from the heat, add the grated chocolate
and beat until the mixture is smooth and glossy. Pour the
fudge into the prepared tin, spreading it into the corners.
Leave for 2 hours or until completely set.
4 Remove the fudge from the tin and peel away the lining
paper. Cut into squares. Store in an airtight container.

NUTRITION PER 25g (1oz) 99 cals | 3g fat (2g sats) | 17g carbs | 0.1g salt Ⓥ

Turkish Delight

Makes 49 squares
Preparation time 15 minutes, plus soaking and
 setting
Cooking time 30 minutes, plus overnight setting

25g (1oz) powdered gelatine
450g (1lb) granulated sugar
¼ tsp citric acid
a few drops of red food colouring
a few drops of rosewater
sunflower oil to grease

For the sherbet mix
50g (2oz) icing sugar
½ tsp bicarbonate of soda
¼ tsp citric acid

1 Pour 300ml (½ pint) water into a heavy-based pan and
sprinkle the gelatine over the surface. Stir gently to ensure
that all the grains are covered. Leave to soak for 10 minutes
or until the gelatine is spongelike.
2 Over a very gentle heat, slowly dissolve the gelatine until
clear and liquid. Add the sugar and citric acid and stir
gently until the sugar dissolves. (Take care not to splash the
sugar up the sides of the pan, as this may cause the mixture
to crystallise.)
3 Bring the contents of the pan to the boil and boil over
a medium heat for 20 minutes or until the mixture is
syrupy and a pale straw colour (do not stir the mixture,
or the scum that appears on the surface will then be
distributed through it and make a cloudy jelly).
4 Remove the pan from the heat, let the bubbles subside,
then skim any scum from the surface of the mixture. Leave
the mixture to stand for 25 minutes or until cool, thick and
almost set. Stir in sufficient red food colouring to give a
pale pink colour and add rosewater to taste.
5 Base line an 18cm (7in) square tin. Oil the base and
sides well. Carefully pour in the Turkish Delight mixture.
Leave until completely cold, then put in the fridge and
leave overnight to set.
6 Meanwhile, sift together the icing sugar, bicarbonate
of soda and citric acid for the sherbet coating. Store in a
polythene bag.
7 The next day, sprinkle half the quantity of sherbet mix
on to a sheet of greaseproof paper. Put the Turkish Delight
on to the sherbert layer. Peel off the lining paper, then turn
the Turkish Delight over to coat the other side.
8 Rinse a large sharp knife in cold running water, then use
to cut the Turkish Delight into 2.5cm (1in) squares. Put in
a bowl, and shake the remaining sherbet mixture over the
top until completely coated.
9 To store, line an airtight container with greaseproof
paper, put in the Turkish Delight squares and sprinkle over
any remaining sherbet.

NUTRITION PER SQUARE 40 cals | 0g fat | 11g carbs | trace salt

Coconut Ice Bars

Makes about 550g (1¼lb), about 21 squares
Preparation time 10 minutes
Cooking time 15 minutes, plus cooling

sunflower oil to grease
450g (1lb) granulated sugar
150ml (¼ pint) milk
150g (5oz) desiccated coconut
a few drops of red food colouring

1 Lightly oil an 18cm (7in) shallow square tin.
2 Put the sugar and the milk in a heavy-based pan and heat gently until the sugar has dissolved. Bring to the boil and boil gently for 10 minutes or until 115°C (soft-ball stage, see right) is reached.
3 Remove from the heat and stir in the coconut.
4 Pour half the mixture quickly into the prepared tin. Add a few drops of food colouring to the second half and pour quickly over the first layer.
5 Leave until half set, mark into bars, then leave to cool completely before cutting or breaking into bars.

SUGAR STAGES
There are five stages in syrup-making. You can test using with a sugar thermometer or by dropping a little of the syrup into cold water.
Thread stage Temperature 110°C; in cold water the syrup forms a fine, soft thread.
Soft-ball stage Temperature 115°C; in cold water the syrup forms a soft ball that you can easily squash between your finger and thumb.
Hard-ball stage Temperature 120°C; in cold water the syrup forms a firmer but still pliable ball.
Soft-crack stage Temperature 125°C; in cold water the syrup forms thick threads which bend a little but then break up.
Hard-crack stage Temperature 145°C; in cold water the syrup forms thick, brittle threads which break immediately when you bend them.

NUTRITION PER 25g (1oz) 92 cals | 3g fat (3g sats) | 16g carbs | trace salt

---

Pecan Praline

Makes about 450g (1lb)
Preparation time 10 minutes
Cooking time 15 minutes, plus cooling

50g (2oz) unsalted butter, plus extra to grease
200g (7oz) granulated sugar
125ml (4fl oz) golden syrup
150g (5oz) pecan halves
½ tsp vanilla extract
¾ tsp bicarbonate of soda
a pinch of salt

1 Grease a large baking sheet. Put the sugar and golden syrup into a large heavy-based pan and heat gently, stirring constantly until the sugar dissolves in the syrup.
2 Increase the heat and boil until the syrup registers 110°C on a sugar thermometer; in cold water it forms a fine, soft thread.

3 Add the pecan halves to the pan and continue to boil until the mixture reaches 140–150°C; in cold water it forms thick, brittle threads which break immediately when you bend them. Immediately remove the pan from the heat and stir in the vanilla extract, butter, bicarbonate of soda and salt. Make sure the ingredients are thoroughly combined.
4 Tip the mixture on to the prepared baking sheet, spreading it thinly. Leave to one side until completely cooled and hardened.
5 Break the pecan praline into pieces and store in an airtight container, layered between sheets of baking parchment, for up to ten days, or gift wrap in cellophane.

NUTRITION PER 25g (1oz) 140 cals | 8g fat (5g sats) | 18g carbs | 0.2g salt Ⓥ

Nutty Chocolate Truffles

Makes 30
Preparation time 20 minutes, plus chilling
Cooking time 12 minutes

100g (3½oz) hazelnuts
200g (7oz) plain chocolate (at least 70% cocoa solids),
 broken into pieces
25g (1oz) unsalted butter
150ml (¼ pint) double cream
3 tbsp cocoa powder, sifted
3 tbsp golden icing sugar, sifted

1 Put the hazelnuts in a frying pan and heat gently for
3–4 minutes, shaking the pan occasionally, until toasted
all over. Put 30 nuts in a bowl and leave to cool. Whiz the
remaining nuts in a food processor until finely chopped.
Put the chopped nuts in a shallow dish.
2 Melt the chocolate in a heatproof bowl over a pan of
gently simmering water, taking care not to let the bowl
touch the water.
3 In a separate pan, melt the butter and cream. Bring just
to the boil, then remove from the heat. Carefully stir into
the chocolate. Whisk until cool and thick, then chill for
1–2 hours.
4 Put the cocoa powder and icing sugar in separate shallow
dishes. Scoop up a teaspoonful of the chilled truffle mixture
and push a hazelnut into the centre. Working quickly,
shape into a ball, then roll in cocoa powder, icing sugar or
chopped nuts. Repeat with the remaining truffle mixture,
then chill until ready to serve.

GET AHEAD
Store the truffles in an airtight container in the fridge for up
to two weeks.

NUTRITION PER TRUFFLE 96 cals | 8g fat (4g sats) | 6g carbs | 0.1g salt Ⓥ

Preserves

Jams

Jams are basically a cooked mixture of fruit and sugar. The high concentration of sugar used effectively preserves the fruit and retards the growth of micro-organisms, allowing the jam to be kept in a cool place for many months without deterioration. Home-made jams taste infinitely better than commercially produced ones.

Choosing fruit

Fruit for jam should be sound – poor quality fruit will not have as much flavour – and either just ripe or slightly underripe. The jam will set only if there are sufficient quantities of pectin, acid and sugar present. Some fruits are naturally rich in pectin (see the chart, page 476) and give a good set, whereas others do not contain as much and may need to have it boosted with added pectin. Lemon juice is most often used for this purpose, since it aids the set and often brings out the flavour of the fruit. Allow 2 tbsp lemon juice to 2kg (4½lb) of a fruit with poor setting properties. Alternatively, you can buy bottled pectin – follow the manufacturer's instructions for how much to use. Sometimes, only an acid is added, such as citric or tartaric acid. These acids contain no pectin but help to extract the natural pectin from the fruit and improve the flavour of fruits lacking in acid. Allow ½ tsp acid for 2kg (4½lb) of a fruit with poor setting properties.

Home-made pectin extracts

A pectin extract can be made from sour cooking apples, crab apples or apple peelings, cores and windfalls.

Wash 1kg (2¼lb) fruit and chop roughly without peeling or coring. Cover with 600–900ml (1–1½ pints) water and simmer gently for about 45 minutes or until well pulped. Strain through a jelly bag or muslin cloth, then carry out a pectin test (see right) to ensure that there is sufficient pectin present. Allow 150–300ml (¼ –½ pint) of this extract to 2kg (4½lb) of fruit which is low in pectin. Pectin extract can also be made using the same method from fresh gooseberries and redcurrants.

Sugar

Sugar acts as a preservative in jam and also affects its setting quality. The exact amount of sugar needed depends on the pectin strength of the fruit, so it is essential to use the amount specified in a recipe. Too little sugar produces a poor set and the jam may go mouldy when stored. Too much sugar makes a dark sticky jam, overpowers the fruit flavour and may crystallise.

Granulated sugar is the most economical for jam making, although less foamy scum is formed on the surface of the jam when lump or preserving sugar is used; however, these are more expensive and the only real benefit is that the end product is slightly clearer than when granulated sugar is used. Caster sugar can be used, but again is more expensive; brown sugar can also be used but will produce a darker jam and will affect flavour.

You can make your own reduced-sugar jams similar to those on the market. Don't reduce sugar content by more than 20 per cent or the jam will be runny. As it doesn't keep well, make it in small batches and store in the fridge (for up to six weeks) or a cool place (three to four weeks).

Testing for pectin content

The chart on page 476 shows the pectin content of fruits and vegetables used in preserving. If you are not sure of your fruit setting qualities, carry out this test.

When the fruit has been cooked until soft, but before you add sugar, take 1 tsp juice, put it in a glass and, when cool, add 1 tbsp methylated spirit. Shake the glass and leave for 1 minute. If the mixture forms a jelly-like clot, the fruit has a good pectin content. If it does not form a single firm clot, the pectin content is too low and you will need extra.

Testing for a set

Thermometer test Dip a sugar thermometer into the pan away from the base and side. Leave it for a few moments. Jams and jellies set when the temperature reaches 105°C.

Saucer test Chill two or three saucers in the freezer. When you think the preserve has reached setting point, take the pan off the heat and spoon a blob of preserve on to a chilled saucer, then put it in the fridge to chill for a minute or so. When the preserve has cooled, push the surface with your finger; it is set if it wrinkles and doesn't break to reveal liquid.

Flake test Using a wooden spoon, lift a little of the preserve out of the pan. Let it cool slightly, then tip the spoon so that the preserve drops back into the pan. If it is set, it will run together along the edge of the spoon and form flakes that will break off.

If the preserve is not ready, return it to the boil for another 5–10 minutes then test again.

The pectin content of fruits and vegetables

GOOD	MEDIUM	POOR
Cooking apples	Apricots	Bananas
Crab apples	Bilberries	Cherries
Cranberries	Blackberries	Elderberries
Currants (red and black)	Cranberries	Figs
Damsons	Dessert or eating apples	Grapes
Gooseberries	Greengages	Japonica
Lemons	Loganberries	Marrows
Limes	Mulberries	Medlars
Quinces	Plums	Melons
Seville oranges	Raspberries	Nectarines
		Peaches
		Pineapples
		Rhubarb
		Strawberries

Potting, covering and storing

Preserves must be potted in scrupulously clean, sterilised containers. Wash jars or bottles in very hot soapy water, rinse thoroughly, then put upturned on a baking sheet in the oven at 140°C (120°C fan oven) mark 1 for 10–15 minutes until completely dry.

Stand the jars upside down on a clean tea towel until the preserve is ready. They should still be warm when you pour in the jam.

As soon as a set has been reached, immediately remove the pan from the heat and, with a slotted spoon, skim off any scum. Don't pot strawberry and other whole-fruit jams immediately or all the fruit will rise to the top. Leave them in the pan for 15–20 minutes before potting. Spoon the jam into the warm jars, filling them right to the top.

Wipe the outside of the jars with a damp cloth while they are still warm, and immediately put wax discs, wax side down, on the surface of the jam, making sure they lie flat. Cover immediately with the screw-top lid or with a dampened round of cellophane and secure with an elastic band or string. Label the jars and store in a cool, dry, dark place. Most jams keep well for about a year after which their flavour starts to deteriorate.

Watchpoints

Problems with jam making can be eliminated if the following simple tips are followed:

- Mould growth usually occurs because the jam has not been covered with a wax disc while still hot, the pots were not cleaned properly or may have been stored in a place where they picked up bacteria. Other possible causes are insufficient evaporation of water while the fruit was being cooked before sugar was added and/or too short a boiling time after the sugar was added. It is important not to eat jam that has mould growth on it, as it produces toxins. Throw away the whole jar if you find any mould on the top surface.
- Bubbles in jam indicate fermentation, which is usually because not enough sugar has been used or because the jam was not reduced sufficiently. Fermented jam can be boiled up again and repotted but thereafter should only be used for cooking.
- Crystallisation is usually caused by lack of enough acid or by under- or over-boiling the jam after the sugar has been added.
- Shrinkage of jam in pots is caused by an inadequate cover or failure to store the jam in a cool, dark, dry place.

Strawberry Jam

Makes about 1.8kg (4lb)
Preparation time 10 minutes, plus standing
Cooking time about 10 minutes

900g (2lb) strawberries, hulled
1kg (2¼lb) sugar with pectin
juice of ½ lemon

1 Put the strawberries into a preserving pan with the sugar and lemon juice. Heat gently, stirring until the sugar has dissolved.
2 Bring to the boil and boil steadily for 4 minutes or until setting point is reached (see page 475).
3 Take the pan off the heat and remove any scum from the surface with a slotted spoon. Leave to stand for 15–20 minutes. Stir the jam gently, then pot and cover in the usual way (see opposite).

NUTRITION PER TABLESPOON
35 cals | 0g fat | 9g carbs | trace salt Ⓥ

Raspberry Jam

Makes about 2.6kg (5¼lb)
Preparation time 10 minutes, plus standing
Cooking time about 45 minutes

1.8kg (4lb) raspberries
1.8kg (4lb) golden caster sugar
a knob of butter

1 Put the raspberries into a preserving pan and simmer very gently in their own juice for 15–20 minutes, stirring carefully from time to time, until soft.
2 Remove the pan from the heat and add the sugar, stirring until dissolved, then add the butter and boil rapidly for 20 minutes or until setting point is reached (see page 475).
3 Take the pan off the heat, remove any scum with a slotted spoon, then leave to stand for 15 minutes. Pot and cover in the usual way (see opposite).

NUTRITION PER TABLESPOON
50 cals | trace fat (0 sats) | 12g carbs | trace salt Ⓥ

Uncooked Freezer Jam

Makes about 3.2kg (7lb)
Preparation time 15 minutes, plus overnight standing

1.4kg (3lb) raspberries or strawberries, hulled
1.8kg (4lb) golden caster sugar
4 tbsp lemon juice
225ml (8fl oz) commercial pectin

1 Put the fruit into a large bowl and very lightly mash with a fork. Stir in the sugar and lemon juice, and leave at room temperature, stirring occasionally, for about 1 hour or until the sugar has dissolved.
2 Gently stir in the pectin and continue stirring for a further 2 minutes.
3 Pour the jam into small freezerproof containers, leaving a little space at the top to allow for expansion. Cover and leave at room temperature for a further 24 hours.
4 Label and freeze for up to six months.
5 To serve, thaw the jam at room temperature for 1 hour.

NUTRITION PER TABLESPOON
35 cals | 0g fat | 9g carbs | trace salt Ⓥ

Blackcurrant Jam

Makes about 4.5kg (10lb)
Preparation time 10 minutes, plus standing
Cooking time 55 minutes

1.8kg (4lb) blackcurrants
2.7kg (6lb) sugar
a knob of butter

1 Put the blackcurrants into a preserving pan with 1.7 litres (3 pints) water. Simmer gently for 45 minutes or until the fruit is soft and the liquid is well reduced, stirring from time to time to prevent sticking.
2 Remove the pan from the heat, add the sugar, stir until dissolved, then add the butter. Bring to the boil and boil rapidly for 10 minutes, stirring frequently or until setting point is reached (see page 475).
3 Take the pan off the heat, remove any scum with a slotted spoon, then leave to stand for 15 minutes. Pot and cover in the usual way (see opposite).

NUTRITION PER TABLESPOON
40 cals | trace fat (0g sats) | 10g carbs | trace salt Ⓥ

Rhubarb Ginger Jam

Makes about 2kg (4½lb)
Preparation time 20 minutes, plus overnight standing
Cooking time 20 minutes

1.1kg (2½lb) rhubarb (prepared weight), chopped
1.1kg (2½lb) sugar
juice of 2 lemons
25g (1oz) fresh root ginger, peeled
125g (4oz) stem or crystallised ginger, chopped

1 Layer the rhubarb in a large bowl with the sugar and lemon juice. Cover and leave overnight at room temperature.
2 Next day, peel and bruise the root ginger slightly, using a weight or rolling pin, and tie it in a piece of muslin. Put the rhubarb mixture in a preserving pan with the muslin bag, bring to the boil, then boil rapidly for 15 minutes, stirring frequently.
3 Remove the muslin bag, add the stem or crystallised ginger and boil for a further 5 minutes.
4 Test for a set and, when setting point is reached (see page 475), take the pan off the heat and remove any scum with a slotted spoon. Pot and cover as usual (see page 476.)

NUTRITION PER TABLESPOON
20 cals | 0g fat | 5g carbs | trace salt Ⓥ

Apricot Jam

Makes about 3kg (6½lb)
Preparation time 20 minutes, plus standing
Cooking time about 40 minutes

1.8kg (4lb) apricots, halved and stoned, stones reserved
juice of 1 lemon
1.8kg (4lb) sugar
a knob of butter

1 Crack a few of the apricot stones with a nutcracker; take out the kernels and blanch them in boiling water for 1 minute; drain.
2 Put the apricots, lemon juice, apricot kernels and 450ml (¾ pint) water into a preserving pan and simmer for about 15 minutes or until well reduced and the fruit is soft.
3 Off the heat, add the sugar and stir until dissolved. Add the butter and boil rapidly for 15 minutes or until setting point is reached (see page 475).
4 Take the pan off the heat, remove any scum with a slotted spoon, then leave to stand for 15 minutes. Pot and cover in the usual way (see page 476).

NUTRITION PER TABLESPOON
40 cals | trace fat (0g sats) | 10g carbs | 0.1g salt Ⓥ

Plum Jam

Makes about 4.5kg (10lb)
Preparation time 15 minutes, plus standing
Cooking time 50 minutes

2.7kg (6lb) plums
2.7kg (6lb) sugar
a knob of butter

TRY SOMETHING DIFFERENT
Greengage Jam Use greengages instead of plums and reduce the water to 600ml (1 pint).
Damson Jam Use 2.3kg (5lb) damsons instead of plums. After adding sugar, boil for 10 minutes only.

1 Put the plums and 900ml (1½ pints) water into a preserving pan. Bring to the boil, then simmer gently for 30 minutes or until well reduced and the fruit is very soft.
2 Remove the pan from the heat, add the sugar, stirring until dissolved, then add the knob of butter. Bring to the boil and boil rapidly for 10–15 minutes or until setting point is reached (see page 475), stirring frequently.
3 Take the pan off the heat. Using a slotted spoon, remove the plum stones and skim off any scum from the surface of the jam, then leave to stand for about 15 minutes. Pot and cover in the usual way (see page 476).

Cook's Tip
If dessert plums are used rather than a cooking variety, add the juice of 1 large lemon.

NUTRITION PER TABLESPOON
40 cals | trace fat (0g sats) | 10g carbs | trace salt

Jellies, Curds and Marmalades

Jellies differ from jams in that only the juice from the fruit is used in the end product. They are a little more difficult to make and the yield is not as high, but they taste delicious and are well worth the effort. Home-made jellies can be served with roast meats to counteract the richness, used as a glaze for flans, and spread on scones or bread in the same way as jam. It isn't practicable to state the exact yield in jelly recipes because the ripeness of the fruit and time allowed for dripping both affect the quantity of juice obtained. As a rough guide, for each 450g (1lb) sugar added, a yield of about 700g (1½lb) will result. It is also difficult to give precise nutritional information for the same reasons, but you can assume that for each of the following recipes 1 tbsp jelly provides roughly 40 calories.

Made with eggs and butter as well as sugar and fruit, curds are not true 'preserves' as they do not keep for long, but they are eaten in the same way as jams and are well worth making. All fruit curds should be made in small quantities, kept in the fridge and eaten within two weeks.

Seville or bitter oranges make the best marmalade, with a good flavour and a clear set, although other citrus fruits, such as limes and grapefruit, can be used. The best time to make marmalade is during January and February when Seville oranges are in season. Buy unwaxed fruit if you possibly can, otherwise wash thoroughly in water with a little washing-up liquid added, then rinse well.

Redcurrant Jelly

Makes 1.3kg (3lb)
Preparation time 30 minutes, plus standing
Cooking time about 1 hour

1.4kg (3lb) redcurrants
sugar (see method)
3 tbsp port (optional)

1 Put the redcurrants into a preserving pan with 600ml (1 pint) water and simmer gently for 30 minutes or until the fruit is very soft and pulpy, stirring from time to time to prevent sticking.
2 Spoon the fruit pulp into a jelly bag suspended over a large bowl and leave to drip through for at least 12 hours (see Cook's Tip, page 480).
3 Discard the pulp remaining in the jelly bag. Measure the juice extract and return it to the pan, adding 450g (1lb) sugar for each 600ml (1 pint) extract.
4 Heat gently, stirring, until the sugar has dissolved, then bring to the boil and boil rapidly for 15 minutes or until setting point is reached (see page 475).
5 Take the pan off the heat and remove any scum with a slotted spoon. Stir in the port if using. Pot and cover in the usual way (see page 476).

TRY SOMETHING DIFFERENT

Bramble Jelly Follow the above using 1.8kg (4lb) slightly under-ripe blackberries with the juice of 2 lemons and 450ml (¾ pint) water.

NUTRITION PER TABLESPOON
39 cals | 0g fat | 10g carbs | trace salt

Quince Jelly

Makes about 1.8kg (4lb)
Preparation time 30 minutes, plus standing
Cooking time about 2 hours

1.8kg (4lb) quinces, washed and roughly chopped
grated zest and juice of 3 lemons
sugar (see method)

1 Put the fruit in a preserving pan with 2.3 litres (4 pints) water and the lemon zest and juice.
2 Cover with foil or a baking sheet and simmer gently for 1 hour or until the fruit is tender. Stir occasionally to prevent sticking.
3 Spoon the fruit pulp into a jelly bag or cloth suspended over a large bowl, and leave to strain into a large bowl for at least 12 hours (see Cook's Tip, page 480).
4 Return the pulp in the jelly bag to the pan and add 1.1 litres (2 pints) water. Bring to the boil, simmer gently for 30 minutes, then strain again through a jelly bag or cloth for at least 12 hours.
5 Discard the pulp remaining in the jelly bag. Combine the two lots of juice extract and measure. Return to the pan with 450g (1lb) sugar for each 600ml (1 pint) extract. Heat gently, stirring, until the sugar has dissolved, then bring to the boil and boil rapidly for about 10 minutes.
6 Test for a set (see page 475) and, when setting point is reached, take the pan off the heat and remove any scum with a slotted spoon. Pot and cover in the usual way (see page 476).

NUTRITION PER TABLESPOON
37 cals | 0g fat | 10g carbs | trace salt Ⓥ

Apple and Mint Jelly

Makes about 1.8kg (4lb)
Preparation time 30 minutes, plus standing
Cooking time about 1¼ hours

2.3kg (5lb) cooking apples, such as Bramleys
a few large fresh mint sprigs
1.1 litres (2 pints) distilled white vinegar
sugar (see method)
6–8 tbsp freshly chopped mint
a few drops of green food colouring (optional)

1 Remove any bruised parts from the apples, then cut into chunks without peeling or coring. Put the apples into a preserving pan with 1.1 litres (2 pints) water and add the mint sprigs.
2 Bring to the boil, then simmer gently for 45 minutes or until soft and pulpy, stirring from time to time to prevent sticking. Add the vinegar and boil for a further 5 minutes.
3 Spoon the pulp into a jelly bag suspended over a large bowl. Leave to drip through for at least 12 hours (see Cook's Tip).
4 Discard the pulp left in the jelly bag. Measure the extract and return to the preserving pan, adding 450g (1lb) sugar for each 600ml (1 pint) extract.
5 Heat gently, stirring, until the sugar has dissolved, then bring to the boil and boil rapidly for 10 minutes or until setting point is reached (see page 475).
6 Take the pan off the heat and remove any scum with a slotted spoon. Stir in the chopped mint and colouring, if you like. Cool slightly, stir well to distribute the mint, then pot and cover in the usual way (see page 476).

Cook's Tip
The easiest way to suspend a jelly bag is from the legs of an upturned stool.

NUTRITION PER TABLESPOON
30 cals | 0g fat | 8g carbs | trace salt Ⓥ

Lemon Curd

Makes about 700g (1½lb)
Preparation time 20 minutes
Cooking time about 25 minutes

grated zest and juice of 4 medium ripe, juicy lemons
4 medium eggs, beaten
125g (4oz) butter, cut into small pieces
350g (12oz) golden caster sugar

1 Put all the ingredients into a double boiler or a large heatproof bowl set over a pan of simmering water. Stir the mixture until the sugar has dissolved. Continue to heat gently, stirring frequently, for about 20 minutes or until thick enough to coat the back of the spoon; do not allow to boil or it will curdle.
2 Strain the lemon curd through a fine sieve. Pot and cover in the usual way (see page 476). Store in the fridge and use within two weeks.

TRY SOMETHING DIFFERENT
Lime Curd Replace the lemons with the grated zest and juice of 5 large ripe, juicy limes.

NUTRITION PER TABLESPOON
60 cals | 3g fat (2g sats) | 8g carbs | 0.1g salt Ⓥ

Mixed Fruit Marmalade

Makes about 4kg (8lb 1.3oz)
Preparation time 30 minutes, plus standing
Cooking time about 2¼ hours

2 Seville oranges
2 yellow grapefruit
2 limes
4 large unwaxed lemons
3kg (6½lb) sugar, warmed

1 Wash any unwaxed fruit thoroughly, rinse well and dry. Weigh the fruit – you need about 1.6kg (3½lb) in total. Cut in half and squeeze to extract as much juice as possible, then pour through a sieve into a jug, reserving any pips in the sieve.
2 Cut the spent fruit halves into quarters. Cut away the membrane and a thin layer of pith and tie these and the pips in a piece of muslin.
3 Cut the peel into very thin strips and tip into a preserving pan.
4 Add all of the citrus fruit juices to the preserving pan, together with 3 litres (5¼ pints) cold water and the muslin bag. Bring to the boil, then simmer for 2 hours or until the peel is very, very tender and the liquid has reduced by about half. Skim off any scum during cooking and discard.
5 Remove the muslin bag from the pan, squeezing well and allowing the juice to run back into the pan. Add the warmed sugar to the pan and stir until dissolved. Bring to the boil, then reduce the heat and bubble until the temperature registers 104°C on a sugar thermometer. Cook at this temperature for about 10 minutes or until setting point is reached. Use the saucer test (see page 475).
6 Take the pan off the heat and remove any scum with a slotted spoon. Leave to stand for 15 minutes, then stir to distribute the peel. Pot and cover in the usual way (see page 476).

NUTRITION PER TABLESPOON
45 cals | 0g fat (0g sats) | 12g carbs | trace salt Ⓥ

Lemon Shred Marmalade

Makes 2.3kg (5lb)
Preparation time 25 minutes, plus standing
Cooking time 2¾ hours, plus standing

900g (2lb) lemons, washed
juice of 2 lemons
2.6 litres (4½ pints) water
1.4kg (3lb) sugar

1 Peel off enough rind from the lemons, avoiding the pith, to weigh 125g (4oz). Cut the rind into thin strips. Cut up the rest of the fruit and simmer it in a covered preserving pan with the lemon juice and 1.4 litres (2½ pints) water for 2 hours or until the fruit is very soft.
2 Put the shredded rind in another pan with 600ml (1 pint) water, cover and simmer gently until this also is very soft.
3 Drain off the liquid from the shreds and put the shreds to one side.
4 Pour the contents of the pan into a jelly bag or cloth suspended over a large bowl for 15 minutes (see Cook's Tip opposite).
5 Return the pulp remaining in the jelly bag to the pan with 600ml (1 pint) water, simmer for a further 20 minutes, then pour into the jelly bag again and leave to drip for several hours.
6 Combine the two lots of extract and test for pectin (see page 475). If the liquid does not clot, reduce it slightly by rapid boiling, then test again. Add the sugar and stir until it has dissolved. Add the reserved lemon peel shreds and boil rapidly for about 15 minutes.
7 Test for a set and, when setting point is reached, take the pan off the heat and remove any scum with a slotted spoon. Leave the marmalade to stand for about 15 minutes, then stir to distribute the peel. Pot and cover in the usual way (see page 476).

NUTRITION PER TABLESPOON
35 cals | 0g fat | 90g carbs | trace salt Ⓥ

Seville Orange Marmalade

Makes about 4.5kg (10lb)
Preparation time 30 minutes, plus standing
Cooking time about 2½ hours

1.4kg (3lb) Seville oranges
juice of 2 lemons
2.7kg (6lb) sugar, warmed

1 Halve the oranges and squeeze out the juice and pips. Tie the pips, and any membrane that has come away during squeezing, in a piece of muslin. Slice the orange peel thinly or thickly, as preferred, and put it into a preserving pan with the orange and lemon juices, muslin bag and 3.4 litres (6 pints) water.
2 Simmer gently for about 2 hours or until the peel is very soft and the liquid has reduced by about half.
3 Remove the muslin bag, squeezing it well and allowing the juice to run back into the pan. Add the sugar and heat gently, stirring until it has dissolved. Bring to the boil and boil rapidly for 15 minutes or until setting point is reached (see page 475). Use the saucer test.
4 Take the pan off the heat and remove any scum with a slotted spoon. Leave to stand for 15 minutes, then stir to distribute the peel. Pot and cover in the usual way (see page 476).

Cook's Tip
It is important to add all the pips and excess pith to the muslin bag as they contain pectin, which helps to set the marmalade.

NUTRITION PER TABLESPOON
40 cals | 0g fat | 10g carbs | trace salt Ⓥ

Pickles

Pickles are a traditional way of preserving fruit and vegetables with vinegar, spices and flavourings. They can be either sweet or sharp, or an interesting blend of both. Fruits for pickling are usually lightly cooked first. For sharp pickles, the vegetables are generally brined first in a salt solution for up to 24 hours, or sometimes longer.

Large, wide-necked bottles are recommended for pickling, although smaller jam jars can be used. Screw-topped jars with tops that have plastic-coated linings, such as those used for coffee jars and bought pickles, are ideal. Metal tops should not be placed in direct contact with the pickle because the vinegar will react with the metal.

Pickled Onions

Makes 1.8kg (4lb)
Preparation time 25 minutes, plus 2 days marinating and maturing

1.1 litres (2 pints) distilled vinegar
2–3 mace blades
1 tbsp whole allspice
1 tbsp cloves
2 cinnamon sticks
6 black peppercorns
1 bay leaf
1.8kg (4lb) pickling onions, unpeeled
450g (1lb) salt

1 To make the spiced vinegar, put the vinegar, spices and bay leaf into a pan, bring to the boil, then leave to cool. Cover and leave to marinate for 2 hours. Strain through a muslin-lined sieve, then pour into sterilised bottles and seal with airtight, vinegar-proof tops until needed.
2 Put the onions in a large bowl. Dissolve half the salt in 2.3 litres (4 pints) water. Pour over the onions and leave to marinate at room temperature for 12 hours.
3 Drain the onions, peel away the skins, then put in a clean bowl. Dissolve the remaining salt in 2.3 litres (4 pints) water. Pour this over the peeled onions and leave for a further 24–36 hours.
4 Drain the onions and rinse well, then pack into sterilised jars. Pour in enough spiced vinegar to cover them completely. Cover with vinegar-proof tops. Store in a cool, dark place for at least one month before using.

NUTRITION PER 25g (1oz)
10 cals | 0g fat | 1g carbs | 0.3g salt Ⓥ

Pickled Red Cabbage

Makes about 1.4kg (3lb)
Preparation time 20 minutes, plus overnight standing

1.4kg (3lb) firm red cabbage, cored and finely shredded
2 large onions, peeled and sliced
4 tbsp salt
2.3 litres (4 pints) spiced vinegar (see Pickled Onions, opposite)
1 tbsp light muscovado sugar

1 Layer the red cabbage and onions in a large bowl, sprinkling each layer with salt, then cover and leave to stand overnight at room temperature.
2 The following day, drain the cabbage and onions, rinse off the surplus salt and drain thoroughly.
3 Pack the cabbage mixture into sterilised jars.
4 Pour the spiced vinegar into a pan and heat gently. Add the sugar and stir until dissolved. Leave to cool.
5 Pour the cooled vinegar over the cabbage and onion, then cover immediately and seal in the usual way (see page 476) with vinegar-proof tops. Use within two to three weeks; thereafter the cabbage tends to lose its crispness.

Cook's Tip

If after a couple of days the cabbage starts to go soft and there are lots of bubbles in the jars, the temperature in the room may be too high.

NUTRITION PER TABLESPOON
10 cals | trace fat (0g sats) | 1g carbs | 0g salt Ⓥ

Piccalilli

Makes 1.8kg (4lb)
Preparation time 25 minutes, plus standing and maturing
Cooking time 25 minutes

1.8kg (4lb) mixed marrow, cucumber, French beans, small onions and cauliflower (prepared weight, see recipe)
225g (8oz) salt
175g (6oz) sugar
2 tsp mustard powder
1 tsp ground ginger
2 garlic cloves, crushed
1 litre (1¾ pints) distilled vinegar
25g (1oz) plain flour
4 tsp ground turmeric

1 Deseed and finely dice the marrow and cucumber; top, tail and slice the French beans; peel and halve the onions; divide the cauliflower into florets.
2 Layer the vegetables in a large bowl, sprinkling each layer with salt. Add 2.4 litres (4¼ pints) water, cover and leave to stand for 24 hours at room temperature.
3 The following day, drain the vegetables, rinse well and drain thoroughly.
4 Combine the sugar, mustard powder, ginger, garlic and 900ml (1½ pints) of the vinegar in a preserving pan. Add the vegetables, bring to the boil, lower the heat and simmer, uncovered, for 20 minutes or until the vegetables are cooked but still crisp.
5 Blend the flour and turmeric with the remaining vinegar and stir into the vegetables. Bring to the boil and cook for 2 minutes.
6 Spoon into sterilised jars, then cover and seal in the usual way (see page 476) with vinegar-proof tops. Store in a cool, dark place for at least one month before using.

NUTRITION PER TABLESPOON
10 cals | trace fat (0g sats) | 2g carbs | 0.7g salt Ⓥ

Chutneys

Chutneys are easy to make – you simply put all the ingredients into a large pan and cook until thick. The fruit and/or vegetables are first chopped or sliced, then cooked slowly for several hours with vinegar and spices to produce a sweet-and-sour mixture, with the texture of a chunky jam. Never leave chutney unattended while it is simmering as it can easily burn, especially towards the end of cooking. The flavour of chutney improves with keeping.

Apple Chutney

Makes 2.7kg (6lb)
Preparation time 30 minutes
Cooking time 3¼ hours

1.4kg (3lb) cooking apples, peeled, cored and diced
1.4kg (3lb) onions, chopped
450g (1lb) sultanas or seedless raisins
grated zest and juice of 2 lemons
700g (1½lb) demerara sugar
600ml (1 pint) malt vinegar

1 Put the apples, onions, sultanas or raisins, lemon zest and juice, sugar and vinegar in a preserving pan.
2 Bring to the boil, then reduce the heat and simmer, uncovered, stirring occasionally, for 3 hours or until the mixture is of a thick consistency with no excess liquid remaining.
3 Spoon the chutney into prepared jars and cover immediately with airtight and vinegar-proof tops.

TRY SOMETHING DIFFERENT

Smooth Apple Chutney A blender or food processor can be used to produce a smoother texture, if you like. In this case, bring all the ingredients, except the sultanas or raisins, to the boil and simmer until really soft. Allow to cool slightly, then whiz in a blender or processor, a little at a time, until smooth. Return to the pan with the sultanas or raisins and cook for a further 15 minutes or until thick. Pot and cover in the usual way (see page 476) with vinegar-proof tops.
Gooseberry Chutney Follow the recipe above, replacing the apples with 1.4kg (3lb) prepared gooseberries.

NUTRITION PER TABLESPOON
28 cals | 0g fat | 7g carbs | trace salt Ⓥ

Tomato Relish

Makes 1.4kg (3lb)
Preparation time 30 minutes, plus overnight salting
Cooking time 1 hour

1.4kg (3lb) tomatoes, peeled and sliced (see page 277)
450g (1lb) cucumber or marrow, peeled, seeded and roughly chopped
50g (2oz) salt
2 garlic cloves, finely chopped
1 large red pepper, seeded and roughly chopped
450ml (¾ pint) malt vinegar
1 tbsp mustard powder
½ tsp ground allspice
½ tsp mustard seeds

1 Layer the tomatoes and cucumber or marrow in a bowl, sprinkling each layer with salt. Cover and leave overnight at room temperature.
2 Next day, drain and rinse well and put in a large pan. Add the garlic and pepper.
3 Blend the vinegar with the dry ingredients and stir into the pan. Bring slowly to the boil, then reduce the heat and simmer gently, uncovered, for about 1 hour, stirring occasionally, until the mixture is soft.
4 Spoon the relish into sterilised jars and cover immediately in the usual way (see page 476) with vinegar-proof tops.

NUTRITION PER TABLESPOON
5 cals | 0g fat | 1g carbs | 0.1g salt Ⓥ

Mango Chutney

Makes 2kg (4½lb)
Preparation time 30 minutes
Cooking time about 1½ hours

1.8kg (4lb) ripe yellow mangoes, peeled and sliced
2 small cooking apples, peeled, cored and chopped
2 onions, chopped
125g (4oz) seedless raisins
600ml (1 pint) distilled malt vinegar
350g (12oz) demerara sugar
1 tbsp ground ginger
3 garlic cloves, peeled and crushed
1 tsp freshly grated nutmeg
½ tsp salt

1 Put all the ingredients into a preserving pan. Bring to the boil, then reduce the heat and simmer gently, uncovered, stirring occasionally, for about 1½ hours or until no excess liquid remains and the mixture is thick and pulpy.
2 Spoon the chutney into sterilised jars and leave to cool.
3 Cover and seal in the usual way (see page 476) with vinegar-proof tops. Once open, store in the fridge and use within a month. Serve with curries, cheese and cold meat.

NUTRITION PER TABLESPOON
20 cals | trace fat (0g sats) | 6g carbs | 0.1g salt Ⓥ

Chilli Jam

Makes 900g (2lb)
Preparation time 25 minutes
Cooking time 55 minutes

550g (1¼lb) caster sugar
200ml (7fl oz) red wine vinegar
900g (2lb) ripe tomatoes, skinned and chopped (see page 277)
8 medium red chillies, seeded and finely chopped (see Cook's Tips, page 69)
6 garlic cloves, crushed
5cm (2in) fresh root ginger, peeled and grated
6 whole cloves, 6 black peppercorns and 4 whole allspice berries, tied in a muslin bag

1 Put the sugar and vinegar into a large pan over a low heat and cook gently to dissolve the sugar.
2 Add the tomatoes, chillies, garlic and ginger, and the spices in a muslin bag. Bring to the boil, then cook very gently for 45–50 minutes, stirring occasionally, until the mixture is thickened. To test, draw a wooden spoon across the base of the pan – it should stay clear for 3 seconds.
3 Pour into sterilised jars, cover and seal in the usual way (see page 476) with vinegar-proof tops. Store in a cool, dark place for one month before eating.

NUTRITION PER TABLESPOON
29 cals | 0g fat | 7g carbs | trace salt Ⓥ

Rhubarb and Ginger Chutney

Makes about 1.6kg (3½lb)
Preparation time 15 minutes, plus 12 hours standing
Cooking time 1¼ hours

1kg (2¼lb) thick rhubarb stems, trimmed and cut into 5cm (2in) pieces
4 tsp salt
225g (8oz) red onions, cut into thick slices
700g (1½lb) dark muscovado sugar
450ml (¾ pint) white wine vinegar
25g (1oz) fresh root ginger, peeled and coarsely grated
¼ tsp ground allspice
125g (4oz) raisins

1 Put the rhubarb in a non-metallic bowl, mix with 1 tsp salt, then cover and leave in a cool place for 12 hours.
2 Drain and rinse the rhubarb, then put it in a preserving pan with all the other ingredients except the raisins. Heat gently until the sugar has dissolved, then increase the heat and bubble for 1 hour, stirring occasionally, until reduced and pulpy. Add the raisins and simmer for 5 minutes.
3 Pot while hot or cool (not warm), cover in the usual way (see page 476) and store for up to six months.

Cook's Tip
This is a useful chutney to have in the cupboard and tastes especially good with mature cheeses and cold meats.

NUTRITION PER TABLESPOON
10 cals | 0g fat | 3g carbs | 0.1g salt Ⓥ

Drinks

Alcoholic Drinks

Brandy Alexander

Serves 1
Preparation time 2 minutes

25ml (1fl oz) brandy
25ml (1fl oz) crème de caçao
25ml (1fl oz) double cream
a pinch of freshly grated nutmeg

1 Mix together the brandy, crème de caçao and cream, and shake well.
2 Dust with a little nutmeg and serve.

TRY SOMETHING DIFFERENT
Gin Alexander Replace the brandy with gin.

NUTRITION PER GLASS
245 cals | 13g fat (8g sats) | 9g carbs | trace salt Ⓥ

Whiskey Sour

Serves 1
Preparation time 2 minutes

juice of ½ lemon
1 tsp sugar
25ml (1fl oz) rye whiskey
crushed ice

1 Mix together the lemon juice, sugar and rye whiskey, and shake well with the ice.
2 Serve in a whiskey tumbler.

NUTRITION PER GLASS
71 cals | 0g fat | 5g carbs | trace salt Ⓥ

Dry Martini

Serves 1
Preparation time 2 minutes

50ml (2fl oz) French vermouth
25ml (1fl oz) dry gin
crushed ice
1 stuffed olive or lemon zest curl

1 Shake the vermouth and gin together with some crushed ice in a shaker.
2 Pour into a glass and float an olive or a lemon zest curl on top. The proportions of a martini are a matter of personal taste; some people prefer 50ml (2fl oz) gin to 25ml (1fl oz) vermouth, others equal quantities of gin and vermouth.

TRY SOMETHING DIFFERENT
Sweet Martini Cocktail Follow the recipe above, but use sweet vermouth and decorate with a cocktail cherry.

NUTRITION PER GLASS
110 cals | 0g fat | 2g carbs | trace salt

Bloody Mary

Serves 4
Preparation time 2 minutes

1 tbsp Worcestershire sauce
1 dash Tabasco sauce
25ml (1fl oz) vodka, chilled
150ml (1¼ pints) tomato juice, chilled
ice cubes
lemon juice to taste
celery salt to taste
1 celery stick, with the leaves left on to serve

1 Pour the Worcestershire sauce, Tabasco sauce, vodka and tomato juice into a tall glass and stir.
2 Add ice cubes and the lemon juice and celery salt to taste. Put the celery stick in the glass and serve.

TRY SOMETHING DIFFERENT
Virgin Mary Omit the vodka for a non-alcoholic cocktail.

NUTRITION PER GLASS
96 cals | 0g fat | 9g carbs | 1.8g salt

Pink Gin

Serves 1
Preparation time 2 minutes

2–3 drops Angostura bitters
25ml (1fl oz) gin
50–75ml (2–2½fl oz) iced water

1 Put the bitters into a glass and turn it until the side is well coated.
2 Add the gin and top up with iced water to taste.

NUTRITION PER GLASS
51 cals | 0g fat | 0g carbs | 0g salt Ⓥ

Daiquiri

Serves 1
Preparation time 2 minutes

juice of ½ lime • 1 tsp sugar • 25ml (1fl oz) white rum
crushed ice • extra lime juice and caster sugar for frosting

1 Mix the fruit juice, sugar and rum and shake well with the crushed ice in a shaker.
2 Dip the edges of the glass in a little more lime juice and then into caster sugar to frost the rim before filling.

NUTRITION PER GLASS
72 cals | 0g fat | 5g carbs | 0g salt

Kir

Serves 1
Preparation time 2 minutes

25ml (1fl oz) crème di cassis
150ml (¼ pint) white wine

1 Pour the crème di cassis and wine into a glass and serve.

TRY SOMETHING DIFFERENT
Kir Royale Use 150ml (¼ pint) sparking white wine.

NUTRITION PER GLASS
165 cals | 0g fat | 9g carbs | 0g salt

Margarita

Serves 1
Preparation time 2 minutes

lemon juice • salt • 125ml (4fl oz) tequila
25ml (1fl oz) curaçao • 25ml (1fl oz) lemon or lime juice

1 Dip the edges of a chilled glass into lemon juice and then salt.
2 In a shaker, mix the tequila, curaçao and lemon juice.
3 Strain into the chilled glass and serve immediately.

NUTRITION PER GLASS
342 cals | 0g fat | 39g carbs | 0g salt Ⓥ

Buck's Fizz

Serves 1
Preparation time 2 minutes

juice from one small orange
150ml (¼ pint) Champagne or sparkling wine

1 Strain the orange juice into a champagne flute.
2 Top up with chilled Champagne or sparkling wine and serve at once.

NUTRITION PER GLASS
132 cals | 0g fat (0g sats) | 7g carbs | 0g salt

Piña Colada

Serves 1
Preparation time 2 minutes

85ml (3fl oz) white rum • 125ml (4fl oz) pineapple juice
50ml (2fl oz) coconut cream • crushed ice
1 pineapple slice and 1 cherry to decorate

1 Blend the rum, juice, coconut cream and crushed ice.
2 Pour into a large goblet or a hollowed-out pineapple half.
3 Decorate with fruit slices and a cherry. Serve with straws.

NUTRITION PER GLASS
382 cals | 17g fat (15g sats) | 13g carbs | trace salt

Irish or Gaelic Coffee

Serves 1
Preparation time 5 minutes, plus standing

25ml (1fl oz) Irish whiskey
1 tsp brown sugar
85–125ml (3–4fl oz) hot double-strength coffee
1–2 tbsp double cream, chilled

1 Gently warm a glass, pour in the whiskey and add the brown sugar.
2 Pour in black coffee to within 2.5cm (1in) of the brim and stir to dissolve the sugar.
3 Fill to the brim with cream, poured over the back of a spoon, and allow to stand for a few minutes.

TRY SOMETHING DIFFERENT
Make these in the same way as Irish Coffee. For one glass, allow 25ml (1fl oz) liqueur or spirit to 125ml (4fl oz) double-strength black coffee, with sugar to taste (about 1 tsp) and thick double cream to pour on top.
• **Cointreau Coffee** Make with Cointreau.
• **Caribbean Coffee** Make with rum.
• **German Coffee** Make with Kirsch.
• **Normandy Coffee** Make with Calvados.
• **Russian Coffee** Make with vodka.
• **Calypso Coffee** Make with Tia Maria.
• **Witch's Coffee** Make with strega and sprinkle a little grated lemon zest on top.
• **Curaçao Coffee** Make with curaçao, stir with a cinnamon stick.

NUTRITION PER GLASS
218 cals | 16g fat (10g sats) | 6g carbs | trace salt

Mulled Wine

Serves 6
Preparation time 10 minutes, plus infusing
Cooking time 10–15 minutes

2 oranges
6 cloves
75cl bottle fruity red wine
50ml (2fl oz) brandy or Cointreau
1 cinnamon stick, broken, plus extra to garnish
½ tsp mixed spice
2 tbsp golden granulated sugar

1 Cut one of the oranges into six wedges and push a clove into each wedge. Using a vegetable peeler, carefully pare the zest of the other orange into strips.
2 Put the clove-studded orange wedges into a stainless-steel pan, along with the red wine, brandy or Cointreau, cinnamon stick, mixed spice and sugar. Warm gently over a low heat for 10–15 minutes, then remove the pan from the heat and set aside for 10 minutes to let the flavours infuse.
3 Strain the wine into a serving jug through a non-metallic sieve to remove the orange wedges and the cinnamon. Serve in heatproof glasses with a strip of orange zest draped over a broken cinnamon stick.

Cook's Tips
Choose a bold, fruity red – nothing too oaky – such as Bordeaux or another wine made from Cabernet Sauvignon or Merlot.

NUTRITION PER GLASS
120 cals | 0g fat | 5g carbs | trace salt

Egg Nog

Serves 1
Preparation time 5 minutes
Cooking time 3 minutes

1 medium egg
1 tbsp sugar
50ml (2fl oz) sherry or brandy
300ml (1½ pints) milk

1 Whisk the egg and sugar and add the sherry or brandy.
2 Heat the milk without boiling and pour it over the egg mixture. Stir well and serve hot in a heatproof glass.

ALCOHOLIC DRINKS AND VEGETARIANS
Animal-derived ingredients, such as gelatine (from cattle) and isinglass (from fish) are often used as fining agents in wine, sherry, port, beer and cider. For this reason some vegetarians prefer to drink only vegetarian alternatives. You can find these in supermarkets and online. Spirits (apart from some malt whiskies, which have been matured in sherry casks) and many liqueurs are generally acceptable to vegetarians.

NUTRITION PER GLASS
356 cals | 11g fat (5g sats) | 38g carbs | 0.5g salt

Non-alcoholic Drinks

Still Lemonade

Serves 6
Makes about 1.1 litres (2 pints)
Preparation time 10 minutes

3 lemons
175g (6oz) sugar

1 Remove the lemon zest thinly using a potato peeler.
2 Put the zest and sugar into a bowl or large jug and pour on 900ml (1½ pints) boiling water. Cover and leave to cool, stirring occasionally.
3 Add the juice of the lemons and strain the lemonade. Serve chilled.

NUTRITION PER GLASS
116 cals | 0g fat | 31g carbs | 0g salt Ⓥ

Warming Ginger Soda

Serves 6
Preparation time 5 minutes
Cooking time 10–15 minutes, plus cooling

300g (11oz) unpeeled fresh root ginger, finely sliced
225g (8oz) caster sugar
zest and juice of 1½ lemons
1 litre (1¾ pints) soda water

1 Put the root ginger into a pan with the sugar and lemon zest and juice. Add about 600ml (1 pint) cold water to cover. Heat gently to dissolve the sugar, then turn up the heat and simmer for 10 minutes.
2 Strain through a fine sieve into a jug. Allow to cool for at least 10 minutes, then top up with soda water.

GET AHEAD
Make syrup up to three days ahead. Chill. Add soda to serve.

NUTRITION PER GLASS
148 cals | 0g fat | 39g carbs | trace salt Ⓥ

Elderflower Cordial

Serves about 30
Makes about 1.1 litres (2 pints)
Preparation time 5 minutes

2kg (4½lb) golden granulated sugar
80g (just over 3oz) citric acid
2 medium lemons, sliced
20 large young elderflower heads, shaken to release any insects

1 Bring 1.1 litres (2 pints) water to the boil, add the sugar and stir until dissolved.
2 Add the citric acid and lemon slices. Stir in the flower heads. Cover and leave overnight.
3 In the morning, strain through a fine sieve. If you want the cordial to be clearer, strain again through muslin or a coffee filter.
4 Bottle, give some away and keep the rest in the fridge – it will last for months!

TRY SOMETHING DIFFERENT
Try this cocktail (everything must be ice cold): put a dribble of elderflower cordial into a Champagne glass, followed by a shot of vodka and a splash of rosewater. Finally, top up with prosecco or cava.

NUTRITION PER GLASS
263 cals | 0g fat | 70g carbs | 0g salt Ⓥ

Summer Berry Smoothie

Serves 6
Preparation time 10 minutes

2 large, ripe bananas, about 450g (1lb)
150g (5oz) natural yogurt
500g (1lb 2oz) fresh or frozen summer berries

1 Peel and chop the bananas, then put into a blender. Add the yogurt and 150ml (¼ pint) water, then whiz until smooth. Add the berries and whiz to a purée.
2 Sieve the mixture into a large jug, using the back of a ladle to press it through the sieve. Pour into six glasses and serve at once.

TRY SOMETHING DIFFERENT
Six ripe apricots or 16 ready-to-eat dried apricots or 400g (14oz) canned apricots in natural juice can be used instead of the berries.

NUTRITION PER GLASS
108 cals | 0.6g fat (trace sats) | 24.3g carbs | 0.1g salt Ⓥ

Mango and Passion Fruit Smoothie

Serves 2
Preparation time 5 minutes

1 small mango
1 passion fruit
150g (5oz) natural yogurt
ice to serve
orange juice (optional)

1 Peel the mango and slice off the flesh from the central stone. Roughly chop. Halve the passion fruit and scoop out the flesh. Rub through a sieve to extract the juice, reserving some of the seeds for decoration, if you like.
2 Put the mango flesh and passion fruit juice into a blender with the yogurt. Whiz until smooth, then serve at once over ice garnished with the passion fruit seeds, if you like. Pour in a little fresh orange juice, if you prefer a thinner smoothie.

NUTRITION PER GLASS
73 cals | 1g fat (1g sats) | 13g carbs | 0.1g salt Ⓥ

Creamy Oat and Raspberry Cooler

Serves 2
Preparation time 5 minutes

175g (6oz) raspberries, thawed if frozen, juices reserved
juice of 1 large orange, about 100ml (3½fl oz)
100ml (3½fl oz) oat milk, well chilled
100ml (3½fl oz) low-fat natural or soya yogurt, well chilled
40g (1½oz) fine oatmeal
2 tsp wheat bran
2 tsp clear honey (optional)

1 If using fresh raspberries, remove the hulls, then wash and pat the fruit dry with kitchen paper. Put into a blender. If the fruit has been frozen, add the juices as well.
2 Pour in the orange juice and oat milk, and spoon in the yogurt. Add the oatmeal and 1 tsp wheat bran. Blend until smooth.
3 Taste and sweeten with honey, if necessary. Pour into two glasses, sprinkle with the remaining wheat bran and serve.

TRY SOMETHING DIFFERENT
Use blackberries or strawberries instead of raspberries.

NUTRITION PER GLASS
82 cals | 3.8g fat (0.6g sats) | 29.4g carbs | 0.2g salt Ⓥ

Entertaining and
Food Storage

Entertaining

Plan ahead and you are more likely to enjoy the occasion. Avoid planning a meal that is too complicated, and don't tackle a recipe that is totally unfamiliar – have a practice run first if you have not cooked it before. When deciding on a menu, keep it as well balanced as possible. Think about the colours, flavours and textures of the foods – rich and light, sweet and savoury, crunchy and smooth, hot and cold – and the cooking methods. Don't have cream or fruit in all the courses; avoid a menu that is all the same colour.

Select produce in season, for the best flavour and value for money. Check whether any of your guests have special dietary needs and plan appropriately. Try to cook an entirely meatless meal even if there is going to be just one vegetarian – it's not as difficult as it sounds, and rarely does anybody notice!

It is worthwhile choosing dishes that can be prepared well in advance or prepared up to a certain point, only needing a little last-minute finishing in the kitchen.

Planning the event

Make a master shopping list and separate lists of dishes to be prepared ahead, with a note of when to make them. Plan fridge and freezer space; for a large party, you may need to make different arrangements such as asking your neighbour to keep some foods in their fridge, or putting bulky items into cool boxes. Check that you have candles if you plan to use them.

Make invitations to a dinner party over the phone about 10–12 days in advance. Mention whether it's a formal or informal occasion, the date and time, address if necessary, and say if there are any special dress requirements so you can be sure that no one is embarrassed by dressing too formally, or informally. If you are sending written invitations, post them two to three weeks in advance.

Check that table linen is laundered and ironed in advance, and that glasses and cutlery are clean. Clean the house a day or two beforehand. Buy or order wine and drinks in advance and avoid doing all the shopping at once.

Cooking in quantity

Decide on the type of party you want to have. A buffet party is ideal if you are entertaining a large number and wish to serve a full meal; make sure that starters and main courses can be eaten with a fork. Choose some recipes that can be prepared and frozen ahead. Many of the recipes in this book can be doubled up easily; however, it isn't usually feasible to prepare a quantity that will serve more than 12 people in one go. So, make up the dishes in batches. On the day, allow plenty of time to reheat dishes and/or arrange serving dishes of cold food. Make sure you have enough people to pass food around – at least one per 20 guests.

Handy hints for entertaining

- Try to strike a balance between hot and cold items, light and substantial ones.
- Most supermarkets have a good selection of ready-to-eat or cook appetisers, if you haven't time to make some. You can also use good-quality bought ingredients, such as mayonnaise and fresh sauces, to save time.
- A freezer is invaluable when entertaining whether on a grand scale or just dinner for two.
- Keep a supply of ready-to-bake bread in the fridge or freezer for quick fresh bread. Freeze packs of half-baked breads to pop in the oven as and when needed.
- Keep a supply of luxury ice cream in the freezer.
- Remember to unwrap cheeses and bring them to room temperature at least an hour before serving, keeping them lightly covered, to prevent drying out, until the last minute.
- Make ice well in advance, and see page 497 for advice on chilling drinks.
- During the winter, if you run out of fridge space, use a greenhouse or garage to keep drinks and other perishables cold.
- Borrow a couple of extra cool boxes, and remember to freeze plenty of cool-box blocks in advance.
- Use the microwave to reheat pre-cooked vegetables, sauces and gravy.
- Decide in advance where you are going to stack dirty plates. A kitchen overflowing with washing-up looks unsightly, so consider paying someone to do this for you on the day.

Approximate quantities for buffet parties

	Ingredients	Portions	Notes
STARTERS			
Fish cocktail	50g (2oz) peeled shrimps, prawns, crab or lobster meat, 2 lettuce leaves, about 40ml (1½fl oz) sauce, 700g (1½lb) fish (as above), 1 large lettuce, 450ml (¼ pint) sauce	1 12	Serve in stemmed glasses, garnished with a shrimp or prawn. Serve with lemon wedges.
Pâtés – allow 3 half slices hot toast per person to serve with the pâté	75–125g (3–4oz) 1.1kg (2½lb)	1 12	
Smoked salmon (serve with toast as above or brown bread)	40–50g (1½–2oz) 550g (1¼lb) 1.1kg (2½lb)	1 12 25	
Other smoked fish, such as smoked trout, mackerel	125g (4oz) 1.1kg (2½lb) 2–2.5kg (4½–5½lb)	1 12 25	
Soups – cream, clear or iced	150–200ml (5–7fl oz) 2.3 litres (4 pints) 4.5 litres (8 pints)	1 12 25	
MAIN DISHES			
Delicatessen meats – ham, tongue, salami	75–125g (3–4oz) 1kg (2¼lb) 2.3kg (5lb)	1 12 25	
Salmon	125–175g (4–6oz) 1.4–1.8kg (3–4lb)	1 12	
Roast turkey	3.6–5kg (8–11lb) 6.8–9kg (15–20lb)	10–15 20–30	
Chicken – whole – joint	Three 2.7kg (6lb) birds 150–225g (5–8oz)	24–26 1	Serve hot or cold
SALAD VEGETABLES			
Carrots	900g (2lb), grated 1.8kg (4lb), grated	12 25	
Celery	2–3 heads 5 heads	12 25	
Cucumbers	1–1½ cucumbers 2–3 cucumbers	12 25	
Lettuce	2–3 lettuces 5–6 lettuces	12 25	Dress at last minute
Boiled potatoes	700g (1½lb) 1.4kg (3lb)	12 25	For potato salads
Tomatoes	700g (1½lb) 1.4kg (3lb)	12 25	
DRESSINGS			
French Dressing	300ml (½ pint) 450–600ml (¾–1 pint)	12 25	
Mayonnaise	600ml (1 pint) 900ml–1 litre (1½–1¾ pints)	12 25	

Approximate quantities for buffet parties

	Ingredients	Portions	Notes
DESSERTS			
Meringues	6 egg whites, 350g (12oz) caster sugar,	40 (small) meringue halves	Sandwich halves together Classic Meringues (page 389)
Trifle	Old-English Trifle Old-English Trifle × 2	6 15	Old-English Trifle (page 382)
Profiteroles	1 quantity of Choux Pastry, 150ml (¼ pint) whipped cream, 1 quantity of Rich Chocolate Sauce 2 quantities of Choux Pastry, 300ml (¼ pint) whipped cream, 2 quantities of Chocolate Sauce	6 12–15	Choux Pastry (page 329) Profiteroles (page 368) Rich Chocolate Sauce (page 25) Fill not more than 2 hours before serving
Lemon Syllabub	Lemon Syllabub × 4	16	Lemon Syllabub (page 380)
Ice cream (bought or home-made)	1 litre (1¾ pints) 2.3 litres (4 pints)	12 25–30	Vanilla Ice Cream (page 393) Transfer from freezer to fridge 30 minutes before serving
SAVOURIES			
Cheese Straws	Cheese Straws × 2	48	Cheese Straws (page 67)
Sausage Rolls	Sausage Rolls × 4	64	Sausage Rolls (page 211)
Tangy Chicken Bites	Tangy Chicken Bites	48	Tangy Chicken Bites (page 70)
Red Pepper Pesto Croûtes	Red Pepper Pesto Croûtes × 2	48	Red Pepper Pesto Croûtes (p. 65).
Mozzarella Nibbles	Mozzarella Nibbles × 2	60	Mozzarella Nibbles (page 66)
Cocktail sausages	450g (1lb)	32	
Quiche	20.5cm (8in) quiche	6–8	Quiche Lorraine (page 340)
BREAD, CRACKERS AND SANDWICHES			
Bread loaves	1 large loaf, about 800g (1lb 12oz) 1 small loaf, about 400g (14oz) 1 long sandwich loaf, 1.4kg (3lb)	20–24 slices 10–12 slices 50 slices	Bread (pages 452–456) Cut into triangles when serving with a meal
Slices of bread	1–1½ slices	1	
French bread	1 large loaf 1 small loaf	12–15 6–8	
Cheese biscuits or crackers	3 biscuits 60 biscuits	1 30	
BUTTER			
	15–25g (½–1oz) butter	1	If bread is served with the meal
	25–40g (1–1½oz) butter	1	If serving cheese as a course
	About 125g (4oz) butter	spreads 10–12 sandwiches	
	About 125g (4oz) butter	spreads 10–12 bread rolls	
CHEESE			
Cheese (for biscuits)	25–40g (1–1½oz) 700–900g (1½– 2lb)	1 25	Serve a selection of at least four types
Cheese (for wine and cheese parties)	75g (3oz) 2–2.3kg (4½–5lb)	1 25	Serve a selection of at least four types

Catering quantities

Approximate quantities to serve 12 people. For 25, multiply the quantities by 2.
For 50, multiply by 4. For 75, multiply by 5½. For 100, multiply by 7.

STARTERS
Soups	2.6 litres (4½ pints)
Pâtés	1.1kg (2½lb)
Smoked salmon	900g (2lb)
Prawns	900g (2lb)

MAIN DISHES
Boneless chicken or turkey	1.8kg (4lb)
Whole chicken	three 1.4kg (3lb) oven-ready birds
Turkey	one 5.4kg (12lb) oven-ready bird
Lamb/beef/pork	
Boneless	2–2.3kg (4½–5lb)
On the bone	3.2–3.6kg (7–8lb)
Mince	2kg (4½ lb)
Fish	
Whole with head	2.3kg (5lb)
Steaks	twelve 175g (6oz) steaks
Fillets	2kg (4½lb)
Prawns (main course)	1.4kg (3lb)

TURKEY
6–10 people	2.3–3.6kg (5–8lb)
10–15	3.6–5kg (8–11lb)
15–20	5–6.8kg (11–15lb)
20–30	6.8–9kg (15–20lb)

ACCOMPANIMENTS
Roast and mashed potatoes	2kg (4½lb)
New potatoes	1.8kg (4lb)
Rice and pasta	700g (1½lb)
Green vegetables	1.4kg (3lb)
Fresh spinach	3.6kg (8lb)

SALADS
Tomatoes	700g (1½lb)
Salad leaves	2 medium heads
Cucumber	1 large
French dressing	175ml (6fl oz)
Mayonnaise	300ml (½ pint)

BREAD
Fresh uncut bread	1 large loaf
Medium sliced loaf	1 large (approximately 24 slices)

CHEESE
For a cheese and wine party	1.4kg (3lb)
To serve at the end of a meal	700g (1½lb)

BUTTER
To serve with bread or biscuits and cheese	225g (8oz)
To serve with bread and biscuits and cheese	350g (12oz)
For sandwiches	175g (6oz) softened butter for 12 rounds

CREAM
For pudding	600ml (1 pint) single cream
For coffee	300ml (½ pint)

COFFEE AND TEA
Ground coffee	125g (4oz) for 12 medium cups
Instant	75g (3oz) for 12 large cups
Milk	allow 450ml (¾ pint) for 12 cups of tea

Approximate coffee and tea quantities

		1 SERVING	24–26 SERVINGS	NOTES
Coffee	ground	200ml (7fl oz)	250–275g (9–10oz) coffee 3.4 litres (6 pints) water 1.7 litres (3 pints) milk 450g (1lb) sugar	If you make the coffee in advance, strain it after infusion. Reheat without boiling.
Tea	Indian	200ml (7fl oz)	50g (2oz) tea 4.5 litres (8 pints) water 900ml (1½ pints) milk 450g (1lb) sugar	It is better to make tea in several pots rather than in one outsized one.
Tea	China	200ml (7fl oz)	50g (2oz) tea 5.1 litres (9 pints) water 2–3 lemons 450g (1lb) sugar	Infuse China tea for 2–3 minutes only. Put a thin lemon slice in each cup before pouring. Serve sugar separately.

Wines and other party drinks

For large gatherings, offer one white and one red wine, sticking to around 12.5 per cent alcohol, and have plenty of different soft drinks. Provide beer and lager if you like, but avoid spirits. Wines, sparkling wines, and hot or cold punches are ideal party drinks.

For very large numbers, buy wines and champagne on a sale-or-return basis from a wine merchant. Mineral water, fruit juices and soft drinks can also be bought in this way. Most supermarkets will also allow this, provided the returned bottles are undamaged – check first.

Wine boxes are good value and it is worth asking your local wine merchant for their advice – some are better than others. If you prefer to serve wine from the bottle, look at the cost-saving potential of buying by the case.

When it comes to choosing wine it makes sense to find a supplier you can trust, whether it be a supermarket, wine merchant or warehouse. If you opt for something different, just buy one bottle and see if you enjoy it.

Generally, red wine goes best with red meats, and white wine is the better complement to fish, chicken and light meats, but there really are no longer any hard-and-fast rules to follow.

For an aperitif, it is nice to serve a glass of chilled champagne or sparkling wine, or perhaps dry sherry.

Avoid sweet drinks, or spirits with a high alcohol content, as these tend to take the edge off the appetite, rather than stimulating it. Wine or sherry can be served with a soup course. A full-bodied red wine is an excellent accompaniment to the cheeseboard, although some people prefer to drink port with their cheese. You may wish to serve a dessert wine, such as Sauternes, or a glass of fruity demi-sec champagne. Coffee follows, with brandy and liqueurs if you like.

How much to buy?

If you allow one 75cl bottle of wine per head you should have more than enough. One standard 75cl bottle of wine, champagne or sparkling wine will give six glasses. A litre bottle will provide eight glasses. For a dinner party, allow one or two glasses of wine as an aperitif, one or two glasses with the first course, two glasses with the main course and another with the dessert or cheese.

Remember to buy plenty of mineral water – sparkling and still – and fresh fruit juices. For every ten guests, buy two 1.5 litre bottles of sparkling water and three similar-sized bottles of still water.

Serving wine

Warm white wine and Champagne is inexcusable, and chilled red wine (unless young and intended for serving cold) is not at all pleasant. The ideal temperature for red wine is around 15–18°C, with the more tannic wines benefiting from the higher temperature. On a warm day, a brief spell in the fridge will help red wine. For whites, the more powerful wines, like Chardonnay, should be served cool rather than cold, at around 11–15°C, while other whites should be properly cold, at around 6–10°C. Party food will probably take up your available fridge space, so you will need plenty of ice to keep drinks cool.

If you have a lot of wine to chill, use the bath, or a large deep sink if you have one. About an hour before the party, half-fill the bath with ice, pour in some cold water and stand the bottles upright, making sure the ice and water come up to their necks. Alternatively, use a clean plastic dustbin or cool boxes as containers. (Some hire companies will loan special plastic bins for cooling wines.)

A large block of ice added to chilled water is a good idea. Make this by filling a large strong plastic bag with water, seal securely and place in the freezer until frozen.

Wine and party drink checklist
- Champagne and sparkling wine
- Red wine
- White wine
- Beer and lager
- Mineral water, sparkling and natural
- Real fruit juices
- Other soft drinks and squashes
- Dessert wine or sweet sparkling wine
- Low-alcohol/alcohol-free wines, beer and lager
- Liqueurs, brandies etc., for cocktails
- Mixers
- Fail-safe corkscrews and wine-bottle stoppers – to re-cork opened wine bottles
- Plenty of ice and reusable ice packs.

Quantity guide: drinks to the bottle
(using a standard size 100ml (3½fl oz) wine glass)

Sherry, port, vermouth	12 glasses
Single measure of spirits	30
'Split' – 200ml (7fl oz) soda, tonic, ginger ale	2–3
Table wine (75cl)	6
Table wine (1 litre)	8
Fruit juices – 600ml (1 pint)	4–6
Fruit cordial – 1 litre (1¾ pints) bottle diluted with 4 litres (7 pints) water	20–26
Punch – 1.7 litres (3 pints)	6–8

Food Storage

Storing food correctly and preparing food in a hygienic way is important to ensure that it remains nutritious and as flavourful as possible, and to reduce the risk of food poisoning. When you are preparing food, always wash your hands thoroughly before and after handling it, particularly raw and cooked meat and poultry. Keep worksurfaces clean and kitchen utensils washed in between preparing raw and cooked foods. Keep raw and cooked foods separate, especially meat, fish and poultry. Never put cooked or ready-to-eat foods directly on to a surface that has just had raw fish, meat or poultry on it. To ensure food safety, remember that foods with a longer shelf life have a best-before date; more perishable items have a use-by date. Make sure items are within either date. When supermarket shopping, pack frozen and chilled items in an insulated cool bag and put them away as soon as possible.

Storage in the fridge

Store day-to-day perishable items, such as opened jams, mayonnaise and bottled sauces, in the fridge along with eggs and dairy products, fruit juices, bacon, fresh and cooked meat (on separate shelves), and salads and vegetables (except potatoes which don't like the cold). The fridge should be kept at 4–5°C. For safe food storage:

- Ensure that all items are well wrapped, and that meat and poultry cannot drip on to other foods.
- Never put hot food into the fridge, as this will raise the temperature.
- Don't leave the door open any longer than necessary, and don't overfill.
- Clean the fridge regularly using a proprietary cleaner or a solution of 1 tbsp bicarbonate of soda to 1 litre (1¾ pints) water.
- Defrost the fridge regularly, if this is not automatic.

Storage in the freezer

Freezing is an excellent way of preserving food. As well as storing bought frozen items, you can cook meals in bulk and freeze portions to be eaten later. You can also freeze concentrated reduced fresh stock. The following prepared items freeze well: bread and scones; pastries and part-baked bread from the supermarket; soups and pizzas. The correct operating temperature for a freezer is -18°C. The following guidelines apply:

- Only freeze food that is very fresh.
- Never put any foods that are still slightly warm into the freezer, or freeze more than one-tenth of your freezer's capacity in any 24 hours, as these will cause a rise in temperature.
- When freezing large quantities, use 'fast-freeze'.
- Pack and seal items well before freezing to avoid moisture or cold air coming into contact with the food,

Maximum fridge storage times

For pre-packed foods, adhere to the use-by date. For other foods the following storage times should apply:

RAW FISH AND MEAT		COOKED MEAT		VEGETABLES AND FRUIT	
fish	1 day	joints	3 days	salad leaves	2–3 days
shellfish	1 day	casseroles/stews	2 days	green vegetables	3–4 days
joints	3 days	pies	2 days	soft fruit	1–2 days
poultry	2 days	sliced meat	2 days	hard and stone fruit	3–7 days
game	2 days	ham	2 days		
raw sliced meat	2 days	vacuum-packed	1–2 weeks	DAIRY FOOD	
minced meat	1 day	(or according to pack		milk	4–5 days
offal	1 day	instructions)		cheese, soft	2–3 days
sausages	3 days			cheese, hard	1 week
bacon	7 days			eggs	1 week

Maximum freezer storage times
Follow the manufacturer's instructions or use the following recommended times:

VEGETABLES		MEAT AND POULTRY		PREPARED FOODS	
blanched vegetables	10–12 months	beef and veal	4–6 months	soups and sauces	3 months
unblanched vegetables	3–4 weeks	lamb	4–6 months	stocks	6 months
tomatoes	6–8 months	pork	4–6 months	prepared meals	4–6 months
vegetable purées	6–8 months	offal	3–4 months	cakes	4–6 months
		sliced bacon	2–3 months	bread	2–3 months
FRUIT		cured meat	2–3 months	sandwiches	2–3 months
fruit in syrup	9–12 months	ham/bacon joints	3–4 months	bread dough	2–3 months
open frozen fruit	6–8 months	chicken/turkey	4–6 months	pastries	3–4 months
fruit purées	6–8 months	duck and goose	4–6 months		
fruit juice	4–6 months	venison	4–6 months	DAIRY PRODUCE	
		rabbit	4–6 months	butter, salted	3–4 months
FISH		sausages	2–3 months	butter, unsalted	6–8 months
white fish	6–8 months	minced beef	3–4 months	ice cream	3–4 months
oily fish	3–4 months				
fish portions	3–4 months				
shellfish	2–3 months				

or cross-flavouring occurring. Wrap awkward-shaped items in foil or freezer film (ordinary clingfilm is not suitable), then seal in a bag. Freezer film can also be used as a lining for acidic foods. Label and date.

- Use square containers to store food, as they stack well and take up less space.
- Interleave items of food that might stick together with greaseproof paper, polythene, foil or freezer film.
- Don't fill containers too full with liquids, allow room for expansion.
- Do not re-freeze food once it has thawed.
- Keep your freezer as full as possible. Empty spaces require more energy to keep cool.

Freezing vegetables and fruit
If you have your own vegetable garden or local farm shop, freezing is the ideal way to preserve vegetables and fruit in peak condition. Most vegetables keep better for longer if they are blanched before freezing although those that will be eaten within a few weeks of freezing do not need to be blanched. Prepare the vegetable as appropriate, then weigh and divide into 450g (1lb) quantities. Blanch by putting the prepared vegetable in a basket and lowering into a large pan of fast-boiling water. Bring to the boil and time 1 minute for most varieties; 2–3 minutes for hard vegetables (carrots and corn-on-the-cob); and 10 seconds for soft vegetables (courgettes, mangetouts and spinach).

Plunge the basket straight into a bowl of ice-cold water, drain and pack.

Not all seasonal fruits freeze well; most berry fruits lose some quality of texture. Always use fruit that is perfectly ripe and in very good condition. Open-freeze small berry fruits, such as raspberries, blackcurrants and redcurrants. Spread them out on a tray lined with baking parchment and freeze until solid, then pack. Fruits that don't freeze well because their texture is spoiled – strawberries, for example – are only suitable for freezing as a purée. Fruits that need to be cooked before eating, such as blackcurrants and gooseberries, should be cooked first. Purée the fresh or cooked fruit, then sieve. Sweeten with sugar to taste if necessary, then pack.

Apricots, damsons, greengages, plums, cooking apples and rhubarb are best frozen in sugar syrup with lemon to avoid discoloration. Dissolve 450g (1lb) sugar in 1 litre (1¾ pints) water over a low heat. Boil for 1 minute, then cool. Add the juice of 1 lemon. Pack the halved or sliced fruit in plastic containers, add sufficient sugar syrup to cover, leaving room for expansion, then seal.

Thawing frozen food
Never leave food to thaw in a warm place but thaw it gradually in the fridge or a cool larder. Cover loosely while thawing and ensure it is thoroughly thawed before cooking. Cook food soon after thawing.

The storecupboard

Having a storecupboard well stocked with the basic essentials will save repeated visits to the shops to pick up missing items. Correct storage is important:

- Always check packaging for storage advice; storage requirements may change if additives, sugar or salt have been reduced.
- Never keep storecupboard foods beyond their use-by date.
- Keep all food cupboards scrupulously clean.
- Once canned foods are opened, transfer the contents to a clean container, cover and keep in the fridge.
- Transfer dry goods such as sugar, rice and pasta to moisture-proof containers. When supplies are used up, wash out and thoroughly dry containers before refilling with fresh stock.

The well-stocked storecupboard

Tailor the following basic guidelines to your own needs and likes:

Baking ingredients Baking powder, bicarbonate of soda and cream of tartar; clear honey and golden syrup; gelatine; easy-blend dried yeast; cocoa powder; instant coffee granules; chocolate with at least 70% cocoa solids (keep wrapped and cool); UHT or dried milk (in case you run out of fresh milk).

Cans, bottles and condiments The following items are most useful: canned tomatoes, cartons of passata, tomato paste and sun-dried tomatoes in oil; jars of pesto; canned coconut milk; tomato ketchup; English, wholegrain and Dijon mustard; Worcestershire, Tabasco, chilli, hoisin, oyster and soy sauces; cans of fruits in natural juice; cartons or cans of ready-made custard; canned chickpeas, red kidney beans and haricot beans; and, of course, baked beans.

Dried fruit and nuts Store all dried fruits and nuts in airtight containers in a cool, dry cupboard. Nuts stale quickly if they are kept in a humid atmosphere. Vacuum-packed chestnuts are a handy time-saver; shelled walnuts, hazelnuts, almonds, pistachio nuts and pinenuts are worth buying; ground almonds and/or hazelnuts; currants, raisins, sultanas, dried apricots and prunes are useful for winter fruit compôtes, cakes and biscuits.

Dried mushrooms There are several different varieties of dried wild mushrooms, including ceps, porcini and morels.

Dried herbs, spices and flavourings Stock a selection from those detailed on pages 32–39, but not too many at once. Whole spices keep their flavour better than ready-ground, but all need to be replaced after a while, as they lose their pungency. Store them in a cool, dark cupboard or in dark jars. Stock up with sea salt, black and green peppercorns; Indian curry and tandoori pastes; Thai green and red curry pastes; vanilla and almond extracts; vanilla pods, whole nutmegs, cloves and cinnamon sticks.

Flours and sugars These should be stored in airtight containers that are easy to access with a spoon or measure. Stock up with plain white flour; self-raising white flour; wholemeal flour; cornflour; golden caster sugar; unrefined granulated sugar; light and dark muscovado sugars and white and golden icing sugar.

Oils are best stored in a dark cupboard away from any heat source, as heat and light can make them turn rancid and affect the colour. Buy olive oil in dark green bottles. Keep a stock of the following: vegetable oil for deep-frying; sunflower oil for frying and salads; light olive oil for cooking; extra virgin olive oil for salad dressings; sesame oil for Chinese cooking; walnut or hazelnut oil for dressings. Vinegars must be kept cool or they can turn bad. Stock up with white and red wine vinegars; balsamic and sherry vinegars for sauces and dressings; cider vinegar and flavoured vinegars for dressings and mayonnaise; distilled malt vinegar for pickles and chutneys; malt vinegar for traditional fish and chips.

Pasta Dried pasta is very useful. Keep at least one long pasta, such as spaghetti, a box of ribbon pasta like tagliatelle; some dried pasta shapes, such as penne, spirals or macaroni; plus lasagne sheets and tiny soup pasta.

Rice, grains and pulses Keep a stock of the following: long-grain rice, pudding rice, mixed wild rice, brown rice and Arborio rice for creamy risottos; couscous, bulgur wheat, rolled oats, oatmeal and polenta; dried kidney beans, haricot beans and flageolets; red, green and Puy lentils.

Other ingredients can be bought as required in small quantities.

Glossary

Acidulated water Water to which lemon juice or vinegar has been added in which fruit or vegetables, such as pears or Jerusalem artichokes, are immersed to prevent discoloration.

Al dente Italian term commonly used to describe food, especially pasta and vegetables, which are cooked until tender but still firm to the bite.

Antipasto Italian selection of cold meats, fish, salads, etc., served as a starter.

Au gratin Describes a dish that has been coated with sauce, sprinkled with breadcrumbs or cheese and browned under the grill or in the oven. Low-sided gratin dishes are used.

Bain-marie Literally, a water bath, used to keep foods, such as delicate custards and sauces, at a constant low temperature during cooking. On the hob, a double pan or bowl over a pan of simmering water is used; for oven cooking, the baking dish(es) are placed in a roasting tin containing enough hot water to come halfway up the sides.

Baking blind Pre-baking a pastry case before filling. The pastry case is lined with greaseproof paper and weighted down with dried beans or ceramic baking beans.

Baking powder A raising agent consisting of an acid, usually cream of tartar and an alkali, such as bicarbonate of soda, which react to produce carbon dioxide. This expands during baking and makes cakes and breads rise.

Bard To cover the breast of game birds or poultry, or lean meat with fat to prevent the meat from drying out during roasting.

Baste To spoon the juices and melted fat over meat, poultry, game or vegetables during roasting to keep them moist. The term is also used to describe spooning over a marinade.

Beat To incorporate air into an ingredient or mixture by agitating it vigorously with a spoon, fork, whisk or electric mixer. The technique is also used to soften ingredients.

Béchamel Classic French white sauce, used as the basis for other sauces and savoury dishes.

Beurre manié Equal parts of flour and butter kneaded together to make a paste. Used to thicken soups, stews and casseroles. It is whisked into the hot liquid a little at a time at the end of cooking.

Bind To mix beaten egg or other liquid into a dry mixture to hold it together.

Blanch To immerse food briefly in fast-boiling water to loosen skins, such as peaches or tomatoes, or to remove bitterness, or to destroy enzymes and preserve the colour, flavour and texture of vegetables (especially prior to freezing).

Bone To remove the bones from meat, poultry, game or fish, so that it can be stuffed or simply rolled before cooking.

Bottle To preserve fruit, jams, pickles or other preserves in sterile glass jars.

Bouquet garni Small bunch of herbs – usually a mixture of parsley stems, thyme and a bay leaf – tied in muslin and used to flavour stocks, soups and stews.

Braise To cook meat, poultry, game or vegetables slowly in a small amount of liquid in a pan or casserole with a tight-fitting lid. The food is usually first browned in oil or fat.

Brochette Food cooked on a skewer or spit.

Brûlée A French term, literally meaning 'burnt' used to refer to a dish with a crisp coating of caramelised sugar.

Butterfly To split a food, such as a large prawn or poussin, almost in half and open out flat, so that it will cook more quickly.

Calorie Strictly a kilocalorie, this is used in dietetics to measure the energy value of foods.

Canapé Small appetiser, served with drinks.

Candying Method of preserving fruit or peel by impregnating with sugar.

Caramelise To heat sugar or sugar syrup slowly until it thickens to a syrup consistency and turns to a rich brown colour.

Carbonnade Rich stew or braise of meat, which includes beer.

Casserole A dish with a tight-fitting lid used for slow-cooking meat, poultry and vegetables, now used to describe food cooked in this way in the oven.

Charcuterie French term for cooked pork products, including hams, sausages and terrines.

Chill To cool food in the fridge.

Chine To sever the rib bones from the backbone, close to the spine. This is done to meat joints, such as loin of pork or lamb, to make them easier to carve into chops after cooking.

Clarify To remove sediment or impurities from a liquid. Stock is clarified by heating with egg white, while butter is clarified by melting and skimming. Butter that has been clarified will withstand a higher frying temperature. To clarify butter, heat until melted and all bubbling stops. Take off the heat and let it stand until the sediment has sunk to the bottom, then gently pour off the fat, straining it through muslin.

Compote Mixture of fresh or dried fruit stewed in sugar syrup. Served hot or cold.

Concassé Diced fresh ingredient, used as a garnish. The term is most often applied to skinned, seeded tomatoes.

Coulis A smooth fruit or vegetable purée, thinned if necessary to a pouring consistency.

Court bouillon Aromatic cooking liquid containing wine, vinegar or lemon juice, used for poaching delicate fish, poultry or vegetables.

Consistency Term used to describe the texture of a mixture, for example: firm, dropping or soft.

Cream To beat together fat and sugar until the mixture is pale and fluffy, and resembles whipped cream in texture and colour. The method is used in cakes and puddings which contain a high proportion of fat and require the incorporation of a lot of air.

Crêpe French term for a pancake.

Crimp To decorate the edge of a pie, tart or shortbread by pinching it at regular intervals to give a fluted effect.

Croquette Seasoned mixture of cooked potato and fish, meat, poultry or vegetables shaped into a small roll, coated with egg and breadcrumbs and shallow-fried.

Croûte Circle or other shaped piece of fried bread, typically used as a base for serving small game birds.

Croûtons Small pieces of fried or toasted bread, served with soups and salads.

Crudités Raw vegetables, usually cut into slices or sticks, typically served with a dipping sauce as an appetiser.

Crystallise To preserve fruit in sugar syrup.

Curdle To cause sauces or creamed mixtures to separate once the egg is added, usually by overheating or over-beating.

Cure To preserve fish, meat or poultry by smoking, drying or salting.

Daube Braising meat and vegetables with stock, often with wine and herbs added.

Deglaze To heat stock, wine or other liquid with the cooking juices left in the pan after roasting or sautéeing, scraping and stirring vigorously to dissolve the sediment on the bottom of the pan.

Dégorge To draw out moisture from a food, eg salting aubergines to remove bitter juices.

Dice To cut food into small cubes.

Draw To remove the entrails from poultry or game.

Dredge To sprinkle food generously with flour, sugar, icing sugar and so on.

Dress To pluck, draw and truss poultry or game. The term is also used to describe tossing a salad in vinaigrette or other dressing.

Dry To preserve food, such as fruit, vegetables, pasta and pulses by dehydration.

Dust To sprinkle lightly with flour, cornflour, icing sugar, etc.

Emulsion A mixture of two liquids, which do not dissolve into one another, such as oil and vinegar. Vigorous shaking or heating will emulsify them, as for a vinaigrette.

En croûte Term used to describe food that is wrapped in pastry before cooking.

En papillote Term used to describe food that is baked in a greaseproof paper or baking parchment parcel and served from the paper.

Enzyme Organic substance in food that causes chemical changes. Enzymes are a complex group. Their action is usually halted during cooking.

Escalope Thin slice of meat, such as pork, veal or turkey, from the top of the leg, usually pan-fried.

Extract Concentrated flavouring, which is used in small quantities, eg yeast extract, vanilla extract.

Ferment Chemical change deliberately or accidentally brought about by fermenting agents, such as yeast or bacteria. Fermentation is utilised for making bread, yogurt, beer and wine.

Fillet Term used to describe boned breasts of birds, boned sides of fish, and the undercut of a loin of beef, lamb, pork or veal.

Flake To separate food, such as cooked fish, into natural pieces.

Flambé Flavouring a dish with alcohol, usually brandy or rum, which is then ignited so that the actual alcohol content is burned off.

Folding in Method of combining a whisked or creamed mixture with other ingredients by cutting and folding so that it retains its lightness. A large metal spoon or plastic-bladed spatula is used.

Frosting To coat leaves and flowers with a fine layer of sugar to use as a decoration. Also an American term for icing cakes.

Fry To cook food in hot fat or oil. There are various methods: shallow-frying in a little fat in a shallow pan; deep-frying where the food is totally immersed in oil; dry-frying in which fatty foods are cooked in a non-stick pan without extra fat; see also Stir-fry.

Galette Cooked savoury or sweet mixture shaped into a round.

Garnish A decoration, usually edible, such as parsley or lemon, which is used to enhance the appearance of a savoury dish.

Glaze A glossy coating given to sweet and savoury dishes to improve their appearance and sometimes flavour. Ingredients for glazes include beaten egg, egg white, milk and syrup.

Gluten A protein constituent of grains, such as wheat and rye, which develops when the flour is mixed with water to give the dough elasticity.

Grate To shred hard food, such as cheese and carrots, with a grater or food processor attachment.

Griddle A flat, heavy, metal plate used on the hob for cooking scones or for searing savoury ingredients.

Grind To reduce foods such as coffee beans, nuts and whole spices to small particles using a food mill, pestle and mortar, electric grinder or food processor.

Gut To clean out the entrails from fish.

Hang To suspend meat or game in a cool, dry place for a number of days to tenderise the flesh and develop flavour.

Hull To remove the stalk and calyx from soft fruits, such as strawberries.

Infuse To immerse flavourings, such as aromatic vegetables, herbs, spices and vanilla, in a liquid to impart flavour. Usually the infused liquid is brought to the boil, then left to stand.

Julienne Fine matchstick strips of vegetables or citrus zest, sometimes used as a garnish.

Knead To work dough by pummelling with the heel of the hand.

Knock back To knead a yeast dough for a second time after rising, to ensure an even texture.

Lard To insert small strips of fat or streaky bacon into the flesh of game birds and dry meat before cooking. A special larding needle is used.

Liaison A thickening or binding agent based on a combination of ingredients, such as flour and water, or oil and egg.

Macerate To soften and flavour raw or dried foods by soaking in a liquid, eg soaking fruit in alcohol.

Mandolin A flat wooden or metal frame with adjustable cutting blades for slicing vegetables.

Marinate To soak raw meat, poultry or game – usually in a mixture of oil, wine, vinegar and flavourings – to soften and impart flavour. The mixture, which is known as a marinade, may also be used to baste the food during cooking.

Medallion Small round piece of meat, usually beef or veal.

Mince To cut food into very fine pieces, using a mincer, food processor or knife.

Mocha Term which has come to mean a blend of chocolate and coffee.

Parboil To boil a vegetable or other food for part of its cooking time before finishing it by another method.

Pare To finely peel the skin or zest from vegetables or fruit.

Pâte The French word for pastry, familiar in pâte sucrée, a sweet flan pastry.

Pâté A savoury mixture of finely chopped or minced meat, fish and/or vegetables, usually served as a starter with bread or toast.

Patty tin Tray of cup-shaped moulds for cooking small cakes and deep tartlets. Also called a bun tin.

Pectin A naturally occurring substance found in most varieties of fruit and some vegetables, which is necessary for setting jams and jellies. Commercial pectin and sugar with pectin are also available for preserve-making.

Pickle To preserve meat or vegetables in brine or vinegar.

Pith The bitter white skin under the thin zest of citrus fruit.

Pluck To remove the feathers from poultry and game birds.

Poach To cook food gently in liquid at simmering point; the surface should be just trembling.

Pot roast To cook meat in a covered pan with some fat and a little liquid.

Prove To leave bread dough to rise (usually for a second time) after shaping.

Purée To pound, sieve or liquidise vegetables, fish or fruit to a smooth pulp. Purées often form the basis for soups and sauces.

Reduce To fast-boil stock or other liquid in an uncovered pan to evaporate water and concentrate the flavour.

Refresh To cool hot vegetables very quickly by plunging into ice-cold water or holding under cold running water in order to stop the cooking process and preserve the colour.

Render To melt fat slowly to a liquid, either by heating meat trimmings, or to release the fat from fatty meat, such as duck or goose, during roasting.

Rennet An animal-derived enzyme used to coagulate milk in cheese-making. A vegetarian alternative is available.

Roast To cook meat by dry heat in the oven.

Roulade Soufflé or sponge mixture rolled around a savoury or sweet filling.

Roux A mixture of equal quantities of butter (or other fat) and flour cooked together to form the basis and thickener for many sauces.

Rub-in Method of incorporating fat into flour by rubbing between the fingertips, used when a short texture is required. Used for pastry, cakes, scones and biscuits.

Salsa Piquant sauce made from chopped fresh vegetables and sometimes fruit.

Sauté To cook food in a small quantity of fat over a high heat, shaking the pan constantly – usually in a sauté pan (a frying pan with straight sides and a wide base).

Scald To pour boiling water over food to clean it, or loosen skin, for example, on tomatoes. Also used to describe heating milk to just below boiling point.

Score To cut parallel lines in the surface of food, such as fish (or the fat layer on meat), to improve its appearance or help it cook more quickly.

Sear To brown meat quickly in a little hot fat before grilling or roasting.

Seasoned flour Flour mixed with a little salt and pepper, used for dusting meat, fish or other ingredients, before frying.

Shred To grate cheese or slice vegetables into very fine pieces or strips.

Sieve To press food through a perforated sieve to obtain a smooth texture.

Sift To shake dry ingredients through a sieve to remove lumps.

Simmer To keep a liquid just below boiling point.

Skim To remove froth, scum or fat from the surface of stock, gravy, stews, jam, etc. Use either a skimmer, a spoon or kitchen paper.

Smoke To cure meat, poultry and fish by exposing it to wood smoke.

Souse To pickle food, especially fish, in vinegar flavoured with spices.

Steam To cook food in steam, usually in a steamer over rapidly boiling water.

Steep To immerse food in warm or cold liquid to soften it, and sometimes to draw out strong flavours.

Sterilise To destroy bacteria in foods by heating.

Stew To cook food, such as tougher cuts of meat, in flavoured liquid which is kept at simmering point.

Stir-fry To cook small even-sized pieces of food rapidly in a little fat, tossing constantly over a high heat, usually in a wok.

Suet Hard fat of animal origin used in pastry and steamed puddings. A vegetarian alternative is readily available.

Sugar syrup A concentrated solution of sugar in water used to poach fruit and make sorbets, granitas, fruit juices, etc.

Sweat To cook chopped or sliced vegetables in a little fat without liquid in a covered pan over a low heat to soften.

Tepid The term used to describe temperature at approximately blood heat, ie 37°C (98.7°F).

Thermometer, sugar/fat Used for accurately checking the temperature of boiling sugar syrups, and fat for deep-frying respectively. Dual-purpose thermometers are obtainable.

Truss To tie with string or to skewer poultry or game into shape prior to roasting.

Unleavened Flat bread, such as pitta, made without using a raising agent.

Vanilla sugar Sugar in which a vanilla pod has been stored to impart its flavour.

Whipping Beating air rapidly into a mixture either with a manual or electric whisk, as below. Whipping usually refers to cream.

Whisking Beating air rapidly into a mixture either with a manual or electric whisk.

Zest The thin coloured outer layer of citrus fruit, which can be removed in fine strips with a zester.

Index

Photographers: Marie-Louise **Avery** (pages 409, 452, 453, 454, 457 and 459); Neil Barclay (pages 79 and 236B); Steve Baxter (pages 99, 128B, 243, 248, 264 and 443); Martin Brigdale (pages 147B, 151, 252, 262B, 269, 355, 438 and 445); Nicki Dowey (pages 14, 45, 47, 49, 50, 52, 60, 65, 66, 69, 70T, 72, 74, 77, 115, 120T, 130, 141, 142, 143B, 144, 145, 146, 148, 149, 154, 156, 167, 170, 179, 182, 184, 189, 190, 200T, 213, 222B, 224, 230T, 232, 233T, 237B, 247B, 250, 262T, 263T, 266, 268B, 284, 285B, 286B, 290T, 292B, 298T, 306, 310, 311, 312B, 313T, 314T, 315, 316, 318B, 319B, 320B, 321T, 322, 333, 334, 337, 344B, 348, 350B, 351, 353T, 358, 364, 366, 367, 368, 391, 396, 402, 406, 408, 410, 420, 442, 444B, 447, 448, 456T, 466 and 473); Will Heap (pages 62, 286T and 375); Emma Lee (page 414); William Lingwood (pages 53T, 55, 164B, 183, 185, 300T, 369, 407, 419 and 427); Gareth Morgans (pages 2, 6, 51B, 80, 98, 120B, 129, 143T, 147T, 165, 169, 198, 214, 233B, 251B, 263B, 265, 268T, 272, 273, 285T, 294T, 297, 331, 387, 389B, 404, 423, 460, 465 and 492); Myles New (pages 46, 137, 341, 359, 430, 474 and 486); Craig Robertson (pages 54, 58B, 82, 85, 95, 108, 136, 139, 153, 155, 162B, 166, 176, 177, 180, 197, 203, 206, 209B, 211B, 242, 270, 277, 299T, 321B, 325–6, 330, 332, 336, 338, 340, 344T, 345B, 352, 356, 360, 361, 362, 365, 394 and 464); Brett Stevens (page 335); Sam Stowell (pages 75T and 202); Lucinda Symons (pages 4T, 28, 30, 32–39, 40, 44, 48, 119, 51T, 53B, 57, 58T, 59, 67, 68, 70B, 71, 76B, 81, 86–9, 90, 92, 93, 94, 96, 97, 102–7, 109, 110, 111, 112, 113, 114, 116, 117, 121, 122, 123, 124, 125, 126, 127, 128T, 134–5, 150, 152, 160–1, 162T, 163, 164T, 168, 174–5, 181, 187, 188, 192, 193, 194–5, 199, 200B, 201, 204–5, 207, 210, 211T, 212, 215, 216, 218–9, 220, 221, 222T, 223, 226, 229, 230B, 231, 234, 235, 236T, 237B, 244, 245, 246, 247T, 249, 256–7, 259–61, 267, 271, 274, 287T, 278–83, 287B, 289, 290B, 291, 292T, 293, 294B, 295, 298B, 299B, 300B, 301, 302, 303, 304, 305, 309, 312T, 313B, 314B, 317, 318T, 319T, 320T, 339, 345T, 346, 347, 349, 350T, 353B, 354, 370, 372, 373, 374, 376, 377, 378, 379T, 380, 381, 382, 383, 384, 385, 388, 389T, 392, 395, 398, 399, 401, 403, 405, 411, 415, 416, 418, 421, 422, 424, 433, 440, 444T, 446, 450, 455, 456B, 458, 461, 463, 468 and 470); Martin Thompson (page 412); Philip Webb (pages 196, 296, 379B, 429 and 441); Jon Whitaker (page 43); Kate Whitaker (pages 4B, 75B, 76T, 138, 208, 288, 342, 357, 363, 390, 413, 417 and 449)

Home Economists: Meike Beck, Anna Burges-Lumsden, Monaz Dumasia, Joanna Farrow, Emma Jane Frost, Teresa Goldfinch, Lizzie Harris, Alice Hart, Zoë Horne, Lucy McKelvie, Jennie Milsom, Kim Morphew, Aya Nishimura, Katie Rogers, Bridget Sargeson, Stella Sargeson, Sarah Tildesley, Kate Trend, Alison Walker, Charlotte Watson, Jennifer White and Mari Mererid Williams

Stylists: Susannah Blake, Tamzin Ferdinando, Lisa Harrison, Jenny Iggleden, Rachel Jukes, Roisin Nield, Wei Tang, Sarah Tildesley, Helen Trent, Fanny Ward, Polly Webb-Wilson and Mari Mererid Williams